SO-ARJ-342

Hungary

Steve Fallon

LONELY PLANET PUBLICATIONS
Melbourne • Oakland • London • Paris

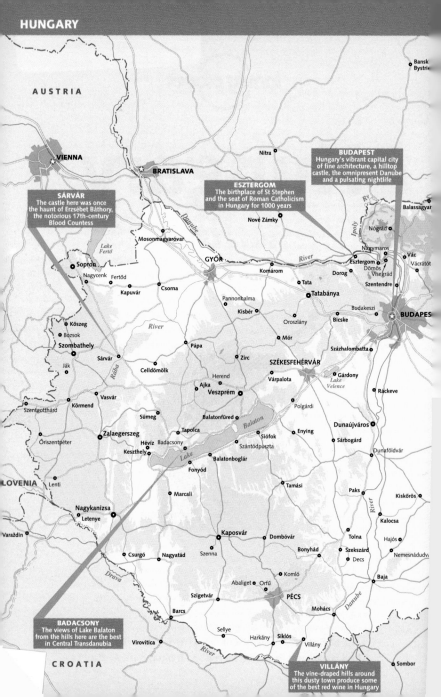

AUSTRIA

VIENNA

BRATISLAVA

Nitra

SÁRVÁR
The castle here was once the haunt of Erzsébet Báthory, the notorious 17th-century Blood Countess

ESZTERGOM
The birthplace of St Stephen and the seat of Roman Catholicism in Hungary for 1000 years

BUDAPEST
Hungary's vibrant capital city of fine architecture, a hilltop castle, the omnipresent Danube and a pulsating nightlife

Balassagyar

Nové Zámky

Danube

Ipoly

Nógrád

Lake Fertő

Mosonmagyaróvár

River

Nagymaros

Vác

Vácrátót

Sopron

GYŐR

Komárom

Esztergom

Dorog

Dömös

Visegrád

Szentendre

Nagycenk

Fertőd

Tata

Kapuvár

Csorna

Pannonhalma

Tatabánya

Budakeszi

BUDAPES

Kisbér

Köszeg

Bozsok

Oroszlány

Bicske

Szombathely

River

Mór

Százhalombatta

Ják

Sárvár

Pápa

Zirc

SZÉKESFEHÉRVÁR

Celldömölk

Herend

Gárdony

Vasvár

Ajka

Veszprém

Várpalota

Lake Velence

Ráckeve

Szentgotthárd

Körmend

Sümeg

Polgárdi

Zalaegerszeg

Tapolca

Balatonfüred

Balaton

Dunaújváros

Őriszentpéter

Hévíz

Badacsony

Siófok

Enying

Sárbogárd

Keszthely

Lake

Szántódpuszta

Dunaföldvár

LOVENIA

Lenti

Fonyód

Balatonboglár

Tamási

Paks

Kiskőrös

Nagykanizsa

Letenye

Marcali

River

Kalocsa

Varaždin

Kaposvár

Dombóvár

Tolna

Hajós

Csurgó

Nagyatád

Szenna

Bonyhád

Szekszárd

Nemesnádudva

Decs

Komló

Baja

Abaliget

Orfű

BADACSONY
The views of Lake Balaton from the hills here are the best in Central Transdanubia

Szigetvár

PÉCS

Barcs

Mohács

Sellye

Harkány

Siklós

Danube

Virovitica

Villány

Sombor

River

CROATIA

VILLÁNY
The vine-draped hills around this dusty town produce some of the best red wine in Hungary

Bansk Bystri

SLOVAKIA

Košice

Užgorod

Mukačevo

UKRAIN

NAGYKÁLLÓ
Final resting place of Isaac
Taub Eizik, the 18th-century
humanistic philosopher known as
the 'Wonder Rabbi'

SZILVÁSVÁRAD
This town in the Bükk Hills region
is the centre of horse breeding
in Hungary, with some
250 Lippizaners in residence

Lučenec

Aggtelek

Sátoraljaújhely

Edelény
Encs
Boldogkőváralja

Sárospatak
River
Dombrád

Ózd
Kazincbarcika

Kisvárda

Somoskő
Szécsény
Salgótarján

Lillafüred
Szilvásvárad
Szerencs

Tokaj

MISKOLC

Vásárosnamény

Mátészalka
Fehérgyarmat

Hollókő
Parád
Eger

Tiszavasvári
NYÍREGYHÁZA

Máriapócs

Mátraháza
Gyöngyös
Füzesabony

Tiszaújváros
Polgár
Hajdúnánás
Nagykálló

Nyírbátor

Mezőkövesd
Tisza

Hajdúböszörmény

Hatvan
Heves

Lake
Tisza
Tiszafüred
Hortobágy

DEBRECEN

Jászberény
Jászapáti

Nádudvar
Hajdúszoboszló

HORTOBÁGY
Home to myths, mirages,
Hungarian cowboys and mor
than 300 species of birds

Berekfürdő
Püspökladány

Berettyóújfalu

Cegléd
Szolnok
Törökszentmiklós
Karcag

Kisújszállás

ORADEA

GREAT
PLAIN
River
Mezőtúr
Szeghalom

KECSKEMÉT
Vésztő

Szarvas
LAKE TISZA
The 'Balaton of the Great Plain'
offers some of the water sports
facilities in Hungary

Kunszentmárton
Mezőberény

Kiskunfélegyháza
Békés
Sarkad

Bugac
Csongrád
Szentes

Békéscsaba
Gyula

Kiskunmajsa
Oroszháza

ROMANIA

Kistelek
Ópusztaszer
Kiskunhalas

Hódmezővásárhely
Tótkomlós

SZEGED
Mezőhegyes

Makó
Nagylak

| | 0 | 25 | 50 km |
| | 0 | 15 | 30 mi |

SZEGED
The Southern Plain's lively capital,
with universities, museums and
more cultural offerings than any other

Subotica

Tisza

ARAD

ELEVATION

	900m
	600m
	300m
	200m
	150m
	0

YUGOSLAVIA

TIMIŞOARA

Hungary
3rd edition – August 2000
First published – February 1994

Published by
Lonely Planet Publications Pty Ltd A.C.N. 005 607 983
192 Burwood Rd, Hawthorn, Victoria 3122, Australia

Lonely Planet Offices
Australia PO Box 617, Hawthorn, Victoria 3122
USA 150 Linden St, Oakland, CA 94607
UK 10a Spring Place, London NW5 3BH
France 1 rue du Dahomey, 75011 Paris

Photographs
Many of the images in this guide are available for licensing from
Lonely Planet Images.
email: lpi@lonelyplanet.com.au

Front cover photograph
The interior dome of Budapest's Parliament building
(Luis Castaneda, The Image Bank)

ISBN 0 86442 685 2

text & maps © Lonely Planet 2000
photos © photographers as indicated 2000

Printed by SNP Offset (M) Sdn Bhd
Printed in Malaysia

Although the authors and Lonely Planet try to make the information as accurate as possible, we accept no responsibility for any loss, injury or inconvenience sustained by anyone using this book.

Contents – Text

Contents – Maps

LAKE BALATON & CENTRAL TRANSDANUBIA

SOUTHERN TRANSDANUBIA

GREAT PLAIN

NORTHERN UPLANDS

THE NORTH-EAST

HUNGARY MAP INDEX

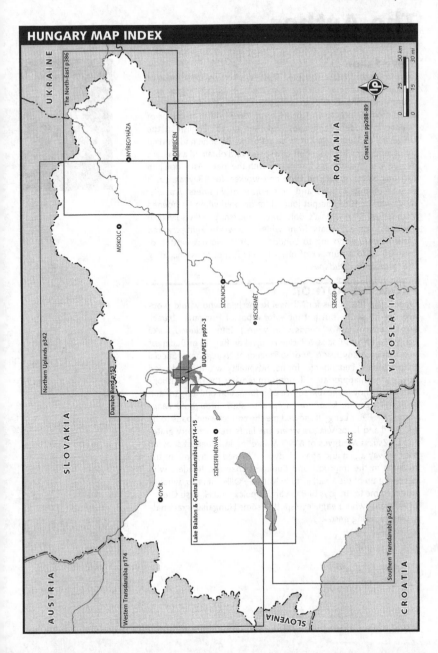

The Author

Steve Fallon

Born in Boston, Massachusetts, Steve worked an assortment of menial but character-building – so his parents said – jobs as a youngster to finance trips to Europe and South America. He graduated from Georgetown University in 1975 with a Bachelor of Science in modern languages and then taught English at the University of Silesia near Katowice in Poland. After he had worked for several years for a Gannett newspaper and obtained a master's degree in journalism, his fascination with the 'new' Asia took him to Hong Kong, where he lived and worked for 13 years for a variety of publications and was editor of *Business Traveller* magazine. In 1987, he put journalism on hold when he opened Wanderlust Books, Asia's only travel bookshop. Steve lived in Budapest for 2½ years from where he wrote *Hungary* and *Slovenia* before moving to London in 1994. He has written or contributed to a number of other Lonely Planet titles, including the forthcoming *Budapest*.

FROM THE AUTHOR

Once again this one is for Michael Rothschild, who would probably sell his soul – but not me – for a pot of Hungarian barack lekvár (apricot jam). Friends who were helpful included Ildikó Nagy Moran and Csaba & Jackie Lengyel de Bagota of Budapest and Mihály Aranyossy & Andrea Szegedi of Nyíregyháza. Special thanks to Jane Leuenberger for her hospitality, warmth and good advice. Much appreciated. Tourinform remains the most authoritative and knowledgeable source of information on Hungary and things Hungarian; köszönöm szépen to staff throughout Magyarország. Péter Lengyel showed me the correct wine roads to be followed and János Vilagosi where the birds are; I am very grateful. Dr Zsuzsa Medgyes of M&G Marketing in Budapest showed me the way again and again. Judy Finn helped with some of the research in the transport and Budapest chapters. Readers who deserve a tip of the kalap include Nathalie Ollier of Paris, who introduced me to the joys of Pápa and Tapolca, and Hamish Gregor of Australia, whose eagle eye spotted some Hungarian grammatical and spelling mistakes.

This Book

From the Publisher

Production of this edition of Hungary was coordinated by Darren O'Connell (editorial) and Birgit Jordan (mapping and design). Kalya Ryan and Yvonne Byron assisted with editing and proofing.

Thanks to Quentin Frayne for laying out the language chapter, Fiona Croyden from LPI for assistance with images, Matt King for coordinating the illustrations and Maria Vallianos for the cover.

THANKS
Many thanks to the travellers who used the last edition and wrote to us with helpful hints, advice and interesting anecdotes. Your names appear in the back of this book.

7

Foreword

ABOUT LONELY PLANET GUIDEBOOKS

The story begins with a classic travel adventure: Tony and Maureen Wheeler's 1972 journey across Europe and Asia to Australia. Useful information about the overland trail did not exist at that time, so Tony and Maureen published the first Lonely Planet guidebook to meet a growing need.

From a kitchen table, then from a tiny office in Melbourne (Australia), Lonely Planet has become the largest independent travel publisher in the world, an international company with offices in Melbourne, Oakland (USA), London (UK) and Paris (France).

Today Lonely Planet guidebooks cover the globe. There is an ever-growing list of books and there's information in a variety of forms and media. Some things haven't changed. The main aim is still to help make it possible for adventurous travellers to get out there – to explore and better understand the world.

At Lonely Planet we believe travellers can make a positive contribution to the countries they visit – if they respect their host communities and spend their money wisely. Since 1986 a percentage of the income from each book has been donated to aid projects and human rights campaigns.

Updates Lonely Planet thoroughly updates each guidebook as often as possible. This usually means there are around two years between editions, although for more unusual or more stable destinations the gap can be longer. Check the imprint page (following the colour map at the beginning of the book) for publication dates.

Between editions up-to-date information is available in two free newsletters – the paper *Planet Talk* and email *Comet* (to subscribe, contact any Lonely Planet office) – and on our Web site at www.lonelyplanet.com. The *Upgrades* section of the Web site covers a number of important and volatile destinations and is regularly updated by Lonely Planet authors. *Scoop* covers news and current affairs relevant to travellers. And, lastly, the *Thorn Tree* bulletin board and *Postcards* section of the site carry unverified, but fascinating, reports from travellers.

Correspondence The process of creating new editions begins with the letters, postcards and emails received from travellers. This correspondence often includes suggestions, criticisms and comments about the current editions. Interesting excerpts are immediately passed on via newsletters and the Web site, and everything goes to our authors to be verified when they're researching on the road. We're keen to get more feedback from organisations or individuals who represent communities visited by travellers.

Lonely Planet gathers information for everyone who's curious about the planet – and especially for those who explore it first-hand. Through guidebooks, phrasebooks, activity guides, maps, literature, newsletters, image library, TV series and Web site we act as an information exchange for a worldwide community of travellers.

Research Authors aim to gather sufficient practical information to enable travellers to make informed choices and to make the mechanics of a journey run smoothly. They also research historical and cultural background to help enrich the travel experience and allow travellers to understand and respond appropriately to cultural and environmental issues.

Authors don't stay in every hotel because that would mean spending a couple of months in each medium-sized city and, no, they don't eat at every restaurant because that would mean stretching belts beyond capacity. They do visit hotels and restaurants to check standards and prices, but feedback based on readers' direct experiences can be very helpful.

Many of our authors work undercover, others aren't so secretive. None of them accept freebies in exchange for positive write-ups. And none of our guidebooks contain any advertising.

Production Authors submit their raw manuscripts and maps to offices in Australia, USA, UK or France. Editors and cartographers – all experienced travellers themselves – then begin the process of assembling the pieces. When the book finally hits the shops, some things are already out of date, we start getting feedback from readers and the process begins again ...

WARNING & REQUEST

Things change – prices go up, schedules change, good places go bad and bad places go bankrupt – nothing stays the same. So, if you find things better or worse, recently opened or long since closed, please tell us and help make the next edition even more accurate and useful. We genuinely value all the feedback we receive. Julie Young coordinates a well travelled team that reads and acknowledges every letter, postcard and email and ensures that every morsel of information finds its way to the appropriate authors, editors and cartographers for verification.

Everyone who writes to us will find their name in the next edition of the appropriate guidebook. They will also receive the latest issue of *Planet Talk*, our quarterly printed newsletter, or *Comet*, our monthly email newsletter. Subscriptions to both newsletters are free. The very best contributions will be rewarded with a free guidebook.

Excerpts from your correspondence may appear in new editions of Lonely Planet guidebooks, the Lonely Planet Web site, *Planet Talk* or *Comet*, so please let us know if you *don't* want your letter published or your name acknowledged.

Send all correspondence to the Lonely Planet office closest to you:

Australia: PO Box 617, Hawthorn, Victoria 3122
USA: 150 Linden St, Oakland, CA 94607
UK: 10A Spring Place, London NW5 3BH
France: 1 rue du Dahomey, 75011 Paris

Or email us at: talk2us@lonelyplanet.com.au

For news, views and updates see our Web site: www.lonelyplanet.com

HOW TO USE A LONELY PLANET GUIDEBOOK

The best way to use a Lonely Planet guidebook is any way you choose. At Lonely Planet we believe the most memorable travel experiences are often those that are unexpected, and the finest discoveries are those you make yourself. Guidebooks are not intended to be used as if they provide a detailed set of infallible instructions!

Contents All Lonely Planet guidebooks follow roughly the same format. The Facts about the Destination chapters or sections give background information ranging from history to weather. Facts for the Visitor gives practical information on issues like visas and health. Getting There & Away gives a brief starting point for researching travel to and from the destination. Getting Around gives an overview of the transport options when you arrive.

The peculiar demands of each destination determine how subsequent chapters are broken up, but some things remain constant. We always start with background, then proceed to sights, places to stay, places to eat, entertainment, getting there and away, and getting around information – in that order.

Heading Hierarchy Lonely Planet headings are used in a strict hierarchical structure that can be visualised as a set of Russian dolls. Each heading (and its following text) is encompassed by any preceding heading that is higher on the hierarchical ladder.

Entry Points We do not assume guidebooks will be read from beginning to end, but that people will dip into them. The traditional entry points are the list of contents and the index. In addition, however, some books have a complete list of maps and an index map illustrating map coverage.

There may also be a colour map that shows highlights. These highlights are dealt with in greater detail in the Facts for the Visitor chapter, along with planning questions and suggested itineraries. Each chapter covering a geographical region usually begins with a locator map and another list of highlights. Once you find something of interest in a list of highlights, turn to the index.

Maps Maps play a crucial role in Lonely Planet guidebooks and include a huge amount of information. A legend is printed on the back page. We seek to have complete consistency between maps and text, and to have every important place in the text captured on a map. Map key numbers usually start in the top left corner.

Although inclusion in a guidebook usually implies a recommendation we cannot list every good place. Exclusion does not necessarily imply criticism. In fact there are a number of reasons why we might exclude a place – sometimes it is simply inappropriate to encourage an influx of travellers.

Introduction

Hungary (Magyarország) is a kidney-shaped country in the heart of Europe whose impact on the continent's history has been far greater than its present size and population would dictate. Hungarians – who call themselves the Magyar – speak a language and form a culture unlike any other in the region; this distinction has been both a source of pride and an obstacle for more than 1100 years. Firmly entrenched in the Communist Soviet bloc until the late 1980s, Hungary is today an independent republic making its own decisions and policies.

Hungarian nationalism has been both the cause and the result of a sometimes almost paranoiac fear of being gobbled up by neighbouring countries – particularly the 'sea of Slavs' that surrounds much of the country. Yet, despite endless occupations and wars,

the Hungarians have been able to retain their own identity without shutting themselves off from the world. Today, Hungary looks at integration with Europe as its future.

Given its geographic situation and its experience in welcoming travellers, Hungary is the best place to enter Central or Eastern Europe. While some of its neighbours may have more dramatic scenery or older and more important monuments, Hungary is the country most geared and stable for tourists, and travel here is essentially hassle-free. Visitors with special interests – horse riding, botany, bird-watching, cycling, thermal spas, Jewish culture – will find Hungary a veritable treasure trove. And, by Western standards, the country remains a bargain destination, with very affordable food, lodging and transport.

11

Under the former regime most of the government's attention and money went to the capital, Budapest. As a result, foreign visitors rarely ventured beyond this splendid city on the Danube, except perhaps on a day trip to the Danube Bend or to Lake Balaton. These places should be visited for sure, but don't ignore other towns and regions off the beaten track, including: a tanya világ, the 'farm world' of the southern Plain; the ethnically rich North-East; the Villány Hills in Southern Transdanubia, awash in vineyards and wine; and the traditional Őrség region of the far west in Transdanubia. This is not a case of 'authentic' versus 'touristy'; a supermarket check-out counter in Budapest is as much a part of the real Hungary today as a village greengrocer's in the Zemplén Hills. But life in the provinces is more redolent of times past – simpler, slower, often more friendly.

The first half of this decade were not glory days for Hungary. Serious economic problems affected all aspects of daily life, and the country's economy was very much in limbo. Gone were the days when job security, free medical insurance and sustainable pensions were a national assumption, and for the first time people had to work very hard for little return. A majority of Hungarians were very disappointed with what the change to a capitalist economy had brought them.

Thankfully, those days (and feelings) appear to be over for most. Foreign investment has increased substantially, living standards have risen, many people have that little bit of extra cash for a new VCR or a winter holiday in the Canary Islands, many historical buildings have received long-overdue face-lifts and the nation is on the fast-track to membership of the European Union – an 'acceptance' that Hungary has craved for a long, long time.

When the Renaissance man they call 'the greatest Hungarian' – a 19th-century reformer and patriot who did more for his nation than any other – wrote the words below, they were but a dream. As the new millennium starts that dream is becoming a reality.

Many people think that Hungary was;
I like to believe that she will be!

Count István Széchenyi, (Credit, 1830)

Facts about Hungary

HISTORY
Early Inhabitants
The Carpathian Basin, in which Hungary lies, has been populated for hundreds of thousands of years. Bone fragments found at Vértesszőlős south-east of Tata in Western Transdanubia in the 1960s and believed to be half a million years old suggest that Palaeolithic and later Neanderthal humans were attracted to the area by the warm-water springs and the abundance of reindeer, bears and mammoths. Stone Age pottery shards were also found at Istállóskő Cave near Szilvásvárad in the Northern Uplands.

During the Neolithic period (around 5000 BC), changes in the climate forced much of the indigenous wildlife to migrate northward. The domestication of animals and the first forms of agriculture appeared, as indeed they did in much of Europe. Remnants of the Körös culture suggest that these goddess-worshipping people lived in the Szeged area at this time.

Indo-European tribes from the Balkans stormed the Carpathian Basin from the south in horse-drawn wheeled carts in about 2000 BC, bringing with them copper tools and weapons. After the introduction of more durable bronze, forts were built and a military elite developed.

Over the next millennium, invaders from the west (Illyrians, Thracians) and east (Scythians) brought iron, but the metal was not in common use until the Celts arrived in the Carpathian Basin in about the 3rd century BC. They introduced glass and crafted some of the fine gold jewellery that can still be seen in museums throughout Hungary.

Around the beginning of the Christian era, the Romans conquered the area west and south of the Danube River and established the province of Pannonia, later divided into Upper (Superior) and Lower (Inferior) Pannonia. Subsequent victories over the Celts extended their domination across the Tisza River as far as Dacia (now Romania). The Romans brought writing, viticulture and stone architecture, and established garrison towns, the remains of which can still be seen in Óbuda, which the Romans knew as Aquincum, Szombathely (Savaria), Pécs (Sophianae) and Sopron (Scarabantia). They also built baths near the region's thermal waters and introduced a new cult: Christianity.

The Great Migrations
The first of the so-called Great Migrations of nomadic peoples from Asia reached the eastern outposts of the Roman Empire late in the 2nd century AD, and in 270 the Romans abandoned Dacia. Within two centuries, they were also forced to flee Pannonia by the Huns, whose short-lived empire was established by Attila. He had earlier conquered the Magyars near the lower Volga River, and for centuries the two groups were (erroneously) thought to have common ancestry. Attila remains a very common given name for males in Hungary.

Germanic tribes such as the Goths, Gepids and Longobards occupied the region for the next century and a half until the Avars, a powerful Turkic people, gained control of the Carpathian Basin in the 6th century. They in turn were subdued by Charlemagne in 796 and converted to Christianity. By that time, the Carpathian Basin was virtually unpopulated except for groups of Turkic and Germanic tribes on the plains and Slavs in the northern hills.

The Magyars & the Conquest
The origin of the Magyars, is a complicated issue, not in the least helped by the similarity – in English at least – of the words 'Hun' and 'Hungary', which are *not* related. One thing is certain: Magyars are part of the Finno-Ugric group of peoples, who inhabited the forests somewhere between the middle Volga River and the Ural Mountains in western Siberia as early as 4000 BC.

By about 2000 BC, population growth had forced the Finnish-Estonian branch to move westward, ultimately reaching the Baltic Sea. The Ugrians moved from the south-eastern slopes of the Urals into the valleys of the region, and switched from hunting and fishing to farming and raising livestock, especially horses. Their equestrian skills proved useful half a millennium later when climatic changes brought drought, forcing them to move northward onto the steppes.

On the grasslands, the Ugrians turned to nomadic herding. After 500 BC, by which time the use of iron had become common among the tribes, a group moved westward to the area of Bashkiria in Central Asia. Here they lived among Persians and Bulgars and began referring to themselves as Magyars (from the Finno-Ugric words *mon*, 'to speak', and *er*, 'man').

After several centuries, another group split away and moved south to the Don River under the control of the Khazars. Here they lived among different groups under a tribal alliance called *onogur* (or '10 peoples'). This is the derivation of the word 'Hungary' in English and 'Ungarn' in German. Their last migration before the conquest of the Carpathian Basin brought them to what modern Hungarians call the Etelköz, the region between the Dnieper and lower Danube Rivers above the Black Sea.

Nomadic groups of Magyars probably reached the Carpathian Basin as early as the mid-8th century, acting as mercenaries for various armies. It is believed that while the men were away during one such campaign in about 889, a fierce people from the Asiatic steppe called the Pechenegs attacked the Etelköz settlements. Fearing a repeat attack, seven tribes under the leadership of Árpád – the *gyula* or chief military commander – struck out for the Carpathian Basin. They crossed the Verecke Pass in today's Ukraine some time between 893 and 895.

The Magyars met almost no resistance and the tribes dispersed in three directions. The Bulgars were quickly dispatched eastward; the Germans had already taken care of the Slavs in the west; and Transylvania was wide open. Known for their ability to ride and shoot – a common Christian prayer

during the so-called Dark Ages was 'Save us, O Lord, from the arrows of the Hungarians' – and no longer content with being hired guns, the Magyars began plundering and pillaging on their own, taking slaves and amassing booty. Their raids took them as far as Spain, northern Germany and southern Italy, but they were stopped by the German King Otto I at the battle of Augsburg in 955.

The defeat left the Magyar tribes in disarray and, like the Bohemian, Polish and Russian princes of the time, they had to choose between their more powerful neighbours – Byzantium to the south and east or the Holy Roman Empire to the west – to form an alliance. Individual Magyar chieftains began acting independently, but in 973, Prince Géza, the great-grandson of Árpád, asked the Holy Roman emperor Otto II to send Catholic missionaries to Hungary. Géza was baptised, as was his son Vajk, who took the Christian name Stephen (István). When Géza died, Stephen ruled as prince, but three years later, on Christmas Day in the year 1000, he was crowned 'Christian King' Stephen I with a crown sent from Rome by Pope Sylvester II. Hungary the kingdom – and the nation – was born.

King Stephen I & the Árpád Dynasty

Stephen ruthlessly set about consolidating royal authority by expropriating the land of the clan chieftains and establishing a system of counties (*megye*) protected by fortified castles (*vár*). Much land was transferred to loyal (mostly Germanic) knights, and the crown began minting coins. Shrewdly, Stephen sought the support of the church throughout and, to hasten the conversion of the populace, he ordered one in every 10 villages to build a church. He also established 10 episcopates, two of which were later made archbishoprics (Kalocsa and Esztergom). Monasteries staffed by foreign scholars were set up around the country. By the time of Stephen's death in 1038 (he was later canonised St Stephen), Hungary was a nascent Christian nation, increasingly westward-looking and multi-ethnic.

But the next two and a half centuries – the reign of the House of Árpád – would test the kingdom to the limit. The period was one of relentless struggles between rival pretenders to the throne, which weakened the young nation's defences against its powerful neighbours. There was a brief hiatus under King Ladislas I (László; ruled 1077-95), who fended off attacks from Byzantium, and under his successor Koloman the Bookish (Könyves Kálmán), who encouraged literature, art and the writing of chronicles until his death in 1116.

Tension flared again when the Byzantine emperor made a grab for Hungary's provinces in Dalmatia and Croatia, which it had attached by the early 12th century. But he was stopped by Béla III, a powerful ruler from 1173 to 1196 who had a permanent residence built at Esztergom (then an alternative royal seat to Székesfehérvár). Béla's son, Andrew II (András; ruled 1205-35), however, weakened the crown when he gave in to local barons' demands for more land in order to fund his crusades. This led to the Golden Bull, a kind of Magna Carta signed at Székesfehérvár in 1222, which limited some of the king's powers in favour of the nobility.

When Béla IV (ruled 1235-70) tried to regain the estates, the barons were able to oppose him on equal terms. Fearing Mongol expansion and realising he could not count on local help, Béla looked to the west and brought in German and Slovak settlers. His efforts were in vain. In 1241 the Mongols raced through the country, virtually burning Hungary to the ground and killing an estimated one-third of its two million people.

To rebuild the country as quickly as possible, Béla again invited Germans and Saxons to settle in Transdanubia and Transylvania and on the Great Plain. He also built a string of defensive hilltop castles (including the ones at Buda and Visegrád). But in a bid to appease the lesser nobility, he handed over large tracts of land to the barons. This enhanced their position and bids for more independence even further. At the time of Béla's death in the late 13th century, anarchy gripped Hungary. The Árpád line died out with the death of the heirless Andrew III in 1301.

Medieval Hungary

The struggle for the Hungarian throne after the death of Andrew III involved several European dynasties, but it was Charles Robert (Károly Róbert) of the French House of Anjou who finally won out (with the pope's blessing) and ruled until 1342. Charles Robert was an able administrator who managed to break the power of the provincial barons (though much of the land remained in private hands) and sought links with his neighbours. In 1335, he met the Polish and Czech kings at the new royal palace in Visegrád to discuss territorial disputes and to forge an alliance that would smash Vienna's control of trade.

Under Charles Robert's son and successor, Louis the Great (Nagy Lajos; ruled 1342-82), Hungary returned to a policy of conquest. A brilliant military strategist, Louis acquired territory in the Balkans as far as Dalmatia and as far north as Poland. But his successes were short-lived and the menace of the Ottoman Turks had begun.

As Louis had sired no sons, one of his daughters, Mary, succeeded him. This was deemed unacceptable by the barons, who rose up against the 'petticoat throne'. Within a short time, Mary's husband, Sigismund (Zsigmond; ruled 1387-1437) of Luxembourg, was crowned king. Sigismund's long reign brought peace at home, and there was a great flowering of Gothic art and architecture in Hungary. But while he managed to procure the coveted crown of Bohemia and was made Holy Roman emperor in 1433, he was unable to stop the march of the Turks up through the Balkans.

A Transylvanian general of Romanian origin, János Hunyadi began his career at the court of Sigismund. When Vladislav I (Ulászló) of the Polish Jagiellon dynasty was killed fighting the Turks at Varna in 1444, Hunyadi acted as regent. His victory over the Turks at Belgrade (Hungarian: Nándorfehérvár) in 1456 checked the Ottoman advance into Hungary for 70 years and assured the coronation of his son

Matthias (Mátyás), the greatest ruler of medieval Hungary.

Wisely, Matthias (ruled 1458-90), called 'the Raven' (Corvinus) from his coat of arms, maintained a mercenary force through taxation of the nobility, and this 'Black Army' conquered Moravia, Bohemia and even parts of Austria. Not only did Matthias Corvinus make Hungary one of Central Europe's leading powers, but under his rule the nation enjoyed something of a golden age. His second wife, the Neapolitan Queen Beatrice, brought artisans from Italy who completely rebuilt and extended the Gothic palace at Visegrád; the beauty and sheer size of the Renaissance residence they built was beyond comparison in Europe at the time. Matthias was celebrated for his fairness and justice, and Hungarian mythology and folk tales are full of stories illustrating 'Good King' Matthias' love of his subjects.

But while Matthias busied himself with centralising power for the crown, he ignored the growing Turkish threat. His successor Vladislav II (Úlászló) was unable to maintain even royal authority as the members of the diet (assembly), which met to approve royal decrees, squandered royal funds and expropriated land. In 1514, what had begun as a crusade organised by the power-hungry archbishop of Esztergom, Tamás Bakócz, turned into a peasant uprising against the landlords under the leadership of one György Dózsa.

The revolt was brutally repressed, some 70,000 peasants were tortured and executed, and Dózsa himself was fried alive on a red-hot iron throne. The retrograde Tripartitum Law that followed codified the rights and privileges of the barons and nobles and reduced the peasants to perpetual serfdom. By the time Louis II (Lajos) took the throne in 1516 at the tender age of nine, he couldn't rely on either side.

The Battle of Mohács & Turkish Occupation

The defeat of Louis' ragtag army by the Ottoman Turks at Mohács in 1526 is a watershed in Hungarian history. On the battlefield near this small town in Southern Transdanubia, a relatively prosperous and independent medieval Hungary died, sending the nation into a tailspin of partition, foreign domination and despair that can still be felt today.

It would be unfair to put all the blame on the weak and indecisive boy-king Louis or on his commander-in-chief Pál Tomori, the archbishop of Kalocsa. Bickering among the nobility and the brutal crackdown of the Dózsa uprising more than a decade earlier had severely weakened Hungary's military power, and there was virtually nothing left in the royal coffers. By 1526, the Ottoman sultan Suleiman the Magnificent had taken much of the Balkans, including Belgrade, and was poised to march on Buda and then Vienna with a force of 100,000 men.

Unable – or unwilling – to wait for reinforcements from Transylvania under the command of his rival John Szapolyai (Zápolyai János), Louis rushed south with a motley army of 25,000 men to battle the Turks, he was soundly thrashed in less than two hours. Along with bishops, nobles and an estimated 20,000 soldiers, the king himself was killed – crushed by his horse while trying to retreat across a stream. John Szapolyai, who had sat out the battle in the castle at Tokaj, was crowned king three months later but, despite grovelling before the Turks, he was never able to exploit the power he had sought so madly. Greed, self-interest and ambition had led Hungary to defeat itself.

After Buda Castle fell to the Turks in 1541, Hungary was divided into three parts. The central part, including Buda, went to the Turks while parts of Transdanubia and what is now Slovakia were governed by the Austrian House of Habsburg and assisted by the Hungarian nobility based at Bratislava (Hungarian: Pozsony). The principality of Transylvania east of the Tisza River prospered as a vassal state of the Ottoman Empire, initially under Szapolyai's son John Sigismund (Zsigmond János). Though heroic resistance continued against the Turks, most notably at Kőszeg (1532), Eger (1552) and Szigetvár (1566), this division would remain in place for more than a century and a half.

The Turkish occupation was marked by constant fighting among the three divisions; Catholic 'Royal Hungary' was pitted against not only the Turks but the Protestant Transylvanian princes. Gábor Bethlen, who ruled Transylvania from 1613 to 1629, tried to end the incessant warfare by conquering Royal Hungary with a mercenary army of Heyduck peasants and some Turkish assistance. But the Habsburgs and the Hungarians themselves viewed the Ottomans as the greatest threat to Europe since the Mongols and stopped the advance.

As Turkish power began to wane in the 17th century, Hungarian resistance to the Habsburgs, who had used Royal Hungary as a buffer zone between Vienna and the Turks, increased. A plot inspired by the palatine Ferenc Wesselényi was foiled in 1670 and a revolt by Imre Thököly (1682) and his army of *kuruc* (anti-Habsburg mercenaries) was put down. But with the help of the Polish army, Austrian and Hungarian forces liberated Buda in 1686. An imperial army under Eugene of Savoy wiped out the last Turkish army in Hungary at the Battle of Zenta (now Senta in Yugoslavia) 13 years later.

Habsburg Rule

The expulsion of the Turks did not result in a free and independent Hungary, and the policies of the Catholic Habsburgs' Counter-Reformation and heavy taxation further alienated the nobility. In 1703, the Transylvanian prince Ferenc Rákóczi II assembled an army of kuruc forces against the Austrians. The war dragged on for eight years, during which time the rebels 'deposed' the Habsburgs as the rulers of Hungary. But superior imperial forces and lack of funds forced the kuruc to negotiate a separate peace with Vienna behind Rákóczi's back. The 1703-11 War of Independence had failed, but Rákóczi was the first leader to unite Hungarians against the Habsburgs.

Though the compromise had brought the fighting to an end, Hungary was now a mere province of the Habsburg Empire. With the ascension of Maria Theresa to the throne in 1740, the Hungarian nobility pledged their 'lives and blood' to her at the diet in Bratislava in exchange for concessions. Thus began the period of enlightened absolutism that would continue under the rule of her son, the 'hatted king' (so-called as he was never crowned in Hungary) Joseph II who ruled for a decade from 1780.

Under the reigns of Maria Theresa and Joseph, Hungary took great steps forward economically and culturally. The depopulated areas in the east and south were settled by Romanians and Serbs while German Swabians went to Transdanubia. Joseph's attempts to modernise society by dissolving the all-powerful (and corrupt) religious orders, abolishing serfdom and replacing 'neutral' Latin with German as the official language of state administration were opposed by the Hungarian nobility, and the king rescinded most of these orders on his deathbed.

Dissenting voices could still be heard, and the ideals of the French Revolution of 1789 began to take root in certain intellectual circles in Hungary. In 1795 Ignác Martonovics, a former Franciscan priest, and six other pro-republican Jacobins were beheaded at Vérmező (Blood Meadow) in Buda for plotting against the crown.

Liberalism and social reform found their greatest supporters among certain members of the aristocracy. Count György Festetics (1755-1819), for example, founded Europe's first agricultural college at Keszthely. Count István Széchenyi (1791-1860), a true Renaissance man and called 'the greatest Hungarian' by his contemporaries, advocated the abolition of serfdom and returned much of his own land to the peasantry, oversaw the regulation of the Tisza and Danube Rivers for commerce and irrigation, and cleverly promoted horse racing among the upper classes in order to improve breeding stock for use in agriculture.

But the proponents of gradual reform were quickly superseded by a more radical faction demanding more immediate action. The group included Miklós Wesselényi, Ferenc Deák and Ferenc Kölcsey, but the predominant figure was Lajos Kossuth (1802-94). It was this dynamic lawyer and journalist who would lead Hungary to its greatest confrontation with the Habsburgs.

Kings, Saints, Strong Men & Premiers

The following is a list of the most important monarchs, rulers, dictators and leaders in Hungarian history. Names are given in English, with the Magyar equivalents in brackets. The dates refer to their reign or term of office.

Árpád Dynasty

Árpád 886-907
Géza 972-97
Stephen I (István) 1000-38
Ladislas I (László) 1077-95
Koloman the Bookish (Könyves Kálmán) 1095-1116
Béla III 1173-96
Andrew II (András) 1205-35
Béla IV 1235-70
Andrew III (András) 1290-1301

Mixed Dynasties

Charles Robert (Károly Róbert) 1307-42
Louis the Great (Nagy Lajos) 1342-82
Mary (Mária) 1383-87
Sigismund (Zsigmond) 1387-1437
János Hunyadi (regent) 1445-56
Matthias (Mátyás) Corvinus 1458-90
Vladislav II (Úlászló) 1490-1516
Louis II (Lajos) 1516-26
John Szapolyai (Zápolyai János) 1526-40

Habsburg Dynasty

Ferdinand I (Ferdinánd) 1526-64
Maximilian II (Miksa) 1564-76
Leopold I (Lipót) 1655-1705
Maria Theresa (Mária Terézia) 1740-80
Joseph II (József) 1780-90
Ferdinand V (Ferdinánd) 1835-48
Franz Joseph (Ferenc József) 1848-1916
Charles IV (Károly) 1916-18

Political Leaders

Mihály Károlyi 1919
Béla Kun 1919
Miklós Horthy (regent) 1920-44
Ferenc Szálasi 1944-45
Mátyás Rákosi 1947-56
János Kádár 1956-88
Károly Grósz 1988-90
József Antall 1990-93
Péter Baross 1993-94
Gyula Horn 1994-98
Viktor Orbán 1998-

1848-49 War of Independence & the Dual Monarchy

The Habsburg Empire began to weaken as Hungarian nationalism increased early in the 19th century. The Hungarians, suspicious of Napoleon's policies, ignored French appeals to revolt against Vienna, and certain reforms were introduced: the replacement of Latin, the official language of administration, with Magyar; a law allowing serfs alternative means of discharging their feudal obligations of service; and increased Hungarian representation in the Council of State.

The reforms carried out were too limited and far too late, however, and the diet became more defiant in its dealings with the crown. At the same time, the wave of revolution sweeping Europe spurred on the more radical faction. In 1848, the liberal count Lajos Batthyány was made prime minister of the new Hungarian ministry, which counted Deák, Kossuth and Széchenyi as members. The Habsburgs also reluctantly agreed to abolish serfdom and proclaim equality under the law. On 15 March, a group calling itself the Youth of March led by the poet Sándor Petőfi took to the streets to press for even more radical reforms and revolution. Habsburg patience was wearing very thin.

In September, the Habsburg forces under the governor of Croatia, Josip Jelačić, launched an attack on Hungary and Batthyány's government was dissolved. The Hungarians hastily formed a national defence commission and moved the government seat to Debrecen, where Kossuth was elected leader. In April 1849, the parliament declared Hungary's full independence and the 'dethronement' of the Habsburgs for the second time.

The new Habsburg emperor, Franz Joseph (1848-1916), was nothing like his feeble-minded predecessor Ferdinand V and quickly took action. He sought the assistance of Russian Tsar Nicholas I, who obliged with 200,000 troops. Support for the revolution was already crumbling, however, particularly in areas of mixed population where the Magyars were seen as oppressors. Weak and vastly outnumbered, the rebel troops had been defeated by the summer of 1849.

A series of brutal reprisals ensued. Batthyány and 13 of his generals were executed (the so-called Martyrs of Arad), and Kossuth went into exile in Turkey. (Petőfi had been killed in battle.) Habsburg troops then went around the country systematically blowing up castles and fortifications lest they be used by resurgent rebels. What little of medieval Hungary that was left after the Turks and the 1703-11 War of Independence was now reduced to rubble.

Hungary was again merged into the Habsburg Empire as a conquered province and 'neo-absolutism' was the order of the day. Passive resistance among Hungarians and disastrous military defeats for the Habsburgs in 1859 and 1865, however, pushed Franz Joseph to the negotiating table with liberal Hungarians under Deák's leadership.

The result was the Compromise of 1867 (*Ausgleich* in German, which actually means 'balance' or 'reconciliation'), which created the Dual Monarchy of Austria (the empire) and Hungary (the kingdom). It was a federated state of two parliaments and two capitals – Vienna and Budapest (the city that would be incorporated six years later when Buda, Pest and Óbuda united). Only defence, foreign relations and customs were shared. Hungary was even allowed to raise a small army.

This 'Age of Dualism' would carry on until 1918 and would spark an economic, cultural and intellectual rebirth in Hungary.

HUNGARY BEFORE THE 1920 TRIANON TREATY

Agriculture developed, factories were established and the composers Franz (Ferenc) Liszt and Ferenc Erkel made beautiful music. The middle class, dominated by Germans and Jews in Pest, burgeoned, and the capital entered into a frenzy of building. Much of what you see in Budapest today – from the grand boulevards and their eclectic-style apartment blocks to the Parliament building and Matthias Church in the Castle District – was built at this time. The apex of this golden age was the six-month exhibition in 1896 celebrating the millennium of the Magyar conquest (*honfoglalás*) of the Carpathian Basin.

But all was not well in the kingdom. The city-based working class had almost no rights, and the situation in the countryside had remained as dire as it was in the Middle Ages. Minorities under Hungarian control – Czechs, Slovaks, Croatians and Romanians – were under increased pressure to 'Magyarise' and viewed their new rulers as oppressors. Increasingly they worked to dismember the empire.

WWI, the Republic of Councils & Trianon

In July 1914, a month to the day after the assassination of Archduke Franz Ferdinand, the heir to the Habsburg throne, by a Bosnian Serb in Sarajevo, the Dual Monarchy entered WWI allied with the German Empire. The result was disastrous, with heavy destruction and hundreds of thousands killed on the Russian and Italian fronts. At the armistice in 1918 the fate of the Dual Monarchy (and Hungary as a multinational kingdom) was sealed.

A republic under the leadership of Count Mihály Károlyi was set up immediately after the war, and the Habsburg monarchy was dethroned for the third and final time. But the fledgling republic would not last long. Widespread destitution, the occupation of Hungary by the Allies, and the success of the Bolshevik Revolution in Russia had radicalised much of the Budapest working class. In March 1919 a group of Hungarian communists under Béla Kun seized power. The so-called Republic of Councils (*Tanácsköztársaság*) set out to nationalise industry and private property and build a fairer society, but mass opposition to the regime unleashed a reign of 'red terror'. Kun and his comrades were overthrown in just five months by Romanian troops, who occupied the capital.

In 1920, the Allies drew up a postwar settlement under the Treaty of Trianon that enlarged some countries, truncated others and created several 'successor states'. As one of the defeated enemy nations and with large numbers of minorities clamouring for independence within its borders, Hungary stood to lose more than most, and it did. The nation was reduced to one-third its historical size and, while it was now largely a uniform, homogeneous nation-state, for millions of ethnic Hungarians in Romania, Yugoslavia and Czechoslovakia, the tables had turned: they were now the minorities.

'Trianon' became the singularly most hated word in Hungary, and the *diktátum* is often reviled today as if it were imposed on the nation just yesterday. Many of the problems it created remain to this day, and it has coloured Hungary's relations with its neighbours for four score years.

The Horthy Years & WWII

In Hungary's first-ever secret-ballot election (1920), parliament chose a kingdom as the form of state and – lacking a king – elected Admiral Miklós Horthy as its regent, who would remain so until the latter days of WWII. The arrangement confused even US President Franklin D Roosevelt in the early days of the war. After being briefed by an aide on the government and leadership of Hungary, he reportedly said: 'Let me see if I understand you right: Hungary is a kingdom without a king run by a regent who's an admiral without a navy?'

Horthy embarked on a 'white terror' – every bit as brutal as the red one of Béla Kun – that attacked communists and Jews for their roles in supporting the Republic of Councils. As the regime was consolidated, it showed itself to be extremely rightist and conservative, advocating the status quo and 'traditional values' – family, state, religion.

Though the country had the remnants of a parliamentary system, Horthy was all-powerful, and very few reforms were enacted. On the contrary, the lot of the working class and the peasantry worsened.

One thing everyone agreed on was that the return of the 'lost' territories was essential for Hungary's development. Early on, Prime Minister István Bethlen was able to secure the return of Pécs, illegally occupied by Yugoslavia, and the citizens of Sopron voted in a plebiscite to return to Hungary from Austria, but that was not enough. Hungary obviously could not count on the victors – France, Britain and the USA – to help recoup its land; instead, it sought help from the fascist governments of Germany and Italy. Hungary's move to the right intensified throughout the 1930s, though it remained silent when WWII broke out in September 1939.

Horthy hoped an alliance would not mean actually having to enter the war, but after recovering northern Transylvania and part of Croatia with Germany's assistance, he was forced to join the Axis in June 1941. The war was as disastrous for Hungary as the 1914-18 one had been, and hundreds of thousands of Hungarian troops died while retreating from Stalingrad, where they'd been used as cannon fodder. Realising too late that his country was again on the losing side, Horthy began negotiating a separate peace with the Allies.

The result was the total occupation of Hungary by the German army in March 1944. Under pressure, Horthy installed Ferenc Szálasi, the deranged leader of the pro-Nazi Arrow Cross Party, and was deported to Germany. (Horthy would later find exile in Portugal, where he died in 1957. Despite some public outcry, his body was returned to Hungary in September 1993 and reburied in the family plot at Kenderes, east of Szolnok.)

The Arrow Cross moved quickly to quash any opposition, and thousands of liberal politicians and labour leaders were arrested. At the same time, its puppet government introduced anti-Jewish legislation similar to that in Germany, and Jews, relatively safe under Horthy, were rounded up into ghettos by Hungarian Nazis. In the summer of 1944, less than a year before the war's end, some 400,000 Jewish men, women and children were deported to Auschwitz and other labour camps, where they were savagely murdered, starved or succumbed to disease.

Hungary now became an international battleground for the first time since the Turkish occupation, and bombs began falling on Budapest. The resistance movement drew support from many sides, including the communists. Fierce fighting continued in the countryside, especially near Debrecen and Székesfehérvár, but by Christmas 1944 the Soviet army had surrounded Budapest. When the Germans and Hungarian Nazis rejected a settlement, the siege of the capital began. By the time the German war machine had surrendered in April 1945, many of Budapest's homes, historical buildings and churches had been destroyed. The vindictive Germans even blew up every bridge spanning the Danube in the capital while retreating.

The People's Republic

When free elections were held in November 1945, the Independent Smallholders Party received 57% of the vote. But Soviet political officers, backed by the occupying Soviet army, forced three other parties – including the Social Democrats and Communists – into a coalition. Limited democracy prevailed, and land-reform laws, sponsored by the communist minister of agriculture, Imre Nagy, were enacted, wiping away the prewar feudal structure.

Within a couple of years, the Communists were ready to take complete control. After a rigged election held under a complicated new electoral law in 1947, they declared their candidate, Mátyás Rákosi, victorious. The Social Democrats were forced to merge with the Communists into the Hungarian Socialist Workers Party.

Rákosi, a big fan of Stalin, began a process of nationalisation and unfeasibly fast industrialisation at the expense of agriculture. Peasants were forced into collective farms, and all produce had to be delivered to state warehouses. A network of spies and informers exposed 'class enemies' (such as Cardinal József Mindszenty) to the secret police (the ÁVO or ÁVH after 1949), who had them jailed for spying, sent into internal exile or condemned to labour camps like the notorious one at Recsk in the Mátra Hills. It is estimated that during this period a quarter of the adult population faced police or judicial proceedings.

Bitter feuding within the party began, and purges and Stalinesque show trials became the norm. László Rajk, the Communist minister of the interior (which also controlled the ÁVO) was executed for 'Titoism'; his successor János Kádár was tortured and jailed. In August 1949, the nation was proclaimed the 'People's Republic of Hungary'.

Following the death of Stalin in March 1953 and Krushchev's denunciation of him three years later, Rákosi's tenure was up and the terror began to abate. Under pressure from within the party, Rákosi's successor, Ernő Gerő, rehabilitated Rajk posthumously and readmitted Nagy, who had been expelled from the party a year earlier for suggesting reforms. But Gerő was ultimately as much a hardliner as Rákosi had been, and by October 1956 during Rajk's reburial, murmured calls for a real reform of the system – 'Communism with a human face' – could already be heard.

The 1956 Uprising

The nation's greatest tragedy – an event that for a while shook the world, rocked Communism and pitted Hungarian against Hungarian – began on 23 October when some 50,000 university students assembled at Bem tér in Buda, shouting anti-Soviet slogans and demanding that Nagy be named prime minister. That night a crowd pulled down the colossal statue of Stalin near Heroes' Square and shots were fired by ÁVH agents on another group gathering outside the headquarters of Hungarian Radio in Pest. Hungary was in revolution.

Two days later Nagy formed a government (which included János Kádár), and for a short time it appeared that he might be successful in transforming Hungary into a neutral, multiparty state. But on 1 November Soviet tanks and troops crossed into Hungary and within 72 hours began attacking Budapest and other centres. Kádár, who had slipped away from Budapest to join the Russian invaders, was installed as leader.

Fierce street fighting continued for several days – encouraged by Radio Free Europe broadcasts and disingenuous promises of support from the West, which was embroiled in the Suez Canal crisis in any case. When the fighting was over, 25,000 people were dead. Then the reprisals – the worst in Hungarian history – began. An estimated 20,000 people were arrested and 2000 – including Nagy and his associates – were executed. Another 250,000 refugees fled to Austria. The government lost what little credibility it had enjoyed and the nation some of its most competent and talented citizens. As for the physical scars, look around you at almost any building in Pest: the bullet holes and shrapnel scorings on the exterior walls still cry out in silent fury.

Hungary under Kádár

The transformation of János Kádár from traitor and most hated man in the land to respected reformer is one of the most astonishing *tours de force* of the 20th century. No doubt it will keep generations of historians busy well into the future.

After the reprisals and the consolidation of his regime, Kádár began a program to liberalise the social and economic structure based on compromise. (His most quoted line is 'Whoever is not against us is with us' – ɔ reversal of the Stalinist adage that 'Those not with us are against us'.) In 1968, he and the economist Rezső Nyers unveiled the New Economic Mechanism (NEM) to introduce elements of a market to the planned economy. But even this proved too daring for many party conservatives. Nyers was ousted and the NEM whittled away.

Kádár managed to survive that power struggle and went on to introduce greater consumerism and market socialism. By the mid-1970s Hungary was light years ahead of any other Soviet bloc country in its standard of living, freedom of movement

Rubik Cubes, Vitamin C & Zsa Zsa

'It is not enough to be Hungarian – one must also have talent.'

Slogan spotted in a Toronto employment office in the early 1960s

The contributions made by Hungarians to any number of fields – from films and toys to science and fine art – both at home and abroad have been enormous, especially when you consider the nation's relatively small population. The following is a list of people whom you may not have known were Hungarian or of Hungarian ancestry:

Brassaï (born Halász Gyula; 1899-1984). French poet, draftsman, sculptor and photographer, known for his dramatic photographs of Paris at night.

Capa, Robert (Friedmann Endre; 1913-54). One of the greatest war photographers and photojournalists of the 20th century.

Cukor, George (1899-1983). Legendary American film producer/director (*The Philadelphia Story*).

Curtis, Tony (Bernard Schwartz; 1925-). Evergreen American actor (*Spartacus*).

Eszterhas, Joe (1944-). American scriptwriter (*Basic Instinct*).

Gabor, Eva (1921-95). American actress chiefly remembered for her starring role as a New York City socialite making her comical life on a farm in the 1960s TV series *Green Acres*; younger sister of Zsa Zsa.

Gabor, Zsa Zsa (?-). Ageless-ish American starlet of grade BBB films and older sister of Eva.

Houdini, Harry (Weisz Erich; 1874-1926). American magician and celebrated escape artist.

Lauder, Estée (1910?-). American fragrance and cosmetics baroness.

Liszt, Franz (Liszt Ferenc; 1811-86). Piano virtuoso and composer.

Lugosi, Béla (Blasko Béla; 1884-1956). The film world's only true Dracula, and Minister of Culture under the Béla Kun regime (see the History section).

Rubik, Ernő (1944-). Inventor of the hottest toy of the 1980 Christmas season – an infuriating plastic cube with 54 small squares that when twisted out of its original arrangement has 43 quintillion variations.

Soros, George (Soros György; 1930-). Billionaire financier and philanthropist.

Szent-Györgyi, Dr Albert (1893-1986). Nobel Prize-winning biochemist who discovered vitamin C.

Vasarely, Victor (Vásárhelyi Győző; 1908-97). French painter of geometric abstractions and father of the op art movement.

Wilder, Billy (Wilder Samuel; 1906-). American film director and producer (*Some Like It Hot*).

and opportunities to criticise the government. People may have had to wait seven years for a Lada car or 12 for a telephone, but most Hungarians could at least enjoy access to a second house in the countryside and a decent material life. The 'Hungarian model' attracted much Western attention – and investment.

But things began to sour in the 1980s. The Kádár system of 'goulash socialism', which had seemed 'timeless and everlasting' as one Hungarian writer has put it, was incapable of dealing with such 'unsocialist' problems as unemployment, soaring inflation and the largest per-capita foreign debt in the region. Kádár and the 'old guard' refused to hear talk about party reforms and the government was dismissed in May 1988.

Renewal & Change

Three reformers – Nyers, Károly Grósz and Imre Pozsgay – took control. Party conservatives at first put a lid on real change by demanding a retreat from political liberalisation in exchange for their support of the new regime's economic policies. But the tide had already turned. Throughout the summer and autumn of 1988, new political parties were formed and old ones revived. In February 1989 Pozsgay, seeing the handwriting on the wall as Mikhail Gorbachev kissed babies and launched his reforms in the Soviet Union, announced that the events of 1956 had been a 'popular uprising', not the 'counter-revolution' that the regime had always said it was. Four months later hundreds of thousands of people attended the reburial of Imre Nagy and other victims of 1956 in Budapest.

In September 1989, again at Pozsgay's instigation, Hungary cut away the electrified wire fence separating it from Austria. The move released a wave of East Germans holidaying in Hungary into the West and the opening attracted thousands more. The collapse of the communist regimes around the region was now unstoppable. What Hungarians now call *az átkos 40 év* ('the accursed 40 years') had come to a withering, almost feeble, end.

The Republic of Hungary Again

In October 1989, on the 33rd anniversary of the 1956 Uprising, the nation once again became the Republic of Hungary. At their party congress the Communists surrendered their monopoly on power, paving the way for free elections in March 1990. The party's name was changed from the Hungarian Socialist Workers' Party to the Hungarian Socialist Party (MSZP).

The MSZP's new program advocated social democracy and a free market economy, but this was not enough to shake off the stigma of its four decades of autocratic rule. The 1990 vote was won by the centrist Hungarian Democratic Forum (MDF), which advocated a gradual transition to capitalism. The social-democratic Alliance of Free Democrats (SZDSZ), which had called for much faster change, came second and the Socialists trailed far behind. As Gorbachev looked on, Hungary changed political systems with scarcely a murmur and the last Soviet troops left Hungary in June 1991.

In coalition with two smaller parties – the Independent Smallholders (FKgP) and the Christian Democrats (KDNP) – the MDF provided Hungary with sound government during its painful transition to a full market economy. Those years saw Hungary's northern (Czechoslovakia) and southern neighbours (Yugoslavia) split apart along ethnic lines. Prime Minister József Antall did little to improve relations with Slovakia, Romania and Yugoslavia by claiming to be the 'emotional and spiritual' prime minister of the large Hungarian minorities in those countries. In mid-1993 the MDF was forced to expel István Csurka, a party vice president, after he made ultranationalistic and anti-Semitic statements that tarnished Hungary's image as a bastion of moderation and stability in a volatile region. Antall died after a long fight with cancer in December 1993 and was replaced by Interior Minister Péter Boross.

Despite initial successes in curbing inflation and lowering interest rates, a host of economic problems slowed the pace of development, and the government's laissez-faire policies did not help. But like most people in the region, Hungarians had unrealistically expected a much faster improvement in their living standards. Most of them – 76% according to a poll in mid-1993 – were 'very disappointed'.

In the elections of May 1994 the Socialist Party, led by Gyula Horn, won an absolute majority in parliament. This in no way implied a return to the past, and Horn was quick to point out that it was in fact his party that had initiated the whole reform process in the first place. (As foreign minister in 1989 Horn had played a key role in opening the border with Austria.) Árpád Göncz of the SZDSZ was elected for a second five-year term as president of the republic in 1995.

After its dire showing in the 1994 elections, the Federation of Young Democrats (FIDESZ), which until 1993 limited membership to those aged under 35 in order to emphasise a past untainted by Communism, privilege and corruption, moved to the right and added the extension 'MPP'

(Hungarian Civic Party) to its name to attract the support of the burgeoning middle class. The Socialist government's renewed support of the Nagymáros project on the Danube (see the boxed text 'The Antediluvian Dam' in the Danube Bend chapter) caused an outcry, something FIDESZ-MPP leader Viktor Orbán milked for everything it was worth.

In the May 1998 parliamentary elections, FIDESZ-MPP won 148 of the 386 seats. Against the wishes of many supporters, it quickly entered into a coalition with the very conservative Independent Smallholders Party (FKgP) and the Hungarian Democratic Forum (MDF) to form a government. Orbán was named prime minister and remains so – but from the looks of it just. He engages in an almost daily squaring off with the FKgP's wily leader, József Torgyán, and is regularly outmanoeuvred, much to the amusement – or despair – of most Hungarians.

GEOGRAPHY

Hungary lies in the Carpathian Basin and almost in the centre of Europe. It shares borders with seven countries: Austria, Slovakia, Ukraine, Romania, Yugoslavia, Croatia and Slovenia. The country covers just over 93,000 sq km.

There are three basic topographies: the low-lying regions of the Great Plain (Nagyföld) in the east, centre and southeast, and of the Little Plain (Kisalföld) in the north-west, which together account for two-thirds of Hungary's territory; the northern mountain ranges; and the hilly regions of Transdanubia in the west and south-west. The biggest rivers are the Tisza (598km in Hungary) and the Danube (417km), which divide the country into thirds; the Rába (190km) in the west and the Dráva (143km), forming the south-western border with Croatia. The country has well over 1000 lakes (of which the largest is by far the Balaton), and is riddled with thermal springs.

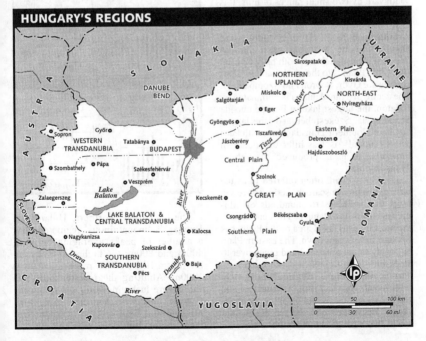

Main Regions

Hungary's topographical divisions do not accurately reflect the country's cultural and subtler geographical differences, nor do the 19 administrative counties (*megye*) help travellers much. Instead, Hungary can be divided into eight main regions: Budapest and its environs; the Danube Bend; Western Transdanubia; Lake Balaton and Central Transdanubia; Southern Transdanubia; the Great Plain; the Northern Uplands; and the North-East.

Greater Budapest, by far Hungary's largest city, with just under two million people, has for its borders Csepel Island in the Danube River to the south, the start of the Great Plain in the east, the Buda Hills to the west and the Danube Bend in the north. The Danube bisects the city, with flat Pest on the east side (or the left bank as you follow the flow of the river) and hilly Buda to the west.

The Danube Bend is the point at which the river, flowing east across Europe, is forced southward by two small ranges of hills. It is an area of great beauty and historical significance and its main city is Esztergom.

Transdanubia – the area 'across the Danube' to the west has great variety. Western Transdanubia is both hilly and flat (the Little Plain is to the north), and its chief centres are Győr, Sopron and Szombathely. The centre of Transdanubia is dominated by Balaton, the largest lake in Europe outside Scandinavia. Székesfehérvár is the largest city here. Southern Transdanubia, with Pécs as its 'capital', is less hilly but richer in minerals. Wine is produced throughout Transdanubia.

The Great Plain, often referred to as the *puszta*, is a prairie scarcely 200m above sea level that stretches for hundreds of kilometres east of the Danube. The central part, the most industrialised area of the Plain, has Szolnok as its major town. The Eastern Plain is largely saline grassland and given over to stock-breeding; Debrecen is the main seat. The Southern Plain is agriculturally rich, with cereal crops and fruit in abundance and the occasional farmstead breaking the monotony. Kecskemét and Szeged are market towns that have grown into cities.

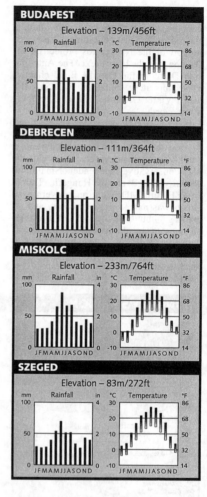

The so-called Northern Uplands is Hungary's 'mountainous' region and has a number of peaks averaging between 400m and 800m; the highest is Kékes in the Mátra Hills, which reaches just over 1000m. Abutting the forested hills and valleys are lush vineyards and sprawling factories, many of them now in decline. Miskolc and Eger are the Northern Uplands' main cities.

North-East Hungary is much lower than the Northern Uplands but not quite as flat as the Great Plain. It is a fruit-growing region and ethnically quite heterogeneous, with the bulk of the nation's Roma population living here. Nyíregyháza is the main centre.

CLIMATE

Hungary has a temperate climate with three climatic zones: Mediterranean in the south, Continental in the east and Atlantic in the country's west.

In Southern Transdanubia, spring arrives early and its famous Indian summers can stretch into early November. Winters are mild and wet.

The Great Plain has the most extreme seasonal differences, with very cold, windy winters and hot, usually dry summers (though sudden storms are a common occurrence on the Plain in summer). The climate of the Northern Uplands is also Continental, but it gets more sun in autumn and winter than any other part of Hungary.

Spring arrives in early April in Budapest and Western Transdanubia and usually ends in showers. Summers can be very hot and humid (especially in the capital). It rains most of November and doesn't usually get cold until mid-December. Winters are relatively short, often cloudy and damp but sometimes brilliantly sunny. What little snow this area gets tends to disappear after a few days.

The climate charts on these pages show you what to expect and when to expect it. For information on specific weather conditions nationwide, ring the national weather forecast service from 8 am to 8 pm daily on ☎ 1-212 2070 or check its Web site at www.met.hu.

ECOLOGY & ENVIRONMENT

Pollution is a large and costly problem in Hungary. Low-grade coal that continues to fuel some industry and heat homes creates sulphur dioxide and acid rain that threatens the forests of the Northern Uplands.

Automobiles manufactured in the former Soviet bloc, especially the two-stroke East German Trabants still commonly seen

Cyanide Spill

The greatest threat to Hungary's environment in recent years came shortly after the start of the new century. A reservoir containing water contaminated with cyanide at a gold mine near Baia Mare in north-western Romania overflowed its banks and spilled into the Someş (Szamos in Hungarian) River. Within days cyanide levels in the Tisza, into which the Szamos flows, were 700 times above acceptable levels, poisoning the drinking water of some two million people and causing ecological havoc.

Less than a month after the mishap some 300 tonnes of dead fish had been collected and, while the cyanide was believed to have been diluted once the Tisza joined the much wider Danube near Novi Sad in Yugoslavia, it was feared that the entire food chain of the Hungarian Tisza had been destroyed. The World Wide Fund for Nature in Budapest said at the time that the Tisza would be affected for at least a decade. Other environmentalists have likened the devastation to that caused by the Chernobyl nuclear reactor meltdown of 1986.

across Hungary, have raised nitrogen oxide levels in some Hungarian cities to among the highest in Europe.

Waste created by the Soviet military, particularly buried toxic chemicals and routinely dumped jet fuel, threatens the soil, the ground-water supply, rivers and lakes. The over-use of nitrate fertilisers in agriculture has caused the ground water beneath the Plain and both Lake Balaton and the Little Balaton to become contaminated with phosphates.

Government funding for the environment has been increased and some work has been carried out in the cities worst hit, including Esztergom, Veszprém and Debrecen. Brown coal, once the nation's main energy source, now accounts for only one-third of energy production; the Soviet-designed nuclear power generator at Paks in Southern Transdanubia produces about one-third of the nation's electricity.

The Birds of Hungary

Grey heron

It may come as a surprise, but Hungary has some of the best bird-watching areas in Europe. Indeed, some 373 of the continent's estimated 395 species have been sighted in Hungary. The country's indigenous populations of great white egrets, spoonbills and red-footed falcons, as well as endangered imperial eagles, white-tailed eagles, corncrakes, aquatic warblers, saker falcons and great bustards are among the most important in Europe. The arrival of the storks in the Northern Uplands and the North-East in spring is a wonderful sight to behold.

The best areas for bird-watching overall are the Hortobágy region, Lake Fertö, the Vertés Hills, Aggtelek, the Little Balaton (Kis-Balaton) and Lake Tisza, but the Pilis and Buda Hills and even small lakes like the ones at Tata and Feher-tó north of Szeged and the Kiskunság salt lakes attract a wide variety of bird life. Spring and autumn are always good seasons for passage sightings, but the best month overall is May.

First of all you should try to get a copy of one of Gerard Gorman's books on the birds of Hungary or at least Eastern Europe, which include *Where to Watch Birds in Eastern Europe* and *The Birds of Hungary*.

The Hungarian Ornithological Society (MME; ☎ 1-395 2605) at XII Költő utca 21 in Budapest may be able to help with general information. A Debrecen-based company called Aquila Nature Tours offers day and week-long bird-watching tours led by ornithologists in and around the Hortobágy (see the Hortobagy section in the Great Plain chapter for details).

Another group offering tours of between three and nine hours in the Hortobágy, Bükk Hills and at Lake Tisza is the Great Bustard Protection Centre (☎/fax 36-441 020, imrefater@externet.hu) at the Fauna Hotel in Besenyőtelek, some 30km north-west of Tiszafüred.

For bird-watching around Lake Fertő, contact Balázs Molnár (☎ 99-355 718, fax 99-334942) at Fő utca 91 in Fertőrákos.

White stork

FLORA

Hungary is home to more than two thousand flowering plant species, many of which are not normally found in regions at this latitude.

A lot of the flora in the Villány Hills of Southern Transdanubia, for example, is usually seen only around the Mediterranean, and the salty Hortobágy region on the Eastern Plain hosts many plants normally found by the seashore. The Gemenc Forest on the Danube near Szekszárd, the Little Balaton in the centre of Transdanubia and the Tisza River backwater east of Kecskemét, are all important wetlands. Most of the trees in the nation's forests are beech, oak and birch, with only a small percentage being fir.

The Birds of Hungary

Hortobágy This area of grassy, saline steppe, fish ponds and marshes on the Great Plain is one of the best bird areas of Europe, with some 334 species sighted, including resident bustards and aquatic warblers. On a recent 10-day springtime tour ornithologists spotted a total of 189 species! Any time of year is good, but September/October is when to spot saker falcons, long-legged buzzards, imperial eagles, cranes and geese. The Hortobágy fishponds are home to four species of grebes and eight species of herons as well as several varieties of terns.

Lake Fertő Some 210 nesting and migrant species have been registered at Fertő-Hanság National Park, which includes the southern end of shallow, saline Lake Fertő, near the Austrian border in Western Transdanubia. April to June sees the most activity in the lake's reedbeds, August the arrival of white and grey storks, and autumn is the best time to sight grey and bean geese and spoonbills.

Vertés Hills This low range of wooded limestone hills west of Budapest, which make up the Vertés Landscape Protection Reserve, supports an incredible variety of woodpeckers and flycatchers (May to July) and in the winter hosts imperial eagles and red-backed and great grey shrikes.

Aggtelek The hilly karst region of Aggtelek is a breeding ground for the strictly protected hazel grouse and black storks, as well as corncrakes and honey buzzards. The best time to visit is April to August though winter attracts resident Ural owls, rock buntings and various woodpeckers.

Great spotted woodpecker

Little Balaton The Kis Balaton, a vast wetland made up of both impenetrable reed-choked ponds and a reservoir created in 1984, is home to about 100 breeding species. The best place to view egrets, spoonbills, terns and warblers is from tiny Kányavári Island. The best time to come is between April and August when tens of thousands of birds stop here on passage.

Lake Tisza The northern third of this vast manmade lake, the area just east of Poroszló, is a bird reserve under the jurisdiction of Hortobágy National Park. The reedbeds and riverine forests along the Tisza River attract large numbers of black-headed gulls, purple herons, little bitterns, great white egrets, cormorants and black kites. Any time is good at Lake Tisza but May and June are best for breeders and August and September for passage birds.

FAUNA

There are a lot of common European animals here (deer, wild hare, boar, otter, wolves) as well as some rare species (wild cat, lake bat, Pannonian lizard). But three-quarters of the country's 450 vertebrates are birds, especially waterfowl, attracted by the rivers, lakes and wetlands. Parts of the Great Plain and the Northern Uplands are important nesting or migratory areas for hundreds of bird species; see 'The Birds of Hungary' boxed text.

NATIONAL PARKS

There are nine national parks in Hungary. The three on the Great Plain – Hortobágy, Kiskunság and Körös-Maros – protect the wildlife and the fragile wetlands, marsh

The wild boar is common to the Gemenc Forest.

and saline grasslands of the puszta. There are two more in the Northern Uplands: the almost completely wooded Bükk Hills and the Aggtelek region with its extensive system of karst caves and streams hewn into the limestone. Other national parks include Danube-Dráva National Park in Southern Transdanubia, which incorporates the Gemenc Forest; Lake Balaton and its surrounding areas; the Danube-Ipoly National Park on the Danube Bend; and Fertő-Hanság, the nation's smallest national park, at Lake Fertő, which Hungarians share with Austrians (who call it Neusiedlersee).

GOVERNMENT & POLITICS

Hungary's 1989 constitution provides for a parliamentary system of government. The unicameral assembly consists of 386 members chosen for four years in a complex, two-round system that balances direct and proportional representation. The head of state, the president, is elected by the house for five years. The prime minister is head of government.

Hungary has six parties represented in parliament: FIDESZ-MPP (148 seats), the MSZP (134), FKgP (48), the SZDSZ (24), the MDF (17) and MIÉP (13) as well as two independent ones. The Christian Democrats (KDNP) currently have no representation in parliament.

ADMINISTRATIVE COUNTIES

The political party in charge of the ruling coalition at present is – in theory – FIDESZ-MPP (see Republic of Hungary Again in the previous History section). The party furthest to the left is the MSZP, the opposition Hungarian Socialist Party. The most right-wing is the conservative and nationalist MIÉP (Hungarian Party for Justice and Life) led by the controversial István Csurka.

In foreign policy, Hungary has taken a more assertive role in recent years as it looks to full integration into Western Europe. It became a fully fledged member of NATO in March 1999, and the government is expected to increase defence spending by some 45% in the first year of the new millennium as it upgrades its military to meet NATO standards.

ECONOMY

Hungary, with the most developed economy in Central Europe, is on the fast-track to EU membership. Political parties are united in ensuring that the country meets economic targets to enable it to join the EU by 2004.

Memories of the transition from a state-controlled economy to market-driven capitalism have dimmed as inflation and unemployment levels approach those of Western Europe. Hungary's 4% growth in gross domestic product is among the highest in Europe as consumers increase purchases of household appliances, cars and television sets made in the country. By comparison, the average growth rate in the EU was 2.2% in 1999.

Hungary's poor endowment of natural resources has proved a blessing, as it means the country isn't saddled with the number of rusting industrial plants processing iron or coal that still plague Poland and neighbouring Slovakia. Instead, manufacturing and brainpower have led to jobs that have reduced unemployment to about 9% and inflation to just over 10% (from 31% in 1995). Over the next few years, inflation is targeted to fall to about 6%.

Economic growth has been driven by foreign exporters like Royal Philips Electronics,

Europe's largest producer of consumer electronics products, and automobile manufacturer General Motors, both of which have factories in the country. They've helped pump about $21 billion in foreign direct investment into the country since 1989, the highest level of foreign money of all the former communist countries.

POPULATION & PEOPLE

When the Italian-American Nobel Prize-winning physicist Enrico Fermi (1901-54) was asked whether he believed extraterrestrial beings existed, he replied: 'Of course they do and they are already here among us. They are called Hungarians'. Dr Fermi was, of course, referring to the Magyars, an Asiatic people of obscure origins who do not speak an Indo-European language and make up the vast majority of Hungary's 10.1 million people. Almost five million Magyars live outside the national borders, mostly as a result of the Trianon Treaty, WWII and the 1956 Uprising. The estimated two million Hungarians in Transylvania (now Romanian) constitute the largest ethnic minority in Europe, and there are another 600,000 in Slovakia, 650,000 in Yugoslavia and Croatia, 200,000 in Ukraine and 70,000 in Austria. Immigrants to the USA, Canada, Australia and Israel add up to over one million people.

Though Hungary is a very homogeneous country, several non-Magyar minorities make their home here. The largest group is the Roma, who number between 150,000 and a quarter of a million people. Much smaller groups include Germans (0.3%), Slovaks (0.1%) and Croatians and Serbs (0.1%). The number of Romanians in Hungary is officially put at about 25,000, but the real total is almost certainly higher.

Life expectancy in Hungary is very low by European standards: 65 years for men, 74 for women. The nation also has one of Europe's lowest rates of natural population increase: -3.2 per 1000 population. Sadly, it also claims the dubious distinction of having the highest suicide rate in the world (see the boxed text 'A Dubious Distinction' in the Great Plain chapter).

EDUCATION

Hungary is a well educated society with a literacy rate of about 98%. School is compulsory for children aged six to 16.

The education system generally follows the German model. Primary or elementary school (*általános iskola*) is followed by four years of secondary education, which can either be in grammar (*gimnázium*) or vocational/trade schools (*szakiskola*). About 30% of those aged over 18 have secondary-school certificates. College and university matriculation is very competitive – places are few and entrance requirements pretty stiff. Still, about 10% of the population hold university degrees, a quarter of which are in engineering and economics.

Hungary has an international reputation in certain areas of specialised education. A unique method of music education devised by the composer Zoltán Kodály (1882-1967) is widespread. The Pető Institute in Budapest has a very high success rate in teaching children with cerebral palsy to walk.

SCIENCE

Hungarians have made great contributions to the sciences and related fields. Albert Szent-Györgyi won the Nobel Prize for Medicine or Physiology in 1937 for his discovery of vitamin C, Georg von Békésy the same prize in 1961 for his research on the inner ear and Eugene Paul Wigner received his Nobel Prize in 1963 for his research in nuclear physics. Both Edward Teller and Leo Szilard worked on the so-called Manhattan Project, which led to the development of the atomic bomb, under Enrico Fermi, who may have drawn his conclusions about the origins of the Magyars at this time (see the previous Population & People section).

ARTS

Hungarian art has been both stunted and spurred on by the pivotal events in the nation's history. King Stephen's conversion to Catholicism brought Romanesque and Gothic art and architecture to Hungary, while the Turkish occupation nipped most of Hungary's Renaissance in the bud. The Habsburgs opened the doors to baroque influences. The arts thrived under the Dual Monarchy, then through truncation and even under fascism. The early days of Communism brought the art celebrating wheat sheaves and muscle-bound steelworkers to a less-than-impressed populace, but much money was spent on music and 'correct art' like classical theatre.

Music & Dance

Hungary has made many contributions to the music world, but one person stands head and shoulders above all: Franz – or Ferenc – Liszt. Liszt (1811-86), who established the Academy of Music in Budapest, liked to describe himself as 'part Gypsy', and some of his works, notably *Hungarian Rhapsodies*, echo traditional Roma music.

Ferenc Erkel (1810-93) is the father of Hungarian opera and two of his works – the stirringly nationalistic *Bánk Bán*, based on József Katona's play, and *László Hunyadi* – are standards at the State Opera House in Budapest. Erkel also composed the music for the Hungarian national anthem.

Imre Kálmán (1882-1953) was Hungary's most celebrated composer of operettas. *The Queen of the Csárdás* is his most popular – and campiest – work.

Béla Bartók (1881-1945) and Zoltán Kodály (1882-1967) made the first systematic study of Hungarian folk music together, travelling and recording throughout the Magyar linguistic region in 1906. Both integrated some of their findings into their own compositions – Bartók in *Bluebeard's Castle*, for example, and Kodály in his *Peacock Variations*.

It is important to distinguish between 'Gypsy music' and real Hungarian folk music. Gypsy music as it is known and played in Hungarian restaurants, from Budapest to Boston, is urban schmaltz and based on recruiting tunes called *verbunkos* played during the Rákóczi independence war. At least two fiddles, a bass and a cymbalom (a curious stringed instrument played with sticks) are *de rigueur*; if you want to hear this saccharine czardas music, almost

Taking the waters at Széchenyi Bath, Pest.

Vorsmarty tér, Pest.

Pest's City Park hosts international speed skating each winter.

Lehel tér market, Pest.

It's standing room only at Capella's drag shows, Pest.

DAVID GREEDY

KIMBERLY GRANT

DAVID GREEDY

STEVE FALLON

DAVID GREEDY

The transport options in Moszkva tér, Buda.

Széchenyi Bridge prepares for the night.

Parliament - from Fisherman's Bastion.

Béla Kun continues to lead the charge on Budapest in Statue Park.

any hotel restaurant in the land can oblige, or you can buy a tape or CD by Sándor Lakatos or his son Déki.

To confuse matters even further, real Roma music does not use instruments but is sung as a cappella (though sometimes it is backed with guitar and percussion); a very good tape of Hungarian Roma folk songs is *Magyarországi Cigány Népdalok*, produced by Hungaroton. The best modern Roma group is Kalyi Jag (Black Fire), led by Gusztav Várga, which comes from the North-East. The group plays all sorts of unconventional instruments and gives performances from time to time at Budapest *táncházak* (dance houses).

Hungarian folk musicians play violins, zithers, hurdy-gurdies, bagpipes and lutes on a five-note scale. There are lots of different groups but ones to watch out for are Méta and Muzsikás (especially when Marta Sebestyén sings). Anyone playing the haunting music of the Csángó region in eastern Transylvania is also a good bet. The Csángó Festival of folk dancing and music in Jászberény in late July attracts aficionados from all over.

Traditional Yiddish music is less known than Gypsy and Roma music but is of similar origin, having once been closely associated with Central European folk music. Until WWI so-called *klezmer* dance bands were led by the violin and cymbalom, but the influence of Yiddish theatre and the first wax recordings inspired a switch to the clarinet, which is the predominant instrument today. Klezmer music is currently going through a great renaissance both in Budapest and abroad.

Hungary has ballet companies based in Budapest, Pécs and Szeged but the best by far is the Győr Ballet. Groups like the State Folk Ensemble perform dances essentially for tourists throughout the year; visit a táncház if you prefer authentic folk dance and not touristy two-stepping.

There are many symphony orchestras both in the capital and provincial cities. Among the best are the Budapest Festival Orchestra and the Hungarian Radio & Television Orchestra.

Literature

No-one could have put it better than the poet Gyula Illyés (1902-83): 'The Hungarian language,' he wrote, 'is at one and the same time our softest cradle and our most solid coffin.'

The difficulty and subtlety of the Magyar tongue has excluded most outsiders from Hungarian literature and, though it would be wonderful to be able to read the swashbuckling odes and love poems of Bálint Balassi (1554-94) or Miklós Zrínyi's *Peril of Sziget* (1651) in the original, most people will have to make do with what they can find in English translation.

Sándor Petőfi (1823-49) is Hungary's most celebrated and accessible poet, and a line from his work *National Song* became the rallying cry for the 1848-49 War of Independence, in which Petőfi fought and died. A deeply philosophical play called *The Tragedy of Man* by Imre Madách (1823-64), published a decade after Hungary's defeat in the War of Independence, is still considered to be the country's greatest classical drama. It is available in English from the Corvinus publishing house.

The defeat in 1849 led many writers to look to Romanticism for inspiration and solace: heroes, winners, knights in shining armour. Petőfi's comrade-in-arms, János Arany (1817-82), whose name is synonymous with impeccable Hungarian, wrote epic poetry (*Toldi Trilogy*) and ballads.

Another friend of Petőfi, the prolific novelist Mór Jókai (1825-1904), wrote of heroism and honesty in such wonderful works as *The Man with the Golden Touch* and *Black Diamonds*. This 'Hungarian Dickens' still enjoys widespread popularity. Another perennial favourite, Kálmán Mikszáth (1847-1910), wrote satirical tales like *The Good Palóc People* and *St Peter's Umbrella* in which he poked fun at the declining gentry.

Zsigmond Móricz (1879-1942) was a very different type of writer. His works, very much in the tradition of the French naturalist Émile Zola (1840-1902), examined the harsh reality of peasant life in late-19th-century Hungary. Corvinus publishes his *Relations* in English. His contemporary, Mihály Babits (1883-1941), poet and the editor of the influential literary magazine *Nyugat* (West), made the rejuvenation of Hungarian literature his lifelong work.

Two 20th-century poets are unsurpassed in Hungarian letters. Endre Ady (1877-1919), who is sometimes described as a successor to Petőfi, was a reformer who ruthlessly attacked the complacency and materialism of Hungary at that time. The socialist Attila József (1905-1937) wrote of alienation and turmoil in a technological age; *By the Danube* is brilliant even in English translation (included in *Winter Night*, an anthology of his poems from Corvinus). József fell afoul of both the underground communist movement and the Horthy regime. Tragically, he threw himself under a train near Lake Balaton at the age of 32.

György Konrád (1933-), Péter Nádas (1942-) and Péter Esterházy (1950-) are three of Hungary's most important contemporary writers. Konrád's *A Feast in the Garden* (1985) is an almost autobiographical account of the fate of the Jewish community in a small eastern Hungarian town. *A Book of Memoirs* by Nádas concerns the decline of Communism in the style of Thomas Mann. In his *The End of a Family Story*, he uses a child narrator as a filter for the adult experience of 1950s communist Hungary. Eszterházy's *A Little Hungarian Pornography* is a difficult but enjoyable read.

Painting & Architecture

The abbey churches at Ják and Lébény are fine examples of Romanesque architecture, and there are important Gothic churches in Nyírbátor and Sopron. For Gothic paintings, have a look at the 15th-century altarpieces done by various masters at the Christian Museum in Esztergom. The Corpus Christi Chapel in the cathedral in Pécs and the Royal Palace at Visegrád contain fine examples of Renaissance stonework.

Baroque abounds in Hungary; you'll see architectural examples in virtually every town in the land. For something on a grand scale, visit the Esterházy Palace at Fertőd or the Minorite church in Eger. The ornately carved altars in the Minorite church at Nyírbátor and the Abbey Church in Tihany are baroque masterpieces. The greatest painters of this style were the 18th-century artists Anton Maulbertsch (Ascension Church frescoes at Sümeg) and István Dorffmeister (Bishop's Palace, Szombathely).

Distinctly Hungarian art and architecture didn't come into its own until the mid-19th century when Mihály Pollack, József Hild and Miklós Ybl were changing the face of Budapest or racing around the country building mansions and cathedrals. The Romantic Nationalist school of heroic paintings, best exemplified by Bertalan Székely (1835-1910) and Gyula Benczúr (1844-1920), gratefully gave way to the realism of Mihály Munkácsy (1844-1900), the painter of the puszta. But the greatest painters from this period were Kosztka Tivadar Csontváry (1853-1919) and József Rippl-Rónai (1861-1927), whose best works are on exhibit at their own museums in Pécs and Kaposvár, respectively. Favourite artists of the 20th century include Victor Vasarely (1908-97), the so-called father of op art, and the sculptor Amerigo Tot (1909-84).

The Romantic Eclectic style of Ödön Lechner (Budapest Museum of Applied Art) and Hungarian Art Nouveau (Reök Palace in Szeged) brought unique architecture to Hungary at the end of the 19th century and the start of the 20th. Fans of Art Nouveau will find in Hungary some of the best examples of that style outside Brussels, Nancy and Vienna.

Postwar architecture in Hungary is almost completely forgettable. One exception is the work of Imre Makovecz, who has developed his own 'organic' style (not always popular locally) using unusual materials like tree trunks and turf. His work is everywhere, but among the best (or strangest) examples are the cultural centres at Sárospatak and Szigetvár and the Lutheran church in Siófok.

Folk Art

Hungary has one of the richest folk traditions in Europe and, quite apart from its music, this is where the country often has

Water jug from the Great Plain

The main centre of cottage weaving has always been the Sárköz region in Southern Transdanubia – its distinctive black and red fabric is copied everywhere. Simpler homespun material can be found in the North-East, especially around the Tiszahát. Because of the abundance of reeds in these once marshy areas, the people here became skilled at cane weaving as well.

Three groups stand out for their embroidery, the pinnacle of Hungarian folk art: the Palóc people of the Northern Uplands, especially around the village of Hollókő; the Mátyó folk from Mezőkövesd; and the women of Kalocsa. The various differences and distinctions are discussed in the appropriate chapters, but to my mind no one works a needle like a Mátyó seamstress. The heavy woollen waterproof coats called *szűr*, once worn by herders on the Great Plain, were masterfully embroidered by men using thick, 'furry' yarn.

Folk pottery is world-class, and no Hungarian kitchen is complete without a couple of pairs of matched plates or shallow bowls hanging on the walls. The centre of this industry is the Great Plain – Hódmezővásárhely, Karcag and Tiszafüred, in particular – though fine examples also come from Transdanubia, especially from the Őrség region. There are jugs, pitchers, plates, bowls and cups, but the rarest and most attractive are the inscribed pots (*írókázás fazékok*) usually celebrating a wedding day or in the form of people or animals like the Miska jugs (*Miska kancsó*) from the Tisza River region. Nádudvar near Hajdúszoboszló specialises in black pottery – striking items and far superior to the greyish stuff produced in Mohács in Southern Transdanubia.

Objects carved from wood or bone – mangling boards, honey-cake moulds, mirror cases, tobacco holders, saltcellars – were usually the work of herders or farmers idle in winter. The shepherds and swineherds of Somogy County south of Lake Balaton and the cowherds of the Hortobágy excelled at this work, and their illustrations of celebrations and the local 'Robin Hood' outlaws are always fun to look at.

come to the fore in art. Many urban Hungarians probably wouldn't want to hear that, considering folk art a bit *déclassé* and its elevation the work of the communist regime, but it's true.

From the beginning of the 18th century, as segments of the Hungarian peasantry became more prosperous, ordinary people tried to make their world more beautiful by painting and decorating objects and clothing. It's important to remember two things when looking at folk art. First, with very few exceptions, eg, the 'primitive' paintings in Kecskemét's Museum of Naive Artists, only practical objects used daily were decorated. Second, this is not 'court art' or the work of artisans making Chinese cloisonné or Fabergé eggs. It is the work of ordinary people trying to express the simple world around them in a new and different way.

Outside museums most folk art in Hungary is all but dead – though the ethnic Hungarian regions of Transylvania in Romania are a different story. Through isolation or a refusal to let go for economic or aesthetic reasons, however, pockets remain throughout the country. Ignore the central *népművészeti bolt* (folk-art shop) you'll find in most towns: they're mostly full of mass-produced kitsch.

Folk woodcarving

Everyone made and decorated their own furniture in the old days, especially cupboards for the *tiszta szoba* (parlour) and trousseau chests with tulips painted on them, the *tulipán láda*. But for my money the best furniture in Hungary are the tables and chairs made of golden spotted poplar from the Gemenc Forest near Tolna. The oaken chests decorated with geometrical shapes from the Ormánság region of Southern Transdanubia are superior to the run-of-the-mill tulip chests.

One art form that ventures into the realm of fine art is ceiling and wall folk painting. Among the best examples of the former can be found in churches, especially in the North-East (eg, at Tákos), the Northern Uplands (Füzér) and the Ormánság (Drávaiványi). The women of Kalocsa also specialise in wall painting, some of them so colourfully over-wrought as to be garish.

Cinema

The scarcity of government grants has limited the production of quality Hungarian films recently, but a handful of good (and even great) ones still get produced every year. For classics, look out for anything by Oscar-winning István Szabó (*Sweet Emma, Dear Böbe, The Taste of Sunshine*), Miklós Jancsó (*The Red and the White*) and Péter Bacsó (*The Witness, Live Show*). György Szomjas' *Junk Film* and more recent *Gangster Movie*, Lívia Gyarmathy's *The Joy of Cheating*, Gábor Dettre's *Diary of the Hurdy-Gurdy Man*, György Molnár's

Anna's Film and Marcell Iványi's award-winning *Wind* are more recent films showing the great talent of their directors.

Other favourites are *Simon Mágus*, the epic tale of two magicians and a young woman directed by Ildikó Enyedi and many of the films of comic director Péter Timár. His *Csinibaba* is a satirical look at life – and film production quality – during the communist regime. *Zimmer Feri*, set on Lake Balaton, pits a young practical joker against a bunch of loud German tourists. Timár's *6:3* takes viewers back to 1953 to that glorious moment when Hungary defeated England in football by that score (see Spectator Sports in the Facts for the Visitor chapter).

SOCIETY & CONDUCT
Traditional Culture

Apart from the Busójárás festival in Mohács, Farsang and other pre-Lenten carnivals are now celebrated at balls and private parties and some people go in costume. The sprinkling of water or perfume on young girls on Easter Monday is now rare (except in Hollókő), though the Christmas tradition of *Betlehemzés*, where young men and boys carry model churches containing a manger from door to door, can still be seen in some parts of the countryside. A popular event for city folk with tenuous ties to the countryside is the *disznótor*, the slaughtering of a pig followed by an orgy of feasting and drinking. (The butchering, gratefully, is done somewhere out the back by an able-bodied peasant.) Wine harvest festivals, now commercial events with rock bands and a late-night outdoor disco, occur throughout the wine-growing regions in September and October.

Social Life

In general Hungarians are not uninhibited like the Romanians or sentimental Slavs who will laugh or cry at the drop of a hat (or a drink). They are reserved, very formal people. Forget the impassioned, devil-may-care Gypsy-fiddling stereotype – it doesn't exist. The national anthem calls Hungarians 'a people torn by fate' and the overall mood is one of *honfibú* (literally 'patriotic sor-row', but really a penchant for the blues with a sufficient amount of hope to keep most people going.)

This mood certainly predates Communism. To illustrate what she calls the 'dark streak in the Hungarian temperament', the veteran US foreign correspondent Flora Lewis recounts a story in *Europe: A Tapestry of Nations* that was the talk of Europe in the early 1930s. 'It was said,' she writes, 'that a song called *Gloomy Sunday* so deeply moved otherwise normal people (in Budapest) that whenever it was played, they would rush to commit suicide by jumping off a Danube bridge.'

Hungarians are almost always extremely polite in social interaction, and the language can be very courtly – even when doing business with the butcher or having your hair cut. The standard greeting for a man to a woman (or youngsters to their elders, regardless of the sex) is *Csókolom* ('I kiss it' – 'it' being the hand, of course). People of

Last Name First

Unusual outside Asia, Hungarians reverse their names in all uses, and their 'last' name (or surname) *always* comes first. For example, 'John Smith' is not 'János Kovács' to Hungarians but 'Kovács János', while 'Elizabeth Taylor' is 'Szabó Erzsébet' and 'Francis Flour' is Liszt Ferenc' for example.

Most titles also follow: 'Mr John Smith' is 'Kovács János úr'. Many women follow the practice of taking their husband's full name. If Elizabeth were married to John, she might be 'Kovács Jánosné' (Mrs John Smith) or, increasingly popular among professional women, 'Kovácsné Szabó Erzsébet'.

To avoid confusion, all Hungarian names in this guide are written in the usual Western manner – including the names of museums, theatres, etc – if they are translated into English. Thus the 'Arany János színház' in Budapest is the 'János Arany Theatre' in English. Addresses are always written in Hungarian as they appear on street signs: 'Kossuth Lajos utca', 'Arany János tér', etc.

all ages – even close friends – shake hands profusely when meeting up.

But while all this gentility certainly oils the wheels that turn a sometimes difficult society, it can be used to keep 'outsiders' (foreigners and other Hungarians) at a distance. Perhaps as an extension of this desire to keep everything running as smoothly as possible, Hungarians are always extremely helpful in an emergency – be it an accident, a pick-pocketing or simply helping someone who's lost their way.

Like Spaniards, Poles and many others with a Catholic background, Hungarians celebrate name days rather than birthdays. Name days are usually the Catholic feast day of their patron saint, but less holy names have a date too.

Drinking is an important part of social life in a country that has produced wine and fruit brandies for thousands of years. Consumption is high; only France and Germany drink more alcohol per capita. Alcoholism in Hungary is not as visible to the outsider as it is, say, in Poland, but it's there nonetheless; official figures suggest that as many as 6% of the population are fully fledged alcoholics, but some experts say that between 40% and 50% of all males drink 'problematically'.

Hungarians let their hair – and most of their clothes – down in summer at lake and riverside resorts; going topless is almost the norm for women. In warm weather you'll see more public displays of affection on the streets than perhaps any place else in the world. It's all very romantic, but beware: in the remoter corners of city parks you may even stumble upon more passionate displays (which always seems to embarrass the stumbler more than the active participants).

Dos & Don'ts

If you're invited to someone's home, bring a bunch of flowers (available in profusion all year and very inexpensive) or a bottle of good local wine. You can talk about anything, but money is a touchy subject. Traditionally, the discussion or manifestation of wealth – wearing flashy jewellery, for example – was considered gauche here (as it was throughout Eastern Europe). Nowadays no one thinks they have enough money, and those still in the low-paying public sector are often jealous of people who have made the leap to better jobs in the private sector. Your salary – piddling as you may think it is back home – will astonish most Hungarians.

Though it's almost impossible to calculate (the 'black economy' being so widespread and important), the average monthly salary in Hungary at time of writing was just under 68,000Ft (US$260/£164/A$418).

RELIGION

Throughout history, religion in Hungary has often been a question of expediency. Under King Stephen, Catholicism won the battle for dominance over Orthodoxy and, while the majority of Hungarians were quite happily Protestants by the end of the 16th century, many donned a new mantle during the Counter-Reformation under the Habsburgs. During the Turkish occupation, thousands of Hungarians converted to Islam – though not always willingly.

As a result, Hungarians tend to have a more pragmatic approach to religion than most of their neighbours, and almost none of the bigotry. It has even been suggested that this generally sceptical view of matters of faith has led to Hungarians' high rate of success in science and mathematics. Except in villages and on the most important holy days (Easter, the Assumption of Mary, Christmas), churches are never full. The Jewish community in Budapest, though, has seen a great revitalisation in recent years.

Of those Hungarians declaring religious affiliation, about 68% say they are Roman Catholic, 21% Reformed (Calvinist) Protestant and 6% Evangelical (Lutheran) Protestant. There are also small Greek Catholic and

Orthodox congregations. Hungary's Jews number about 80,000, down from a prewar population of almost 10 times that size. Some 400,000 died during deportation under the fascist Arrow Cross in 1944 or were murdered in Nazi concentration camps. Many others emigrated after 1956.

LANGUAGE

The national language is Hungarian (Magyar), and Hungarians like to boast that it ranks with Japanese and Arabic as among the world's most difficult. All languages are hard for non-native speakers to master, but it's true, Hungarian is extraordinarily difficult. Don't let this put you off attempting a few words and phrases, however. Partly as a reaction to the compulsory study of Russian in all schools until the late 1980s, Hungarians prefer to speak only Hungarian – attempt a few words in Magyar and they'll be impressed, take it as a compliment and be extremely encouraging.

The second most useful language for getting around in Hungary is German. Historical ties, geographical proximity and the fact that it was the preferred language of the literati up until the turn of the twentieth century have given it almost semi-official status. Still, outside Budapest and Transdanubia, the frequency and quality of spoken German is low.

While English is slowly becoming more common, it's rarely heard outside the capital. If you're desperate, look for someone young, preferably under the age of 25. Familiarity with Italian is increasing due to tourism, but French and Spanish will be of little use.

For more on what to say and how to say it Magyarul (in Hungarian – literally 'Hungarian-ly'), see the Language chapter at the back of this book.

Facts for the Visitor

HIGHLIGHTS
Historic Towns
Many of Hungary's historic towns, including Eger, Győr, Székesfehérvár and Veszprém, were rebuilt in the baroque style during the 18th century after being destroyed by the Turks. Sopron and Kőszeg are among the few Hungarian towns with a strong medieval flavour. The greatest monuments of the Turkish period are in Pécs. Kecskemét and Budapest have wonderful examples of Art Nouveau and Secessionist architecture.

Castles, Palaces & Manors
Hungary's most celebrated castles are those that resisted the Turkish onslaught in Eger, Kőszeg and Szigetvár. Though in ruins, the citadel at Visegrád evokes the power of medieval Hungary. The fortresses at Siklós, Sümeg, Hollókő and Boldogkőváralja have dramatic locations.

Among Hungary's finest palaces and manor houses are:

- Esterházy Palace at Fertőd
- Festetics Palace at Keszthely
- Széchenyi Manor at Nagycenk
- restored Royal Palace at Gödöllő

Museums & Galleries
The following museums stand out not just for the treasures they contain but also for the presentation of their exhibits:

- Christian Museum in Esztergom (Gothic paintings)
- Storno Collection in Sopron (Romanesque and Gothic furnishings)
- Zsolnay Museum (Art Nouveau and Secessionist porcelain)
- Csontváry Museum in Pécs
- Palóc Museum in Balassagyarmat (folklore)
- Ferenc Móra Museum in Szeged (Avar finds)
- Imre Patkó Collection (Asian and African art) in Győr
- Applied Arts Museum (furniture and decorative items) in Budapest.

Churches & Synagogues
Among Hungary's most beautiful houses of worship are:

- baroque Minorite church in Eger
- Gothic Calvinist church in Nyírbátor
- Art Nouveau synagogue in Szeged
- baroque cathedral at Kalocsa
- Sümeg's Church of the Ascension for its frescoes
- Gothic Old Synagogue in Sopron
- Abbey Church in Tihany
- Minorite church in Nyírbátor for its carved wooden altars
- Romantic Nationalist synagogue in Szolnok (now the Szolnok Gallery)
- Romanesque church at Őriszentpéter
- Pécs Synagogue

Outdoor Activities
Among the top outdoor activities in Hungary are:

- bird-watching in the Hortobágy region
- hiking in the Zemplén
- riding the narrow-gauge railway from Miskolc into the Bükk Hills
- canoeing on the Tisza River
- caving in Aggtelek
- cycling in the Danube Bend area

SUGGESTED ITINERARIES
Depending on the length of your stay and the season, you might want to visit the following places in Hungary:

Two days Budapest
One week Budapest, the Danube Bend and one or two of the following: Eger, Pécs, Sopron, Kecskemét
Two weeks Budapest, the Danube Bend, the north shore of Lake Balaton, Kőszeg, and two or three of the following: Eger, Pécs, Sopron, Kecskemét, Szeged

PLANNING
When to Go
Every season has its attractions in Hungary, but do yourself a favour and drop the

romantic notion of a winter on the *puszta* (Great Plain). Aside from being cold and often bleak, winter sees museums and other tourist sights closed or their hours sharply curtailed.

Though it can be pretty wet in May and early June, spring is just glorious in Hungary. The Hungarian summer is warm, sunny and unusually long, but the resorts at Lake Balaton and the Mátra Hills can get very crowded in late July and August.

As elsewhere in Europe, Budapest and other Hungarian cities come to a grinding halt in August, which Hungarians traditionally call 'the cucumber-growing season' (because that's about the only thing happening), although lots more festivals are now scheduled in that month.

Autumn is beautiful, particularly in the hills around Budapest and in the Northern Uplands. In Transdanubia and on the Great Plain it's harvest and vintage time. November is one of the rainiest months of the year, however.

For more information on Hungary's climate, see the Climate section in the Facts about the Country chapter.

Maps

Cartographia, Hungary's largest mapmaking company, produces national, regional and hiking maps (average scales: 1:40,000 or 1:60,000) as well as city plans, though newer companies like DiMap, Magyar Térképház (MT) and Nyír-Karta also produce city and specialised maps. A company called Top-Gráf produces dozens of useful little city maps that are no bigger than a cigarette packet.

Cartographia publishes a useful 1:450,000 scale sheet map to Hungary (300Ft) and its *Magyarország autóatlasza* (Road Atlas of Hungary) is indispensable if you plan to do a lot of travelling in the countryside, especially by car. The map comes in two sizes and scales – 1:360,000 (1200Ft) and 1:250,000 (1500Ft). The smaller scale atlas from Cartographia has thumbnail plans of virtually every community in the land while the larger one has 24 city maps.

What to Bring

There are no particular items of clothing to remember – an umbrella in late spring and autumn, perhaps, and a warm hat in winter – unless you plan to do some serious hiking or other sport. A swimsuit for use in the mixed-sex thermal spas and pools is a good idea as are plastic sandals or thongs (flip-flops).

In general, Hungarian dress is very casual – daringly brief, even by European standards in summer and many people attend even the opera in denim. Men needn't bother bringing a tie; it will never be used.

If you plan to stay at hostels and college dormitories, pack or buy a towel and a plastic soap container when you arrive. Bedclothes and padlocks are usually provided, though you might want to take along your own sheet bag and lock.

Other items you might need include a torch (flashlight), an adapter plug for electrical appliances (such as a cup or coil immersion heater to make your own tea or instant coffee), a universal bath/sink plug (a plastic film canister sometimes works), sunglasses, a few clothes pegs and premoistened towelettes or a large cotton handkerchief that you can soak in fountains and use to cool off while touring cities and towns in the warmer months.

TOURIST OFFICES
Local Tourist Offices

The Hungarian National Tourist Office (HNTO) has a chain of almost 100 tourist information bureaus called Tourinform in many parts of Hungary. These are the best places to ask general questions and pick up brochures – and can sometimes provide more comprehensive assistance. The main Tourinform office (☎ 1-317 9800, fax 317 9656, @ hungary@tourinform.hu) is in Budapest at V Sütő utca 2. Check its Web site at www.hungarytourism.hu.

If your query is about private accommodation, international train transport or changing money, you may have to turn to a commercial travel agency; almost every Hungarian town has at least one of them. The oldest, Ibusz, is the best for private accommodation. Cooptourist has reduced the number of its offices substantially in recent years. Travel agencies in provincial centres (Dunatours, Balatontourist, Mecsek Tourist, etc) are often more familiar with their own local areas.

The travel agency Express used to serve the youth and student market exclusively, but it now also sells outbound package tours. It issues student, youth, teachers and hostel cards and sells discounted BIJ train tickets. Some local Express offices can tell you about the availability of university accommodation.

Tourist Offices Abroad

The HNTO has offices in some 16 countries, including the following:

Austria (☎ 01-585 201210, fax 585 201221, ✉ htvienna@hungarytourism.hu), Opernring 3-5, A-1010 Vienna
Czech Republic (☎ 02-2109 0135, fax 2109 0139, ✉ htpragaue@hungarytourism.hu), Rumunská 22, 22537 Prague 2
France (☎ 01-53 70 67 17, fax 47 04 83 57, ✉ htparis@hungarytourism.hu), 140 Avenue Victor Hugo, 75116 Paris
Web site: www.hongrie.org
Germany (☎ 030-243 146 0, fax 243 146 13, ✉ htberlin@hungarytourism.hu), Karl Liebknecht Strasse 34, D-10178 Berlin
Netherlands (☎ 070-320 9092, fax 327 2833, ✉ htdenhaga@hungarytourism.hu), Postbus 91644, 2509 EE The Hague
Romania (☎/fax 064-414 520, ✉ htcluj@hungarytourism.hu), Consulate of Hungary, Piata Unirii, CP 352, 3400 Cluj-Napoca
Ukraine (☎ 044-229 9628, fax 229 9661, ✉ htkiev@hungarytourism.hu), vul Striletska 16, 252034 Kiev 34
UK (☎/fax 020-7823 1032, fax 823 1459, ✉ htlondon@hungarytourism.hu), 46 Eaton Place, London SW1X 8AL
USA (☎ 212-355 0240, fax 207 4103, ✉ htnewyork@hungarytourism.hu), 150 East 58th St, 33/F, New York, NY 10155-3398
Web site: www.gotohungary.com

In countries without an HNTO, contact Malév Hungarian Airlines, which has offices or associated agencies in some four dozen countries worldwide, including the following seven:

Australia (☎ 02-9244 2111, fax 9290 3306, ✉ wassyd@worldaviation.com.au), World Aviation Systems, 403 George St, Sydney 2000 NSW
Canada (☎ 416-944 0093, fax 944 0095, ✉ toronto@malev.hu), 175 Bloor St East, Suite 909, Toronto, Ont M4W 3R8
Croatia (☎ 01-483 6935/36, fax 01-483 6937), Hotel Inter-Continental, Krsnjavoga 1, 10000 Zagreb
Ireland (☎ 01-844 6127, fax 01-844 6092), South Apron, Gategourmet Building, Dublin Airport, Dublin
New Zealand (☎ 09-379 4455, fax 377 5648), World Aviation Systems, Trustbank Building, 6/F, 229 Queen St, Auckland 1
Slovakia (☎ 07-531 0130, fax 531 0132), Satur Travel Agency, ul Jeseskeho 5-9, Bratislava
Yugoslavia (☎ 011-323 9673, fax 323 0224), Ul Nusiceva 4, 3/F, Belgrade

VISAS & DOCUMENTS
Passport

Almost everyone entering Hungary must have a valid passport, though citizens of Austria, Belgium, France, Italy, Liechtenstein, Luxembourg, Germany, Slovenia, Spain and Switzerland need only produce their national identity card. It's a good idea to carry your passport or other identification at all times.

Visas

Citizens of the USA, Canada, all European countries (except Albania and Turkey) and South Africa do not require visas to visit Hungary for stays of up to 90 days. Nationals of Australia, Hong Kong, Singapore, Taiwan and New Zealand (among others) still do need them. If you hold a passport from one of these countries, check current visa requirements at an embassy or consulate or any HNTO or Malév office.

A single-entry visa can be purchased at a Hungarian consulate or foreign mission in your country of residence upon receipt of US$40 and three photos (it costs US$65 if purchased at a foreign mission outside your country of residence or at the border). A double-entry tourist visa costs US$75/100 and you must have five photos. A multiple-entry visa is US$180/200. Some consulates charge US$15 extra for express service (10 minutes as opposed to overnight). Single and double-entry visas are valid for six months prior to use. Multiple entries are good for a year.

Be sure to get a tourist rather than a transit visa; the latter – available for single (US$38/50), double (US$65/90) and multiple (US$150/180) crossings – is only good for a stay of 48 hours and cannot be extended. On a transit visa you must enter and leave through different border crossings and have a visa (if required) for the next country you visit. A tourist visa can be extended (3000Ft) at the central police station (*rendőrkapitányság*) of any city or town, provided you do so 48 hours before it expires. Rather than face the bureaucracy, most travellers just go to a neighbouring country like Austria and then re-enter.

Visas are issued at most international highway border crossings (see Border Crossings under Land in the Getting There & Away chapter) and the airport, but this usually involves a wait and there are not always photo booths nearby if you've forgotten your mug shots. Visas are never issued on trains and seldom to passengers on international buses.

You are supposed to register with the police if staying in one place for more than 30 days, and your hotel, hostel, camping ground or private room booked through an agency will do this for you. In other situations, eg, if you're staying with friends or relatives, you have to take care of this yourself within 72 hours. Don't worry if you haven't got round to it; it's a hangover from the old regime, and enforcement has been fairly lax. Address registration forms for foreigners (*lakcímbejelentő lap külföldiek részére*) are available at main post offices.

Travel Insurance

You should seriously consider taking out travel insurance. This not only covers you for medical expenses and luggage theft or loss but also for cancellation or delays in your travel arrangements. (You could, for example, fall seriously ill two days before departure.) Cover depends on your insurance and type of airline ticket, so ask both

your insurer and your ticket-issuing agency to explain where you stand. Ticket loss is also covered by travel insurance.

Paying for your airline ticket with a credit card often provides limited travel accident insurance, and you may be able to reclaim the payment if the operator doesn't deliver. In the UK, for instance, institutions issuing credit cards are required by law to reimburse consumers if a company goes into liquidation and the amount in contention is more than UK£100. Ask your credit card company what it's prepared to cover.

Driving Licence & Permits

If you don't hold a European driving licence and plan to drive in Hungary, obtain an International Driving Permit from your local automobile association before you leave – you'll need a passport photo and a valid local licence. It is usually inexpensive and valid for one year only.

Hostel Card

A hostel card is sometimes useful in Hungary. No hostels require that you be a Hostelling International (or associated) member, but sometimes charge less if you have a card. Express, with offices around Hungary, will issue you an HI card for 1250Ft.

Student, Youth & Teacher Cards

The International Student Identity Card (ISIC), a plastic ID-style card with your photograph, provides discounts on some forms of transport and cheap admission to museums, sights and even films. If you're aged under 26 but not a student, you can also apply for a GO25 card issued by the Federation of International Youth Travel Organisations (FIYTO), which gives much the same discounts and benefits. An ITIC card identifies the holder as a teacher and offers similar deals. Express sells all these cards for 800Ft each.

Seniors' Cards

Many attractions offer reduced-price admission for people over 60 or 65 (sometimes as low as 55 for women) but this is usually just for Hungarian *nyugdíjasok* (pensioners). For a fee of around €15, European residents aged over 60 can get a Rail Europe Senior (RES) card as an add-on to their national rail senior pass. It entitles the holder to reduced European fares of about 30%.

Hungary Card

The Hungary Card (3920Ft), which is valid for 13 months, offers savings of between 5% and 25% on hotels, pensions, camp sites and restaurants throughout Hungary, up to 50% on train, bus and boat travel, and some museums and cultural events are free to card-holders. It even gives you a 15% discount on the Budapest Card (see Information in the Budapest chapter). The Hungary Card is available at Tourinform offices, petrol and major train stations and the Hotelinfo travel agency (☎ 1-267 0896) at V Váci utca 78-80 in Budapest.

Copies

The hassles brought on by losing your passport can be considerably reduced if you have a record of its number and issue date, or even better, photocopies of the relevant data pages. A photocopy of your birth certificate can also be useful. Also add the serial numbers of your travellers cheques (cross them off as you cash them) and photocopies of your credit cards, airline ticket and other travel documents.

EMBASSIES & CONSULATES
Hungarian Embassies & Consulates

Hungarian embassies and consulates around the world include the following:

Australia
  Embassy: (☎ 02-6282 3226) 17 Beale Crescent, Deakin, ACT 2600
  Consulate: (☎ 02-9328 7859) Edgecliff Centre, Suite 405, 203-233 New South Head Road, Edgecliff, NSW 2027
Austria
  Embassy: (☎ 0222-533 2631) 1 Bankgasse 4-6, 1010 Vienna
Canada
  Embassy: (☎ 613-230 9614) 299 Waverley St, Ottawa, Ont K2P 0V9
  Consulate: (☎ 416-923 8981) 121 Bloor St East, Suite 1115, Toronto, Ont M4W 3M5

Croatia
  Embassy: (☎ 01-422 296) Ul Krlezin Gvozd 11/a, 41000 Zagreb
Czech Republic
  Embassy: (☎ 02-365 041) Ul Badeniho 1, 12537 Prague 6
France
  Embassy: (☎ 01 43 54 66 96) 92 Rue Bonaparte, 75006 Paris
Germany
  Embassy: (☎ 030-220 2561) Unter den Linden 72, 10177 Berlin
  Consulate: (☎ 0228-371 112) Turmstrasse 30, 53175 Bonn
  Consulate: (☎ 089-911 032) Vollmannstrasse 2, 81927 Munich 8
Ireland
  Embassy: (☎ 01-661 2902) 2 Fitzwilliam Place, Dublin 2
Netherlands
  Embassy: (☎ 070-350 0404) Hogeweg 14, 2585 JD The Hague
New Zealand
  Consulate: (☎ 04-938 0427) 151 Orangi Kaupapa Road, Wellington 6005
Romania
  Embassy: (☎ 01-311 0062) Strada Jean-Louis Calderon 63-65, Bucharest
Slovakia
  Embassy: (☎ 07-533 0541) Sedlarska ul 3, 81425 Bratislava
Slovenia
  Embassy: (☎ 061-152 1882) Ul Konrada Babnika 5, Ljubljana-Sentvid 1210
South Africa
  Embassy: (☎ 012-433 030) 959 Arcadia St, 0132 Pretoria
  Consulate: (☎ 021-641 547) 14 Fernwood Ave, Rondeboch, 7701 Cape Town
UK
  Embassy: (☎ 020-7235 5218) 35 Eaton Place, London SW1X 8BY
Ukraine
  Embassy: (☎ 044-212 4134) Ul Rejterskaya 33, 252901 Kiev
USA
  Embassy: (☎ 202-362 6730) 3910 Shoemaker St NW, Washington, DC 20008
  Consulate: (☎ 212-752 0661) 223 East 52nd St, New York, NY 10022
Yugoslavia
  Embassy: (☎ 011-444 0472) Ul Ivana Milutinovica 74, Belgrade 11000

Foreign Embassies in Hungary

Selected countries with representation in Budapest (where the telephone code is 1) follow. The Roman numerals preceding the street name indicates the *kerület*, or district, in the capital.

Australia (☎ 201 8899) XII Királyhágó tér 8-9 (open 9 am to noon weekdays)
Austria (☎ 352 6913) VI Benczúr utca 16 (open 9 to 11 am weekdays)
Canada (☎ 275 1200) XII Budakeszi út 32 (open 8 am to noon weekdays)
Croatia (☎ 249 2215) XII Arató utca 22/b (open weekdays 10 am to 2 pm)
Czech Republic (☎ 351 0539) VI Székely Bertalan utca 4 (open 8.30 am to 12.30 pm weekdays)
France (☎ 332 4980) VI Lendvay utca 27 (open 9 am to 12.30 pm weekdays)
Germany (☎ 467 3500) XIV Stefánia út 101-103 (open 9 am to noon weekdays)
Ireland (☎ 302 9600) V Szabadság tér 7 (open 9.30 am to 12.30 pm and 2.30 to 4.30 pm weekdays)
Netherlands (☎ 326 5301) II Füge utca 5-7 (open 10 am to noon weekdays)
Romania (☎ 352 0271) XIV Thököly út 72 (open 8.30 am to noon Monday to Wednesday, to 11.30 am on Friday)
Slovakia (☎ 251 7973) XIV Gervay utca 44 (open 8.30 to 11.30 am and 2 to 3.30 pm weekdays)
Slovenia (☎ 335 6694) II Cseppkő utca 68 (open 9 am to noon weekdays)
South Africa (☎ 392 0999) II Gárdonyi Géza út 17 (open 9 am to 12.30 pm weekdays)
UK (☎ 266 2888) V Harmincad utca 6 (open 9.30 to noon and 2 to 4 pm weekdays)
Ukraine (☎ 355 9609) XII Nógrádi utca 8 (open 9 am to noon weekdays)
USA (☎ 475 4400 or ☎ 475 4703 after hours) V Szabadság tér 12 (open 8.15 am to 5 pm weekdays)
Yugoslavia (☎ 322 9838) VI Dózsa György út 92/b (open 10 am to 1 pm weekdays)

CUSTOMS

You can bring into Hungary the usual personal effects as well as 250 cigarettes, 2L of wine and 1L of spirits duty-free. When leaving the country, you are not supposed to take out valuable antiques without a 'museum certificate' (available from the place of purchase).

Restrictions on the import/export of forint won't affect most travellers; the limit now is 350,000Ft.

MONEY
Currency

The Hungarian forint (Ft) was once divided into 100 fillér, worthless little aluminium coins that have now been withdrawn from circulation. There are coins of one, two, five, 10, 20, 50 and 100Ft.

Notes come in six denominations: 200, 500, 1000, 2000, 5000 and 10,000Ft.

Exchange Rates

Exchange rates at the time of going to press were:

country	unit		forint
Australia	A$1	=	160
Austria	AS10	=	180
Canada	C$1	=	184
euro	€1	=	258
France	10FF	=	394
Germany	DM1	=	132
Ireland	IR£1	=	328
Japan	¥100	=	252
Netherlands	1f	=	117
New Zealand	NZ$1	=	134
South Africa	R1	=	40
UK	£1	=	427
USA	US$1	=	269

Exchanging Money

Cash & Travellers Cheques Nothing beats cash for convenience – or risk. However, it's always prudent to carry a little foreign cash – US$50 or DM100, say – in case you can't find an automatic teller machine (ATM) nearby or there's no bank or travel office open to cash your travellers cheques.

You can exchange cash and travellers cheques – American Express (AmEx), Visa and Thomas Cook are the most recognisable brands in Hungary – at most banks and post offices; the National Savings Bank (Országos Takarékpénztár; OTP) has branches almost everywhere and charges no commission on travellers cheques. Travel agents usually take a commission of 1% to 2%. Using private money-change bureaus can be convenient but expensive. Shops never accept travellers cheques in Hungary.

Though the forint is now a totally convertible currency, you should avoid

The Euro

On 1 January 1999 a new currency, the euro (denoted with the symbol €), was introduced in 11 EU countries, including Germany and Austria. Euro banknotes and coins will be introduced on 1 January 2002, ushering in a period of dual use of euros and local currency. By July 2002 local currency in the 11 countries will be withdrawn and only euros will remain. The effect of the euro's introduction on travel in Hungary will mainly be restricted to the replacement of the Deutschmark, the currency used by many hotels when they quote their prices, by the euro. Many places to stay and travel agencies may also show prices in euros, while the euro may well replace the US dollar as the best hard currency to travel with in Europe. The full effect of the euro's introduction on travel in Hungary, and Europe for that matter, is hard to predict and you should check with your travel agent before you leave.

changing too much. You are allowed to change leftover forint back into foreign currency without limit, but you must have official receipts for anything over US$150. It might be difficult exchanging forint beyond the borders of Hungary's neighbours.

ATMs & Credit Cards The hassle of trying to change travellers cheques at the weekend, rip-off *bureaux de change* and the allure of the black market have all gone the way of the dodo in Hungary, with the arrival of ATMs that accept most credit and cash cards in even the tiniest of villages. All the banks listed under Information in this guide have ATMs unless noted otherwise.

Credit cards are still not as commonly used in Hungary as in Western Europe but are gaining ground, especially AmEx, Visa and MasterCard. You'll be able to use them at upmarket restaurants, shops, hotels, car-rental firms, travel agencies and petrol stations.

K&H banks and post offices will give a cash advance on major credit cards; AmEx is at V Deák Ferenc utca 10 in Budapest.

International Transfers Having money wired to Hungary through Thomas Cook or AmEx is fairly straightforward; for the latter you don't need to be a cardholder and it takes less than a day. You should know the sender's full name, the exact amount and the reference number when you're picking up the cash. With a passport or other ID you'll be given the amount in US dollars or forint. The sender pays the service fee, eg, US$20 for US$100, US$40 for US$500, US$60 for US$1000.

Guaranteed Cheques Many banks, including OTP branches, and some 300 post offices will cash up to three Eurocheques worth 35,000Ft each per transaction.

Black Market It's senseless to make use of the black market to change money. The advantage – 5% to 10% on the outside – is not worth the bother. It's illegal and you are almost sure to be ripped off anyway.

Costs

Relatively high inflation and the systematic devaluation of the forint has made life very difficult for Hungarians earning local salaries, but for foreign travellers the country remains a bargain destination for food, lodging and transport.

If you stay in private rooms, eat at medium-priced restaurants and travel 2nd-class on trains, you should get by easily on less than US$25 a day without scrimping. Those putting up in hostels, dormitories or camping grounds and eating at self-service restaurants or food stalls will cut costs substantially.

Because of the rapidly changing value of the forint, many hotels quote their rates in Deutschmarks – at least until July 2002 when that currency will cease to exist in favour of the euro (See 'The Euro' boxed text.) Also the national rail company MÁV has begun to list its prices in euros. In such cases, we have followed suit.

Tipping & Bargaining

Hungary is a very tip-conscious society and virtually everyone routinely tips waiters, hairdressers and taxi drivers. Doctors and dentists accept 'gratitude money' (see Health later in this chapter), and even petrol station and thermal spa attendants expect 50Ft to 100Ft. If you were less than impressed with the service at the restaurant, the joyride in the taxi or the way someone cut your hair, leave next to nothing or nothing at all. He or she will get the message.

The way you tip in restaurants is unusual. You never leave the money on the table – this is considered both rude and stupid in Hungary – but tell the waiter how much you're paying in total. If the bill is 1540Ft, you're paying with a 2000Ft note and you think the waiter deserves the extra 10%, first ask if service is included (some restaurants in Budapest and other big cities add it to the bill automatically). If it isn't, say you're paying 1700Ft or that you want 300Ft back.

Bargaining was never the done thing under the old regime; except for the privileged class, everyone paid the same amount by weight and volume for items freely available, including a scoop of ice cream. Though you'll never be able to do it in shops, you may haggle in flea markets or with individuals selling folk crafts. But even this is not as commonplace as it is in other parts of Eastern Europe.

Taxes & Refunds

ÁFA, a value-added tax of between 12% and 25%, covers the purchase of all new goods in Hungary. It is almost always included in the quoted price but sometimes it is on top, so be wary. Visitors are not exempt, but they can claim refunds for total purchases of more than 50,000Ft on one invoice. However, claiming your money is a bit complicated.

You must take the goods out of the country within 90 days, the ÁFA receipts (available from the shops where you made the purchases) should be stamped by customs at the border and the claim has to be made

within six months of the purchase. No ÁFA is refunded on the purchase of works of art and antiques. Cash refunds are made at the following points before departure: Ferihegy Airport, the Mahat International Landing Stage on Belgrád rakpart in Budapest, Keleti train station and Ibusz branch offices at international border crossings.

Two outfits in Budapest that can help with refunds are Global Refund Tax Free Shopping (☎/fax 1-212 4906) at II Bég utca 3-5 and Inteltrade (☎ 1-356 9800, fax 375 0616) at I Csalogány utca 6-10.

POST & COMMUNICATIONS

The Hungarian Postal Service (Magyar Posta) has improved somewhat in recent years; perhaps its jaunty logo of a stylised St Stephen's Crown has helped kick-start it into the 21st century. But post offices are usually still crowded, service is slow and the exclusively Magyar-speaking staff would put the fear of God in Margaret Thatcher herself.

Postal Rates

A letter sent within any Hungarian city or town costs 27Ft, while for the rest of Hungary and neighbouring countries it's 32Ft (add 79/160Ft if you want to send it as registered/express).

Postcards within/outside a city and to neighbouring countries cost 24/27Ft. Foreign airmail is 100Ft to 110Ft for up to 20g and 190Ft to 210Ft for 20g to 100g base rate plus 15Ft per 10g for airmail charge. Thus a standard 20g letter to most of Western Europe costs 130Ft and to the rest of the world 140Ft. Postcards are 130Ft and 140Ft respectively.

Sending & Receiving Mail

To beat the crowds at the post office, ask at kiosks, newsagents or stationery shops if they sell stamps (*bélyeg*). If you must deal with the post office, you'll be relieved to learn that most people are there to pay electric, gas and telephone bills or parking fines. To get in and out with a minimum of fuss (and tears), look for the window marked with the symbol of an envelope.

Make sure the destination of your letter is written clearly, and simply hand it over to the clerk, who will apply the stamps for you, postmark it and send it on its way.

If you are sending a parcel, look for the sign '*Csomagfeladás*' or '*Csomagfelvétel*'. Packages must not weigh more than 2kg or else you'll face a Kafkaesque nightmare of permits and queues; try to send small packages. Books and printed matter are exceptions. You can send up to 2kg in one box for between 2200Ft and 2800Ft and up to 5kg for 5500Ft to 6900Ft.

Hungarian addresses start with the name of the recipient, followed on the next line by the postal code and city or town and then the street name and number. The postal code consists of four digits. The first indicates the city or town, the second and third the district and the last the neighbourhood.

Mail addressed to poste restante in any town or city will go to the main post office (*főposta*), the address of which you'll find under Information in the relevant entry. All mail marked 'Poste Restante, Budapest' goes to the post office at V Petőfi Sándor utca 13-15. When picking up mail, look for the sign '*Postán maradó*', and make sure you have identification. Since the family name always comes first in Hungarian usage, have the sender underline your last name, as letters are often misfiled under foreigners' first names.

You can have your mail delivered to AmEx (1052 Budapest, Deák Ferenc utca 10) if you have an AmEx credit card or travellers cheques.

Telephone

You can make domestic and international calls from most public telephones, which are usually in good working order. To avoid having to carry a purse or pocket full of change, buy a telephone card from any post office or newsagent. These come in message units of 50/120 and cost 800/1800Ft. Telephone boxes with a black and white arrow and red target on the door and the word '*Visszahívható*' display a telephone number, which can be phoned back; place a call and have the party phone you back.

All areas of Hungary have a two-digit telephone area code, except for Budapest, which simply has a '1'. Local codes appear in small point type under the name of each city and town in this book.

To make a local call, pick up the receiver and listen for the neutral and continuous dial tone. Then dial the local number (seven digits in Budapest, six elsewhere). For a trunk call in Hungary, dial ☎ 06 and wait for the second, 'brrrring', tone. Then dial – and don't forget the two-digit area code. You must *always* dial ☎ 06 if ringing a mobile telephone, whose area codes are usually ☎ 209, ☎ 309 or ☎ 609.

The procedure for making an international call is the same except that you dial ☎ 00, followed by the country and area codes and then the number. Charges for international phone calls are: 132/99Ft per minute to all neighbouring countries from a public/private telephone; 180/135Ft for most of Europe; 185/139Ft to North America, Australia and New Zealand; 450/338Ft to much of east Asia and the Pacific; 524/393Ft to the Middle East; and 625/469Ft to south Asia. The country code for Hungary is ☎ 36.

There's a wide range of local and international phonecards. Lonely Planet's eKno Communication Card is aimed specifically at independent travellers and provides budget international calls, a range of messaging services, free email and travel information – for local calls, you're usually better off with a local card. You can join online at www.ekno.lonelyplanet.com, or by phone from Hungary by dialling ☎ 00-800 13572. Once you have joined, to use eKno from Hungary, dial ☎ 00-800 13568. Check the eKno Web site for joining and access numbers from other countries and updates on super budget local access numbers and new features.

The AmCard (☎ 00 800 01213), a smart card with a face value of 3000Ft, will save you between 17% and 43% on phone calls to Europe, the USA and Asia.

You can also get straight through to an operator based in your home country by dialling the 'country direct' number from a public phone (charges are reversed), but you need a coin or phone card for the initial connection and these services can be very expensive.

Australia Direct	☎ 00-800 11573
Australia (Telstra)	☎ 00-800 06111
Britain Direct (BT)	☎ 00-800 04411
Britain (Mercury)	☎ 00-800 04412
Canada Direct	☎ 00-800 01211
New Zealand Direct	☎ 00-800 06411
South Africa Direct	☎ 00-800 02711
USA Direct (AT&T)	☎ 00-800 01111
USA MCI	☎ 00-800 01411
USA Sprint Express	☎ 00-800 01877

Other numbers you may find useful include:

domestic operator (English spoken)
  ☎ 198
international operator (English spoken)
  ☎ 199
mobile phone directory assistance
  ☎ 1-464 6020 for area code 209,
  ☎ 265 8585 for area code 309,
  ☎ 265 8585 for area code 609
time in Hungarian
  ☎ 080

Fax
You can send faxes from most main post offices and telephone centres in towns and cities around Hungary.

Email & Internet Access
Travelling with a portable computer is a great way to stay in touch with family and friends back home, but unless you know what you're doing it's fraught with potential problems. If you plan to carry your notebook or palmtop computer with you, remember that the power supply voltage in the countries you visit may vary from that at home, risking damage to your equipment. The best investment is a universal AC adaptor for your appliance, which will enable you to plug it in anywhere without frying its innards. You'll also need a plug adaptor for each country you visit – often it's easiest to buy these before you leave home.

Also, your PC-card modem may or may not work once you leave your home country

– and you won't know for sure until you try. The safest option is to buy a reputable 'global' modem before you leave home, or buy a local PC-card modem if you're spending an extended time in any one country. Keep in mind that the telephone socket in each country you visit will probably be different from that at home, so ensure that you have at least a US RJ-11 telephone adaptor that works with your modem. You can almost always find an adaptor that will convert from RJ-11 to the local variety. For more information on travelling with a portable computer, see www.teleadapt.com or www.warrior.com.

Major Internet service providers have dial-in nodes throughout Europe such as AOL (☎ 1-457 8888, ☎ 1-457 8888 in Budapest) and CompuServe (☎ 1-291 9999); it's best to download a list of the dial-in numbers from the Web sites at www.aol.com or www.compuserve.com before you leave home. If you access your Internet email account at home through a smaller ISP or your office or school network, your best option is either to open an account with a global ISP, like those mentioned above, or to rely on cybercafes and other public access points to collect your mail.

INTERNET RESOURCES
The World Wide Web is a rich resource for travellers. You can research your trip, hunt down bargain air fares, book hotels, check on weather conditions or chat with locals and other travellers about the best places to visit (or avoid!).

Budapest Week Online Events, music and movie listings, is not necessarily limited to the capital
  www.budapestweek.com
Businessweb A wealth of information on business and economics
  www.businessweb.hu
Hotels Information on hotels throughout Hungary
  www.miwo.hu
  www.hotels.hu
  www.hotelshungary.com
  www.hotelinfo.hu
Hungary.com This site offers a broad range of topics on its Exhibition Hall pages – from links to government offices to hotels.
  www.hungary.com

Hungary-Info Basic information on Hungary with business and travel links www.hungary-info.com.

HVG Weekly news magazine *HVG* (see Newspapers & Magazines) with summaries of its lead stories www.hvg.hu

Inside Hungary National news www.insidehungary.com

Lonely Planet There's no better place to start your Web explorations than the Lonely Planet Web site (www.lonelyplanet.com). Here you'll find succinct summaries on travelling to most places on earth, postcards from other travellers and the Thorn Tree bulletin board, where you can ask questions before you go or dispense advice when you get back. You can also find travel news and updates to many of our most popular guidebooks, and the subWWWay section links you to the most useful travel resources elsewhere on the Web.
www.lonelyplanet.com

Tourinform Tourist information and links www.tourinform.hu (only in Hungarian) www.hungarytourism.hu

BOOKS

There's no shortage of books on Hungary and things Hungarian – from travel guides and histories to travelogues and cookery books. Once regarded as one of Hungary's biggest bargains, books have become more expensive, though haven't reached Western prices yet.

Lonely Planet

Both Lonely Planet's *Eastern Europe* and *Central Europe* contain Hungary chapters. The Lonely Planet *Eastern Europe phrasebook* contains lengthy sections of useful words and expressions in Hungarian. The new *Budapest* guide takes an in-depth look at the capital.

Guidebooks

Jewish Heritage Travel: A Guide to Central and Eastern Europe by Ruth Gruber. Contains a comprehensive chapter on Hungary.

Where to Watch Birds in Eastern Europe by Gerard Gorman. For assistance in spotting the best of Hungary's feathered friends. Contains a 40-page chapter on Hungary. His *The Birds of Hungary* is unfortunately now out of print but you may find copies in second-hand bookshops.

The Wines & Vines of Hungary (New World Publishing) by Stephen Kirkland. Positively the best guide to Hungarian wine, leaving no leaf, grape or bottle unturned.

Travel

Travellers writing diary accounts usually treat Hungary rather cursorily as they make tracks for 'more exotic' Romania or points beyond.

Between the Woods and the Water by Patrick Leigh Fermor. In describing his 1933 walk through Hungary en route to Constantinople, Fermor wrote the classic account of Hungary.

Stealing from a Deep Place by Brian Hall. Sensitive but never cloying, the author describes his tempered love affair with the still communist Budapest of the 1980s.

The Double Eagle: Vienna, Budapest and Prague by Stephen Brook. A cultural and political commentary on the three major Habsburg cities through the eyes of a modern traveller. It has just gone out of print but can often be found at second-hand bookshops.

The City of the Magyar by Miss Julia Pardoe. One of the best sources for contemporary views of early 19th-century Hungary is published in 1840. You'll only find this three-volume set in a library or antiquarian bookshop.

History & Politics

Hungary: A Brief History by István Lázár. A light, almost silly, history by geologist-cum-journalist.

The Magyars: Their Life & Civilisation by Gyula László. A dense anthology of the beliefs, traditions and culture of the Hungarians at the time of the conquest.

A History of Modern Hungary by Jörg K Hoensch. Covers the period from 1867 to 1994 in a balanced, though somewhat dry, way.

A History of Hungary by Peter F Sugar (ed). Arguably the best single-volume history of Hungary in English by one of the most incisive historians of Central and Eastern Europe.

We the People by Timothy Garton Ash; and, *The Rebirth of History* by Misha Glenny. Clear insightful interpretations of what led to the collapse of Communism in 1989.

Hungary's Negotiated Revolution by Rudolf L Tőkés. On the same subject but more specific to Hungary this book is based on interviews with former top communist leaders and transcripts of the Hungarian Socialist Workers Party Central Committee.

Eclipse of the Crescent Moon (Corvina) by Géza Gárdonyi. More in the spirit of *Boy's Own* and written in 1901 this swashbuckling tale is an excellent fictionalised account of the 1552 siege of Eger Castle.

General

The Architecture of Historic Hungary by Dora Wiebenson & József Sisa. A very serious look at important buildings and their place in history throughout the country, with lavish photos and schematic drawings.

The Cuisine of Hungary by restaurateur George Lang. Offers a comprehensive history of Magyar cooking and examination of its regional differences.

Homage to the Eighth District by Giorgio & Nicola Pressburger (Readers International). Poignant account of life in what was a Jewish working-class section of Budapest during and after WWII. The twin brothers emigrated to Italy in 1956.

Under the Frog by Tibor Fischer. An amusing account of a basketball team's antics in the Hungary of the early 1950s.

Hungarian Folk Art (Corvina) by Tamás Hofer & Edit Fél. Oversized picture book that offers a good introduction to the subject.

Hungarian Ethnography and Folklore by Iván Balassa & Gyula Ortutay. This real gem is an 800-page opus that weighs in at 3kg and leaves no question on traditional culture unanswered. It's out of print but can still be found in Budapest and some provincial bookshops. Highly recommended.

NEWSPAPERS & MAGAZINES

Since the demise of *Budapest Week* in print in favour of the company's Web site at www.budapestweek.com, Hungary counts only two weekly English-language newspapers: the fluffy *Budapest Sun* (158Ft) tabloid, with a particularly useful Style supplement of entertainment listings, and the *Budapest Business Journal* (450Ft), an almost archival publication of financial news and business features. The monthly *Budapest Style* magazine has features, interviews, etc.

English-language newspapers available on the day of publication at many large kiosks, newsagents and hotels in Budapest include the *International Herald Tribune*, the European edition of the *Wall Street Journal*, the *Financial Times* and the weekly *Guardian International*.

Other English-language periodicals include the erudite *Hungarian Quarterly* (US$8), which examines a wide variety of issues in great depth and is a valuable source of current Hungarian thinking in translation; the *Central European Business Weekly* (200Ft); and the *Central European Economic Review* (330Ft) published monthly by the *Wall Street Journal*.

RADIO & TV

With the sale of state-owned TV2, Magyar Televízió (MTV) controls only one channel (MTV1) though there's a host of cable and satellite stations (Duna Televizió, RTL Klub, M Sat, ZTV, etc) broadcasting everything from game shows and Top 40 hits to the Flintstones – all in (or dubbed into) Hungarian. Most larger hotels and pensions now subscribe to satellite channels that receive stations like Sky News, CNN, Eurosport and MTV (the music – not the Magyar – one).

Hungarian Radio has stations named after Lajos Kossuth (news; 98.6 FM), Sándor Petőfi ('60s to '80s music, news; 94.8 FM) and Béla Bartók (classical music, news; 105.3 FM) and there's a whole range of stations playing trashy pop and mixes. The one exception is Rádió Tilos (98 FM), a former pirate station that has the best music line-up in Hungary.

VIDEO SYSTEMS

If you want to record or buy video tapes to play back home, you won't get the picture if the image registration systems are different. Like most of Australia and Europe, Hungary uses PAL, which is incompatible with the North American and Japanese NTSC system or the SECAM system used in France.

PHOTOGRAPHY & VIDEO

All major brands of film are readily available in Hungary and you can have your film developed in one hour at many shops in Budapest, including any of the dozen or so Fotex outlets (VII Rákóczi út 2, V Váci utca 9, etc).

Film prices vary, but basically 24 exposures of 100 ASA Kodacolor II, Agfa or Fujifilm will cost from 690Ft to 799Ft and 36 exposures between 880Ft and 1090Ft. Ektachrome 100 is 1490Ft. Developing print film costs about 699Ft a roll; for the prints themselves, you choose the size and pay accordingly (10x15cm prints cost 79Ft each). Slide film costs 799Ft to process. Video film like TDK EHG 30/45 minutes costs 990/1310Ft.

TIME

Hungary lies in the Central European Time Zone. Winter time is GMT plus one hour and in summer it's GMT plus two hours. Clocks are advanced at 2 am on the last Sunday in March and set back at the same time on the last Sunday in October. Without taking daylight-saving times into account, when it's noon in Budapest, it's:

11 am	in London
6 am	in New York
3 am	in San Francisco
9 pm	in Sydney

An important note on the complicated way Hungarians tell time: 7.30 is 'half eight' (*fél nyolc óra*) and the 24-hour system is often used in giving times of movies, concerts, etc. So a film at 7.30 pm could appear on a listing as 'f8', 'f20', '-½ 8' or '-½ 20'. A quarter to the hour has a ¾ in front ('¾ 8' means 7.45) while quarter past is ¼ of the next hour ('¼ 9' means 8.15).

ELECTRICITY

The electric current in Hungary is 220V, 50 Hz AC. Plugs are the European type with two round pins.

WEIGHTS & MEASURES

Hungary uses the metric system – there's a conversion table at the back of this book. In supermarkets and outdoor markets, fresh food is sold by weight or by piece (*darab*). When ordering by weight, you specify by kilos or *deka* (decagrams – 50dg is equal to 0.5kg or a little more than 1lb).

Beer at a *söröző* (pub) is served in a *pohár* (0.3L) or a *korsó* (0.4L or 0.5L). Wine in an old-fashioned *borozó* (wine bar) is ladled out by the *deci* (decilitre, 0.1L),

but in more modern places it comes by the ill-defined 'glass'.

LAUNDRY

Laundries (*patyolat*) are fairly common in Hungary, especially in Budapest, though they're never self-service. You can elect to have your laundry done in six hours or one, two or three days – and pay accordingly – though the Top Clean chain in Budapest (see Laundry under Information in that chapter) claims it can do so in just an hour. Dry-cleaning is appalling except at big international hotels.

TOILETS

Public toilets in Hungary are invariably staffed by an old *néné* (auntie), who mops the floor continuously, hands out sheets of grade AAA sandpaper and has seen it all. The usual charge is 50Ft a go and even restaurants and cafes sometimes charge their patrons.

HEALTH

Mosquitoes are a real scourge around lakes and rivers in summer, so be armed with insect repellent (*rovarírtó*). One insect that can bring on more than just an itch, though, is the forest tick (*kullancs*), which burrows under the skin causing inflammation and even encephalitis. It has become a common problem in parts of Central and Eastern Europe, especially eastern Austria, Germany, Hungary and the Czech Republic. You might consider getting an FSME (meningoencephalitis) vaccination if you plan to do extensive hiking and camping in Transdanubia or the Northern Uplands between May and September.

The numbers of registered AIDS cases in Hungary and those who are HIV-positive are relatively low – 210 and 600 respectively – though the Hungarian epidemiologists estimate the actual number of those infected with HIV to be between 3500 and 4000. Those could multiply in a very short time, particularly as Budapest has become the sex industry capital of Eastern and Central Europe. Two AIDS lines operate in Budapest: a 24-hour information line at ☏ 1-338 4555 and a help line (some English

Shiver Me Timbers: Malaria in Hungary

Though it could hardly be called typical, my only experience with a Hungarian hospital was an unqualified success. I had been living in Hungary for six months by then, enjoying things I'd scarcely dreamed about during a dozen or so years in Hong Kong, like attending organ concerts in 18th-century baroque churches and buying raspberries by the kilogram. And at last my partner and I had found a flat with character – a large one perched on the side of Gellért Hill, within neck-craning view of the lovely bronze lady proclaiming liberty throughout the city.

Then I began to feel sick. Really sick. It came fast, as these things often do, and in a matter of days I was running fevers of almost 41°C (that's a delirium-inducing 105.8°F) that would then plummet, throwing me into chilling spasms and sweats. My doctor was phlegmatic as I dripped great puddles onto the floor of his surgery. 'These summer flus are hard to shake,' he said, cautioning me to rest, take vitamins, drink plenty of fluids etc.

After one particularly severe bout of fever, I found myself flipping through an Asian guidebook and reminiscing about a 'farewell' trip we'd made to a remote part of Indonesia the previous winter. I read the health section and the penny dropped. Sure the symptoms were familiar, but aren't they always when you're sick? And it had been over half a year...

Still, I sought advice by telephone from staff at the Hospital for Tropical Diseases in London, who told me to be tested immediately, and the US embassy directed me to the only hospital in Budapest – in Hungary for that matter – dealing with tropical illnesses. Three hours after arriving at the Szent László Hospital in central Pest I had the positive results in hand: two types of malaria contracted in the swamps of south-western Irian Jaya.

It was a speedy, well-nursed recovery and with a half-dozen Lariam tablets in me and a prescribed follow-up course of primaquine to zap the *plasmodium vivax* and *plasmodium falciparum* in their deepest lairs, I was up in no time. My ward mates – a Cambodian student called Sowan suffering from appendicitis and 91-year-old Péter with jaundice – and I would stroll through the old gardens dressed only in our dressing gowns, looking like characters from a Thomas Mann novel.

So a *maláriás beteg* (the malaria patient) – a rare breed indeed in Hungary – became the resident 'talking dog' and an odd mix of doctors and nurses would stop me for a look, a quick examination and a lot of free advice. 'You are *sure* you took all of the prophylactics faithfully – the chloroquine and the Paludrine?' one asked with doubt in her eyes. Did I know about resistant strains, that malaria could lie dormant for up to a year, that a cold shower directly on the kidneys could 'coax' it out? (That last one made me wince as I remembered the ice-cold plunge pool at my favourite Turkish bath.)

The head physician examined me after three days and told me to get dressed. Once I'd paid the relatively modest fee for the private room, board, care and drugs, he said I could return to Gellért Hill and start rearranging the furniture.

---

spoken) on ☎ 1-338 2419 open 8 am to 4 pm weekdays (to 1 pm on Friday).

First-aid and ambulance services are free of charge for citizens of the UK as well as Scandinavian and most Eastern European countries and former republics of the USSR, though follow-up treatment and medicine must be paid for. Treatment at a public outpatient clinic (*rendelő intézet*) costs little, but doctors working privately sometimes charge much more. Very roughly, a consultation in a Hungarian doctor's surgery (*orvosi rendelő*) costs 3000Ft to 5000Ft while a home visit is 8000Ft to 10,000Ft. Consultations and treatment are much more expensive in the new 'Western-style' clinics in Budapest (see Medical Services under Information in that chapter).

Dental work is usually of a high standard and cheap by Western standards (at least the Austrians seem to think so, judging from the numbers who regularly cross the border to have their teeth cleaned or fixed). Some dentists advertise in the English-language press in Budapest.

Most large towns and all of Budapest's 23 districts have a rotating all-night pharmacy open every day; a sign on the door of any pharmacy will help you locate the closest 24-hour one.

WOMEN TRAVELLERS
Hungarian men can be sexist in their thinking, but women do not suffer any particular form of harassment (though rape and domestic violence get little media coverage). Most men – even drunks – are effusively polite with women. Women may not be made to feel especially welcome when eating or drinking alone; really no different than in many other countries in Europe.

Try calling the Women's Line (Nővonal) on ☎ 06-80 505 303 or contact one of the following organisations dealing with women's issues:

Women for Women against Violence (NANE)
(help line ☎ 1-267 4900) PO Box 660, Budapest 1462, open from 6 to 10 pm daily
Feminist Network PO Box 701, Budapest 1399

GAY & LESBIAN TRAVELLERS
There's not much gay life beyond Budapest (see Gay & Lesbian Budapest under Entertainment in that chapter for listings in the capital) unless you take it with you, but there are magazines for both gay men (*Mások*) and lesbians (*Labrisz*) published sporadically. A couple of help lines will provide further information. Visit the gay Web site at www.gayguide-net/europe/hungary/budapest or call the following:

Háttér Gay & Lesbian Association (help line ☎ 1-329 3380) open daily from 6 to 11 pm
Gay Switchboard (help line mobile ☎ 06-309 323 334, fax 1-351 2015) open 4 to 8 pm weekdays

DISABLED TRAVELLERS
Most of Hungary has a very long way to go before it becomes accessible to the physically challenged (one positive step: the 5000Ft and

10,000Ft notes have markings in Braille). Wheelchair ramps, toilets fitted for the disabled and so on are virtually nonexistent though audible traffic signals for the blind are becoming increasingly commonplace.

For more information, contact:

Hungarian Disabled Association (MEOSZ)
(☎ 1-368 1758) San Marco utca 76, Budapest 1035

SENIOR TRAVELLERS
Seniors are sometimes entitled to discounts in Hungary on things like public transport, museum admission fees, etc, provided they show proof of their age. See Seniors' Cards under Visas & Documents earlier in this chapter for more information.

TRAVEL WITH CHILDREN
Successful travel with young children requires planning and effort. Don't try to overdo things; even for adults, packing too much into the time available can cause problems. Make sure the activities include the kids as well – balance that morning at Budapest's Museum of Fine Arts with an afternoon at the nearby Grand Circus or a performance at the puppet theatre. Include children in the trip planning; if they've helped to work out where you will be going, they will be much more interested when they get there. Lonely Planet's *Travel with Children* by Maureen Wheeler is a good resource. Most car-rental firms in Hungary have children's safety seats for hire at a nominal cost, but it is essential that you book them in advance. The same goes for highchairs and cots (cribs); they're standard in many restaurants and hotels but numbers are limited. The choice of baby food, infant formulas, soy and cow's milk, disposable nappies (diapers) and the like can be as great in Hungarian supermarkets these days as it is back home, but the opening hours may be quite different. Don't get caught out at the weekend.

DANGERS & ANNOYANCES
Hungary is hardly a violent or dangerous society. Crime has increased fourfold over the

past decade (notably theft), but violence is seldom directed against travellers. Having said that, attacks – including stabbings – have occurred in the central 5th as well as the dodgy 8th and 9th districts of Budapest (all areas of prostitution – both male and female), and racially motivated attacks by skinheads against Roma, Africans and Arabs are not unknown in other parts of Hungary. The tit-for-tat gangland bombings in Budapest, one of which killed four people in July 1998, have not affected foreigners.

As a traveller, you are most vulnerable to car thieves, pickpockets, taxi louts and the scams of the capital's *konzum lányok*, attractive young women in collusion with rip-off bars and clubs who will see you relieved of a serious chunk of money. These scams have become as common as the stars judging from the number of readers' letters and complaints filed with foreign embassies in Budapest. To learn how to keep out of the clutches of these 'consume girls', see Dangers & Annoyances in the Budapest chapter.

Most Hungarian car thieves are not after fancy Western models because of the difficulty in getting rid of them. But Volkswagens, Audis and the like are very popular, and are easy to dismantle and ship abroad. Don't leave anything of value inside the car, even if it is hidden.

Pickpocketing is most common in flea markets and on certain forms of transport in Budapest (see Dangers & Annoyances in that chapter). Always put your wallet in your front pocket, hold your purse close to your body and keep your backpack or baggage in sight. And watch out for tricks. The usual method on the street is for someone to distract you by running into you and then apologising profusely – as an accomplice takes off with the goods.

Taking a taxi in the provinces is seldom a problem. For information about arriving at your destination in a Budapest taxi without tears (or bruises), see Getting Around in the Budapest chapter.

In the event of an emergency anywhere in Hungary, the following numbers are the most important national ones:

Police	☎ 107
Fire	☎ 105
Ambulance	☎ 104 (☎ 1-111 1666 in English)
Car assistance	☎ 188

BUSINESS HOURS

With rare exceptions, the opening hours (*nyitvatartás*) of a business, museum or government office are posted on the front door (*nyitva* is 'open' and *zárva* is 'closed'). Grocery stores and supermarkets are usually open from 7 am to 7 pm on weekdays and to 1 pm on Saturday, but a few huge supermarkets in Budapest and on the outskirts of provincial cities even open to 1 or 2 pm on Sunday nowadays. There's always at least one 'nonstop' around – convenience stores open round the clock and selling basic food items, bottled drinks and cigarettes, which have sprung up all over the country.

Department stores, clothiers and bookshops keep shorter hours: roughly from 10 am to 6 pm on weekdays (though some stay open until 7 or 8 pm on Thursday) and 9 am to 1 pm on Saturday. Many private shops close early on Friday and throughout most of August. Restaurants in Budapest can stay open till midnight or even later, but don't arrive at one in the provinces after 9 or 9.30 pm and expect to get much to eat.

Bank hours vary but generally they're open from 8 am to 3 or 4 pm Monday to Thursday and to 1 pm on Friday. The main post office in any town, city or Budapest district (usually the ones listed in the Information sections of this book) is open from 8 am to 7 or 8 pm on weekdays and till noon or even 2 pm on Saturday. Branch offices close much earlier – usually at 4 pm – and are never open at the weekend.

PUBLIC HOLIDAYS & SPECIAL EVENTS

Hungary celebrates nine public holidays (*ünnep*) a year:

New Year's Day 1 January
1848 Revolution/National Day 15 March
Easter Monday March/April
Labour Day 1 May

Whit Monday May/June
St Stephen's/Constitution Day 20 August
1956 Remembrance/Republic Day 23 October
Christmas holidays 25-26 December

Hungary's most outstanding annual events
include:

February
Busójárás pre-Lenten carnival Held in
Mohács on the Sunday before Ash Wednesday

March
Budapest Spring Festival
Debrecen Jazz Days

May
Balaton Festival Held in Keszthely

June
World Music Festival Held in Budapest
Savaria International Ballroom Dancing
Competition Held in Szombathely
Szentendre Summer Festival of Arts
Sopron Festival Weeks
Győr Summer International Cultural Festival

July
Hortobágy International Equestrian Days
Held in Hortibágy
Winged Dragon International Street Theatre
Festival Held in Nyírbátor
Kaláka Folk Festival of Music Held in
Miskolc
Danube Folklore Festival Held in Kalocsa,
Baja and Szekszárd
Pannonian Summer Arts Festival Held in
Pécs
Szeged Open-Air Festival
Martonvásár Days Held in Martonvásár
Csángó Festival A festival of folk dancing and
music held in Jászberény

August
Pepsi Island (Pepsi-sziget) Festival of Music
Held on Óbuda Island in Budapest
Hungarian Formula-1 Grand Prix Held in
Magyoród
St Stephen's Day Celebrated with sporting
events, parades and fireworks nationwide
Floral Carnival Held in Debrecen
Zemplén Arts Days

September
Vintage and grape harvest festivals Held
throughout Hungary

October
Budapest Marathon Held in early October
Budapest Autumn Festival Held in Budapest
from mid-October to early November

ACTIVITIES
While Hungary is more of an 'educational'
experience than an 'active' one, when
compared with, say, Australia or Canada,
there's still plenty to do here. You could
forsake many of the country's sights and
spend your entire time boating, bird-
watching or folk dancing.

Hungarians love a day out in the country
to escape their relatively cramped quarters
and the pollution of the towns and cities, and
nothing is more sacred than the *kirándulás*
(outing), which can be a day of horse riding
or just a picnic of *gulyás* cooked in a *bogrács*
(kettle) in the open air by a river or lake.

Cycling
Hungary now counts 1200km of dedicated
bicycle lanes around the country, with another 800km planned over the next few
years. In addition there are another 4000km
or so of roads with light traffic and dikes
suitable for cycling. The HNTO publishes
the useful 1:835000-scale *Bicycle Tour
Map* with eight recommended routes and
descriptions, including Lake Tisza, the
Hortobágy and the North-East. The larger
and more detailed 1:550,000-scale *Hungary
Cycle Route Map* (Paulus; 500Ft) can be
found in Budapest bookshops, as can *Hungary by Bicycle* (NL & Nyír-Karta; 980Ft),
with places of interest, maps and service
centres in Hungarian, German and English.

In Budapest, the Hungarian Bicycle
Touring Association (MKTSZ; ☎ 1-316
5867) at II Bem rakpart 51 can supply more
information as can the Hungarian Cyclists'
Association (☎ 1-302 1463), V Vadász utca
29. For bike tours around Hungary, contact
Velo-Touring (☎ 1-302 1648) at VI Vörösmarty utca 61.

Hiking
Though Hungary does not have high mountains, you can enjoy good hiking in the forests
around Visegrád, Esztergom, Badacsony,

Kőszeg and Budapest. North of Eger are the Bükk Hills and, south of Kecskemét, the Bugac Puszta, both national parks with marked hiking trails.

Cartographia (☎ 1-312 6001) publishes three dozen hiking maps (average scales 1:40,000 and 1:60,000) to the hills, forests, rivers and lakes of Hungary. Most are available from its outlet in Budapest at VI Bajcsy Zsilinszky ut 37 for 250Ft to 700Ft. On hiking maps, paths appear as a red line and usually with a letter, or an abbreviation in Hungarian, indicating the colour-coding of the trail. Colours are painted on trees and markers and are 'K' for *kék* (blue), 'P' for *piros* (red), 'S' for *sárga* (yellow) and 'Z' for *zöld* (green).

The Hungarian Friends of Nature Federation (MTSZ; ☎ 1-311 2467 or ☎ 332 7177) in Budapest at VI Bajcsy-Zsilinszky út 31 organises hiking competitions around the country.

Swimming

Swimming is extremely popular in Hungary, and most towns have both a covered and outdoor pool, allowing enthusiasts to get into the water all year. The entry fee is low (about 200Ft), and you can often rent swimming costumes and bathing caps (the latter are mandatory in some indoor pools for both sexes). All pools have a locker system. Find one, get changed in it (or beside it) and call over the attendant. He or she will lock the door with your clothes inside and hand you a numbered tag to tie on your costume. Lakes and rivers of any size have a grassy *strand* (beach), usually with showers and changing facilities.

Thermal Baths

Since Roman times settlers have been enjoying Hungary's ample thermal waters, and today there are no fewer than 100 spas open to the public throughout the country. Many spas, such as those at Hajdúszoboszló, Sárvár, Gyula and Balatonfüred, are very serious affairs indeed, and people come to 'take the waters' for specific complaints, be it respiratory, muscular, cardiac or gynaecological. Many spa hotels at such places offer cure packages (including accommodation, board, use of the spa and other facilities, medical examination, etc) that last a week or longer. Danubius Travel (☎ 1-317 3562, ✉ danubtra@hungary.net) at V Szervita tér 8 in Budapest is the expert in this field and can book the best packages. Check out its Web site at www.danubiusgroup.com.

The procedure for getting into the warm water is similar to the one for swimming pools, though in Budapest's baths you will sometimes be given a number and will have to wait until it's called or appears on the electronic board. Though some of the local spas and baths look a little rough around the edges, they are clean and the water is changed regularly. You might consider taking along a pair of plastic sandals or flip-flops, however.

Windsurfing

Wherever there's water, a bit of wind and a camp site, you'll find sailboards for rent, eg, on Lake Tisza at Tokaj, on Lake Pécs at Orfű or on Lake Velence. However, the main place for the sport is Lake Balaton, especially at Kilián-telep and Balatonszemes. The best time for the sport is early and late summer, as the wind tends to die down in July and August.

Boating & Kayaking

Qualified sailors can rent boats at locations around Lake Balaton, including Balatonfüred, Tihany, Siófok, Fonyód and Balatonboglár. Only sailing boats and those with electric motors are allowed on the lake.

There are many canoe and kayak trips available. Following the Danube from Rajka to Mohács (386km) or the Tisza River from Tiszabecs to Szeged (570km) are popular runs, but there are less congested waterways and shorter trips such as the 210km stretch of the Körös and Tisza Rivers from Békés to Szeged or the Rába River from Szentgotthárd to Győr (205km).

The HNTO publishes a brochure titled *Great Lakes and Rivers*, which introduces what's available on Hungary's waterways and gives the rules and regulations for boaters. The water tours section of the

Hungarian Friends of Nature Federation (☎ 1-311 9289), VI Bajcsy-Zsilinszky út 31 in Budapest, organises hiking competitions around the country. Nyír-Karta publishes some 16 water-sport maps (*Vízitúrázók térképei*) to the rivers and lakes of Hungary (eg, the 1:50,000 *Sajó* for 400Ft, the 1:20,000 *Duna* for 800Ft etc).

Bird-watching

For details on the excellent possibilities for bird-watching in Hungary, see The Birds of Hungary special section in the Facts about the Country chapter.

Fishing

You'll see people fishing in waterways everywhere. Permits can be bought locally but the best source for information is the Hungarian National Angling Association (Mohosz; ☎ 1-319 1443) in Budapest at XII Korompai utca 17. The cyanide spill into the Tisza River will have changed conditions in that river (see 'Cyanide Spill' in Facts about Hungary chapter).

Horse Riding

There's a saying in Hungarian that the Magyars were 'created by God to sit on horseback'. Judging from the number of stables, riding schools and courses around the country, that is still true today. The HNTO produces a useful brochure called *Riding in Hungary* with both general and very detailed information.

A lot of the riding in Hungary is the follow-the-leader variety up to a castle or through open fields, but larger schools have horses for more advanced equestrians that can be taken into the hills or across the puszta. These schools also offer lessons. Not surprisingly, the best centres are on the Great Plain – at Máta near Hortobágy, Lajosmizse and Bugacpuszta near Kecskemét and Solt, north of Kalocsa. In Transdanubia you'll find good schools at Nagycenk and Szombathely while around Lake Balaton they're at Szántódpuszta and Keszthely. Gizellatelep near Visegrád has some of the best horse flesh in the country, but nothing beats mounting a Lipizzaner at

the stud farm at Szilvásvárad in the Northern Uplands.

It's risky – particularly in the high season – to show up at a riding centre without a booking. Book through the local tourist office or the Hungarian Equestrian Tourism Association (☎ 1-317 1644) at V Ferenciek tere 4 in Budapest. You can also contact Pegazus Tours (☎ 1-317 1644, fax 267 0171, ✉ pegazus@mail.datanet.hu) at V Ferenciek tere 5, which organises riding tours of between three and 10 days in Transdanubia, the Great Plain and around Lake Balaton. Prices range from DM218 per person for a five-day tour of Somogy County in Southern Transdanubia to DM1685 for 10 days of the Bugacpuszta on the Great Plain.

Hunting

Whether you like it or not, hunting is big business in Hungary, and roe and red deer, mouflon, wild pig, hare, pheasant and duck abound in wooded areas like the Gemenc Forest in Southern Transdanubia. Strict rules apply, and you must do your hunting through one of the large hunting agencies such as Budapest-based Pannonvad (☎ 1-375 4089), I Várfok utca 15/b, or MAVAD (☎ 1-375 9611), I Úri utca 39, Budapest.

LANGUAGE COURSES

Schools teaching Hungarian to foreigners have proliferated – at least in Budapest – over the past five years.

Reliable schools in the capital include:

Arany János Language School (☎ 1-311 8870) VI Csengery utca 68
Danubius Language School (☎ 1-269 1537) VI Bajcsy-Zsilinszky köz 1
Hungarian Language School (☎ 1-312 5899) VI Rippl-Rónai utca 4

The granddaddy of all Hungarian language schools is the Debrecen Summer University, which organises intensive two- and four-week courses in July and August and 80-hour, two-week advanced courses in winter. The emphasis is not just on language but the whole Magyar picture: art, history, culture, literature. The two-week

(60-hour)/four-week (120-hour) summer courses cost US$250/490; board and lodging accommodation in a triple room (singles and doubles are available at extra cost) is US$350/180. For more information, contact the Debrecen Summer University (Debreceni Nyári Egyetem; ☎/fax 52-489 117, ✉ nyariegy@tigris.klte.hu), PO Box 35, Debrecen 4010.

WORK

Travellers on tourist visas in Hungary are not supposed to accept employment, but many end up teaching, doing a little writing for the English-language press or even working for foreign firms without permits. Check the English-language telephone book or advertisements for English-language schools in the *Budapest Sun*, which also has job listings but the pay is generally pretty low. You can do much better teaching privately (1000Ft to 2000Ft per 45-minute 'hour') once you've built up the contacts.

Obtaining an official work permit involves a Byzantine paper chase with Hungarian bureaucracy and, at the end of it all, you'll have to pay Hungarian income tax. First you'll need a letter of support from your prospective employer to get a one-year renewable residency. You'll need copies of your birth certificate and school transcript or academic record officially translated into Hungarian (3000Ft per page). A medical exam and AIDS test (12,000Ft) is also mandatory. The office in Budapest dealing with foreigners' registrations is KEOKH (☎ 1-343 0034) at VI Városligeti fasor 46-48.

ACCOMMODATION

Except during the peak summer season – July and August – in places like Budapest, parts of Lake Balaton, the Danube Bend and the Mátra Hills, you should have no problem finding accommodation to fit your budget in Hungary. Camp sites are plentiful; university and college dormitories open their doors to guests during summer and other holiday periods; large trade-union holiday homes have been converted into hostels and hotels; and, family-run pensions have sprung up everywhere. It's unusual for

even a small town not to have a hotel, and the paying-guest service (see Private Rooms later in this chapter) is as common as B&Bs are in the UK and Ireland.

The price quoted should be the price you pay, but it is not as cut-and-dried as that. There's a 10% turnover tax on all hotels, though this should definitely be included in the price you've been told. In the past, all hotels and pensions included breakfast in their rates, but this is changing and now quite a few do not. Certain places insist on a 'mandatory breakfast' and charge you from 500Ft even if you don't want it (and it's never the huge buffet served in other Eastern European countries).

Tourist offices and bureaus charge you a small fee for booking a private room or other accommodation, and there's usually a surcharge if you stay for less than three or four nights. Many cities and towns levy a local tourist tax of between 150Ft and 250Ft per person per night – sometimes only after the first 48 hours though. People under 18 years of age or staying at camping grounds may be exempt.

It is usually difficult to get a single room. Outside expensive hotels, a room is designated a single, double or triple according to how many beds it has and not by the number of occupants. If you are travelling solo and the owners try to charge you for a double, insist – pleasantly – that you are alone. You should be able to negotiate the price down depending on the location, season and staff.

Inflation is running at just over 14%, so prices will almost certainly be higher than those quoted in this book, although they shouldn't change much when quoted in Deutschmarks, and the relative differences between various establishments in forint should stay the same. The room rate usually increases in April for the summer season – sometimes by as much as 30%. Where possible, we've indicated seasonal price differences in this book, eg, 'doubles are 1800Ft to 3200Ft').

Camping

Hungary counts upwards of 400 camping grounds, and these are the cheapest places to stay. Small, private camping grounds accommodating as few as six tents are usually preferable to the large, noisy, 'official' camping grounds. Prices for two adults plus tent vary from as low as 400Ft, off the beaten track in the Northern Uplands, to 10 times that amount on Lake Balaton in summer.

Most camping grounds are open from May to September (though some open in April and close in October) and rent small bungalows (*üdölőház* or *faház*) from around 1200Ft per person to those without tents. In midsummer the bungalows may all be booked, so it pays to check with the local tourist office before making the trip. Holders of the Camping Card International sometimes get a discount of 5% to 10%. Camping 'wild' is prohibited in Hungary.

For more information, contact the Hungarian Camping and Caravaning Club (MCCC; ☎ 1-317 3703), VIII Üllői út 6, in Budapest.

Hostels & University Accommodation

Despite all the 'hostels' listed in the HI/Hungarian Youth Hostel Federation handbook available at Tourinform offices everywhere, an HI card doesn't get you very far in Hungary. With the exception of those in Budapest, most of the youth hostels (*ifjúsági szálló*) are in places well off the beaten track. Generally, the only year-round hostels are in Budapest.

Hostel beds cost 1200Ft to 4000Ft, depending on room size, in Budapest and considerably less elsewhere. An HI card is not required, although you occasionally get 10% off with one or not be required to pay the tourist tax if there is one. There's no age limit at the hostels, which remain open all day and are often good places to meet other travellers. The hostels almost always have cooking facilities and Internet access is becoming more and more common.

From 1 July to 20 August *only*, Hungary's cheapest rooms are available in vacant student dormitories, known as *kollégium* or *diákszálló*, where beds in double, triple and quadruple rooms begin at around 600Ft per person. There's no need to show a student or

hostel card, and it usually won't get you any discount anyway.

The Hungarian Youth Hostel Federation (MISZSZ; ☎ 1-352 1572) is based in Budapest at VII Almássy tér 6.

Private Rooms

Hungary's 'paying-guest service' (*fizető-vendég szolgálat*) is a great deal and still relatively cheap. Expect to pay from 1200Ft to 3000Ft per person, depending on the class and location of the room. Private rooms at Lake Balaton are always more expensive, even in the shoulder seasons. Single rooms are often hard to come by, and you'll usually have to pay a 30% supplement if you stay less than three or four nights. Some agencies also have entire flats or holiday homes for rent without the owner in residence. These can be a good deal if there are four or more of you travelling together and you want to stay put for a while.

Private rooms are assigned by travel agencies, which take your money and give you a voucher bearing the address or sometimes even the key to the flat. If the first room you're offered seems too expensive, ask if there is something cheaper. There are usually several agencies offering private rooms, so ask around if the price seems higher than usual or the location inconvenient.

If you decide to take a private room, you'll share a house or flat with a Hungarian widow, couple or family. The toilet facilities are usually communal, but otherwise you can close your door and enjoy as much privacy as you please. All 1st and some 2nd and 3rd-class rooms have shared kitchen facilities. In Budapest you may have to take a room far from the centre of town, but public transport is good and inexpensive.

Individuals at train stations in Budapest may offer you an unofficial private room. The prices these people ask are often higher than those at the agencies, and you will have nowhere to complain in case of problems. Sometimes these people misrepresent the location or quality of their rooms to convince you to go with them. In resort areas look for houses with signs reading '*szoba kiadó'* or *'Zimmer frei'*, advertising private rooms in Hungarian or German.

Village Tourism Village tourism (*falusi turizmus*), which means staying at a farmhouse, is in no way as developed as it is in, say, Slovenia, and most of the places are truly remote, but the price is right: from 500Ft to 1700Ft per person per night. The National Village Tourism Association (FTOSZ; ☎ 1-352 9804, fax 268 0592) at Király utca 93 in Budapest publishes a comprehensive catalogue, available at Tourinform offices, that lists farmhouses accepting paying guests. By their very nature, these places are well off the beaten track, and you'll usually need your own transport.

Pensions

Privately run pensions (*panzió*), which have formed the biggest growth area in the Hungarian hospitality trade over the past decade, are really just little hotels of up to a dozen or so rooms charging from 4000Ft in the provinces and twice that in Budapest for a double with shower. They are usually new and very clean and usually have an attached restaurant.

Most pensions in Budapest (where there are as many pensions as there are hotel rooms) are up in the Buda Hills, while in the provinces they're often 2km to 3km out of town. Thus they're best for people travelling under their own steam, and visitors from Austria and Germany seem to favour them. But that's changing too, and you'll sometimes find them downtown in cities like Budapest, Győr, Sopron and Pécs, along the Danube Bend and on Lake Balaton. Always ask to see a room first as they can vary. Those under the roof – so-called 'mansard rooms' – are cramped but cheaper. You are sometimes allowed to use the kitchen at a pension.

Hotels

Hotels, called *szálló* or *szálloda*, can run the gamut from luxurious five-star palaces like the Kempinski Corvinus in Budapest to the derelict Béke (Peace) hotel you can still find in a few Hungarian towns and small cities. The cheapest hotel rooms are more expensive than private rooms, but they are a real bargain by international standards (from 3000Ft single, 5000Ft double). A hotel may be the answer if you're only staying one night, or if you arrive too late to get a private room through an agency.

Two-star hotels usually have rooms with private bathroom, whereas at one-star hotels the bathroom is usually down the hall. Breakfast – a meal at which the Hungarians decidedly do not excel – is usually (but not always) included in the room price. Expect ersatz coffee, weak tea, unsweetened lemon 'juice', tiny triangles of processed 'cheese' and stale bread.

For the big splurge, if you're romantically inclined, or if you're travelling with a rich uncle or aunt, check Hungary's network of castle and mansion hotels, *kastély szálló* or *kúria szálló*. These need not break the bank: the one at Esterházy Palace in Fertőd, for example, charges 2800/3300/3700Ft for doubles/triples/quads with shared bath and the hotel at the Zichy family's country manor house at Seregélyes near Székesfehérvár costs 9900Ft for a double. But most of the fancy castle hotels have at least three stars and charge accordingly. The HNTO brochure *Historic Mansions, Castles and Palaces* lists more than two dozen of the nation's finest residences, including those that accept guests.

FOOD

Much has been written about Hungarian food – some of it silly, much of it downright false. It's true that Hungarian cuisine has had many outside influences and that it makes great use of paprika. But that spice is pretty mild stuff; a taco with salsa or chicken vindaloo from the corner takeaway will taste a lot more 'fiery' to you. Paprika in its many varieties is used predominantly with sour cream or in *rántás*, a heavy roux of pork lard and flour added to cooked vegetables. Most meat dishes – and Hungarians eat an astonishing amount of flesh – are breaded and fried or baked.

Hungary's reputation as a food centre dates partly from the last century and partly from the chilly days of Communism. In the heady days following the advent of the Dual Monarchy and right up to WWII, food became a passion among well-to-do city folk, and writers and poets sang its praises. This was the 'gilded age' of the famous chefs and confectioners Károly Gundel and József Dobos and of Gypsy violinists like Jancsi Rigo and Gyula Benczi, an age when nothing was too extravagant. The world took note and Hungarian restaurants sprouted up in cities around the world – including a 'Cafe Budapest' in Boston, Massachusetts – complete with imported Gypsy bands and waiters who sounded like Bela Lugosi and Zsa Zsa Gabor.

After the war, Hungary's gastronomic reputation lived on – most notably because everything else in the region was so very bad. Hungarian food was, as one observer noted, 'a bright spot in a culinary black hole'. But most of the best chefs, including Gundel himself, had voted with their feet and left the country in the 1950s, and restaurants were put under state control. The reputation and the reality of food in Hungary had diverged.

Although inexpensive by Western standards and served in huge portions, Hungarian food today remains heavy and, frankly, can be unhealthy. Meat, sour cream and fat abound and, except in season, saláta means a plate of pickled beets, cabbage and peppers. There are a few bright spots, though. Vegetarian restaurants (or ones at least halfway there) are opening up, and ethnic food – from Middle Eastern and Italian to fast-food Thai and Chinese is very popular. And even Hungarian food seems to be going through a transformation at many middle-level and upmarket restaurants; many Magyars have tried 'New Hungarian' cuisine and seem to like it – judging from the bookings at the establishments serving it.

On the whole, Hungarians are not big breakfast eaters at home, preferring a cup of tea or coffee with an unadorned bread roll at the kitchen table or on the way to work. (It is said that Hungarians will 'eat bread with bread'.) Lunch, eaten at 1 pm, is often the main meal and can consist of two or three courses, though this is changing in the cities. Dinner – supper, really – is less substantial when eaten at home, often just sliced meats, cheese and some pickled vegetables.

It is important to note the various sauces and cooking methods unique to Hungarian food. Pörkölt (stew) is what almost everyone calls 'goulash' abroad; the addition of sour cream makes the dish, whatever it may contain, paprikás. Gulyás or gulyásleves is a thickish soup of beef, usually eaten as a main course. Halászlé, fish soup with paprika and one of the spicier dishes around, is also a main dish. Items such as cabbage or peppers, are stuffed with meat and rice and cooked in rántás, tomato sauce or sour cream (töltött). As a savoury, palacsinta (pancakes) can be prepared in a similar way, but they also appear as a dessert with chocolate and nuts. Lecsó is a tasty stewed sauce of peppers, tomatoes and onions served with meat.

Pork is the preferred meat, followed by beef. Chicken and goose legs and turkey breasts – though not much else of the birds – make it on to most menus. Freshwater fish from Lake Balaton, such as the indigenous fogas (pike-perch), or from the Tisza River is plentiful, but quite expensive and often overcooked. Lamb and mutton are rarely eaten in Hungary.

A main course usually comes with some sort of starch and a little garnish of pickles. Vegetables and salads must be ordered separately. A typical menu will have up to 10 pork and beef dishes, a couple of fish ones and usually only one poultry dish.

Vegetarian Food

In restaurants, vegetarians can usually order fried mushroom caps (gombafejek rántva), pasta dishes with cheese like túrós csusza and sztrapacska, or plain little dumplings (galuszka). Salad as it's usually known around the world is called vitamin saláta here and usually available when in season; everything else is savanyúság (literally 'sourness') or pickled things. Boiled, vegetables (zöldség) are 'English-style' or angolos zöldség. The traditional way of preparing vegetables is in főzelék, where they're fried or boiled and then mixed into a roux with cream.

Lángos, a deep-fried dough with various toppings, is a cheep meatless snack sold on streets throughout the land. Plain/sour cream/cheese lángos usually cost 70/90/110Ft.

Eating Out

It's useful to know the names of the types of Hungarian eateries though distinctions can sometimes be a bit blurred.

An *étterem* is a restaurant with a large selection, including international dishes, and is usually relatively expensive. A *vendéglő* or *kisvendéglő* is smaller and is supposed to serve regional dishes or 'home cooking', but the name is now 'cute' enough for a lot of large places to use it. An *étkezde* is something like a vendéglő but cheaper, smaller and often with counter seating. The overused term *csárda* originally signified a country inn with a rustic atmosphere, Gypsy music and hearty local dishes. Now any place that strings dry paprikas on the wall is a csárda. Most restaurants offer a good-value set menu (*menü*) of two or three courses at lunch.

A *bisztró* is a much cheaper sit-down place that is usually *önkiszolgáló* (self-service). A *büfé* is cheaper still with a very limited menu. Here you eat while standing at counters.

Most butcher shops (*hentesáru bolt*) have a büfé on the side selling boiled or fried *kolbász* (sausage), *wirsli* (frankfurters), roast chicken, bread and pickles. Point to what you want; the staff will weigh it all and hand you a slip of paper with the price. You usually pay at the *pénztar* (cashier) and hand the stamped receipt back to the staff for your food. Food stalls, known as *Laci konyha* (Larry's kitchen) *pecsenyesütő*, sell the same sorts of things, as well as fish when located beside lakes or rivers. At these last few places you pay for everything, including a dollop of mustard for your kolbász, and eat with your hands.

An *eszpresszó* is essentially a coffee house, but usually also sells alcoholic drinks and light snacks. A *cukrászda* serves cakes, pastries and ice cream.

It is not unknown for waiters to try to rip you off once they see you are a foreigner. They may try to bring you an unordered dish or make a 'mistake' when tallying the bill. If you think there's a discrepancy, ask for the menu and check the bill carefully. The most common ruse is to bring you the most expensive beer or wine when you order a draught or a glass. Ask the price before you order. If you've been taken for more than 15% or 20% of the bill, call for the manager. Otherwise just don't leave a tip (see the section on Tipping & Bargaining earlier in this chapter).

DRINKS
Nonalcoholic Drinks

Most international soft drink brands are available in Hungary, but mineral water seems to be the most popular libation for teetotallers in pubs and bars. Fruit juice is usually canned or boxed fruit 'drink' with lots of sugar added.

Hungarians drink a tremendous amount of coffee (*kavé*) – as a single black (*fekete*), a double (*dupla*) or with milk (*tejes kávé*). Most better cafes now serve some variation of cappuccino. Decaffeinated coffee is *koffeinmentes káve'*.

Black tea (*tea*, pronounced 'TAY-ah') is not popular in Hungary (though teahouses seem to be all the rage in the trendier neighbourhoods of Budapest these days). In fact it can often be difficult to find 'English' tea in small grocery stores, though you'll always be able to choose from a wide range of herbal teas and tisanes. When Hungarians do drink tea they never add milk, preferring lemon, honey or even rum.

Alcoholic Drinks

Wine See the special section The Wines of Hungary starting on page 65..

Brandy & Liqueur An alcoholic drink that is as Hungarian as wine is *pálinka*, a strong brandy distilled from a variety of fruits but most commonly from plums or apricots. There are many different types and qualities but the best is Óbarack, the double-distilled 'Old Apricot', and anything with *kóser* (kosher) on the label.

Hungarian liqueurs are usually unbearably sweet and taste artificial, though the Zwack brand is reliable. Zwack also produces Unicum, a bitter apéritif that has been around since 1790. The Austrian emperor Joseph II christened the liqueur when he tasted it and supposedly exclaimed '*Das ist ein Unikum!*' (This is a unique drink!). It's an acquired taste.

Beer Hungary produces a number of its own beers for national distribution (eg, Dreher and Kőbanyai), though some are usually found only near where they are brewed such as Kanizsai in Nagykanizsa and Szalon in Pécs. Bottled Austrian and German beer like Gösser, Holstein and Zipfer – either imported or brewed here in Hungary under licence – are readily available as are Czech imports like Pilsner Urquell, Budweiser and Staropramen.

Beer is available in pubs and shops in half-litre bottles and imported cans, and many licensed pubs and bars now sell their own draught beers in half or one-third litre glasses. Locally brewed and imported beer in Hungary is almost always lager, though occasionally you'll find Dreher stout.

ENTERTAINMENT

Hungary is a very culture-oriented society, and the arts – especially music – are dear to the hearts (and ears) of most people. Many cities and even some large towns have a symphony or chamber orchestra, a theatre where plays and musicals are staged, and a cultural centre where other events take place. Outside Budapest, cultural life is especially active in Debrecen, Eger, Győr, Kecskemét, Pécs, Sopron, Szeged and Szombathely. Festivals in spring, summer and autumn are scheduled in cities throughout the country (see Public Holidays & Special Events earlier in this chapter), and some of them, like the Budapest Spring Festival, attract many visitors from abroad. Some useful words to remember are *színház* (theatre), *pénztár* (box office), *jegy* (ticket) and *elkelt* (sold out).

In the first few years after the fall of Communism, the loss of state subsidies forced many smaller festivals and groups to cut back their events and performances. Theatre troupes, which now had to rely on box-office receipts, abandoned classical and avant-garde drama in favour of imported musical productions like *Macskák* (Cats) or *Sakk* (Chess) – and the crowds loved it. But things seem to have gone full circle and along with popular musicals and classic and modern Hungarian plays by Mihály Babits and István Örkény, theatregoers can choose anything and everything from Chekhov's *Ványa bácsi* (Uncle Vanya) and Shakespeare's *Sok Hűhó Semmiért* (Much Ado about Nothing) to Edward Albee's *Három Magas Nő* (Three Tall Women).

Your best single source of information for performances nationwide is *Programme in Hungary*, which is available in German and English. Complete listings of plays, concerts, exhibitions and films for the capital can be found in the weekly *Pesti Műsor* and the freebie *Pesti Est*, available in Hungarian only. The latter publishes editions to almost 20 other cities and regions – from *Békés Est* to *Zalai Est*. You can pick them up for free in tourist offices.

Tickets, for as little as 500Ft (except during special festivals), can be purchased at the venue. It's always safer to get tickets in advance, particularly in smaller towns where the production may be the big event of the month and the place 'to be seen'. You'll find the addresses of ticket offices and information sources under individual cities and towns.

Of course, it's not all Mozart and Brecht. Hungary is now on the circuit for many pop and rock bands – hey, the Stones, Michael Jackson and Tina Turner were all there within a year of each other in the mid-1990s and more recent acts have included Massive Attack, Jamiroquai, the Red Hot Chilli Peppers and Chumbawumba.

The summertime Pepsi-sziget Festival in Budapest in August (see Public Holidays & Special Events) is now Europe's largest outdoor music festival.

The *táncház* (literally 'dance house'), an evening of Hungarian folk music and some traditional dance, is great entertainment and an excellent way to meet Hungarians. You'll seldom find táncház outside the capital though.

Be aware that many foreign films are dubbed into Hungarian, so try asking the ticket seller if the film you plan to see is dubbed (*szinkronizált* or *magyarul beszélő*), or only has Hungarian subtitles (*feliratos*) and retains the original soundtrack. All films listed under their English titles are in the latter category. Seats are assigned in most cinemas, and admission is usually 500Ft to 700Ft. In theatres, there are *bal* (left) and *jobb* (right) seats with the same numbers so make sure you know which one you are. To make sure you arrive at the correct time, see the Time section earlier in this chapter.

Discos and clubs – which range from those in Budapest's rollicking rave houses to unpretentious get-togethers in provincial sport halls – are the most popular form of entertainment for young people and are always good fun. Striptease and sex shows attract foreigners and the well-heeled Hungarian *új gazdag* (nouveau riche).

SPECTATOR SPORTS

Swimming is extremely popular, as is water polo, a sport at which Hungary excels. For its size, Hungary has done extremely well in the Olympics. At the 1996 Olympic Games in Atlanta, for example, they finished 12th overall out of 197 countries, with 21 medals, including seven gold. (They ranked eighth in 1992 at Barcelona with 30 medals, 11 of them gold.) Chess is also hugely popular – even as a spectator sport!

Football is far and away the nation's favourite sport, and people still talk about the 'match of the century' at Wembley in 1953 when the Magic Magyars beat England 6-3 – the first time England lost a home match. The Hungarian Formula-1 Grand Prix in August is the sporting event of the year for those in and around the capital.

For more information on Hungarian sports and where and when to watch them see the Spectator Sport section in the Budapest chapter.

SHOPPING

Hungarian shops are well stocked with generally high quality products. Food, alcohol, books and folk-music recordings are affordable, and there is an excellent selection. Traditional products include folk art embroidery and ceramics, wall hangings, painted wooden toys and boxes, dolls, all forms of basketry and porcelain (especially Herend and Zsolnay). Feather or goose down goods like pillows and duvets (comforters or doonas) are of superb quality.

Foodstuffs that are expensive or difficult to buy elsewhere – goose liver (both fresh and potted), caviar and some prepared meats like Pick salami – make nice gifts as do the many varieties of paprika (if you're allowed to take them home).

Some of Hungary's new 'boutique' wines – especially the ones with imaginative labels – make good, relatively inexpensive gifts. A bottle of sweet Tokaj dessert wine always goes down a treat – again and again.

The Wines of Hungary

Previous page: Fine new Hungarian wine. (Photo by David Greedy.)

Top: Wines from the Tokaj region are probably the most famous in Hungary and are readily available in Budapest.

Bottom: An owner of one of the wine cellars in Eger's 'Valley of the Beautiful Women' pours Egri Bikavér (Bull's Blood) from a flute.

Wine has been produced in Hungary for thousands of years, and it remains very important both economically and socially. You'll find it available by the glass or bottle everywhere in Budapest – at *borozó* (wine bars, but very basic affairs by international standards), food stalls, restaurants, supermarkets and 24-hour grocery stores – at very reasonable prices. In summer, spritzers (wine coolers) of red or white wine and mineral water are consumed in large quantities.

Before WWII Hungarian wine was much in demand throughout Europe, but with the advent of socialism and mass production, foreign wine enthusiasts were generally disappointed by the Hungarian product. Most of what wasn't consumed at home went to the Soviet Union where, frankly, they were happy to drink anything. This and state control offered little incentive to upgrade antiquated standards of wine-making and to apply modern methods to traditional grape varieties.

All of that is changing – and fast. Small to medium-sized upscale family-owned wineries such as Tiffán, Bock, Szeremley, Thummerer and others are now producing very good wines indeed. Joint ventures with foreign vintners (eg, GIA in Eger partnered with Italians, the Hungarian-Austrian Gere-Weninger winery in Villány, and Disznókő with French vintners in Tokaj) are helping to reshape the industry, arguably the most exciting and fastest-growing in Hungary.

When choosing wine here, look for the words *minőségi bor* (quality wine) or *különleges minőségű bor* (premium quality wine), Hungary's version of *appellation controlée*. Generally speaking, vintage (*évjárat*) is not as important here as it is in France or Germany, and the quality of a label can sometimes vary widely from bottle to bottle.

On a Hungarian wine label, the first word indicates where the wine comes from while the second word is the grape variety (eg, Villányi Kékfrankos) or the type or brand of wine (eg, Tokaji Aszú, Szekszárdi Bikavér etc). To decipher other words on Hungarian wine labels, see Drinks in the Language section at the back of this book.

With the inclusion of two new ones in 1998 (Zala and Tolna), Hungary now counts 22 wine-growing areas in Transdanubia, the Northern Uplands and on the Great Plain. They range in size from tiny Somló (essentially just one hill) in Western Transdanubia to the vast vineyards of the Kiskunság on the Southern Plain, with its sandy soil nurturing more than a third of all the vines growing in the country. The wines from the latter are mass-produced, however, and inferior to those from other parts of Hungary.

Of course it's all a matter of taste, but the most distinctive red wines come from Villány and Szekszárd in Southern Transdanubia and the best whites are produced around Lake Balaton and in Somló. However, the reds from Eger and sweet whites from Tokaj are much better known abroad.

TOKAJ

The volcanic soil, sunny climate and protective mountain barrier of the Tokaj-Hegyalja region in the Northern Uplands make it ideal for wine-making. Tokaj wines were exported to Poland and Russia in the Middle Ages and reached the peak of their popularity in Western Europe in the 17th and 18th centuries, gaining some illustrious fans along the way. King Louis XIV famously called Tokaj 'the wine of kings and the king of wines', while Voltaire wrote that 'this wine could only be given by the boundlessly good God'.

Tokaj dessert wines are rated according to the number – from three to six – of *puttony* (butts, or baskets for picking the grapes) of sweet Aszú essence added to the base wines. This essence comes from a grape infected with 'noble rot', a mould called *botrytis cinera* that almost turns it into a raisin on the vine. But Tokaj also produces less-sweet wines: dry Szamorodni (an excellent aperitif); sweet Szamorodni, which is not unlike an Italian *vin santo*; Furmint; and, the driest of them all, Hárs-levelű (Linden Leaf). Some Hungarian wine connoisseurs believe Furmint to be potentially the best white wine in the country – Hungary's own Chardonnay. It has a flavour vaguely reminiscent of apples.

For Tokaji Aszú *the* name to look out for is István Szepsy, one of Hungary's most innovative winemakers, who concentrates on the

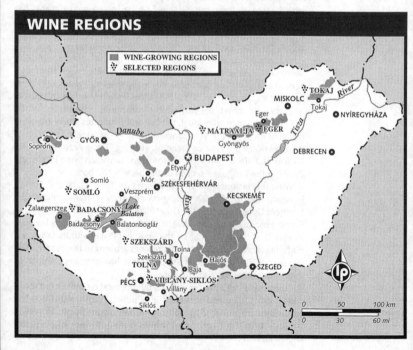

WINE REGIONS

- **WINE-GROWING REGIONS**
- ❖ **SELECTED REGIONS**

❖ TOKAJ
MISKOLC
Tokaj
❖ NYÍREGYHÁZA
Eger
❖ MÁTRAALJA   ❖ EGER
Gyöngyös
DEBRECEN
Danube
GYŐR
Sopron
❖ BUDAPEST
Etyek
Mór
Somló   SZÉKESFEHÉRVÁR
❖ SOMLÓ   Veszprém
KECSKEMÉT
Zalaegerszeg   ❖ BADACSONY   Lake Balaton
Badacsony   Balatonboglár
❖ SZEKSZÁRD
Szekszárd   Tolna
TOLNA   Hajós
Baja   SZEGED
PÉCS   ❖ VILLÁNY-SIKLÓS
Villány
Siklós

0   50   100 km
0   30   60 mi

upscale six-puttony variety as well as the *Aszúesszencia* itself; his 1995 six-puttony Aszú currently retails for a cool 13,000Ft. Château Pajzos has produced a *natúresszencia*, with such a high concentration of honey-sweet free-run juice that it is almost a syrup. Disznókő produces a six-puttony 1993 Aszú that tastes of apricots (5000Ft to 7000Ft) and a fine sweet Szamorodni. Other good names to watch out for are Oremus and Hétszőlő.

Vintage plays a more important role in Tokaj than elsewhere in Hungary, and it is said that there is only one truly excellent year each decade. The wines produced in 1972, 1988 and 1999 were superb, though 1993 and 1995 were also good years.

EGER

This lovely city flanked by two of the Northern Uplands' most beautiful ranges of hills (the Bükk and the Mátra) is the home of the celebrated Egri Bikavér (Eger Bull's Blood), a wine known the world over. By law, Hungarian winemakers must spell out the blend on the label; the sole exception is Bikavér, though it is usually Kékfrankos (Blaufränkisch) mixed with other reds, sometimes including Kadarka. The only winemaker's blend of Bikavér known for sure is that of Tibor Gál. His is 50% Kékfrankos and 50% Cabernet and it is excellent.

Eger produces Pinot Noir but it is a far cry from that of Burgundy, its true home. Still, Vilmos Thummerer's 1999 Pinot Noir (6000Ft) promises to be one of the finest produced in Hungary. You'll also find several decent whites in Eger, including Leányka (Little Girl), Olaszrizling (Italian Riesling) and Hárslevelű from Debrő.

VILLÁNY

Villány is one of Hungary's principal producers of wine, noted especially for its red Oportó, Cabernet Sauvignon, Merlot and Cabernet Franc wines. They are almost always big-bodied Bordeaux-style wines high in tannin. Many are *barrique* wines – those aged in new oak barrels that are then discarded or passed on to other wineries – and remain a favourite of Hungarian yuppies, who like its 'big' flavour and the fact that it is so easy to recognise.

Among the best vintners in Villány is József Bock, whose Cuvée Barrique is a smoky, earthy special blend of Kékfrankos (Blaufränkisch), Cabernet and Merlot. Other wines to try include Attila Gere's elegant and complex Cabernet Sauvignon and the austere, tannic Kékoportó (Blue Oporto or Blue Portuguese) and Cabernet Franc produced by Ede Tiffán.

Because of their international exposure, Villány wines tend to be overpriced. At present there is not much competition as the government slaps a 70% duty on all imported wine. But once Hungary joins the European Union and the barriers come down, Villány wine will no doubt be the first to suffer.

SZEKSZÁRD

Mild winters and warm, dry summers combined with favourable loess soil help Szekszárd in Southern Transdanubia to produce some of the best red wines in Hungary. They are not like the big-bodied reds of Villány but softer, less complex and easier to drink. And in general they are much better value, with an excellent, premium-quality Szekszárd retailing for 1500Ft to 2000Ft.

The premier grape here is Kadarka, a late-ripening and vulnerable variety that is produced in limited quantities. Franz Schubert is said to have been inspired to write his *Trout Quintet* after a glass or two, and Franz Liszt, a frequent visitor to Szekszárd in the 1840s, preferred to 'drink it until his death' some 40 years later. The best is made by Ferenc Takler (1000Ft).

Kadarka originated in the Balkans and is a traditional ingredient in making Bikavér, a wine that is usually associated with Eger but is also produced in Szekszárd. In fact, many wine aficionados in Hungary prefer the Szekszárd variety of Bull's Blood. The best Merlot and Kékfrankos (1500Ft to 2000Ft) from Szekszárd is produced by Ferenc Vesztergombi, who also makes an excellent Bikavér.

BADACSONY

The Badacsony region is named after the 400m basalt massif that rises like a loaf of bread from the Tapolca Basin along the north-western shore of Lake Balaton. Wine has been produced here for centuries, and the region's Olaszrizling, especially that produced by Huba Szeremley (under 1000Ft), is arguably the best dry white wine for everyday drinking to be had in Hungary.

Olaszrizling, a straw-blond 'Italian Riesling' high in acid that is related to the famous Rhine vintages in name only, is drunk young – in fact, the younger it is, the better.

The area's volcanic soil gives the unique Kéknyelű (Blue Stalk) wine its distinctive mineral taste; it is a blunt, complex and age-worthy tipple wine. Szeremley's version of Kéknyelű (2000Ft) is the only reliably authentic example.

SOMLÓ

The entire region of Somló is a single volcanic dome, and the soil helps to produce wine that is mineral-tasting, almost flinty.

The region can boast two great and indigenous varieties: Hárslevelű and Juhfark (Sheep's Tail); the latter takes its name from the shape of its grape cluster. Firm acids give 'spine' to this wine, and it is best when five years old.

Foremost among the producers of Somló Hárslevelű and Juhfark (under 1000Ft) is Béla Fekete. Another big name in these parts is Imre Györgykovács, whose Olaszrizling (1000Ft to 1500Ft) is a big wine with a taste vaguely reminiscent of burnt almonds.

WINE & FOOD

The pairing of food with wine is as great an obsession in Hungary as it is elsewhere. Everyone agrees that sweets like strudel (*rétes*) go very well indeed with a Tokaji Aszú but what is less appreciated is the wonderful synergy that this wine enjoys with savoury foods like *foie gras*. A bone-dry Olaszrizling from Badacsony is a superb accompaniment to any fish dish, but especially the *fogas* (pike-perch) indigenous to nearby Lake Balaton.

It would be a shame to 'waste' a big wine like a Villány Cabernet on traditional but simple Hungarian dishes like *gulyás* or *pörkölt*; save it for a more complex or sophisticated meat dish. Instead, try Kékfrankos, a wine that never seems to fail. Cheese and cream-based dishes stand up well to late-harvest Furmint, and pork dishes are nice with new Furmint.

For those who would like to learn more about Hungarian wines, the best sources of information are *The Wines and Vines of Hungary* by Stephen Kirkland; the *Wine Guide Hungary*, published annually by the Borkollégium (Wine College) in Budapest; and *Borbarát* (Friends of Wine), a bilingual, fully illustrated quarterly magazine (600Ft) published by Spread Press (✉ borbarat@starkingnet.hu), PO Box 104, 1506 Budapest.

Left: A fine accompaniment to a traditional meal.

Right: Some goulash with your wine, perhaps?

DAVID GREEDY

VERONICA GARBUTT

Getting There & Away

AIR
Airports & Airlines

Malév Hungarian Airlines, the national carrier, flies nonstop to Budapest's Ferihegy International Airport from North America, the Middle East, Asia and more than three dozen cities in Continental Europe and the British Isles.

Malév flights arrive and depart from Ferihegy Terminal 2A; all other international airlines use the new Terminal 2B. (The old Terminal 1, about 5km to the west, is now used only for cargo or special flights.) The general information number for both terminals at Ferihegy is ☎ 1-296 9696. Otherwise, call ☎ 1-296 7000 or ☎ 296 6578 for departures and ☎ 1-296 8000 or ☎ 296 8268 for arrivals at Terminal 2A. For Terminal 2B call ☎ 1-296 5882/83/84 for departures and ☎ 1-296 5052/53/54 for arrivals.

Malév has a ticketing desk at Terminal 2A (☎ 1-296 7179 or 296 7211) and one at Terminal 2B (☎ 1-296 7544 or ☎ 296 5767) as well.

Check out its Web site at www.malev.hu.

Departure Tax

An air passenger duty (*illeték*) of between 3000Ft and 6500Ft is levied on all air tickets written in Hungary. The one exception is JFK International Airport in New York, which attracts a tax of 12,000Ft. This duty is almost always incorporated in the quoted fare. There are no other departure or port taxes.

The UK & Continental Europe

Malév flies nonstop to Budapest from the following destinations: Amsterdam, Athens, Barcelona, Berlin, Brussels, Bucharest, Cologne, Copenhagen, Dublin, Düsseldorf, Frankfurt, Hamburg, Helsinki, Istanbul, Kaunas, Kiev, Larnaca, London, Madrid, Milan, Moscow, Munich, Oslo, Paris, Prague, Riga, Rome, St Petersburg, Sarajevo, Skopje, Sofia, Stockholm, Stuttgart, Thessaloniki, Tirana, Vienna, Warsaw, Zagreb and Zürich.

Other airlines serving Budapest from European gateways include:

Aeroflot	Moscow
airBaltic	Riga
Air France	Paris
Air Malta	Malta
Alitalia	Rome and Milan
Austrian Airlines	Vienna
Balkan	Sofia
British Airways and British Midland	London
Czech Airlines	Prague
Finnair	Helsinki
Iberia	Madrid
KLM Royal Dutch Airlines	Amsterdam
LOT	Warsaw
Lufthansa	Düsseldorf, Frankfurt, Hamburg, Munich, Stuttgart
Olympic Airways	Athens

Air Travel Glossary

Cancellation Penalties If you have to cancel or change a discounted ticket, there are often heavy penalties involved; insurance can sometimes be taken out against these penalties. Some airlines impose penalties on regular tickets as well, particularly against 'no-show' passengers.

Courier Fares Businesses often need to send urgent documents or freight securely and quickly. Courier companies hire people to accompany the package through customs and, in return, offer a discount ticket which is sometimes a phenomenal bargain. However, you may have to surrender all your baggage allowance and take only carry-on luggage.

Full Fares Airlines traditionally offer 1st class (coded F), business class (coded J) and economy class (coded Y) tickets. These days there are so many promotional and discounted fares available that few passengers pay full economy fare.

Lost Tickets If you lose your airline ticket an airline will usually treat it like a travellers cheque and, after inquiries, issue you with another one. Legally, however, an airline is entitled to treat it like cash and if you lose it then it's gone forever. Take good care of your tickets.

Onward Tickets An entry requirement for many countries is that you have a ticket out of the country. If you're unsure of your next move, the easiest solution is to buy the cheapest onward ticket to a neighbouring country or a ticket from a reliable airline which can later be refunded if you do not use it.

Open-Jaw Tickets These are return tickets where you fly out to one place but return from another. If available, this can save you backtracking to your arrival point.

Overbooking Since every flight has some passengers who fail to show up, airlines often book more passengers than they have seats. Usually excess passengers make up for the no-shows, but occasionally somebody gets 'bumped' onto the next available flight. Guess who it is most likely to be? The passengers who check in late.

Promotional Fares These are officially discounted fares, available from travel agencies or direct from the airline.

Reconfirmation If you don't reconfirm your flight at least 72 hours prior to departure, the airline may delete your name from the passenger list. Ring to find out if your airline requires reconfirmation.

Restrictions Discounted tickets often have various restrictions on them – such as needing to be paid for in advance and incurring a penalty to be altered. Others are restrictions on the minimum and maximum period you must be away.

Round-the-World Tickets RTW tickets give you a limited period (usually a year) in which to circumnavigate the globe. You can go anywhere the carrying airlines go, as long as you don't backtrack. The number of stopovers or total number of separate flights is decided before you set off and they usually cost a bit more than a basic return flight.

Transferred Tickets Airline tickets cannot be transferred from one person to another. Travellers sometimes try to sell the return half of their ticket, but officials can ask you to prove that you are the person named on the ticket. On an international flight tickets are compared with passports.

Travel Periods Ticket prices vary with the time of year. There is a low (off-peak) season and a high (peak) season, and often a low-shoulder season and a high-shoulder season as well. Usually the fare depends on your outward flight – if you depart in the high season and return in the low season, you pay the high-season fare.

Sabena	Brussels
SAS	Copenhagen
Swissair	Geneva, Zürich
Tarom Romanian	Bucharest
Turkish Airlines	Istanbul

At the time of writing, British Airways offered basic return excursion tickets with fixed dates (and heavy penalties if you changed them) from London to Budapest for about UK£235 to UK£280, depending on whether you wanted to travel on a weekend; those under 26 paid UK£20 less. British Midland had a discount fare for UK£170. Of course, you can always fly to Prague on BA's budget airline, Go (☎ 0845 605 4321), or to Vienna with KLM's Buzz (☎ 0870 240 7070) for around UK£100 and then cover the last leg by bus or train. For details, check out the Web sites at www.go-fly.com and www.buzzaway.com.

From Budapest, most destinations in Europe on Malév cost from 40,000Ft to 55,000Ft return, including Warsaw and Prague (46,000Ft each). A return flight to Moscow is 64,000Ft and to London is 60,000Ft.

The USA & Canada

Malév and Delta Air Lines run a daily joint service to/from New York (JFK Airport); Malév runs a direct flight to/from Toronto twice a week. From New York with Malév, the standard return fare hovers around US$900 though a discount one with the usual restrictions costs about US$420.

From Budapest you should be able to fly return to New York for 109,000Ft (75,000Ft for those under 26).

Australia

The easiest way to get to Hungary from Australia is to fly Qantas from Sydney or Melbourne to London and connect with a Malév or British Airways flight to Budapest. Another option is Sydney to Frankfurt and then Malév or Lufthansa to Budapest. A less frequently served routing is Sydney or Melbourne to Bangkok and then the thrice-weekly nonstop Malév flight to Budapest. A return flight to Sydney or Melbourne from Budapest costs about 168,000Ft.

Africa & the Middle East

Malév flies nonstop four times a week to Tel Aviv while El Al has a thrice-weekly service. Malév and Egyptair serve Cairo three times a week. Malév also flies nonstop twice a week to Beirut. There are two Malév flights a week to Damascus and one to Tripoli. Tunisair flies nonstop once a week to Budapest.

Asia

Malév flies nonstop to/from Bangkok (145,000Ft return, 104,000Ft under 26) three times a week and runs a direct flight six times weekly to Beijing with Air China (via Helsinki) and Swissair (via Zürich). From Hong Kong there are two weekly flights on Lauda Air to Vienna and three a week from Bangkok. Lufthansa (via Frankfurt) and British Airways (via London) also offer good deals to Budapest from Asia.

A return excursion ticket valid for six months on Lauda Air from Bangkok to Vienna is US$1200. From the same gateway British Airways flies to Budapest via London and Lufthansa via Frankfurt for about US$1600. From Bombay to Budapest on Swissair (via Zürich) costs from US$1000.

LAND

Budapest is well connected with all seven of its neighbours by road, rail and even some river ferries. Trains arrive in Budapest from every neighbouring capital, and in summer there's a hydrofoil service between Vienna, Bratislava and Budapest.

Timetables for both domestic and international trains and buses use the 24-hour system. Remember that 0.05 means five minutes past midnight (or 12.05 am).

On many (though not all) bus and train timetables, Hungarians tend to use the Hungarian name for cities and towns in neighbouring countries. Many of these are in what once was Hungarian territory and the names are used by the Hungarian-speaking minorities who live there. You should at least be familiar with the more important ones to help decipher bus and (less so) train timetables. See the Alternative Place Names appendix in the back of this book.

Border Crossings

Bus There's a bus service to/from all neighbouring countries from Budapest as well as from cities and towns closer to the borders. This is often the cheapest – if not the easiest – way to enter a neighbouring country.

For example, from Pécs, you can catch one of three buses a day to Osijek in Croatia and there are an equal number from Barcs, 32km south-west of Szigetvár, to Zagreb.

From Balassagyarmat, one bus a day goes to Lučenec in Slovakia, and there's bus service from Nyíregyháza twice a day to Užgorod in Ukraine and twice a week to Satu Mare in Romania.

From Szeged, buses cross the Romanian border for Arad and Timişoara, and buses go to Ljubljana in Slovenia from Lenti.

Train The main entry points for international trains to Hungary include the following (clockwise from the north-west):

Entry points

entry point	from
Szombathely	Graz
Sopron and	Vienna and much of
Hegyeshalom	Western Europe
Komárom and Szob	Prague and Berlin
Miskolc	Košice, Kraków and
	Warsaw
Nyíregyháza	Lvov, Moscow and
	St Petersburg
Békéscsaba	Bucharest via Arad
	and Timişoara
Szeged	Subotica
Kiskunhalas	Belgrade
Pécs	Sarajevo and Osijek
Nagykanizsa	Zagreb and Ljubljana

Car & Motorcycle Of the 55 road crossings that Hungary maintains with its seven neighbours, about 20 of the crossings (mostly in the north and north-east) are restricted to local citizens from both sides of the border (or, in the case of Austria, Hungarian and EU citizens).

See the table on page 73 for a list of border crossings that are open to all motorists (clockwise from Austria).

The Hungarian checkpoint appears first, the foreign checkpoint (or closest town) follows, and references to cities or big towns are inserted in brackets after each.

Bicycle Cyclists may have a problem crossing Hungarian stations connected to main roads since bicycles are banned on motorways and national highways with single-digit route numbers.

Hitching To save the cost of an international ticket, or just for fun, you may consider walking across the frontier into or out of Hungary. But many border guards frown on this practice, particularly in Romania, Yugoslavia and Ukraine; try hitching a ride instead.

There are three crossings to/from Slovakia where you won't have any problems. At Komárom, 88km north-west of Budapest, a bridge over the Danube connects the city with Komárno.

At Sátoraljaújhely, north-east of Miskolc, another highway border crossing over the Ronyva River links the centre of town with Slovenské Nové Mesto. For information on the ferry from Esztergom to Štúrovo, see the River section later in this chapter.

To/from Romania, the easiest place to cross on foot is Nagylak/Nădlac between Szeged and Arad. There are eight local trains a day from the train station at Újszeged across the Tisza River from Szeged proper to Nagylak (47km, 1¼ hours) near the border. After crossing into Romania you must walk, cycle or hitch for 6km to Nădlac, where you can connect with up to four local trains a day to Arad (52km, 1½ hours).

If you're bound for Slovenia, take one of up to 10 trains a day from Zalaegerszeg to Rédics (49km, 1½ hours), which is only a couple of kilometres from the main highway border crossing from Hungary into Slovenia. From the border it's a 5km walk south to the Lendava bus station, where you'll have a choice of five buses daily to Ljubljana (212km, four hours) and many more to Maribor (92km).

Border Crossings

The following is a list of border crossings between Hungary and its neighbouring countries that are open to all motorists (beginning in Austria and heading clockwise from there). The Hungarian checkpoint appears first, the foreign checkpoint (or closest town) follows, and references to cities or big towns are inserted in brackets after each.

Austria

Rábafüzes (5km north of Szentgotthárd)/Heiligenkreuz in Lafnitztal
Bucsu (13km west of Szombathely)/Schachendorf
Kőszeg/Rattersdorf
Kópháza (11km north of Sopron)/Deutschkreutz
Sopron (7km north-west of the city)/Klingenbach
Fertőrákos (open April to October to pedestrians & cyclists only)/Mörbisch
Fertőd/Pamhagen
Jánossomorja (14km south-west of Mosonmagyaróvár; open April to October to pedestrians & cyclists only/Andau
Hegyeshalom (51km north-west of Győr)/Nickelsdorf

Slovakia

Rajka (18km north-west of Mosonmagyaróvár)/Rusovce
Vámosszabadi (13km north of Győr)/Medvedov
Komárom/Komárno
Parassapuszta (40km north of Vác)/Šahy
Balassagyarmat/Slovenské Darmoty
Somoskőújfalu (8km north of Salgótarján)/Filakovo
Bánréve (43km north-west of Miskolc)/Král
Tornyosnémeti (60km north-east of Miskolc)/Milhost
Sátoraljaújhely/Slovenské Nové Mesto

Bus

In Budapest, buses to/from Western and Central Europe and several neighbouring countries use the bus station at V Erzsébet tér (metro: Deák tér). Volánbusz (literally 'steering-wheel bus') has an international office (☎ 1-317 2562) upstairs at the station, which is open from 6 am to 7 pm (6 pm in winter) on weekdays and 6.30 am to 4 pm at the weekends.

Buses serving most – but not all – Eastern European countries leave from the station at Népstadion (☎ 1-252 1896, metro: Népstadion), XIV Hungária körút 48-52. The international ticket office there is open from 5.30 am to 6 pm weekdays and from 5.30 am to 4 pm on Saturday. On Sunday try paying the driver. The staff at Népstadion speak no English, so study the posted timetables and then write down where you want to go. Be advised that the names of Romanian destinations are in Hungarian; refer to the Alternative Place Names appendix.

Bus Passes Volánbusz, in conjunction with Eurolines, sells 30 and 60-day passes allowing unlimited travel to/from some 21 European countries, including Hungary.

For a 30-day pass adults pay 71,000/60,000Ft in the high/low season; the youth and senior passes for the same periods cost 59,000/48,000Ft.

For 60 days in the high/low season adults pay 85,000/76,000Ft while the reduced-priced passes are 76,000/60,000Ft in those seasons.

Border Crossings

Ukraine
Záhony (23km north of Kisvárda)/Čop (23km south of Užgorod)
Beregsurány (21km north-east of Vásárosnamény)/Beregove)
Tiszabecs (27km north-east of Fehérgyarmat)/Vylok

Romania
Csengersima (40km south-east of Mátészalka)/Petea (11km north-west of Satu Mare)
Ártánd (25km south-east of Berettyóújfalu)/Borş (14km north-west of Oradea)
Méhkerék (24km north of Gyula)/Salonta
Gyula/Varşand (66km north of Arad)
Battonya (45km south-east of Orosháza)/Turnu
Nagylak (52km west of Szeged)/Nădlac (54km west of Arad)

Yugoslavia
Rözske (16km south-west of Szeged)/Horgoš (30km north-east of Subotica)
Tompa (30km south of Kiskunhalas)/Kelebija (11km north-west of Subotica)
Hercegszántó (32km south of Baja)/Bački Breg (28km north-west of Sombor)

Croatia
Udvar (12km south of Mohács)/Doboševica
Drávaszabolcs (9km south of Harkány)/Donji Miholjac (49km north-west of Osijek)
Barcs (32km south-west of Szigetvár)/Terezino Polje
Berzence (24km west of Nagyatád)/Gola
Letenye (26km west of Nagykanizsa)/Gorican

Slovenia
Rédics (9km south-west of Lenti)/Dolga Vas
Bajánsenye (60km west of Zalaegerszeg)/Hodoš

Western & Central Europe From Erzsébet tér there's a Volánbusz/Eurolines service on Monday, Friday and Saturday throughout the year to Amsterdam via Frankfurt, Düsseldorf and Rotterdam (1615km, 22 hours) costing 28,500Ft (about US$121) one way and 44,000Ft (US$187) return, with a 10% discount for those under 26 or over 60 years of age. From early June to late September the Amsterdam bus runs four times a week and in July and early August it goes daily at slightly higher rates: 29,700Ft (US$125) one-way, 46,700Ft (US$198) return. In summer this bus is often full, so try to book ahead.

The Budapest-Amsterdam bus goes through Austria, precluding the need for a Czech or Slovakian visa. In Amsterdam tickets are sold by Eurolines Nederland (☎ 020-560 87 87), Rokin 10, and at Amstel bus station, Julianaplein 5. In Budapest you can buy them upstairs at the Erzsébet tér bus station.

A similar service to Brussels (1395km, 19 hours, 18,900Ft/US$77 one way, 30,900Ft/US$126 return) also operates three times a week (Wednesday, Thursday, Sunday) with an additional trip on Monday from July to mid-September. In Brussels, seek information and buy tickets from Eurolines' Belgian office (☎ 02-203 07 07) at 80 Rue du Progrès near the Gare du Nord.

Other buses departing from Erzsébet tér station between two and four times a week from May to September include those to: Venice (770km, 12 hours, 12,800Ft/US$55);

Bologna (945km, 16½ hours, 16,800Ft/US$72); Florence (1045km, 18½ hours, 19,400Ft/US$83); and Rome (1330km, 22½ hours, 23,300Ft/ US$99). There are also buses to Hamburg via Berlin (two to four times a week, 1215km, 18½ hours, 24,570Ft/ US$104); Milan (one or two a week, 1080km, 19 hours 19,400Ft/US$83); Munich (three to six a week, 700km, 10 hours, 19,400Ft/ US$83); Paris (two to three times weekly, 1525km, 22½ hours, 29,250Ft/ US$125); Zurich (twice a week, 1045km, 17½ hours, 20,670Ft/US$88). A bus to Oslo with a transfer in Göteborg runs once a week (1915km, 34½ hours, 42,500Ft/US$180).

Buses run between Budapest and London via Vienna and Brussels on Wednesday, Thursday and Sunday (1770km, 26 hours, 35,000Ft/US$149 one way, 50,600Ft/US$215 return). From June to October the bus also runs on Monday and from July to early September it runs on Saturday too. In London check with Eurolines (☎ 020-7730 8235 for information, ☎ 0990-143219 for bookings), 52 Grosvenor Gardens SW1. In Paris inquire about Hungary-bound buses at Eurolines France (☎ 01 49 72 51 51) at the Gare Routière Internationale, 28 Avenue du Général de Gaulle.

Three daily buses make the run between Erzsébet tér and Vienna's Autobusbahnhof Wien-Mitte, departing from Budapest at 7 am, noon and 5 pm and from Vienna at 7 am and 5 and 7 pm and (254km, 3½ hours, 6800Ft/US$29 one way, 8500Ft/ US$36 return). From July to September an additional bus leaves Budapest at 9 am and Vienna at 3 pm daily and on Friday only the rest of the year. Still another bus departs Budapest at 7 pm and Vienna at 11 am Sunday to Friday during the same period. In Vienna, Eurolines (☎ 0222-712 0453) is at Autobusbahnhof Wien-Mitte, Landstrasser Hauptstrasse 1b.

Czech Republic, Slovakia & Poland

From Erzsébet tér there are buses to Bratislava (daily, 207km, 2990Ft/US$13) and Prague (two to three times weekly, 535km, 8½ hours, 8500Ft/US$36). An extra night bus from Budapest to Prague runs on Sunday in summer, leaving Budapest at 10 pm and arriving at 6 am. From Népstadion buses head twice a week for Krakow via Zakopane (475km, 12 hours, 5200Ft/US$22).

Romania By far the cheapest way to get to Romania is by bus from Népstadion, from where there are buses to Oradea (two a week, 260km, six hours 2800Ft/US$12), Arad (six a week, 282km, seven hours 3100Ft/US$13), Timişoara (one a week, 334km, eight hours, 3800Ft/US$16) and Cluj-Napoca (two a week, 413km, 9½ hour, 4500Ft/US$19). A return ticket is about 50% more than a one-way ticket.

Yugoslavia & Greece To reach Yugoslavia, you can catch a daily bus from Népstadion to Subotica (224km, 4½ hours, 2450Ft/US$11). There are also buses three times a week in summer from Népstadion to Athens (1570km, 23,500Ft/US$100.

Croatia & Slovenia From June to mid-September a bus leaves Erzsébet tér on Friday for Riejka (10,500Ft/US$45) on Croatia's Istrian Peninsula, stopping at Ljubljana, Koper and Piran in Slovenia along the way.

Train

Magyar Államvasutak, which translates as Hungarian State Railways and is universally known as MÁV, links up with the European rail network in all directions, running trains as far as London (via Cologne and Brussels), Paris (via Frankfurt), Stockholm (via Hamburg and Copenhagen), Moscow, Rome and Istanbul (via Belgrade). MÁV's Web site is at www.mav.hu.

The international trains listed below are expresses, and many – if not all – require seat reservations. On long hauls, sleepers are almost always available in both 1st and 2nd class, and couchettes are available in 2nd class. Surprisingly, not all express trains have dining or even buffet cars. Make sure you bring along some snacks and drinks as vendors can be few and far between. Hungarian trains are hardly luxurious but are generally clean and punctual.

Most international trains now arrive and depart from Budapest-Keleti (Eastern) train station (☎ 1-314 5010 or ☎ 313 6835); trains to some destinations in Romania leave from Budapest-Nyugati (Western) station (☎ 1-349 0115), while Budapest-Déli (Southern) station (☎ 1-375 6293 or ☎ 355 8657) handles trains to/from Zagreb and Rijeka in Croatia. But these are not hard-and-fast rules, so always make sure you check which station the train leaves from when you buy a ticket. The central number for international train information is ☎ 1-461 5500.

To reduce confusion, specify your train by its name (these are listed in the following section and on the posted schedule) when requesting information or buying a ticket. You can get information and buy tickets directly at the three train stations, but it's easier to communicate with the information staff at MÁV's central ticket office (☎ 1-322 8082 or ☎ 322 9035) at VI Andrássy út 35. The office is open from 9 am to 6 pm weekdays from April to September and to 5 pm the rest of the year. It accepts credit cards though the train stations do not.

If you just want to get across the border, local trains are cheaper than international expresses, especially if you're on a one-way trip. Concession fares between cities of the former socialist countries are only available on return tickets.

Tickets & Discounts Everyone gets a 30% to 55% discount on return fares to the Czech Republic, Croatia, Poland, Russia, Ukraine, Belarus, Lithuania and Latvia; it's a generous 55% to Slovakia and 70% to certain destinations in Romania. Also, there's a 40% concession on return fares from Budapest to six selected cities: Prague and Brno in the Czech Republic, and Warsaw, Kraków, Katowice and Gdynia in Poland. Sample 2nd-class return fares in euros/forint include the following: Prague €54/13,959Ft; Moscow €93/24,154Ft; Warsaw €52/13,424Ft.

For tickets to destinations in Western Europe you'll pay the same as everywhere else unless you're aged under 26 and qualify for a BIJ (Billet International de Jeunesse) ticket, which cuts international fares by 25% to 35%; ask at MÁV, Express or the Wasteels office (☎ 1-210 2802) in Keleti train station. The following are sample return fares in euros/forint from Budapest: Amsterdam €199.50/51,870Ft; Berlin €183/47,643Ft; London €274/71,098Ft; Munich €88/23,000Ft; Rome €152/39,395Ft; Vienna €54/14,040Ft. There's a 30% discounted return fare to Vienna of €41/10,608Ft if you come back to Budapest within four days. Three daily EuroCity (EC) trains to Vienna and points beyond charge a supplement of 1000Ft to 1500Ft. Seats in 1st class are always 50% more expensive than 2nd class.

An international seat reservation costs 650Ft. Fines are levied on passengers without tickets (400Ft) or seat reservations (1000Ft plus the reservation fee) where it is compulsory. Costs for sleepers depend on the destination, but a two-berth 2nd-class sleeper to Berlin/Prague/Venice/Moscow costs 5000/5460/7800/15,000Ft per person; 1st-class sleepers always cost 50% more than the ones in 2nd class. A 2nd-class couchette in a compartment for six people costs 4500Ft. Tickets are valid for 60 days from purchase and stopovers are permitted.

Budapest is no longer the bargain basement that it once was for tickets on the Trans-Siberian or the Trans-Mongolian railways. In fact, MÁV will only write you a ticket to Moscow; you have to buy the onward ticket from there (from about US$285, depending on the route). Of course, if you are coming back to Budapest from Moscow you get a 40% discount.

When pricing train tickets from Western Europe remember that airfares (especially those out of London) often match or beat surface alternatives (especially trains) in terms of cost. For example, a return airfare from London to Budapest is available through discount travel agents off season for around UK£170 or less. By comparison, a two-month return ticket by rail to Budapest available from Rail Europe (☎ 0990 848 848) costs UK£375/365 for adults/youths, though there are discounted fares of UK£240/230 available if the tickets are purchased a month in advance. Rail Europe's Web site is at www.raileurope.com.

Rail Passes MÁV sells Inter-Rail passes from one to seven zones to those under 26 years of age, provided they are EU citizens or resident in Europe for at least six months. The price for any one zone is about US$180 and passes are valid for three weeks; Hungary is in Zone D along with the Czech Republic, Slovakia, Poland, Croatia, Bulgaria and Romania. Multizone passes are better value and are valid for one month: two zones is US$239, three zones US$272, and all zones – a 'Global' pass – is US$310. For travellers over 26 years of age, a one-zone pass costs US$258, a Global one is US$436.

Travel in Hungary is also valid using a Eurail pass, sold to non-European residents only. Several types of Eurail passes are available, but the cheapest is a Eurail Flexipass good for 10/15 days' 1st-class travel in 17 countries over two months for US$654/US$862 (children aged four to 12 pay half of the adult price). Those under 26 years of age can get the 2nd-class Eurail Youthpass, which allows from 15 days (US$388) to three months (US$1089) of consecutive travel. It's almost impossible for a Eurail pass to pay for itself in Hungary, and it's not valid in the Czech Republic, Slovakia, Bulgaria or Romania so plan your Eurail travel days carefully. Eurail's Web site is at www.eurail.com.

Both Inter-Rail and Eurail have country-specific passes available as well. See Rail Passes under Train in the Getting Around chapter.

Western & Central Europe Some eight trains a day link Vienna with Budapest (three hours) via Hegyeshalom. Most of them leave from Vienna's Westbahnhof, including the *Orient Express* arriving from Paris (18 hours from Budapest) via Munich, the *Arrabona*, the EC *Bartók Béla* from Munich (eight hours) via Salzburg, the EC *Liszt Ferenc*

from Cologne (11 hours) via Frankfurt, the *Dacia Express* bound for Bucharest (13 hours) and the IC *Avala* bound for Belgrade (6½ hours). The early-morning EC *Lehár*, however, departs from Vienna's Südbahnhof and the *Beograd Express* arrives and departs in the wee hours from Budapest's 'fourth' station – Kelenföld in Buda. None requires a seat reservation, though it is highly recommended in summer.

In addition, up to seven weekday trains (three at the weekend) leave Vienna's Südbahnhof for Sopron (75 minutes) via Ebenfurth; as many as 10 weekday (five at the weekend) trains also serve Sopron from Wiener Neustadt, which is easily accessible from Vienna. Some seven trains on weekdays (five at the weekend) make the three-hour trip from Graz to Szombathely.

There are two or three trains a day from Berlin (Zoo, Ostbahnhof, and Schnefeld stations) to Budapest (12½ hours) via Dresden, sometimes Prague and Bratislava: the *Spree-Donau Kurier*, the EC *Hungária* and the EC *Comenius*, which originates in Hamburg, a central point for trains from Malmö, Copenhagen and Amsterdam.

Czech Republic, Slovakia & Poland In addition to being served by the EC trains *Hungária* and *Comenius* from Berlin, Prague (7½ to nine hours) also sees the IC *Csárdás*, the *Slovan*, and the *Pannónia Express* from Bucharest daily. Each day two trains, the EC *Polonia* and the *Báthory*, leave Warsaw for Budapest (12 hours) passing through Katowice and Bratislava and/or Štúrovo. The *Amicus* runs directly to/from Bratislava (three hours) every day.

The *Karpaty* from Warsaw bound for Bucharest passes through Kraków and Košice before reaching Miskolc, where you can change for Budapest. The *Cracovia* runs from Kraków to Budapest (13 hours) and Pécs via Košice. Another train, the *Rákóczi*, links Budapest (four hours) with Košice and Poprad Tatry, 100km to the north-west. The *Bem* connects Szczecin in north-western Poland with Budapest (17 hours) via Poznań, Wrocław and, in Slovakia, Lučenec.

Two additional local trains cover the 90km from Miskolc and Košice (two hours) every day. The 2km hop from Sátoraljaújhely to Slovenské Nové Mesto (three a day) is only a four-minute ride by train.

Ukraine & Russia From Moscow to Budapest (38½ hours) there's only the *Tisza Express*, which travels via Kiev and Lviv in Ukraine. Most nationalities require a transit visa to travel through Ukraine.

Romania From Bucharest to Budapest (12 to 14 hours) you can choose among four trains: the EC *Traianus*, the *Dacia*, the *Ister*, the *Pannónia* and the *Muntenia*, all of which go via Arad and require seat reservations. The *Karpaty* goes to Bucharest from Miskolc.

There are three connections daily from Cluj-Napoca to Budapest (seven hours, via Oradea): the IC *Ady Endre*, the *Corona* (from Brașov) and the *Claudiopolis*. These trains require a seat reservation as does the *Partium*, which links Budapest and Oradea only.

There are two local trains a day linking Baia Mare in northern Romania with Budapest (eight hours) via Satu Mare and Debrecen. Otherwise you'll have to take one of two additional local trains from Debrecen across the border to Valea lui Mihai and catch a Romanian train there.

Bulgaria & Yugoslavia The *Balkán Express*, originating in Istanbul (32 hours), links Budapest with Sofia (22 hours) via Belgrade. Other trains between Budapest and Belgrade via Subotica (seven to eight) include the *Beograd Express*, the *Ivo Andrić*, the IC *Avala* and the *Hellas*, which runs from Thessaloniki in Greece, via Skopje in Macedonia, and takes just over a day to arrive. Be warned that the *Beograd* arrives and departs from Kelenföld station in Buda. You must reserve your seats on some of these trains.

Two additional local trains (no reservations necessary) make the journey (1¾-hour, 45km) between Subotica and Szeged every day.

Croatia & Slovenia You can get to Budapest from Zagreb (six hours) on three trains, all of them via Siófok on Lake Balaton's southern shore: the *Maestral*, which originates in Split in summer (17¼ hours); the *Avas*; and, the *Venezia Express* via Ljubljana (eight hours). The *Dráva*, which originates in Venice, also travels via Ljubljana but not Zagreb. The *Kvarner* from Rijeka (nine hours) to Budapest via Zagreb follows the route to the north of the Balaton.

RIVER

Hungary's two main international river crossings involve – naturally enough – the Danube.

A hydrofoil service on the Danube from Budapest to Vienna (282km, 5½ hours) via Bratislava (on request) operates daily from early April to October with an extra sailing on certain days from early July to late August. Fares to Vienna are high: US$71/102 one way/return. Adult one-way/return fares to Bratislava are US$64/91.

Ferries arrive and depart from the International Landing Stage *(Nemzetközi hajóállomás)* on Belgrád rakpart in Pest, just north of Szabadság Bridge. From early April to early July and from late August to October there's a daily sailing at 9 am from both Budapest and Vienna. From early July to late August boats leave both cities at 8 am. An additional one departs from Budapest at 1 pm Thursday to Sunday and at the same time from Vienna from Friday to Monday. Tickets are available in Budapest from Mahart Tours (☎ 1-318 1953) at the International Landing Stage on V Belgrád rakpart, just north of Szabadság Bridge in Budapest. The small office there is open from 8 am to 4 pm on weekdays. At weekends the ticket window is open from 8 am to noon. In Vienna, get them from Mahart Tours (☎ 0222-729 2161) at Karlsplatz 2-8.

The second way of getting out of Hungary is much more, well, pedestrian – and cheaper. It's the passenger and car ferry linking Esztergom with Štúrovo and is one of the easiest ways to enter Hungary from Slovakia. For more information see Esztergom in the Danube Bend chapter.

Getting Around

Hungary's domestic transport system is efficient, comprehensive and very inexpensive. In general most everything runs to schedule, and the majority of Hungary's towns and cities are easily negotiated on foot.

AIR

There are no scheduled flights within Hungary. The cost of domestic air taxis is prohibitive, eg, 87,000Ft/DM680 from Budapest to Szeged and back, and the trips can take almost as long as the train when you add the time required to get to/from the airports. Several better known firms with offices in Budapest are: Indicator (☎ 1-202 6284), XII Városmajor utca 30; Air Service Hungary (☎ 1-385 1344), XI Kőérberki út 36; and Avia-Express (☎ 1-296 7092 or ☎ 296 6383) at Ferihegy Terminal 1.

BUS

Hungary's Volánbusz network is a good – and sometimes necessary – alternative to the trains. In Southern Transdanubia and many parts of the Great Plain, buses are essential unless you are prepared to make several time-consuming changes on the train. For short trips around the Danube Bend or Lake Balaton areas, buses are recommended over trains.

In most cities and large towns it is usually possible to catch at least one direct bus a day to fairly far-flung areas of the country (Pécs to Sopron, for example, or Debrecen to Szeged).

Of course, not everyone likes bus travel, but in Hungary it's a better way to see the deep countryside than from a train – the areas 'somewhere behind the back of God', as the Magyars say. Seats on Volánbusz are spaced far enough apart for you to be able to fit your pack between your knees. A few large bus stations have luggage rooms, but they generally close early, eg, 6 pm. Check your bag in at the train station, which is almost always nearby.

National buses arrive and depart from Budapest's long-distance bus stations (*távolságiautóbusz pályaudvar*), not the local stations, which are called *helyiautóbusz pályaudvar*. But these are often found side by side or share the same space. Arrive early to confirm the correct departure bay or stand (*kocsiállás*), and be sure to check the individual schedule posted at the stop itself; the times shown can be different from those shown on the main board (*tábla*).

Tickets are usually purchased directly from the driver, who gives change and will hand you a receipt as ticket. There are sometimes queues for intercity buses (especially on Friday afternoon) so it's wise to arrive early. Smoking is not allowed on buses in Hungary, though a 10-minute rest stop is made about every 1½ hours.

People in the countryside use intercity buses for short hops, and there are always many stops, which drivers usually do not announce. If you plan to do a lot of travelling by bus, buy a copy of the national road atlas (see Maps in the Planning section of the Facts for the Visitor chapter), and watch for signs when entering or leaving a settlement. Otherwise get the attention of your fellow passenger and point both to your destination on the map and this sentence: *Szóljon kérem, mikor kell leszállnom?* ('Could you tell me when to get off?').

Posted bus schedules and timetables can be horribly confusing if you don't speak Hungarian. The basics to remember when reading a timetable are that *indulás* means 'departures' and *érkezés* means 'arrivals'. Timetable symbols include the following:

Numbers one to seven in a circle refer to the days of the week, beginning with Monday. Written footnotes you might see include *naponta* (daily), *hétköznap* (weekdays), *munkanap* (workdays), *munkaszünetes nap kivételével naponta* (daily except holidays), *szabadnap kivételével naponta* (daily except Saturday), *szabadés munkaszünetes nap* (Saturday and holidays), *munkaszunetes nap*

Bus Timetable Symbols

✕	Monday to Saturday (except public holidays)
⊗	Monday to Friday (except public holidays)
☒	Monday to Thursday (except public holidays)
☐	first working day of the week (usually Monday)
⊺	last working day of the week (usually Friday)
⊙	Saturday
⊕	Saturday, Sunday and public holidays
✛	Sunday and public holidays
⊞	day before the first working day of the week (usually Sunday)
▼	school days
▽	on working days during school holidays (mid-June to August; Christmas and New Year; two weeks in April)

(holidays), *iskolai nap* (school days) and *szabadnap* (Saturday).

For bus services to inland destinations south and west of Budapest, go to the bus station on V Erzsébet tér (☎ 1-317 2345 or ☎ 317 2318, metro: Deák tér). The Népstadion bus station (☎ 1-252 4496 or ☎ 252 4498, metro: Népstadion), at XIV Hungária körút 48-52, serves cities and towns to the north and the east of the capital. The bus station on the Pest side of Árpád Bridge (☎ 1-329 1682 or ☎ 329 1450, metro: Árpád híd) just off XIII Róbert Károly körút is the place to catch buses for the Danube Bend and parts of the Northern Uplands.

Costs

Bus fares are slightly more expensive than comparable 2nd-class train fares. At present Volánbusz charges:

68Ft	for up to 5km
90Ft	for 10km
124Ft	for 15km
910Ft	for 100km
1740Ft	for 200km
2570Ft	for 300km

TRAIN

MÁV operates reliable and relatively comfortable train services on some 8000km of track. All main railway lines converge on Budapest, though many secondary lines link provincial cities and towns. There are three main stations in Budapest: Keleti station (for destinations in the Northern Uplands and the North-East), Nyugati (for the Great Plain and the Danube Bend) and Déli (for Transdanubia and Lake Balaton). The central number for domestic train information is ☎ 1-461 5400.

Tickets for one-way (*egy útra*) and return (*oda-vissza*) journeys in 1st and 2nd class are available at stations, MÁV's main ticket office (☎ 1-322 8082 or ☎ 322 9035) at VI Andrássy út 35 and at certain travel agencies.

There are several types of trains: Expressz ('Ex' on the timetable), of which there are only a handful; InterCity (IC), which number about two dozen and stop at main centres only; *gyors* and *sebesvonat* (fast and swift trains), indicated on the timetable by boldface type, a thicker route line and/or an 'S'; and *személyvonat* (passenger trains). These last ones are the real milk runs and stop at every city, town, village and hamlet along the way.

Depending on the station, departures and arrivals are announced by loudspeaker/ Tannoy or on an electronic board and are always on a printed timetable – yellow for departures (*indul*) and white for arrivals (*érkezik*). On these, fast trains are marked in red, local trains in black. The number (or sometimes letter) next to the word *vágány* indicates the 'platform' from which the train departs or arrives; for symbols and abbreviations used, see under Bus, earlier in this chapter. The huge paper rolls in glass cases that you'll see in some stations show the schedules for every train in the country; look for the route number on the map posted nearby. If you plan to do a lot of travelling by train, get yourself a copy of

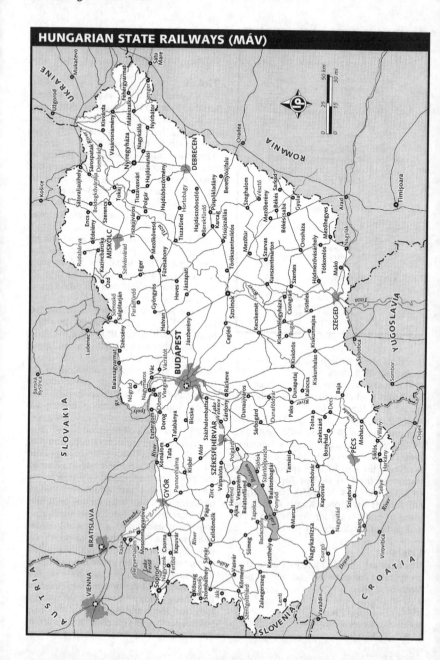

MÁV's official timetable (*menetrend*), which is available at most large stations, at the MÁV office on Andrássy út or at GWK-Mávtours (☎ 312 0472), VI Teréz körút 62, for 600Ft. It has explanatory notes in six languages, including English and – wait for it – Esperanto.

All railway stations have left-luggage offices, many of which stay open 24 hours a day. You often have to pay the fee (from 140Ft to 280Ft per day) at another office or window (usually marked *pénztár*).

Some trains have a dedicated carriage for bicycles; on other trains, bicycles must be placed in the first or last cars. You are able to freight a bicycle for 176Ft per 100km.

Trains within Hungary

from Budapest to	distance	duration (hrs) slow	express
Danube Bend			
Esztergom	53km	1¾	1½
Szentendre	20km	40 min.*	
Transdanubia			
Győr	131km	2	–
Sopron	216km	3	–
Szombathely	236km	3½	–
Pécs	228km	3½	2½
Balaton			
Siófok	115km	2½	1½
Balatonfüred	132km	2½	–
Veszprém	112km	2½	1¾
Székesfehérvár	67km	1½	50 min
Great Plain			
Szolnok	100km	2½	1½
Kecskemét	106km	1½	–
Debrecen	221km	4½	3
Békéscsaba	196km	3½	2½
Szeged	191km	3½	2½
The North			
Nyíregyháza	270km	4½	3
Eger	142km	3	2
Miskolc	183km	2¾	2
Sátoraljaújhely	266km	4½	3½
*HÉV commuter railway			

The following are distances and approximate times to provincial cities from Budapest via express trains (on which you might expect to cover from 65 to 70km/h) or slow passenger trains, which take much longer:

Rail Passes

An unlimited travel pass for trains in Hungary is available from MÁV for 11,622/17,433Ft in 2nd/1st class for seven days and 16,744/25,116Ft for 10 days, but you'd have to travel like the wind to make it pay for itself. Reservation charges are additional. A much better deal is available from Inter-Rail and Eurail.

Inter-Rail has a Euro Domino pass for Hungary available to residents of Europe aged under 26 that allows three to eight days of travel over a month period for between UK£29 and UK£69.

Eurail's Hungarian Flexipass, available to non-European residents only, costs US$64 for five days' 1st-class travel in a 15-day period or US$80 for 10 days' travel within a month.

Reservations

Seat reservations on trains may be compulsory (indicated on the timetable by a boxed 'R'), mandatory on trains departing from Budapest (an 'R' in a circle) or simply available (just plain 'R').

Express trains usually require a seat reservation costing 120Ft while the Inter-City ones levy a surcharge of 320Ft that includes the seat reservation.

Costs

In Hungary 2nd-class train fares are 353Ft for 50km; 706Ft for 100km; 1412Ft for 200km; 3530Ft for 500km.

To travel 1st class costs 50% more: 530/1059/2118/5295Ft respectively.

Passengers holding a ticket of insufficient value must pay the difference plus a fine of 200Ft. If you buy your ticket on the train rather than at the station, there's a 400Ft surcharge. You can be fined 1000Ft for travelling on a train without a seat reservation when it is compulsory.

Special Trains

Narrow-gauge trains (*keskenynyomközű vonat*) run by Állami Erdei Vasutak (ÁEV; United Forest Railways) can be found in many wooded and hilly areas of the country. They are usually taken as a round-trip excursion by holiday-makers, but in some cases can be useful for getting from A to B, eg, Miskolc to Lillafüred and the Bükk. MÁV passes are not valid on these trains.

An independent branch of MÁV runs vintage steam trains (*nosztalgiavonat*), in summer, generally along the northern shore of the Balaton (eg from Keszthely to Talpoca via Badacsonytomaj) and along the Danube Bend in summer. For information contact MÁV Nostalgia (☎ 1-317 1665, fax 318 1704) at V Belgrád rakpart 26 in Budapest or visit the company's Web site at www.miwo.hu/old_trains).

The only other private train line in Hungary is called GySEV and links Győr and Sopron with Ebenfurth in Austria. MÁV pass-holders have to buy a ticket (minus 20%) when using this line.

CAR & MOTORCYCLE

Roads in Hungary are generally good – sometimes excellent nowadays – and there are several basic types. Motorways, preceded by an 'M' (including the curious M0), total seven and link Budapest with Lake Balaton and with Vienna and run part of the way to Miskolc and Szeged. Some of these levy a toll, eg, 1250Ft for the 64km from Győr to Hegyeshalom on the Austrian border. National highways (dual carriageways) are designated by a single digit and fan out mostly from the capital. Secondary and tertiary roads have two or three digits.

Almost every large town or city has a 24-hour petrol station – look for it as you enter (or sometimes leave) the limits. Petrol (*benzin*) of 91 and unleaded (*ólommentes*) of 95 and 98 octane is available everywhere and costs 195/199/207Ft respectively. Most stations also have diesel fuel (*gázolaj*) costing 170Ft per litre. Payment by credit card is now standard at Hungarian petrol stations.

Foreign drivers' licences are valid for one year after entering Hungary. Third-party liability insurance is compulsory. If your car is registered in the EU, it is assumed you have it; all other motorists must be able to show a Green Card or will have to buy insurance at the border.

The Yellow Angels (*Sárga Angyal*) of the Hungarian Automobile Club do basic repairs free of charge in the event of a breakdown if you belong to an affiliated organisation such as AAA in the USA or AA in the UK, but towing is still very expensive even with these reciprocal memberships. It can be reached 24 hours a day nationwide at ☎ 188 or ☎ 1-212 2938 in Budapest.

Road Rules

You must drive on the right. Speed limits for cars and motorbikes are consistent throughout the country and strictly enforced: 50km/h in built-up areas (from the town sign as you enter to the same sign with a red line through it as you leave); 80km/h on secondary and tertiary roads; 100km/h on most highways/dual carriageways; and 120km/h on motorways. Exceeding the limit will earn you a fine of between 5000Ft and 30,000Ft, which is no longer payable on the spot but at the post office or with a postal cheque.

The use of seat belts in the front (and in the back – if fitted – outside built-up areas) is compulsory in Hungary, but this rule is often ignored. Motorcyclists must wear helmets, a law strictly enforced. Another law taken very seriously indeed is the one requiring *all* drivers to use their headlights throughout the day outside built-up areas. Motorcycles must illuminate headlights at all times. Using a mobile phone while driving is prohibited in Hungary.

There is a complete ban on alcohol when you are driving in Hungary, and this rule is *very* strictly enforced. Do not think you will get away with even a few glasses of wine at lunch; if caught with any alcohol in the blood, you will be fined up to 60,000Ft. If the level is high, you will be arrested and your licence taken away. In the event of an accident, the drinking party is automatically regarded as guilty.

Road Distances (km)

	Békéscsaba	Budapest	Debrecen	Dunaújváros	Eger	Győr	Kaposvár	Kecskemét	Miskolc	Nyíregyháza	Pécs	Sopron	Szeged	Székesfehérvár	Szolnok	Szombathely	Veszprém	Zalaegerszeg
Békéscsaba	---																	
Budapest	203	---																
Debrecen	130	226	---															
Dunaújváros	210	67	277	---														
Eger	220	128	130	194	---													
Győr	327	123	350	142	251	---												
Kaposvár	314	189	381	146	317	201	---											
Kecskemét	124	85	191	86	158	208	190	---										
Miskolc	228	179	98	246	61	303	368	199	---									
Nyíregyháza	179	245	49	311	145	368	434	240	93	---								
Pécs	283	198	367	131	326	241	67	176	377	416	---							
Sopron	414	217	436	229	338	87	220	295	390	455	287	---						
Szeged	94	171	224	158	245	294	251	86	286	273	189	381	---					
Székesfehérvár	258	66	292	55	194	87	126	134	245	310	153	174	206	---				
Szolnok	107	97	129	148	121	220	252	62	162	179	238	307	130	163	---			
Szombathely	404	222	448	211	350	105	178	280	402	467	245	70	352	156	319	---		
Veszprém	292	110	336	99	238	77	127	168	289	355	166	143	240	44	207	111	---	
Zalaegerszeg	392	224	450	216	352	154	124	268	403	468	190	124	342	161	321	54	119	---

Mind you, when driving in Hungary you'll want to keep your wits about you; Hungary can be quite a trying place for motorists. It's not that drivers don't know the road rules; everyone has to attend a driver's education course and pass an examination. (A 'T' on the roof or back of a vehicle indicates *tanuló vezető* or 'learner driver', by the way – not 'taxi'!) But overtaking on blind curves, making turns from the outside lane, running stop signs and lights, and jumping lanes in roundabouts are everyday occurrences. That means a lot of car accidents and you'll probably see your fair share of them. Be careful at level crossings; they are particularly dangerous and you must decrease to 30km/h as you approach them.

All accidents should be reported to the police (☎ 107) immediately. Several insurance companies handle auto liability and minor claims can be settled without complications. Any claim on insurance policies bought in Hungary can also be made to Hungária Biztosító (☎ 1-301 6565) in Budapest at V Vadász utca 23-25. It is the largest insurance company in Hungary and deals with foreigners all the time.

Though many cities and towns have a confusing system of one-way streets, pedestrian zones and bicycle lanes, parking is not a big problem in the provinces. Most now require that you 'pay and display' when parking your vehicle – parking disks, coupons or stickers are available at newsstands, petrol stations or, increasingly, automated ticket machines. In smaller towns and cities a warden (usually a friendly pensioner) will approach you as soon as you emerge from the car and collect 40Ft to 60Ft for each hour you plan to park. In Budapest parking now costs between 140Ft and 240Ft per hour on the street and in covered car parks.

For information on traffic and public road conditions nationwide, ring Útinform on ☎ 1-322 2238 or ☎ 322 7643.

Rental

In general, you must be at least 21 years of age and have had your licence for a year or longer to rent a car in Hungary. All the big international firms have offices in Budapest, and there are scores of local companies throughout the country, but don't expect many bargains. For more details, see Car & Motorcycle in the Getting There & Away section of the Budapest chapter.

BICYCLE

The possibilities for cyclists are many in Hungary. The slopes of northern Hungary can be challenging, while the terrain of Transdanubia is much gentler; the Great Plain is flat though windy (and in summer, hot). The problem is bicycle rentals: which are hard to come by in Hungary. Your best bets are camping grounds, resort hotels and – very occasionally – bicycle repair shops. See the Things to See & Do or Activities sections under the various cities and towns for guidance.

Remember when planning your itinerary that bicycles are banned from all motorways and national highways with a single digit (Nos 1 to 9), and it must be equipped with lights and reflectors. Bicycles can be taken on trains but not on buses.

For more information, see Cycling in the Activities section of the Facts for the Visitor chapter.

HITCHING

Hitching is never entirely safe in any country in the world, and we don't recommend it. Travellers who decide to hitch should understand that they are taking a small but potentially serious risk. However, many people do choose to hitch, and the advice that follows should help to make their journeys as fast and safe as possible.

Hitchhiking is legal everywhere in Hungary except on motorways. Though this form of transport is not as popular as it once was (and can be very difficult in Hungary, according to readers), the road to Lake Balaton is always jammed with hitchhikers in the holiday season. There is a service in the capital called Kenguru that matches drivers

and passengers. For details, see Getting There & Away in the Budapest chapter.

BOAT

In summer the boat company Mahart runs regular passenger ferries on Lake Balaton and on the Danube from Budapest to Szentendre, Visegrád and Esztergom. Mahart services on certain sections of the Tisza River – Sárospatak to Tokaj (36km, 2¼ hours), for example, and Szeged to Csongrád (72km, 4¼ hours) – are now available only to groups of at least 40 people between April and mid-October and cost 30,000Ft an hour. The Budapest transport company BKV runs passenger ferries on the Danube within the capital in summer. Full details on these are given in the relevant chapters.

LOCAL TRANSPORT
Public Transport

Urban transport is well developed in Hungary, with efficient buses and, in many cities and towns, trolley buses. Budapest, Szeged, Miskolc and Debrecen also have tram lines, and there's an extensive metro (underground or subway) system and a suburban railway known as the HÉV in the capital.

You'll probably make extensive use of public transport in Budapest but little (if any) in provincial towns and cities: with very few exceptions, most places are quite manageable on foot, and bus services are not all that frequent except in the largest cities. Generally, city buses meet incoming long-distance trains; hop onto anything standing outside and you'll get close to the centre of town.

You must purchase your ticket (generally 70Ft to 100Ft) at newsstands or ticket windows beforehand and cancel it once aboard. Passes which are valid from a day to a month are available in the capital; these are very convenient as single-journey tickets are not always easy to buy and excellent value if you're moving around a lot. In the provinces, such passes (if available) are only useful if you're staying a long time.

Boarding without a ticket ('riding black', as the Hungarians say) is an offence and

A Street by Any Other Name...

After WWII, most streets, squares and parks were renamed after people, dates or political groups that have since become anathema to independent, democratic Hungary. From April 1989, names were changed at a frantic pace and with a determination that some people felt was almost obsessive; Cartographia's *Budapest Atlas* lists almost 400 street name changes in the capital alone. Sometimes it's just been a case of returning a street or square to its original (perhaps medieval) name – from Lenin útja, say, to Szent korona útja (Street of the Holy Crown). Other times the name is new.

The new (or original) names are now pretty much in place all these years later, the old street signs with a red 'X' drawn across them have all but disappeared and virtually no one refers to Ferenciek tere (Square of the Franciscans) in Budapest, for example, as Felszabadulás tér (Liberation Square), which honoured the Soviet Army's role in liberating Budapest in WWII.

you'll be put off and fined on the spot. Don't try to argue; the inspector has heard it all before.

Taxi

Taxis are plentiful and, if you are charged the correct fare, very reasonably priced. Flag fall varies, but a fair price is anything between 100Ft and 150Ft, with the charge per kilometre between 150Ft and 200Ft (higher late in the night). The best places to find taxis are in ranks at bus and railway stations, outside big hotels, near markets and on the main square.

You can flag down cruising taxis anywhere at any time. At night, taxis illuminate their sign on the roof when vacant. But to minimise the chances of being ripped off, try to book a cab with a reliable company by telephone; numbers are listed in the Getting Around sections of most towns and cities. You don't have to call from a private phone; Hungarian taxi companies use a 'reverse' telephone directory, with cabs dispatched to the address of where the phone is listed – including phone boxes, which post numbers either above the handset or on the door outside.

While taking a taxi is almost always without incident in the provinces, this is not always the case in Budapest. See the Getting Around section of that chapter for special advice.

ORGANISED TOURS

A number of travel agencies, including Vista, Ibusz and Cityrama (see that section under Information in the Budapest chapter) offer excursions and special interest guided tours (horse riding, cycling, bird-watching, Jewish culture, etc) to every corner of Hungary.

A 4½-hour tour by boat and bus to Szentendre or to Gödölö by bus with Cityrama or Ibusz costs about 9000Ft (children half-price) while a 10-hour tour of the Danube Bend by coach and boat with stops at Visegrád and Esztergom costs 15,000Ft. It also offers day trips to Lake Balaton (Balatonfüred, Tihany and the southern shore), the Southern Plain (Lajosmizse or Bugacpuszta in Kiskunság National Park and Kecskemét), Eger and Hollókő for about 16,000Ft. Vista tours of the countryside start at DM57 per person.

If you're interested in touring the North-East (a difficult area to appreciate without your own wheels), contact Nyíregyháza-based Air Mediterrán (☎/fax 42-314 303, ✉ mail@airmed.hu); no one knows that part of the country better than it does. All-inclusive tours include an eight-day one along the Tisza River to Tokaj on horseback (DM900), four days of riding narrow-gauge trains in Dombrád, Pálháza and Hármas (about DM500), an eight day tour of the churches, synagogues and holy sites in Nagykálló, Máriapócs, Tákos and Tarpa (DM970) and an eight-day bicycle tour of the North-East (DM730), including bicycle rental. It also does shorter wine-tasting tours in and around Tokaj for between DM20 and DM85.

Budapest

There's no other city in Hungary like Budapest. With some two million inhabitants, the metropolis is home to 20% of the total population. As Hungary's capital (*főváros*), it is the administrative, business and cultural centre; virtually everything in Hungary starts, finishes or is taking place in Budapest.

But the beauty of Budapest is what really makes it stand apart. Straddling a gentle curve in the Danube, the city is flanked by the Buda Hills on the west bank and what is essentially the start of the Great Plain to the east. Architecturally, it is a gem. Though it may lack the medieval buildings so ubiquitous in cities like Prague, there is enough baroque, neoclassical, Eclectic and Art Nouveau/Secessionist architecture here to satisfy anyone.

Overall, however, Budapest has a *fin de siècle* feel to it, for it was then – during the industrial boom and the capital's 'golden age' – that most of today's city was built. In some places, particularly along the two ring roads and up Andrássy út to the City Park, Budapest's nickname – 'the Paris of Central Europe' – is well deserved. Nearly every building in this district has some interesting or unusual detail – from Art Nouveau glazed tiles and neoclassical reliefs to bullet holes left over from WWII or the 1956 Uprising.

In fact, Budapest's scars are not well hidden. Industrial and automobile pollution have exacerbated the decay, but in recent years the rebuilding and renovations have been nothing short of astonishing.

Budapest is at its best in the spring and summer or just after dark when Castle Hill is bathed in a warm yellow light. Stroll along the Danube embankment (Duna korzó) on the Pest side or across any of the bridges past young couples embracing passionately. It's then that you'll feel the romance of a city that, despite all attempts both from within and outside to destroy it, has never died.

HIGHLIGHTS

- The view of Pest from Fishermen's Bastion on Castle Hill
- A night at the State Opera House
- A soak at any of the following thermal baths: Gellért, Rudas, Király, or Széchenyi
- The two icons of Hungarian nationhood: the Crown of St Stephen at the National Museum and the saint-king's mortal remains in the Basilica of St Stephen
- The wonderfully restored Central Market Hall
- The Old Masters at the Museum of Fine Arts

Budapest pp92-3
Budapest Districts p89
Castle Hill & Watertown p98
Óbuda & Margaret Island p104
Central Pest p110
City Park p114
University Area p128
Budapest Metro & Rail p147

HISTORY

Strictly speaking, the story of Budapest begins in 1873 when hilly, residential Buda and historic Óbuda to the north merged with flat, industrial Pest to form what was first called Pest-Buda. But like everything here, it's not that simple.

The Romans had an important colony here called Aquincum until the early 5th century, when they were forced to flee the settlement by the Huns. The Magyars arrived nearly half a millennium later, but Buda and Pest were no more than villages until the 12th century, when foreign merchants and tradespeople settled here. In the late 13th century, King Béla IV built a fortress in Buda, but it was King Charles

Robert (Károly Róbert) who moved the court from Visegrád to Buda 50 years later. His son Louis the Great (Nagy Lajos) began the construction of a royal palace.

The Mongols had burned Buda and Pest to the ground in 1241, and thus began a pattern of destruction and rebuilding that would last until the 20th century. Under the Turks, the two towns lost most of their populations, and when the Turks were defeated by the Habsburgs in the late 17th century, Buda Castle was in ruins. The 1848 Revolution, WWII and the 1956 Uprising all took their toll. In the final days of WWII,

for example, all seven bridges linking the two sides of the river were blown up by the retreating Germans, and a large part of the city was in ruins.

ORIENTATION

Budapest lies in the north-central part of Hungary, some 250km south-east of Vienna. It is a large, sprawling city measuring 525 sq kms and, with few exceptions, eg, Buda Hills, City Park and some excursions, the areas beyond the Nagykörút (literally the 'big ring road') in Pest and west of Moszkva tér in Buda are residential or

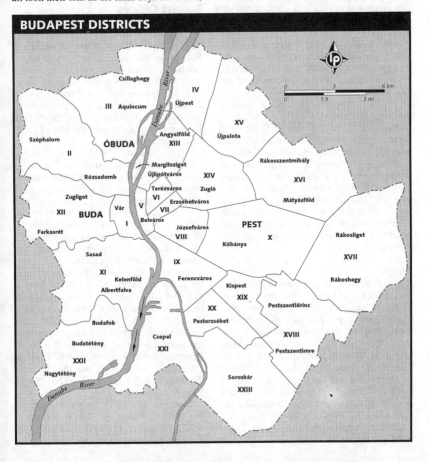

BUDAPEST DISTRICTS

industrial and of little interest to visitors. It is a well laid-out city, so much so that it is almost difficult to get lost in Budapest.

If you look at a map of the city you'll see that two ring roads – Nagykörút (the big one) and the semicircular Kiskörút (the 'little ring road') – link three of the bridges across the Danube and essentially define central Pest. The Nagykörút consists of Szent István körút, Teréz körút, Erzsébet körút, József körút and Ferenc körút. The Kiskörút comprises Károly körút, Múzeum körút and Vámház körút. Important boulevards like Bajcsy-Zsilinszky út, leafy Andrássy út, Rákóczi út and Üllői út fan out from the ring roads, creating large squares and circles.

Buda is dominated by Castle and Gellért Hills. The main roads in this district are Margit körút (the only part of either ring road that crosses the river), Fő utca and Attila út on either side of Castle Hill, and Hegyalja út and Bartók Béla út running west and south-west.

Budapest is divided into 23 *kerület*, or districts, which usually also have traditional names like Lipótváros (Leopold Town) or Víziváros (Watertown). While these can sometimes help visitors negotiate their way around (all of Castle Hill is in district I, for example, and the Inner Town is district V), we've divided the city into a dozen walks for easy touring. The Roman numeral appearing before each street address signifies the district.

Maps

The best folding maps to the city are Cartographia's 1:20,000 (350Ft) and 1:28,000 (300Ft) *Budapest City* maps available everywhere. If you plan to explore the city thoroughly or stay more than just a few days, the *Budapest Atlas*, also from Cartographia, is indispensable for long-term stayers. It comes in two scales: 1:25,000 (1000Ft) and the larger sized 1:20,000 (1300Ft). Both have indexes with all the new street names and some descriptive information in English. There is also a 1:25,000 pocket atlas of the Inner Town available for 390Ft.

Cartographia has its own outlet at VI Bajcsy-Zsilinszky út 37 (Map 4; ☎ 1-312 6001, metro: Arany János utca), but it's not self-service, which can be annoying. A better bet if you're looking for maps is the small Párisi Udvar Bookshop (Párisi udvari könyvesbolt) in the Párisi Udvar at V Petőfi Sándor utca 2 (Map 4; ☎ 1-318 3136, metro: Ferenciek tere) or the larger Libri Map Shop at VII Nyár utca 1 (Map 4; ☎ 322 0438, metro: Blaha Lujza tér) open weekdays from 9.30 am to 5.30 pm.

INFORMATION
Tourist Offices

The best single source of information is Tourinform (Map 4; ☎ 1-317 9800, fax 1-317 9656, @ hungary@tourinform.hu) in Pest at V Sütő utca 2, just off Deák tér (metro: Deák tér). It's open from 9 am to 7 pm weekdays and until 4 pm at the weekend. Though the staff can't book your accommodation, they'll send you somewhere that does and will help with anything else – from maps and ferry schedules to where to find vegetarian food.

Other Tourinform offices include the branch at Nyugati train station in Pest (☎/fax 1-302 8580, @ budapest2@tourinform.hu) next to platform No 10, which is open from 7 am to 8 pm daily (metro: Nyugati pályaudvar), and also another office located in Pest (Map 4; ☎ 1-352 1433, fax 352 9804, @ budapest3@tourinform.hu) at VII Király utca 93 (metro: Vörösmarty utca), which is open from 9 am to 6 pm daily.

Another option for tourist information is the Budapest Tourist Office (BTO; Map 2; ☎ 1-488 0453, fax 488 0474) at I Tárnok utca 9-11 in the Castle District, can point you in the right direction, organise tours and change money from 8 am to 8 pm daily from April to October and from 9 am to 6 pm the rest of the year. The BTO office can easily be reached via the Várbusz minibus from Moszkva tér or bus No 16 from Erzsébet tér in Pest.

Budapest Tourist Office has another office close to Roosevelt tér in Pest (Map 4; ☎ 322 4098, fax 342 2541) at VI Liszt Ferenc tér 11 (metro: Oktogon).

Money

Automatic teller machines (ATMs) can be found outside banks everywhere in the capital these days; the National Savings Bank (OTP) alone counts some 210 machines in the capital. If you have problems withdrawing cash from an ATM, any branch of K&H bank will give you a cash advance on your Visa, American Express card, Eurocard or MasterCard. The ATM at V Vörösmarty tér 4 tends to be more reliable than most as does the nearby K&H bank at V Váci utca 40.

Though credit cards are widely accepted nowadays in Budapest – even at some youth hostels – it is always more prudent to consider plastic an option rather than the rule. The Tribus agency (Map 4; ☎ 1-266 8042, @ tribus.hotel.service@mail.datanet.hu), at V Apáczai Csere János utca 1 near the Budapest Marriott Hotel (metro: Ferenciek tere), has a 24-hour facility that includes exchange.

The American Express office (Map 4; ☎ 1-235 4330) at V Deák Ferenc utca 10, a block up from Vörösmarty tér towards Deák tér, will change its own travellers cheques into eight different currencies and other travellers cheques into forint based on its daily rate, which is usually about 3% lower than bank rates.

To convert US dollar Amex travellers cheques into cash here incurs a 6% commission. Amex is open from 9 am to 6.30 pm daily in summer but on weekdays and till 2 pm on Saturday only the rest of the year. Citibank cardholders should go to Citibank (Map 4; ☎ 1-458 2351 or 266 9895) at V Vörösmarty tér 4. Cash advances are not available, but cardholders can get emergency cash in case of a lost or stolen card (24-hr helpline ☎ 06-80 488 888).

Whatever you do, avoid the big commercial bureaux de change, such as Interchange in Vörösmarty tér or on Castle Hill. Some deduct exorbitant 10% commissions while others have huge signs reading 'no commission' and advertise a rate – forgetting to mention you have to change the equivalent of US$1000 or more to get it or receive 10% below the bank rate. Moneychangers on the street come with the usual risks (if you can even find them these days). See Money in the introductory Facts for the Visitor chapter for more information about the black market.

Keleti Train Station As elsewhere in Hungary, OTP changes travellers cheques without commission, but get there at least an hour before closing to be sure the foreign-exchange counter is still open. The OTP branch closest to Keleti (metro: Keleti pályudvar) is at VIII Rákóczi út 84. The Ibusz office inside the station itself also changes travellers cheques at a good rate and takes credit cards. It's open from 8 am to 6 pm weekdays and to 4 pm at the weekend.

Nyugati Train Station The OTP branch with foreign exchange facilities closest to Nyugati train station (metro: Nyugati pályudvar) is at XIII Nyugati tér 9. The GWK-Mávtours exchange bureau at VI Teréz körút 62, near the street entrance at the station, is a good bet and keeps long hours: 7 am to 8pm daily.

Déli Train Station The OTP branch closest to Déli (metro: Déli pályudvar) is at I Alagút utca 3, on the corner of Attila út (Map 2). The GWK-Mávtours bureau in the concourse is a good place to change certain Eastern European currencies into forint (open 8 am to 6 pm weekdays, from 9 am to 1 pm on Saturday).

Erzsébet Tér Bus Station Not far from the international bus station on Erzsébet tér (metro: Deák tér) is the OTP bank at V József nádor tér 10 (Map 4). The big OTP branch opposite American Express on V Deák Ferenc utca doesn't do exchange, but it has two ATMs and currency-exchange machines outside. The K&H bank at V Váci utca 40 will change US dollar travellers cheques into cash dollars for a 3% commission. Exclusiv at No 12 of the same street is centrally located and quite reliable.

Post

The main post office, where you can buy stamps, mail letters and send packages and

BUDAPEST

MAP 1 - GREATER BUDAPEST

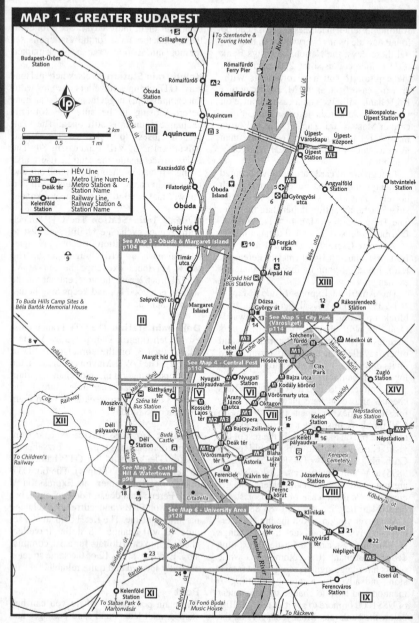

1 Csillaghegy
To Szentendre & Touring Hotel

Budapest-Üröm Station

Rómaifürdő Ferry Pier
Rómaifürdő
2
Óbuda Station
Rómaifürdő
Váci út

Aquincum

IV Rákospalota-Újpest Station

III Aquincum 3

Danube River

Újpest-Városkapu
Újpest-Központ
Újpest Station M3

Kaszásdülő
Angyalföld Station
Istvántelek Station

Filatorigát 4
5 Gyöngyösi utca
6
M3

Béla út

Óbuda Island
Óbuda

Árpád híd

See Map 3 - Óbuda & Margaret Island p104
10 Forgách utca

Timár utca
11 Árpád híd
Árpád híd Bus Station

XIII

Szépvölgyi út
Margaret Island
Dózsa György út
12 Rákosrendező Station

To Buda Hills Camp Sites & Béla Bartók Memorial House
7
9
8

III

13 See Map 5 - City Park (Városliget) p114
14
Lehel utca
Széchenyi fürdő
Mexikói út

Szilágyi Erzsébet fasor

Margit híd
Lehel tér
M1
Hősök tere
City Park
Hungária körút
Zugló Station

Cog Railway
Moszkva tér
See Map 4 - Central Pest p110
Nyugati pályaudvar Nyugati Station
Bajza utca
Kodály körönd
XIV

Batthyány tér
V
Arany János utca
VI Vörösmarty utca
Thököly
Népstadion Bus Station

Margit körút
Fő
Széna tér Bus Station
Kossuth Lajos tér
M1
Oktagon
VII
Keleti Station

I
M2 M3
Opera
15
Keleti pályaudvar
Népstadion
M2

XII
Déli pályaudvar
Bajcsy-Zsilinszky út
16

To Children's Railway
Déli Station
Buda Castle
Deák tér
M2 Blaha Lujza tér
17
Kerepesi Cemetery

M1 M Vörösmarty tér
Astoria

Ferenciek tere
Kálvin tér
Józsefváros Station

18
See Map 2 - Castle Hill & Watertown p98
20
M3 Ferenc körút
VIII

19
Citadella
Ferenc körút
Kőbányai út

See Map 6 - University Area p128
Klinikák

Villányi út
Boráros tér
21
Népliget

Budafoki út
23
Nagyvárad tér
22

Bartók
Béla út
Danube River
Népliget
M3

24
Fehérvári út
Ecseri út

Kelenföld Station XI
To Fonó Budai Music House
Ferencváros Station
IX

To Statue Park & Martonvásár
To Ráckeve

Legend:
HÉV Line
M3 — M Metro Line Number, Metro Station & Station Name
Deák tér
Kelenföld Station Railway Line, Railway Station & Station Name

0   1   2 km
0   0.5   1 mi

1 Csillaghegy Bath & Pools
2 Római Camping & Baths
3 Aquincum Museum
4 Dokk Backstage
5 International Medical Services
6 Duna Plaza Shopping Mall
7 Pál-völgy Cave
8 Szép Ilona & Remíz Restaurant
9 Szemlő-hegy Cave
10 Dagály Pools
11 Central Police Station
12 Góliát & Flandria Hotels
13 Ibis Volga Hotel &
   Americana Rent-a-Car
14 Diáksport Hostel
15 Ananda Hostel
16 Park Hotel
17 Erkel Theatre
18 Budapest Congress Centre
19 Kis Gellért Hotel
20 Royal Guesthouse
21 SOTE Klub
22 Planetarium; Laser Theatre
23 Back Pack Guest House
24 Folklór Centrum &
   Municipal Cultural House

XV

XVI

Nagy Lajos király útja
Fogarasi út

To Gödöllő

Kerepesi út
Nagyicce

Pillangó M2 Örs vezér tere
utca   Rákosfalva

Racetrack

Kőbánya
felső Station

Jászberényi út
Rákos Station

Kőbánya
alsó Station

X

Új köztemető
(Municipal Cemetery)

Gyömrői út

Pöttyös utca M
Határ út

Kőbánya-
Kispest
Station

Határ út Üllői út
M3

To Ferihegy
Airport

faxes, is in Pest at V Petőfi Sándor utca 13-15 (Map 4; metro: Deák tér). It sells boxes of varying sizes for 300Ft to 600Ft. All post marked 'Poste Restante, Budapest' also arrives here but pick it up from the entrance at V Városháza utca 18. It is open from 8 am to 8 pm weekdays and to 2 pm on Saturday. The post office at Nyugati train station, VI Teréz körút 51 (Map 4), is open from 8 am to 8 pm daily while the one at Keleti station, VIII Baross tér 11, keeps even longer hours: from 7 am to 9 pm but Monday to Saturday only.

Telephone

The best place to make international telephone calls in Hungary is from a phone box with a telephone card; a card with 50 units (800Ft) is worth about five minutes of conversation to North America. The Inner Town Telephone Centre (Map 4; ☎ 1-317 5500), run by Matáv at V Petőfi Sándor utca 17-19, has international telephone, email and fax services and is open from 8 am to 8 pm weekdays, from 9 am to 3 pm Saturday. There's also a call centre at the Vista Visitor Centre (see the following Travel Agencies section). You can also make calls and send or receive faxes at hotel business centres like the one at the Kempinski Corvinus hotel (Map 4; ☎ 1-429 3777), V Erzsébet tér 7-8.

Budapest's telephone code is ☎ 1.

Email & Internet Access

Budapest counts up to a dozen cybercafes, which are often crowded and reservations are not just advisable but essential at some. Many hostels also have at least one terminal. See that section under Places to Stay.

Budapest Net
(Map 4; ☎ 328 0292, fax 328 0294, ✆ info@budapestnet.hu), V Kecskeméti utca 5 (metro: Kálvin tér). With more than 30 terminals, this is the largest Internet cafe in Central Europe. It costs 700Ft to log on for the first hour, 500Ft thereafter. It's open from 10 am to 10 pm daily.

Cafe Eckermann
(Map 4; ☎ 374 4076, fax 374 4080), Goethe Institute, VI Andrássy út 24 (metro: Opera). Free access to one of three terminals is limited to one hour a week. Open from 2 to 10 pm weekdays, from 10 am to 10 pm on Saturday.

Vista Internet Cafe
(Map 4; ☎ 267 8603, fax 267 5568, ❷ incoming@
vista.hu), VII Paulay Ede utca 7. Six terminals
are available from 8 am to 10 pm weekdays and
from 10 am to 10 pm at the weekend (11/660Ft
per minute/hour).

Internet Resources
Budapest Week Online, with events, music
and movie listings, can be found at
www.budapestweek.com. The *Budapest
Sun* weekly newspaper has an informative
site at www.budapestsun.com. For Hungarian Web sites with Budapest links, see
Internet Resources in the introductory
Facts for the Visitor chapter.

Travel Agencies
Many of the offices listed under Travel
Agencies below and those under Private
Rooms in the Places to Stay section later in
this chapter also provide information and
often brochures and maps. But Unless noted
otherwise, travel agencies in Budapest are
open from 8 or 8.30 am to 5 pm weekdays
and in summer till noon or 1 pm on Saturday.

An outfit called Vista has the most comprehensive array of services of any travel
agency in Hungary – and one of only three
such outfits in the world. It's an amazing
place and the staff do everything – from
room bookings and chauffeured Trabant
service to adventure sport and discounted
student air fares (but *not* domestic train
tickets). For all your outgoing needs (air
tickets, package tours, etc) go to the Vista
Travel Centre (Map 4; ☎ 1-269 6032, fax
267 5568, ❷ info@vista.hu) at VI Andrássy
út 1 (enter from VI Paulay Ede utca), which
is open from 9 am to 6.30 pm weekdays and
to 2.30 pm on Saturday. The nearby Vista
Visitor Centre (Map 4; ☎ 1-268 0888, fax
267 5568) VI Paulay Ede utca 7, does all
the incoming stuff – tourist information,
study and eco tours in Hungary, etc – and
has a popular cafe, a bookshop called Bamako and a call centre. It is open 24 hours
a day, seven days a week. Visit Vista's Web
site at www.vista.hu.

In Central Pest, the main Ibusz office
(Map 4; ☎ 317 1806 or ☎ 318 1763,

❷ reservation@ibusz.h), V Ferenciek tere
10, supplies travel brochures, and the staff
are usually very good about answering general questions. The office also changes
money, books all forms of accommodation
and.accepts credit card payments. Another
Ibusz office (Map 4; ☎ 1-321 2932 or 322
2452), also good for train tickets, is at VII
Dob utca 1 (metro: Astoria).

Express (Map 4; ☎ 1-317 6634, fax 317
6823) at V Semmelweis utca 4 (metro: Astoria), open from 8.30 am to 4 pm weekdays
(to 5 pm Thursday and, from June to September, from 9 am to noon on Saturday)
sells BIJ train tickets with discounts of up to
35% on international trains to those under
the age of 26. There's another Express office
(Map 4; ☎ 1-331 7777, fax 331 6393) at V
Szabadság tér 16 (metro: Kossuth tér).

The Wasteels agency (☎ 1-210 2802) on
platform No 9 at Keleti train station (metro:
Keleti pályaudvar) also sells BIJ tickets.
You must have an ISIC or GO25 card
(available from Express or Vista for 900Ft)
to get the student fare. It is open from 8 am
to 7 pm weekdays and to 1 pm on Saturday.

Other helpful agencies in Pest are Budapest Tourist (Map 4; ☎ 1-318 6167, fax 318
6062), V Roosevelt tér 5, and Cooptourist
(Map 4; ☎ 1-374 6229 or 332 6387) nearby
at Kossuth Lajos tér 13-15. In Buda, there's
a Cooptourist (Map 6; ☎ 1-209 6667) at XI
Bartók Béla út 4.

Bookshops
One of the best English-language bookshops in Budapest is Pendragon (Map 3; ☎
340 4426) at XIII Pozsonyi út 21-23 (tram
No 4 or 6), which has an excellent selection
of guidebooks (including Lonely Planet titles) and fiction. It's open from 10 am to 6
pm on weekdays.

Another bookshop particularly strong in
English-language fiction is Bestsellers
(Map 4; ☎ 312 1295), V Október 6 utca 11
(metro: Arany János) open from 9 am till
6.30 pm weekdays, from 10 am to 6 pm on
Saturday and from 10 am to 4 pm on Sunday. It also runs the nearby CEU Academic
Bookshop (Map 4; ☎ 327 3096) at the Central European University, V Nádor utca 9,

which has an excellent selection of serious titles with a regional focus. It's open from 9 am to 6 or 6.30 pm weekdays and from 10 am to 4 pm on Saturdays.

The new kid on the block is the huge Libri Könyvpalota (Book Palace; Map 4; ☎ 267 4844) at VII Rákóczi út 12 (metro: Astoria) south-east of the Great Synagogue – Budapest's answer to Waterstone's or Borders – with some 6000 foreign-language titles. It is open from 10 am to 8 pm weekdays and to 3 pm on Saturday.

The Libri Studium (Map 4; ☎ 318 5680), V Váci utca 22, has an excellent selection of English books (including guides), as has the Kódex Bookshop (Map 4; ☎ 331 6350) at V Honvéd utca 5, where you'll find Hungarian books on the ground floor, foreign books on the 1st floor and a decent selection of classical and jazz CDs. The Párisi Bookshop in the Párisi Udvar (see the previous Maps section) and the Bamako bookshop at the Vista Travel Centre (see Travel Agencies) stock both maps and guides.

For Hungarian authors in translation, try the Writers' Bookshop (Írók boltja; Map 4; ☎ 322 1645), VI Andrássy út 45 (metro: Oktogon). With coffee and tables for use while browsing, it is one of the most comfortable bookshops in the city and was a popular literary cafe for most of the first half of the 20th century. It's open from 10 am to 6 pm weekdays and to 1 pm on Saturday.

For antique and second-hand books in Hungarian, German and English try Központi Antikvárium (Map 4; ☎ 317 3514) at V Múzeum körút 13-15 (metro: Kálvin tér), established in 1881 and the largest antiquarian bookshop in Budapest. Another good *antikvárium* is Kárpáti és Szőnyi (Map 4; ☎ 311 6431), V Szent István körút 1-3 (tram No 4 or 6), with an excellent selection of antique prints and maps.

Convenient places for foreign-language newspapers and magazines are the small bookshop in the Kempinski Corvinus Hotel at V Erzsébet tér 7-8; the outdoor kiosk on V Deák Ferenc utca as you enter Vörösmarty tér; the Hírker newsstand in the subway below Nyugati tér and the Világsajtó háza (World Press House) at V Városház utca 3-5

(open 7 am to 7 pm weekdays, to 6 pm Saturday and from 8 am to 4 pm on Sunday).

Cultural Centres

The Institut Français (Map 2; ☎ 202 1133) at I Fő utca 17 is open Tuesday to Friday from 1 to 7 pm and Saturday from 10 am to 1 pm while the Italian Institute of Culture (☎ 318 8144) is at VIII Bródy Sándor utca 8. It is open from 10 am to 6 pm weekdays. The Goethe Institute's Eckermann Cafe (see Email & Internet Access) is the place for German culture and periodicals.

Laundry

There are no self-service laundries in Budapest though some of the hostels (see Places to Stay) have washing machines and dryers. Generally you select to have your laundry done in one or six hours or the following day and pay accordingly (from about 1100Ft).

The Top Clean chain (☎ 227 5648) does a fairly reliable and affordable job on both laundry and dry cleaning and has some 40 locations around the city, including ones at V Arany János utca 34 (Map 4; metro: Arany János utca) and at the new Westend City Centre shopping mall, VI Váci út 3 (Map 4; metro: Nyugati pályaudvar). In general it is open from 7 am to 6.30 pm weekdays, from 8 am to 1 pm on Saturday.

Central full-service laundries include the Nádor Szalon (☎ 317 1542) at V József nádor tér 9 (metro: Vörösmarty tér) and Irisz Szalon (Map 4; ☎ 269 6840) at VII Rákóczi út 8/b (metro: Astoria) or a branch (☎ 317 2092) near Ferenciek tere at V Városház utca 3-5.

Left Luggage

Budapest's three major train stations, two international bus stations and the terminals at Ferihegy Airport all have left-luggage offices or lockers. For more information see those sections under Getting There & Away.

Medical Services

International Medical Services (Map 1; ☎/fax 329 9349, 📧 imskekes@euroweb.hu), XIII Váci út 202 (metro: Gyöngyösi utca) in Pest, is a flash private medical clinic, the first but not necessarily the best in Hungary, where consultations start at 6700Ft and home visits at 11,700Ft. It is open from 7.30 am to 8 pm. There's another branch (☎/fax 250 3829) open 24 hours a day in Óbuda at Vihar utca 29.

In addition to dental care the Interako Dental Co-op (☎ 175 1455 or 349 2243), XII Zugligeti út 60 (bus No 158 from Moskva tér) offers a whole range of medical services. It is open from 8 am to 8 pm weekdays and 9 am to 3 pm on Saturday. A more conveniently located clinic and open 24 hours to boot is the SOS Dental Service (Map 4; ☎ 267 9602) at VI Király utca 14 (metro: Deák tér).

The Teréz Patika (Teréz Pharmacy; Map 4; ☎ 311 4439) at VI Teréz körút 41 (metro: Nyugati pályaudvar) has a 24-hour window (ring for service).

Emergency

If you need to report a crime or a lost or stolen passport or credit card, first call the emergency police help number at ☎ 107 or go to the police station of the district (*kerület*) you're in. In the Inner Town that would be the station (Map 4; ☎ 302 5935) at V Szalay utca 11-13 (metro: Kossuth Lajos tér). If possible, ask a Hungarian speaker to accompany you. In the high season, police officers pair up with university students, who act as translators, and patrol the busiest areas.

In the event of an emergency, the following are currently the most important telephone numbers:

Police	☎ 107
Fire	☎ 105
Ambulance	☎ 104 or ☎ 311 1666
24-hour car assistance	☎ 188 (nationwide)
	☎ 1-212 2821 or 212 2938 (Hungarian Automobile Club) in Budapest

Dangers & Annoyances

No parts of Budapest are 'off-limits' to visitors, although some locals now avoid Margaret Island after dark and you may want to give the dodgier parts of the 8th and 9th districts (areas of prostitution) a wide berth.

As in the rest of Hungary, you are most vulnerable to car thieves, pickpockets, taxi louts, and scammers. To avoid having your car ripped off, follow the usual security procedures. Don't park it in a darkened street, make sure the burglar alarm is armed and have a steering-wheel lock in place.

Pickpocketing is most common in markets, the Castle District, Váci utca and Hősök tere, and on certain buses (eg, No 7) and trams (Nos 2, 4, 6, 47 & 49); in the past, metro No 1 (the little yellow line) has been plagued by thieves who work in pairs and even gangs, though this has decreased with the presence of police officers on board metro trains and on the platforms.

Scams involving attractive young women, gullible guys, expensive drinks in nightclubs and a frog-marching to the nearest ATM by gorillas in residence are all the rage these days – and we get letters from male readers complaining they've been ripped off all the time. Guys, please: if it seems too good to be true, it is, and the tab in these cases has run into hundreds and even thousands of dollars for such vanity. A list of these rip-off cafes and restaurants (it changes all the time) is available at tourist offices and the US Embassy, which circulates the information to hotels and hostels.

Taking a taxi in Budapest can be an expensive – even violent – experience. Always call a taxi from a phone – private, mobile or public – and give the number (almost always somewhere in the phone box) to the dispatcher. For more information, see Taxi in Getting Around in this chapter.

If you've left something on any form of public transport in Budapest contact the Budapest Transport Company (BKV) lost and found office (Map 4; ☎ 267 5299), VII Akácfa utca 18, between 7 am and 3 pm weekdays.

Discount Cards

For information on the Hungary Card and the Budapest Card, both of which offer general discounts or even free entry to museums and other tourist sights as well as reductions on hotel rates, menu prices, etc, see Documents in the Facts for the Visitor chapter.

Vajdahunyad Castle sunset, Pest.

Margaret Island in winter.

Chain Bridge at dusk, Budapest.

A snowwoman plays hide-and-seek with winter revellers on Budapest's Margaret Island.

The roof and door of the Geology Institute provide a colourful look at the world of rocks, Pest.

The Applied Arts Museum's ornate ceiling, Pest.

Primary school, Budapest - colourful start to life.

The Elephant House at City Zoo.

WALKING TOURS

Budapest is an excellent city for walking, and there are sights around every corner – from a brightly tiled gem of an Art Nouveau building to peasant women fresh in from the countryside hawking their home-made *barack lekvár* (apricot jam) or colourful embroidery.

The city's museums and other important sights are described in detail and listed in alphabetical order following this section for those of you who just want to visit a handful of places not close to one another and/or are not into walking.

Walking Tour 1: Castle Hill (Map 2)

Castle Hill, a 1km-long limestone plateau in Buda, 170m above the Danube, contains Budapest's most important medieval monuments and some of its best museums. It sits on a 28km network of caves formed by thermal springs that were supposedly used by the Turks for military purposes and then as air-raid shelters during WWII.

The walled Castle area consists of two distinct parts: the Old Town (Vár), where commoners lived in the Middle Ages (the current owners of the coveted burgher houses here are no longer so common) and the Royal Palace (Budavári palota), the original site of the castle built by Béla IV in the 13th century. To get to the former (where we'll start), take bus No 16 from Erzsébet tér in Pest, which terminates at Dísz tér. If you're already in Buda, find your way to Moskva tér on the red metro line and up Várfok utca (south-east above the square) to Vienna Gate, the northern entrance to the Old Town. A small bus labelled 'Várbusz' follows the same route from the start of Várfok utca.

If you want to begin with all the museums in the Royal Palace, there are a number of transport options. The easiest is the Sikló, a funicular built in 1870 that takes passengers up in two minutes from Clark Ádám tér to Szent György tér between 7.30 am and 10.30 pm daily (closed on the Monday of every even-numbered week). It costs 300/150Ft (adults/children under 10) to ascend and is 250/100Ft to ride back down. Al-

ternatively, you can walk up the Király lépcső, the 'Royal Steps' that lead from Hunyadi János út north-west of Clark Ádám tér, or the wide staircase that goes to the southern end of the Royal Palace from Szarvas tér.

The best way to see the Old Town is to stroll along the four medieval streets that more or less run parallel to one another and converge on Szentháromság tér, poking your head into the attractive little courtyards (an acceptable activity) and visiting the odd museum. A brief tour of the Old Town in one of the *fiáker* (horse-drawn hackney cabs), standing in Szentháromság tér, will cost 1000Ft to 1500Ft per person.

You can start your tour by climbing to the top of **Vienna Gate** (Bécsi kapu), rebuilt in 1936 to mark the 250th anniversary of the retaking of the castle from the Turks.

Táncsics Mihály utca is a narrow street of little houses painted in lively hues and adorned with statues. The one at No 9 is where Lajos Kossuth was imprisoned from 1837 to 1840 'for his homeland' (as the plaque says). In the entrances to many of the courtyards, you'll notice lots of **sedilia** – stone niches dating as far back as the 13th century. Historians are still debating their function. Some say they were merchant stalls, while others think servants cooled their heels here while their masters (or mistresses) paid a visit to the occupant.

Parts of the **medieval Jewish prayer house** (középkori zsidó imaház) at Táncsics Mihály utca 26 date from the 14th century; there's a small museum inside. Across the road to the south-east at No 7 is the **Museum of Music History** in an 18th-century palace with a lovely courtyard. Concerts are sometimes held in the Kodály Hall inside for a modest 400Ft. The controversial **Budapest Hilton Hotel**, which incorporates parts of a 14th-century Dominican church and a baroque Jesuit college, is farther south at Hess András tér 1. Have a look at the little red hedgehog in the relief above the doorway at house No 3, which was an inn in the 14th century.

If you walk north along Fortuna utca, another street of decorated houses, you'll soon reach one of Budapest's most interesting

BUDAPEST

MAP 2 - CASTLE HILL & WATERTOWN

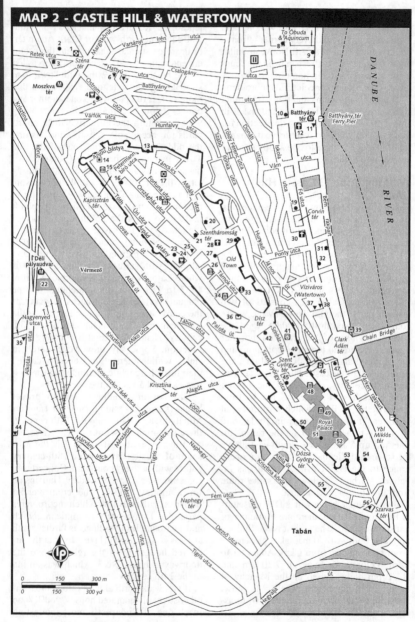

CASTLE HILL & WATERTOWN

PLACES TO STAY
3 Büro Pension &
   Söröző a Szent Jupáthoz
20 Budapest Hilton Hotel
21 Kulturinnov Hotel
31 Victoria Hotel

PLACES TO EAT
6 Nagyi Palacsintázója
7 Macbeth Sandwich Shop
11 Angelika Café
24 Café Miró
25 Ruszwurm Café
35 Il Treno Pizzeria
37 Taverna Ressaikos
38 Seoul House
43 Déryné Café
44 Mongolian Barbecue
55 Tabáni Kakas
56 Aranyszarvas

OTHER
1 Mammut Shopping Mall
2 Fény Utca Market

4 Oscar's Café & Pub
5 Budapest Wine Society
8 Military Court of Justice &
   Fő utca Prison
9 Herend Village Pottery
10 Supermarket
12 St Anne's Church
13 Vienna Gate
   (Bécsi Kapu)
14 Tomb of Abdurrahman
15 Military History Museum
16 Magdalene Tower
17 Medieval Jewish
   Prayer House
18 Museum of Commerce &
   Catering
19 Budai Vigadó
   (Concert Hall)
22 Déli Train Station
23 Judit Gift Shop
26 Golden Eagle
   Pharmacy Museum
27 Hackney Stand
28 Matthias Church

29 Fishermen's Bastion
30 Capuchin Church
32 Institut Français
33 BTO Information Centre
34 Labyrinth
36 Post Office
39 Tram Stop No 19
40 Sándor Palace
41 Castle Theatre
   (Vár Színház)
42 Former Defence Ministry
45 Corvinus Gate
46 Funicular
   (Lower Station)
47 0km Stone
48 Ludwig Museum
49 National Gallery
50 Lift to Dózsa György tér
51 Széchenyi National
   Library
52 Budapest History
   Museum
53 Ferdinand Gate
54 Turkish Cemetery

small museums: the **Commerce & Catering Museum** at No 4. This street leads back into Bécsi kapu tér, but if you continue west along Petermann bíró utca you'll reach Kapisztrán tér, a square named after John Capistranus (St John of Capistrano; 1386-1456), a charismatic Franciscan monk who raised an entire army for János Hunyadi in his campaign against the Turks.

The large white building to the north of the square houses the **Military History Museum**. Around the corner, along the so-called **Anjou Bastion** (Anjou bástya), with displays detailing the development of the cannon, lies the turban-topped **Tomb of Abdurrahman**, the last Turkish governor of Budapest, who was killed here in 1686 at the age of 70 on the day Buda was liberated. 'He was a heroic foe,' reads the tablet. 'May he rest in peace.'

The large steeple on the south side of Kapisztrán tér, visible for kilometres to the west of Castle Hill, is the **Magdalene Tower** (Magdolna torony). A reconstructed window and a bit of foundation is all that is left of the church once reserved for Hungarian-speakers in this district. It was used as a

mosque during the Turkish occupation and was destroyed in an air raid in WWII. Travellers not worried about claustrophobia or nose bleeds can climb the 163 steps for a great view of Castle Hill and beyond.

From Kapisztrán tér, walk south on Országház utca, being careful not to miss the sedile (that's one of the sedilia described earlier) in the entrance to No 9 and the medieval houses painted white, lime and tangerine at Nos 18, 20 & 22.

The next street to the west, running parallel, Úri utca, has some interesting courtyards, especially No 19 with a sundial and what looks like a tomb. There are more Gothic sedilia at Nos 32 and 36. The **Telephony Museum** at Úri utca 49 is housed in an old Clarist monastery. At No 9 of the same street is the entrance to the **Labyrinth** of Buda Castle.

Tree-lined Tóth Árpád sétány, the next 'street' over, follows the west wall from the Anjou Bastion to Dísz tér and has some great views of the Buda Hills.

In the centre of Szentháromság square there's a **Holy Trinity statue** (Szentháromság szobor), another one of the 'plague pillars' put up by grateful, healthy citizens in the early 18th century. Szentháromság tér is dominated by the Old Town's two most famous sights: Matthias Church, originally reserved for German-speakers, and beyond it the Fishermen's Bastion.

Bits of **Matthias Church** (Mátyás templom) – so named because the 15th-century Renaissance king Matthias Corvinus was married here – date back some 500 years, notably the carvings above the southern entrance. But basically the church is a neo-Gothic creation designed by the architect Frigyes Schulek in the late 19th century. The church has a colourful tile roof and a lovely tower; the interior is remarkable for its stained-glass windows, frescoes and wall decorations by the Romantic painters Károly Lotz and Bertalan Székely.

Escape the crowds by walking down the steps to the right of the main altar to the crypt, which leads to the **Collection of Ecclesiastical Art**. There are organ concerts in the church on certain evenings, continuing a tradition that began in 1867 when Franz Liszt's *Hungarian Coronation Mass* was first played here for the coronation of Franz Joseph and Elizabeth as king and queen of Hungary.

The **Fishermen's Bastion** is another neo-Gothic masquerade that most visitors (and Hungarians) believe to be much older. But who cares? It looks medieval and still offers among the best views in Budapest (200/100Ft). Built as a viewing platform in 1905 by Schulek, the bastion's name was taken from the guild of fishermen responsible for defending this stretch of the wall in the Middle Ages. The seven gleaming white turrets represent the Magyar tribes who entered the Carpathian Basin in the late 9th century.

Nearby is an equestrian **statue of St Stephen** (977-1038), the ornate detailing reflects sculptor Alajos Stróbl's deep leap into 11th-century art history.

The **Golden Eagle Pharmacy** (Aranysas patikaház), just south of Szentháromság tér at Tárnok utca 18, probably looks exactly the way it did in Buda Castle in the 16th century, though it was moved to its present site 100 years later. Today it houses a museum.

From Dísz tér, walk south along Színház utca to Szent György tér. Along the way you'll pass the **Castle Theatre** (Vár színház) on the left, built in 1736 as a Carmelite church and monastery, and across from it the bombed-out **Ministry of Defence**, another wartime casualty. During the Cold War, this site was NATO's nuclear target for Budapest, we're told. To the east is the **Sándor Palace** (Sándor palota), restored on the outside, while inside an important archaeological excavation continues.

On the south-east side of Szent György tér is an enormous **statue of the turul**, an eagle-like totem of the ancient Magyars (see boxed text 'Blame it on the Bird' in the Western Transdanubia chapter) honoured as the ancestor of the Magyars. The steps, beyond Corvinus Gate with its big black raven symbolising King Matthias Corvinus, lead to the Royal Palace.

The **Royal Palace** has been burned, bombed, razed, rebuilt and redesigned at least a half-dozen times over the past seven centuries.

The first part of the palace (Wing A) houses the **Ludwig Museum** of modern Hungarian and foreign (Andy Warhol, Roy Liechtenstein, etc) art. In the middle of the square, a Hortobágy *csikós* (cowboy) in full regalia tames a mighty *bábulna* steed.

Return to the square facing the Danube to get to Wing C or walk under the massive archway protected by snarling lions to Wing D to enter the National Gallery. Those choosing the former will enter what was once the palace terrace and gardens. In the centre stands a **statue of Eugene of Savoy**, who is credited with driving the Turks out of Hungary in 1686.

If you take the second route, you'll pass a Romantic-style fountain called **Matthias Well** with the young King Matthias Corvinus in his hunting garb. On the right is Szép Ilonka (Beautiful Helen), a protagonist of a Romantic ballad by Mihály Vörösmarty. The poor girl fell in love with the dashing 'hunter' and, upon learning his true identity and feeling unworthy, she died of a broken heart. On the left is Galeotto Marzio, an Italian chronicler at Matthias' court.

If you want to bail out of the tour now, there's a lift to the right of the archway that will take you down to Dózsa György tér and the bus stop (No 16) for Pest.

The **National Gallery**, spreading out through Wings B, C & D, is devoted almost exclusively to Hungarian art from the Middle Ages onward, though there are a few German artists represented. Wing F of the palace on the west side of Lion Court contains the **Széchenyi National Library** (☎ 355 6967), which has occasional exhibits. It is open from 1 to 9 pm on Monday and from 9 am Tuesday to Saturday. The **Budapest History Museum** is in Wing E.

From the Budapest History Museum, exit through the rear doors, have a look around the castle walls and enter the palace gardens. **Ferdinand Gate** under the conical **Mace Tower** will bring you to a set of steps. These descend to Szarvas tér in the Tabán district via the Turkish cemetery dating from that decisive battle of 1686.

Walking Tour 2: Víziváros (Map 2 & 3)

Víziváros (Watertown) is the narrow area between the Danube and Castle Hill that widens as it approaches Rózsadomb (Rose Hill) and Óbuda to the north-west and north, spreading as far west as Moszkva tér, one of the main transport hubs in Buda. In the Middle Ages, those involved in trades, crafts and fishing – the commoners who couldn't make the socio-economic ascent to the Old Town on Castle Hill – lived here. Under the Turks many of the district's churches were used as mosques, and baths were built, one of which is still functioning. Today Víziváros is the heart of urban Buda.

Sights in this section can be found initially on Map 2 (see p 100).

Víziváros actually begins at Ybl Miklós tér, but the best place to begin a stroll is at **Clark Ádám tér**. You can reach it on foot from Batthyány tér by walking south along the river or via tram No 19, which links it with Szent Gellért tér. Bus No 16 from Deák tér stops here on its way to/from Castle Hill.

The square is named after the Scottish engineer who supervised the building of

Chain Bridge (Lánchíd), leading from the square, and who designed the tunnel, which took eight months to carve out of the limestone. (The bridge was actually the idea of Count István Széchenyi and is officially named after him.) When the bridge opened in 1849, it was unique for two reasons: it was the first link between Buda and Pest, and the nobility – previously exempt from all taxation – had to pay up like everybody else to use it. The curious sculpture hidden in the bushes to the south that looks like a elongated doughnut is the **0km stone**; all Hungarian roads to and from the capital are measured from this point.

Fő utca is the main street running through Víziváros and dates from Roman times. The medieval house (now a French restaurant) below street level at No 20 has interesting Chinese reliefs above and below the windows. At the former **Capuchin church** at No 30, turned into a mosque by the Turks, you can see the remains of Islamic-style ogee-arched doors and windows on the south side. Around the corner there's the seal of King Matthias Corvinus – a raven and a ring – and the little square is called Corvin tér. The Eclectic building on the north side at No 8 is the **Budai Vigadó** (Buda Concert Hall), much less grand than its Pest counterpart and home to the State Folk Ensemble.

The next square is **Batthyány tér**, the centre of Víziváros and the best place to snap a picture of the Parliament building across the Danube. In the centre of this rather shabby space is the entrance to both the red metro and the HÉV suburban line to Szentendre.

On the south of Batthyány tér is **St Anne's Church** (Szent Ana templom), with one of the loveliest baroque interiors of any church in Budapest. The attached building at No 7 was an inn until 1724, then the church presbytery and now a fine cafe. Batthyány tér was called Upper Market Square in the Middle Ages, but the **market hall** (1902) to the west now contains just a supermarket and department store.

A couple of streets north is Nagy Imre tér, with the enormous **Military Court of Justice** on the northern side. Here Imre Nagy and others were tried and sentenced to death in 1958. It was also the site of the notorious Fő utca prison where many lesser mortals (but victims nonetheless) were incarcerated and tortured.

From here on, sights can be found on Map 3 (see p 104).

Király Bath (Király Gyógyfürdő), parts of which date from 1580, is one block up at II Fő utca 84. Next to it, across Ganz utca, is the Greek Catholic **St Florian Chapel** (Szent Flórián kápolna), built in 1760 and dedicated to the patron saint of firefighters. The whole chapel was raised more than a metre in the 1930s after earlier flooding had washed up dirt and silt. Opposite is the new (and quite attractive) **Foreign Ministry building**.

The next square up is **Bem tér**, named after the Pole József Bem who fought on the Hungarian side in the 1848-49 War of Independence. In 1956 students from the Technical University rallied in front of the statue here at the start of the Uprising. Bem József utca leads westward from the square and at No 20 is the **Foundry Museum** – perhaps not to everyone's taste but a lot more interesting than it sounds.

At Bem tér, Fő utca turns into Frankel Leó út, a tree-lined street of pricey antique shops. If you cross Margit körút and continue north, you'll reach Gül Baba utca on the left. This steep, narrow lane leads to the nicely renovated **Tomb of Gül Baba**, named after a Muslim holy man who died in 1548.

Walking north along Frankel Leó út, you'll pass the **Lukács Bath** (Lukács Gyógyfürdő), one of the city's dirtier spas, at No 25-29. At No 49 and tucked away in an apartment block is the **Újlak Synagogue** built in 1888 on the site of an older prayer house. It is the only functioning synagogue left on the Buda side.

Walking Tour 3: Óbuda & Aquincum (Map 3)

Ó means ancient in Hungarian and, as its name suggests, Óbuda is the oldest part of Buda. The Romans established Aquincum here (see History earlier in this chapter) and when the Magyars arrived, they named it Buda, which became Óbuda when the Royal Palace was built on Castle Hill.

Flórián tér is the historic centre of Óbuda. You can reach it on the HÉV train from Batthyány tér (Árpád-híd stop) or bus No 86 from many points along the Danube on the Buda side. Most people coming from Pest will catch the red metro line to Batthyány tér and board the HÉV. But if you're up near the City Park (Városliget), walk south-east to the intersection of Hungária körút and Thököly út and catch the No 1 tram, which avoids Buda and crosses Árpád Bridge into Óbuda.

Archaeology buffs taking the No 86 bus should descend at Nagyszombat utca (for HÉV passengers, it's the Tímár utca stop), about 800m south of Flórián tér on Pacsirtamező utca, to explore the **Roman Military Amphitheatre** (Római katonai amfiteátrum) built in the 2nd century for the garrisons. It could accommodate up to 15,000 spectators and was larger than the Colosseum in Rome. The rest of the military camp extends north to Flórián tér.

The yellow baroque **Óbuda Parish Church** (Óbudai plébániatemplom; 1749) dominates the east side of Flórián tér. There's a massive rococo pulpit inside. The large neoclassical building beside the Aquincum Hotel at III Lajos utca 163 is the former **Óbuda Synagogue** and now houses sound studios of Hungarian Television (MTV).

A branch of the **Budapest Gallery** directly opposite at Lajos utca 158 has some of the more interesting avant-garde exhibitions in Budapest.

In the subway below Flórián tér are Roman objects discovered in the area (many of them vandalised and covered in graffiti), including ancient **military baths**. Still more Roman ruins can be found in the park outside (including a reconstructed temple).

Two squares north-east of Flórián tér contain Óbuda's most important museums. In the former Zichy Mansion at III Szentlélek tér 6 is the **Vasarely Museum** devoted to the works of the 'Father of Op Art', Victor Vasarely (or Vásárhelyi Győző before he emigrated to Paris in 1930). In the back of the same building, facing the courtyard (enter at Fő 1), is the **Kassák Museum**, a three-room art gallery with some real gems of early 20th-century avant-garde art.

Fő tér is a restored square of baroque houses, public buildings and restaurants. At No 4, the **Zsigmond Kun Collection** of the Óbuda Museum displays folk art amassed by a wealthy ethnographer in his 18th-century townhouse. Walking east from Fő tér, in the middle of the road, you'll see a group of odd metal statues of rather worried-looking women with umbrellas. The statues are the work of prolific sculptor Imre Varga. The **Imre Varga Collection** is housed in a charming townhouse nearby at III Laktanya utca 7.

The HÉV or bus Nos 34 and 43 from Szentlélek tér head north for a few stops to **Aquincum** (Map 1), the most complete Roman civilian town in Hungary.

Aquincum had paved streets and fairly sumptuous single-storey houses with court-yards, fountains and mosaic floors as well as sophisticated drainage and heating systems. Not all that is easily apparent today as you walk among the ruins, but you can see its outlines as well as those of the big public baths, market, an early Christian church and a temple dedicated to the god Mithra.

The **Aquincum Museum**, Szentendrei út 139 (Map 1), tries to put it all in perspective – unfortunately only if you have a good grasp of Hungarian.

Walking Tour 4: Margaret Island (Map 3)

Neither Buda nor Pest, 2.5km-long Margaret Island (Margit sziget) in the middle of the Danube was always the domain of one religious order or another until the Turks came and turned what was then called the Island of Rabbits into – appropriately enough – a harem, from which all infidels were barred. It's been a public park open to everyone since the mid-19th century.

Cross over to Margaret Island from Pest or Buda via tram No 4 or 6. Bus No 26 covers the length of the island as it makes the run between Nyugati station and Árpád Bridge. Cars are allowed on Margaret Island from Árpád Bridge only as far as the two big hotels at the north-eastern end. The rest is reserved for pedestrians and cyclists. If you follow the shoreline in winter, you'll see thermal water gushing from beneath the island into the river.

You can walk the length of Margaret Island in one direction and return on bus No 26. Or you can rent a bicycle from one of two stands. The first, open from March to October, is on the west side just past the stadium as you walk from Margaret Bridge. It charges 360/1300Ft per hour/day for a basic three-speed and a pedal coach is 1100Ft an hour. The other is Bringóhintó (☎ 329 2073), refreshment stand near the Japanese Garden in the north of the island and open all year. A bicycle/mountain bike costs 480/650Ft per hour and a pedal coach from 890Ft to 2090Ft, depending on how many adults and kids it seats. A twirl around the island in one of the horse-drawn coaches near the hotels costs from 1000Ft per person.

In the flower-bed roundabout at the end of the access road, the **Centennial Monument** marks the union of Buda, Pest and Óbuda in 1873. It was unveiled a quarter of a century ago, which was an entirely different era, and the sculptor filled the strange cone with all sorts of socialist symbols. They remain as if contained in a partially open time capsule.

Margaret Island boasts two popular swimming pools on its west side. The first is the indoor/outdoor **National Sports Pool** (Nemzeti Sportuszoda), officially named after the Olympic swimming champion Alfréd Hajós, who won the 100m and 1200m races at the first modern Olympiad in 1896 and actually built the place. Amateur water polo league play takes place here at the weekend. The **Palatinus**, a large complex of outdoor pools, huge water slides and strands to the north, is a madhouse on a hot summer afternoon.

Just before you reach the Palatinus, you'll pass the ruins of the 13th-century **Franciscan church and monastery** (Ferences templom és kolostor) of which only the tower and a wall still stand. The Habsburg archduke Joseph built a summer residence here when he inherited the island in 1867. It was later converted into a hotel that ran until after WWII.

The octagonal **water tower** (víztorony; 1911) to the north-east rises above the

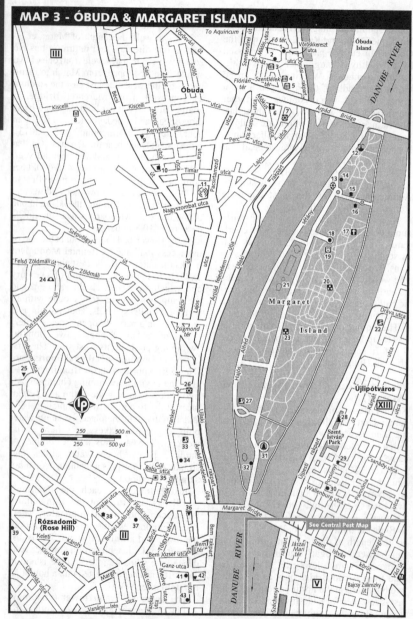

MAP 3 - ÓBUDA & MARGARET ISLAND

ÓBUDA & MARGARET ISLAND

PLACES TO STAY
10 San Marco Pension
15 Margitsziget Thermal Hotel & Bath
16 Grand Hotel
38 Papillon Pension

PLACES TO EAT
9   Kisbuda Gyöngye
25 Vadrózsa
29 Móri Borozó
36 Hong Kong Pearl Garden
40 Marxim Pizzeria
42 Kacsa

OTHER
1   Imre Varga Sculptures
2   Town Hall
3   Zsigmond Kun Collection (Óbuda Museum)
4   Kassák Museum
5   Vasarely Museum
6   Óbuda Parish Church
7   Former Óbuda Synagogue (TV Studios)
8   Kiscelli Museum
11 Roman Military Amphitheatre
12 Musical Fountain
13 Japanese Garden
14 Bringóhintó Bike Rentals
17 Premonstratensian Church
18 Water Tower
19 Open-Air Theatre
20 Dominican Church & Convent Ruins
21 Palatinus Pools
22 Helia Baths & Pools
23 Franciscan Church & Monastery Ruins
24 Szemlő-hegy Cave
26 Újlak Synagogue
27 Alfréd Hajós National Sports Pool & Danubius National Boating Association
28 Raoul Wallenberg Memorial
30 Pendragon Bookshop
31 Centennial Monument
32 Bike Rentals & Stadium
33 Béla Komjádi Swimming Pool
34 Lukács Bath
35 Gül Baba's Tomb
37 Magyar Autóklub
39 Marczibányi Tér Cultural Centre
41 Király Baths
43 Military Court of Justice

---

open-air theatre (szabadtéri színpad), used for opera and plays in summer. Beyond the roundabout is the **Japanese Garden** with lily pads, carp and a small wooden bridge. The raised gazebo in front of you is called the **Musical Fountain**, a replica of one in Transylvania.

The Romans used the thermal springs in the north-eastern part of the island. Today the springs lie below the Margitsziget Thermal hotel (entrance on the south side). The **thermal spa** here is one of the cleanest, most modern in Budapest, but lacks atmosphere because of that.

South of the posh Grand is the reconstructed Romanesque **Premonstratensian Church** (Premontre templom) dedicated to St Michael. Its 15th-century bell is real enough, though; it mysteriously appeared one night in 1914 under the roots of a walnut tree that had been knocked over in a storm. It was probably buried there by monks at the time of the Turkish invasion.

More ruins – but more important ones – lie a few steps south. These are the former **Dominican convent** (Domonkos kolostor) built by Béla IV whose scribes played an important role in the continuation of Hungarian scholarship. Its most famous resident was Béla's daughter, St Margaret (1242-71), who has something of a cult following

in Hungary. A red marble sepulchre cover marks her original resting place.

Walking Tour 5: Gellért Hill & the Tabán (Map 4)

Gellért-hegy, a 235m rocky hill south-east of the Castle, is crowned with a fortress of sorts and the Independence Monument, Budapest's unofficial symbol. From Gellért Hill, you can't beat the views of the Royal Palace or the Danube. The Tabán, the area between the two hills and stretching north-west as far as Déli train station, is associated with the Serbs, who settled here after fleeing from the Turks in the early 18th century. Later it became known for its restaurants and wine gardens – a kind of Montmartre for Budapest – but it burned to the ground at the turn of the 20th century.

If you're starting the tour from Castle Hill, exit via Ferdinand Gate and walk south from Szarvas tér to **Elizabeth Bridge** (Erzsébet híd), the big white span rebuilt after the war and opened to great fanfare in 1964. To the west is a large gushing fountain and a **statue of St Gellért**, an Italian missionary invited to Hungary by King Stephen. The stairs lead to the top of the hill. Though bus No 27 runs from Móricz Zsigmond körtér almost to the top of the hill, we'll begin at Szent Gellért tér, which is accessible from Pest on bus No 7 or tram Nos 47 and 49 and from the Buda side on bus No 86 and tram Nos 18 and 19.

Bartók Béla út runs south-west from the square and leads to Móricz Zsigmond körtér, a busy 'circular square' or circus.

Szent Gellért tér faces **Independence Bridge** (Szabadság-híd), which opened for the millenary exhibition in 1896. It was destroyed by German bombs during WWII and then rebuilt in 1946. The square is dominated by the **Gellért Hotel**, an Art Nouveau pile (1918) and the city's favourite old-world hotel and spa.

Directly north on the small hill above the hotel is the **Cliff Chapel** (Sziklakápolna) built into a cave in 1926. It was the seat of the Paulite order until the late 1940s when the priests were arrested and the cave sealed off. It was reopened in the early 1990s and re-consecrated.

From the chapel, a small path called Verejték utca (Perspiration Street) leads to **Jubilee Park** (Jubileum park). Another route to follow from Gellért tér is along Kelenhegyi út.

Towering above you is the **Citadella**, a fortress that never went to battle. Built by the Habsburgs after the 1848-49 War of Independence to 'defend' the city from further insurrection, by the time it was ready in 1851 the political climate had changed and the Citadella had become obsolete. It was given to the city in the 1890s and parts of it were symbolically blown to pieces. There's not much inside the Citadella today except for a hotel/hostel, a casino, a restaurant and a pleasant outdoor cafe.

To the east along Citadella sétány stands the **Independence Monument** (Szabadság szobor), the lovely lady with the palm frond proclaiming freedom throughout the city and the land. It was erected in 1947 in tribute to the Soviet soldiers who died liberating Budapest in 1945, but the victims' names in Cyrillic letters on the plinth and the statues of the Soviet soldiers were removed in the early 1990s. If you walk west a few minutes, you'll come to what is the best vantage point in Budapest.

A short distance to the north-east is the second of the area's three thermal spas, the

Rudas Bath (Rudas gyógyfürdő) at Döbrentei tér 9, and the most Turkish of them all with its octagonal pool, domed cupola with coloured glass and massive columns. If you don't like getting wet you can try a 'drinking cure' by visiting the **pump house** (ivócsarnok), which is below the bridge and within sight of the bath. A half-litre of the smelly hot water – meant to cure whatever ails you – is just 20Ft. To the north through the underpass is a statue of the Habsburg empress and Hungarian queen, Elizabeth (1837-98), the consort of Franz Joseph much beloved by Hungarians because, among other things, she learned to speak Hungarian.

Walking Tour 6: Szent István körút & Bajcsy-Zsilinszky út (Map 4)

This relatively brief walk crosses over into Pest and follows Szent István körút, the northernmost stretch of the Big Ring Road, to Nyugati tér and then south to Deák tér. You can reach Jászai Mari tér, the start of the walk, via tram No 4 or 6 from either side of the river or simply by walking over the bridge from Margaret Island. If you're coming from the Inner Town in Pest, hop on the waterfront tram No 2 to the terminus.

Two buildings of very different styles and functions face Jászai Mari tér, which is split in two by the foot of the bridge. To the north is an elegant 19th-century block of flats called **Palatinus House**. The modern building south of the square is the **White House**, the former headquarters of the Central Committee of the Hungarian Socialist Workers' Party. It now contains the offices of ministers of Parliament.

The area north of Szent István körút is called **Újlipótváros** (New Leopold Town) to distinguish it from Lipótváros around Parliament. (Archduke Leopold was the grandson of Habsburg Empress Maria Theresa.) The area was upper middle class and Jewish before the war, and many of the 'safe houses' organised by the heroic Swedish diplomat Raoul Wallenberg during WWII were here (see boxed text 'Raoul Wallenberg, Righteous Gentile'). A street named after this great man, two blocks to the north, bears a commemorative plaque and in 1999 a **statue** (Map 3) of a man (Wallenberg) doing battle with a snake (evil) was erected in Szent István Park, replacing the one torn down in 1948.

Szent István körút is an interesting street to stroll along. As elsewhere on the Big Ring Road, most of the Eclectic-style buildings, decorated with Atlases, reliefs and other details, were erected in the last part of the 19th century. Don't hesitate to explore the inner courtyards here and farther on – if Dublin is celebrated for its doors and London for its squares, Budapest is known for its lovely *udvar* (courts).

The attractive little theatre on your left as you continue east along Szent István körút is the **Vígszínház** (Gaiety Theatre), a popular venue for comedies and musicals. When it was built in 1896, the new theatre's location was criticised for being too far out of the city.

The large iron and glass structure on Nyugati tér (once known as Marx tér) is the **Nyugati train station** (Nyugati pályaudvar) built in 1877 by the Paris-based Eiffel company. In the early 1970s a train actually crashed through the enormous glass screen on the main facade when its brakes failed, coming to rest at the tram line.

From Nyugati tér, walk south on Bajcsy-Zsilinszky út for about 800m to the **Basilica of St Stephen** (Szent István-bazilika), the main sight on this street. This neoclassical structure was built over the course of half a century and not completed until 1906. Much of the interruption had to do with the fiasco in 1868 when the dome collapsed. No one was killed but it certainly must have frightened the horses. The basilica is rather dark and gloomy inside; disappointing for the city's largest and most important Catholic church, but take a walk to the top of the dome which offers one of the best views in the city. It is open from 10 am to 6 pm daily from April to October (300/200Ft).

To the right as you enter is a small **treasury** (kincstár) of ecclesiastical objects. Behind the main altar in a small chapel rests the basilica's major draw card: the **Holy**

Raoul Wallenberg, Righteous Gentile

Of all the 'righteous gentiles' honoured by Jews around the world, one of the best-known is Raoul Wallenberg, the Swedish diplomat and businessman who rescued as many as 35,000 Hungarian Jews during WWII.

Wallenberg, who came from a long line of bankers and diplomats, began working in 1936 for a trading firm whose president was a Hungarian Jew. In July 1944 the Swedish Foreign Ministry, at the request of Jewish and refugee organisations in the USA, sent the 32-year-old Wallenberg on a rescue mission to Budapest as an attaché to the embassy there. By that time, almost half a million Jews in Hungary had been sent to Nazi death camps.

Wallenberg immediately began issuing Swedish safe-conduct passes (called 'Wallenberg passports') and set up a series of 'safe houses' flying the flag of neutral countries where Jews could seek asylum. He even followed German 'death marches' and deportation trains, distributing food and clothing and actually pulling some 500 people off the cars along the way.

When the Soviet army entered Budapest in January 1945, Wallenberg went to Debrecen to report to the authorities, but in the wartime confusion was arrested for espionage and sent to Moscow. In the early 1950s, responding to reports that Wallenberg had been seen alive in a labour camp, the Soviet Union announced that he had in fact died of a heart attack in 1947. Several reports over the next two decades suggested Wallenberg was still alive, but none were ever confirmed.

TONY FANKHAUSER

Right (Szent Jobb), also known as the Holy Dexter. It is the mummified right hand of St Stephen (King Stephen I) and an object of great devotion. Like the Crown of St Stephen in the National Museum, it too was snatched by the bad guys after WWII but was soon, er, handed back.

To view it, follow the signs for 'Szent Jobb' (yes, it's to the right). You have to put a coin into a little machine in front of it to light up the glass casket containing the Holy Right. At almost 1000 years of age, it is – unsurprisingly – not a pretty sight. The treasury and chapel are open from 10 am to 5 pm (to 4 pm in winter) daily. Concerts are held at 7 pm on Monday from July to September.

Walking Tour 7: Northern Inner Town (Map 4)

This district, also called Lipótváros (Leopold Town), is full of offices, ministries and 19th-century apartment blocks.

From Deák tér, walk north-west through Erzsébet tér and west on József Attila utca toward the Danube. **Roosevelt tér**, named in 1947 after the long-serving (1933-45) American president, is at the foot of Chain Bridge and offers the best view of Castle Hill.

In the middle of the square is a **statue of Ferenc Deák**, the Hungarian minister largely responsible for the Compromise in 1867, which brought about the Dual Monarchy of Austria and Hungary. The statues on the west side are of an Austrian and a Hungarian child holding hands in peaceful bliss.

The Art Nouveau building with the gold tiles to the east (Nos 5-6) is the **Gresham Palace**, built by an English insurance company in 1907. After much ado, plans to turn it into a hotel are under way. The **Hungarian Academy of Sciences** (Magyar Tudományos Akadémia), founded by Count István Széchenyi, is at the northern end of the square.

Szabadság tér (Independence Square), one of the largest squares in the city, is a few minutes' walk to the north-east. It has one of Budapest's few remaining monuments to the Soviets in the centre. On the east side at No 12 is the US Embassy, where

Cardinal József Mindszenty took refuge for 15 years until leaving for Vienna in 1971 (see boxed text 'Cardinal Mindszenty' in the Danube Bend chapter).

South of the embassy is the former **Post Office Savings Bank** building, now part of the **Hungarian National Bank** (Magyar Nemzeti Bank; MNB) next door. The former, an Secessionist extravaganza of colourful tiles and folk motifs built by Ödön Lechner in 1901, is completely restored; go around the corner for a better view from Hold utca.

The large white and yellow building on the west side of the square housed the Budapest Stock Exchange when it was built in 1906. It is now the **headquarters of Magyar Televízió** (Hungarian Television; MTV).

North-west of Szabadság tér is Kossuth Lajos tér, the site of Budapest's most photographed building: the **Parliament**. This is where the national government sits and tourists are allowed in on certain days when Parliament is not in session.

Opposite Parliament at V Kossuth Lajos tér 12 is the **Ethnography Museum** (Néprajzi Múzeum). As Hungary's largest indoor folk collection, it is somewhat disappointing, but it has some excellent rotating exhibits and the building itself, designed in 1893 to house the Supreme Court, is worth a look – especially the massive central hall with its marble columns and ceiling fresco of *Justice* by Károly Lotz. South of the museum and past the Ministry of Agriculture in Vértanúk tere is a **statue of Imre Nagy**, the reformist Communist prime minister executed in 1958 for his role in the Uprising two years before. It was unveiled to great ceremony in the summer of 1996.

Walking Tour 8: Inner Town (Map 4)

The Inner Town (Belváros) is the heart of Budapest and contains the most expensive property in the city. But it has something of a split personality. North of Ferenciek tere is the 'have' side with the flashiest boutiques, the biggest hotels, some expensive restaurants and the most tourists. You'll often hear more German, Italian and English spoken here than Hungarian. Until recently the south was the 'have not' section – studenty, quieter and more Hungarian. Now it too has been reserved for pedestrians and is full of trendy clubs, cafes and restaurants.

You can decide which part of the Belváros you want to explore first; we'll start with the latter. Busy Ferenciek tere, which divides the Inner Town at Szabadsajtó út (Free Press Avenue), is on the blue metro line and can be reached by bus No 7 from Buda or points east in Pest. To get here from the end of the last tour, take tram No 2 along the Danube and get off at Elizabeth Bridge.

The centre of this part of the Inner Town is Egyetem tér (University Square), a five-minute walk south along Károly Mihály utca from Ferenciek tere. The square's name refers to the branch of the prestigious **Loránd Eötvös Science University** (ELTE) at No 1-3. Next to the university building is the **University Church**, a lovely baroque structure built in 1748.

Leafy Kecskeméti utca runs south-east from the square to Kálvin tér. At the end of it, near the Korona hotel on Kálvin tér, there's a plaque marking the location of the **Kecskemét Gate** (Kecskeméti-kapu), part of the medieval city wall that was pulled down in the 1700s. Ráday utca, which leads south from Kálvin tér and is full of full of cafes, clubs and restaurants, is where university students entertain themselves.

South-west of Egyetemi tér, at the corner of Szerb utca and Veres Pálné utca, stands the **Serbian Orthodox church** built by Serbs fleeing the Turks in the 17th century. The iconostasis is worth a look.

There are a couple of interesting sights along **Veres Pálné utca**. The building at No 19 has bronze reliefs above the 2nd floor illustrating various stages of building in the capital. At the corner of the next street, Pap-növelde utca, the enormous university building at No 4-10 is topped with little Greek temples on either side of the roof.

The best way to see the posher – the 'have' – side of the Inner Town is to walk up pedestrian **Váci utca**, the capital's premier – and most expensive – shopping street, with designer clothes, antique jew-

ellery shops, pubs and some bookshops for browsing. This was the total length of Pest in the Middle Ages. At V Ferenciek tere 5, walk through the **Párisi Udvar** (Parisian Court) built in 1909, a decorated arcade wiíh a domed ceiling, out onto tiny Kigyó utca. Váci utca is immediately to the west.

Many of the buildings on Váci utca are worth a closer look, but as it's a narrow street you'll have to crane your neck or walk into one of the side lanes for a better view. **Thonet House** at No 11/a is another masterpiece built by Ödön Lechner (1890), and the **Philanthia** flower shop at No 9 has an original Art Nouveau interior. The **Polgár Gallery** at No 11/b in a building dating from 1912 has recently undergone a spectacular renovation and contains a stained glass domed ceiling.

Váci utca leads into **Vörösmarty tér**, a large square of smart shops, galleries, airline offices, cafes and an outdoor market of stalls selling tourist schlock and artists who will draw your portrait or caricature. Suitable for framing – maybe.

In the centre is a statue of the 19th-century poet after whom Vörösmarty tér was named. It is made of Italian marble and is protected in winter by a bizarre plastic 'iceberg' that kids love sliding on. The first – or last – stop of the little yellow metro line is also in the square, and at the northern end is **Gerbeaud**, Budapest's fanciest and most famous cafe and cake shop.

The despised modern building on the west side of Vörösmarty tér (No 1) contains a music shop and ticket office for concerts in the city. South of it at Deák utca 5 is the sumptuous **Bank Palace**, built in 1915 and completely renovated. It now houses the Budapest Stock Exchange.

The **Pesti Vigadó**, the Romantic-style concert hall built in 1865 but badly damaged during the war, faces the river on Vigadó tér to the west. But before proceeding, have a look in the foyer at Vigadó utca 6, which has one of those strange lifts called Pater Noster.

A pleasant way to return to Ferenciek tere is along the **Duna korzó**, the riverside 'Danube Promenade' between Chain and Elizabeth Bridges and above Belgrád rakpart.

MAP 4 - CENTRAL PEST

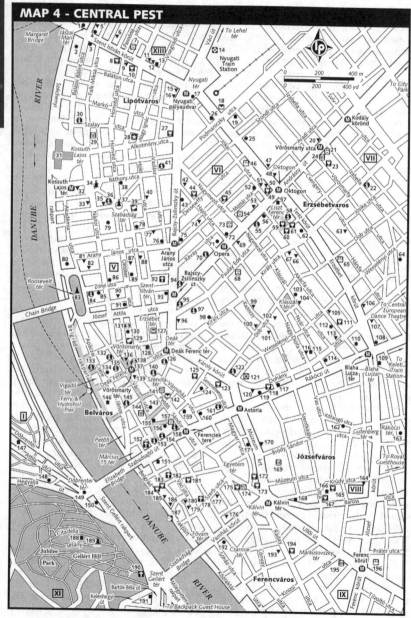

CENTRAL PEST

PLACES TO STAY
- 13 City Ring Pension
- 19 Best Hostel
- 26 Yellow Submarine Lotus Hostel
- 52 Medosz Hotel
- 57 Caterina Guesthouse
- 109 Nemzeti Hotel
- 110 Emke Hotel
- 115 Marco Polo Hostel
- 128 Kempinski Corvinus Hotel
- 146 Budapest Marriott Hotel
- 147 Orion Hotel
- 151 City Mátyás Pension
- 159 City Pilvax Pension
- 166 Museum Guesthouse
- 188 Citadella Hostel & Hotel
- 191 Gellért Hotel & Baths

PLACES TO EAT
- 5 Bambusz
- 6 Mézes Kucko Bakery
- 9 Turkish-Chinese Restaurant (Török-Kinai Büfé)
- 11 Okay Italia I
- 12 Három Testvér
- 15 Okay Italia II
- 16 Don Pepe Pizzeria
- 20 Lukács Café
- 32 Pick Ház
- 33 Tulipán
- 35 Iguana Mexican Restaurant
- 40 Hold Utca Market
- 42 Marquis de Salade
- 47 Arigato
- 48 McDonald's (24-Hour)
- 50 Butterfly Ice-Cream Shop
- 51 Teahouse at the Red Lion
- 53 Bombay Palace
- 63 Jorgosz
- 66 Bisquine Crêperie
- 67 Papa Frank's Canteen (Frici Papa Kifőzdéje)
- 69 Művész Café
- 74 Articsóka
- 77 Happy Bank
- 81 Self-Service Restaurant
- 82 Lou Lou & Gandhi
- 87 Kisharang Canteen
- 88 Café Kör
- 90 La Fontaine & National Philharmonic Ticket Office
- 96 Durcin Sandwich Shop
- 99 Kővári Kosher Delicatessen
- 100 Fröhlich Cakeshop
- 101 Kosher Bakery
- 102 Hanna Kosher Restaurant
- 104 Kádár Canteen
- 105 La Bodega
- 106 Gül Baba
- 107 New York Café
- 113 Grill 99
- 116 King's Restaurant & Hotel
- 120 Fausto's Restaurant
- 136 Café Gerbeaud
- 139 Cyrano & Cosmo Restaurants
- 164 Centrál Self-Service Restaurant
- 170 Múzeum Restaurant
- 176 Chan-Chan
- 177 CD Fű Teahouse
- 179 Fatál
- 180 1000 Tea
- 185 Govinda
- 186 Taverna Dionysos
- 193 Coquan's Café

BARS & CLUBS
- 8 Süss Fél Nap
- 10 Trocadero Club
- 23 Hades Jazztaurant
- 27 Becketts Pub
- 44 Picasso Point
- 45 Piaf
- 49 Cactus Juice
- 59 Incognito Café
- 60 PestiEst Café
- 61 Café Vian
- 111 Old Man's Music Pub
- 118 Portside Pub
- 123 Café Eklektika
- 125 Merlin Club & Theatre
- 165 Darshan Udvar
- 167 Fél Tíz Jazz Club
- 172 Action Bar
- 173 Irish Cat
- 175 Janis Pub
- 181 Fat Mo's
- 183 Kalamajka Táncház
- 184 Capella
- 194 Paris, Texas (Club)

TOURIST OFFICES & BOOKING AGENCIES
- 22 Tourinform Branch Office
- 30 Cooptourist
- 36 Express (Train Tickets)
- 41 Cityrama Bus Tours
- 55 MÁV Ticket Office
- 58 BTO Information Branch
- 70 Színházak Központi Jegyiroda (Central Ticket Office)
- 84 Gresham Palace & Budapest Tourist
- 94 Budatours
- 95 Vista Travel Centre; Internet Cafe
- 97 Vista Visitor Centre
- 122 Ibusz (Train Tickets)
- 126 Tourinform
- 132 Malév Office
- 133 Mahart Ticket Office
- 135 Vigadó Ticket Office
- 140 Avis
- 145 Tribus (24-Hour Accommodation Office)
- 153 Music Mix Ticket Office
- 154 Charles Tourist Service
- 158 Ibusz Main Office (Private Rooms) & Párisi Udvar Bookshop
- 161 Express (Hostel Bookings); Puskin Cinema

MUSEUMS
- 24 Ferenc Liszt Museum
- 29 Ethnography Museum
- 121 Great Synagogue & Jewish Museum
- 169 National Museum
- 195 Museum of Applied Arts

OTHER
- 1 Palatinus House
- 2 White House
- 3 Kárpáti és Szőnyi & BÁV Shop
- 4 Rothschild Supermarket
- 7 Vigszínház (Gaiety Theatre)
- 14 Westend City Centre Shopping Mall
- 17 Kaiser's Supermarket
- 18 Post Office
- 21 Budapest Puppet Theatre
- 25 Teréz Pharmacy (24-Hour)
- 28 Inner Town Police Station
- 31 Parliament
- 34 Imre Nagy Monument
- 37 Soviet Army Memorial
- 38 Kódex Bookshop
- 39 US Embassy
- 43 Cartographia Map Shop
- 46 Művész Cinema
- 54 Budapest Operetta Theatre
- 56 Writers' Bookshop
- 62 Franz Liszt Academy of Music
- 64 Almássy tér Leisure Centre
- 65 Örökmozgó Cinema & Film Museum
- 68 New Theatre
- 71 State Opera House
  (continued next page)

CENTRAL PEST

OTHER (cont.)		
72 Goethe Institute & Eckermann Cybercafé	114 Libri Map Shop	150 Rudas Baths; Cinetrip Vízi-Mozi
73 Thália Theatre	117 Libri Book Shop	152 Inner Town Parish Church
75 Haas & Czjzek Shop	119 Irisz Szalon Laundry	155 Libri Studium Bookshop
76 Top Clean Laundry	124 Holló Atelier (Folk Craft)	156 Zsolnay
78 Hungarian National Bank Building	127 Erzsébet Tér Bus Station	157 József Katona Theatre
79 MTV Building	129 UK Embassy	160 World Press House
80 Academy of Science	130 Herend	162 Kenguru Ride Service
83 Ferenc Deák Statue	131 OTP Bank	163 Rákóczi Tér Market
85 Duna Palota	134 Pesti Vigadó (Concert Hall)	168 Ervin Szabó Library
86 Central European University	137 Citibank	171 Központi Antikvárium
89 Bestsellers Bookshop	138 American Express	174 Budapest Net Cybercafé
91 La Boutique des Vins (Wine Shop)	141 Inner Town Telephone Centre	178 Serbian Orthodox Church
92 Basilica of St Stephen	142 Main Post Office (Poste Restante)	182 Church of St Michael
93 Inka Car Rental	143 Folkart Centrum	187 International Landing Stage (Nemzetközi hajóállomás)
98 SOS Dental Service	144 Polgár Gallery	189 Independence Monument
103 Ghetto Market	148 Rác Baths	190 Cliff Chapel & Monastery
108 Julius Meinl Supermarket	149 Ivócsarnok (Pump House)	192 Central Market Hall (Nagycsarnok)
112 BKV Office		196 Corvin Filmpalota (Cinema)

It's full of cafes, musicians and handicraft stalls by day and hookers and hustlers by night. The Duna korzó leads into **Petőfi tér**, named after the poet of the 1848-49 War of Independence and the scene of political rallies (both legal and illegal) over subsequent years. **Március 15 tér**, which marks the date of the outbreak of the revolution, abuts it to the south.

On the east side of Március 15 tér, sitting uncomfortably close to the Elizabeth Bridge flyover, is the **Inner Town parish church** (Belvárosi plébániatemplom), where a Romanesque church was first built in the 12th century within a Roman fortress. You can see a few bits of the fort, **Contra Aquincum**, in the square to the north. The church was rebuilt in the 14th and 18th centuries, and you can easily spot Gothic, Renaissance and baroque elements both inside and out.

Walking Tour 9: Andrássy út & the City Park (Map 4 & 5)

This is a rather long tour starting at Deák tér and following the most attractive boulevard in Budapest. The yellow metro runs just beneath Andrássy út from Deák tér to the City Park (Városliget), so if you begin to lose your stamina, just go down the short flight of steps and jump on board.

The listed sights can first be found on Map 4 (see p 110).

Join Andrássy út a short way north of Deák tér as it splits away from Bajcsy-Zsilinszky út. This section of Andrássy is lined with plane trees – cool and pleasant on a warm day.

The neo-Renaissance **Hungarian State Opera House** on the left at No 22 was designed by Miklós Ybl in 1884, and for many it is the city's most beautiful building. The interior is especially lovely and sparkles after a total overhaul in the 1980s. If you cannot attend a concert or an opera, at least join one of the guided tours (see the listing under Museums and other Sights).

The building across from the Opera House, the so-called **Drechsler House**, was designed by the Art Nouveau master builder Ödön Lechner in 1882. Until recently it housed the State Ballet Institute but is now being redeveloped. You can explore the interior courtyard from the west side (Dalszínház utca), but go around the corner for something even more magical: a Secessionist gem (1909) embellished with monkey faces, globes and geometric designs that is now the **New Theatre** (Új Színház) at VI Paulay Ede utca 35.

The old-world **Művész** (Artist) cafe at Andrássy út 29 is one of the most atmospheric in the city. Across the street is Nagymező utca, 'the Broadway of Budapest', with a number of theatres, including the lovingly restored **Thália** (formerly the Arizona) at No 22-24.

The Big Ring Road meets Andrássy út at **Oktogon**, a busy intersection full of fast-food joints, shops, honking cars and pedestrians. Teréz körút runs to the north-west and for a block to the south-east where it becomes Erzsébet körút.

Beyond Oktogon, Andrássy út is lined with very grand buildings, housing such institutions as the **Budapest Puppet Theatre** at No 69, the **Academy of Fine Arts** at No 71 and **MÁV** headquarters at No 73-75. The former **secret police building** at No 60 has a ghastly history, for it was here that many activists of whatever political side (including Cardinal Mindszenty) that was out of fashion before and after WWII were taken for interrogation and torture. The walls were apparently made doubly thick to mute the screams. The **Franz Liszt Memorial Museum** is across the street at No 69 (but enter from VI Vörösmarty utca 35).

From here on, listed items can be found on Map 5 (see p 114).

The next square (more accurately a circus) is **Kodály körönd**, one of the most beautiful in the city, though the four neo-Renaissance townhouses are in varying states of decay, including the former residence of the composer Zoltán Kodály at No 1.

The **Ferenc Hopp Museum of East Asian Art** is at VI Andrássy út 103 in the former villa of its collector and benefactor. Some of the collection on exhibit is at the nearby **György Ráth Museum** at VI Városligeti fasor 12, a few minutes walk south on Bajza utca and then west.

Andrássy út ends at **Hősök tere** (Heroes' Square), which has the nation's most solemn monument – an empty coffin representing one of the unknown insurgents from the 1956 Uprising lies beneath a stone tile – and a guard of honour. The **Millenary Monument** (Ezeréves emlékmű), a 36m pillar backed by colonnades to the right and left defines the square. About to take off from the top of the pillar is the Angel Gabriel, who is offering Vajk – the future King Stephen – the Hungarian crown. At the base are Árpád and the six other Magyar chieftains who occupied the Carpathian Basin in the late 9th century. The statues and reliefs in and on the colonnades are of rulers and statesmen. The four allegorical figures atop are (from left to right): Work & Prosperity, War, Peace and Knowledge & Glory.

On the northern side of the square is the **Museum of Fine Arts** (1906), housing the city's outstanding collection of foreign works. To the south is the **Műcsarnok**, the ornate 'Art Gallery' or 'Palace of Art' built around the time of the millenary exhibition in 1896 and renovated a century later. It is used for temporary (usually modern) art exhibits.

Heroes' Square is in effect the entrance to the **City Park** (Városliget), an open space measuring almost a square kilometre that hosted most of the events during Hungary's 1000th anniversary celebrations in 1896.

The **City Zoo** is a five-minute walk to the west along Állatkerti út, past **Gundel**, Budapest's – and Hungary's – most famous restaurant. A short distance to the east is the permanent **Grand Circus** (see the Entertainment section) and **Vidám Park** (XIV Állatkerti körút 14-16), a 150-year-old fun fair on 2½ hectares with a couple of dozen new rides as well as a vintage wooden roller coaster, go-karts and dodgem cars (100/50Ft per ride). It is open from 10 am to 8 pm daily between April and September and to 7 pm the rest of the year.

The gigantic wedding cake-like building south of the circus, just off XIV Kós Károly sétány, is the **Széchenyi Bath**, which has indoor and outdoor thermal pools open year round (see the boxed text 'Taking the Waters in Budapest' in the Activities section).

Due south of the large castle on the little island in the lake, which is transformed into a skating rink in winter, is **Vajdahunyad Castle** (Vajdahunyad vára), partly modelled after a fortress in Transylvania and erected for the millenary exhibition in 1896. It now houses the **Agricultural Museum**.

The little church opposite the castle is called **Ják Chapel** (Jáki-kápolna), but only

MAP 5 - CITY PARK (VÁROSLIGET)

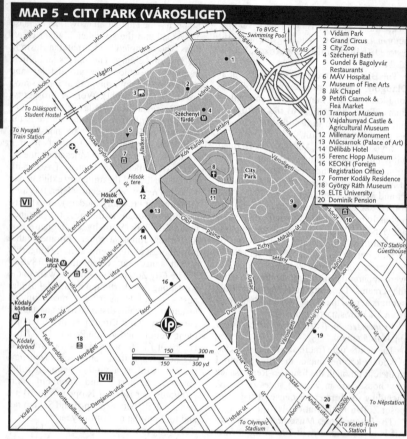

1 Vidám Park
2 Grand Circus
3 City Zoo
4 Széchenyi Bath
5 Gundel & Bagolyvár
  Restaurants
6 MÁV Hospital
7 Museum of Fine Arts
8 Ják Chapel
9 Petőfi Csarnok &
  Flea Market
10 Transport Museum
11 Vajdahunyad Castle &
  Agricultural Museum
12 Millenary Monument
13 Műcsarnok (Palace of Art)
14 Délibáb Hotel
15 Ferenc Hopp Museum
16 KEOKH (Foreign
  Registration Office)
17 Former Kodály Residence
18 György Ráth Museum
19 ELTE University
20 Dominik Pension

its portal is copied from the 13th-century Abbey Church in Ják in Western Transdanubia. The statue of the hooded scribe south of the chapel is that of **Anonymous**, the unknown chronicler at the court of King Béla III who wrote a history of the early Magyars. Writers (both real and aspirant) touch his pen for inspiration.

Walking Tour 10: Oktogon to Blaha Lujza tér (Map 4)

The Big Ring Road slices district VII (also called Erzsébetváros or Elizabeth Town) in half between these two busy squares. The eastern side is a rather poor area with little of interest to visitors except the Keleti train station on Baross tér. The western side, bounded by the Little Ring Road, has always been predominantly Jewish, and this was the ghetto where Jews were forced to live behind wooden fences when the Nazis occupied Hungary in 1944.

Your starting point, Oktogon, is on the yellow metro line. It can also be reached via tram Nos 4 and 6 from both Buda and the rest of Pest.

The **Liszt Academy of Music** (Liszt Zeneakadémia) is one block south-east of

Oktogon just off Király utca at Liszt Ferenc tér 8. Built in 1907, the academy attracts students from all over the world and is one of the top venues in Budapest for concerts. The interior, richly embellished with Zsolnay porcelain and frescoes, is worth a look even if you're not attending a performance. **Klauzál tér**, the heart of the old Jewish quarter, is a couple of streets to the south-west down Csányi utca.

The square and surrounding streets retain a feeling of prewar Budapest. Signs of a continued Jewish presence are still evident – in a kosher bakery at Kazinczy utca 28, the Kővári delicatessen at Kazinczy utca 41 and the Frölich cake shop and cafe at No 22, which has old Jewish favourites.

There are about half a dozen synagogues and prayer houses in the district once reserved for conservatives, the orthodox, Poles, Sephardics, etc. The **Orthodox Synagogue**, at VII Kazinczy utca 29-31 (or enter from Dob utca 35), has been given a face-lift as has the Moorish **Conservative Synagogue** (1872) at VII Rumbach Sebestyén utca 11.

But none compares with the **Great Synagogue** (Nagy zsinagóga) at VII Dohány utca 2-8, the largest in the world outside New York. Built in 1859 with Romantic and Moorish elements, the copper-domed synagogue was renovated with funds raised by the Hungarian government and a New York-based charity headed by the actor Tony Curtis, whose parents emigrated from Hungary in the 1920s. The **Jewish Museum** is in the annexe to the left.

The **Holocaust Memorial** (Imre Varga, 1989) on the Wesselényi utca side of the synagogue stands over the mass graves of those murdered by the Nazis in 1944-45. On the leaves of the metal 'tree of life' are the family names of some of the 400,000 victims.

Rákóczi út, a busy shopping street, leads to **Blaha Lujza tér**, named after a leading 19th-century stage actress. The subway under the square is one of the most lively in the city, with hustlers, beggars, peasants selling their wares, Peruvian musicians and, of course, pickpockets.

North of Blaha Lujza tér at Erzsébet körút 9-11 is the Art Nouveau **New York Palace** and its famous **New York Cafe**, scene of many a literary gathering over the years. Find your way through the scaffolding; it's been here since the 1956 Uprising when a tank smashed into it.

Rákóczi út ends at Baross tér and **Keleti train station**. It was built in 1884 and renovated a century later. About 500m south on Fiumei út (tram No 23 or 24) is the entrance to **Kerepesi Cemetery** (Kerepesi temető; Map 1), VIII Fiumei út 16, Budapest's Highgate or Père Lachaise and last resting place of such greats as Lajos Kossuth, Ferenc Deák, Lajos Batthyány, Lujza Blaha and Endre Ady. Plot 21 contains the graves of many who died in the 1956 Uprising. The cemetery is open from 8 am to 7 pm daily.

Walking Tour 11: Blaha Lujza tér to Petőfi Bridge (Map 4)

From Blaha Lujza tér, the Big Ring Road runs through district VIII, also called Józsefváros (Joseph Town). The west side transforms itself from a neighbourhood of lovely 19th-century townhouses and villas around the Little Ring Road to a large student quarter. East of the boulevard is the rough-and-tumble district so poignantly described in the Pressburger brothers' *Homage to the Eighth District*. It is the area where much of the fighting in October 1956 took place.

Rákóczi tér, the only real square on the Big Ring Road, is as good a place as any to get a feel for this area. It is the site of a busy **market hall** (*vásárcsarnok*), erected in 1897 and renovated in the early 1990s after a bad fire.

Across the boulevard, Bródy Sándor utca runs west from Gutenberg tér (with a lovely Art Nouveau building at No 4) to the old **Hungarian Radio** (Magyar Rádió) building at No 5-7, where shots were first fired on 23 October 1956. Beyond it, at VIII Múzeum körút 14-16, is the **Hungarian National Museum**, the largest historical collection in the country. Designed by Mihály Pollack, this purpose-built museum opened in 1847 and just a year later was the scene of a momentous event (see the History section in the Facts about Hungary chapter). The national museum contains the most cherished object in Hungary: the **Crown of St Stephen** (see boxed text 'The Crown of St Stephen').

You can wander back to the Big Ring Road through any of the small streets. If you follow Baross utca eastward from Kálvin tér, drop into the **Ervin Szabó Library**, VIII Reviczky utca 3, built in 1887. With its gypsum ornaments, faded gold tracery and enormous chandeliers, you'll never see another public reading room like it (open from 9 am to 9 pm Monday and Tuesday and Thursday and Friday and to 1 pm at the weekend).

The Art Deco **Corvin Film Palace** (Corvin Filmpalota) sits at the southern end of Kisfaludy utca in the middle of a square flanked by Regency-like houses and has been restored to its former glory.

Directly to the west at IX Üllői út 33-37 is Hungary's Victoria & Albert: the **Applied Arts Museum**. In fact, the London museum was the inspiration when this museum was founded in 1864. The building, designed by Ödön Lechner and decorated with Zsolnay ceramic tiles, was completed for the Millenary Exhibition but was badly damaged during WWII and again in 1956.

The neighbourhood south of Üllői út is **Ferencváros** (Francis Town), home of the city's most popular football team, Ferencvárosi Torna Club (FTC), and many of its rougher supporters dressed in green and white. (Its stadium at IX Üllői út 129 is the only one in the city where booze is banned.) Most of the area was washed away in the Great Flood of 1838. The area to the west toward the Little Ring Road is dominated by the **Budapest Economics University** (Budapesti Közgázdaságtodományos Egyetem) on Fővám tér and is full of hostels, little clubs and inexpensive places to eat. The imposing **Great Market Hall** (Nagycsarnok), built for the Millenary Exhibition, reopened in 1996 after a major face-lift. It is now the nicest covered market in the city.

The Crown of St Stephen

Legend tells us that it was Asztrik, the first abbot of the Benedictine monastery at Pannonhalma in Western Transdanubia, who presented a crown to Stephen as a gift from Pope Sylvester II around the year 1000, thus legitimising the new king's rule and assuring his loyalty to Rome rather than Constantinople. It's a nice (and convenient) story, but has nothing to do with the object temporarily on display in the Parliament building. That two-part crown with its characteristic bent cross, pendants hanging on either side and enamelled plaques of the Apostles probably dates from the 12th century. Regardless, the Crown of St Stephen has become the very symbol of the Hungarian nation.

The crown has disappeared several times over the centuries, only to reappear later. During the 13th-century Mongol invasions, the crown was dropped while being transported to a safe-house, giving the crown its jaunty, skewed look. More recently in 1945 Hungarian fascists fleeing the Soviet army took it to Austria. Eventually the crown fell into the hands of the US Army, which transferred it to Fort Knox in Kentucky. In 1978 the crown was returned to Hungary with great ceremony – and relief. Because legal judgements had always been handed down 'in the name of St Stephen's Crown' it was considered a living symbol and had thus been 'kidnapped'.

MARTIN HARRIS

Walking Tour 12: Buda Hills (Map 1)

With 'peaks' reaching over 500m, a comprehensive system of trails and no lack of unusual transport, the Buda Hills are the city's true playground and a welcome respite from hot, dusty Pest in summer. If you're walking, take along a copy of Cartographia's 1:30,000 *A Budai-hegység* map (No 6; 500Ft).

Heading for the hills is more than half the fun. From the Moszkva tér metro station in Buda, walk westward along Szilágyi Erzsébet fasor for 10 minutes (or take tram No 18 or bus No 56 for two stops) to the circular high-rise Budapest hotel at No 47. Opposite is the terminus of the **Cog Railway** (Fogaskerekű). Built in 1874, the cog climbs for 3.5km to **Széchenyi-hegy** (427m), one of the prettiest residential areas in the city. The railway runs all year from 5 am to 11 pm and costs the same as a tram or bus.

At Széchenyi-hegy, you can stop for a picnic in the park south of the station or board the narrow-gauge **Children's Railway** (Gyermekvasút), two minutes to the south on Hegyhát út. The railway was built in 1951 by Pioneers (socialist Scouts) and is staffed entirely by children aged 10 to 14 – the engineer excepted (120/60Ft). The little train chugs along for 12km, terminating at **Hűvös-völgy** (Chilly Valley). There are walks fanning out from any of the stops along the way, or you can return to Moszkva tér on tram No 56 from Hűvösvölgy. The train operates about once an hour daily from mid-March to October but Tuesday to Sunday only the rest of the year.

A more interesting way down, though, is to get off at **János-hegy**, the fourth stop and the highest point (527m) in the hills. There's an old lookout tower (1910) here, with excellent views of the city, and some good walks. About 700m west of the station is the **chair lift** (*libegő*), which will take you down to Zugligeti út. From here bus No 158 returns to Moszkva tér. The chair lift runs from 9 am till 5 pm between April and September and 9.30 am till 4 pm the rest of the year; it is closed on Monday of every odd-numbered week. The one-way fare is 200/100Ft.

MUSEUMS & OTHER ATTRACTIONS

The museums and some other sights mentioned on the 12 walking tours are listed alphabetically, in English, and described in detail below.

Agricultural Museum (Map 5)

The Hungarian Agricultural Museum (Magyar Mezőgazdasági Múzeum; ☎ 343 0573) in the stunning baroque wing of Vajdahunyad Castle, XIV Vajdahunyad sétány (metro: Hősök tere), Europe's largest such collection, has permanent exhibits on cattle breeding, winemaking, hunting and fishing. After a visit here there's not much you won't know about Hungarian fruit production, cereals, wool, poultry and pig slaughtering – if that's what you want. It's open from 10 am to 5 pm Tuesday to Saturday and to 6 pm on Sunday from March to mid-November but closes one hour earlier on the same days the rest of the year (200/50Ft adults/students and children).

Applied Arts Museum (Map 4)

The galleries of the Museum of Applied Arts (Iparművészeti Múzeum; ☎ 217 5222) at IX Üllői út 33-37 (metro: Ferenc körút), which surround a white-on-white main hall, supposedly modelled on the Alhambra in southern Spain, contain Hungarian furnishings and bric-a-brac from the 18th to 19th centuries and the history of trades and crafts (glass making, bookbinding, gold smithing, leatherwork etc).

Don't miss the collection of Art Nouveau and Secessionist artefacts, the painted 18th-century coffered ceiling in the room with the old printing presses, or the stained-glass skylight in the entrance hall. The museum is open from 10 am to 6 pm Tuesday to Sunday mid-March to mid-December and to 4 pm the rest of the year (300/100Ft). English-language tours (2000Ft) can be arranged in advance.

Aquincum Museum (Map 1)

The Aquincum Museum (Aquincumi Múzeum; ☎ 368 8241), III Szentendrei út 139 (HÉV: Aquincum), in the centre of what remains of this Roman civil settlement, tries to put the ruins in perspective, but unfortunately only in Hungarian. Keep an eye open for the portable 3rd-century water organ (and the mosaic illustrating how it was played), pottery moulds, and floor mosaics from the governor's palace across the river on Óbuda Island. Most of the big sculptures and stone sarcophagi are outside to the left of the museum or behind it along a covered walkway.

The museum and complex are open from 9 am to 6 pm Tuesday to Sunday from May to September, to 5 pm in April and October (400/200Ft, family 600Ft). English-language tours (2000Ft) by arrangement.

Budapest History Museum (Map 2)

The Budapest History Museum (Budapesti Történeti Múzeum; ☎ 355 8849) in Wing E of the Royal Palace, I Szent György tér (bus No 16 or Várbusz), traces the 2000 years of the city on three floors of jumbled exhibits. Restored palace rooms dating from the 15th century can be entered from the basement, which contains an exhibit on the Royal Palace in medieval Buda.

Three vaulted halls, one with a magnificent door frame in red marble bearing the seal of Queen Beatrice and tiles with a raven and a ring (the seal of her husband King Matthias Corvinus), lead to the **Gothic Hall**, the **Royal Cellar** and the 14th-century **Tower Chapel**.

On the ground floor is an exhibit entitled Budapest in the Middle Ages as well as Gothic statues discovered in 1974 during excavations. The exhibit on the 1st floor traces the history of the city from the expulsion of the Turks in 1686 to the present day. The museum, sometimes called the Castle Museum (Vár Múzeum), is open from 10 am to 6 pm daily from mid-May to mid-September, the same times Wednesday to Monday only from March to mid-May and mid-September to mid-October and from 10 am to 4 pm Wednesday to Monday the rest of the year (300/150Ft, family 600Ft).

Commerce & Catering Museum (Map 2)

The catering section of the Museum of Commerce & Catering (Kereskedelmi és Vendéglátóipari Múzeum; ☎ 375 6249), I Fortuna utca 4 (bus No 16 or Várbusz) contains an entire 19th-century cake shop in one of its three rooms, complete with a pastry kitchen. There are moulds for every occasion, a marble-lined icebox and an antique ice-cream maker. Much is made of those great confectioners Emil Gerbeaud of *cukrászda* fame and József Dobos, who gave his name to Dobos torta, a layered chocolate and cream cake with a caramelised brown sugar top.

The commerce collection traces retail trade in the capital. Along with electric toys and advertisements that still work, there's an exhibit on the hyperinflation that Hungary suffered after WWII when a basket of money would buy no more than four eggs. The museum is open from 10 am to 5 pm Wednesday to Friday, to 6 pm at the weekend (100/50Ft).

Ethnography Museum (Map 4)

As the nation's largest indoor folk collection, the Hungarian collection of the Museum of Ethnography (Néprajzi Múzeum; ☎ 312 4878), V Kossuth Lajos tér 12 (metro: Kossuth tér), contained in more than a dozen rooms on the 1st floor, is somewhat disappointing. However, it's an easy introduction to traditional Hungarian life.

The labels are also in English, the mock-ups of peasant houses from the Őrség and Sárköz regions of Transdanubia are pretty well done and there are some excellent rotating exhibits. On the 2nd floor are displays dealing with the other peoples of Europe and farther afield.

The building itself, designed in 1893 to house the Supreme Court, is worth a look – especially the massive central hall with its marble columns and ceiling fresco of *Justice* by Károly Lotz. The museum is open from 10 am to 6 pm Tuesday to Sunday from March to October, to 4 pm the rest of the year (300/150Ft).

Fine Arts Museum (Map 5)

The Museum of Fine Arts (Szépművészeti Múzeum; ☎ 343 9759), XIV Hősök tere (metro: Hősök tere) houses the city's outstanding collection of foreign works in a renovated building dating from 1906. The Old Masters collection is the most complete, with thousands of works from the Dutch & Flemish, Spanish, Italian, German, French and British schools between the 13th and 18th centuries, including seven paintings by El Greco. Other sections include Egyptian and Greco-Roman artefacts and 19th and 20th-century paintings, watercolours and graphics, and sculpture, including some important impressionist works. The museum is open from 10 am to 5.30 pm Tuesday to Sunday (500/200Ft).

Golden Eagle Pharmacy Museum (Map 2)

The Golden Eagle Pharmacy Museum (Aranysas Patikamúzeum; ☎ 375 9772), just north of Dísz tér at I Tárnok utca 18 (bus No 16 or Várbusz), contains an unusual miniature of Christ as a pharmacist; the mock-up of an alchemist's lab with dried bats, tiny crocodiles and what appears to be eye of newt in jars is straight out of the *Addams Family*. There's also a 2000-year-old mummy's head and a small 'spice rack' used by 17th-century travellers for their daily fixes of herbs and other elixirs. The pharmacy museum is open from 10.30 am to 5.30 pm Tuesday to Sunday (60/20Ft).

Gül Baba's Tomb (Map 3)

The reconstructed Tomb of Gül Baba (Gül Baba türbéje; ☎ 355 8849), II Mecset utca 14 (HÉV Margit híd or tram No 4 or 6), contains the remains of Gül Baba, a Ottoman Dervish who took part in the capture of Buda in 1541 and is known in Hungary as the 'Father of Roses'. To reach it, walk up Gül Baba utca to the set of steps just past No 14, which will lead to a small octagonal building and a lookout tower. The tomb is still a pilgrimage place for Muslims, and you must remove your shoes. It contains Islamic furnishings and is open from 10 am to 5.30 pm Tuesday to Sunday from May to September and to 4 pm in October (150/50Ft).

Ferenc Hopp East Asian Art Museum (Map 5)

The Ferenc Hopp Museum of East Asian Art (Hopp Ferenc Kelet-ázsiai Művészeti Múzeum; ☎ 322 8476) is in the former villa of its benefactor and namesake at VI Andrássy út 103 (metro: Bajza utca). Founded in 1919, the museum has a good collection of Indonesian *wayang* puppets, Indian statuary and lamaist sculpture and scroll paintings from Tibet. There's an 18th-century Chinese moon gate in the back garden, but most of the Chinese and Japanese collection of ceramics and porcelain, textiles and sculpture is housed in the György Ráth Museum (see later in this section). The museum is open from 10 am to 6 pm Tuesday to Sunday from mid-March to December (160/50Ft).

Jewish Museum (Map 4)

The Jewish Museum (Zsidó Múzeum; ☎ 342 8949), in an annexe of the Great Synagogue at VII Dohány utca 2 (metro: Astoria) contains objects related to religious and everyday life, and an interesting handwritten book of the local Burial Society from the 18th century. The Holocaust Memorial Room – dark and sombre – relates the events of 1944-45, including the infamous mass murder of doctors and patients at a hospital on Maros utca. The museum is open from 10 am to 3 pm Monday to Friday and to 1 pm on Sunday (400/200Ft).

Kassák Museum (Map 3)

The unique Kassák Museum (☎ 368 7021), III Fő tér 1 (HÉV Árpád híd or bus No 86), is a three-room art gallery with some real gems of early 20th-century avant-garde art as well as the complete works of the artist and writer Lajos Kassák (1887-1967). It's open from 10 am to 6 pm and costs 200/100Ft.

Kiscelli Museum & Municipal Gallery (Map 3)

Housed in an 18th-century monastery, later a barracks that was badly damaged in WWII and again in 1956, the exhibits at the Kiscelli

Museum (☎ 388 8560), III Kiscelli utca 106 (tram No 17 or bus No 60), painlessly tell the story of Budapest since liberation from the Turks. The museum counts among its best exhibits a complete 19th-century apothecary moved here from Kálvin tér, but my favourites are the rooms furnished in Empire, Biedermeier and Art Nouveau furniture. The Municipal Gallery (Fővárosi Képtár), with its impressive art collection (József Rippl-Rónai, Lajos Tihanyi, István Csók, Lázsló Károly, etc) is also here. The museum is open from 10 am to 6 pm Tuesday to Sunday from April to October and to 4 pm the rest of the year (200/100Ft).

Labyrinth (Map 2)

The Labyrinth (Labirintus; ☎ 375 6858), I Úri utca 9 (bus No 16 or Várbusz), a 1200m-long cave system some 16m under the Castle District, is another one of those rip-off tourist sites you'll find from London to Los Angles and Lhasa – and everywhere in between. Ogle at the damp rooms masquerading as one-time dungeons. Marvel at how fake the wax figures of historical figures look. Wince at the entry fee: 800/700Ft. The Labyrinth is open from 9.30 am to 7.30 pm daily, with tours leaving every 30 minutes.

Franz Liszt Memorial Museum (Map 4)

The Franz Liszt Memorial Museum (Liszt Ferenc Emlékmúzeum; ☎ 322 9804), VI Vörösmarty utca 35 (metro: Vörösmarty utca) is in the house where the great composer lived, in an apartment on the 1st floor from 1881, until his death in 1886, and the four rooms are filled with his pianos (including a tiny glass one), composer's table, portraits and personal effects. It's open from 10 am to 6 pm on weekdays and from 9 am to 5 pm on Saturday with a 'free' piano recital at 11 am (150/80Ft).

Ludwig Museum (Map 2)

The Ludwig Museum, also known as the Museum of Contemporary Art (Kortárs Művészeti Múzeum; ☎ 375 9175), in Wing A of the Royal Palace, I Szent György tér (bus No 16 or Várbusz) surveys American Pop art as well as works by German, French and North American artists of the 1980s and Hungarian contemporary art. It is open from 10 am to 6 pm from Tuesday to Sunday (300/150Ft).

Medieval Jewish Prayer House (Map 2)

This small museum at the medieval Jewish prayer house (középkori zsidó imaház; ☎ 355 8849), I Táncsics Mihály utca 26 (bus No 16 or Várbusz), contains documents and items linked to the Jewish community of Buda as well as Gothic stone carvings and tomb stones. It is open from 10 am to 6 pm Tuesday to Sunday from May to October (100/50Ft).

Military History Museum (Map 2)

The Museum of Military History (Hadtörténeti Múzeum; ☎ 356 9586), I Tóth Árpád sétány 40 (bus No 16 or Várbusz), has more weapons inside than a Los Angeles crack house but also does a pretty good job with uniforms, medals, flags and battle-themed fine art. Exhibits focus on the 15th-century fall of Buda Castle, the Hungarian Royal Army up to the time of Admiral Miklós Horthy and the 1956 Uprising. The museum is open from 10 am to 6 pm Tuesday to Sunday from April to September, to 4 pm from October to mid-December and February and March (250/80Ft).

Műcsarnok (Map 5)

The opulent Műcsarnok (☎ 343 740), XIV Hősök tere (metro: Hősök tere), which simply means 'Art Gallery' in English, is the country's largest exhibition hall and hosts temporary exhibits of works by Hungarian and foreign artists in fine and applied art, photography and design. It is open 10 am to 6 pm Tuesday to Sunday (300/100Ft).

National Gallery (Map 2)

The Hungarian National Gallery (Magyar Nemzeti Galéria; ☎ 375 7533), in Wings B, C & D of the Royal Palace, I Szent György tér (bus No 16 or Várbusz), is an overwhelmingly large collection and traces the development of Hungarian art from the 10th century to the present day. The largest collections include medieval and Renaissance stonework, Gothic wooden sculptures and panel paintings, late Gothic winged altars, late Renaissance and baroque art. On no account should you miss the restored Altar of St John the Baptist from Kisszebes (a town now in Romania) and the 16th-century painted wooden ceiling in the next room.

The museum also has an important collection of Hungarian paintings and sculpture from the 19th and 20th centuries. You won't recognise many names, but keep an eye open for works by the Romantic painters József Borsos, Gyula Benczúr and Mihály Munkácsy and the impressionists Jenő Gyárfás and Pál Merse Szinyei. Personal favourites include the harrowing depictions of war and the dispossessed by László Mednyánszky, the unique portraits by József Rippl-Rónai, the mammoth canvases by Tivadar Csontváry and the paintings of carnivals by the modern artist Vilmos Aba-Novák. The national gallery is open from 10 am to 6 pm Tuesday to Sunday from March to November and to 4 pm the rest of the year (300/100Ft).

National Museum (Map 4)

The Hungarian National Museum (Magyar Nemzeti Múzeum; ☎ 338 2122), VIII Múzeum körút 14-16 (metro: Kálvin tér), is the nation's largest historical collection. The Crown of St Stephen, the single-most important object in the nation's patrimony, is on display in a darkened room to the left and past the Roman mosaics as you enter the museum just past the enormous 3rd-century Roman mosaic from Balácapuszta, near Veszprém, at the foot of the steps. Also here are the ceremonial sword, orb, and the oldest object among the coronation regalia, the 10th-century sceptre with a crystal head, In another glass case is the crimson silk coronation robe stitched by nuns at Veszprém in 1031. The silver chests in the room were used to carry the regalia during the coronations of Franz Joseph in 1867 and of the last Habsburg king of Hungary, Charles IV, in 1916.

Other exhibits trace the history of the Carpathian Basin from earliest times, of the Magyar people to 1849 and of Hungary in the 19th and 20th centuries in 16 comprehensive rooms. Watch out for the reconstructed 3rd-century Roman villa from Pannonia, the treasury room with pre-Conquest gold jewellery, a second treasury room with later gold objects (including the 11th-century Monomachus crown), the Turkish tent, the stunning baroque library and Beethoven's Broadwood piano that toured world capitals in 1992. The Ceremonial Hall (Dísz terem) on the 2nd floor has been reserved for temporary exhibitions in the past. The national museum is open from 10 am to 6 pm Tuesday to Sunday from mid-March to mid-October and to 5 pm the rest of the year (300/150Ft).

Natural History Museum

The Hungarian Natural History Museum (Magyar Természettudományi Múzeum; ☎ 333 0655), VIII Ludovika tér 6 (metro: Klinikák), the city's newest museum, is not on any of the 12 walks described earlier but is worth a look and is close to a metro stop on the blue line. It has lots of hands-on interactive displays, the geological park in front of the museum is well designed and there's a new exhibit focusing on both the natural resources of the Carpathian Basin and the flora and fauna of Hungarian legends and tales. The museum is open from 10 am to 6 pm Wednesday to Monday from April to September and to 5 pm the rest of the year (240/120Ft; free on Friday afternoon).

Óbuda Museum (Map 3)

The Zsigmond Kun Folk Art Collection (Kun Zsigmund Népművészeti Gyűtemény; ☎ 250 1020), part of the Óbuda Museum at III Fő tér 4 (HÉV Árpád híd or bus No 86), displays folk art amassed by a wealthy ethnographer in his 18th-century townhouse. Most of the pottery and ceramics are from his hometown, Mezőtúr, near the Tisza River, but there are some rare Moravian and Swabian pieces and Transylvanian furniture and textiles. It's open from 2 to 6 pm Tuesday to Friday and from 10 am to 6 pm at the weekend (200/150Ft).

Opera House (Map 4)

The neo-Renaissance Hungarian State Opera House (Magyar Állami Operaház; ☎ 332 8197), VI Andrássy út 22 (metro: Opera), offers guided tours at 3 and 4 pm daily. Tickets (900/450Ft) are available from the office on the east side of the building (Hajós utca), and the tour includes a brief musical performance.

Parliament (Map 4)

Budapest's colossal Parliament building (Országház; ☎ 317 9800 or 268 4904), V Kossuth Lajos tér (metro: Kossuth tér), built in 1902, has almost 700 rooms and 18 courtyards. It is a blend of many architectural styles and in sum works very well.

The ornate structure was surfaced with a porous form of limestone that does not resist pollution very well; renovations began almost immediately after it opened and will continue until the building crumbles.

Guided tours (800/500Ft) in English lasting 45 minutes are available at 10 am and 2 pm Wednesday to Sunday from July to September and at 10 am only the rest of the year. Buy your tickets at gate No 10 and expect a lot of airport-style security checks.

György Ráth Museum (Map 5)

The György Ráth Museum (☎ 342 3916), housed in an incredibly beautiful Art Nouveau residence at VI Városligeti fasor 12 (metro: Bajza utca), contains most of the Chinese and Japanese collection of ceramics and porcelain, textiles and sculptures belonging to the Ferenc Hopp Museum of East Asian Art (see the listing earlier in this section). To reach it from there walk south on Bajza utca and then west. It is open from 10 am to 6 pm Tuesday to Sunday from April to October and to 4 pm the rest of the year (160/50Ft).

Transport Museum (Map 5)

OK, it doesn't sound like a crowd-pleaser, but the Transport Museum (Közlekedési Múzeum; ☎ 343 0565) at XIV Városligeti körút 11 in the City Park (metro: Széchenyi fürdő or trolleybus No 72), is one of the most enjoyable in Budapest and great for children.

In an old and a new wing there are scale models of ancient trains (some of which run), classic late 19th-century automobiles and lots of those old wooden bicycles called 'bone-shakers'. There are a few hands-on exhibits and lots of show-and-tell from the attendants. Outside are pieces from the original Danube bridges that were retrieved after the bombings of WWII. The Transport Museum is open from 10 am to 5 pm Tuesday to Friday and to 6 pm at the weekend May to September and closes an hour earlier the rest of the year (150/50Ft).

Vasarely Museum (Map 3)

The Vasarely Museum (☎ 250 1540), housed in the crumbling Zichy Mansion at III Szentlélek tér 6 (HÉV Árpád híd or bus No 86), is devoted to the works of Victor Vasarely, the 'Father of Op Art'. The works, especially ones like *Dirac* and *Tlinko-F*, are excellent and fun to watch as they swell and move around the canvas. On the 1st floor are some of the unusual advertisements Vasarely did for French firms before the war. The museum is open from 10 am to 6 pm Tuesday to Sunday from mid-March to October and to 5 pm the rest of the year (50/20Ft).

Zoo (Map 5)

The large and recently renovated City Zoo (Városi Állatkert; ☎ 343 6882), XIV Állatkerti út, has a good collection of animals (big cats, rhinos, hippopotamuses), but some visitors come here just to look at the Secessionist animal houses built in the early part of this century, such as the Elephant House with pachyderm heads in beetle-green Zsolnay ceramic and the Palm House erected by the Eiffel company of Paris. The zoo is open from 9 am to 7 pm daily from May to August and to between 4 and 6 pm the rest of the year, depending on the season (700/500Ft).

ACTIVITIES
Cycling

Parts of Budapest, including City and Népliget Parks, Margaret, Óbudai and Csepel Islands and the Buda Hills, are excellent places for cycling. At present bike paths in the city total about 100km, including the path along Andrássy út, which includes little bicycle traffic signals. There are places to rent bicycles on Margaret Island (see Walking Tour 5: Margaret Island for details) and in City Park. Both the Best Hostel and Charles Tourist Service in Pest (see Places to Stay) rent bicycles. Bicycles can be transported on the HÉV and Cog Railway but not on the metro, buses or trams.

The Friends of the City Cycling Group (☎ 280 0888), V Curia utca 3, publishes the useful four-sheet *Budapesti bringás térkép* (Budapest Map for Bikers; 580Ft). Frigoria publishes a number of useful guides and maps, including *By Bike in Budapest*. One that takes in the surrounding areas and describes 30 different routes is *Kerékparral Budapest környéken* (1200Ft), also published by Frigoria and available in most bookshops.

Horse Riding

In a nation of equestrians, the chances for riding in the capital are surprisingly limited. Wait till you get to the *puszta* or Transdanubia if you're looking for a serious gallop.

Riding schools in Budapest include the Budapesti Lovas Klub (☎ 313 5210), VIII Kerepesi út 7, and Petneházy Lovascentrum (☎ 397 5048) at II Feketefej utca 2-4 near Budakeszi. The latter offers beginner's lessons (1200Ft per half-hour), paddock practice (2000Ft per hour), trail riding (2500Ft per hour) and carriage rides. Prices increase by 500Ft at the weekend. The riding school is open from 9 am to noon and 2 pm to 4 pm Tuesday to Sunday.

Thermal Baths & Swimming

For information see the boxed text 'Taking the Waters in Budapest' on page 124 and 125.

Boating

Kayaking and canoeing on the Danube is not as popular a pursuit as it once was but it's still possible. Most rowing clubs will rent you a boat without prior booking, including the Danubius National Boating Association (Map 3; ☎ 329 3142) at XIII Hajós Alfréd sétány 2 on Margaret Island (bus No 26) and the Technical University Rowing Club (☎ 284 2126) at XX Vízisport

utca 44 opposite Csepel Island (HÉV Torontál utca).

Caving

Budapest has a number of caves, two of which are open for walk-through guided tours in Hungarian language. Pál-völgy Cave (Map 1; ☎ 325 9505) at II Szépvölgyi út 162 (bus No 65 from Kolosy tér in Óbuda), the third-largest in Hungary, is noted for its stalactites and bats. Unfortunately, visitors only get to see about 500m of it on half-hour guided tours (250/150Ft), which run every hour from 10 am to 4 pm Tuesday to Sunday. A more beautiful cave, with stalactites, stalagmites and weird grape-like formations, is the one at Szemlőhegy (Map 3; ☎ 325 6001), about a kilometre south-east of Pál-völgyi at II Pusztaszeri út 35 (bus No 29 from Kolosy tér). It is open from 10 am to 3 pm on Monday and Wednesday to Friday and to 4 pm at the weekend (250/150Ft).

More adventurous caving possibilities can be booked through the adventure sports department of the Vista Visitor Centre (see Travel Agencies in the Information section as well as various hostels, under Places to Stay, including Diáksport, Yellow Submarine and the Back Pack Guesthouse. The Best hostel (see Places to Stay) has a 2½-hour excursion to a cave opposite Pál-völgy at 11 am every Tuesday and Thursday for 1900Ft.

ORGANISED TOURS
Bus

Many travel agencies, including Ibusz (Map 4; ☎ 317 8343) and Cityrama (Map 4; ☎ 302 4382), V Báthory utca 22, offer three-hour city tours from 5200/2600Ft. It also has excursions farther afield to the Danube Bend, Lake Balaton, the Southern Plain, etc. See Organised Tours in the Getting Around chapter for details.

Budatours (Map 4; ☎ 331 1585), VI Andrássy út 2, runs seven tour buses a day in July and August (between two and three the rest of the year) from the Gresham Palace at V Roosevelt tér 5. The company runs a two-hour nonstop tour with taped commentary in 16 different languages and costs

Taking the Waters in Budapest

Budapest is blessed with an abundance of hot springs – some 123 thermal and more than 400 mineral springs come from 14 different sources. As a result 'taking the waters' at one of the city's many spas or combination spa and swimming pools is a real Budapest experience, so try to go at least once. Some date from Turkish times, others are Art Nouveau wonders, while a few more are spic-and-span modern establishments.

Thermal Baths Generally, entry to the baths starts at 500Ft, which usually allows you to stay for two hours on weekdays and 1½ hours at weekends, though this rule is not always enforced. They offer a full range of serious medical treatments as well as services like massage (750/1500Ft for 15/30 minutes) and pedicure. Specify what you want when buying your ticket(s). For the procedure for getting out of your street clothes and into the water, see Thermal Baths in the Facts for the Visitor chapter. The baths may sometimes look a bit rough around the edges, but they are clean and the water is changed continuously. You may want to wear rubber sandals though.

Please note that some of the baths become gay venues on male-only days – especially the Király and Rác and, to a lesser extent, the Gellért. Not much actually goes on except for some intensive cruising, but those not into it may feel uncomfortable.

Gellért
(Map 4; ☎ 466 6166), XI Kelenhegyi út 2-4 (tram No 18, 19, 47 or 49, bus No 7 or 86). Soaking in this Art Nouveau palace has been likened to taking a bath in a cathedral. It is open to men and women (separate sections) from 6 am to 7 pm weekdays and to 5 pm at the weekend (to 3 pm from October to April). 1200Ft.

Király
(Map 3; ☎ 202 3688 or 201 4392), II Fő utca 82-86 (bus No 60 or 86). The four pools, including the main one with a fantastic skylit dome, date from 1570. Open to men only from 9 am to 9 pm on Monday, Wednesday and Friday, to women only from 6.30 am to 7 pm Tuesday and Thursday and to 12.30 pm on Saturday. 500Ft.

Lukács
(Map 3; ☎ 326 1695), II Frankel Leó út 25-29 (tram No 17 or bus No 60 or 86). This sprawling 19th-century establishment has everything from thermal and mud baths to a swimming pool. The thermal baths are open to both men and women from 6 am to 7 pm Monday to Saturday and to 5 pm on Sunday (6 am to 5 pm on both Saturday and Sunday from October to April). The mud and weight baths are segregated: men are welcome on Tuesday, Thursday and Saturday, women on Monday, Wednesday and Friday. 500Ft.

Rác
(Map 2; ☎ 356 1322 or 356 1010), I Hadnagy utca 8-10 (tram No 18 or bus No 78). The 19th-century exterior of this spa in a lovely park in the Tabán hides a Turkish core. Open to men only from 6.30 am to 7 pm on Tuesday, Thursday and Saturday and to women only the same hours on Monday, Wednesday and Friday. 500Ft.

Rudas
(Map 4; ☎ 375 8373), I Döbrentei tér 9 (tram No 18 or 19 or bus No 7 or 86). This is the most Turkish of all the baths in Budapest. The thermal baths are open to men only from 6 am to 7 pm weekdays and to 1 pm at the weekend (500Ft).

Széchenyi
(Map 5; ☎ 321 0310), XIV Állatkerti út 11 (metro: Széchenyi fürdő). This bath is unusual for three reasons: its immense size; its bright, clean look; and its water temperatures, which really are what the wall plaques say they are. It is open to men and women (separate sections) from 6 am to 7 pm on weekdays and to 5 pm at the weekend. 500Ft.

Thermal
(Map 3; ☎ 329 2300), Margitsziget Thermal hotel, XIII Margaret Island (bus No 26). This thermal bath, on leafy Margaret Island, is the most upmarket (and expensive) in town. It is open to men and women from 7 am to 8 pm daily. 1800Ft (2300Ft at the weekend).

Taking the Waters in Budapest

Széchenyi Bath - the largest medicinal waters in Europe

Swimming Pools At the same time, every town of any size in Hungary has at least one indoor and outdoor swimming pool (*uszoda*), and Budapest boasts dozens. They're always excellent places to get in a few laps (if indoor), cool off on a hot summer's day (if outdoor) or watch all the posers strut their stuff.

The system inside is similar to that at the baths except that rather than a cabin or cubicle, there are sometimes just lockers. Get changed and call the attendant, who will lock it, write the time on a chalkboard and hand you a key. Many pools require the use of a bathing cap, so bring your own or wear the plastic one provided, rented or sold for a nominal fee.

The following is a list of the best outdoor and indoor pools in the city. The former are usually open from May to September unless specified. Addresses for the swimming pools attached to the thermal baths can be found in the previous Thermal Baths section.

Csillaghegyi
(off Map 1; ☎ 250 1533), III Pusztakúti út 3 (HÉV: Csillaghegy). The outdoor pools, with a capacity for 3000 bathers, are open from 7 or 8 am to 7 pm daily from May to September, the indoor pool from 6 am to 7 pm weekdays, to 4 pm on Saturday and to 1 pm on Sunday. There's a nudist section on the southern slope in summer. 400Ft.

Dagály
(Map 1; ☎ 320 2203), XIII Népfürdő utca 36 (metro: Árpád híd or tram No 1). This huge complex has a total of 12 pools, with plenty of grass and shade. The outdoor pools are open from 6 am to 7 pm daily from May to September, the indoor ones from 6 am to 7 pm weekdays and to 5 pm at the weekend the rest of the year. 500Ft.

Gellért
The indoor and outdoor pools, with a wave machine and nicely landscaped gardens, are open from 6 am till 7 pm. On Friday and Saturday in July and August the pools reopen from 8 pm to midnight. In winter the indoor pools close at 5 pm at the weekend (1800/750Ft).

Alfréd Hajós (National)
(Map 3; ☎ 340 4946), XIII Margaret Island (bus No 26). The pools, one indoor and two outdoor are open from 6 am to 5 pm on weekdays and to 6 pm at the weekend (provided no competitions are on). 350Ft.

Helia
(Map 3; ☎ 350 3277), Helia Thermal hotel, XIII Kárpát utca 62-64 (metro: Dósza György út or trolleybus No 79). This ultra modern four-star hotel boasts three pools, sauna and steam room and a health-food bar. 1800Ft.

Béla Komjádi
(Map 3; ☎ 212 2750), II Árpád fejedelem útja (tram No 17 or bus No 60 or 86). This very serious pool is where the Hungarian Water Polo Association holds some of its matches. It's open from 6 am to 9 pm weekdays and to 7 pm at the weekend. 350/200Ft.

Palatinus
(Map 3; ☎ 340 4505), XIII Margaret Island (bus No 26). The largest series of pools in the capital, seven in all plus a wave pool, are open from 8 am to 7 pm daily from May to August and from 10 am to 6 pm the first half of September. There are separate-sex roof decks for nude sunbathing. 500Ft.

Rómaifürdő
(Map 1; ☎ 388 9740), III Rozgonyi Piroska utca 2 (HÉV Rómaifürdő or bus No 34). The outdoor cold-water thermal pools are open from 8 am to 7 pm daily in season. 400Ft.

Széchenyi
The enormous and recently renovated pools of the Széchenyi baths, the largest medicinal bath extant in Europe, contain thermal water and open year-round: 6 am to 7 pm May to September and from 6 am to 7 pm weekdays and to 5 pm at the weekend the rest of the year. 500Ft.

Thermal
The indoor pool at the spa complex is open from 7 am to 8 pm daily. (1800Ft, 2300Ft at the weekend).

4400/2200Ft. Queenybus (☎ 247 7159) departs twice daily (11 am and 2.20 pm) from St Stephen's Basilica, V Bajcsy-Zsilinszky út, for three-hour tours of the city (4800/3600/2400Ft for adults/students/children). Both Budatours and Queenybus also have Parliament tours for 2800/1400Ft.

For those who prefer the hop-on, hop-off style of tour bus, N Bus (☎ 06-60 560 001) makes 1½-hour circuits (3500Ft) of the city from 9 am to 6 pm daily, stopping at 10 different sights.

Boat

From April to September Mahart (Map 4; ☎ 318 1704) has 1½-hour cruises on the Danube at noon and 7 pm daily for 800/400Ft. In April the cruise at noon operates on Sunday and holidays only, and in July and August the evening program begins at 7.45 pm and includes music and dance (900/450Ft). You can buy your ticket at the small ticket office by the river at Vigadó tér 3 (metro: Vörösmarty tér). Other more expensive cruises such as the ones on the Legenda (☎ 266 4190) for 2800/1400Ft for adults/children during the day and 3200/1600Ft in the evening are heavily promoted around town ('selection of 24 languages!'), but try to find the much cheaper Mahart boat.

Walking

Budapest Walks, organised by Robinson Travel (☎ 340 4232), offers a 2½-hour 'Gems of Buda Castle' tour departing from Matthias Church in I Szentháromság tér at 2.30 pm Tuesday to Sunday from May to September and a 'Highlights of Pest' one leaving from Gerbeaud in V Vörösmarty tér at 10.30 am on the same days. The tours cost 3200/1600Ft for adults/students and include museum entry fees. IA Tours (☎ 06-30 211 8861) has a number of three-hour tours in English (2500/2000Ft) departing from in front of the Műcsarnok in XIV Hősök tere at 10 am to 2 pm daily from mid-June to September. Castle Walks (☎ 488 0453, for information) will lead you through the winding ways and tortuous tales of the historic Castle District starting from

Matthias Church for 1500Ft. Tours leave at 11 am daily from late June to September and at the weekend only from late September to late October.

Jewish Walking Tour

Hungaria Koncert (☎ 317 2754) has a 2½-hour tour that focuses on Budapest's Jewish heritage, available at 11 am and 2 pm most weekdays from August to October (at 11.30 am on Sunday in October too). The tour includes a visit to the Great Synagogue, a walking tour of the ghetto, cantor music, a nonkosher meal and a concert in the synagogue by the Budapest Klezmer Band for 6000/5400Ft adults/students (3900Ft for the concert alone). Tickets are available from locations throughout the city, including the Duna Palota at V Zrínyi utca (Map 4) and at the entrance to the synagogue.

SPECIAL EVENTS

Countless festivals and events are held in and around Budapest each year; look out for the tourist board's annual *Events in Hungary from January to December* for a complete listing. Among the most important annual events are the following:

January
New Year Operetta Gala Held at the Vigadó on 1 January

February
Opera Ball Held at the Opera House

March
Budapest Spring Festival Held at venues throughout the capital

April
Welcome Marathon

June
World Music Festival
Búcsú (Farewell) Festival A festival of rock and pop music
Duna Carnival Folklore Festival
Ferencváros Summer Festival Held in late June and July
Jewish Summer Festival Held in late June/early July

August
BudaFest Summer Opera & Ballet Festival
Pepsi Island (Pepsi-sziget) Festival A festival
  of music and culture on Óbuda Island
Hungarian Formula-1 Grand Prix Held in
  Magyoród near Budapest

September
International Wine Festival
European Heritage Days

October
Budapest Marathon
Autumn Festival Held at venues throughout the
  city

December
New Year's Eve masked ball Held at the
  Opera House on 31 December

PLACES TO STAY – BUDGET
Camping

The largest camping ground in Budapest is
*Római Camping (Map 1; ☎ 368 6260 or
242 1934, fax 250 0426, III Szentendrei út
189, HÉV Rómaifürdő)*, with space for
more than 2500 happy campers in a shady
park north of the city. Though the facility is
open all year, the 45 cabins are available
from mid-April to mid-October only for between 3600Ft and 6000Ft per double, depending on the category. Pitching a tent
costs 715/920/1220Ft per person/tent/
caravan. Use of the adjacent swimming
pool, with lots of green grass on which to
stretch out, is included.

Up in the Buda Hills *Niche Camping
(Map 1; ☎ 200 8346, XII Zugligeti út 101,
bus No 158 from Moszkva tér)* at the bottom
station of the Buda Hills chair lift charges
2200Ft for two people to camp on one of
the small hillside terraces or 1700Ft for a
caravan plus 850Ft extra per person.
There's also one on-site caravan at 2400Ft
for a double, one bungalow at 3800Ft for
two people and two rooms at 3300Ft for a
double or 4950Ft for four people. Additional charges are 700Ft to park, 1700Ft for
a trailer, and additionally 850Ft per person.
Its reception area and snack bar are in a
couple of old Budapest trams parked at the

entrance. The site is open all year. Also in
the hills, the *Csillebérc Youth Centre* (see
Hostels – Buda) has tent sites and charges
DM6/7/18 per person/tent/car.

Hostels

Though you can go directly to all the hostels mentioned below, the Travellers Youth
Hostels-Mellow Mood group, a member of
Hostelling International (HI), runs eight different hostels for individual travellers and
has an office (☎ 343 0748) at Keleti train
station open daily from 7 am to 11 pm (to
10 pm in winter). It will make bookings or
you can go directly to its main hostel *Diáksport Hostel* (see Hostels – Pest later in this
section); there's no difference in price.

The Vista Visitor Centre (see Travel
Agencies in the Information section) is
open 24 hours a day and makes room bookings. The Express office (Map 4; ☎ 331
7777) for booking hostel beds is at V Szabadság tér 16, a block from the Kossuth
Lajos tér (metro: Kossuth tér).

Hostel or student cards are not required at
any of the hostels, although it'll sometimes
get you a discount of up to 10%. Most hostels have laundry facilities (about 700Ft to
1000Ft for a load), breakfast for around
300Ft and a few now have Internet access.
There's almost always an eat-in kitchen,
storage lockers, TV lounge and no curfew.

Hostels – Pest Earning high marks for atmosphere, though a tad off the beaten
track, is the friendly *Station* guesthouse
*(Map 5; ☎ 221 8864, ✉ station@mail
.matav.hu, XIV Mexikói út 36/b, metro:
Mexikói út or bus No 7)*. It's a party place
with a 24-hour bar, pool tables and occasional live entertainment, and staff will
pick you up from the station. Accommodation costs 1600/2000/2400Ft, depending on
whether you're in a room with eight/four/
three or two beds.

There are several much more central
places in Pest though most are not nearly as
nice as the Station. The 38-bed *Yellow Submarine Lotus* hostel *(Map 4; ☎ 331 9896,
✉ yellowsubmarine@mail.imperware.hu,
3/F, VI Teréz körút 56, metro: Nyugati*

MAP 6 - UNIVERSITY AREA

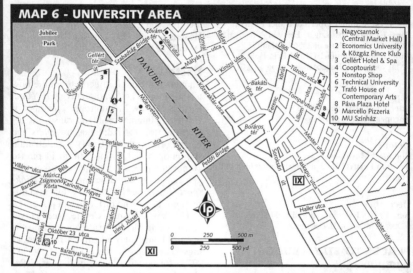

1 Nagycsarnok
   (Central Market Hall)
2 Economics University
   & Közgáz Pince Klub
3 Gellért Hotel & Spa
4 Cooptourist
5 Nonstop Shop
6 Technical University
7 Trafó House of
   Contemporary Arts
8 Páva Plaza Hotel
9 Marcello Pizzeria
10 MU Színház

pályaudvar) is a very central place to stay, almost opposite Nyugati train station, and has a lot of facilities: laundry, Internet access, TVs in some rooms. It costs 2500/2000/1800Ft per person in rooms with two/four/up to 10 beds. The nearby *Best* hostel *(Map 4;* ☎ *332 4934,* **@** *bestyh@mail .datanet.hu, I/F, VI Podmaniczky utca 27, metro: Nyugati pályaudvar)* has rooms with two to nine beds costing between 1700Ft and 2300Ft (nine to two beds) per person in large airy rooms, some of which have balconies. Staff will do your laundry for 700Ft, rent you a bike for 900Ft and organise a caving excursion to the Buda Hills (see Caving under Activities).

The *Caterina* guesthouse *(Map 4;* ☎ *342 0804,* **@** *caterina@mail.inext.hu, 3/F, VI Andrássy út 47, metro: Oktogon),* run by an affable English-speaking woman, charges 2400/1500Ft per person in a double/dorm room. The *Museum* guesthouse *(Map 4;* ☎ *318 9508,* **@** *museumgh@freemail.c3.hu, I/F, VIII Mikszáth Kálmán tér 4, metro: Kálvin tér),* with 22 beds in a pretty square in the centre of town, charges 1800Ft per person in rooms with six to eight beds. It is a little cramped and grungy (in the not-so-cool

sense) but certainly its proximity to the night life of VIII Krúdy utca and IX Ráday utca is a plus. It has an even smaller though more salubrious sister-hostel called *Ananda (Map 1;* ☎ *322 0502,* **@** *anandayh@freemail.c3.hu, 2/F, VII Alsóerdősor utca 12, metro: Keleti pályaudvar)* north-west of Keleti train station, with accommodation in rooms with four/six or eight beds costing 2000/1800Ft per person.

The *Royal* guesthouse *(Map 1;* ☎ *303 8302,* **@** *royalh@freemail.hu, 2/F, VIII Német utca 13, tram No 4 or 6),* in a large converted flat with a central courtyard, is another hostel where the night life is close by and the rooms (four or six beds) are even cheaper at 1600Ft per person.

The *Diáksport Hostel (Map 1;* ☎ *340 8585,* **@** *travellers@matavnet.hu, XIII Dózsa György út 152, metro: Dózsa György út)* is the flagship of the Travellers Youth Hostels-Mellow Mood group and the only one of its hostels open all year. Although this 140-bed hostel is impersonal and the most crowded (hordes of backpackers), it offers a free minibus transfer from Keleti train station and in summer will take you to any of its other hostels that still have beds

Night falls on the western side of Buda Castle.

Gül Baba stands proudly over Rózsadomb.

Holy Trinity statue, Buda.

Relatives remember loved ones on All Saints Day at Farkasréti Cemetery, Buda.

The Danube slides peacefully by Buda Castle and the Old Town, Buda.

Gellert Bath - Budapest's most lavish bathhouse.

The splendid Parliament interior.

available, so this is probably the best place to go first. The Diáksport charges 2500Ft per person in rooms with between six and 12 beds and 2600Ft per person in triples and quads. The singles (3500Ft) and doubles (2700Ft to 3400Ft per person) are almost always full in summer. There's a 24-hour pub here called the Travellers Bar.

The powder-blue **Marco Polo** hostel (*Map 4;* ☎ *344 5367, fax 344 5368,* ✆ *universumhostels@mail.matav.hu, VII Nyár utca 6, metro: Blaha Lujza tér)*, the swish flagship of the Universum hostel chain with five branches and the only one open year-round, is the place to choose if you want to splurge on a hostel. It is clean, centrally located, with a small restaurant, a stray pool table, an outdoor terrace, Internet access and telephones in the rooms. Even the 12-bed dorm rooms are spotless and 'private', with beds separated by lockers and curtains. Prices in rooms with one/two/three/four/five or six/12 beds are DM78/52/43/36/32/28 per person including breakfast.

Hostels – Buda A very popular hostel, which is located in Buda but quite a long way out is the brightly coloured **Back Pack Guesthouse** (*Map 1;* ☎ *385 9946,* ✆ *backpackguest@hotmail.com, XI Takács Menyhért utca 33, bus No 7 or 7/a – black number – from Keleti train station or Ferenciek tere)*, with 50 beds. A place in a dorm with seven to 11 beds is 1300Ft, one with four or five beds is 1600Ft and a double is 1900Ft per person. There's Internet access, a nice back garden with a gazebo and a very relaxed clientele who appreciate all the gifts of Mother Nature.

If you've always dreamed of staying in a castle on the Danube you'll like the **Citadella** (*Map 4;* ☎ *466 5794, fax 386 0505, XI Citadella sétány, bus No 27 from XI Móricz Zsigmond körtér)* in the fortress on Gellért Hill. In addition to hotel rooms (see the following section), it has 24 dorm beds for 1400Ft per person. The dorms are usually booked by groups a week ahead, so call well in advance for a reservation. Also, this area is something of a tourist trap and

you may feel more like a prisoner than a prince or princess. If you're travelling alone try something more central.

One of Budapest's nicest yet least known places to stay is the **Csillebérc** (*off Map 1;* ☎ *395 6537,* ✆ *csill@mail.datanet.hu, XII Konkoly Thege Miklós út 21)*, a hotel and youth centre in the Buda Hills. This huge complex was once a Pioneer camp, and it's in a quiet, wooded location. Csillebérc offers a 73-room hostel with doubles/triples for DM22/30 (lower in the off season). Bungalows for two with private bath are DM64 (DM52 in off season). The dormitory accommodation at Csillebérc is available in summer only.

To reach here take bus No 21 (black number) from Moszkva tér to the end of the line, then bus No 90 to the first stop after the railway tracks (or a 10-minute downhill walk).

In addition to the 180 beds on offer in summer, the **Martos** hostel usually has about 20 beds available during the university year. See Hostels – Buda for details.

Hotels

Hotels in Budapest run the gamut from converted worker hostels to five-star properties charging well over DM500 a night for a double. The low season for hotels in the capital runs roughly from mid-October or November to March (not including the Christmas/New Year holidays).

A one-star hotel room will cost more than a private room, though the management doesn't mind if you stay only one night. There are no cheap hotels right in the city centre, but in Pest there's the **Flandria** (*Map 1;* ☎ *350 3181,* ✆ *flandria@eravishotels.hu, XIII Szegedi út 27, bus No 4 or tram No 14 from Lehel tér)* has singles/doubles/triples in the high season for DM32/44/54/64 including breakfast. In the low season, rooms are about DM10 less. Rates at the enormous, 11-storey **Góliát** (*Map 1;* ☎ *350 1456,* ✆ *goliat@eravishotels.hu, XIII Kerekes utca 12-20, bus No 4)*, two blocks away from the Flandria, are similar.

In Buda, the 12-room **Citadella** (*Map 4;* ☎ *466 5794, fax 386 0505, XI Citadella sétány, bus No 27 from XI Móricz Zsigmond* *körtér)* on Gellért Hill charges 7400Ft for a double room with shared bath, 8200Ft for one with shower and 9000Ft for a double with bath.

Several inexpensive places are accessible on the HÉV line to Szentendre from Batthyány tér in Buda. The two-star *Touring (off Map 1;* ☎ *250 3184,* ☻ *touring@ touring.hu, Pünkösdfürdő utca 38, HÉV Békásmegyer),* in Csillaghegy, has basic singles/doubles/triples for 7000/9500/ 11,500Ft, including breakfast – good value for small groups.

PLACES TO STAY – MID-RANGE
Private Rooms

The private rooms assigned by travel agencies are reasonable value for money in Budapest. The rooms generally cost from about 3000/5000Ft per single/double plus 3% tourist tax and a 30% supplement if you stay less than four nights. To get a single or a room in the centre of town, you may have to try several offices. There are lots of rooms available, and even in July and August you'll be able to find something. You'll probably need to buy an indexed city map to find your room though.

Individuals on the street outside the train stations and the 24-hour Tribus office (see later in this section) may offer you an unofficial private room, but its prices are usually higher than those asked by the agencies, and there is no quality control. The quality varies considerably and cases of travellers being promised an idyllic room in the centre of town, only to be taken to a dreary, cramped flat in some distant suburb are not unknown. On the other hand, we've received dozens of letters extolling the virtues of the landlords they've dealt with directly in this way. You really have to use your own judgement here. Tourinform in Budapest does not arrange private accommodation but will send you to the Vista Visitor Centre (see Travel Agencies under Information) or to To-Ma Tour (☎ 353 0819, ☻ tourismo@mail.elender.hu) at V Október 6 utca 22.

Some of Budapest's least expensive private rooms are available from Ibusz's main office

(Map 4; ☎ 317 3500) at V Ferenciek tere 10 (metro: Ferenciek tere). It is open from 8 am to 4 pm weekdays, to 1 pm on Saturday and it accepts Visa and MasterCard. The Tribus accommodation office (Map 4; ☎ 318 5776, ☻ tribus.hotel.service@mail.datanet.hu), V Apáczai Csere János utca 1 near the Budapest Marriott hotel (metro: Ferenciek tere), is open 24 hours. Charles Tourist Service (Map 4; ☎ 318 0677, ☻ infoserv@elender.hu) near Ferenciek tere at Szabadsajtó utca 6 has rooms and even bicycles for rent. It is open from 9 am to 9 pm daily.

Pensions

In Pest, the *Dominik (Map 5;* ☎ *343 4419, fax 343 7655, XIV Cházár András utca 3),* beside a large church on Thököly út, is just two stops north-east of Keleti train station on bus No 7 (black number). The 36 rooms with shared bath are DM40/DM50 for a single/double. It also has a five person apartment for DM100. This friendly pension includes an all-you-can eat breakfast buffet and is a convenient place to stay for a few nights.

A more expensive (but central) place in Pest is the 39-room *City Ring (Map 4;* ☎ *340 5450,* ☻ *ring@taverna.hu, XIII Szent István körút 22, metro: Nyugati pályaudvar),* with singles that range from DM81 to DM126, doubles from DM122 to DM162, depending on the season. Two other pensions in the same group, charging the same prices, are the *City Mátyás (Map 4;* ☎ *338 4711,* ☻ *matyas@taverna.hu, Március 15 tér 8, metro: Ferenciek tere or tram No 2),* with 53 rooms near Elizabeth Bridge, and the 32-room *City Pilvax (Map 4;* ☎ *266 7660,* ☻ *pilvax@taverna.hu, Pilvax köz 1-3, metro: Ferenciek tere),* just off Váci utca.

In Buda, the *Büro* pension *(Map 2;* ☎ *212 2929, fax 212 2928, II Dékán utca 3, metro: Moskva tér),* just a block off the north side of Moszkva tér, looks basic from the outside but its 10 rooms (9840/12,300Ft for a single/double with bath) are comfortable and have TVs and telephones.

The friendly *Papillon (Map 3;* ☎ *212 4750,* ☻ *rozsahegy@mail.matav.hu, II Rózsahegy utca 3/b),* one of Buda's best-kept accommodation secrets, has 20 rooms with bath costing 6000Ft to 10,000Ft for singles and 7000Ft to 13,000Ft for doubles, depending on the season. There is quite a good little restaurant attached.

The 10-room *Kis Gellért (Map 1;* ☎ *209 4211 or mobile* ☎ *06-209 332 236, XI Otthon utca 14, bus No 8 or 112 or tram No 61)*, named after the 'Little Gellért' hill to the west of the more famous bigger one, has doubles/triples with bath for 7000/12,000Ft in the high season and 5000/7000Ft in the low season.

A comfortable, very friendly place in Óbuda is the small, family-run *San Marco (Map 3;* ☎/*fax 388 9997, III San Marco utca 6, tram No 17)*. It has five spic-and-span rooms on the 2nd floor (three with private bath), a pleasant courtyard out the back and air conditioning. Singles/doubles are 9000/10,000Ft, including breakfast.

Hotels

In Pest, the old *Park* hotel *(Map 1;* ☎ *313 1420, fax 313 5619, VIII Baross tér 10, metro: Keleti pályaudvar)*, with 170 rooms directly opposite Keleti train station, charges 5950/7500Ft for a single/double without bath, or 7500/14,000Ft with shower, but it is often full. The 74-room *Emke (Map 4;* ☎ *322 9230,* ✉ *emke@pannoniahotels.hu, VII Akácfa utca 1-3, metro: Blaha Lujza)* has singles for DM80 to DM130 and doubles for DM100 to DM150, depending on the season.

A much better-value, medium-priced hotel than these, though, is the 70-room *Medosz* hotel *(Map 4;* ☎ *353 1700, fax 332 4316, VI Jókai tér 9, metro: Oktogon)*. Singles/doubles/triples with bath are DM56/80/120.

The *Délibáb (Map 5;* ☎ *342 9301, VI Délibáb utca 35, metro: Hősök tere)*, across from Heroes' Square and the City Park, is housed in an old Jewish orphanage and its 34 rooms (all with showers) are 9245/10,900/14,830Ft for singles/doubles/triples.

PLACES TO STAY – TOP END
Hotels

In Pest, the *Nemzeti (Map 4;* ☎ *477 2000,* ✉ *nemzeti@pannoniahotels.hu, VIII József*

körút 4, metro: Blaha Lujza), with a beautifully renovated Art Nouveau exterior and inner courtyard, has 76 rooms (all with shower or bath) with singles/doubles starting at DM159/199.

For location and price in Buda, you can't beat the *Kulturinnov (Map 2;* ☎ *355 0122,* ✉ *mka3@mail.matav.hu, I Szentháromság tér 6, bus No 16 or Várbusz)*, a 16-room hotel in the former Finance Ministry in the Castle District. Chandeliers, artwork and a sprawling marble staircase greet you on entry and the halls often host art exhibitions or concerts. The rooms, though clean and with private baths, are not so nice. Singles/doubles are DM100/130.

The friendly *Victoria (Map 2;* ☎ *457 8080,* ✉ *victoria@victoria.hu, I Bem rakpart 11, tram No 19 or bus No 86)* has 27 rooms with larger-than-life views of the Parliament building and the Danube, and gets high marks for service and facilities. Singles/doubles are DM144/154 in the low season and DM189/199 in summer – good value for a four-star hotel.

The *Orion* hotel *(Map 4;* ☎ *356 8583,* ✉ *orionhot@mail.matav.hu, I Döbrentei utca 13, tram No 18 or 19 or bus No 7 or 7/a)*, tucked away in the Tabán district, is a cosy, 30-room hotel with a relaxed atmosphere and within walking distance of the castle. Most importantly, unlike most three-star hotels in Budapest, it has central air conditioning. Rooms are DM145/185.

Budapest's *grande dame* of hotels, the 233-room *Gellért (Map 4;* ☎ *385 2200,* ✉ *sales@gellert.hu, XI Szent Gellért tér 1, tram No 18, 19, 47 or 49)*, is looking less tattered these days as renovations progress; some rooms are now very attractive. It's a four-star hotel but with loads more personality than most. The thermal baths are free for guests, but with the exception of the terrace restaurant on the Kelenhegyi út side, its other facilities are forgettable. Prices change depending on which way your room faces and what sort of bathroom it has, but singles range from DM200 to DM260, doubles from DM352 to DM410. Lower-level rooms which face the river can be noisy.

The 322-room **Budapest Hilton** *(Map 2;* ☎ *488 6600,* ✉ *hiltonhu@hungary.net, I Hess András tér 1, bus No 16 or Várbusz)* on Castle Hill was built carefully in and around a 14th-century church and baroque college (though it still has its detractors). It has great views of the city and the Danube and some good facilities, including a medieval wine cellar serving a good range of Hungarian vintages. Singles are a minimum DM360, doubles from DM410. A more central branch, the 260-room **Hilton West-end City Centre** *(Map 4;* ☎ *238 9000, fax 238 9005, VI Váci út 3, metro: Nyugati pályaudvar)* was scheduled to open early in the first year of the new millennium at the massive new Westend City Centre shopping mall (Map 4) near Nyugati station.

The **Kempinski Corvinus** *(Map 4;* ☎ *429 3777,* ✉ *hotel@kempinski.hu, V Erzsébet tér 7-8, metro: Deák tér)* is Budapest's (and Hungary's) most expensive hotel, with singles/doubles from DM480/560 (or DM520/600 for a 'superior' room). Essentially for business travellers on hefty expense accounts, the hotel has European service, American efficiency and Hungarian charm.

The new 186-room **Páva Plaza** hotel *(Map 6;* ☎ *477 7282 or 459 0065,* ✉ *tomotel@ hotelgloria.hu, IX Tompa utca 30-34, metro: Ferenc körút)*, on a newly pedestrianised street in unlikely Ferencváros, counts a number of distinctions. It's the first entirely new hotel built in the capital in almost a decade and has complete state-of-the-art technology and philosophy, with ISDN lines to every room, full access for the disabled, allergen-free rooms and a bio-cuisine restaurant. Doubles start at DM239.

The 164-room **Grand Hotel** *(Map 3;* ☎ *329 2300,* ✉ *margotel@hungary.net, XIII Margitsziget, bus No 26)*, built in 1873 on Margaret Island, is posh, quiet, has all the mod cons and is connected to the Thermal spa via an underground corridor. Of course it ain't cheap: singles are from DM180 to DM280, doubles DM230 to DM330, depending on the season and the view. The views of this narrow stretch of the Danube and Pest from this hotel are

hardly what you would call spectacular, however.

PLACES TO EAT
Restaurants

Very roughly, a two-course meal for one person with a glass of wine or beer for between 900Ft and 1100Ft in Budapest is 'cheap', while a 'moderate' meal hovers around 1500Ft (or slightly more). There's a pretty big jump to an 'expensive' meal (from 2500Ft to 3000Ft per head), and 'very expensive' is anything over that – from 5000Ft to as much as 7000Ft per person. Most restaurants are open till midnight, but it's best to arrive by 9 or 10 pm. It is advisable to book tables at medium to expensive restaurants.

Traditional Hungarian The *Arany-szarvas (Golden Stag; Map 2;* ☎ *375 6451, I Szarvas tér 1)*, set in an old 18th-century inn perched above Döbrentei tér, serves – what else? – game dishes and has a lovely outside terrace at the foot of Castle Hill in summer. If your cholesterol is down, the nearby *Tabáni Kakas (Map 2;* ☎ *375 7165, I Attila út 27)*, will raise it for you – almost everything is cooked in flavour-enhancing goose fat.

Kacsa (Map 3; ☎ *201 9992, II Fő utca 75)* is the place for duck, which is what its name means. It's a fairly elegant place with good service and pricey mains (1800Ft to 2900Ft). Open from 6 pm to midnight daily.

The *Vadrózsa (Map 3;* ☎ *326 5817,* ✉ *vadrozsa@hungary.com, II Pentelei Molnár út 15)*, in a beautiful neo-Renaissance villa in the Rózsa-domb district, remains one of the swishest restaurants in Buda and should be one of your first choices if you've got the rich uncle or aunt in tow. It's filled with roses, antiques and soft piano music, and there's no menu – you choose off the cart of raw ingredients and specify the cooking style. Open daily for lunch and dinner to 11 pm. Very expensive.

In the Buda Hills, *Szép Ilona (Map 1;* ☎ *275 1391, II Budakeszi út 1-3)* opposite Remíz (see International later in this section) is the place to come for heavy, indigenous Hungarian cuisine at very modest prices.

In Óbuda, my favourite expensive restaurant in this neck of the woods is the *Kisbuda Gyöngye* *(Map 3;* ☎ *368 6402, III Kenyeres utca 34)*, an attractive, cosy place decorated with antiques that manages to create the *fin-de-siècle* atmosphere of Óbuda and serves excellent goose liver dishes (around 1600Ft) and more pedestrian things like *csirke paprikás* (1280Ft). It's open for lunch and dinner till midnight Monday to Saturday.

In Pest, *Fatál (Wooden Platter; Map 4;* ☎ *266 2607, V Váci utca 67)* serves massive Hungarian meals on wooden platters or in iron cauldrons in three rustic rooms daily from 11.30 am to 2 pm.

Try to have lunch at the little *Móri Borozó (Map 3;* ☎ *349 8390, XIII Pozsonyi út 39)*, a wine bar and restaurant a short walk north of Szent István körút that has arguably the best home-cooked Hungarian food in Budapest. It's cheap (160Ft to 190Ft for soups, 340Ft to 390Ft for *főzelék* and 580Ft to 860Ft for mains) and very popular with local customers (open weekdays from 10 am till 8 pm (to 3 pm on Friday).

Modern Hungarian For lighter, more up-to-date Hungarian food it's hard to beat the newly renovated *Múzeum* cafe-restaurant *(Map 4;* ☎ *338 4221, VIII Múzeum körút 12)*, which is still going strong after more than a century at the same location, just up from the National Museum. It has very good fish and duck with fruit (specify this over the usual potatoes and cabbage) and is open from noon to 1 am Monday to Saturday. Expensive.

If you're not discouraged by the prospect of spending something like 7000Ft per person for dinner, *Gundel (Map 5;* ☎ *321 3550,* ✉ *gundel@mail.datanet.hu, XIV Állatkerti út 2)*, next to the zoo and directly behind the Museum of Fine Arts, is the city's fanciest (and most famous) restaurant, with a tradition dating back to 1894. Indeed, it still feeds the Habsburgs when they visit. It's open from noon to 4 pm and 6.30 pm to midnight daily. Very expensive.

Budapest cognoscenti, though, leave this place to the expense-account brigade and head for *Bagolyvár (Owl's Castle; Map 5;* ☎ *343 0217, XIV Állatkerti út 2)*, Gundel's little sister restaurant next door, run entirely by women who endeavour to lighten up granny's traditional recipes (open from noon to 10.30 pm daily).

French One of the most popular places with expat *français* in Pest is *Lou Lou (Map 4;* ☎ *312 4505, V Vigyázó Ferenc utca 4)*, a lovely bistro with excellent daily specials; try the *très* garlicky lamb. *La Fontaine (Map 4;* ☎ *317 3715, V Mérleg utca 10)* is a Parisian-style brasserie celebrated for its beef and goose liver dishes and *mousse au chocolat*. It's open from 10 am to 11 pm Monday to Saturday.

The French-owned *Bisquine Crêperie (Map 4;* ☎ *351 7473, VI Kertész utca 48)* has its flour specially milled for its savoury *galettes* (spinach, egg, cheese, bacon etc; 380Ft to 590Ft) and sweet *crêpes* (chocolate, vanilla, banana, rum, etc; 230Ft to 590Ft). Wash it all down with the champagne of ciders, Bretagne (open from noon to 10 pm weekdays, till midnight at the weekend).

Italian Arguably the best budget Italian food is to be had at the Italian-owned *Okay Italia* chain, with one branch (Map 4; ☎ 349 2991) at XIII Szent István körút 20 and another (Map 4; ☎ 332 6960) at V Nyugati tér 6. Pizzas, pastas and Italian main courses range from 800Ft to 1500Ft.

Articsóka (Map 4; ☎ *302 7757, VI Zichy Jenő utca 17)* – more Hungo-Mediterranean than Italian but in that direction – is an impressive arrival, with great decor, an atrium and roof-top terrace (the only one in the city) and a small theatre for post-prandial entertainment. The food (starters 490Ft to 990Ft, pastas 890Ft to 1000Ft), however, is only just above average while the atmosphere wins the trophy.

The most upmarket Italian restaurant in town is still *Fausto's (Map 4;* ☎ *269 6806, VIII Dohány utca 5)* with excellent (though pricey) pasta dishes, daily specials and desserts. There's lots of choices for vegetarians. It's open from noon to 3 pm and 7 pm to midnight. Expensive.

Happy Bank (Map 4; ☎ none, V Bank utca 3) is a great place for inexpensive home-made pasta and pizzas (400Ft to 650Ft), but is only open 11 am to 9 pm weekdays.

Greek *Jorgosz* (Map 4; ☎ 351 7725, VII Csengery utca 24), a cellar restaurant just east of Erzsébet körút, has an extensive menu (from 700Ft for mains) but average food. The occasional live bazouki music helps, though. It's open noon till midnight daily. Moderate. A better choice would be the more expensive *Taverna Ressaikos* (Map 2; ☎ 212 1612, I Apor Péter utca 1) in Buda, where lunch is 990Ft to 1490Ft and dinner platters range from 1000Ft to 4000Ft. *Taverna Dionysos* (Map 4; ☎ 318 1222, V Belgrád rakpart 16) is always crowded but has an excellent view of Gellért Hill; a table on the terrace here should be your first choice in summer. Main courses are 890Ft to 1390Ft.

Mexican & Latin American *Iguana* (Map 4; ☎ 331 4352, Zoltán utca 16) serves decent enough Mexican food (not a difficult task in these parts) but it's hard to say whether the pull is chicken and prawn *fajitas* (1730Ft and 2390Ft), 'whoop ass' enchiladas and burritos (1290Ft and 1490Ft) and tortilla chips with salsa (270Ft) or the frenetic, 'we-always-party' atmosphere. It's open daily from 11.30 am to 12.30 am. Moderate.

La Bodega (Map 4; ☎ 267 5048, VII Wesselényi utca 35) is a bright and airy place serving Latin American and Spanish specialities (600Ft to 1700Ft). There's Spanish guitar music in the evenings (open noon to 1 am weekdays, from 6 pm at the weekend).

Kosher *Hanna* (Map 4; ☎ 342 1072, VII Dob utca 35 or VI Kazinczy utca 21), housed in an old school behind the Orthodox Synagogue, is the more atmospheric of Budapest's two kosher restaurants. Be wary of the hours, though; it opens for lunch only from 11.30 am to 3 pm weekdays and to 2 pm on Saturday. The restaurant at the *King's* hotel (Map 4; ☎ 352 7675, VII Nagy Diófa 25-27)

the next block over is as soul-less a kosher eatery as any, though the food is not half bad.

Chinese Some of the best Chinese food in the city (and priced accordingly) is served at the *Hong Kong Pearl Garden* (Map 3; ☎ 212 3131, II Margit körút 2) in Buda, with dishes for 980Ft to 1400Ft. Try the Peking duck, Sichuan eggplant or the Singapore noodles. The *Mongolian Barbecue* (Map 2; ☎ 212 1859, XII Márvány utca 19/a) is another one of those all-you-can-eat pseudo-Asian places found the world over. The big difference here is that for 1490/2590Ft at lunch/dinner you also get to *drink* as much beer or wine as you like. Open from noon to midnight daily.

Thai The standards at *Chan-Chan* (Map 4; ☎ 318 4266, V Só utca 3) have fallen considerably over the past few years, but the food does retain something of a Thai/Laotian taste. 'Stick to the spring rolls with peanut sauce,' I've been told by residents – as Thai a dish as peanut butter is French. Chan-Chan is open from noon to 11 pm daily. Expensive. A much cheaper alternative is *Bambusz* (Map 4; ☎ 359 3124, XIII Hollán Ermő utca 3), a Thai place by way of Ho Chi Minh City (eg, *pho* for 1050Ft). It's open from noon to 11 pm daily.

Japanese & Korean *Arigato* (Map 4; ☎ 353 3549, VI Teréz körút 23) has an inexpensive sushi lunch menu (1180Ft) and plenty of other choices but eating alongside a car showroom – a Suzuki one at that – may not be everyone's idea of a Budapest experience. It's open from noon to 11 pm Monday to Saturday. *Seoul House* (Map 2; ☎ 201 9607, I Fő utca 8), in Buda, serves excellent Korean food from *bulgogi* and *kalbi grills* to *kimchi* and *bibimbop* rice; some would argue that it serves the most authentically Asian dishes in Budapest. Expensive.

Indian For Indian food, you might try the flashy *Bombay Palace* (Map 4; ☎ 332 8363, VI Andrássy út 44), with curries and tandoors from 1400Ft, or *Govinda* (see the following Vegetarian section) instead.

Vegetarian The *Gandhi* cellar restaurant *(Map 4;* ☎ *269 1625, V Vigyázó Ferenc utca 4)* has a diverse and fresh salad bar where you pay by the weight or choose set menu plates in two sizes: 'moonplate' (660Ft) and 'sunplate' (880Ft). Gandhi (non-smoking) opens from noon till 10.30 pm Monday to Saturday. Even more strictly veg is *Govinda (Map 4;* ☎ *318 1144, V Belgrád rakpart 18)*, part of the Krishna chain. Why must the children of God make and eat such boring food though?

Nonstop In Buda, hearty Hungarian meals – consider splitting a dish – are served round the clock at *Söröző a Szent Jupáthoz (Map 2;* ☎ *212 2923, II Retek utca 16)*, a block north of Moszkva tér. Nearby, the *Nagyi Palacsintázója (Granny's Palacsinta Place; Map 2;* ☎ *201 8605, I Hattyú utca 16)* serves Hungarian pancakes and *Macbeth (Map 2;* ☎ *224 9004, I Hattyú utca 14)* next door has sandwiches 24 hours a day.

The *Grill 99 (Map 4;* ☎ *352 1150, VIII Dohány utca 52)* is a popular place for late, late meals or early, early post-club breakfast. Very cheap. *Tulipán (Map 4;* ☎ *269 5043, V Nádor utca 34)* is another nonstop, also popular with after-club crowds and taxi drivers, which may be a good thing or a bad thing.

International In Buda, *Remíz (Map 1;* ☎ *394 1896, II Budakeszi út 5)*, next to an old tram depot (*remíz*), remains excellent both for its food (try the grilled dishes, especially the ribs) and prices, despite the hype. Great atmosphere. It's open from 9 am to 1 am daily (the fabulous fresh plum pastries are ready after 9.30 am).

In Pest, *Cafe Kör (Map 4;* ☎ *311 0053, V Sas utca 17)* near St Stephen's Basilica is a great place for a light meal at any time between 10 am and 10 pm Monday to Saturday. Salads, desserts, and daily specials (740Ft to 1690Ft) are very good.

If you really want to be in the thick of things hip though, head for the upscale *Cosmo (Map 4;* ☎ *266 4747, V Kristóf tér 7-8)*, a postmodern, minimalist restaurant above the more established *Cyrano* and favourite chi-chi hangout of the city's best

actors (well, the best paid ones anyway). Very expensive.

Marquis de Salade (Map 4; ☎ *302 4086, VI Hajós utca 43)* is a serious hybrid, with dishes from as far apart as Russia and China, Greece and Azerbaijan. (Did he say Azerbaijan?). There's lots of quality vegetarian choices too in this beautifully decorated place with a salad bar (650Ft) and cheap lunch menu (750Ft).

Cafes & Teahouses

For the past two centuries, Budapest has been as famous as Vienna for it's cafes, cake shops and cafe life; at the start of the 20th century, the city counted more than 300 cafes but by the time of the change in 1989, there were scarcely a dozen left. In recent years, a new breed of cafe has developed – all polished chrome, neon lighting and straight lines. But the coffee is just as good as ever. Teahouses have made the biggest splash in recent years in Budapest, the capital of a country not usually associated with *cha*.

Traditional Cafes The most famous of the famous cafes in Budapest – bar none – is *Gerbeaud (Map 4;* ☎ *429 9000, V Vörösmarty tér 7)*, a fashionable meeting place for the city's elite, on the west side of Budapest's busiest square since 1870. It's still not the place for fast service, a problem even the new German management can't seem to solve.

The *Művész (Map 4;* ☎ *322 4606, VI Andrássy út 29)*, almost opposite the Opera House, is a more interesting place to people-watch than Gerbeaud and has a better selection of cakes (try the apple *torta*) at lower prices. It is open from 9 am to midnight daily.

The *Cafe New York (Map 4;* ☎ *322 3849, VII Erzsébet körút 9-11)*, has been a Budapest institution since 1895 (and for other reasons since 1956 when the scaffolding surrounding it first went up). The *belle époque* decor and memories of the cafe's literary associations are fading – but not yet extinguished (open 10 am to midnight daily).

Lukács (Map 4; ☎ 302 8747, VI Andrássy út 70) has reopened its doors after a major renovation and is again dressed up in the finest of divine decadence – all mirrors and gold and soft piano music (with a no-smoking section too). It is open 9 or 10 am to 8 pm daily.

In Buda, the perfect place for coffee and cakes up in the Castle District is the tiny (and crowded) *Ruszwurm (Map 2; ☎ 375 5284, I Szentháromság utca 7)* near Matthias Church. Two more good cafes on the Buda side are the atmospheric and service-oriented *Angelika (Map 2; ☎ 201 4847, I Batthyány tér 5-7)* and the un-touristy *Déryné (Map 2; ☎ 212 3824, I Krisztina tér 3)*.

Modern Cafes *Cafe Miró (Map 2; ☎ 375 5458, I Úri utca 30)* is a safe bet in the Castle District, with heavy wrought-iron chairs, light snacks and local artwork on the walls. There's live music here every night (open 9 am to midnight).

Leafy VI Liszt Ferenc tér is surrounded by hip cafes generally open from 10 or 11 am to 1 or 2 am. If there not playing music, you can catch strains from musicians practising in the Music Academy at the southern end of the square.

Artsy *Cafe Vian (Map 4; ☎ 342 8991)* at No 9 is the royal court of Budapest 'it' girls and guys though the new *PestiEst (Map 4; ☎ 344 4381)* at No 5 should make an impact with its overall Magyar-ness (read crap service), funky house music and cutting-edge interior. It's a good place to try Unicum (380Ft). *Incognito (Map 4; ☎ 342 1471)* at No 3 was the first on the square and is still going strong; seek out the sofa in back and sip an Irish coffee (open 9.30 am to midnight weekdays and from 11.30 am at the weekend).

Cafe Eklektika (Map 4; ☎ 266 3054, V Semmelweis utca 21) has some of the most comfortable chairs in Budapest and a pleasant clutter of 1950s and 60s bric-a-brac, with artwork on the walls and low lighting. It's a great place for writing post-cards or an early evening *rendez-vous* (open 10 am to midnight).

Teahouses *1000 Tea (Map 4; ☎ 337 8217, V Váci utca 65)*, in a small courtyard, is the place to go if you want to sip a soothing blend, made by tea-serious staff, and lounge on pillows in a Japanese-style tearoom (open noon to 9 pm weekdays, from 11 am on Saturday). There are several other tea-house around, including the funky *Teaház a Vörös Oroszlánhoz (Teahouse at the Red lion; Map 4; ☎ 269 0579, VI Jókai tér 8)* north of Liszt Ferenc tér, but my absolute favourite is *CD Fű (Map 4; ☎ 317 5094, V Szerb utca 15)* a popular studenty place in a big old cellar whose name means 'CD Grass'. It's open from 11 am to 11 pm weekdays and to 2 pm at the weekend.

Fast Food & Cheap Eats

Fast-food places like McDonald's (the one at Teréz körút 19 near Oktogon on Map 4 is open almost 24 hours a day), Pizza Hut, KFC, Dunkin' Donuts, Wendy's and the local Paprika abound in Budapest (Oktogon is full of them) but old-style self-service restaurants, the mainstay of both white and blue-collar workers in the old regime, where full meals cost 400Ft, are disappearing fast. One of just a few left in Pest is the *self-service restaurant* at V Arany János utca 5 (Map 4) open from 11.15 am to 3 pm weekdays only. A bit more up-scale is the self-service upstairs at the *Pick Ház (Map 4)* beside the metro entrance on Kossuth Lajos tér (open from 9 am to 6 pm week-days, from 8 am to 1 pm on Saturday). One of the cleanest, most upbeat in this genre is the *Centrál Önkiszolgáló (Map 4; ☎ 267 4955, VIII Krúdy Gyula utca)* open 11 am to 9 pm weekdays, to 8 pm Saturday and Sunday.

Even better value are the wonderful little restaurants called *étkezde* – canteens not un-like British 'caffs' that serve simple dishes that change every day. A meal easily costs under 800Ft. Some of the best ones are *Kisharang (Map 4; ☎ 269 3861, V Október 6 utca 17)* open from 11 am to 9 pm week-days, from 11.30 am to 4 pm at the week-end; *Kádár (Map 4; ☎ 321 3622, X Klauzál tér 9)* in the former Jewish district (open 11.30 am to 3.30 pm weekdays); and *Frici*

Papa Kifőzdéje (Papa Frank's Canteen; Map 4; ☎ 351 0197, VI Király utca 55), which is larger than the usual étkezde and opens from 11 am to 9 pm Monday to Saturday (mains under 400Ft).

Pizza Among the best places in Buda for pizza are *Il Treno (Map 2; ☎ 356 4251, XII Alkotás utca 15)*, with pizzas from 690Ft to 1080Ft and a cheap 750Ft menu, and *Marcello (Map 6; ☎ 466 6231, XI Bartók Béla út 40)*, which is popular with students from the nearby university (open from noon to 10 pm and nonsmoking). Pizzas cost 480Ft to 620Ft, salads 330Ft to 600Ft.

Marxim (Map 3; ☎ 316 0231, II Kisrókus utca 23), a short walk from the Mammut shopping mall on Széna tér is a hangout for teens who have added a layer of their own graffiti to the communist memorabilia. Okay, we all know Stalin *szuksz*, but it's still a curiosity for those who appreciate the Gulag, Kulák, Lenin and Anarchismo pizzas and the campy Stalinist decor.

There are several pizza places on Nyugati tér, including *Okay Italia* (see Italian under Restaurants) at No 6 and *Don Pepe (Map 4; ☎ 322 2954)* at No 8, open till the very wee hours.

Middle Eastern A very inexpensive place for gyros is the *Török-Kinai Büfé (Turkish-Chinese Buffet; Map 4; ☎ 269 3128, XIII Szent István körút 13)*. Husband (the Turk) beats wife (the Chinese) in the culinary contest here, however (open every day 11.30 am to 10 pm daily).

Három Testvér (Three Brothers; Map 4; ☎ 329 2951, XIII Szent István körút 22) is great anytime but especially for a late-night snack. *Gül Baba (Map 4; ☎ 342 2377, Erzsébet körút 17)* is a hybrid takeaway/sit-down gyro place near Blaha Lujza tér (open 10 am to 4 am).

Food Markets & Self-Catering

Budapest counts some 20 markets and, while the *Nagycsarnok (Great Market Hall; Map 6; IX Fővám tér)* is the largest, it has become something of a tourist trap since it was renovated for the millecentenary in

1996. There are some good food stalls on the upper level serving everything from Chinese spring rolls to German sausages, though, and the best and cheapest wine spritzers at a little stall hidden among the table cloth vendors. Among other colourful *food markets* in the city are the ones at VIII Rákóczi tér 34; V Hold utca 11 near V Szabadság tér (Map 4; with a stall selling tasty, inexpensive croissant sandwiches); and at II Fény utca alongside Mammut shopping mall (Map 2). Markets are usually open from 6 or 6.30 am to 6 pm weekdays and till 2 pm on Saturday. Monday is always very quiet (if the market isn't closed altogether).

There are large supermarkets everywhere in Budapest, including the *Julius Meinl* on VIII Blaha Lujza tér (Map 4) and the *Kaiser's* opposite Nyugati train station at VI Nyugati tér 1-2 (Map 4). *Rothschild* is another large chain with outlets throughout the city including one at XIII Szent István körút 4 (Map 4).

If you've got the urge for something sweet, head for the tiny bakery called *Mézes Kuckó (Honey Nook; Map 4; XIII Jászai Mari tér 4/a)*; its nut and honey cookies are to die for (open from 9 am to 6 pm weekdays and to 1 pm on Saturday). For ice cream, no one but no one does it better than the little *Butterfly* shop at Teréz körút 20 (Map 4; *not* the pastry shop next door called Vajassütemények boltja). It is open from 10 am to 6 pm weekdays and to 2 pm Saturday 45Ft per scoop).

There are 24-hour *nonstop shops* selling everything from cheese and cold cuts to cigarettes and beer all over Budapest, including the ones at the Nyugati train station (next to track No 13), VIII Baross tér 3 near Keleti station and V Apáczai Csere János utca 5 near Marriott hotel in Pest and at I Attila utca 57 and XI Bartók Béla utca 16 in Buda.

ENTERTAINMENT

For a city its size, Budapest has a huge choice of things to do and places to go after dark – from opera and folk dancing to jazz and cattle-market clubs. It's almost never difficult to get tickets or to get in; the hard part is deciding what to do.

Listings

Your best sources of general information in the city are the weekly freebies *PestiEst* (in Hungarian but easy to follow) and the English-language *Scene*. The free bilingual publications *Programme in Ungarn/in Hungary* and its scaled-down version for the capital, *Budapest Panorama*. The most thorough listings magazine – from clubs and films to art exhibits and classical music – is the weekly *Pesti Műsor* (Budapest Program), also called *PM Magazin*, available at newsstands every Thursday (59Ft). The free *Koncert Kalendrium*, published once a month, lists concerts, opera and dance.

Booking Agencies

For concerts of all types try the Vigadó Ticket Office (Map 4; ☎ 327 4322), V Vörösmarty tér 1 (metro: Vörösmarty tér). It's open from 9 am to 7 pm on weekdays. You can also buy tickets to the philharmonic and other classical concerts at the Nemzeti Filharmónia Jegypénztára (National Philharmonic Ticket Office; Map 4; ☎ 318 0281) at V Mérleg utca 10 (open from 10 am to 6 pm weekdays).

The busiest ticket agency is the Színházak Központi Jegyiroda (Central Ticket Office; Map 4; ☎ 312 0000), VI Andrássy út 18 (metro: Opera), which is open from 10 am to 6 pm (5 pm on Friday) on weekdays. It has tickets to numerous theatres and events, although the best are gone a couple of days in advance. For opera or ballet tickets, go to the office (☎ 353 0170) two doors down at VI Andrássy út 22. It is open 11 am (10 am on Monday) to 5 pm weekdays.

Music Mix (Map 4; ☎ 338 2237), V Váci utca 33 (metro: Ferenciek tere), has tickets to special events such as rock spectaculars, appearances by foreign superstars, etc. It's open from 10 am to 6 pm daily and to 1 pm on Saturday. Ticket Express (☎ 353 0692), VI Jókai utca 40, is another option with extended hours: it's open from 9.30 am to 9.30 pm daily.

Pubs & Bars

Budapest is loaded with pubs and bars and there are enough venues to satisfy all tastes. Inevitably the capital has a number of 'Irish' pubs on offer; if you're into these McDonald's of drinking venues head for *Becketts (Map 4; ☎ 311 1035, V Bajcsy-Zsilinszky út 72)* or the *Irish Cat (Map 4; ☎ 266 4085, V Múzeum körút 41)*, which has Guinness and Kilkenny on tap.

Oscar's Cafe & Pub (Map 2; ☎ 212 8017, I Ostrom utca 12), with film memorabilia on the wood-panelled walls and leather director's chairs on the floor, is open from 5 pm to 2 am weekdays, till 4 am at the weekend.

The *Cactus Juice (Map 4; ☎ 302 2116, VI Jókai tér 5)* is supposed to be 'American rustic' but it's really Wild West out of Central Casting. The Juice is a good place to sip and sup with no distractions. Quite the opposite is *Portside (Map 4; ☎ 351 8405. VII Dohány utca 7)*, which is open till 2 am on weekdays, to 4 am at the weekend. This place absolutely packs in a yuppie mingle-and-meat crowd nightly.

The *Janis Pub (Map 4; ☎ 266 2619, V Királyi Pál utca 8)*, near Ferenciek tere, is usually a stop for a quick few on the way to somewhere else, but some people linger here for the choice of imported beer. *Picasso Point (Map 4; ☎ 269 5544, VI Hajós utca 31)* shocked a fair few when it closed and re-emerged *sans* cellar disco and Hungarian pre-teens.

Paris, Texas (Map 4; ☎ 218 0570, IX Ráday utca 22) has a coffee house feel to it and pool tables downstairs; the crowds arrive later in the evenings. *Darshan Udvar (Map 4; ☎ 266 5541, VIII Krúdy Gyula utca 7)* is a cavernous new complex of two bars, a restaurant with lots of vegetarian choices (mains 600Ft to 750Ft) and a courtyard terrace cafe with decor that combines cutting-edge Euro-techno with Seattle grunge and Eastern flair. It's open from 10 am to 1 pm Sunday to Thursday and to 3 am at the weekend.

Discos & Clubs

Budapest's top disco at the moment (see clock) is *Dokk Backstage (Map 1; ☎ 457 1023, II Obudai hajógyári-sziget 122)*, a club in a converted warehouse on Óbuda Island in the Danube, that attracts the capital's *szép ember* (beautiful people) and is at its hottest, grinding-est best on Saturday night.

Discos run by the medical and economics universities – the *SOTE Klub* (Map 1; ☎ 210 4419, IX Nagyvárad tér 4) and the *Közgaz Pince Klub* (Map 6; ☎ 218 6855, IX Fővám tér 8) – have fewer frills, cheaper covers and but plenty of room to dance.

Trocadero (Map 4; ☎ 311 4691, VI Szent István körút 15) attracts one of the most diverse crowds in Budapest with its great canned Latin, salsa Afro, reggae and soul nights.

Süss Fél Nap (Map 4; ☎ 374 3329, cnr V Honvéd utca and Szent István körút) attracts a student crowd and hosts student bands; it's a lot of fun and less expensive than many of the other clubs. Go to *Piaf* (Map 4; ☎ 312 3823, VI Nagymező utca 25) for dancing and action well into the new day, when everything else has slowed down. This place is always a trip and a half.

Gay & Lesbian Venues

There are no women-only clubs in Budapest, but lesbians (and straights) frequent the *Capella* (Map 4; ☎ 318 6231, V Belgrád rakpart 23), which hosts some really bad – in the real sense of the word – nudge-nudge, wink-wink drag shows. *Angel* (☎ 351 6490, VII Szövetség utca 33), sometimes called by its Hungarian name Angyal, is the largest gay disco with a cavernous dark room in the cellar. It's open from 10 pm to 5 am from Thursday to Sunday. The name of the *Action Bar* (Map 4; ☎ 266 9148, V Magyar utca 42) says it all; take the usual precautions and have fun.

Rock & Pop Music

The *Petőfi Csarnok* (Map 5; ☎ 343 4327, XIV Zichy Mihály utca 14, metro: Széchenyi fürdő or trolleybus No 72 or 74), the city's main youth centre, is in the City Park and *the* place for smaller rock concerts in Budapest as the hall is small enough to get really close to the performers. It produces a monthly program available at the information counter and at night spots around Budapest.

The *Almássy téri Szabadidő Központ* (Almássy tér Leisure Centre; Map 4; ☎ 352 1572, VII Almássy tér 6) is a venue for just about anything that's in and/or or interesting; the DJs from the very popular Tilos Rádió (Forbidden Radio) often hold events.

The *Laser Theatre* (Lézerszínház; Map 1; ☎ 263 0871, X Népliget, metro: Népliget) at the Planetarium in Népliget (People's Park) has a mixed bag of video concerts with laser and canned music featuring the likes of Pink Floyd, Queen, U2, Led Zeppelin and Mike Oldfield. There are usually shows at 7.30 pm from Monday to Saturday, which cost 1190/790/500Ft for adults/students/children.

You simply can't miss a *Cinetrip Vízi-Mozi* (Cinetrip Water-Movie; Map 4) event at the Rudas Bath (see the boxed text 'Taking the Waters') if one is taking place during your visit. It combines partying and dancing with music, film and bathing and is just short of being all-out orgies. The events are held monthly or bimonthly (usually from 8 am to 2 pm on Saturday); schedules are available at tourist offices and other venues around town (1500Ft).

Jazz & Blues

Old Man's Music Pub (Map 4; ☎ 322 7645, VII Akácfa utca 13) pulls in the best live blues and jazz acts in town; shows are from 9 to 11 pm. A dinner reservation is usually required to score a table, though the food is pretty good. The dance floor really gets going after midnight.

The *Merlin Club* (Map 4; ☎ 317 9338, V Gerlóczy utca 4) has live music most nights from 10 pm and a good crowd, especially if the club is staging something at the adjoining English-language theatre (see the Theatre section).

Hades (Map 4; ☎ 352 1503, VI Vörösmarty utca 31) calls itself (shudder) a 'jazztaurant', but as much for the food as the low-key music. *Fat Mo's* (Map 4; ☎ 267 3199, V Nyáry Pál utca 9) plays the blues early in the evening before the small bar gets too packed for anything but schmoozin' and cruisin'. Another place for jazz is the *Fél Tíz Jazz Club* (Map 4;

☎ 333 7721, VIII Baross utca 30), with red velvet and black wrought-iron decor, an eclectic mix of people and dancing later in the evening.

Folk & Traditional Music

Authentic *táncház*, literally 'dance house' but really folk-music workshops, are held at least once a week at several locations around Budapest (350Ft to 500Ft), including three in Buda: the *Fonó Budai Zeneház* (*Fonó Buda Music House; off Map 1;* ☎ 206 5300, XI Sztregova utca 3); the *Folklór Centrum* (*Map 1;* ☎ 203 3868, XI Fehérvári út 47-51) at the Municipal Cultural House; and the *Marczibányi tér Cultural Centre* (Marczibányi téri Művelődési Központ; Map 3; ☎ 212 4885, II Marczibányi tér 5/a), where the popular folk group Muzsikás usually jams at 8 pm on Thursday. In Pest, there's the fabulous *Kalamajka Táncház* at the Inner Town Youth House (*Belvárosi Ifjúság Ház; Map 4;* ☎ 317 5928 or 266 3378, V Molnár utca 9) from 5 pm to midnight on Saturday. Also, look in any of the listings mentioned at the start of this section for táncház evenings at the *Petőfi Csarnok* or the *Almássy téri Szabadidő Központ*.

Classical Music

The *Koncert Kalendárium* (see Listings at the start of this section) highlights all concerts in Budapest each month, and most nights you'll have several to choose from. Budapest's main concert halls are the stunning *Franz Liszt Academy of Music* (Liszt Ferenc Zeneakadémia; Map 4; ☎ 342 0179, VI Liszt Ferenc tér 8) in Pest, and the modern *Budapest Congress Centre* (Budapesti Kongresszusi Központ; Map 1; ☎ 209 1990, XII Jagelló út 1-3) in Buda. The *Pesti Vigadó* (Map 4; ☎ 318 9903, V Vigadó tér 2) has light classical music and touristy musical revues.

Cinemas

A couple of dozen movie houses show English-language films with Hungarian subtitles. Consult the listings in *Scene* or *Budapest Sun* newspapers. See anything at the fantastically renovated *Corvin Filmpalota* (*Corvin Film Palace; Map 4;* ☎ 459 5050, VIII Corvin köz 1), which saw a lot of action during the 1956 Uprising and led a revolution of a different sort four decades later: the introduction of state-of-the-art sound systems and comfortable seating.

The *Örökmozgó Filmmúzeum* (Map 4; ☎ 342 2167, VII Erzsébet körút 39), part of the Hungarian Film Institute, shows an excellent assortment of foreign and classic films in their original languages. *Művész* (Map 4; ☎ 332 6726, VI Teréz körút 30) shows artsy and cult films. The *Puskin* (Map 4; ☎ 429 6080, V Kossuth Lajos utca 18) has a mix of art and popular releases. All three have cafes *in situ*.

Theatre

In Pest, the *Merlin Theatre* (☎ 317 9338, V Gerlóczy utca 4) stages numerous plays in English, often put on by the local English Theatre Company (ETC). Tickets (around 600Ft to 2000Ft) should always be booked in advance.

If you want to brave a play in Hungarian, go to the *József Katona Theatre* (Map 4; ☎ 318 3725, V Petőfi Sándor utca 6) for the best acting in the city, the *New Theatre* (Új Színház; Map 4; ☎ 351 1406, VI Paulay Ede utca 35) for the amazing Art Deco decor or the newly renovated *Thália* (Map 4; ☎ 312 4230, VI Nagymező 22-24).

You won't have to understand Hungarian to enjoy what's going on at the *Budapest Puppet Theatre* (Budapest Bábszínház; Map 4; ☎ 321 5200, VI Andrássy út 69). It presents shows designed for children during the day and occasional evening programs for adults.

Opera

You should pay at least one visit to the *Opera House* (Map 4; ☎ 353 0170 or 331 2550, VI Andrássy út 22) both to see a production and admire the murals and incredibly rich decoration inside. Tickets range in price from 300Ft to 3000Ft.

Budapest's second opera house, the modern (and ugly) *Erkel Theatre* (Map 1; 333 0108, VIII Köztársaság tér 30) south-west of Keleti train station. Tickets are sold just inside the main door (open from 11 am to 7 pm Tuesday to Saturday, from 10 am to 1 pm and 4 to 7 pm on Sunday).

Operettas – always a riot, especially one like the campy *Queen of the Csárdás* by Imre Kálmán – are presented at the *Budapest Operetta Theatre (Budapesti Operettszínház; Map 4;* ☎ *269 3870, VI Nagymező utca 17)*. Tickets are sold at the box office at No 19 (☎ 353 2172) of the same street (open 10 am to 6 pm weekdays).

Dance

Budapest's two ballet companies perform at the Opera House and the Erkel Theatre but you really want to be in Győr (see the Western Transdanubia chapter) to see world-class classical dance.

For modern dance fans, Budapest has a few good options. The best stage in which to see it is the *Trafó Kortárs Művészetek Háza (Trafó House of Contemporary Arts; Map 6;* ☎ *456 2040, IX Liliom utca 41)*, which has the cream of the crop, including a good pull of international acts, but everyone there got their start at *MU Színház (Map 6;* ☎ *209 4014 or 466 4627, XI Kőrösy utca 17)*. At the *Kamra (Chamber; Map 4;* ☎ *318 2487, V Ferenciek tere 4)*, the studio theatre of the József Katona Theatre, watch for performances by contemporary dance darling Yvette Bozsik.

The *Közép-Európai Táncszínház (Central European Dance Theatre; off Map 4;* ☎ *342 7163, VII Bethlen Gábor tér 3)* has both folk and contemporary performances. The *Thália Színház* (see the Theatre section) usually hosts the Honvéd dancers, one of the city's best folk troupes and now experimenting with modern choreography as well.

Folk Dancing Many people attend táncház evenings (see Folk & Traditional Music above) to learn the folk dances that go with the music, and you can become part of the program as well, instead of merely watching others perform. At the height of summer many of the main táncház mentioned earlier may not be taking place and you may have to seek them out in more remote locations.

To access the most up-to-date information, check the listings of the Dance Music Guild, a sub-section of just about any Hungary tourist information Web site under 'Folk'.

Every Monday and Friday from about May to mid-October at 8.30 pm, the much more Folklór Centrum presents a program of Hungarian dancing accompanied by a Gypsy orchestra at the Municipal Cultural House (see Folk & Traditional Music earlier in this section).

During the same period, the 30 dancers of the Hungarian State Folk Ensemble (Állami Népi Együttes) and two other groups perform at the *Puppet Theatre* (see the Theatre section), the *Budai Vigadó (Map 2; I Corvin tér 8)* in Buda, and the *Duna Palota (Map 4; V Zrínyi utca 5)*, just off Roosevelt tér in Pest, on alternative days. The 1½-hour programs begin at 8 pm daily and cost 3900/3500Ft for adults/students. Ring Hungaria Koncert (☎ 317 2754 or 201 5928) for information and bookings. The folk ensemble's Gypsy Orchestra performs at the Budai Vigadó at 8 pm on Monday from July to October (5000/4500Ft).

Circus

The *Municipal Grand Circus (Fővárosi Nagycirkusz; Map 5;* ☎ *343 9630, XIV Állatkerti körút 7, metro: Széchenyi fürdő)* has performances at 7.30 pm on Wednesday, at 3.30 and 7.30 pm on Thursday and Friday, at 10 am and 3.30 and 7.30 pm on Saturday and at 10 am and 3.30 pm on Sunday from mid-April to August. Although the matinees are occasionally booked out by school groups, there's almost always space in the evening. Advance tickets (400Ft to 800Ft) are sold at the circus itself.

SPECTATOR SPORT
Water Polo

Hungary has dominated the European water-polo championships for decades so it's worthwhile catching a professional or amateur match of this exciting seven-a-side sport. The Magyar Vízilabda Szövetség (Hungarian Water Polo Association) is based at the Alfréd Hajós National Sports

Pool (Map 3; ☎ 340 4946 or 239 3989) on Margaret Island and matches take place here and at two other pools – the Béla Komjádi (Map 3; ☎ 212 2750, II Árpád fejedelem útja) and the BVSC (off map 5; ☎ 251 v1670, XIV Szőnyi út) – during the spring and autumn seasons. Get a local Hungarian to look at the match schedule for you in the *Nemzeti Sport* (National Sport) daily (50Ft).

Football

Hungary's descent from being on top of the heap of world football to *a béka segge alatt*, or 'under the arse of the frog' as the Hungarians say to describe something *really* low, remains one of life's great mysteries. Hungary's defeat of the England team both at Wembley (6-3) in 1953 and at home (7-1) the following year, is still talked about as if the matches were yesterday.

There are four premier league football teams in Budapest out of a total 18 nationwide including: Kispest-Honvéd which plays at Bozsik stadium (☎ 282 9789); MTK at Hungária körút stadium (☎ 333 6758); and Újpesti TE at UFC stadium (☎ 369 7333). But none dominates Hungarian football like Ferencváros (FTC), the country's loudest and brashest team and its only hope. You either love the boys in white and green from Fradi or you hate them. Watch them play at FTC stadium (☎ 215 1013). The daily sports paper *Nemzeti Sport* has the game schedules.

Horse Racing

The descendants of the nomadic Magyars are keen about horse racing. For trotting, go to the Ügetőpálya (☎ 334 2958, VIII Kerepesi út 9), about 10 minutes south of Keleti train station via bus No 95. About 10 races are held on Saturday from 2 pm and on Wednesday from 4 pm. The Lóversenytér (☎ 263 7858, X Albertirsai út 2), which is also called the Galopp-pálya, has flat racing from 2 pm on Thursday and Sunday between April and November. It's in Kincsem Park about a 15-minute walk (follow the signs) south of the Pillangó utca metro station.

SHOPPING

Before you do any shopping for handicrafts at street markets, have a look in the Folkart Centrum (Map 4; ☎ 318 5840, V Váci utca 14), a large store where everything Magyar-made is available and prices are clearly marked. It's open daily from 9.30 am to 4 am (!) for all your chotchky needs. Another good bet is Judit (Map 2; ☎ 212 7050, I Tarnok utca 1) in the castle District.

In the far back corner, upstairs in the Nagycsarnok (see Food Markets & Self-Catering under Places to Eat) are a group of stalls where vendors sell Hungarian folk costumes, dolls, painted eggs, embroidered tablecloths, etc. Holló Atelier (Map 4; ☎ 317 8103, V Vitkovics Mihály utca 12), near Váci utca, has attractive folk art with a modern look and remains one of my favourite places.

If you don't have time to head all the way out to the Ecseri or Petőfi Csarnok flea markets (see the following section), check out any of the BÁV shops, essentially a chain of pawn and second-hand shops with several branches around town. Try VI Andrássy út 43 for old jewellery and bric-a-brac; V Bécsi utca 1-3 for knick-knacks, porcelain and glassware; and XIII Szent István körút 3 for chinaware and textiles (Map 4).

For fine porcelain, check out the Zsolnay (Map 4; ☎ 318 3712, V Kigyó utca 4) and Herend (Map 4; ☎ 317 2622, V József nádor tér 11) outlets. Haas & Czjzek (Map 4; ☎ 311 4094, VI Bajcsy-Zsilinszky út 23), just off Deák tér, sells more affordable Hungarian-made Hollóháza and Alföldi porcelain.

Herend Village Pottery (Map 2; ☎ 356 7899, II Bem rakpart 37) is an alternative to prissy, fragile flatware; it stocks ceramic pottery for the kitchen with bold fruit patterns.

There's an excellent selection of Hungarian wines at La Boutique des Vins (Map 4; ☎ 317 5919, V József Attila utca 12, but enter from Hild tér), which is owned by the former sommelier at Gundel. Ask the staff to recommend a label if you feel lost. Serious oenophiles, however, will travel to the Budapest Wine Society shop (Map 2; ☎ 212 0262, I Batthyány utca 59), south-east of Moskva tér. No one but no one knows Hungarian wines likes these guys. It's open from 10 am to 8 pm weekdays and to 6 pm on Saturday; and it offers free tastings on Saturday afternoon.

Flea Markets

Ecseri (XIX Nagykőrösi út 156), often just called the piac (market), is one of the biggest and best bolhapiac (flea markets) in Central Europe, selling everything from antique jewellery and Soviet army watches to old musical instruments and Fred Astaire-style top hats. It's open from 6 am to about 1 pm Tuesday to Saturday (the best day to go). To get there, take bus No 54 from Boráros tér in Pest near the Petőfi Bridge or, better, the red express bus No 54 from the Határ utca stop on the blue metro line and get off at the Fiume utca stop and walk over the pedestrian bridge.

The Petőfi Csarnok Bolhapiac (Map 5; ☎ 251 7266, XIV Zichy Mihály utca) is a huge outdoor flea market in City Park, a Hungarian boot or garage sale if you will. The usual diamonds-to-rust on offer – from old records and draperies to candles, honey and herbs. It's open from 7 am to 2 pm on Saturday and Sunday, though the latter is said to be the better day.

GETTING THERE & AWAY

Air

Malév Hungarian Airlines has its main ticket office (Map 4; ☎ 235 3565 or 266 5616) near Vörösmarty tér at V Dorottya utca 2. Other major carriers and locations include:

Aeroflot (☎ 318 5955) V Váci utca 4
Air Canada (☎ 317 9109) V Vörösmarty tér 6
Air France (☎ 318 0441) V Kristóf tér 6
Alitalia (☎ 373 7782) V Ferenciek tere 2
Austrian Airlines (☎ 327 9080) V Régiposta utca 5
British Airways (☎ 318 4041) VIII Rákóczi út 1-3
Delta Air Lines (☎ 294 4400) V Apáczai Csere János utca 4
KLM Royal Dutch Airlines (☎ 373 7737) VIII Rákóczi út 1-3
Lauda Air (☎ 266 3169) V Aranykéz utca 4-6
Lufthansa (☎ 266 4511) V Váci utca 19-21
SAS (☎ 266 2633) V Bajcsy-Zsilinszky út 12
Swissair (☎ 328 5000) V Kristóf tér 7-8

For more details see To/From the Airport in the Getting Around section.

Bus

There are three important bus stations in Budapest. Most buses to/from Western and Central Europe as well as several neighbouring countries and destinations in Hungary south and west of Budapest leave from the station at V Erzsébet tér (Map 4; ☎ 317 2562 for international inquiries, ☎ 317 2345 for domestic ones, metro: Deák tér). The international ticket office upstairs is open from 6 am to 7 pm weekdays and from 6.30 am to 4 pm on Saturday from June to August, to 6 pm weekdays and 4 pm Saturday the rest of the year. There's a left-luggage office inside the station open from 6 am to 7 pm daily (to 8 pm on Monday and Friday).

In general, buses to/from Eastern Europe as well as Greece and Turkey and destinations north and east of the capital leave from the bus station in Népstadion (Map 1; ☎ 252 1896 for international buses, ☎ 252 4498 for domestic ones), XIV Hungária körút 48-52 (metro: Népstadion). The international ticket office is open from 6 am to 6 pm weekdays, to 4 pm on Saturday. The left-luggage office here is open from 6 am to 6 pm daily.

Most buses to the Danube Bend and parts of the Northern Uplands (Balassagyarmat, Széchenny, etc) arrive at and leave from the Árpád híd bus station (Map 1; ☎ 329 1682 or 329 1450) just off XIII Róbert Károly körút on the Pest side of Árpád Bridge (metro: Árpád híd). A small bus station (Map 1; ☎ 201 3688) at I Széna tér 1/a (metro: Moszkva tér) in Buda handles some traffic to and from the Pilis Hills and towns north-west of the capital, including a few departures to Esztergom, as an alternative to the Árpád híd bus station. For details of international bus services, see the introductory Getting There & Away chapter.

Train

Budapest also has three main train stations. Keleti train station at Baross tér (Map 1; ☎ 314 5010 or 333 6342; metro: Keleti pályaudvar) handles most international trains and domestic ones to and from the north and north-east. Trains for some destinations in Romania as well as the Great Plain and the Danube Bend arrive and depart from Nyugati train station (Map 4; ☎ 349 0115; metro: Nyugati pályaudvar). For trains bound for Zagreb and Rijeka in Croatia as well as Transdanubia and Lake Balaton, go to Déli train station (Map 2; ☎ 375 6593 or 355 8657; metro Déli pályaudvar). The central number for international train information is ☎ 461 5500; for domestic train information it's ☎ 461 5400.

The handful of secondary train stations are of little importance to long-distance travellers. Very occasionally, though, a through train will stop at Kőbánya-Kispest train station (Map 1; ☎ 357 5754) in summer only, which is the terminus of the blue metro line, or Kelenföld train station (Map 1; ☎ 313 6835, tram No 19 or 49) in Buda.

The stations are pretty dismal places, with unsavoury-looking characters hanging about day and night, but all have some amenities. Keleti and Nyugati stations have left-luggage sections open round the clock and from 5 am to midnight respectively (140Ft to 280Ft), post offices and grocery stores that are open late or even round the clock. Déli has coin-operated lockers (200Ft) and a 24-hour convenience store nearby on I Alkotás utca.

All the stations are on metro lines, and there's a rail minibus service between stations (☎ 353 2722, 700Ft) for when the metro is closed. If you need to take a taxi, avoid the sharks hovering around. At Déli, cross over to I Alkotás utca and hail one there. At Keleti station, get into one of the legal cabs at the rank on VIII Kerepesi út, south of the terminal. Nyugati tér is a major intersection, so you'll have no problem finding a legitimate taxi.

You can buy tickets and reserve seats directly at all three stations, but the queues are often long, passengers are in a hurry and salespeople are not the most patient in the city. Many of the travel agencies listed in this chapter will get you train tickets, and you can buy advance tickets for express trains at MÁV's central ticket office (Map 4;

☎ 322 8082 or 461 5400), VI Andrássy út 35 (metro: Opera). It is open from 9 am to 6 pm weekdays from April to September and to 5 pm the rest of the year. It accepts credit cards though the train stations do not.

For more information about international train travel, see the introductory Getting There & Away chapter.

Car & Motorcycle

Prices at the big international car-rental firms in Budapest are very high. An Opel Corsa from Avis (Map 4; ☎ 318 4158, fax 318 4859), V Szervita tér 8, for example, costs US$222 a week plus US$0.37 per kilometre and US$20 a day insurance (CDW/TP). The same car with unlimited kilometres and insurance costs US$131 a day or US$158 for a weekend. The 25% ÁFA (value-added tax) doesn't apply to nonresidents paying with foreign currency or credit card.

One of the cheapest outfits for renting cars is Inka (Map 4; ☎ 317 2150, fax 318 1843, ✆ inka@mail.hungary.net) at V Bajcsy-Zsilinszky út 16 or XIII Váci út 41 (☎ 350 1091, fax 349 4154). An Opel Corsa here costs US$155 a week plus US$0.26 per kilometre and US$8 for insurance (or US$80 a day with unlimited kilometres or US$100 for a weekend. Though more expensive than Inka, Americana Rent-a-Car (Map 1; ☎ 320 8287, ✆ americana@mail.matav.hu), in the Ibis Volga at XIII Dózsa György út 65, is reliable and has American cars with automatic transmissions. A Suzuki Swift with unlimited kilometres costs US$49 a day or US$97 for a three-day weekend.

Assistance and/or advice for motorists is available 24 hours a day at the Magyar Autóklub (Map 3; ☎ 212 2821), II Rómer Flóris utca 4/a off Margit körút near Margaret Bridge. Motorists anywhere in Hungary can call the automobile club on ☎ 188.

For information on traffic and public road conditions in the capital ring Főinform on ☎ 317 1173.

Hitching

There's a service in Budapest called Kenguru (Map 4; ☎ 266 5837 or 338 2019,

@ kenguru@elender.hu), VIII Kőfaragó út 15 (metro: Blaha Lujza tér), that matches up drivers and riders for a fee – mostly to points abroad. Kenguru gets 2Ft per kilometre and the driver 6Ft. Sample one-way costs are: Amsterdam 11,050Ft, London 12,900Ft, Munich 5750Ft, Paris 11,750Ft, Prague 4250Ft and Vienna 2150Ft. Kenguru is open from 8 am till 6 pm weekdays and from 10 am to 2 pm at the weekend.

Boat

Mahart ferries and hydrofoils (Map 4; ☎ 318 1953, @ mahartpass@aux.net) to Vienna depart from the International Landing Stage (Nemzetközi hajóállomás) on V Belgrád rakpart, just north of Szabadság Bridge in Pest. For details of schedules and fares, see the introductory Getting There & Away chapter.

From early April to seasonal shutdown, Mahart river ferries link Budapest with Szentendre, Visegrád and Esztergom on the Danube Bend; see that chapter for details. In the capital the boats leave from the pier off V Vigadó tér (metro: Ferenciek tere) on the Pest side (Map 4; ☎ 318 1223). The first stop is usually I Batthyány tér on the Buda side, which is on the red metro line.

GETTING AROUND
To/From the Airport

There are two terminals side by side at Budapest's Ferihegy International Airport, which is 24km south-east of the capital. Malév flights arrive and depart from Ferihegy Terminal 2A; all other international airlines use Terminal 2B, which opened in late 1998. Terminal 2B has an ATM, car rental and hotel booking desks, a post office open from 8 am to 3.30 pm weekdays and a 24-hour left-luggage facility (250/800/5000Ft per hour/day/week).

With three much cheaper options for getting to/from Ferihegy (soon to be four – a light rail connecting Ferihegy with central Pest is under construction), it would be senseless to take a taxi and risk a major rip-off. If you do want to take a taxi, call one of the companies listed under Taxi below with a mobile phone or from a phonebox at arrivals; you'll save between 1000Ft and 1500Ft on the posted airport fares of 3900Ft to 4600Ft. The Tele 5 taxi company (☎ 355 5555) has a fare of 2555Ft to the airport from the city centre.

The Airport Minibus Service (☎ 296 8555 or 296 6283) picks up passengers wherever they're staying – be it hotel, hostel or private home. But there are drawbacks: you have to book 24 hours in advance on departure and, as the van seats eight people, it can be a time-consuming process (and nerve-wracking if you're running late). The fare is 1500/2500Ft one way/return per person. Tickets into the city are available in the airport arrivals hall.

An easier way to go is with the airport-run Centrum Bus (☎ 296 8555), which links V Erzsébet tér (board the bus outside the Kempinski Corvinus with both Ferihegy every half-hour between 5.30 am and 9.30 pm (6 am to 10 pm from the airport). The fare is 600Ft (pay on the bus), and you are advised to count on 30 to 40 minutes' travel.

The cheapest way to go in either direction is to take the blue metro to the end of the line (Kőbánya-Kispest station) and board bus No 93 (the one with the red number). Total cost at the moment: 180Ft.

The general flight information phone number at the airport is ☎ 296 9696 or 296 8000.

Public Transport

Budapest has an ageing but safe, inexpensive and efficient transport system that will never have you waiting more than five or 10 minutes. There are five types of vehicles in use: metro trains, green HÉV trains, blue buses, yellow trams and red trolleybuses.

Public transport in Budapest runs from 4.30 am till between 11.20 and 11.30 pm depending on the station. There are also about 16 night buses (marked with an 'É' after the designated number) running every half-hour or so on the main routes. After 8 pm, you must board buses from the front entrance and show the driver your ticket or pass.

Single Fares & Passes To travel on trams, trolleybuses, regular buses and the

HÉV (as far as the city limits, which is the Békásmegyer stop) you must have a ticket, which you can buy at kiosks, newsstands or metro entrances. The basic fare is 90Ft, allowing you to travel as far as you want on the same metro line without changing; it drops to 60Ft if you are just going three stops within 30 minutes. For 95Ft you can travel five stops and make a change (transfer) at Deák tér to another metro line within one hour. Unlimited stations travelled with one change within one hour is 135Ft. You must always travel in one continuous direction on a metro ticket; return trips are not allowed. Blocks of 10/20 single tickets cost 810/1500Ft.

You can get travelcards valid on all trams, buses, trolleybuses, HÉV (to the city limits) and metro lines for one day (700Ft) or three days (1400Ft). Others include a weekend family travelcard (two adults and two children under 14 1750Ft). None of these require a photograph. Seasonal passes good for a week (1650Ft), a fortnight (2250Ft) or a month (3400Ft) require a mug shot. All but the monthly passes are valid from midnight to midnight, so buy them in advance and specify the date(s) you want. The most central places to get them are at the Deák tér metro station and the Nyugati tér metro concourse.

Travelling 'black' (ticketless) is more risky than ever in Budapest; with increased surveillance (including a big crackdown in the metro), there's a good chance you'll get caught. Tickets are always checked on the HÉV. The on-the-spot fine is 1200Ft, which rises to 3000Ft if you pay later at the BKV office, VII Akácfa utca 22. It's your call, but if you do get nabbed, do us all a favour: shut up and pay up. The inspectors – and your fellow passengers – hear the same boring (and false) stories every day of the year.

Bus, Tram & Trolleybus There's an extensive network of tram, trolleybus and bus services run by the BKV (☎ 342 2335); you'll seldom wait more than a few minutes for any of them. On certain bus lines the same numbered bus may have a black or a red number. In this case, the red-numbered bus is the express, which makes limited stops and is faster. An invaluable transit map detailing all services is available at most metro ticket booths.

Buses and trams are much of a muchness, though the latter are often faster and generally more pleasant for sightseeing. Trolley buses go along cross-streets in central Pest and are of little use to most visitors, with the sole exception of the ones to the City and Népliget Parks.

The most important tram lines (always marked red on a Budapest map) are:

- Nos 2 and 2/a, scenic trams that travel along the Pest side of the Danube as far as Jászai Mari tér
- Nos 4 and 6, which start at Fehérvári út and Móricz Zsigmond körtér in district XI (southern Buda) respectively and follow the entire length of the Big Ring Road in Pest before terminating at Moszkva tér
- No 18, which runs from southern Buda along Bartók Béla út through the Tabán to Moszkva tér
- No 19, which covers part of the same route but then runs along the Buda side of the Danube to Batthyány tér
- Nos 47 and 49 linking Deák tér in Pest with points in southern Buda
- No 61 connecting Móricz Zsigmond körtér with Déli station and Moszkva tér

Buses you might take are:

- the black No 4, which runs from northern Pest via Heroes' Square to Deák tér (the red No 4 follows the same route but crosses over Chain Bridge into central Buda)
- No 7, which cuts across a large swathe of central Pest and southern Buda from Bosnyák tér and down Rákóczi út to Kelenföld station in southern Buda
- No 86, which runs the length of Buda from Kosztolányi Dezső tér to Óbuda
- No 105 from Heroes' Square to Deák tér

The 6É night bus follows the route of tram No 6 along the Big Ring Road and the No 14É follows the line of the blue metro.

Metro (see Metro Map) Budapest has three underground metro lines intersecting (only) at Deák tér: M1, the little yellow line from Vörösmarty tér to Mexikói út; M2, the red line from Déli train station to Örs vezér tere; and M3, the blue line from Újpest-Központ to Kőbánya-Kispest. A possible source of confusion on the yellow line (no-

one calls it the 'M1') is that one stop is called Vörösmarty tér and another is Vörösmarty utca. The metro is the fastest (but obviously the least scenic) way to go. Though it only has three stops in Buda, the green HÉV suburban railway functions almost

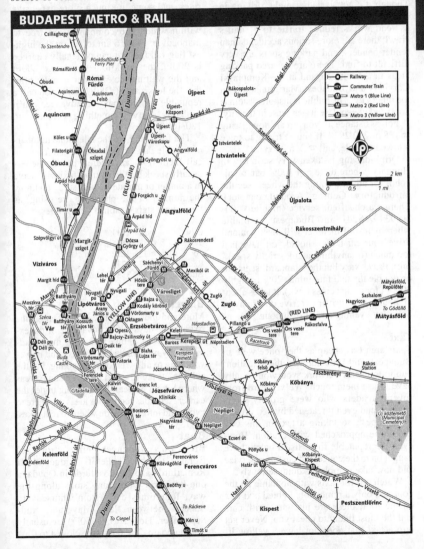

BUDAPEST METRO & RAIL

Legend:
- Railway
- Commuter Train
- Metro 1 (Blue Line)
- Metro 2 (Red Line)
- Metro 3 (Yellow Line)

0   1   2 km
0   0.5   1 mi

like a fourth metro line. It has four lines, but only one is of real use to most travellers: from Batthyány tér in Buda via Óbuda and Aquincum to Szentendre.

Car & Motorcycle

Though it's not so bad at night, driving in Budapest during the day can be a nightmare as road works reduce traffic to a snail's crawl; there are more serious accidents than fender-benders; and parking spots are very difficult to find. There are covered parking areas in Szervita tér and at the Kempinski Corvinus and Budapest Marriott hotels in the inner city. The public transport system is good and cheap. Use it – at least in the city.

For assistance if you break down, ring ☎ 188 or 212 2938. If you're trying to trace a towed vehicle, call ☎ 286 0163.

Drink-driving is taken very seriously in Hungary, where there is a 100% ban on alcohol for anyone taking the wheel (see the introductory Getting Around chapter). There's a chauffeur service (mobile ☎ 06-30-9349 824) in Budapest available whereby a staff member will meet you and drive your car home should you have had too much (or anything at all, strictly speaking). Prices vary but the 'standard' seems to be double the taxi fare minus 20% (roughly 2000Ft for a trip across town). It takes about an hour for the driver to arrive on Friday or Saturday evening and at rush hour.

Taxi

Taxis aren't as cheap as they once were in Budapest and, considering the excellent public transport network, you won't really have to use them much. We've heard from several readers who were grossly overcharged and even threatened by taxi drivers in Budapest, so taking a taxi in this city should be approached with caution. However, the reputable firms listed below have caught on to the concept of customer service and now take complaints quite seriously.

Watch out for taxis with no name on the door and only a removable lighted taxi box on the roof; these are just guys with cars and the most likely to cheat you. Never get into a taxi that does not have a yellow li-

cence plate and an identification badge displayed on the dashboard (required by law), the logo of one of the reputable taxi firms we list on the side doors and a table of fares posted on the dashboard inside.

Not all taxi meters are set at the same rates, and some are much more expensive than others, but there are price ceilings within which cab companies are free to manoeuvre. From 6 am to 10 pm the highest flag-fall fee that can be legally charged is 200Ft, the per-kilometre charge 200Ft and the waiting fee 50Ft per minute; after that the fees are 280/280/70Ft. If you call a reputable cab company in advance, you'll probably pay something closer to 120/160/50Ft.

The following are the telephone numbers of reliable taxi firms in Budapest. You can call them from anywhere (the dispatchers usually speak English), and a taxi will arrive in a matter of minutes. Make sure you know the number of the phone you're using, as that's how staff establish your address.

City	☎ 211 1111
Tele 5	☎ 355 5555
Fő	☎ 222 2222
Rádió	☎ 377 7777
Buda	☎ 233 3333

Bicycle

More and more cyclists can be seen on the roads these days taking advantage of the excellent network of bike paths. The main roads in the city might be a bit too busy and nerve-wracking to allow enjoyable cycling, but the side streets are fine and there are some areas where biking is ideal. See Cycling under the earlier Activities section for ideas on where to cycle, and information on where to rent bikes.

Boat

BKV runs passenger ferries from IX Boráros tér, beside Petőfi Bridge, to III Rómaifürdő and Pünkösdfürdő in Óbuda, a one-hour trip with many stops along the way, four times daily from Thursday to Sunday between late May and mid-September. Tickets (300/150Ft) are usually sold on board. The ferry stop closest to Castle Hill is I Batthyány tér, and V Petőfi tér is not far from Vörösmarty tér, a convenient place to pick up the boat on the Pest side.

See Boat under the previous Organised Tours section for information about river cruises.

Around Budapest

Let's be honest: an awful lot in Hungary is 'around Budapest' and many of the towns and cities in the Danube Bend, Transdanubia, Northern Uplands and even the Great Plain could be day trips from the capital. You can be in Szentendre (19km) in a half-hour, for example, and Gyöngyös, the gateway to the bucolic Mátra Hills, is only 80km to the east. But here are four easy day or even half-day trips from the capital.

STATUE PARK

A truly mind-blowing experience is a visit to Statue Park (Szobor Park; ☎ 227 7446) in district XXII, home to three dozen busts, statues and plaques of Lenin, Marx, Béla Kun and 'heroic' workers that have ended up on trash heaps in other former socialist countries. Ogle at the socialist realism and try to imagine that at least four of these monstrous monuments were erected as recently as the late 1980s; many were still in place when I first moved to Budapest in early 1992. The shop at the entrance sells fabulously kitsch communist memorabilia, statues, pins and tapes.

Statue Park is at the corner of XXII Szabadkai út and Balatoni út (the old route No 7 towards Lake Balaton). It can be reached on the yellow bus to Érd, which can be boarded from bay No 6 at the little station on the south side of XI Kosztolányi Dezső tér in Buda; get there from Pest on bus No 7 (black number). The park is open from 10 am to dusk daily from March to December and at the weekend only in January and February (250/150Ft; family 400Ft).

RÁCKEVE

☎ 24 • postcode 2300 • pop 8100

The lures of this town on the south-east end of Csepel Island, the long island in the Danube south of Budapest, are its pretty riverside park and strand, a Gothic Serbian Orthodox church (rác is the old Hungarian word for 'Serb') and the former Savoy Mansion, now a lovely hotel.

Savoy Mansion

From the HÉV station in Ráckeve, walk south along Kossuth Lajos utca to the Savoy Mansion (Savoyai-kastély), now a 30-room hotel at No 95, which faces the Ráckeve-Danube River branch. The domed manse with two wings was built in 1702 for Prince Eugene of Savoy by an Austrian architect who would later design the Schönbrunn Palace in Vienna. The mansion was completely renovated and turned into a pricey hotel and conference centre in 1982.

Serbian Orthodox Church

As you carry on south toward the centre of town, you can't miss the blue belfry of the Serbian Orthodox Church (Görög-keleti szerb templom) to the west at Viola utca 1. The church was originally built in 1487 by Serbs who fled their town of Keve ahead of the invading Turks. It was enlarged in the following century. The free-standing clock tower was added in 1758.

The walls and ceiling of the church interior are covered with colourful murals painted by a Serbian master from Albania in the mid-18th century. The walls depict scenes from the Old and New Testaments and were meant to teach the Bible to illiterate parishioners. The first section of the nave is reserved for women; the part beyond the separating wall is for men. Only the priest and his servers enter the sanctuary beyond the iconostasis, the richly carved and gilded gate festooned with icons.

The church is open from 10 am till noon and 2 till 5 pm Tuesday to Saturday and from 2 pm on Sunday.

Places to Eat

Unless you have the dosh to stay at the hotel, the closest you'll get inside the Savoy Manor is the *Pince* cellar restaurant. The *Fekete Holló* restaurant and cellar bar (*Kos-*

suth Lajos utca 129) is in a renovated 16th-century townhouse in the centre of town.

Getting There & Away

The easiest way to reach Ráckeve, about 40km south of Budapest, is on the HÉV suburban train departing from the Közvágóhíd terminus in district IX on the Buda side. You can get to that station on tram No 2 or from Keleti train station on tram No 24. The HÉV trip takes about 1¼ hours. The last HÉV train back to Budapest leaves Ráckeve at about 11.20 pm.

MARTONVÁSÁR

☎ 22 • postcode 2462 • pop 4350

Lying almost exactly halfway between Székesfehérvár and Budapest and easily accessible by train, Martonvásár is the site of **Brunswick Mansion** (Brunszvik-kastély), one of the loveliest summertime concert venues in Hungary. The mansion was built in 1775 for Count Antal Brunswick (Magyarised as Brunszvik), the patriarch of a family of liberal reformers and patrons of the arts (Teréz Brunszvik established Hungary's first nursery school in Pest in 1828).

Beethoven was a frequent visitor to the manse, and it is believed that Jozefin, Teréz's sister, was the inspiration behind the *Appassionata* and *Moonlight* sonatas, which the great Ludwig van composed here.

Brunswick Mansion, at Brunszvik út 2 just off Dózsa György utca, was rebuilt in neo-Gothic style in 1875 and restored to its ivory and sky-blue glory another century later. It now houses the Agricultural Research Institute of the Academy of Sciences, but you can see at least part of the mansion by visiting the small **Beethoven Memorial Museum** (Beethoven Emlékmúzeum) to the left of the main entrance. It is open from 10 am to noon and 2 to 4 pm Tuesday to Sunday (80/40Ft).

A walk around the grounds – one of Hungary's first 'English parks' to be laid out when these were all the rage in the early 19th century – is a pleasant way to spend a warm summer's afternoon. It's open every day from 8 am to 4 pm (80/40Ft). Concerts are held on the small island in the middle of the lake (reached by a wooden footbridge) during the Martonvásár Summer (Martonvásári Nyár) festival from May to October. The climax is the 10-day Martonvásár Days (Martonvásár Napok) festival in late July. For information contact Tourinform in Székesfehérvár.

The baroque **Catholic church**, attached to the mansion but accessible from outside the grounds, has frescoes by Johannes Cymbal. There's also a small **Nursery Museum** (Óvodamúzeum) in the park open the same hours as the Beethoven museum.

Places to Eat

In the centre, the *Postakocsi* restaurant (*Fehérvári utca 1*) is a convenient place for lunch and has courtyard seating. The restaurant at the *Macska (Cat)* pension (*Budai út 21*), just north of town, serves not feline under glass but the standard Hungarian csárda dishes and has a good wine cellar.

Getting There & Away

Dozens of trains between Budapest-Déli and Székesfehérvár stop at Martonvásár every day and, if you attend a concert, you can easily make your way back to Velence town and Székesfehérvár or on to Budapest on the last trains (11.17 pm and 11.23 pm respectively). The station is a 10-minute walk along Brunszvik út, north-west of the main entrance to the mansion.

GÖDÖLLŐ

☎ 28 • postcode 2100 • pop 28,200

Just 29km north-east of the Belváros and easily accessible on the HÉV, Gödöllő (pronounced, very roughly, 'GOOD-duh-ler') is an easy day trip from Budapest. The main draw here is the Royal Mansion, which rivaled Esterházy Palace at Fertőd in Western Transdanubia (see that chapter) in splendour and size when it was completed in the 1760s, but the town itself, full of lovely baroque buildings and monuments and home to the seminal Gödöllő Artists' Colony (1901-20) is worth the trip alone. For information contact Tourinform (☎ 415 402, ✆ godollo@tourinform.hu) at the entrance to the Royal Mansion.

Royal Mansion

Construction of the Royal Mansion (Királyi Kastély; ☎ 410 124), Szabadság tér 1, sometimes called the Grassalkovich Mansion after its commissioner, Antal Grassalkovich, count and confidante of Empress Maria Theresa, was designed by Antal Mayerhoffer in 1741. After the formation of the Dual Monarchy, the mansion (or palace) was enlarged as a summer retreat for Emperor Franz Joseph and soon became the favoured residence of his consort, the much beloved Habsburg empress and Hungarian queen, Elizabeth (1837-98) affectionately known as Sissy. Between the two world wars, the regent, Admiral Miklós Horthy, also spent time here regularly, but after the communist takeover, part of the mansion was used as an old people's home and as temporary housing. The rest was left to decay.

Partial renovation of the mansion began in 1994 and today more than a dozen rooms are open to the public. The rooms have been restored (some would say too heavily) to when the imperial couple were in residence, and Franz Joseph's suites (done up in manly greys and golds) and Sissy's lavender-coloured private apartments are impressive, if not as evocative of the past as the rooms at the Esterházy Palace. Check out the **Decorative Hall** (Díszterem), all gold tracery and chandeliers, where chamber music concerts are held in July; **Elizabeth's salon**, with a Romantic-style oil painting of Sissy repairing the cloak of St Stephen with needle and thread; and the **study annexe**, with a restored ceiling painting and an 18th-century tapestry of the huntress Diana.

The mansion is open from 10 am to 6 pm Tuesday to Sunday from April to October and to 5 pm the rest of the year. Entry to the reconstructed rooms costs 250/150Ft for adults/students and seniors and a guide costs 350Ft per hour. A guided tour that also includes rooms and outbuildings not yet reconstructed (the palace chapel, theatre, stables, etc) costs 400/250Ft.

Places to Eat

Tourinform at the palace has sample menus from restaurants around town and distributes discount vouchers. Two convenient and inexpensive pizzerias are *Carnevale* (*Dózsa György utca 12*) and *Pizza Joe* (*Szabadság tér 2*), both a short distance north of the palace car park. For decent Hungarian dishes, try the nearby *Pelikán* (*Kossuth Lajos utca 31*).

Getting There & Away

HÉV trains from Örs vezér tere at the terminus of the red metro link Budapest with Gödöllő (45 minutes) about once every half-hour throughout the day. Make sure you get off at the Szabadság tér stop, which is the third from the last. In addition, buses leave Népstadion about every 30 minutes for Gödöllő.

Other destinations served by bus and their daily frequencies include Eger (one to three), Gyöngyös (nine), Hatvan (half-hourly), Jászberény (three to five), Szolnok (one or two) and Vác (six). The bus station is on Szabadság út, some 600m north-east of the palace.

Danube Bend

The Danube (Hungarian: Duna), the second-longest river in Europe after the Volga, rises in the Black Forest in south-western Germany and flows eastward until it reaches a point about 40km north of Budapest. Here the Börzsöny Hills on the left bank and the Pilis Hills on the right force it to bend sharply southward through Budapest and the rest of Hungary for just more than 400km before it again resumes its easterly flow, finally emptying into the Black Sea in Romania.

The Danube Bend (Dunakanyar) is, strictly speaking, the S-shaped curve that begins just below Esztergom and twists for 20km past Visegrád to where it splits in two, forming the long and narrow Szentendre Island. But the name has come to describe the entire region of peaks, resorts and river towns to the north and north-west of the capital. The Bend is the most beautiful stretch of the Danube along its entire course of almost 3000km and should not be missed.

The right bank (that is, the area south and west of the Danube) has the lion's share of the Bend's historical towns and parkland. This was the northernmost region of Rome's colonies; Esztergom was the first seat of the Magyar kings and has been the centre of Roman Catholicism in the region for more than a millennium.

Visegrád was Central Europe's 'Camelot' and the royal seat during Hungary's short-lived flirtation with the Renaissance in the 15th century. Szentendre, which has its origins in Serbian culture, is an important centre for art and culture. And then there's the Pilis Park Forest, once a royal hunting ground, and the Visegrád Hills which, together with the Börzsöny Protected Area on the opposite bank, form the new 51,500-hectare Danube-Ipoly National Park.

The river's left bank (north and east of the Danube) is far less developed, though the ancient town of Vác and, of course, the hills, gorges and trails of the Börzsöny have much to offer visitors.

HIGHLIGHTS

- The medieval hilltop citadel at Visegrád with its wonderful views of the Danube
- A trip by ferry from Budapest to Szentendre, Visegrád or even Esztergom
- The splendid Gothic altarpieces and paintings at the Christian Museum in Esztergom
- The Margit Kovács Museum of ceramic art in Szentendre
- A visit to the Vácrátót arboretum on a warm spring afternoon
- Any of a number of hikes in the Börzsöny Hills from 12th-century Nográd Castle

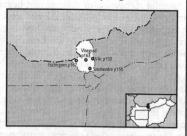

SZENTENDRE
☎ 26 • postcode 2000 • pop 19,350

Just 19km north of Budapest, Szentendre (St Andrew) is the southern gateway to the Danube Bend. As an art colony turned lucrative tourist centre, Szentendre strikes many as a little too 'cute', and the town can be crowded and relatively expensive. Still, it's an easy train trip from the capital, and the town's dozens of art museums, galleries and churches are well worth the trip. Just try to avoid it at weekends in summer.

Like most towns along the Danube Bend, Szentendre was home first to the Celts and then the Romans, who built an important border fortress here called Ulcisia Castra (Wolf's Castle). The area was overrun by a succession of tribes during the Great Migrations until the Magyars arrived late in the 9th century and established a colony here. By the 14th century, Szentendre was a prosperous estate under the supervision of the royal castle at Visegrád.

It was about this time that the first wave of a people who would build most of Szentendre's churches and give the town its unique Balkan feel, the Serbian Orthodox Christians, came from the south in advance of the Turks. They settled here, and many were employed as boatmen and border soldiers under King Matthias Corvinus. But the Turkish occupation of Hungary brought this peaceful coexistence to an end, and by the end of the 17th century Szentendre was deserted. Though Hungary was liberated from the Ottomans not long afterward, fighting continued in the Balkans and a second wave of Serbs, together with Greeks, Dalmatians and others, fled to Szentendre. Believing they would eventually return home, but enjoying complete religious freedom under the relatively benevolent rule of the Habsburgs (a right denied Hungary's Protestants at the time), a half-dozen Orthodox clans each built their own wooden churches.

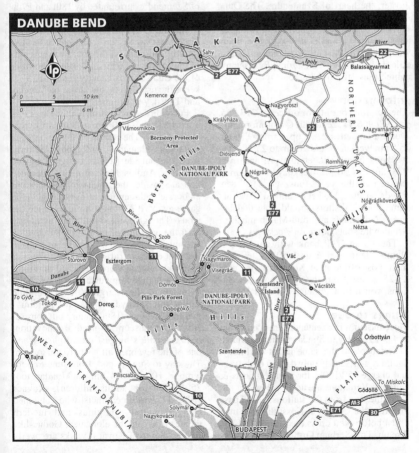

DANUBE BEND

Szentendre's delightful location began to attract day-trippers and painters from Budapest early in the 20th century; an artists' colony was established here in the 1920s. It has been known for its art and artists ever since.

Orientation

The HÉV commuter train and bus stations lie side by side south of the town centre at the start of Dunakanyar körút (Danube Bend Ring Road). From here walk through the subway and north along Kossuth Lajos utca, veer right into Dumtsa Jenő utca onto Fő tér, the heart of Szentendre. The Duna korzó promenade along the Danube and the ferry to Szentendre Island are a few minutes' walk east and north-east respectively of Fő tér. The Mahart ferry pier is about a kilometre north-east on Czóbel Béla sétány, which runs off Duna korzó.

Information

The helpful Tourinform office (☎ 317 965, fax 317 966, @ szentendre@tourinform.hu), Dumtsa Jenő utca 22, is open from 9.30 am to 5 pm weekdays and 10 am to 2 pm at the weekend from October to April and from 9.30 am to 4.30 pm weekdays only during the rest of the year. Ibusz (☎ 310 181), Bogdányi utca 11, keeps almost the exact same hours. Visitors should note that between November and mid-March much of Szentendre shuts down on weekdays.

There's an OTP bank with an ATM at Dumtsa Jenő utca 6, just off Fő tér. The main post office is at Kossuth Lajos utca 23-25 across from the HÉV and bus stations; you'll find a branch at Fő tér 15.

Things to See

Most museums in Szentendre are open 10 am to 4 pm Tuesday to Sunday from mid-March to October and the same hours on Friday, Saturday and Sunday only the rest of the year and charge 150/100Ft for adults/students & children. Variations are noted below.

On the way from the stations, you'll pass **Požarevačka Church** at Kossuth Lajos utca 1 just before you cross the narrow Bükkös Stream. This Serbian Orthodox church was dedicated in 1763; the lovely iconostasis inside (1742) is the oldest in Szentendre. The church is open for visitors from 11 am to 5 pm Friday to Sunday (80Ft).

To the north, the **Sts Peter and Paul Church** at Péter-Pál utca 6 off Dumtsa Jenő utca began life as the Čiprovačka Orthodox Church in 1753, but was later taken over by Dalmatian Catholics. The **Barcsay Collection** (Barcsay Gyüjtemény), to the east at Dumtsa Jenő utca 10, contains the work of one of the founders of Szentendre's art colony, Jenő Barcsay (1900-88).

In the centre of **Fő tér**, the colourful heart of Szentendre surrounded by 18th and 19th-century burghers' houses, stands the **Memorial Cross** (1763), an iron cross decorated with icons on a marble base. The **Kmetty Museum** on the south-western side of the square at Fő tér 21 displays the work of the Cubist János Kmetty (1889-1975). It keeps the usual hours but closes on Monday and Tuesday in summer.

For a little less rational thought, cross over the square to **Blagoveštenska Church**, built in 1754. The church, with fine baroque and rococo elements, hardly looks 'eastern' from the outside (it was designed by the architect András Mayerhoffer), but once you are inside, the ornate iconostasis and elaborate 18th-century furnishings give the game away. It's interesting to examine the icons. Though painted only half a century after the ones in Požarevačka Church, they are much more realistic and seem to have lost that other-world spiritual feel.

If you descend Görög utca and turn right onto Vastagh György utca, you'll reach the entrance to the **Margit Kovács Ceramic Collection** (Kovács Margit Kerámiagyüjtemény) in an 18th-century salt house at No 1. The museum, in need of renovation, is Szentendre's biggest crowd-pleaser and one of the few open all year (10 am to 6 pm Tuesday to Sunday and, from June to September, 10 am to 4 pm on Monday too; 250/150Ft for adults/children). Kovács (1902-77) was a ceramicist who combined Hungarian folk, religious and modern themes to create the elongated, Gothic-like figures. Some of Kovács' works are overly

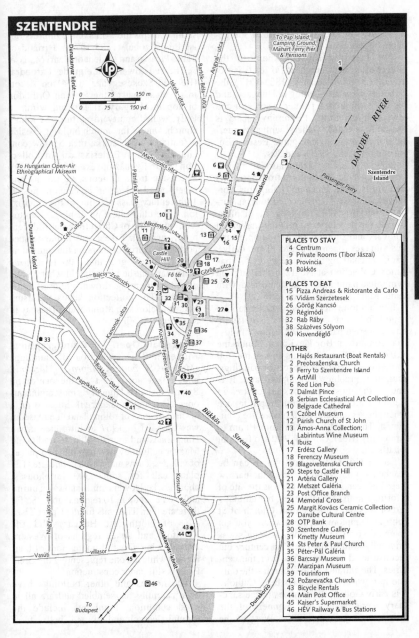

SZENTENDRE

PLACES TO STAY
4 Centrum
9 Private Rooms (Tibor Jászai)
33 Provincia
41 Bükkös

PLACES TO EAT
15 Pizza Andreas & Ristorante da Carlo
16 Vidám Szerzetesek
26 Görög Kancsó
29 Régimódi
32 Rab Ráby
38 Százéves Sólyom
40 Kisvendéglő

OTHER
1 Hajós Restaurant (Boat Rentals)
2 Preobraženska Church
3 Ferry to Szentendre Island
5 ArtMill
6 Red Lion Pub
7 Dalmát Pince
8 Serbian Ecclesiastical Art Collection
10 Belgrade Cathedral
11 Czóbel Museum
12 Parish Church of St John
13 Ámos-Anna Collection;
   Labirintus Wine Museum
14 Ibusz
17 Erdész Gallery
18 Ferenczy Museum
19 Blagoveštenska Church
20 Steps to Castle Hill
21 Artéria Gallery
22 Metszet Galéria
23 Post Office Branch
24 Memorial Cross
25 Margit Kovács Ceramic Collection
27 Danube Cultural Centre
28 OTP Bank
30 Szentendre Gallery
31 Kmetty Museum
34 Sts Peter & Paul Church
35 Péter-Pál Galéria
36 Barcsay Museum
37 Marzipan Museum
39 Tourinform
42 Požarevačka Church
43 Bicycle Rentals
44 Main Post Office
45 Kaiser's Supermarket
46 HÉV Railway & Bus Stations

sentimental, but many are very powerful, especially the later ones in which she became obsessed with mortality.

The **Ferenczy Museum** next to the Blagoveštenska Church at Fő tér 6 is devoted to Károly Ferenczy (1862-1917), the father of *plein air* painting in Hungary, and his three children: a painter, a sculptor and a weaver. Just north, at Bercsényi utca 3, is the sublime **Erdész Gallery**, with a wonderful collection of avante-garde Eastern European art of the 1920s and 30s.

Bogdányi utca, Szentendre's busiest pedestrian street, leads north from here. The **Labirintus Wine Museum** (Labirintus Bormúzeum) at No 10, connected to a restaurant, charges 100Ft to look at displays tracing the development of wine-making in Hungary and another 700Ft to sample various vintages (open 10 am to 11 pm daily). Far more challenging is the excellent **Anna-Ámos Collection** at No 12 displaying the symbolist paintings of husband and wife team, Margit Anna & Imre Ámos.

In a bid to recapture its past as a serious centre for artists and the arts, Szentendre has converted part of a 19th-century industrial complex at Bogdányi utca 32 into the **ArtMill** (MűvészetMalom), with some 700 sq metres of exhibition space for paintings, sculpture, graphics and applied arts. It is one of the most ambitious art centres in Central Europe and will quadruple in size when the second and third phases are completed. The ArtMill is open from 10 am to 6 pm daily (free); call ☎ 319 128 to find out what's on.

Castle Hill (Vár-domb), which can be reached via the Váralja lépcső, the narrow steps between Fő tér 8 and 9, was the site of a fortress in the Middle Ages, but all that's left of it is the walled **Parish Church of St John** in Templom tér, from where you get splendid views of the town. St John's was originally built in the late 13th century but reconstructed several times over the centuries. The entrance to the church – the only one in town that has always been Catholic – is early Gothic; the frescoes in the sanctuary were painted by members of the artists' colony in the 1930s. West of the

church at Templom tér 1, the **Czóbel Museum** contains the works of the impressionist Béla Czóbel (1883-1976), a friend of Pablo Picasso and student of Henri Matisse.

The red tower of **Belgrade Cathedral** (Belgrád Székesegyház; 1764) on Alkotmány utca, seat of the Serbian Orthodox bishop in Hungary, rises from within a leafy, walled courtyard north of St John's church. One of the church buildings beside it (entrance at Pátriárka utca 5) now contains the **Serbian Ecclesiastical Art Collection** (Szerb Egyházművészeti Gyűjtemény), a treasure trove of icons, vestments and other sacred objects in precious metals. A 14th-century glass painting of the crucifixion is the oldest item on display; a 'cotton icon' of the life of Christ from the 18th century is unusual. Take a look at the defaced portrait of Christ upstairs on the right-hand wall. The story goes that a drunken *kuruc* mercenary slashed it and, told what he had done next morning, drowned himself in the Danube. The collection keeps the usual hours but closes on Monday and Tuesday in summer (100/50Ft).

Hungarian Open-Air Ethnographical Museum

This collection of buildings (*Magyar Szabadtéri Néprajzi Múzeum*), about 3km north-west of the centre on Sztaravodai út, is Hungary's most ambitious open-air museum (*skanzen*). Situated on a 46-hectare tract of rolling land, the museum was founded in 1967 to introduce urban Hungarians and tourists alike to traditional Magyar culture by bringing bits and pieces of villages, farms and towns to one site. The plans call for some 300 farmhouses, churches, bell towers, mills and so on ultimately to be set up in 10 regional units. So far there are four. The units for the Upper Tisza area of North-East Hungary and the Kisalföld and Őrség regions of Western Transdanubia give full impressions of their regions while the one representing the Great Plain is still under construction.

The houses and other buildings have been carefully reassembled and are all in good condition; highlights include the Calvinist church and 'skirted' belfry from the Erdőhát of the North-East, the German 'long house' from Harka outside Sopron, the curious heart-shaped gravestones from the Buda Hills and the lovely whitewashed facade of the thatched house from Sükösd on the Great Plain. Craftspeople and artisans do their thing on the first and third Sunday of each month and on holidays, and the open-air museum hosts festivals throughout the season (see the following Special Events section). For information ring ☎ 312 304 or visit the museum's Web site at www.sznm.hu.

The museum is open from 9 am to 5 pm Tuesday to Sunday from mid-March to October. Entry costs 350/150Ft or 800Ft for a family ticket.

Activities

Pap Island (Pap-sziget), 2km north of the centre, is Szentendre's playground and has a grassy strand for sunbathing, a swimming pool (open from 8 am to 7 pm daily from May to September), tennis courts and rowing boats for hire.

You can rent bicycles from the Holdas Udvar next to the post office at Kossuth Lajos utca 19; take the hourly ferry across to Szentendre Island to enjoy many kilometres of uncrowded cycling paths. The Hajós restaurant on a boat moored in the Danube north of the centre rents boats and jet skis.

Places to Stay

Szentendre is so close to Budapest that there's no point in spending the night here unless you want to continue on to other towns on the Danube Bend without backtracking. What little is on offer in the centre of town can be expensive in season.

Some 2km north of Szentendre on Pap Island is *Pap-sziget Camping* (☎ *310 697, fax 313 777*), where two people and a tent pay 1000Ft to 1200Ft and a *bungalow* for four people with bath costs 7000Ft. Also on Pap Island is a 20-room *motel* with rooms for three/four people and shared bath for 3000/3300Ft; and the *Paprika* pension which costs 4000/4500Ft for a double/triple. All prices include admission to the swimming pool next door; other facilities include

a small supermarket, a snack bar and a restaurant. Pap-sziget Camping is open from May to mid-October.

Ibusz can organise private rooms in town for 1500Ft to 2000Ft per person. Readers have recommended the private rooms let by *Tibor Jászai* (☎ *310 657, Céh utca 3*), 400m north-west of Fő tér, and there are a lot more rooms available on this street.

The *Centrum* (☎ *302 500, fax 315 151, Bogdányi utca 15*) is just a few minutes walk from Fő tér and overlooks the Danube and Duna korzó (where the main entrance is actually located). A double without breakfast is DM60.

Farther afield, the *Apollo* pension (☎ *310 909, fax 313 777, Méhész utca 3*), just off the ring road, has six double rooms with shower for DM45. The nearby *Cola* (☎/fax *310 410, Dunakanyar körút 50*), with 12 terraced rooms, charges from 6200/8500Ft for a double/triple.

The friendly 16-room *Bükkös* (☎ *312 021, fax 310 782, Bükkös part 16*), halfway between the bus and HÉV stations and Fő tér, is more like a pension than a hotel but what's in a name? Singles/doubles with bath are 7150/8500Ft. The 24-room *Provincia* (☎ *301 081, fax 301 085, Paprikabíró utca 21-23*) is a not-unattractive, modern structure hard up against the noisy ring road with singles/doubles for DM97/100.

Places to Eat

There are *food stalls* at the bus and HÉV stations – very convenient if you're going directly on to the open-air museum, where the choice is limited to a pricey restaurant called the *Öregpatak* (Old Stream). A cheap Hungarian restaurant on the way into town is the *Kisvendéglő* (Jókai Mór tér) just over the Bükkös Stream.

The *Régimódi* (Dumtsa Jenő utca 2), just down from the Margit Kovács museum, occupies an old Szentendre house. Another old stand-by is the *Rab Ráby* (Kucsera Ferenc utca 1), housed in an 18th-century smithy and wine press.

There are a couple of Italian places along the Danube. *Ristorante da Carlo* (Duna korzó 6-8) is a relatively expensive restaurant with tables outside in summer, while *Pizza Andreas (Duna korzó No 5/a)* is a simpler affair. The ambitiously named *Görög Kancsó (Greek Jug; Görög utca 1)* manages tsatsiki and Greek salads but serves mostly standard (and pricey) Hungarian fare.

The *Vidám Szerzetesek (Merry Monks; Bogdányi utca 3-5)* is a pretty touristy restaurant, but it has outside tables in summer and you're sure to make yourself understood here: the menu is written in 19 languages. The new kid in town is the posh *Százéves Sólyom (Dumtsa Jenő utca),* opposite the Marzipan Museum at No 12. The 'Centenary Falcon' serves upmarket Hungarian dishes at Budapest prices: 800Ft to 1600Ft for main courses.

Entertainment
The *Danube Cultural Centre (☎ 312 647, Duna korzó 11/a)* stages theatrical performances, concerts and folk dance gatherings and can tell you what's on elsewhere in Szentendre. The *Dalmát Pince (Malom utca 5),* up the steps from Bogdányi utca, is a music coffee house and bar with blues, jazz and folk programs almost every night in season. The *Red Lion* pub *(Szerb utca 2/1),* just off Bogdányi utca, has five beers on tap.

Things to Buy
Szentendre is a shopper's town – from souvenir embroidery to the latest fashions – and although prices are at Budapest levels, not everything you see is available in the capital. For glassware and ceramics, try the Péter-Pál Galeria at Péter-Pál utca 1. The Metszet Gallery at Fő tér 15 has wonderful old engravings, maps and prints. For fine art, try the Szentendre Gallery at Fő tér 20 or the Artéria Gallery, which is a few steps to the west at Városháza tér 1.

Getting There & Away
Bus Buses from Budapest's Árpád híd station, which is on the blue metro line, run to Szentendre at least once an hour throughout the day. Onward service to Visegrád (seven buses Monday to Saturday, four on Sunday) and Esztergom (16 buses Monday to Saturday, hourly on Sunday) is good.

Train The easiest way to reach Szentendre from Budapest is to catch the HÉV suburban train from Batthyány tér in Buda, which takes just 40 minutes. You'll never wait longer than 20 minutes (half that in rush hour), and the last train leaves Szentendre for Budapest at 11.30 pm. Remember that a yellow city bus/metro ticket is good only as far as the Békásmegyer stop on the way up; you'll have to pay extra to get to Szentendre. Also, many HÉV trains run only as far as Békásmegyer, where you must cross the platform to board the train for Szentendre.

Boat From late May to late August, three daily Mahart river boats leave from Vigadó tér in Pest (five minutes later from Batthyány tér in Buda) at 7.30 and 9 am and 2 pm) for Visegrád (two carry on to Esztergom) via Szentendre. From April to late May and September till seasonal shutdown, one boat operates on weekdays (9 am) with an additional one sailing at 8 am on Saturday and Sunday. The one-way/return fare is 600/900Ft for adults and 300/450Ft for children aged four to 14.

Getting Around
Any bus heading north on route No 11 to Visegrád and Esztergom will stop near some of the pensions and the camp site on Pap Island mentioned earlier. Ring the bell after you pass the Danubius hotel at Ady Endre utca 28 on the left.

Between 14 and 16 buses daily leave bus stop No 7 for the open-air ethnographical museum.

You can call a taxi on ☎ 313 131 or 301 111.

VÁC
☎ 27 • postcode 2600 • pop 34,000
Vác lies 34km north of Budapest on the left (east) bank of the Danube opposite Szentendre Island. To the north-west and stretching as far as Slovakia are the Börzsöny Hills, the start of Hungary's mountainous northern region. The Cserhát Hills are to the east.

Unlike most Hungarian towns, Vác can prove its ancient origins without putting a spade into the ground: Uvcenum – the

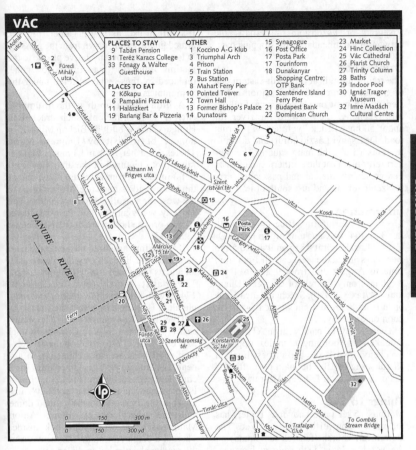

VÁC

PLACES TO STAY
9 Tabán Pension
31 Teréz Karacs College
33 Fónagy & Walter Guesthouse

PLACES TO EAT
2 Kókapu
6 Pampalini Pizzeria
11 Halászkert
19 Barlang Bar & Pizzeria

OTHER
1 Koccino Á-G Klub
3 Triumphal Arch
4 Prison
5 Train Station
7 Bus Station
8 Mahart Ferry Pier
10 Pointed Tower
12 Town Hall
13 Former Bishop's Palace
14 Dunatours

15 Synagogue
16 Post Office
17 Posta Park
17 Tourinform
18 Dunakanyar Shopping Centre; OTP Bank
20 Szentendre Island Ferry Pier
21 Budapest Bank
22 Dominican Church

23 Market
24 Hinc Collection
25 Vác Cathedral
26 Piarist Church
27 Trinity Column
28 Baths
29 Indoor Pool
30 Ignác Tragor Museum
32 Imre Madách Cultural Centre

DANUBE BEND

town's Latin name – is mentioned by Ptolemy in his 2nd-century *Geographia* as a river crossing on an important road. King Stephen established an episcopate here in the 11th century, and within 300 years Vác was rich and powerful enough for its silver mark to become the realm's legal tender. The town's medieval centre and Gothic cathedral were destroyed during the Turkish occupation; reconstruction under several bishops in the 18th century gave Vác its present baroque appearance.

No more than a sleepy provincial centre in the middle of the 19th century, Vác (German: Wartzen) was the first Hungarian town to be linked with Pest by train (1846), but development didn't really come until after WWII. Sadly, for many older Hungarians the name Vác conjures up a single frightening image: the notorious prison on Köztársaság út, where political prisoners were incarcerated and tortured both before the war under the rightist regime of Miklós Horthy and in the 1950s under the communists.

Today you'd scarcely know about that as you enjoy the breezes along the embankment of the Danube, a more prominent feature here than in the Bend's other towns. Vác is also far less touristed than Szentendre, Visegrád or Esztergom – perhaps the strongest recommendation for stopping over.

Orientation

The train station is at the north-eastern end of Széchenyi utca, the bus station a few steps south-west on Galcsek utca. Following Széchenyi utca toward the river for about 500m will take you across the ring road (Dr Csányi László körút) and down to Március 15 tér, the main square. The Mahart ferry pier is at the northern end of Liszt Ferenc sétány; the car and passenger ferry to Szentendre Island just south of it.

Information

There's a Tourinform office (☎ 316 160, fax 316 464, ✉ vac@tourinform.hu) at Dr Csányi László körút 45 open 9 am to 5 pm weekdays and at the weekend till 1 pm from June to August and from 9 am to 4 pm weekdays only the rest of the year. Dunatours (☎/fax 310 950), Széchenyi utca 14, is open from 8 am to 4 pm weekdays and till noon on Saturday.

There's an OTP bank with an ATM in the Dunakanyar shopping complex opposite Széchenyi utca 8 and a Budapest Bank at Köztársaság út 10. The main post office is at Posta Park 2 off Görgey Artúr utca.

Things to See

Március 15 tér (also known as Fő tér) has the most colourful buildings in Vác. The **Dominican church** (fehérek temploma) on the south side is 18th-century baroque; there's a lively **market** to the east. The seals held by the two figures on the gable of the magnificent baroque **Town Hall** (1764) at No 11 represent Hungary and Bishop Kristóf Migazzi, the driving force behind Vác's reconstruction more than 200 years ago. The building next door at No 9 has been a hospital since the 18th century. Opposite at Március 15 tér 6, the former **Bishop's Palace**, parts of which belong to the oldest building in Vác, is now a school.

If you walk north along Köztársaság út to No 62-64, you'll see the enormous 18th-century school that was turned into the

town's infamous **prison** in the 19th century. It's still in use, as you'll gather from the armed guard staring down from the glassed-in tower. The commemorative plaque to the victims of the Horthy regime is now gone, replaced by those who suffered under the communists.

A little farther north is the **Triumphal Arch** (Diadaliv), the only such structure in Hungary. It was built by Bishop Migazzi in honour of a visit by Empress Maria Theresa and her husband Francis of Lorraine (both pictured in the arch's oval reliefs) in 1764. From here, dip down one of the narrow side streets (eg, Molnár utca) to the west for a stroll along the Danube. The **old city walls** and Gothic **Pointed Tower** (now a private home) are near Liszt Ferenc sétány 12.

If you climb up Fürdő utca near the pool complex, you'll reach tiny Szentháromság tér and its renovated **Trinity Column** (1755). The **Piarist church** (piarista templom; 1741), with a stark white interior and marble altar, is to the east across the square.

Tree-lined Konstantin tér to the southeast is dominated by **Vác Cathedral** (Vaci Székesegyház; 1775), one of the first examples of neoclassical architecture to appear in Hungary. This imposing grey church designed by the French architect Isidore Canevale is not to everybody's liking, but the frescoes on the vaulted dome and the altarpiece by Franz Anton Maulbertsch are worth the look inside. There's a display of stone fragments from the medieval cathedral in the **crypt**.

If you continue walking south along Budapesti főút, you'll reach the small stone **Gombás Stream Bridge** (Gombás-patak hídja; 1757) lined with the statues of seven saints – Vác's modest response to Charles Bridge in Prague.

The weed-choked, decrepit **synagogue** at Eötvös utca 5 off Széchenyi utca was designed by an Italian architect in the Romantic style in 1864.

There are a couple of museums in Vác of only marginal interest to visitors, including the **Ignác Tragor Museum**, Múzeum utca 4, and the related **Hinc Collection** (Hinc

Exploring Sopron's backstreets with its Gothic and baroque architecture can be a step back in time.

Statue of St Leonard in Kőszeg.

All smiles at Grassalkovich Mansion, Gödöllő.

Graffiti on a Renaissance-style house in Kőszeg.

JON MURRAY

Taking a stroll around Győr's old town.

STEVE FALLON

Őriszentpéter's well-maintained church.

JON MURRAY

Surrounded by water, Győr was a difficult city to conquer for many invaders.

Gyüjtemény), Káptalan utca 16, which trace the history of Vác from earliest times (open 10 am to 6 pm Tuesday to Sunday; 150/100Ft).

Activities

The Vác Strandfürdő behind the Trinity statue at Szentháromság tér 3 has outdoor pools open from 7 am to 7 pm daily from June to September. The indoor pool on the southern edge of the 'beach', accessible from Ady Endre sétány, is open from 5.30 am to 7.30 pm weekdays, from 7 am to 7 pm on Saturday and from 7 am to 5 pm on Sunday all year. Both cost 300/150Ft.

Places to Stay

Dunatours has *private rooms* for 3400Ft (double), and the *Teréz Karacs College* (☎ 315 480, Budapesti főút) opposite Migazzi tér sometimes lets out dormitory rooms in July and August. You'll see lots of *szoba kiadó* and *Zimmer frei* signs along Budapesti főút.

The *Tabán* (☎ 315 607, Dombay utca 11), an attractive five-room pension just up from Liszt Ferenc sétány, charges 3500/5000Ft for a single/double. The three-room *Fónagy & Walter* (☎ 310 682, @ fonagy@maildunaweb.westel.hu, Budapesti főút 36) is a cosy guesthouse about 850m south-east of Március 15 tér. Singles/doubles are 2500/4800Ft.

Places to Eat

Pampalini Pizzeria (Széchenyi utca 40) is convenient to the bus and train stations but a more interesting place for a pizza (270Ft to 570Ft) is the *Barlang Bar* in a medieval wine cellar below Március 15 tér (entrance in the centre of the square). It's open to 11 pm (till 1 am on Friday and Saturday).

Kőkapu (Dózsa György út 5) near the Triumphal Arch is one of the older restaurants in Vác with solid Hungarian fare on offer. The *Halászkert* (Liszt Ferenc sétány 9) is a fine place for fish soup in warm weather (main dishes from 620Ft to 1250Ft), when you can sit outside and watch the ferries cross over to Szentendre Island.

Entertainment

The circular *Imre Madách Cultural Centre* (☎ 316 411, Dr Csányi László körút 63) can help you with what's on in Vác. Concerts are sometimes held in Vác Cathedral and the Dominican church and at the arboretum in Vácrátót at 7 pm on certain Saturdays in July and August (800Ft to 1200Ft). Don't miss the chance to hear the Vox Humana, Vác's award-winning mixed choir.

The *Koccino Á-G Klub* (Dózsa György út 8) is a divey little pub opposite the Kőkapu restaurant. I've heard good things about the *Trafalgar Club* (Budapesti főút), south-east of the centre.

Getting There & Away

Bus Buses depart for Árpád híd Bridge station in Budapest every half-hour or so. From Vác count on between eight and 14 buses a day to Vácrátót, at least a dozen to Balassagyarmat, up to 10 to Diósjenő and Nógrád and between three and five to Rétság. You can also reach the county capital, Salgótarján, four times a day. Two buses a week (on Wednesday and Saturday at 7.35 am) leave for the Polish city of Kraków.

Train Trains depart from Budapest-Nyugati station almost every half-hour for Szob via Vác, and some five of these continue along the eastern bank of the Danube to Štúrovo, across the Danube from Esztergom in Slovakia. Slow trains north to Balassagyarmat (five a day) from Vác stop at Nógrád and Diósjenő in the Börzsöny Hills.

From the first Saturday in May to the last one in September MÁV Nostalgia (☎ 1-317 1665, Belgrád rakpart 26) runs a vintage steam train (*nosztalgiavonat*) from Budapest-Nyugati (departing at 9.45 am) to Szob (two hours) via Vác and Nagymaros-Visegrád and returning from Szob at 4.35 pm (Nagymaros-Visegrád at 4.59 pm, Vác at 5.23 pm). But verify this service and schedule with MÁV Nostalgia or check the Web site at www.miwo.hu/old_trains before making plans.

Car & Motorcycle Car ferries (350/100Ft per car/bicycle) cross over to Szentendre

DANUBE BEND

Island hourly from 6 am to 9 pm; a bridge connects the island's west bank with the mainland at Tahitótfalu. From there hourly buses run to Szentendre, about 10km south.

Boat From late May to August, one daily Mahart river boat sails between Pest's Vigadó tér (at 7.30 am, 7.35 am from Batthyány tér in Buda) and Vác via Szentendre. The same boat continues on to Visegrád and Esztergom at 9.55 am. From April to late May and late September till winter shutdown, the boat leaves Budapest at 8 am on Saturday and Sunday only and departs Vác for Visegrád and Esztergom at 10.25 am.

AROUND VÁC
Börzsöny Hills
These hills begin the series of six ranges that make up Hungary's Northern Uplands, and – along with the Pilis Park Forest and the Visegrád Hills on the opposite bank of the Danube – form Hungary's new Danube-Ipoly National Park. Vác is the best starting point for a visit to the Börzsöny, which sees surprisingly few visitors. There's very good hiking, but make sure you get hold of Cartographia's 1:40,000 map *A Börzsöny* (No 5; 400Ft).

Nógrád, with the ruins of a hilltop castle dating back to the 12th century, could be considered the gateway to the Börzsöny; at Diósjenő, 6km north, there's *Diósjenő Camping* (☎ 35-364 134) with four-bed bungalows open May to September. From here you can strike out west along marked trails to 864m **Nagy Hideg** or 739m **Magas-Tax**. The Börzsöny's highest peak, 938m **Csóványos**, lies to the west of Diósjenő and is a much more difficult climb.

If you're under your own steam, take the beautiful restricted road (a small fee may be charged) from Diósjenő to Kemence via Királyháza, where you'll find the 10-room *Matthias* riding pension (☎ 27-365 139), with accommodation from 4000Ft and 6000Ft. The road follows the Kemence Stream almost the entire way – a great place for a cool dip or a picnic in summer. Just before you reach Kemence, there's a turn south into the **Fekete-völgy**, the beautiful

'Black Valley' and the 18-room *Vilati Fekete-völgy* pension (☎ 27-365 153) with doubles for 4000Ft.

An easy and excellent excursion is the 5km walk south-west from Nógrád to **Királyrét**, the royal hunting grounds of King Matthias Corvinus. Here a **narrow-gauge train** runs 12km south to Kismaros, where you can catch a train back to Vác, Budapest or even Štúrovo in Slovakia. The train departs two times a day weekdays and five times at the weekend from April to October but only three times a day on Saturday and Sunday the rest of the year.

VISEGRÁD
☎ 26 • postcode 2025 • pop 1780
Situated on the Danube's abrupt loop, Visegrád (from the Slavic words for 'high castle') is the most beautiful section and the very symbol of the Bend. As you approach Visegrád from Szentendre, 23km to the south, keep your eyes open for the citadel high up on Castle Hill. With the palace at the base, it was once the royal centre of Hungary.

The Romans built a border fortress on Sibrik Hill just north of the present castle in the 4th century, and it was still being used by Slovak settlers 600 years later. After the Mongol invasion in 1241, King Béla IV began work on a lower castle by the river and then on the hilltop citadel. Less than a century later, King Charles Robert of Anjou, whose claim to the local throne was being fiercely contested in Buda, moved the royal household to Visegrád and had the lower castle converted into a palace.

For almost 200 years, Visegrád was Hungary's 'other' (often summer) capital and an important diplomatic centre. But Visegrád's real golden age came during the reign of King Matthias Corvinus (ruled 1458-90) and Queen Beatrice, who had Italian Renaissance craftsmen rebuild the Gothic palace. The sheer size of the residence, its stonework, fountains and hanging gardens were the talk of the 15th century.

The destruction of Visegrád came with the Turks and later in 1702 when the Habsburgs blew up the citadel to prevent

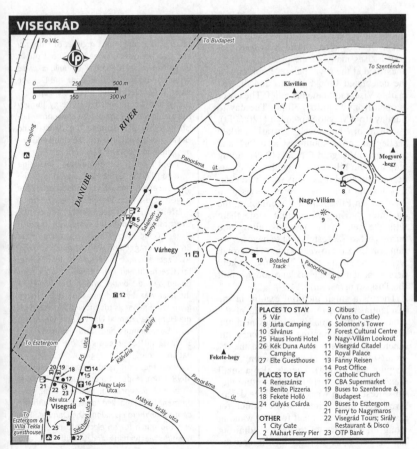

VISEGRÁD

To Vác
To Budapest
To Szentendre

Kisvillám

Mogyoró-hegy

DANUBE BEND

DANUBE RIVER

Panoráma út

Camping

Nagy-Villám

Salamon tornya utca

Várhegy

Bobsled Track

Panoráma út

To Esztergom

Kálvária

Fekete-hegy

Panoráma út

Nagy Lajos utca

Rév utca

Mátyás király utca

Visegrád

Széchenyi utca

To Esztergom & Villa Tekla guesthouse

PLACES TO STAY		
5	Vár	
8	Jurta Camping	
10	Silvánus	
25	Haus Honti Hotel	
26	Kék Duna Autós Camping	
27	Elte Guesthouse	

PLACES TO EAT		
4	Reneszánsz	
15	Benito Pizzeria	
18	Fekete Holló	
24	Gulyás Csárda	

OTHER		
1	City Gate	
2	Mahart Ferry Pier	
3	Citibus (Vans to Castle)	
6	Solomon's Tower	
7	Forest Cultural Centre	
9	Nagy-Villám Lookout	
11	Visegrád Citadel	
12	Royal Palace	
13	Fanny Reisen	
14	Post Office	
16	Catholic Church	
17	CBA Supermarket	
19	Buses to Szentendre & Budapest	
20	Buses to Esztergom	
21	Ferry to Nagymaros	
22	Visegrád Tours; Sirály Restaurant & Disco	
23	OTP Bank	

Hungarian independence fighters from using it as a base. All trace of the palace was lost until the 1930s when archaeologists, following descriptions in literary sources, uncovered the ruins.

Orientation & Information

The Mahart ferry pier on route No 11, just south of the city gate and opposite the Vár hotel, is one of two stops where the bus from Szentendre or Budapest will drop you off. Across the street to the right of the Vár hotel are steps to Salamon-torony utca, which leads to the lower castle and the

citadel. There is also a bus stop near the village centre and the car ferry about a kilometre south on Fő utca. Visegrád Tours (☎ 398 160) is at Rév utca 15 near the Nagymaros ferry pier, but the staff are singularly unhelpful and disinterested. Seek assistance instead from Fanny Reisen (☎ 398 268), Fő utca 55. There's a small OTP bank branch (no ATM) at Rév utca 9. The post office is at Fő utca 77.

Things to See

The first thing you'll see as you walk north up Salamon-torony utca to the lower castle is the 13th-century **Solomon's Tower**, a stocky, hexagonal keep with walls up to 8m thick. Once used to control river traffic, it now houses many of the precious objects unearthed at the royal palace. Look out for the celebrated Lion Fountain and the red marble Visegrád Madonna relief. The tower is open from 9 am to 4.30 pm Tuesday to Sunday from May to September (120/60Ft).

North of the tower, a trail marked 'Fellegvár' turns south-east at a fork and leads up to **Visegrád Citadel** (1259), sitting atop a 350m hill and surrounded by moats hewn from solid rock. This was the repository for the Hungarian crown jewels until 1440, when Elizabeth of Luxembourg, the daughter of King Sigismund, stole them with the help of her lady-in-waiting and hurried off to Székesfehérvár to have her infant son László crowned king. (The crown was returned to the citadel in 1464 and held here – under a stronger lock no doubt – until the Turkish invasion.)

There's a small pictorial exhibit in the residential rooms on the west side of the citadel and two smaller displays near the east gate: one on hunting and falconry, the other on traditional occupations in the region (stone-cutting, charcoal-burning, beekeeping and fishing). There's also a small **wax museum** of fairly life-like torture victims. Restoration work on the three defensive levels of the citadel will continue for many years, but it's great fun just walking along the ramparts of this eyrie, admiring the views of the Börzsöny Hills and the Danube. Across the Danube from Visegrád lies Nagymaros and the abandoned site of what was to have been Hungary's section of the Gabčikovo-Nagymaros dam project (see boxed text 'Dam Nations'). The citadel is open from 8.30 am to 6 pm daily from mid-March to mid-November (200/160Ft).

If you're walking to the citadel from the village centre, Kálvária sétány, a trail beginning from behind the 18th-century Catholic church on Fő tér, is less steep than the trail from Solomon's Tower. You can also reach it by minibus (see Getting Around).

The **Visegrád Royal Palace** (Visegrádi királyi palota) at Fő utca 29, the 15th-

Dam Nations

In 1977 the communist regimes of Hungary and Czechoslovakia agreed – without public or parliamentary debate – to build a canal system and power station along the Danube River. The project would produce cheap electricity and be financed by energy-hungry Austria. It wasn't long before environmentalists foresaw the damage the dam would cause, and the public outcry was loud and unmitigated. In 1989 Hungary's last reform government under communism, including Foreign Minister Gyula Horn, caved in to the pressure and halted all work on its part of the project across from Visegrád at Nagymaros.

Efforts to convince newly democratic Czechoslovakia to do the same with its much larger Gabčikovo Canal upstream near Bratislava dragged on without much success. As Czechoslovakia came closer to dividing, the Czechs turned a blind eye on what continued by the Slovaks, and in October 1992 the river was diverted into the canal. Energy gains were minor as the project depended on the Hungarian dam at Nagymaros, which has now been demolished. Both Hungary and Slovakia put their cases before the International Court in The Hague.

When the court handed down its ruling in 1998, Horn, leader of the reinvented Socialist Party and now prime minister, said his government felt compelled to go ahead with the dam somewhere else along the Danube. This was too much for an electorate tired of old regime-style waffling and untruths. He and the socialists were swept from office in the national elections later that year. The new government has said it will not go ahead with the damn project.

century seat of King Matthias, once had 350 rooms and was said to be unrivalled in Europe in size and splendour. Everything you see at the terraced palace today – the Court of Honour with its Renaissance Hercules Fountain in the centre, the arcaded Gothic hallways, the Lion Fountain and the foundations of St George's Chapel (1366) – are reconstructions or replicas. The palace is open from 9 am to 4.30 pm Tuesday to Sunday (120/60Ft).

Activities

There are some easy walks and hikes in the immediate vicinity of Visegrád Citadel – to the 377m Nagy-Villám Lookout Tower, for example. Across from the Jurta camping ground is the sod and wood Forest Cultural Centre designed by Imre Makovecz. It contains a small wildlife exhibit.

A 700m bobsled track (*bobpálya*), on which you wend your way down a metal chute while sitting on a felt-bottomed cart, is on the hillside below the lookout; rides are available from 10 am to 4 pm daily March to November. There are tennis courts for hire from 7 am to 9 pm daily near the Royal Palace at Fő utca 41.

About 3km south of Visegrád on route No 11 to Esztergom, the Villa Tekla guesthouse (☎ 397 051), Berkenye utca 12, in Gizellatelep has a horse-riding school and some of the finest stock in Hungary.

Places to Stay

Up on Mogyoró-hegy (Hazelnut Hill), about 2km north-east of the citadel, *Jurta Camping* (☎ 398 217) has relatively expensive bungalows and sites (250/600/360Ft per tent/caravan/person). It's nicely situated but far from the centre, and bus service is infrequent. *Kék Duna Autós Camping* (☎ 398 102, Fő utca 70), by the highway south of the Nagymaros ferry, charges 360Ft per person, 200Ft to 400Ft per tent and 500Ft per caravan, but there are no bungalows. Both sites are open May to September.

Visegrád Tours and Fanny Reisen can organise private rooms for between 1200Ft and 1600Ft per person. Many houses along Fő utca (eg, Nos 55, 60 & 107) and Széchenyi utca (Nos 16/a & 21) have signs advertising rooms. Almost as cheap as a private room but open April to September only is the accommodation at the *Elte* (☎/fax 398 165, Fő utca 117), a four-storey guesthouse with 33 basic rooms costing 2240/1120Ft for adults/students per person in singles and doubles.

The *Haus Honti* (☎ 398 120, Fő utca 66), a friendly, 28-room hotel with a new building just off the main road to Esztergom and an older one next to a picturesque little stream, has singles/doubles with shower for 5000/6500Ft.

The 22-room *Vár* (☎ 397 522, fax 397 572, Fő utca 9), a new hotel in a lovely, renovated old building, is convenient to the Mahart boat pier but also faces busy, noisy route No 11. Singles/doubles cost DM55/70.

The *Silvánus* hotel (☎/fax 398 311, @ hotelsilvanus@mail.matav.hu), a 94-room hotel on Fekete-hegy (Black Hill), a few minutes' walk east of the citadel, has a great location, terrace restaurant and bar, swimming pool, tennis and squash courts and 10-pin bowling. But it's expensive: singles with bath and breakfast are DM78 to DM98, doubles DM108 to DM136, depending on the season and the view.

Places to Eat

Benito Pizzeria (Fő utca 83) is a reasonable place for a cheap pizza (450Ft to 600Ft). The medieval banquet-themed *Reneszánsz* restaurant (Fő utca 11), next to the Vár hotel, feeds tourists wearing paper crowns by the bus load. In the village, the *Fekete Holló* (Rév utca 12) is a somewhat touristy fish restaurant opposite the Nagymaros ferry pier.

Most people here say the best restaurant is the *Gulyás Csárda* (Nagy Lajos király utca 4) across from the church.

Entertainment

The *Sirály* (Rév utca 15) restaurant and disco is about the only place open at night in these parts.

Getting There & Away

Bus & Train Buses are very frequent – as often as twice an hour – to/from Budapest's Árpád híd station, Szentendre and Esztergom. No railway line reaches Visegrád, but you can take one of two dozen daily trains to Szob from Budapest-Nyugati. Get off at Nagymaros-Visegrád, and hop on the ferry to Visegrád.

Boat Between late May and late August, three daily Mahart boats from Budapest stop at Visegrád (650/975Ft one way/return for adults, 375/485Ft for children), with two of them carrying on to Esztergom at 10.55 am and 5 pm. The boats depart for Szentendre and Budapest at 10.30 am and 5.30 pm.

Hourly ferries cross the Danube between Visegrád (from 5.35 am to 8.35 pm) and Nagymaros (5.45 am and 8.45 pm) year round except when the Danube freezes over or fog descends (80/80/420Ft per person/bicycle/car). From Nagymaros-Visegrád train station, just inland from the ferry pier, there are trains to Budapest-Nyugati about every hour.

Getting Around

Citibus, a taxi van service, leaves from the Mahart boat pier three times a day (9.26 am and 12.26 and 3.26 pm) from April to September (and sometimes more often in high season), stopping at the Nagymaros ferry pier two minutes later before carrying on to Jurta Camping via the citadel. Ring ☎ 397 372 for information.

AROUND VISEGRÁD
Pilis Hills

If you want to explore the protected forest in the Pilis, the limestone and dolomite hills south-west of Visegrád, take the Esztergom bus for 6km to Dömös, where there is an excellent river beach and **Dömös Camping** (☎ 33-482 319), with two four-bed cabins (8000Ft) along the Danube is open from May to mid-September. Camping at the same location costs 500/600/530/380 per tent/caravan/adult/child.

If you follow Duna utca across from the camp for 3km, you'll reach the entrance to the 25,000-hectare **Pilis Park Forest**, where Matthias Corvinus once hunted and Hungary's first hiking trails were laid in 1869. It now forms part of the Danube-Ipoly National Park. Marked trails lead to **Prédikálószék** (Pulpit Seat), a 639m crag for experienced hikers and climbers only, and to **Dobogókő**, a much easier ascent of about three hours via the Rám-szakadék (Rám Precipice).

At Dobogókő there's an excursion centre with further trails mapped out, or you can catch a bus to Esztergom (there are four or five a day) or to the HÉV station in Pomáz, two stops before Szentendre.

Alternatively, you can take the small ferry across the Danube from Dömös to Dömösi átkelés (on the train line two stops from Visegrád), then climb to the caves that are visible on the hillside and hike back into the hills behind Nagymaros. Cartographia's 1:40,000 *A Pilis és a Visegrádi-helység* (The Pilis and Visegrád Hills) map (No 16; 400Ft) outlines the many hiking possibilities in this area.

Some of the best bird-watching in western Hungary is in the Pilis Hills.

ESZTERGOM
☎ 33 • postcode 2500 • pop 30,000

Esztergom, 25km from Visegrád and 66km from Budapest via route No 11, is one of Hungary's most historical and sacred cities. For more than 1000 years it has been the seat of Roman Catholicism – the archbishop of Esztergom is the primate of Hungary. The country's first king, St Stephen, was born here in 975, and it was a royal seat from the late 10th to mid-13th centuries. For these and other reasons, Esztergom has both great spiritual and temporal significance for most Hungarians.

Esztergom lies on a high point above a slight curve of the Danube across from the Slovakian city of Štúrovo (Hungarian: Párkány), which can be reached by ferry and, in future, via the rebuilt Mária Valéria Bridge (see Other Attractions). Vár-hegy (Castle Hill) was the site of the Roman settlement of Solva Mansio in the 1st century, and it is thought that emperor-to-be Marcus Aurelius finished his *Meditations* in a camp nearby during the second half of the 2nd century.

Prince Géza chose Esztergom as his capital, and his son Vajk (as he was known before his baptism) was crowned King Stephen here in 1000. Stephen founded one of the country's two archbishoprics and a basilica at Esztergom, bits of which can be seen in the palace.

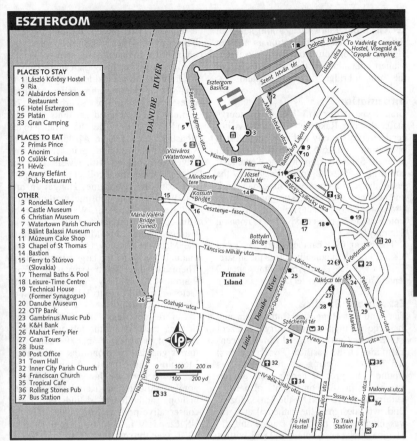

ESZTERGOM

PLACES TO STAY
1 László Kőrösy Hostel
9 Ria
12 Alabárdos Pension & Restaurant
16 Hotel Esztergom
25 Platán
33 Gran Camping

PLACES TO EAT
2 Primás Pince
5 Anonim
10 Csülök Csárda
21 Hévíz
29 Arany Elefánt Pub-Restaurant

OTHER
3 Rondella Gallery
4 Castle Museum
6 Christian Museum
7 Watertown Parish Church
8 Bálint Balassi Museum
11 Múzeum Cake Shop
13 Chapel of St Thomas
14 Bastion
15 Ferry to Štúrovo (Slovakia)
17 Thermal Baths & Pool
18 Leisure-Time Centre
19 Technical House (Former Synagogue)
20 Danube Museum
22 OTP Bank
23 Gambrinus Music Pub
24 K&H Bank
26 Mahart Ferry Pier
27 Gran Tours
28 Ibusz
30 Post Office
31 Town Hall
32 Inner City Parish Church
34 Franciscan Church
35 Tropical Cafe
36 Rolling Stones Pub
37 Bus Station

DANUBE BEND

Esztergom (German: Gran) lost its political significance when King Béla IV moved the capital to Buda following the Mongol invasion in 1241. It remained an important trading centre and the ecclesiastical seat, however, vying with the royal court for power and influence. Esztergom's capture by the Turks in 1543 interrupted the church's activities, and the archbishop fled to Nagyszombat (now Trnava in Slovakia).

The church did not re-establish its base here – the 'Hungarian Rome' – until the early 19th century. It was then that Esztergom went on a building spree that transformed it into a city of late baroque and, in particular, neoclassical buildings.

Orientation

The modern centre of Esztergom is Rákóczi tér, a few steps east of the Kis-Duna (Little Danube), the tributary that branches off to form Prímás-sziget (Primate Island). Up Bajcsy-Zsilinszky utca to the north-west is Castle Hill. To the south-west of Rákóczi tér is Széchenyi tér, the town centre in the Middle Ages and site of the rococo Town Hall.

Esztergom's bus station is near the market on Simor János utca, 700m south of Rákóczi tér. The train station is another 1200m farther south on Bem József tér. Mahart boats dock at the pier just south of the 'broken bridge' on Primate Island.

Information

Gran Tours (☎/fax 413 756, ✆ grantour@ mail.holop.hu), Rákóczi tér 25, is the visitor centre run by the city and very helpful. It is open from 8 am to 6 pm weekdays and till noon on Saturday from May to September and from 8 am to 4 pm weekdays only the rest of the year. If you speak Hungarian check out the Web site at www.esztergom.hu. Ibusz (☎/fax 411 643), Kossuth Lajos utca 5, opens from 8 am to 5 pm weekdays and to noon on Saturday.

There's an OTP bank on Rákóczi tér and a K&H branch diagonally across the square. The post office is at Arany János utca 2 (enter from Széchenyi tér).

Esztergom Basilica

The centre of Hungarian Catholicism and the largest church in the country is in Szent István tér on Castle Hill, and 72m-high central dome of the basilica (*főszékesegyház*) can be seen soaring up for kilometres around. The present neoclassical church was begun in 1822 on the site of a 12th-century one destroyed by the Turks. József Hild, who designed the cathedral at Eger, was involved in the final stages, and the basilica was consecrated in 1856 with a sung Mass composed by Franz Liszt.

The grey church is colossal (118m long and 40m wide) and rather bleak inside, but the white and red marble **Bakócz Chapel** on the south side is a splendid example of Italian Renaissance stone-carving and sculpture. It was commissioned by Archbishop Tamás Bakócz who, failing in his bid for the papacy, launched a crusade that turned into the peasant uprising under György Dózsa in 1514 (see the History section in the Facts about Hungary chapter). The chapel escaped most – though not all – of the Turks' axes; notice the smashed-in faces of Gabriel and other angels above the altar. It was disman-

tled into 1600 separate pieces and then reassembled in its present location in 1823. The copy of Titian's *Assumption* over the cathedral's main altar is said to be the world's largest painting on a single canvas.

On the north-west side of the church, to the left of the macabre relics of three priests martyred in Košice early in the 17th century and canonised as saints by Pope John Paul II in 1995, lies the entrance to the **treasury** (*kincstár*), an Aladdin's cave of vestments and religious plates in gold and silver and studded with jewels. It is the richest ecclesiastical collection in Hungary and contains Byzantine, Hungarian and Italian objects of sublime workmanship and great artistic merit. Watch out for the 13th-century Coronation Oath Cross, the Garamszentbenedek Monstrance (1500), the Matthias Calvary Cross of gold and enamel (1469) and the large baroque Maria Theresa Chalice. The treasury is open from 9 am to 4.30 pm daily from mid-March to October, from 11 am to 3.30 pm the rest of the year (200/100Ft).

Before you leave the cathedral, go through the door on the left and down to the **crypt**, a series of spooky vaults with tombs guarded by monoliths representing Mourning and Eternity. Among those at rest down here are János Vitéz, Esztergom's enlightened Renaissance archbishop, and József Mindszenty, the conservative primate who holed up in the US Embassy in Budapest from 1956 to 1971 (see boxed text 'Cardinal Mindszenty'). The crypt is open from 9 am to 5 pm daily from April to October and from 10 am to 3 pm the rest of the year (50Ft).

Castle Museum

This comprehensive museum at the southern end of Castle Hill is housed in a dozen or so rooms of the former Royal Palace, which was built mostly by French architects under Béla III (ruled 1172-96) during Esztergom's golden age. The palace was the king's residence until the capital was relocated to Buda – at which time the archbishop moved in. Most of the palace was destroyed and covered with earth for

Cardinal Mindszenty

Born József Pehm in the village of Csehimindszent, near Szombathely, in 1892, Mindszenty was politically active from the time of his ordination in 1915. Imprisoned under the short-lived regime of communist Béla Kun in 1919 and again when the fascist Iron Cross came to power in 1944, Mindszenty was made archbishop of Esztergom (and thus primate of Hungary) in 1945 and cardinal the following year.

When the new cardinal refused to secularise Hungary's Roman Catholic schools under the new communist regime in 1948, he was arrested, tortured and sentenced to life imprisonment for treason. Released during the 1956 Uprising, Mindszenty took refuge in the US Embassy on Szabadság tér when the communists returned to power. There he would remain until 1971.

As relations between the Kádár regime and the Holy See began to thaw in the late 1960s, the Vatican made several requests for the cardinal to leave Hungary, which he refused. Following the intervention of US President Richard Nixon, Mindszenty left for Vienna, where he continued to criticise the Vatican's relations with the regime in Hungary. He retired in 1974 and died the following year. But as he had vowed not to return to Esztergom until the last Soviet soldier had left Hungarian soil, Mindszenty's remains were not returned until May 1991 – several weeks before the last soldier had actually left.

TONY FANKHAUSER

DANUBE BEND

defensive purposes under the Turks; it did not see the light of day again until excavations began in the 1930s. It is currently undergoing extensive renovation and rebuilding overseen by the same architectural firm that worked on the palace at Gödöllő; don't expect everything described here to be open or in the same place.

Among the most interesting of the museum's rooms are the vaulted 12th-century room said to be the oldest 'living room' in Hungary; the study of János Vitéz, with 15th-century murals of the Virtues; and the 12th-century royal chapel, with a rose window and frescoes of lions and a tree of life. You can climb the narrow steps to the terrace for a windswept view of the palace, the Danube and Štúrovo in Slovakia, and the basilica. The **Rondella Gallery** to the east is housed in a corner bastion with rotating exhibits and hosts touristy song and dance performances in summer. The Castle Museum (Vármúzeum) is open from 9 am to 4.30 pm Tuesday to Sunday from April to October, from 10 am to 4 pm the rest of the year (160/60Ft).

Other Attractions

Below Castle Hill on the banks of the Little Danube is **Víziváros**, the colourful 'Watertown' district of pastel town houses, churches and museums. The easiest way to get there is to walk over the palace drawbridge and down the grassy hill to Batthyány Lajos utca. Turn west onto Pázmány Péter utca.

The **Bálint Balassi Museum**, in an 18th-century baroque building at Pázmány Péter utca 13, has objects of local interest, with much emphasis on the churches and monasteries of medieval Esztergom (open 9 am to 5 pm Tuesday to Sunday; 100/50Ft). The museum is named in honour of the general and lyric poet who was killed during an unsuccessful attempt to retake Esztergom Castle from the Turks in 1594.

Past the Italianate **Watertown parish church** (Víziváros plébániatemplom; 1738), which is vaguely reminiscent of the glorious Minorite church in Eger, you'll come to the former Bishop's Palace at Mindszenty hercegprímás tere 2. Today it houses the **Christian Museum** (Keresztény Múzeum), the finest collection of medieval religious art in Hungary and one of the best museums in the country. Established by Archbishop János Simor in 1875, it contains Hungarian Gothic triptychs and altarpieces, later works by German, Dutch and Italian masters, tapestries, and what is arguably the most beautiful object in the nation: the sublime **Holy Sepulchre of Garamszentbenedek** (1480). It's a sort of wheeled cart in the shape of a cathedral with richly carved figures of the 12 Apostles (above) and Roman soldiers (below) guarding Christ's tomb. It was used at Easter Week processions and was painstakingly restored in the 1970s.

Be sure to see Tamás Kolozsvári's *Calvary* altar panel (1427), which was influenced by Italian art, the late Gothic *Christ's Passion* by 'Master M S', the gruesome *Martyrdom of the Three Apostles* (1490) by the so-called Master of the Martyr Apostles, and the *Temptation of St Anthony* (1530) by Jan Wellens de Cock, with its drug-like visions of devils and temptresses. The museum's displays are labelled in five languages, and a guided tour in English can be booked by ringing the museum (☎ 413 880) in advance. The museum is open from 10 am to 6 pm Tuesday to Sunday (200/100Ft).

If you cross the little Kossuth Bridge, past the pier where ferries head for Štúrovo in Slovakia, and on to Primate Island, you can't help noticing the ruins of **Mária Valéria Bridge**, with the jagged spans on both sides of the river failing to meet in the middle. The bridge was destroyed during WWII and was never rebuilt. But in late 1999 the prime ministers of both countries signed an agreement to rebuild the span, which should be up in place by 2005.

The so-called **Technical House** (Technika Háza; 1888) at Imaház utca 4 once served as a synagogue for Esztergom's Jewish community, the oldest in Hungary, and now houses a science association. It was designed in 'Moorish romantic' style by Lipót Baumhorn, the master architect who also engineered the synagogues in Szeged, Szolnok and Gyöngyös, and is currently under renovation.

Activities

Between the still vacant Fürdő hotel and the Little Danube at Bajcsy-Zsilinszky utca 14-18, there are outdoor thermal pools open May to September from 9 am to 7 pm (200/100Ft). You can use the indoor pool the rest of the year from 6 am to 6 pm on weekdays, 9 am to 1 pm on Saturday and 9 am till noon on Sunday.

Places to Stay

Camping The most central camp site is the small *Gran Camping* (☎/fax 489 563, Nagy-Duna sétány 3) on Primate Island open May to mid-October. It also has a *hostel* for students costing 1050Ft per person and *bungalows* with two to six beds; a double costs 4800Ft to 5300Ft, depending on the season. *Gyopár Camping* (☎ 311 401, Vaskapui út), open mid-April to mid-October, is on Sípoló-hegyy, some 3km to the east (bus No 1); it has *bungalows* for 1150Ft per person. *Vadvirág Camping* (☎ 312 234, route No 11, 63km stone) is at Bánomi dűlő, 3km on the way to Visegrád (bus No 6) and costs 400Ft per tent, car and person. Accommodation in the site's *motel* and *bungalow* costs 950Ft to 1150Ft. Vadvirág Camping is open May to September.

Private Rooms & Hostel See Gran Tours for private rooms (1500Ft per person) or apartments (4500Ft). From July to late August, the *trade school* (☎ 411 746, Budai Nagy Antal utca 38) near the train station has dormitory rooms available for 950Ft per person while the László Kőrösy College opposite the basilica becomes the *Kőrösy* hostel (☎ 312 813, Szent István tér 16), with singles/doubles/triples costing 1620/2800/3840Ft. The József Károly Hell College 6km south of the centre in Esztergom-Kertváros becomes – what else? – the *Hell* hostel (☎/fax 319 144, Wesselényi utca 40-42) in summer but often has three/four-bed rooms (2100/2800Ft) available at school holidays and the weekend.

Pensions The friendly 24-room *Platán* (☎/fax 411 355, Kis-Duna sétány 11) is more like a small, budget hotel; doubles with bath cost 3300Ft. The entrance is to the right as you walk into the courtyard.

Closer to the sights, the very comfortable 21-room *Alabárdos* (*☎/fax 312 640, Bajcsy-Zsilinszky utca 49*) has singles/doubles for 5500/6500Ft (500Ft cheaper in the low season). The 13-room *Ria* (*☎ 313 115, fax 401 429, Batthyány utca 11-13*), a much more homely *panzió* only a short distance north, charges 4800/6500Ft for singles/doubles in both a new and an older building.

Hotel The 36-room *Hotel Esztergom* (*☎ 412 555, fax 412 853, ✉ hotelesz@ mail.elender.hu, Nagy-Duna sétány*) is a modern block of a hotel on Primate Island, with singles from DM46 to DM76 and doubles from DM71 to DM103, depending on the season. There's a rather fancy restaurant, a roof terrace and a sports centre with a tennis court and canoes for rent.

Places to Eat

The *Hévíz (Aradi vétanúk tere 4/b)* on the 1st level of the Bástya shopping centre is the cheapest place in town for a meal – and looks, smells and feels it. If you're a little more flush than that head for the charming *Csülök Csárda (Batthyány Lajos utca 9)* next to the Ria pension; it has very good home cooking and huge main courses from 800Ft.

The *Anonim (Berényi Zsigmond utca 4)*, in an attractive historical town house and convenient to the museums in Watertown, is open daily to midnight. The attractive *Arany Elefánt* pub-restaurant *(Petőfi Sándor utca 15)* is just east of the market area and open daily till 10 pm (most mains around 500Ft). The *Primás Pince (Szent István tér)* is an atmospheric restaurant in an old cellar beneath the basilica by the Dark Gate (Sötétkapu). The *Múzeum (corner of Bajcsy-Zsilinszky utca & Batthyány utca)* is one of the better cake shops in Esztergom.

Entertainment

Organ concerts take place in the cathedral in summer, and the Esztergom Chroniclers sometimes perform ancient Hungarian music at the palace; check with Gran Tours or any of the other agencies for more information. The *Leisure-Time Centre (Szabadidőközpont; ☎ 312 446, Bajcsy-Zsilinszky utca 4)* has a cinema and rotating exhibits. It's open from 8 am to 9 pm on weekdays, 8 am to 1 pm and 2 to 5 pm on Saturday and 8 am to noon on Sunday.

A miniature strip of activity after dark is the street market on Simor János utca, which continues south from Bajcsy-Zsilinszky utca. The *Tropical Cafe* at No 44 is popular with students from the nearby trade school; the *Rolling Stones* at No 64 attracts a more mature crowd, plays decent canned music and has a back courtyard. The *Gambrinus Music Pub (Vörösmarty utca 3)* is a popular place with live acts (open till 2 am).

For up-to-date entertainment, check the listings in the freebie weekly *Esztergomi Est*.

Getting There & Away

Bus Buses to/from Budapest's Árpád híd station run about every half-hour from 4 or 4.30 am to just after 7 pm; count on as many as 20 buses on Sunday. The buses may go via Dorog (75 minutes) or Visegrád (two hours). Buses from Esztergom to Visegrád and Szentendre depart almost hourly between 5.40 am (6.50 am) and 9 pm. Other important destinations served are limited: Balatonfüred (one bus per day); Dobogókő (four to five); Komárom (two), Pilisszentlélek (four to five); Sopron (one), Tata via Tatabánya (hourly); and Veszprém (one).

Train Trains to Esztergom depart from Budapest-Nyugati train station up to a dozen times a day. To get to Western Transdanubia from Esztergom, take one of the three daily trains to Komárom, where you can change for Győr, Székesfehérvár, Vienna and Bratislava (via Komárno on the Slovakian side).

Boat Mahart river boats travel from Vigadó tér in Pest and Batthyány tér in Buda to Esztergom (690/1035Ft one way/return, 50% discount for children aged four to 14) twice a day from late May to late August, but it's a very slow trip of more than five hours.

During the low season, from April to late May and September to seasonal shutdown, there's only one boat on Saturday and Sunday. A year-round ferry crosses the Danube from Esztergom, just north of Mária Valéria Bridge, to Štúrovo in Slovakia 12 times a day from June to August with the first at 7.20 am and the last at 6.20 pm (from Štúrovo: on the hour from 8 am to 7 pm). During the rest of the year there are nine sailings starting at the same times. Adults/children pay 110/50Ft, and it costs another 300/200Ft to take a car or motorcycle/bicycle along.

Western Transdanubia

As its name suggests, Western Transdanubia (Nyugat-Dunántúl) lies 'across the Danube' from Budapest, stretching west and southwest to the borders with Austria and Slovenia. It is a region of hills and plains, with some of the most historically important towns, castles, churches and monuments in Hungary. As the nation's 'window on the West', it has always been the richest and most developed region of Hungary and popular with Austrian day-trippers in search of cheaper goods and services.

The Danube River was the limit of Roman expansion in what is now Hungary, and most of Western Transdanubia formed the province of Upper Pannonia. The Romans built some of their most important military and civil towns here – Arrabona (Győr), Scarbantia (Sopron), Savaria (Szombathely), Adflexum (Mosonmagyaróvár) and Brigetio (Komárom). Because of their positions on the trade route from northern Europe to the Adriatic and Byzantium, and the influx of Germans, Slovaks and other ethnic groups, these towns prospered in the Middle Ages. Episcopates were established, castles were built and many of the towns were granted special royal privileges.

A large part of Western Transdanubia remained in the hands of the Habsburgs during the Turkish occupation, and it was thus spared the ruination suffered in the south or on the Great Plain. As a result, some of the best examples of Romanesque and Gothic architecture can be found here. Because the influence of Vienna continued throughout the 16th and 17th centuries, Western Transdanubia received Hungary's first baroque churches and public buildings. That domination by Austria continued, with parts of the region changing hands several times over the following centuries.

Western Transdanubia took a pounding during WWII, and though many of the town centres were spared, the outlying districts were demolished. As a result, they have distinctly similar appearances: a medieval or

HIGHLIGHTS

• The Imre Patkó Collection of Asian and African art and the Herm of László reliquary at the cathedral in Győr

• Colourful Jurisics tér in Kőszeg

• The opulent Esterházy Palace at Fertőd

• The neoclassical Széchenyi Mansion at Nagycenk

• Sopron's Storno Collection of Romanesque and Gothic furnishings

• The massive Benedictine abbey complex at Pannonhalma and its treasures

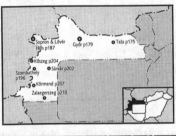

baroque core ringed with concrete housing blocks, factories and sometimes farmland. The region was industrialised after the war, especially around Tatabánya and Győr. Agriculture is less important here, though Sopron and Mór are wine centres.

TATA
☎ 34 • postcode 2890 • pop 25,000
Tata, situated west of the Gerecse Hills, is a pleasant town of springs, canals and lakes, a castle and a lot of history. Tatabánya, on the other hand, is a heavily industrial city 14km to the south-east whose only real claim to fame is a giant statue of the symbolic *turul* (see boxed text 'Blame it on the Bird').

Much of the action in Tata (German: Totis) has focused in and around the 14th-century Öregvár (Old Castle) perched on a

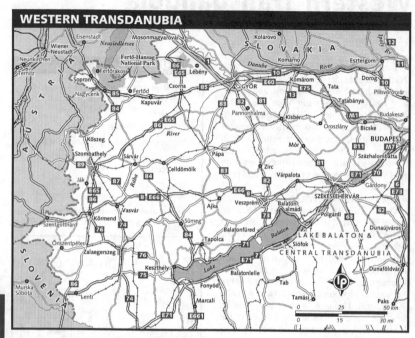

WESTERN TRANSDANUBIA

rock at the northern end of a large lake. It was a favourite residence of King Sigismund, who added a palace in the 15th century; his daughter, Elizabeth of Luxembourg, lingered here in 1440 with the purloined crown of St Stephen en route to Székesfehérvár where her newly born son would be crowned king. King Matthias Corvinus turned Tata into a royal hunting reserve attached to Visegrád, and his successor, Vladislav (Úlászló) II, convened the Diet here to escape from plague-ravaged Buda. Tata Castle was badly damaged by the Turks in 1683, and the town did not begin its recovery until it was acquired by a branch of the aristocratic Esterházy family in the 18th century. They retained the services of Moravian-born architect Jakab Fellner, who designed most of Tata's fine baroque buildings.

Tata is as much a town of recreation as of history. Tata's two lakes offer ample opportunities for sport, and there's a spa complex to the north. Tata is also a convenient gateway to Budapest and the Danube Bend for other Western Transdanubian towns.

Orientation & Information

Tata's busy main street (Ady Endre utca), a section of route No 100, separates the larger Öreg-tó (Old Lake) from Cseke-tó (Tiny Lake).

The bus station is north-west of the castle on Május 1 út. There are two train stations. The main one is a couple of kilometres north of the city centre. The second station, Tóvároskert, which is used only by local trains, is to the south-east and closer to the Fáklya utca camp site and hotel.

The helpful Tourinform office (☎/fax 384 806, ✉ komarom-m@tourinform.hu), Ady Endre utca 9, is open from 8 am to 6 pm weekdays and till noon on Saturday from June to August. During the rest of the year it is open from 8 am to 4 pm weekdays only. Cooptourist (☎/fax 381 602) is off Kodály tér at Tópart setány 18. It's open from 8 am to 4 pm weekdays only.

There's an OTP bank branch at Ady Endre utca 17 opposite the Spar supermarket. The main post office is at Kossuth tér 19, west of the Old Lake.

Öregvár

The remains of the medieval Old Castle – one of four original towers and a palace wing – were rebuilt in neo-Gothic style at the end of the 19th century just before Emperor Franz Joseph came to visit. Today they house the **Domokos Kuny Museum**,

open from 10 am to 6 pm Tuesday to Sunday from May to October and to 4 pm the rest of the year (150/100Ft). On the ground floor are archaeological finds from nearby Roman settlements, bits of the 12th-century Benedictine monastery near Oroszlány and contemporary drawings of the castle in its heyday. The exhibit on the 1st floor entitled 'Life in the Old Castle' is interesting; don't miss the cathedral-like Gothic stove that takes pride of place in the **Knights' Hall**. Material on the 2nd floor examines the work of a dozen 18th-century artisans, including Kuny, a master ceramist. Tata

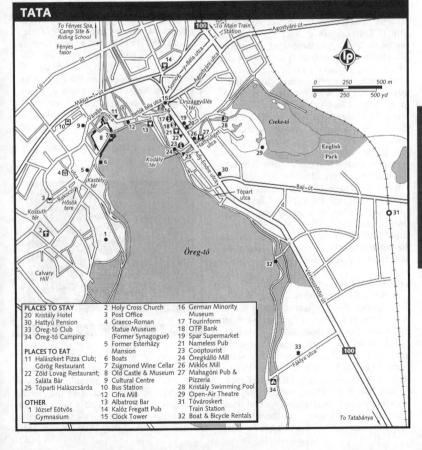

TATA

WESTERN TRANSDANUBIA

PLACES TO STAY	2 Holy Cross Church	16 German Minority
20 Kristály Hotel	3 Post Office	Museum
30 Hattyú Pension	4 Graeco-Roman	17 Tourinform
33 Öreg-tó Club	Statue Museum	18 OTP Bank
34 Öreg-tó Camping	(Former Synagogue)	19 Spar Supermarket
	5 Former Esterházy	21 Nameless Pub
PLACES TO EAT	Mansion	23 Cooptourist
11 Halászkert Pizza Club;	6 Boats	24 Öregkálló Mill
Görög Restaurant	7 Zsigmond Wine Cellar	26 Miklós Mill
22 Zöld Lovag Restaurant;	8 Old Castle & Museum	27 Mahagóni Pub &
Saláta Bár	9 Cultural Centre	Pizzeria
25 Tóparti Halászcsárda	10 Bus Station	28 Kristály Swimming Pool
	12 Cifra Mill	29 Open-Air Theatre
OTHER	13 Albatrosz Bar	31 Tóvároskert
1 József Eötvös	14 Kalóz Fregatt Pub	Train Station
Gymnasium	15 Clock Tower	32 Boat & Bicycle Rentals

porcelain was well known for centuries (the lobster or crayfish was a common decoration here) and the craft indirectly led to the foundation of the porcelain factory at Herend near Vezprém (see boxed text 'Herend Porcelain' in the Lake Balaton & Central Transdanubia chapter). The castle's neoclassical **chapel** (1822) is also open to the public.

Mills

Öregvár, attractively reflected in the lake, is surrounded by a moat, and a system of locks and sluices regulates the flow of water into nearby canals. Tata made good use of this water power; it was once known as the 'town of mills'. The shell of the 16th-century **Cifra Mill** (Cifra-malom), east of the castle at Bartók Béla utca 3, is interesting only for its red marble window frames and five water wheels visible from the north side.

The magnificently restored **Nepomucenus Mill** (1758), a bit farther on at Alkotmány utca 1, now houses the **German Minority Museum** (60/40Ft), which keeps the same hours as the Domokos Kuny Museum. Like Pécs and Székesfehérvár, Tata was predominantly German-speaking for several centuries – there's still a German-language weekly called the *Schwäbische Post* – and all aspects of the German experience in Hungary are explored here. The collections of festive clothing and musical instruments are in very good condition. Other mills on or around the lake include the **Öregkálló Mill** on Tópart sétány and the **Miklós Mill** at Ady Endre utca 26.

Other Attractions

Walking south-west from the castle for a few minutes through leafy Kastély tér to Hősök tere, you'll pass a Zopf-style former **Esterházy Mansion** designed by Jakab Fellner (1764-69); it is just one of four in the town and served as a hospital for some years. At Hősök tere 3, in the old Romantic-style former synagogue, is the weird **Greco-Roman Statue Museum**, with displays of plaster copies of stone sculptures that lined the walkways of Cseke-tó in the 19th century. It's open from 10 am to 6 pm Tuesday

Blame it on the Bird

The ancient Magyars were strong believers in magic and celestial intervention, and the *táltos* (shaman) enjoyed an elevated position in their society. Certain animals – for example, bears, stags and wolves– were totemic, and it was taboo to mention them directly by name. Thus the wolf was 'the long-tailed one' and the stag the 'large-antlered one'. In other cases the original Magyar word for an animal deemed sacred was replaced with a foreign loan word: *medve* for 'bear' comes from the Slavic *medved*.

No other totemic animal is better known to modern Hungarians than the *turul*, an eagle or hawk-like bird that had supposedly impregnated Emese, the grandmother of Árpád. That legend can be viewed in many ways: as an attempt to foster a sense of common origin and group identity in the ethnically heterogeneous population of the time; as an effort to bestow a sacred origin on the House of Árpád and its rule; or just as a nice story.

In the recent past the fearsome-looking turul has been used as a symbol by the far right – much to the distress of average Hungarians, who simply look upon it as their heraldic 'eagle' or 'lion'.

to Sunday May to October (80/50Ft). At Bercsényi utca 1, just before you enter Kossuth tér, stands the birthplace of Mór Farkasházi Fischer, founder of the Herend porcelain factory and Tata's most famous son. Dominating the square is another of Fellner's works, the 18th-century **Holy**

Cross Church (Szent Kereszt-templom), also called the Great Church. If you're up to it, a sadly neglected crucifixion shrine, 14th-century Gothic chapel and a 45m look-out tower (80/60Ft) await at the top of **Calvary Hill** (Kálvária-domb), a short distance to the south. You can look east to the Gerecse Hills, north into Slovakia and south to the urban wasteland of Tatabánya.

Cseke-tó, surrounded by the protected 200-hectare Angolpark, built in 1780 and Hungary's first 'English park' (a landscaped garden), is a relaxing place for a walk or a day of fishing.

The octagonal wooden **clock tower** (óratorny) in Országgyűlés tér is a lot older than it looks. It was designed by – guess who? – Fellner in 1763, and at one time it housed the town's tiny prison.

Activities

As odd as it may seem with a main highway only 100m away, Öreg-tó (a nature conservation area) attracts a considerable number and variety of waterfowl; between 20,000 and 40,000 bean and white-fronted geese pass through in February alone. The best spot for bird-watching, in winter, is the southern end of the lake where a warm spring prevents that part of the lake from freezing over.

The lake has several swimming beaches, and pleasure boats (150/100Ft) depart from the pier just south-west of the castle and on the eastern shore of the lake, where you can also rent bicycles (mobile ☎ 06-209-287 958), in season, from 1 to 9 pm daily. Horses are available from the riding school (mobile ☎ 06-309-579 016) north of the centre in Fényes düllő from 10 am till noon and 2 to 8 pm daily.

The Kristály swimming pool near the English Park is open from 9 am to 7 pm May to September (200/120Ft), but you'll probably enjoy the complex at Fényesfürdő, north of the centre, more (see Places to Stay). It has thermal spas and several huge pools open the same hours.

If you plan on doing any hiking in the Gerecse Hills east of Tata and tailor-made, get a head start by taking a bus to Tardos,

Tarján or Dunaszentmiklós. Cartographia publishes a 1:40,000 map of the area with clear trail markings called *A Gerecse* (No 10; 400Ft).

Places to Stay

There are two camp sites in Tata, both with bungalows. *Fényesfürdő Camping* (☎ *381 591, Fényes fasor*), about 2km north of the city centre near the spa complex, is open from May to September. Camping for a couple costs 600Ft to 1000Ft; one of eight bungalows sleeping four people is 4000Ft. *Öreg-tó Camping* (☎ *383 496, Fáklya utca 1*), south of town and on the big lake, has the same season.

Nearby, the *Öreg-tó Club* hotel (☎/fax *487 960, Fáklya utca 4*) is both a 24-room hotel with singles/doubles/triples for 2000/4000/4700Ft and a hostel with dormitory accommodation for as little as 680Ft a night.

Cooptourist can find you a *private room* for 1500Ft to 2000Ft per person. You'll also find private rooms available near the Kristály swimming pool at Hattyúliget utca 2.

The 26-room *Kristály* hotel (☎ *383 577, fax 383 614, Ady Endre utca 22*), a 200-year-old former Esterházy holding, charges an outrageous DM70/80 for very noisy singles/doubles with modern bath (though there are three double rooms with washbasin for DM45). Instead head a couple of hundred metres south to the cheaper six-room *Hattyú* pension (☎ *383 653, fax 383 322, Ady Endre utca 56*), which has doubles for 3500Ft.

Places to Eat

The *Saláta Bár* (Ady Endre utca 17) in a courtyard called Parizsi Udvar has salads, burgers and gyros and opens to 10 pm weekdays and till midnight at the weekend. The *Mahagóni* (Ady Endre utca 28) takes a stab at real Italian dishes and misses by just a hair. The *Halászkert Pizza Club* (Váralja utca 18) in an attractive restored Esterházy mansion is open daily from 10 am to 10 pm. The *Görög* (Váralja utca 20), next door, serves Greek-ish food in pseudo-Hellenic splendour.

The *Tóparti Halászcsárda (Tópart sétány 10)*, south of Kodály tér, is a quaint little lakeside eatery serving fish. It's open to 10 pm weekdays and till midnight at the weekend. Try the Baja fish soup.

The *Zöld Lovag* (Green Knight) in the same courtyard as the Saláta Bár is another one of those 'medieval-style' restaurants, with colourful banners, large rough-hewn tables and chairs, a menu in Old Hungarian and men in tights. But the food (soups from 350Ft, mains from 1000Ft) ain't half bad at this one and its open daily till midnight.

Entertainment

The *Zoltán Magyary Cultural Centre* (☎ 380 811, *Váralja utca 4*), between the castle and the bus station, will provide you with up-to-date information on what's going on in this culturally active town. Venues include the atmospheric but cramped *Knights' Hall* in the castle, *Holy Cross Church* and the *József Eötvös Gymnasium (Eötvös utca)* on the lake's western shore. Concerts are sometimes held in summer at the *open-air theatre* in the English Park.

The *Albatrosz* bar *(Tópart utca 3)*, in an attractive old house near the castle, attracts a lively young crowd till midnight. The *Zsigmond* cellar in the castle is a great place for a glass of wine. It's open daily till midnight (to 2 am Friday and Saturday). The *Kalóz Fregatt* pub *(Almási út 2)* northeast of the castle has live music at the weekend and stays open to 2 am. A very central place is the nameless *pub (Ady Endre utca 19-21)* in a pavilion connected to the Pán Európa Cinema.

Getting There & Away

Buses leave very frequently for Tatabánya and Dunaszentmiklós, and there are up to eight departures a day to Komárom, Esztergom, Tarján in the Gerecse Hills and Oroszlány, the gateway to the Vértes Hills. Buses to Győr and Budapest (via Visegrád or Tatabánya) depart three or four times a day.

Tata is on the train line linking Budapest-Déli or Keleti with Győr and Vienna. A few daily trains go directly to Sopron and Szombathely via Tata, but you usually have to

change at Győr. If you're travelling by train to Esztergom, change at Almásfüzitő. To get to Slovakia, take the train to Komárom and walk across the border.

Getting Around

Bus No 1 links the main train station with the bus station and Kossuth tér. Bus No 3 will take you to Fényesfürdő; No 5 goes to Tóvároskert train station and Fáklya utca.

You can also order a local taxi on ☎ 489 808 or 489 080.

GYŐR

☎ 96 • postcode 9000 • pop 129,500

Most travellers see no more of Győr (German: Raab) than what's visible in the distance from the highway between Vienna and Budapest. It's usually pegged as 'that big industrial city with the funny name' (it's pronounced something like 'jyeur') and, well, neither can be denied. An important producer of trucks, rolling stock and textiles, Győr is the nation's third-largest industrial centre.

But Győr is also an historical city; in fact, after Budapest and Sopron, no place in the country can boast as many important buildings and monuments. Stroll 100m up pedestrian Baross Gábor utca, and you'll enter a world that has changed little since the 17th and 18th centuries.

Situated in the heart of the so-called Little Plain (Kisalföld) at the meeting point of the Mosoni-Duna and Rába rivers, Győr was settled by the Celts and later the Romans who called it Arrabona. The Avars came here too and built a circular fort (called *gyűrű* from which the town took its name) before the arrival of the Magyars.

King Stephen established a bishopric at Győr in the 11th century, and 200 years later the town was granted a royal charter, allowing it to levy taxes on goods passing through it.

A castle was built here in the 16th century and, being surrounded by water, was an easily defended outpost between Turkish-held Hungary and Vienna, the seat of the Habsburg Empire, until late in the century. When the Ottomans did manage to take

GYŐR

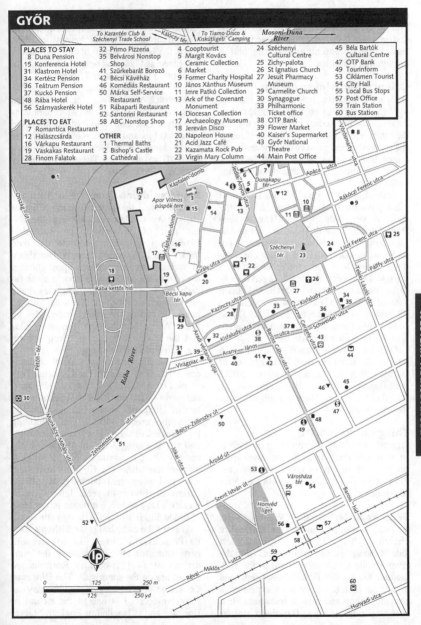

PLACES TO STAY
- 8 Duna Pension
- 15 Konferencia Hotel
- 31 Klastrom Hotel
- 34 Kertész Pension
- 36 Teátrum Pension
- 37 Kuckó Pension
- 48 Rába Hotel
- 56 Szárnyaskerék Hotel

PLACES TO EAT
- 7 Romantica Restaurant
- 12 Halászcsárda
- 16 Várkapu Restaurant
- 19 Vaskakas Restaurant
- 28 Finom Falatok
- 32 Primo Pizzeria
- 35 Belvárosi Nonstop Shop
- 41 Szürkebarát Borozó
- 42 Bécsi Kávéház
- 46 Komédiás Restaurant
- 50 Márka Self-Service Restaurant
- 51 Rábaparti Restaurant
- 52 Santorini Restaurant
- 58 ABC Nonstop Shop

OTHER
- 1 Thermal Baths
- 2 Bishop's Castle
- 3 Cathedral
- 4 Cooptourist
- 5 Margit Kovács Ceramic Collection
- 6 Market
- 9 Former Charity Hospital
- 10 János Xánthus Museum
- 11 Imre Patkó Collection
- 13 Ark of the Covenant Monument
- 14 Diocesan Collection
- 17 Archaeology Museum
- 18 Jereván Disco
- 20 Napoleon House
- 21 Acid Jazz Café
- 22 Kazamata Rock Pub
- 23 Virgin Mary Column
- 24 Széchenyi Cultural Centre
- 25 Zichy-palota
- 26 St Ignatius Church
- 27 Jesuit Pharmacy Museum
- 29 Carmelite Church
- 30 Synagogue
- 33 Philharmonic Ticket office
- 38 OTP Bank
- 39 Flower Market
- 40 Kaiser's Supermarket
- 43 Győr National Theatre
- 44 Main Post Office
- 45 Béla Bartók Cultural Centre
- 47 OTP Bank
- 49 Tourinform
- 53 Ciklámen Tourist
- 54 City Hall
- 55 Local Bus Stops
- 57 Post Office
- 59 Train Station
- 60 Bus Station

WESTERN TRANSDANUBIA

Győr, they were able to hold on for only four years and were evicted in 1598. For that reason Győr has been praised as the 'dear guard', watching over the nation through the centuries.

Orientation &Information

Győr's train station lies south of Honvéd liget (Soldier Park) on Révai Miklós utca. To reach the bus station in Hunyadi utca on the other side of the railway line go through the subway (underpass) east of the main entrance. Baross Gábor utca leads to Belváros, the historic Inner Town, and the river runs to the north.

Tourinform (☎/fax 311 557) is in a small glass pavilion at Árpád utca 22, and the staff are very helpful. The office is open from 8 am to 8 pm daily from June to August, from 8 am to 6 pm weekdays, to 3 pm on Saturday and from 9 am to 1 pm on Sunday in April, May and September and from 9 am to 4 pm weekdays and to 2 pm on Saturday from October to March. Ciklámen Tourist (☎ 311 557) at Aradi Vértanúk útja 22 and Cooptourist (☎/fax 329 533) at Jedlik Ányos utca 8, are open from 8 am to 4 or 4.30 pm on weekdays only.

OTP has a bank branch at Árpad út 36 next to the Rába hotel and another one at Baross Gábor utca 16. The main post office is at Bajcsy-Zsilinszky út 46, opposite the Kisfaludy Theatre. There's a branch near the train station.

Things to See & Do

Almost everything worth seeing in Győr is in or around three areas just minutes apart on foot. Museums in Győr usually cost 80Ft or 100Ft for adults and 40Ft or 50Ft for students.

Bécsi kapu tér Baroque 'Viennese Gate Square' is dominated by the **Carmelite church**, built in 1725. On the north-west side of the square and cutting it off from the river are the fortifications built in the 16th century to stop the Turkish onslaught, and a bastion that has served as a prison, a chapel, a shop and now a restaurant. Just east at Király utca 4 is **Napoleon House**.

One of the more unusual footnotes in Hungarian history is that Napoleon entered Hungarian territory very briefly in 1809, and actually spent the night of 31 August in this house as Győr was near a battle site. An inscription on the Arc de Triomphe in Paris recalls 'la bataille de Raab'.

A branch of the János Xánthus Museum – an **archaeology museum** of cellars containing a rich collection of Roman and medieval bits and pieces – is housed in the castle casemates at Bécsi kapu tér 5 (open from 10 am to 6 pm Tuesday to Sunday from April to October).

Káptalan-domb From the archaeology museum, walk up Káptalan-domb (Chapter Hill) to Apor Vilmos püspök tere, the oldest part of the city. The **cathedral** (Székesegyház), whose foundations date back to the 11th century, is an odd amalgam of styles, with Romanesque apses (have a look from the outside), a neoclassical facade and a Gothic chapel riding piggyback on the south side. But most of what you see inside, including the stunning frescoes by Franz Anton Maulbertsch, the main altar and the bishop's throne, is baroque from the 17th and 18th centuries.

The Gothic **Héderváry Chapel** contains one of the most beautiful (and priceless) examples of medieval gold work in Hungary, the **Herm of László**. It's a bust reliquary of one of Hungary's earliest king-saints and dates from around 1400. If you're looking for miracles, though, move to the north aisle and the **Weeping Icon of Mary**, a 17th-century altarpiece brought here from Galway by the Bishop of Clonfert in Ireland who had been sent packing by Oliver Cromwell. Some 40 years later – on St Patrick's Day no less – it began to cry tears of blood and is still a pilgrimage site.

West of the cathedral is the **Bishop's Castle** (Püspökvár), a fortress-like structure with parts dating from the 13th century; the foundations of an 11th-century Romanesque chapel are on the south side. The **Diocesan Collection** (Egyházmegyei Gyüjtemény) at Káptalan-domb 1 is one of the richest in Hungary and is labelled in English. Marvel at the heavy chasubles in gold thread, the bishops' crooks of solid silver and pieces of the True Cross, but the collection of manuscripts (some illuminated) is ultimately more impressive. It is open from 10 am to 4 pm Tuesday to Sunday.

Széchenyi tér A couple of blocks southeast of Káptalan-domb is Széchenyi tér, a large square in the heart of Győr and the market in the Middle Ages currently being excavated for archaeological treasures. Along the way, at the bottom of the hill on Jedlik Ányos utca, you'll pass the outstanding **Ark of the Covenant** (Frigyláda emlékmű), a large statue dating from 1731. Local tradition has it that the king erected the city's finest baroque monument to appease the angry people of Győr after one of his soldiers accidentally knocked the Eucharist out of a priest's hands during a Corpus Christi procession.

The renovated **Column of the Virgin Mary** (Mária-oszlop) in Széchenyi tér was raised in 1686 to honour the recapture of Buda Castle from the Turks. The Jesuit and later Benedictine **Church of St Ignatius**, the city's finest, dates from 1641. The 17th-century white-stucco side chapels and the ceiling frescoes painted by the Viennese artist Paul Troger in 1744 are worth a look. The **Szécheny Pharmacy Museum** (Szécheny Patikamúzeum), next door at Széchenyi tér 9, was established by the Jesuits in 1667 and is a fully operational baroque institution. You can inspect the rococo vaulted ceiling and the frescoes with religious and herbal themes during opening hours (8 am to 4.30 pm on weekdays, from 10 am on Wednesday).

If time is limited, skip the main branch of the **János Xánthus Museum** (open from 10 am to 6 pm Tuesday to Sunday) across the square at Széchenyi tér 5 (Győr history, stamps and coins, antique furniture, natural history) and head for the **Imre Patkó Collection** in the 17th-century **Iron Stump House** (Vastuskós Ház) at No 4, a former caravanserai that still sports the log into which itinerant artisans would drive a nail to mark their visit. The museum is one of the best of its size anywhere in Hungary and has an excellent collection of 20th-century fine art on the first two floors; the 3rd floor is given over to objects collected by the journalist and art historian Imre Patkó during his travels in India, Tibet, Vietnam and west Africa.

Just off Széchenyi tér at Apáca utca 1 is the **Margit Kovács Ceramic Collection** (Kovács Margit kerámiagyűjtemény), a branch of the more famous one found in Szentendre. It's open from 10 am to 6 pm Tuesday to Sunday.

Other Attractions

One of the nicest things about Győr is its atmospheric old streets. Take a stroll down Bástya utca, Apáca utca, Rákóczi Ferenc utca, Liszt Ferenc utca and Király utca (east and north-east of Széchenyi tér), where you'll see many fine buildings. The late Renaissance **palace** at Rákóczi Ferenc utca 6 was once a charity hospital. Go inside to see the courtyards.

The richly decorated octagonal cupola, galleries and tabernacle of the city's **synagogue** (1869), across the river at Kossuth Lajos utca 5, are well worth a look if you can get into the decrepit old building. Try at the entrance to the music academy (formerly a Jewish school) next door.

Have a look at the colourful **flower market** held most mornings on Virágpiac south of Bécsi kapu tér.

Activities

On the left bank of the Rába River are Győr's well-maintained thermal baths (Ország út 4). To get there, cross Rába kettős híd (Rába Double Bridge) over the little island and walk north along Radó sétány. The covered pool is open from 6 am to 8 pm weekdays, 7 am to 6 pm at weekends year round. The strand pools are open between May and September.

Places to Stay

Camping *Kiskútligeti Camping* (☎ *318 986)*, near the stadium and some 3km northeast of town in Kiskútliget (Little Well Park), has a *motel* which is open all year

(2300/3500Ft singles/doubles) and horrid little *bungalows* for up to four people (3400Ft) open between mid-April and mid-October. Camping costs 500Ft per person.

Private Rooms & Hostels Private rooms for two are available from Ibusz for about 3000Ft. Dormitory accommodation is available year round at the huge *István Széchenyi Trade School* (*Héderváry út 3*) north of the centre. Contact Tourinform for details.

Pensions Unusually for a Hungarian city, Győr is full of small private pensions and, while not the cheapest places to stay, they are usually very central and in some of the city's most colourful old buildings. The *Kuckó* (☎ *316 260, fax 319 459, Arany János utca 33*) in an old townhouse has nine rooms with bath for 6000/7400Ft singles/doubles. The smaller (and cheaper) *Kertész* (☎/*fax 317 461, Iskola utca 11*) to the east has eight rooms for 5400/6700Ft. The picks of the crop, though, and under the same management, are the 10-room *Teátrum* (☎ *310 640, fax 328 827, Schweidel utca 7*) on an attractive pedestrian street and its sister pension, the Regency-blue *Duna* (☎/*fax 329 084, Vörösmarty utca 5*), with 14 rooms and antique furniture in some of the common rooms. Singles/doubles/triples at both are 5300/6500/7500Ft.

Hotels The four-storey, 30-room *Szárnyaskerék* hotel (☎ *314 629, fax 317 844, Révai Miklós utca 5*) opposite the noisy train station charges 3750Ft for a double with washbasin, 6300Ft for one with bath.

The *Rába* hotel (☎ *315 533, fax 311 124,* ✉ *hhtours1@hungary.net, Árpád utca 34*), a 166-room colossus with old and new wings close to busy Szent István út, charges DM130/160 for singles/doubles. If you can afford that kind of money, though, book into the three-star *Klastrom* hotel (☎ *315 611, Zechmeister utca 1*) south of Bécsi kapu tér. It has 42 rooms with bath (DM105 to DM120, according to the room and the season) in a 250-year-old Carmelite convent and boasts a sauna, a solarium, a pub with a vaulted ceiling, and a rather cramped restaurant. The best rooms face the inner courtyard.

The modern carbuncle on Káptalandomb next to the cathedral is the 20-room *Konferencia* hotel (☎ *314 011, fax 316 993, Apor Vilmos püspök tere 3*), once a company guesthouse and now one of Győr's most expensive (and pretentious) places to stay. Singles/doubles at the hotel are a budget-destroying DM130/155.

Places to Eat

For a cheap self-service meal, try the modernised *Márka* (*Bajcsy-Zsilinszky út 30*), which is open weekdays from 11.30 am to 3.30 pm weekdays, to 2 pm on Saturday. It has a popular *cukrászda* attached. Another inexpensive place is *Finom Falatok* (*Kazinczy utca 12*) east of Bécsi kapu tér and open from 7 am to 6 pm weekdays and to 1 pm on Saturday.

A decent wine cellar restaurant is the *Szürkebarát Borozó* (*Arany János utca 20 or Baross Gábor utca 18*) in a small courtyard, with mains from 500Ft and pizzas for 310Ft to 480Ft. In the same courtyard you'll also find the *Bécsi* coffee house, which is a pleasant place to sit and read. A younger crowd favours *Primo Pizzeria* (*Aradi vértanúk útja 3*) open Monday to Saturday till midnight.

The *Rábaparti* (*Zehmeister utca 18*) serves tasty Hungarian fare in an unpretentious (though rather gloomy) restaurant at very reasonable prices. The cellar-like *Vaskakas* (*Bécsi kapu tér 2*), in the former castle casemates near the Rába River, has loads of atmosphere as long as you don't mind long tables of German-speaking pensioners to your left and right. Instead, try the charming little *Várkapu* (*Bécsi kapu tér 7*), overlooking the Carmelite church. It lists its dishes on a blackboard outside (650Ft to 1450Ft).

A typical inn with fish dishes is the *Halászcsárda* (*Apáca utca 4*), near the market. More expensive places include the *Santorini* (*Munkácsy Mihály utca 6*), a Greek/Mediterranean restaurant south-west of the centre, and *Komédiás* (*Czuczor Gergely utca 30*), a cellar eatery decorated in postmodern greys and blacks opposite the cultural centre (mains 580Ft to 800Ft). I would vote the upmarket *Ristorante Romantica (Dunakapu tér 5)* as the most authentic Italian restaurant in Hungary (including the capital). But it's not cheap, with pastas from 900Ft to 1200Ft and mains 1300Ft to 2200Ft.

A colourful *open-air market* unfolds on Dunakapu tér most mornings. There's an *ABC nonstop shop* down to the steps of the subway to the train station. The *Belvárosi nonstop* is at Schweidel utca 19.

Entertainment

The celebrated Győr Ballet and the city's opera company and philharmonic orchestra all perform at the modern *Győr National Theatre (Győri Nemzeti Színház; ☎ 314 800, Czuczor Gergely utca 7)*, a technically advanced, though unattractive, structure covered in op art tiles by Victor Vasarely. Another important venue for classical music is the *Zichy Palace (Zichy-palota; ☎ 320 289, Liszt Ferenc utca 20)*. The box office at the theatre is open from 10 am till noon and 1 to 6 pm weekdays (mornings only on Monday). The ticket office for the philharmonic (☎ 326 323) is at Kisfaludy utca 25.

Unusual places for a pint in the centre are the *Kazamata Rock Pub (Szabadsajtó utca 9)* and the *Acid Jazz Café (Baross Gábor utca 3)* around the corner. The *Jereván (Radó sétány)* on the little island in the Rába River and the *Tiamo Club (Héderváry út 22/a)* and *Karantén (Kálóczy tér 6)* north of the centre are popular clubs.

Getting There & Away

Bus There are at least a dozen departures a day to Budapest, Kapuvár, Pannonhalma, Pápa and Veszprém, and half as many go to Balatonfüred, Mosonmagyaróvár and Székesfehérvár. Other destinations from Győr : Dunaújváros (five buses daily), Esztergom (one), Hévíz (two), Keszthely (five), Lébény (from eight to 12), Pécs (two), Szombathely (three to five), Tapolca (three), Tata (three), and Zalaegerszeg (five). Three to four buses run to Vienna daily (the first at 8.40 am, the last at 6.25 pm), and there's a daily one to Bratislava at 9.15 am.

Train Győr is the main rail junction after Budapest and has convenient connections with both Budapest-Keleti and Budapest-Déli stations and Vienna via Hegyeshalom. Trains to Ebenfurth in Austria via Sopron, which are run by a private concern called GySEV and not part of the MÁV system, are not as frequent.

From Győr, you can also reach Szombathely by train via Pápa and the gateway to the Balaton region, Veszprém, via Pannonhalma and Zirc. If you're heading for Slovakia, change at Komárom.

Getting Around

You can reach the Kiskútligeti camp site on bus No 8 from beside the colossal city hall on Városház tér.

Local taxis can be ordered on ☎ 312 222.

AROUND GYŐR
Lébény
☎ 96 • postcode 9155 • pop 3200

This village 15km north-west of Győr contains the most important example of Romanesque architecture still standing in Hungary: the Benedictine **Abbey Church of St James** (Szent Jakab apátsági templom). Though not as intimate or evocative of medieval Hungary as the Abbey Church at Ják near Szombathely, it is nonetheless worth a visit for its sheer size and superb condition.

The church was begun by two Győr noblemen in 1199 and consecrated in 1212 under the authority of Pannonhalma Abbey. Though the Lébény church managed to escape destruction during the Mongol invasion, it was set aflame twice by the Turks. The abbey hired Italian stonemasons to raze the structure in 1563, but apparently they were so impressed with it that they refused to carry out the task. In the 17th century the church passed into the hands of the Jesuits, who renovated it in the baroque style 100 years later. In the late 19th century, when neo-Romanesque and neo-Gothic architecture was all the rage in Transdanubia, the church was restored by a German architect.

Take a close look at the carved-stone west portal and the south entrance portal; they're in excellent condition. The fresco fragment of the Three Magis above the west portal dates from the mid-17th century.

Between eight and 12 buses make the run every day from Győr. The bus stop is on Fő utca, a two-minute walk east of the church.

PANNONHALMA
☎ 96 • postcode 9090 • pop 3700

Since late in the 10th century, this small village 21km south-east of Győr has been the site of a Benedictine abbey, which even managed to continue functioning during the darkest days of Stalinism. Its secondary school, attended by some 360 students, is tops in the nation; oddly, the only other Hungarian Benedictine monastery in operation today is in the Brazilian city of São Paolo.

The abbey celebrated its millennium to great fanfare in 1996 and was also added to UNESCO's World Heritage List, the fourth site in Hungary to be so honoured.

The monastery was founded by monks from Venice and Prague with the assistance of Prince Géza. The Benedictines were considered a militant order, and Géza's son King Stephen made use of the order to help Christianise Hungary.

The abbey and associated buildings have been razed, rebuilt and restored many times over the centuries. Under the Turks, the basilica did not sustain as much damage as it could have for the simple reason that it faced east and was turned into a mosque. As a result the complex is a crazy patchwork of architectural styles.

Orientation & Information

The village is dominated by 282m Castle Hill (Várhegy) and the abbey. The bus from Győr stops in the centre of the village; from here, follow Váralja up to the abbey. Some buses – between four and five a day – continue up the eastern side of the hill and stop at the abbey's main entrance.

The train station is a couple of kilometres west of the village off Petőfi utca in the direction of route No 82.

The Tourinform office (☎/fax 471 733, @ pannonhalma@tourinform.hu) at Petőfi utca 25 is inconveniently located about 600m south of Szabadság tér and – in theory

– opens from 9 am to 6 pm daily from June to August and from 10 am to 4 pm weekdays only the rest of the year. A much better bet is Pax Tourist (☎ 570 191, fax 570 192), the only agency here, just south of the abbey's main entrance at Vár utca 1. There's an OTP bank at Dózsa György utca 1 opposite the Pax hotel. The main post office is on the same street at No 7.

Pannonhalma Abbey

Pannonhalma Abbey (Pannonhalmi főapátsád) at Vár utca 1 was thoroughly spruced up for its 1000th birthday in 1996 and is now one of the most impressive historical complexes in Hungary. You'll begin your guided tour in the central courtyard, with its statue of the first abbot, Asztrik, who brought the crown of King Stephen to Hungary from Rome, and a relief of King Stephen presenting his son Imre to the tutor Bishop Gellért. To the north there are dramatic views over the Kisalföld while looming behind you are the abbey's modern wings and neoclassical clock tower built in the early 19th century.

The entrance to **St Martin's Basilica** (Szent Márton-bazilika), built early in the 12th century, is through the **Porta Speciosa**. This arched doorway in red limestone was recarved in the mid-19th century by the Stornos, a controversial family of restorers who imposed 19th-century Romantic notions of Romanesque and Gothic architecture on ancient buildings (see the Sopron section). It is beautiful despite the butchery. The fresco above the doorway by Ferenc Storno depicts the church's patron, St Martin of Tours, giving half his cloak to a crouching beggar. Look down to the right below the columns and you'll see what is perhaps the oldest graffiti in Hungary: 'Benedict Padary was here in 1578' it reads in Latin.

The interior of the long and sombre church contains more of the Stornos' handiwork, including the neo-Gothic pulpit and raised marble altar. The Romanesque niche in the wall of the 13th-century crypt is called the **Seat of St Stephen**; legend says that it contains the saint-king's throne.

The 13th-century seal of Pannonhalma Abbey

As you walk along the cloister arcade (or ambulatory), notice the little faces carved in stone on the wall. They represent human emotions and vices such as wrath, greed and conceit. In the cloister garden a Gothic sundial offers a sobering thought: 'Una Vestrum, Ultima Mea' (One of you will be my last).

The most beautiful part of the abbey is the neoclassical **abbey library** (főapátság könyvtára) built in 1836 by János Packh, who helped design the cathedral at Esztergom. It contains some 300,000 volumes – many of them priceless historical records – making it the largest private library in Hungary. But the rarest and most important document is in the **abbey archives**. It is the *Deed of Foundation* of Tihany Abbey and dates from 1055. Though in Latin, it contains about 50 Hungarian place names and is the earliest surviving example of written Hungarian. The library's interior may look like marble, but it is made entirely of wood. An ingenious system of mirrors within the skylights reflect and direct natural light throughout the room.

The **gallery** (képtár) off the library contains works by Dutch, Italian and Austrian masters from the 16th to 18th centuries. The oldest work, however, goes back to 1350. The most valuable piece is the 17th-century *Dead Christ* by Teniers the Younger. Below the library are the rooms of the **Millennium Exhibition** tracing the development of the abbey in Hungarian, German and English as well as liturgical objects from the abbey treasury.

The abbey is open from 8.30 am to 6 pm daily from June to September and 8.30 or 9.30 am to 4.30 or 5 pm Tuesday to Sunday the rest of the year. Because it is a working monastery, the abbey must be visited with a guide. From late March to mid-November they are available between seven and nine times a day in Hungarian (9 am to 4 or 5 pm) but only at 11 am and 1 pm in English and four other languages (Italian, German, French and Russian). In winter, tours leave in Hungary five times a day (10 am to 3 pm); those in other languages are on a request basis only. If there's no guide available in your language, the ticket office will provide you with a leaflet to follow.

For foreign languages you must pay 300Ft above the usual entry fee, so it's 800/400Ft in English and the four other foreign languages and 500/150Ft in Hungarian but the tour is well worth it.

After you've admired the abbey follow the paved path south of Pax Tourist and the ticket office up the hill to two lovely chapels and a lookout tower, which offers expansive views of the region.

Special Events

There are a half-dozen organ and choral concerts scheduled between April and December in the basilica always at the same time – 3.30 pm – and on the same dates: Easter Monday, Whit Monday, 20 August (St Stephen's Day), the Saturday before/after 8 September (Virgin Mary's Birthday), 23 October (National Day) and 26 December (Boxing Day).

Places to Stay & Eat

Panoráma Camping (☎ 471 240, Fenyvesalja utca 4a) to the east of Castle Hill also has a couple of bungalows sleeping four people (4500Ft), a small *büfé* and a salad bar. Open from May to September, the camp site is in a good location for visiting the abbey – just go through the gate in the back and climb the hill to the car park.

There are two small pensions in town: the five-room *Família* (☎/fax 470 192, Béke utca 61) as you enter town from the north on route No 82 (3500Ft per double), and the less-than-welcoming *Pannon* (*☎/fax 470 041, Hunyadi út 7/c*), with seven rooms on the way up to the abbey. Singles/doubles are DM40/50. The *Pax* (*☎ 470 006, fax 470 007, Dózsa György utca 2*) is a 25-room hotel in the centre. Singles/doubles with bath are 6700/6900Ft, suites are 9100Ft.

In the village, the *Kolostor* restaurant (*Szabadság tér 1*) near Dózsa György utca may do in a pinch and is open to 10 pm, but the *István Vendéglő* (*Szabadság tér 24*) is a better choice. You might also try the *Borpince* (*corner of Hunyadi utca & Szabadság tér*) for a glass of local wine. It's open daily from 11 am to 7 pm.

The *Szent Márton* complex (*Vár utca 1*) below the abbey near the car park has a snack bar, restaurant, pub and gift shop.

Getting There & Away

Buses to/from Győr are frequent with two or three an hour passing through on weekdays (between 12 and 17 at the weekend). Six trains a day stop at Pannonhalma on their way to Veszprém from Győr.

SOPRON

☎ 99 • postcode 9400 • pop 55,000

Sopron, at the foot of the Lővér Hills and a mere 6km from the Austrian border, is one of the most charming medieval cities in Hungary. With its preponderance of Gothic and early baroque architecture, Sopron is the closest thing the country has to Prague and exploring the backstreets and courtyards of the thumb-shaped Inner Town is like a step back in time.

Sopron (German: Ödenburg) has had a long and tumultuous past, with more wars and decisions thrust upon its population than most cities. Indeed, as recently as 1921 the citizens of Sopron had to vote whether to stay in Austria's Bürgenland as a result of the Trianon Treaty or be re-annexed by Hungary. They resoundingly chose the latter, and that explains the little knot of Hungarian territory that juts into Austria.

The Celts arrived in the area first and then came the Romans, who lived in a settlement called Scarbantia (now Sopron's Inner Town) between the 1st and 4th centuries. The Germans, Avars, Slavs and the Magyars followed. In medieval times, Sopron was ideally situated for trade along the so-called Amber Route from the Baltic Sea to the Adriatic and Byzantium. By the 1300s, after a century of struggle between the Hungarians and the Austrians for hegemony over the city, Sopron had been made a royal free town – its mixed population able to pursue their trades without pressure from feudal landlords. Thus a strong middle class of artisans and merchants emerged here, and their wealth contributed to making Sopron a centre of science and education.

Neither the Mongols nor Turks were able to penetrate the heart of Sopron, which is why so many old buildings still stand. But damage during WWII was severe, and restoration continued apace in the 1960s.

Sopron is an anomaly in Hungary – a city with a Gothic heart and a modern mind. It's true that it attracts enormous amounts of tourists, but most of the visitors who flock to the streets on a Saturday are Austrians in search of cut-rate haircuts, dental work and enough sausage to open their own delicatessens. Come nightfall, the city is once again in the hands of the loyal citizens of Sopron.

Orientation

The medieval Belváros (Inner Town) contains almost everything of interest in Sopron, though there are a few worthy sights across the narrow Ikva Stream to the north-east just beyond the city walls. The Lővér Hills start about 4km south-west of the city.

Sopron's main train station is on Állomás utca south of the shoeprint-shaped Inner Town. Walk north along Mátyás király utca and past Széchenyi tér to reach Várkerület and Hátsókapu (Back Gate), one of the few entrances to the Inner Town. Várkerület and Ógabona tér beyond it form a ring around the Inner Town, roughly following the city's Roman and medieval walls. Sopron-Déli station, through which trains to/from Szombathely also pass, is to the north-west. The bus station is north-west of the Inner Town on Lackner Kristóf utca.

SOPRON & LŐVÉR HILLS

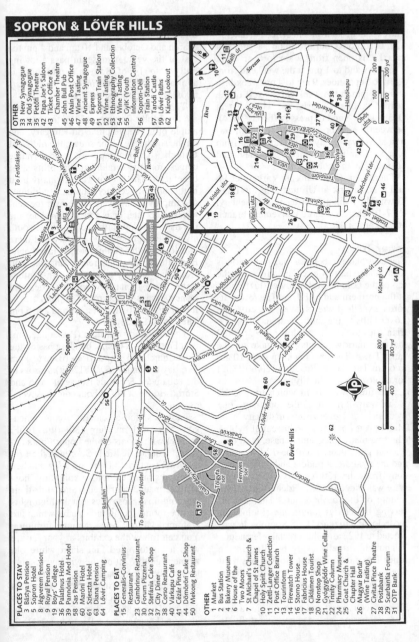

WESTERN TRANSDANUBIA

PLACES TO STAY
3 Bástya Pension
5 Sopron Hotel
8 Jégverem Pension
9 Royal Pension
19 Boys' College
36 Palatinus Hotel
39 Pannónia Med Hotel
58 Sas Pension
60 Maróni Hotel
61 Szieszta Hotel
63 Diana Pension
64 Lővér Camping

PLACES TO EAT
15 Generalis-Corvinius
   Restaurant
23 Gambrinus Restaurant
30 Forum Pizzeria
32 Stefánia Cake Shop
37 City Diner
38 Corso Restaurant
40 Várkapu Café
41 Cézár Pince
44 Dömörői Cake Shop
50 Mekong Restaurant

OTHER
1 Market
2 Bus Station
4 Bakery Museum
6 House of the
   Two Moors
7 St Michael's Church &
   Chapel of St James
10 Holy Spirit Church
11 Zettl-Langer Collection
12 Post Office Branch
13 Tourinform
14 Firewatch Tower
16 Storno House
17 Fabricius House
18 Ciklámen Tourist
20 Nonstop Shop
21 Gyógygödör Wine Cellar
22 Trinity Column
24 Pharmacy Museum
25 Goat Church &
   Chapter Hall
26 Magyar Bortár
   (Wine Tasting)
27 Civitas Pince Theatre
28 Postabank
29 Scarbantia Forum
31 OTP Bank

OTHER
33 New Synagogue
34 Old Synagogue
35 Petőfi Theatre
42 Papa Joe's Saloon
43 Ticket Office &
   Chamber Theatre
45 John Bull Pub
46 Main Post Office
47 Wine Tasting
48 Ancient Synagogue
49 Express
51 Sopron Train Station
52 Wine Tasting
53 Ethnography Collection
54 Wine Tasting
55 Cyík (Youth
   Information Centre)
56 Sopron-Deli
   Train Station
57 Tarodi Castle
59 Lővér Baths
62 Károly Lookout

Information

The excellent Tourinform office (☎/fax 338 892, ☒ sopron@tourinform.hu), at Előkapu utca 11, is open from 9 am to 6 or 7 pm weekdays and to 1 pm at the weekend from April to September; 9 am to 4 pm weekdays and to 1 pm at the weekend the rest of the year. Ciklámen Tourist (☎ 312 040) at Ógabona tér 8 and Express (☎/fax 312 024), between the Inner Town and the train station at Mátyás király utca 7, are open from 8 or 8.30 am to 4.30 pm on weekdays and on Saturday to noon or 1 pm.

There's an OTP bank at Várkerület 96 and a Postabank at Új utca 3 in the Inner Town. The main post office is at Széchenyi tér 7-10; there's a more convenient branch at Várkerület 37.

Inner Town

The best place to begin a tour of Sopron is to climb the narrow circular staircase to the top of the 60m **firewatch tower** (tűztorony) at the northern end of Fő tér. The tower affords excellent views over the city, the Lővér Hills to the south-west and the Austrian Alps to the west. Below are Fő tér and the four narrow streets that make up the Inner Town. The tower is open from 10 am to 6 pm Tuesday to Sunday (120/60/180Ft for adults/children/family).

The fire tower, from which trumpeters would warn of fire, mark the hour (now done by chimes) and greet visitors to the city in the Middle Ages, is a true architectural hybrid. The two-metre thick square base, built on a Roman gate, dates from the 12th century, and the cylindrical middle and arcaded balcony from the 16th century. The baroque spire was added in 1681. **Fidelity Gate** at the bottom of the tower pictures Hungary receiving the *civitas fidelissima* (Latin: 'the most loyal citizenry') of Sopron. It was erected in 1922 after that crucial referendum.

Though virtually every building in the Inner Town is of interest, Sopron has relatively few specific monuments of importance. Fő tér contains the lion's share of what there is and most of the museums. The choice is great and each charges a separate admission fee, so choose carefully. In general, the museums are open from 10 am to 5 or 6 pm Tuesday to Sunday between March and October and 10 am and 4 pm the rest of the year. A museum pass allowing entry into 14 of Sopron's museums is available from Tourinform and costs 500/250Ft for adults/children.

The focal points of this graceful square are the **Trinity Column** (1701), the best example of a 'plague pillar' in Hungary, and on the south side of the square the old **Goat Church** (Kecsketemplom), whose name comes from the heraldic animal of its chief benefactor. The church was originally built in the late 13th century, but many additions and improvements were made over the centuries. The interior is mostly baroque, the red marble pulpit in the centre of the south aisle dates from the 15th century and there is a lovely little Gothic domed tabernacle. Beneath the Goat Church is **Chapter Hall** (Káptalan-terem), part of a 14th-century Benedictine monastery with frescoes and stone carvings. Enter from Templom utca 7. It is open from 10 am till noon and 2 to 5 pm Tuesday to Sunday (free).

The **Pharmacy Museum** (Patikamúzeum) is at Fő tér 2 in a Gothic building beside the Goat Church and is open from 10 am to 4 pm Tuesday to Sunday (60/30/120Ft). Across to the square are **Fabricius House** at No 6 and **Storno House** at No 8; both contain several exhibits.

Fabricius House contains a comprehensive historical museum (80/40Ft, 140Ft family) with rooms on the upper floors devoted to domestic life in Sopron in the 17th and 18th centuries. There are a few kitchen mock-ups and exhibits explaining how people made their beds and did their washing-up in those days, but the highlights are the rooms facing the square, which are crammed with priceless antique furniture. You can follow the exhibits at your leisure with a photocopied fact sheet while old women 'guides' sit by the window making lace in the afternoon sunlight. Scarbantia-era statues reconstructed from fragments found in the area, including enormous ones of Juno, Jupiter and Minerva, guard the lapidarium (kőtar) in the cellar of house No 7, once a Gothic chapel, with vaulted ceilings 15m high.

On the 1st floor of Storno House (1417), there's a less-than-enthralling exhibit on Sopron's more recent history, but on the floor above is the wonderful **Storno Collection** (Storno Gyűjtemény; 150/80/250Ft), which belonged to a 19th-century Swiss-Italian family of restorers whose recarving of Romanesque and Gothic monuments throughout Transdanubia is frowned upon today. To their credit, the much maligned Stornos did rescue many altarpieces and church furnishings from oblivion, and their house is a Gothic treasure trove. Highlights include the beautiful enclosed balcony with leaded windows and frescoes, leather chairs with designs depicting Mephisto with his dragons, and door frames made from pews taken from 15th-century St George's Church on Szent György utca. It is open from 10 am to 6 pm Tuesday to Sunday from May to September and to 2 pm the rest of the year.

Beneath the building at Új utca 1 is the **Scarbantia Forum**, an original marketplace dating from Roman times; parts have been incorporated into the tourist office there (open 9 am to 4.30 pm Monday to Saturday). If you continue walking down Új utca – known as Zsidó utca (Jewish Street) until the Jews were evicted from Sopron in 1526 – you'll reach the **Old Synagogue** (Ózsinagóga) at No 22 and the **New Synagogue** (Új Zsinagóga) across the street at No 11. Both were built in the 14th century and are among the greatest Jewish Gothic monuments in Europe and unique in Hungary. The Old Synagogue is now a museum (100/50/160Ft) and can be visited from 9 am to 5 pm Wednesday to Monday. The New Synagogue forms part of a private house and offices, though you can see the exterior quite clearly by entering the courtyard at Szent György utca 12. The Old Synagogue contains two rooms, one for each sex (note the women's windows along the west wall). The main room contains a medieval 'holy of holies' with geometric designs and trees carved in stone, and some ugly new stained-glass windows. The inscriptions on the walls date from 1490. There's a reconstructed *mikvah* (ritual bath) in the courtyard.

Other Attractions

Sopron's sights are not entirely confined to the Inner Town. Walk back to Fő tér, past the old Roman walls, under Előkapu and over a small bridge leading to Ikva, once the district of merchants and artisans. At Balfi út 11 the excellent **Zettl-Langer Private Collection** (Zettl-Langer Magángyűjtemény) contains ceramics, paintings and furniture. It's open from 10 am to noon only Tuesday to Sunday (150Ft).

To the north, on Dorfmeister utca, is the 15th-century **Church of the Holy Spirit** (Szentlélek-templom). Farther north at Szent Mihály utca 9 is the **House of the Two Moors** (Két mór ház). It was fashioned from two 17th-century peasant houses and is guarded by two large and very black statues.

At the top of the hill is **St Michael's Church** (Szent Mihály-templom), built between the 13th and 15th centuries, and behind it the Romanesque-Gothic **Chapel of St James** (Szent Jakab-kápolna), the oldest structure in Sopron. Not much escaped the Stornos' knives when they 'renovated' St Michael's (they also added the spire).

If you return to the House of the Two Moors and walk west along Fövényverem utca, you'll soon reach Bécsi út and the **Bakery Museum** (Pékmúzeum) at No 5, the second-best museum in Sopron. It's actually the completely restored home, bakery and shop of a successful 19th-century bread and pastry maker named Weissbeck and contains some interesting gadgets and work-saving devices. It's open from 10 am to 2 pm on Wednesday, Friday and Sunday, and from 2 to 6 pm on Tuesday, Thursday and Saturday (80/40/140Ft).

The city museum's **Ethnography Collection** (Néprajzi Gyűjtemény), with an interesting array of implements used in winemaking, baking and weaving is at Deák tér 1 and is open from 10 am to 6 pm Tuesday to Sunday (100/50/160Ft).

There's an ancient **synagogue**, barely standing, east of the Inner Town at Paprét 14.

Special Events

Sopron is a musical town – the child prodigy Franz Liszt gave concerts here in

1820 – and the highlights of the season are the Spring Days (Tavaszi Napok) in March, the Ancient Music Days (Régi Zenei Napok) in late June, the International Chorus & Orchestra Festival (Nemzetközi Kórus és Zenekari Fesztivál) in early July and German Culture Week (Német Kultúra Hete) in early September. Tickets to the various events are available from the box office (☎ 511 730) at Széchenyi tér 17-18 from 9 am to 5 pm weekdays and till noon on Saturday.

Places to Stay

Camping *Lővér Camping* (☎ 311 715, Kőszegi út), on Pócsi-domb about 5km south of the city centre, has more than 100 bungalows, though we've had complaints from readers about the condition of them. Doubles with shared bath are 2200Ft and camping costs from 580Ft. The site is open from mid-April to mid-October.

Hostels The *Brennbergi* hostel (☎/fax 313 116, Brennbergi út) is pretty far to the west of the city centre, but a bed is under 1000Ft a night and there's also a pension here charging 1300Ft per person. It's open from mid-April to mid-October. A half-dozen different colleges and schools in the Sopron area offer accommodation in July and much of August for about 800Ft, including the *Boys' College* (☎ 312 105, Lackner Kristóf utca 7) near the bus station.

Private Rooms Ciklámen Tourist has private rooms for about 1500Ft per person. You can also find quite a few private rooms by taking bus No 1 from the train station to the *Szieszta hotel*, (Lővér körút 37), then walking back down the hill looking for houses with *szoba kiadó* and *Zimmer frei* signs.

Pensions Most of the pensions in Sopron are expensive, but there are a couple of exceptions. The 16-room *Bástya* (☎/fax 325 325, Patak utca 40), a 10-minute walk north of the Inner Town up Szélmalom utca, charges 7800Ft for a double. The more central and excellent *Jégverem* (☎/fax 312 004, Jégverem utca 1), with five suite-like rooms

in an 18th-century ice cellar in the Ikva district, charges only 3000/6000Ft for singles/doubles. They serve a fabulous breakfast (no mean feat in Hungary) with – wait for it – real coffee. The nearby *Royal* (☎/fax 314 481, Sas tér 13), with seven rooms in a renovated old townhouse, has singles/doubles for 4000/8000Ft.

Hotels The 32-room *Palatinus* (☎/fax 311 395, Új utca 23) couldn't be more central, but it's in a badly renovated building that doesn't fit in well with its surrounds. Small, dark singles/doubles are DM75/110. Sopron's grand old hotel is the 100-year-old *Pannónia Med* hotel (☎ 312 180, fax 340 766, ✆ pannonia_med_hotel@sopron.hu, Várkerület 73). Its 60 renovated rooms cost DM120 for a single, DM150 for double.

Up on Coronation Hill with views of the city and the Lővér Hills is the sprawling 113-room *Sopron* hotel (☎ 314 254, fax 311 090, ✆ hotel-sopron@sopron.hu, Fövényverem utca 7), with bars, a restaurant, clay tennis courts, an outdoor swimming pool and singles/doubles for DM120/160.

Places to Eat

The best place in Sopron for an inexpensive lunch or light meal is the *Cézár Pince* (Hátsókapu 2) in a medieval cellar in a historical building off Orsolya tér (open till 10 pm). The platter of sausages and salad for under 500Ft attracts locals; chase it with a glass of Soproni Kékfrankos (a red) or the young white Zöldveltelini. If you want to stay in this century visit the *City Diner* (Várkerület 104) a short distance away, with burgers and Mexican dishes from 300Ft to 550Ft.

The *Generális-Corvinus* restaurant (Fő tér 7-8), with its cafe tables on the Inner Town's main square, is a great place for a pizza in the warmer months. For an attempt at Greek food, try *Gambrinus* (Fő tér 3), open till 10 pm. The *Forum* (Szent György utca 3) does decent pizza.

For Hungarian fare try the *Corso* restaurant (Várkerület 73) in the Korona shopping arcade next to the Pannónia Med hotel. The *Mekong* (Deák tér 46), south of the Inner

Town, pretends – in both senses – to serve Chinese food. Mains average 600Ft, and it's open nightly till midnight.

You'll find good ice cream at a little cake shop called *Stefánia (Szent György utca 12)* in a medieval courtyard backed by the New Synagogue. Check the ancient Gothic windows above you as you sit and lick your tutti-frutti. Other excellent places for sweets are the *Várkapu Café (Várkerület 108a)* on the corner of Hátsókapu (open till 9 pm weekdays and to 10 pm on Saturday) and the *Dömöröri (Széchenyi tér 13)*, an old world cukrászda next to the John Bull pub.

There's a *nonstop shop* at Ógabona tér 12.

Entertainment

The *Hungarian Cultural House (☎ 511 700, Liszt Ferenc tér 1)*, just off Széchenyi tér, is the place to go for music and other cultural events; many are staged at the *Chamber Theatre* (Kamara Színház) where you'll find the ticket office (☎ 511 730), Széchenyi tér 17-18, open weekdays from 9 am to 5 pm and till noon on Saturday. The beautiful *Petőfi Theatre (☎ 511 700, Petőfi tér 1)*, with its National Romantic-style decor, is just around the corner. The *Civitas Pince Theatre (☎ 332 098, Templom utca 16)* has cabaret on Friday and Saturday nights. For more up-to-date entertainment, check the listings in the freebie weekly *Soproni Est*. The GyIK youth information office (☎ 311 571) at Ady Endre utca 10 also has information on concerts, clubs, etc.

The Sopron region is noted for red wines like Kékfrankos and Merlot. They're pretty cheap even in restaurants but particularly high in acid and tannin, so watch your intake if you don't want a massive *macskajaj* ('cat's wail' – the Hungarian term for a hangover) the next day. A convenient place to sample them is in the *Gyógygődőr (Fő tér 4)*, a deep, deep cellar open to 10 pm Tuesday to Sunday, but there are smaller places around town with bunches of leaves hanging outside to signify they're serving wine. Look for them at Zsilip utca 18, Balfi út 16, III Rákóczi Ferenc utca 17 and at the Magyar Bortár (Hungarian Wine Store) at Ógabona tér 34.

The *John Bull (Széchenyi tér 12)* is a pricey pub and part of a chain. More individual – well, sort of – is *Papa Joe's Saloon (Várkerület 108)*.

Getting There & Away

Bus The bus service is good to and from Sopron. Buses leave up to twice an hour for Fertőd, Fertőrákos, Győr, Kapuvár and Nagycenk, and departures are frequent to Kőszeg (eight a day) and Szombathely (nine). Other destinations to/from Sopron include: Balatonfüred (two), Budapest (six), Esztergom (two), Lake Fertő (eight), Hévíz and Keszthely (four), Kaposvár (one), Komárom (one or two), Nagykanizsa (two), Pécs (one), Sárvár (two), Székesfehérvár (two), Tapolca (one), Tatabánya (two), Veszprém (five) and Zalaegerszeg (two).

There's a daily bus to Vienna at 7.15 pm and an extra one on Friday at 5.50 pm. There is also a bus which leaves for Munich and Stuttgart at 6.25 am on Tuesday and 4.25 am on Saturday.

Train Express trains en route to Vienna's Südbahnhof via Ebenfurth pass through Sopron between three and seven times a day; between two and three local trains a day go to Wiener Neustadt (where you can transfer for Vienna). There are up to eight express trains a day to Budapest-Keleti via Győr and Komárom, and eight to 10 local trains to Szombathely.

Getting Around

Buses No 12 and 12a, from both the bus and train stations, stops directly in front of Lővér Camping. If you take bus No 1 from the bus station or No 2 from the train station, get off at Citadella Park and walk down Sarudi utca to Kőszegi utca. The camp site is just south. For the Brennbergi hostel take bus No 3 or 10 from the bus station.

Local taxis can be ordered on ☎ 312 222 or ☎ 333 333.

AROUND SOPRON
Lővér Hills

This range, 300m to 400m high foothills of the Austrian Alps some 5km south and south-west of the city centre, is Sopron's playground. It's a great place for hiking and walks, but is not without bitter memories, for it was here that partisans and Jews were executed by Nazis and the fascist Hungarian Arrow Cross during WWII. You can climb to the top of **Károly Lookout** (Károly kilátó) on the 394m hill west of the Lővér hotel, or visit the **Lővér Baths** at Lővér körút 82, with outside pools open from 9 am to 8 pm daily from late May to mid-September and a covered pool, sauna and solarium open from 6 am to 8 pm weekdays and 9 am to 8 pm at the weekend year round.

Places to Stay The *Diana* (*π/fax 329 075, Lővér körút 64*) is a nine-room, family-run pension with doubles for 7100Ft while the nearby *Sas* pension (*π 316 183, fax 341 068, Lővér körút 69*) with the same number of rooms charges 6000Ft.

There are several big hotels here as well, including the 180-room *Maróni* (*π 312 549, fax 341 182, @ hmaroni@sopron.hu, Lővér körút 74*), which has rooms in several different categories, with superior ones from 8400Ft, and the *Szieszta* (*π 314 260, fax 316 923, @ reserve@hotelszieszta.hunguest.hu, Lővér körút 37*), a huge former trade-union holiday house and now a 288-room with doubles from 9300Ft.

FERTŐD
π 99 • postcode 9431 • pop 2700

Some 27km east of Sopron, Fertőd has been associated with the aristocratic Esterházy family since the mid-18th century when scion Miklós, proclaiming that 'Anything the (Habsburg) emperor can afford, I can afford too' began construction of the largest and most opulent summer palace in Central Europe. When completed in 1766, it boasted 126 rooms, a separate opera house, a hermitage (complete with a cranky old person in a sack cloth who wanted to be left alone), temples to Diana and Venus, a Chinese dance house, a puppet theatre and a 250-hectare garden laid out in the French manner. Fertőd – or Esterháza as it was known until the middle of the 20th century – had made it on the map.

Much has been written about the Esterházy Palace and many hyperbolic monikers bestowed on it (the 'Hungarian Versailles' is the most common). But the fact remains that this baroque and rococo structure – its architects unknown except for the Austrian Melchior Hefele – is the most beautiful palace in Hungary. While the rooms are mostly bare, history is very much alive here: in the Concert Hall, where many of the works of composer Franz Joseph Haydn, a 30-year resident of the palace, were first performed, including the *Farewell Symphony*; in the Chinoiserie Rooms, where Empress Maria Theresa attended a masked ball in 1773; and in the French Garden, where Miklós 'the Splendour Lover' threw some of the greatest parties of all time for friends like Goethe, complete with fireworks and tens of thousands of Chinese lanterns.

After a century and a half of neglect (it was used as a stables in the 19th century and a hospital during WWII), the palace has been partially restored to its former glory.

Orientation & Information
The palace and its gardens on Bartók Béla utca dominate the town; the bus will let you off almost in front of the main gate. The town centre is a few minutes' walk to the west. The closest train station (on the Sopron-Győr line) is at Fertőszentmiklós, 4km to the south.

Tourinform (*π/fax 370 544*) in the east wing of the Music House at Madách sétány 1 is open from 8 am to 6 pm weekdays and till noon at the weekend from April to September and from 8 am to 4 pm weekdays only the rest of the year. There's an OTP bank branch at Fő utca 7. The post office is at No 6 of the same street diagonally opposite the Music House.

Esterházy Palace
Some 26 renovated rooms at the horseshoe-shaped Esterházy Palace are open to the public; the rest of the complex houses a hotel, a secondary school and a horticultural research centre.

As you approach the main entrance to the so-called **Courtyard of Honour**, notice the

The Old Lake at Tata provides an attractive setting for the medieval castle.

The Vázsonykő Castle at Nagyvázsony was an important border fortress under the Turks.

The twin spires of the Abbey Church are landmarks of the Lake Balaton town of Tihany.

Wine connoisseurs flock to the cellars that line the streets of Villánykövesd.

ornamental wrought-iron gate, a rococo masterpiece. You can only tour the palace with a guide, but armed with a fact sheet in English available from the ticket office, lag behind and explore the rooms away from the crowds.

On the ground floor of the palace you'll pass through several rooms done up in mock Chinese style (all the rage in the late 18th century); the pillared **Sala Terrena**, with its floor of glimmering marble and Miklós Esterházy's initials in floral frescoes on the ceiling; and the Prince's Bed Chamber, with paintings of Amor. On the 1st floor are more sumptuous baroque and rococo salons, as well as the lavish **Concert Hall** and **Ceremonial Hall**, which give on to each other. There's also an exhibit dedicated to the life and times of Haydn.

The palace is open from 9 am to 5 pm Tuesday to Sunday from mid-April to mid-October. It closes an hour earlier the rest of the year. Entry costs 600/250Ft.

The apartment where Haydn lived, off and on, from 1761 to 1790 in the west wing of the baroque **Music House**, south-west of the palace at Madach sétány 1, has been turned into a temple to the great composer. It is open Tuesday to Friday from 9.30 am to 4 pm and 10 am to 3 pm at the weekend from May to mid-October.

Special Events

From May to mid-October there are piano and string quartets performing in the palace Concert Hall on most Saturdays at 6 pm and some Sundays at 4 and/or 7 pm.

The Haydn Festival in early September is usually booked out months in advance, but try your luck at Tourinform.

Places to Stay

The *Aladár Porpáczy College* (☎ *370 966, Kossuth Lajos utca*) has 32 rooms with four/six beds which cost 1000/800Ft per person, available in summer and at the weekend year round. There are plenty of pensions (1800Ft to 2000Ft per person) in and around Fertőd, including the *Újvári* (☎/fax *371 828, Kossuth Lajos utca 57a*) in Sarród, just 130m north of Tourinform. But one of the main reasons people come to

Fertőd is to stay at the 19-room *Kastély* hotel (☎ *370 971, fax 370 120, Bartók Béla út 2*) in the east wing of the palace, which must be booked well in advance. You won't be sleeping in anything like the Prince's Bed Chamber but for a palace price is right: 2800/3300/3700Ft for doubles/triples/quads with shared bath. The truly romantic (or flush) will choose to stay at the *Bagatelle*, a separate pavilion in the garden with two apartments.

Places to Eat

The *Gránátos* cafe in the west wing of Grenadier House, the former living quarters of the grenadier guards is directly across from the palace's main entrance on Bartók Béla út and is pleasant enough (not to be confused with the dumpy *Árkád* restaurant in the east wing). In summer *food stalls* dispensing *lángos* and the like fill the nearby car park. The *Haydn* restaurant (*Fő utca 3*) located in Udvaros-ház has standard Hungarian favourites and garden seating in summer. It's open till 10 pm. The *Elit* cafe (*Fő utca 1*), next door, is a nice place for a cuppa and cake.

Getting There & Away

Some two dozen buses a day link Sopron with Fertőd on weekdays and 15 or so on Saturday and Sunday. There are also buses to Győr and Kapuvár. Eight trains a day link Sopron and Győr with Fertőszentmiklós to the south.

NAGYCENK

☎ 99 • postcode 9485 • pop 1650

Only 14km west of Fertőd and the Esterházy Palace, but light-years away in spirit, lies Nagycenk, site of the ancestral mansion of the Széchenyi clan. No two houses – or families – could have been more different than these. While the privileged, often frivolous Esterházys held court in their imperial palace, the Széchenyis – democrats and reformers all – went about their work in a sombre neoclassical manor house that aptly reflected their temperament and sense of purpose. The mansion has been completely renovated and part of it has been turned into a superb museum dedicated to the Széchenyis.

The Greatest Hungarian

The contributions Count István Széchenyi made to Hungary were enormous and extremely varied.

In his seminal 1830 work *Hitel* (meaning 'credit' and based on *hit*, or 'trust'), he advocated sweeping economic reforms and the abolition of serfdom (he himself had distributed the bulk of his property to landless peasants two years earlier).

The Chain Bridge, the design of which Széchenyi helped push through Parliament, was the first link between Buda and Pest and for the first time everyone, nobles included, had to pay a toll.

Széchenyi was instrumental in straightening the serpentine Tisza River, which rescued half of Hungary's arable land from flooding and erosion, and his work made the Danube navigable as far as the Iron Gates in Romania.

He arranged the financing for Hungary's first railway lines (from Budapest north and east to Vác and Szolnok and west to what is now Wiener Neustadt in Austria) and launched the first steam transport on the Danube and Lake Balaton.

A lover of all things English, Széchenyi got the upper classes interested in horse racing with the express purpose of improving breeding stock for farming.

A large financial contribution made by Széchenyi led to the establishment of the nation's prestigious Academy of Science.

Széchenyi joined Lajos Batthyány's revolutionary government in 1848, but political squabbling and open conflict with Vienna caused him to lose control and he suffered a nervous breakdown. Despite a decade of convalescence in an asylum, Széchenyi never fully recovered and tragically he took his own life in 1860.

For all his accomplishments, Széchenyi's contemporary and fellow reformer, Lajos Kossuth, called him 'the greatest Hungarian'. This dynamic but troubled visionary retains that accolade to this day.

The family's public-spiritedness started with Ferenc Széchenyi, who donated his entire collection of books and *objets d'art* to the state in 1802, laying the foundations for the National Library named in his honour. But it was his son, István (1791-1860), who made the greatest impact of any Hungarian on the economic and cultural development of the nation (see boxed text 'The Greatest Hungarian').

Orientation

The train station is near the centre of Nagycenk, not far from neo-Romanesque St Stephen's Church, designed by Miklós Ybl in 1864, and the Széchenyi family's mausoleum. The bus from Sopron stops at the mansion's main gate.

Széchenyi Manor

The entrance to the **István Széchenyi Memorial Museum** in the mansion is through the Sala Terrena – almost austere compared with the one at the Esterházy Palace in Fertőd. Guided tours on cassette are available in several languages (including English) from the ticket office for 300Ft. You would do well to rent one: as excellent as this museum is, the labels are only in Hungarian.

The rooms on the ground floor of the museum, with furniture contemporary with the times, deal with the history of the Széchenyi family and their political development, from typical baroque aristocrats in the 18th century to key players in the 1848 War of Independence and István's involvement in the ill-fated government of Lajos Batthyány. A sweeping baroque staircase leads to the exhibits on the 1st floor – a veritable temple to István's many accomplishments – from Budapest's Chain Bridge and the Danube and Tisza River engineering works through to steamboat and rail transport. The museum is open from 10 am to 6 pm Tuesday to Sunday from April to September and to 2 pm the rest of the year (150/70Ft).

It is fitting that the mansion of a railway developer like István Széchenyi lies near an open-air **Train Museum**, with steam engines that were still in use on main lines as late as 1950, and you can actually ride a 100-year-old **narrow-gauge steam train** for 3.5km to Fertőboz and back (108/216Ft one way/return for adults and 54/108Ft for children). Departures between May and late September from the Kastély station at Nagycenk are at 10.05 and 11.30 am and 3.20 and 5.40 pm on Saturday and Sunday only. All but the last one turn around at Fertőboz in less than a half-hour for the return trip to Kastély.

A 2.5km **row of linden trees** opposite the mansion and planted by István's grandmother in 1754 leads to a **hermitage**. Like the Esterházys, the Széchenyi family had a resident loner who, in this case, was expected to earn his keep by ringing the chapel bell and tending the garden.

The **Széchenyi Mausoleum**, the final resting place of István and other family members, is in the village cemetery across the road from St Stephen's Church.

Cross-country riding and coach tours are available at the 200-year-old Nagycenk Stud Farm (☎ 360 026), which has 60 horses. You can also rent horses at the Nemet Riding School (☎ 360 196) in the village.

Places to Stay & Eat

The only game in town nowadays is the *Kastély* hotel (☎ *360 061*, **@** *hotel@ syneco.hu, Kiscenki utca 3*) in the west wing of the mansion. It is a beautifully appointed 19-room inn, but it may exceed your budget: singles are DM88 to DM144 and doubles DM110 to DM158, depending on the season and room type. If you can afford between DM116 and DM194, opt for No 106 or No 107, large suites with period furniture and restful views of the six-hectare garden.

The splendid dining room at the *Kastély* hotel is the place for lunch in these parts, and there are outside tables in the courtyard in summer. The Terrace cafe at the hotel has a beautiful interior and serves excellent cakes and ice cream. The *Gyura* restaurant

in the renovated little train station near the Train Museum is more affordable and will be almost as crowded at weekends with local tourists. If you can't get a seat, snack at the *Park* or one of the other food stalls in the Train Museum car park.

Getting There & Away

Nagycenk is accessible from Sopron by bus every half-hour. The village is on the railway line linking Sopron and Szombathely, and eight to 10 trains arrive and depart each day.

If you time it right, you can reach Nagycenk by the toy train. Take the bus from Sopron to Fertőboz and board the train for Kastély station at 10.50 am, 12.30 or 4.15 pm.

SZOMBATHELY
☎ 94 • postcode 9700 • pop 85,600

Szombathely (German: Steinamanger) is a major crossroads in western Hungary. Its name (pronounced roughly as 'SOM-bot-hay') translates as 'Saturday place' and refers to the important weekend markets held here in the Middle Ages. For many Austrians who cross the border in search of cheap edibles and services, it remains just that.

Szombathely got an earlier start than most. In 43 AD the Romans established a trade settlement called Savaria here on the all-important Amber Route. By the start of the 2nd century it was important enough to become the capital of Upper Pannonia. Over the next few centuries, Savaria prospered and Christianity arrived; Martin of Tours, the patron saint of France, was born here in 316. But attacks by Huns, Longobards and Avars weakened its defences. It was destroyed by an earthquake in 455.

Szombathely began to develop in the early Middle Ages, but the Mongols, then the Turks and the Habsburgs, put a stop to that. It was not until 1777, when János Szily was appointed Szombathely's first bishop, that the city really began to flourish economically and culturally. The building of the railway line to Graz brought further trade. In 1945 Allied bombers levelled much of the town, which has since been rebuilt (not very successfully in many parts).

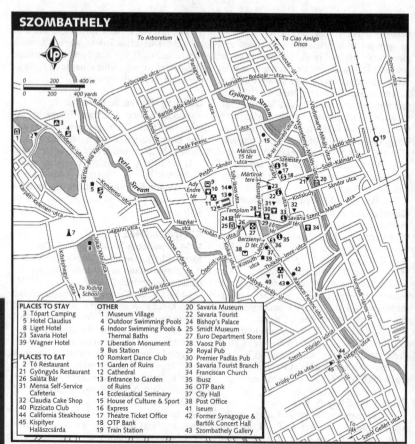

SZOMBATHELY

To Arboretum

To Ciao Amigo
Disco

0   200   400 m
0   200   400 yards

PLACES TO STAY	OTHER	20 Savaria Museum
3 Tópart Camping	1 Museum Village	22 Savaria Tourist
5 Hotel Claudius	4 Outdoor Swimming Pools	24 Bishop's Palace
8 Liget Hotel	6 Indoor Swimming Pools &	25 Smidt Museum
23 Savaria Hotel	Thermal Baths	27 Euro Department Store
39 Wagner Hotel	7 Liberation Monument	28 Vaosz Pub
	9 Bus Station	29 Royal Pub
PLACES TO EAT	10 Romkert Dance Club	30 Premier Padlás Pub
2 Tó Restaurant	11 Garden of Ruins	33 Savaria Tourist Branch
21 Gyöngyös Restaurant	12 Cathedral	34 Franciscan Church
26 Saláta Bár	13 Entrance to Garden	35 Ibusz
31 Mensa Self-Service	of Ruins	36 OTP Bank
Cafeteria	14 Ecclesiastical Seminary	37 City Hall
32 Claudia Cake Shop	15 House of Culture & Sport	38 Post Office
40 Pizzicato Club	16 Express	41 Iseum
44 California Steakhouse	17 Theatre Ticket Office	42 Former Synagogue &
45 Kispityer	18 OTP Bank	Bartók Concert Hall
Halászcsárda	19 Train Station	43 Szombathely Gallery

Orientation & Information

Szombathely is made up of narrow streets
and squares with the centre at enormous,
leafy Fő tér, one of the largest squares in
Hungary. To the west are Berzsenyi Dániel
tér and Templom tér, the administrative and
ecclesiastical centres of town. The train station is on Éhen Gyula tér, five blocks east
of Mártírok tere at the end of Széll Kálmán
út. The bus station is on Petőfi Sándor utca.

Two tourist agencies are just a block
apart from one another: Savaria Tourist
(☎ 312 348) at Mártírok tere 1 and Express
(☎ 311 230) at Király utca 12. Savaria

Tourist (☎ 325 831) has a second branch at
Király utca 1. Ibusz (☎ 314 141, fax 310
440) is at Fő tér 44. All are open from 8 or
8.30 am to 5 pm weekdays and, in summer,
to noon on Saturday.

There's an OTP bank branch diagonally
opposite Savaria Tourist at Király utca 10
and another south of Fő tér on Bejczy István
utca. The main post office is at Kossuth
Lajos utca 18.

Things to See

Allied bombing in the final days of WWII did
not spare Zopf-style **Szombathely Cathedral**

(1797) on Templom tér. Designed by Melchior Hefele for Bishop Szily in 1791, the cathedral was once covered in stucco work and frescoes by Franz Anton Maulbertsch and supported by grand marble columns. They're now gone, of course, though a couple of Maulbertsch originals and a glorious red and white marble pulpit remain, breaking the monotony of this sterile place.

Maulbertsch frescoes in the upstairs Reception Hall at the **Bishop's Palace** (Püspöki palota; 1783), south of the cathedral at Berzsenyi Dániel tér 3, miraculously survived the air raids, but these are not usually open to the public. You can, however, admire the frescoes of Roman ruins and gods (1784) by István Dorffmeister in the Sala Terrena on the ground floor. Other rooms contain more prewar photographs of the cathedral and the **Diocesan Collection** (Egyházmegyei Gyüjtemény), including missals and Bibles from the 14th to 18th centuries, Gothic vestments and a beautiful 15th-century monstrance from Kőszeg. The palace is open from Tuesday to Friday and on Sunday from 9.30 am till noon and 12.30 to 3.30 pm and on Saturday to 11.30 am. The late-baroque **Ecclesiastical Seminary** (Papi szeminárium), Szily János utca 1, contains a library of some 70,000 volumes, including incunabula and medieval codices, but is open to groups only.

The **Smidt Museum**, in a baroque mansion behind the Bishop's Palace at Hollán Ernő utca 2, contains the private collection of one Lajos Smidt, a pack-rat physician who spent most of his adult life squirrelling away antique weapons, furniture, fans, pipes, clocks, Roman coins and so on. None of it looks like it's worth very much, but the volume and zaniness of it all makes the museum worth a visit. It's open from 10 am to 5 pm Tuesday to Sunday (100Ft).

Szombathely has some of the most important Roman ruins in Hungary, and many of them are on display. The **Garden of Ruins** (Romkert), behind the cathedral and accessible from Templom tér, contains a wealth of Savaria relics excavated here since 1938 and is open from 10 am to 6 pm Tuesday to Sunday from April to October

and to 4 pm the rest of the year (80Ft). Don't miss the beautiful mosaics of plants and geometrical designs on the floor of what was **St Quirinus Basilica** in the 4th century, and there are also remains of Roman road markers, a customs house, shops and the medieval castle walls.

The **Iseum**, south of Fő tér at Rákóczi Ferenc utca 12 is part of a grand 2nd-century complex of two temples dedicated to the Egyptian goddess Isis by Roman legionnaires. When the smaller temple was excavated in the 1950s, the city decided to reconstruct it – with cement blocks. The result is grotesque and should be removed. The frieze on the sacrificial altar depicts Isis riding the dog Sirius; it's spoiled by the location.

The **Szombathely Gallery** overlooking the temple at Rákóczi Ferenc utca 12 is one of the best modern art galleries in Hungary. It is open from 10 am to 5 pm Tuesday and Friday to Sunday and to 7 pm on Thursday. The lovely twin-towered Moorish building across the street at No 3 is the former **synagogue** designed in 1881 by the Viennese architect Ludwig Schöne. Today it houses a music school and the **Béla Bartók Concert Hall**. A plaque points out the spot from which '4228 of our Jewish brothers and sisters were deported to Auschwitz on 4 July 1944'.

The **Savaria Museum**, fronting a little park at Kisfaludy Sándor utca 9 east of Mártírok tere, is worth a short look around. The ground floor is devoted to highly decorative but practical items carved by 19th-century shepherds to while away the hours; the cellar is full of Roman altars, stone torsos and blue-glass vials found at Savaria excavation sites. There's a local history exhibit on the 1st floor. It's open from 10 am to 5 pm Tuesday to Thursday, to 7 pm on Friday and to 4 pm on Saturday and Sunday (100Ft)

The **Vas Museum Village** (Vasi Múzeumfalu), on the western bank of the fishing lake at Árpád utca 30, is an open-air museum with a dozen 18th and 19th-century *porták* (farmhouses) moved from various villages in the Őrség region. They are arranged around a semicircular street, as was usual on the western border. The most interesting of these are the Croatian, German and 'fenced' houses. Nettles from a strange plant called *kővirózsa* (stone rose) growing on the thatch were used to pierce little girls' ears. The museum village is open from 10 am to 5 pm Tuesday to Sunday from May to October (100Ft).

Some 3km north-east of the centre at Szent Imre herceg útja 102 is the rich **Kámoni Arboretum** established in the 19th century with some 3000 species of trees and shrubs. It is open from 8 am to 6 pm Tuesday to Sunday from March to October and to 4 pm the rest of the year (100/50Ft).

Activities

The rowing and fishing lakes north-west of the centre along Kenderesi utca cover an area of 12 hectares and make up Szombathely's playground; boats can be hired from the western side of the little island in the middle. There's a huge outdoor swimming pool on Kenderesi utca on the east bank open to the public from 9 am to 8 pm daily from mid-May to mid-September. The city's thermal baths and indoor pools are next to the Claudius hotel (open 1.30 to 8 pm on Monday, 5.30 am to 8 pm Tuesday to Friday and 9 am to 6 pm Saturday and Sunday; 280/200Ft).

A well-established horse-riding school (☎ 313 461) lies south-west of the Liget hotel on Középhegyi út.

Places to Stay

Camping From May to September you can stay at *Tópart Camping* (☎ *314 766, Kenderesi utca 6)* by the lakes north-west of town. From the bus stop (bus No 7) walk along the causeway between the lakes. Bungalows for two with shared shower are 3000Ft, for four people with shower the cost is 7500Ft. Camping costs 375Ft per person and 250Ft for a tent.

Private Rooms Private rooms (4000Ft a double) are assigned by staff at Savaria Tourist and Ibusz.

Hotels The 38-room *Liget* hotel (☎*/fax 314 168, Szent István park 15)* west of the centre

has singles/doubles with shower for 5200/6000Ft. It's effectively a motel but convenient to the lakes, the museum village and the riding school. The monstrous *Liberation* monument – the two concrete 'wings' on the hill to the north-west – was once topped with a big red star.

Szombathely's old world hotel is the *Savaria* (☎ *311 440, Mártírok tere 4)*. It's a 90-room Art Nouveau gem built in 1917 and, while the rooms are dark and unexceptional, its restaurant with antique *kocsma* (saloon) furniture and Winter Garden function room are easy places to conjure up ghosts of a more elegant past. Depending on the size of the room and what facilities are in them, singles with washbasin/shower/bath are 3900/5900/8400Ft, doubles 6000/8000/10,100Ft. Room No 318 with bath and views of the square is the best.

The loveliest hotel in the city is the new *Wagner* hotel (☎*/fax 322 208, Kossuth Lajos utca 15)*, with a dozen rooms just south-west of Fő tér. Singles/doubles are 8800/14,600Ft and the hotel restaurant is excellent. The 102-room *Claudius* (☎ *313 760, fax 313 545, Bartók Béla körút 39)* is a three-star hotel near the lakes with singles/doubles from 8400/14,600Ft.

Places to Eat

For its size, Szombathely has surprisingly few restaurants – good, bad or otherwise. The cheapest place around is the *Mensa* self-service cafeteria *(Mártírok tere 5b)* open from 9 am to 7 pm weekdays, 7 am to 2 pm on Saturday.

The *Pizzicato Club* *(Thököly Imre utca 14)* is popular for its pastas (590Ft to 790Ft) and salads (290Ft to 790Ft). The *Saláta Bár* *(Belsikátor utca)* on a tiny pedestrian street connecting Berzsenyi Dániel tér with Fő tér is a good place for a cheap lunch and is open 9 am to 6 pm weekdays and to 2 pm on Saturday.

The *Gyöngyös* *(Széll Kálmán út 8)* has mains from 600Ft and an inexpensive set menu (990Ft). It closes on Monday. The *Kispityer Halászcsárda (Rumi út 18)*, 1.5km south-west of Fő tér, is worth the trip if you're in search of fish. It's open till 11 pm (midnight at the weekend). Carnivores can cross the road to the *California Steakhouse (Rumi út 21)*, an almost authentic American restaurant with a salad bar.

If you're messing around in boats on the lake or visiting the museum village and get hungry, head for the *Tó* restaurant *(Rajki sétány)* on the narrow isthmus separating the two lakes and grab a table on the terrace.

The *Claudia (Savaria tér 2)* has decent cakes and ice cream and is open daily from 9 am to 7 pm.

Entertainment

The Savaria Symphony Orchestra performs throughout the year at the *Bartók Hall (Bartók Terem;* ☎ *314 472, Rákóczi Ferenc utca 3)*. Another important venue is the ugly 1960s *House of Culture & Sport* (☎ *312 666, Március 15 tér 5)*. The ticket office (☎ 312 579) is at Király utca 11.

For a less-mannered evening, start at the *Royal (Fő tér)*, a pub with sidewalk tables on the northern side of the main square. The *Vaosz* pub, opposite, is also good. The *Premier Padlás* cafe-pub in the Uránia Udvar shopping arcade has pool tables and is open most nights till 4 am.

The House of Culture & Sport has a popular cafe-bar called *Club Mylos*. Other popular night spots are the *Romkert Dance Club (Ady Endre utca)* behind the bus station (open Tuesday and Thursday to Saturday) and *Ciao Amico (Arad utca)* north of the centre just off 11es Huszár út. A good source of information is the weekly entertainment guide *Szombathelyi Est*, distributed free.

Getting There & Away

Bus The bus service is not so good to/from Szombathely, though up to 16 buses leave every day for Ják and there are frequent departures for Kőszeg (15), Sárvár (12) and Velem (eight). Other destinations to/from Szombathely include Budapest (three departures daily), Győr (five), Kaposvár (two), Keszthely via Hévíz (three), Körmend (nine), Nagykanizsa (eight), Pécs (two), Sopron (four), Sümeg (three), Szeged (one), Szentgotthárd (four), Veszprém (three) and Zalaegerszeg (seven). One bus a week departs for Graz (Friday at 7 am) and Vienna (Wednesday at 6.40 am).

Train Express trains to Budapest-Déli and Budapest-Keleti go via Veszprém and Székesfehérvár. Other express trains run to Győr via Celldömölk. There are frequent local trains to Kőszeg, Sopron and Körmend and three express trains a day to/from Pécs. There are also up to seven direct trains to/from Graz.

Getting Around

Szombathely is simple to negotiate on foot, but bus No 7 will take you from the train station to the museum village, lakes, camp site and the Liget hotel. No 2 is good for the Kámoni Arboretum. You can order a taxi on ☎ 311 300 or ☎ 333 666.

AROUND SZOMBATHELY
Ják
☎ 94 • postcode 9798 • pop 2100

Try to visit Ják, 12km south of Szombathely and an easy half-day trip by bus. This sleepy village boasts the **Benedictine Abbey Church** (Bencés apátsági templom), one of the finest examples of Romanesque architecture in Hungary. Its main feature, a magnificent portal carved in geometric patterns 12 layers deep and featuring carved stone statues of Christ and his Apostles, on the west side, was renovated for the Millecentenary in 1996. The decorative sculptures on the outside wall of the sanctuary and the church's interior are also worth a look.

The two-towered structure was begun as a family church in 1214 by Márton Nagy and dedicated to St George four decades later in 1256. Somehow the partially completed church managed to escape destruction during the Mongol invasion, but it was badly damaged during the Turkish occupation. The church has had many restorations, the most important being in the mid-17th century, between 1896 and 1904 (when most of the statues in the portal were recut or replaced, rose windows added and earlier baroque additions removed) and from 1992 to 1996.

Enter through the south door, once used only by the monks based here. The interior, with its single nave and three aisles, has a much more graceful and personal feel than most later Hungarian Gothic churches. To the west and below the towers is a gallery reserved for the benefactor and his family. The faded rose and blue frescoes on the wall between the vaulting and the arches below could very well be of Márton Nagy and his progeny. If you slip a coin into the machine nearby, you'll illuminate the church, transforming the cold grey stone to soft yellow. The Abbey Church is open from 8 am to 6 pm daily April to October.

To the west of the Romanesque church is the tiny clover-leaf **Chapel of St James** (Szent Jakab-kápolna) topped with an onion dome. It was built around 1260 as a parish church since the main church was monastic. Note the paschal lamb (symbolising Christ) over the main entrance, and the baroque altar and frescoes inside.

In the unlikely event that you've missed the last bus and need a place to stay, two *private rooms* (☎ 356 304) are available at the house on Széchenyi utca 16 for 1200Ft per person. For something to eat there's a *snack bar* at the ticket office, and the simple *Falatozó* (*Szabadság utca*) is on the way to/from the church as you walk up/down the hill.

Buses from Szombathely are very frequent and will drop you off at the bottom of the hill a few minutes' walk from the church. From Ják you can return to Szombathely on one of up to 16 daily buses or continue on to Szentpéterfa (15 a day), Körmend (four) or Szentgotthárd (one).

SÁRVÁR
☎ 95 • postcode 9600 • pop 15,800
Some 27km east of Szombathely on the Rába River, the quiet town of 'Mud Castle' has experienced some good and some very bad times. During the Reformation, Sárvár's fortified castle was a centre of Calvinist culture and scholarship, and its owners, the Nádasdy family, a respected dynasty in statecraft and military leadership. In 1537, Tamás Nádasdy set up a press

that published the first two printed books in Hungarian – a Magyar grammar in Latin and a translation of the New Testament. Ferenc Nádasdy II, the so-called Black Captain, fought heroically against the Turks, and his grandson Ferenc III, a lord chief justice, established one of the greatest libraries and private art collections in Central Europe.

But everything began to sour at the start of the 17th century. It seems that while the Black Captain was away at war, his wife Erzsébet Báthory, as mad as a hatter and blood-thirsty to boot, was up to no good (see boxed text 'The Blood Countess'), and then Ferenc III's involvement in a plot led by Ferenc Wesselényi to overthrow the Habsburgs was exposed. He was beheaded in Vienna in 1671.

Sárvár is not all bloody history. It is equally well known for its 44°C thermal waters, discovered in the 1960s during experimental drilling for oil.

Orientation & Information
The train station is on Selyemgyár utca. To reach the town centre, walk south along Hunyadi János utca and turn east on Batthyány Lajos utca, which leads to Kossuth tér and the castle. The bus station is at the western end of Batthyány Lajos utca.

The less-than-helpful Savaria Tourist office (☎/fax 320 578), almost opposite the castle entrance at Várkerület 33, is open on weekdays from 8 am to 5 pm and on Saturday to 12.30 pm.

There's an OTP bank branch at Batthyány Lajos utca 2 and a K&H Bank and foreign currency exchange machine at Kossuth tér 1. The main post office is at Várkerület 32.

Nádasdy Castle
The entrance to the **Ferenc Nádasdy Museum**, Várkerület 1, in pentagonal Nádasdy Castle (Nádasdy-vár) is across a brick footbridge from Kossuth tér and through the gate of a 14th-century tower. Though parts of the castle date from the 13th century, most of it is in 16th-century Renaissance style and in remarkably good condition despite Erzsébet

The Blood Countess

It was the scandal of the 17th century. On the night of 29 December 1610, the Lord Palatine of Hungary, Count György Thurzó, raided the castle at Csejta (now Čachtice in western Slovakia) and caught the lady of the house, Countess Erzsébet Báthory, literally red-handed – or so he and history would later claim. Covered in blood and screaming like a demon, the widow of the celebrated Black Captain was in the process of consuming (as in chomp-chomp) one of her servant girls.

Yet another one – or so it would seem... By the time Thurzó had finished collecting evidence from household staff and the townspeople at Čachtice and at Sárvár, some 300 depositions had accused the countess of torturing, mutilating, murdering and – worst of all – disposing of the bodies of more than 600 girls and young women without so much as a Christian burial.

The case of the so-called Blood Countess has continued to catch the imagination of everyone from writers (Erzsébet is believed to have been the model for Bram Stoker's *Dracula*) and musicians (remember the Goth group Bathory?) to filmmakers and fetishists over the centuries, and some pretty crazy theories as to why she did it have emerged. Some say she considered the blood of young maidens to be an *elixir vitae* and bathed in it to stay young. Others claim she suffered from acute iron deficiency and just had to have those red corpuscles. Still others point to the high incidence of lunacy in the two, much intermarried branches of the Báthory dynasty. Most likely, however, Erzsébet Báthory herself was the victim of a conspiracy.

When the Black Captain died in 1604, his widow inherited all his estates – properties coveted by both Thurzó and Erzsébet's son-in-law Miklós Zrínyi, the poet and great-grandson of the hero of Szigetvár, who themselves were linked by marriage. Worse, the election of the countess' nephew Gábor Báthory as prince of Transylvania, a vassal state under Ottoman rule, threatened to unite the two Báthory families and strengthen the principality's position. It was in the interest of the Palatine – and the Habsburgs – to get this matriarch of the Báthorys out of the way.

Gábor was murdered in a power struggle in 1613 and the 'Bathory faction' in Hungary ceased to be a threat. The case against the Blood Countess never came to trial, and she remained interned 'between stones' (ie, in a sealed chamber) at the castle until she died in 1614 at the age of 54.

Was Erzsébet as blood-thirsty as history has made her out to be? Did she really bite great chunks out of the girls' necks and breasts and mutilate their genitals? Much of the villagers' testimony does appear to be consistent, but to form your own conclusions read Tony Thorne's well-researched *The Blood Countess* published by Bloomsbury.

Báthory's shenanigans and all the plundering by the Habsburgs. As punishment for their involvement in the rebellion of 1670, the Nádasdy estate was confiscated by the Austrian crown and the castle's contents – including much of the library – were carted off to Vienna. As a result, many of the furnishings, tapestries and *objets d'art* you see in the museum's three wings today were collected from other sources.

What the Habsburgs could not take away were the magnificent ceiling frescoes in the **Knight's Hall** (Lovag terme) picturing Hungarians – the Black Captain included – doing battle with the Turks at Tata, Székesfehérvár, Győr, Pápa, Kanizsa and Buda. They were painted by Hans Rudolf Miller in the mid-17th century. The biblical scenes (1769) on the walls, depicting Samson and Delilah, David and Goliath, Mordechai and Esther and so on, are by István Dorffmeister. There's a particularly beautiful 16th-century cabinet of gilded wood and marble to the right of the hall as you enter.

The Nádasdy Museum contains one of the finest collections of weapons and armour in Hungary, and almost an entire wing is given over to the Hussars, a regiment of which was named after the family. The uniforms, all buttons and ribbons and fancy epaulets, would do any Gilbert & Sullivan operetta proud.

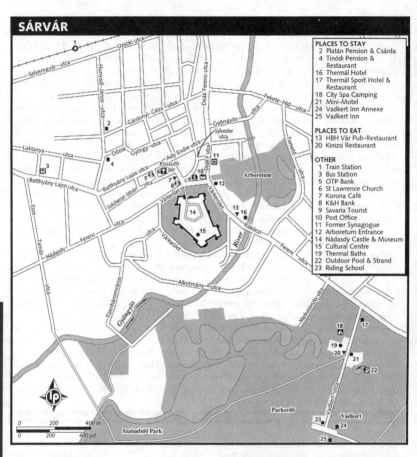

SÁRVÁR

PLACES TO STAY
2 Platán Pension & Csárda
4 Tinódi Pension & Restaurant
16 Thermál Hotel
17 Thermál Sport Hotel & Restaurant
18 City Spa Camping
21 Mini-Motel
24 Vadkert Inn Annexe
25 Vadkert Inn

PLACES TO EAT
13 HBH Vár Pub-Restaurant
20 Kinizsi Restaurant

OTHER
1 Train Station
3 Bus Station
5 OTP Bank
6 St Lawrence Church
7 Korona Café
8 K&H Bank
9 Savaria Tourist
10 Post Office
11 Former Synagogue
12 Arboretum Entrance
14 Nádasdy Castle & Museum
15 Cultural Centre
19 Thermal Baths
22 Outdoor Pool & Strand
23 Riding School

Among the exhibits about the castle and Sárvár is the printing press established here, and some of the then inflammatory Calvinist tracts it published. One work in Hungarian, emphatically entitled *The Pope Is Not the Pope – That's That* and dated 1603, was later vandalised by a Counter-Reformationist who defiantly wrote 'Lutheran scandal' across it in Latin.

A superb (and priceless) collection of some 60 antique Hungarian maps donated by an Oxford-based expatriate Magyar in 1986 is on exhibition in a room at the end of the west wing.

The museum and castle are open from 9 am to 5 pm Tuesday to Sunday (120/60Ft).

Other Attractions

The **arboretum** at Várkerület 30a east of the castle and bisected by the Gyöngyös, a tributary of the Rába River, was planted by the Nádasdys' successors, the royal Wittelsbach family of Bavaria (the castle's last royal occupant was Ludwig III, who died in exile in 1921).

The **Church of St Lawrence** (Szent Lőrinc-templom) on Kossuth tér, originally medieval but rebuilt in the 19th century, is of little interest, though there are some contemporary frescoes inside.

Only the circular window and ornamentation around the door and windows of the Romantic-style private home (1850) at Deák utca 6 north of the castle betray it as the town's former **synagogue**.

Activities

The thermal baths at Vadkert utca 1, southeast of the castle, have both indoor and outdoor hot pools and full medical facilities. It is open from 8 am to 6 pm daily and costs 400Ft. The outdoor swimming pools at the strand across the street are open from 9 am to 7 pm daily from mid-May to mid-September.

There are tennis courts and the Vadkert Major riding school (☎ 320 045) at the end of Vadkert utca. Ask the staff at the Vadkert inn about rentals (1500Ft an hour and 5000Ft for a coach seating four).

Places to Stay

You can pitch a tent at *Városi Gyógyfürdő Kemping (City Spa Camping;* ☎ *320 228, Vadkert utca 1)* 660/500/700Ft for adults/children/tent, but there are no bungalows. They do run the less-than-salubrious *Mini Motel* (☎ *same, Vadkert utca 1),* opposite, during the warmer months and charge 4000Ft for a double.

Savaria Tourist can organise *private rooms* for 1500Ft per person. If they're closed or you want to strike out on your own, look for 'Zimmer frei' signs among the stately homes on Rákóczi utca (especially Nos 23, 25 and 57a).

Two restaurants – the *Platán* (☎ *320 623, Hunyadi János utca 23)* and the *Tinódi* (☎*/fax 323 606, Hunyadi János utca 11)* – have four and eight rooms respectively for about 4500Ft to 5000Ft for a double. The Platán is in a neoclassical building between the train station and the town centre; the Tinódi is more in the thick of things but pleasant, with a lovely (and leafy) back courtyard.

Most of the reasonably priced hotels are on or near Vadkert utca. The 20-room *Thermál Sport* (☎*/fax 320 656, Rákóczi utca 46a)* at the start of Vadkert utca is a friendly place

but surprisingly expensive at DM54/77 for singles/doubles with bath.

The most atmospheric place to stay is the *Vadkert* inn (☎*/fax 320 045, Vadkert utca),* a 19th-century royal hunting lodge with 25 rooms in an old building and newer annexe. The older rooms are furnished in rustic pine, and the common sitting room with the large hearth looks straight out of an Agatha Christie whodunnit. Singles/doubles with bath are DM50/65.

The 136-room *Thermál* hotel (☎ *323 999, fax 320 406,* ❸ *thermal@savaria.hu, Rákóczi utca 1)* is Sárvár's poshest hostelry with all the mod cons, indoor and outdoor thermal pools and complete curative facilities. Singles are a whopping DM142, doubles DM199.

Places to Eat

The *csárda* at the *Platán* pension (see Places to Stay) is open till midnight; the cheaper *Tinódi* closes at 10 pm. The German-Hungarian *HBH Vár* pub-restaurant *(Rákóczi utca)* just before the Thermál hotel is open daily to midnight. The *Kinizsi (Vadkert utca),* next to the thermal spa, is there if you're hungry after a soak, but the health-conscious will head for the *restaurant* at the Thermál Sport hotel, which serves salads and a couple of vegetarian dishes.

The *Korona (Kossuth tér 3)* is a great choice for cakes and ice cream.

Entertainment

Concerts are occasionally held in the Knight's Hall in the castle; check with Savaria Tourist or the *Lajos Kossuth Cultural Centre* (☎ *320 063),* in the castle, for dates.

Getting There & Away

Destinations served by bus to/from Sárvár and their daily frequencies include Budapest (one or two departures a day), Bük and Celldömölk (10), Győr (one or two), Keszthely (two), Pápa (thr ee), Sitke (12), Sopron (three), Sümeg (four), Szombathely (eight to 10), Veszprém (three) and also Zalaegerszeg (two to three). Buses to Vienna on Friday at 3.35 am and Saturday at 7.50 am.

Sárvár is on the railway line linking Szombathely with the towns of Veszprém, Székesfehérvár and Budapest-Déli (and sometimes Budapest-Keleti). You can expect up to two-dozen trains a day to Szombathely, from where up to seven continue on to Graz in Austria via Szentgotthárd. Between 10 and 12 trains reach the other three cities every day.

KŐSZEG
☎ 94 • postcode 9730 • pop 11,900

The tranquil little town of Kőszeg (German: Güns) is sometimes called 'the nation's jewellery box', and as you pass under the pseudo-Gothic Heroes' Gate into Jurisics tér, you'll understand why. What opens up before you is a treasure trove of colourful Gothic, Renaissance and baroque buildings that together make up one of the most delightful squares in Hungary.

In the shadow of Mt Írottkő – at 882m, the highest point in Transdanubia – and just 3km from the Austrian border, Kőszeg has played pivotal roles in the nation's defence. The best known story is the storming of the town's castle by Suleiman the Magnificent's troops in August 1532, which sounds all too familiar but has a surprise ending. Miklós Jurisics' 'army' of fewer than 50 soldiers and the town militia held the fortress for 25 days against 100,000 Turks. An accord was reached when Jurisics allowed the Turks to run up their flag over the castle in a symbolic declaration of victory provided they then left town immediately thereafter. The Turks kept their part of the bargain (packing their bags at 11 am on 30 August), and Vienna was spared the treatment that would befall Buda nine years later. To this day church bells in Kőszeg peal an hour before noon to mark the withdrawal.

Orientation & Information
Kőszeg's thumbprint-shaped historic district, the Belváros (Inner Town), is ringed

KŐSZEG

PLACES TO STAY
1 Gyöngyvirág Camping & Pension
6 Jurisics Castle Hostel
15 Írottkő Hotel
20 Miklós Jurisics College
21 Kóbor Macska Pension
26 Aranystrucc Hotel
32 Children's Holiday & Tourist Hotel

PLACES TO EAT
7 Bécsikapu Restaurant
9 Garabonciás Cafe
13 Korona Eszpresszó
14 Kulacs Restaurant
30 Szarvas Restaurant
31 Golden Wreath Restaurant

OTHER
2 Synagogue
3 Bastion Ruins
4 Ponzichter Wine Cellar
5 Jurisics Castle & Museum
8 Churches of St James & St Henry
10 Golden Unicorn Pharmacy
11 Ibusz
12 Outdoor Pools
16 Városkapu Bookshop
17 Heroes' Gate
18 General's House & Museum
19 Town Hall
22 Old Tower
23 Post Office
24 Savaria Tourist
25 Church of the Sacred Heart
27 Black Moor Pharmacy
28 OTP Bank
29 Bus Station

by the Várkör, which follows the old castle walls. The city's bus 'station' is a half-dozen stands on Liszt Ferenc utca a few minutes' walk to the south-east, the train station about 1.5km in the same direction on Alsó körút.

Savaria Tourist (☎ 360 238), Várkör 69, and Ibusz (☎/fax 360 376) at Várkör 35-37 are open from 8 am to 4.30 or 5 pm on weekdays and to noon on Saturday.There's an OTP bank branch and a foreign currency exchange machine at Kossuth Lajos utca 8. The main post office is just west of Savaria Tourist at Várkör 65. The Városkapu bookshop at Városház utca 4 has a decent English-language section.

Things to See

Heroes' Gate (Hősök kapuja) leading into Jurisics tér was erected in 1932 (when these nostalgic portals were all the rage in Hungary) to mark the 400th anniversary of Suleiman's departure. The tower above is open to visitors and offers wonderful views (and photo opportunities) of the square. The **General's House** (Tábornokház), next to the gate at Jurisics tér 4-6, contains a branch of the **Miklós Jurisics Museum**, with exhibits on folk art, trades and guilds and the natural history of the area. Like all of the museums in Kőszeg it is open from 10 am to 5 pm Tuesday to Sunday. Entry is 100/50Ft.

Almost all of the buildings on Jurisics tér are interesting. The red and yellow **town hall** (Városháza) at No 8, a mixture of Gothic, Renaissance, baroque and neoclassical styles, has oval paintings on its facade of worldly and heavenly worthies. The Renaissance house at No 7, built in 1668 and now housing a pub, is adorned with graffiti etched into the stucco. No 11 is the **Golden Unicorn Pharmacy** (Arany Egyszarvú Patikaház) – one of two pharmacy museums in little Kőszeg. For those of you who can't get enough of controlled substances under glass is the other, the **Black Moor Pharmacy** (Fekete Szerecseny Patikaház), at Rákóczi Ferenc utca 3. The latter is open from 1 to 5 pm on weekdays only.

A statue of the Virgin Mary (1739) and the town fountain (1766) in the middle of

the square adjoin two fine churches. The Gothic **Church of St James** (Szent Jakab-templom; 1407), to the north, contains very faded 15th-century frescoes, on the east wall, of a giant St Christopher carrying the Christ Child, Mary Misericordia sheltering supplicants under a massive cloak and the Three Magi with their gifts. The altars and pews are masterpieces of baroque wood-carving, and Miklós Jurisics and two of his children are buried in the crypt. The baroque **Church of St Henry** (Szent Imre-templom) with the tall steeple has two art treasures: a painting of the church's patron above the altar by István Dorffmeister and one of Mary visiting her cousin Elizabeth on the north wall by Franz Anton Maulbertsch.

Just off Rajnis József utca to the north-west is a path leading to **Jurisics Castle**. Originally built in the mid-13th century, but reconstructed again and again (most recently in 1962), the four-towered fortress is now a hotchpotch of Renaissance arcades, Gothic windows and baroque interiors. The **Castle Museum** (Vármúzeum) on the 1st floor has exhibits on the history of Kőszeg (with the events of 1532 taking up most of the space) and on local wine production. Among the latter is the curious *Szőlő jővés-nek könyve* (Arrival of the Grape Book), a kind of gardener's log of grape shoot and bud sketches begun in 1740 and updated every year on St George's Day (23 April). You can climb two of the towers, from which a brass ensemble entertained the townspeople in the Middle Ages.

Walking south along narrow Chernel utca with its elegant baroque facades and saw-toothed rooftops (which allowed the defenders a better shot at the enemy), you'll pass the remains of the **old castle walls** and the **Old Tower** (Öreg Zwinger) at No 16, an 11th-century corner bastion.

The neo-Gothic **Church of the Sacred Heart** (Jézus Szíve-templom; 1894) in Fő tér is unexceptional save for its refreshingly different geometric frescoes and those 'midday' bells at 11 am. The circular **synagogue** (1859) with its strange neo-Gothic towers once served one of the oldest Jewish communities in Hungary, but now sits abandoned and in decay at Várkör 38 to the north-east of Jurisics tér.

Activities

Walking up to the baroque chapel on 393m Kálvária-hegy (Calvary Hill) north-west of the town centre or into the vineyards of Király-völgy (King's Valley) west of the castle is a pleasant way to spend a few hours, or you can follow Temető utca south-west and then south up to Szabó-hegy (Tailor's Hill). A copy of Cartographia's *A Kőszegi-hegység és környéke* (The Kőszeg Hills & Surrounds) 1:40,000 map (No 13; 400Ft) will prove useful if you plan to do more adventurous hiking or visit the new Írottkő Nature Park (☎/fax 562 532 for information) to the west. The Kőszeg Hills are known for their rare Alpine flora.

The pool and 'beach' on Strand sétány is open from 10 am to 6 pm from mid-June to August.

Special Events

Events to watch out for include the Arrival of the Grape Book festival (see Things to See) in late April, the Kőszeg Castle Games (Kőszegi Várjátékok) held in the castle yard throughout the summer and the Kőszeg Vintage (Kőszegi Szüret) festival in late September. Some of the events of the Pannon Autumn (Pannon Ősz) arts festival (September to early October) are held in Kőszeg.

Places to Stay

Camping *Gyöngyvirág Camping* (☎/fax 360 454, Bajcsy-Zsilinszky utca 6) by the little Gyöngyös River has tent sites and a pension (see later in this section) open all year.

Hostels & Private Rooms The nine-room *Jurisics Castle* hostel (☎ 360 227, Rajnis József utca 9), in a small building in the fore-court of the castle, is pretty decrepit but the location and price make it attractive: 950Ft a head in multi-bed rooms (though they make you pay 500Ft for a shower). Check-in time is 5 pm, check out at 8 am. The *Miklós*

Jurisics College (☎ 361 404, Hunyadi János utca 10) has dormitory accommodation for 1000Ft to 1300Ft (700Ft for students) in summer, as does the **Children's Holiday & Tourist Hotel** *(Gyermeküdülő és turistasza-szálló; ☎ 360 169, Ürhajósok útja 2)*. Dormitory rooms (four to six beds) at the latter cost 1500Ft per person while singles/doubles are 2200/3500Ft. Savaria Tourist can arrange rooms for about 1500Ft to 1800Ft per person.

Pensions The 12-room *Gyöngyvirág* pension *(☎/fax 360 454, Bajcsy-Zsilinszky utca 6)* at the camping ground has singles for 2000Ft to 3000Ft, doubles for 2800Ft to 3800Ft and studios for two for 4500Ft.

The *Kóbor Macska* (Stray Cat) inn *(☎/fax 362 273, Várkör 100)* is a charming eight-room place just outside the Inner Town with doubles for 3600Ft.

Hotels One of the best places to stay in Kőszeg is at the 16-room *Aranystrucc* hotel *(☎/fax 360 323, Várkör 124)* in an 18th-century building near the entrance to the Inner Town. Doubles with bath at the 'Golden Ostrich' are 5500Ft (6500Ft for larger rooms with antique furnishings). Room No 7, on the corner, with balcony views over the main square is the biggest and the best.

The 52-room *Írottkő* hotel *(☎/fax 360 373, Fő tér 4)* is Kőszeg's main hotel but, with an uninspiring restaurant, ugly concrete galleries and a dental clinic for visiting Austrians, it has little to recommend itself. Singles/doubles are 5000/7000Ft.

Places to Eat

The *Bécsikapu (Rajnis József utca 5)*, almost opposite the Church of St James, is a pleasant little place with a back garden looking toward the castle (open daily to 10 pm) though the *Kulacs (Várkör 12)* is more convenient to the bus stops. The *Garabonciás* cafe *(Jurisics tér 7)*, in a lovely historical building in the main square, serves pizza.

Other options include the *Szarvas (Rákóczi Ferenc utca 12)* in an attractive dusky pink 19th-century house with main courses from 650Ft, and the **Betérő az Aranykoszorúhoz** *(Temető utca 59)*. The 'Visitor at the Sign of the Golden Wreath' has excellent food and closes at 10 pm Tuesday to Friday, 11 pm on Saturday, 9 pm on Sunday and all day Monday.

For coffee and cakes you can't beat the **Korona** *(Várkör 18)*, a little *presszó* open from 8 am to 6 pm daily.

Entertainment

The city's *cultural centre* (☎ *360 113)* is in the castle.

For wine (mostly common Sopron vintages), go to the old **Ponzichter** wine cellar *(Rajnis József utca 10)* with vaulted ceilings and high Gothic windows (complete with extractor fan stuck into one of them).

Getting There & Away

At least half a dozen buses a day run to Sopron, Szombathely, Sárvár and Velem, but there's only two a day to Nagykanizsa and one each to Körmend and Keszthely. Two buses a week (on Friday at 8.10 am and Wednesday at 7.05 am) head for Oberpullendorf and Vienna in Austria and there's a daily bus to Lenti, the gateway to Slovenia.

Kőszeg is at the end of an 18km railway spur from Szombathely; there are 15 arrivals/departures each day (the only express – at 8.15 am – takes just 15 minutes).

KÖRMEND

☎ 94 • postcode 9900 • pop 12,100

Though certainly not worth a detour, this town 25km south of Szombathely is considered the gateway to the Őrség, a region on the border with Austria and Slovenia that retains many of its folk traditions and characteristics. Körmend was for many years the seat of the Batthyány family, an aristocratic clan that once owned much of the Őrség and would later change its spots to support the independence struggles during the mid-19th century.

Orientation & Information

Körmend's bus and train stations are five minutes apart north of the town centre on Vasútmellék utca. Walk south on Deák

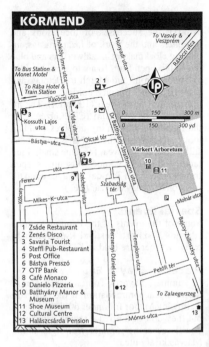

KÖRMEND

1 Zsáde Restaurant
2 Zenés Disco
3 Savaria Tourist
4 Steffi Pub-Restaurant
5 Post Office
6 Bástya Presszó
7 OTP Bank
8 Café Monaco
9 Danielo Pizzeria
10 Batthyány Manor & Museum
11 Shoe Museum
12 Cultural Centre
13 Halászcsárda Pension

Ferenc utca or Kossuth Lajos utca to reach the main thoroughfare, Rákóczi utca. The shopping area and town centre is Szabadság tér (also called Fő tér) to the south-east.

Savaria Tourist (☎/fax 410 161) is at Rákóczi utca 11. Its opening hours are from 9 am to noon and 1 to 5 pm on weekdays and till noon on Saturday. There's an OTP bank branch on pedestrians-only Vída utca at No 6. The post office is at Dr Batthyány-Strattmann utca 2.

Batthyány Manor & Museums

Batthyány Manor (Batthyány kastély), east of Szabadság tér at Dr Batthyány-Strattmann utca 3 and buffered by an arboretum (Várkert), is a typically Hungarian mix of medieval, baroque and neoclassical elements that together form a very pleasing but decaying edifice. It houses a student dormitory and the **Rába Local History Museum** (Rába Helytörténeti Múzeum), which focuses on town history through old photographs (the splendid synagogue was bombed to bits in WWII), the successes of local sons and daughters and the work of local artisans, including clockmakers, metalworkers and blue dyers. It is open from 10 am to 5 pm Tuesday to Sunday from mid-March to October and from 10 am to 3 pm on Saturday and Sunday only the rest of the year (100/50Ft). The interesting **Shoe Museum** (Cipőmúzeum) in the manor's 18th-century archives building looks exclusively at the cobbler's trade and is still producing footwear from the small Marc factory there. The Shoe Museum is open from 9 am to 5 pm Tuesday to Sunday and till noon on Saturday all year (free).

Special Events

Some of the events of the Pannon Autumn (Pannon Ősz) arts festival (September to early October) are held in Körmend.

Places to Stay & Eat

In summer, Savaria Tourist can organise dormitory accommodation at the *hostel* in Batthyány Manor for under 600Ft per head, but they don't do private rooms. However, you'll see some *Zimmer frei* signs along Mátyás király utca.

The 21-room *Rába* hotel (☎ *410 089, Bercsényi utca 24)*, in an interesting neoclassical building not far from the bus and train stations, charges 2400/4500Ft for singles/doubles. The nearby *Monet* motel (☎ *414 282, Arany János utca 8)* is a new place with singles/doubles for 2200/3950Ft. The *Halászcsárda* pension (☎*/fax 410 069, Bajcsy-Zsilinszky utca 20)* is a friendly place with nine doubles for about 4000Ft but a bit away from everything. The back rooms have restful views of the Rába River.

The *Steffl* pub-restaurant (*cnr of Rákóczi utca and Vída utca)* won't win any awards for originality, but it's convenient, inexpensive and open to 11 pm daily. For pizza and/or burgers, try *Zsáde* (*Rákóczi utca 4)*, which is open seven days a week to 10 pm and popular with students, or *Danielo* (*Kölcsey Ferenc utca 1)* with pizzas for 500Ft to 600Ft and pasta dishes from 390Ft. If you crave spicy fish soup, head for the popular *Halászcsárda* pension.

Entertainment

The small *Körmend Cultural Centre* (☎ *410 132, Berzsenyi Dániel utca 11)* has a list of events, including summertime theatre performances in the courtyard of Batthyány Manor. The *Café Monaco* (*Vída utca 8)* is a popular bar open daily till midnight (to 2 am on Friday and Saturday). The *Zenés* (*Rákóczi utca 6)* is a popular dance club open to 2 am (4 am on Friday and Saturday). From September to May the *Bástya Presszó* (*Bástya utca 4)* hosts a disco every Friday night.

Getting There & Away

Bus service to/from Körmend is relatively limited, although the seven daily departures to Zalaegerszeg cut travel time considerably. Other services to/from Körmend include Szentgotthárd (four buses daily), Zalalövő (seven), Lenti (one), Kaposvár (two), Pécs (two), Szigetvár (one) and Szombathely (one). Some Őrség towns served by bus from Körmend are Őriszentpéter (nine), Pankasz (five) and Szalafő (two).

Körmend is linked by train with Szombathely and Szentgotthárd, from where you can continue on to Graz in Austria on one of seven trains a day. To reach Zalaegerszeg by train, you must change at Zalalövő.

ŐRSÉG REGION

This westernmost region, where Hungary, Austria and Slovenia come together, has for centuries been the nation's 'sentry' (*őrség)*, and its houses and villages, spaced unusually far apart on the crests and in the valleys of the Zala foothills, once served as the national frontier. For their service as guards, the inhabitants of the region were given special privileges by the king, which they were able to retain until the arrival of the Batthyány family.

Őriszentpéter

☎ 94 • postcode 9941 • pop 1200

Őriszentpéter, the centre of the Őrség, is a pretty village of timber and thatch-roofed houses and large gardens; it is the best Őrség town in which to base yourself. Its prime sight, a remarkably well-preserved

13th-century **Romanesque church** at Templomszer 15, is an easy 2km walk north-west of the village centre. On the southern extension of the church is a wonderful carved portal and small fragments of 15th-century frescoes. The writing on the south walls inside are Bible verses in Hungarian from the 17th century. The 18th-century altarpiece was painted by a student of Franz Anton Maulbertsch.

A series of hiking trails link Őriszentpéter with other Őrség villages, including Szalafő, Velemér and Pankasz. The entrance (with map) is on Városszer just west of the Őrségi hostel/camp site (see Places to Stay & Eat later in this section).

Szalafő
☎ 94 • postcode 9942 • pop 280
Energetic travellers may want to continue along Templomszer for another 4km, past arcaded old peasant houses and abandoned crank wells to Szalafő, the oldest settlement in the Őrség. In Szalafő-Pityerszer, 2km west of the village, is the **Open-Air Ethnographical Museum** (Szabadtéri Néprajzi Múzeum), the grandiose name given to a mini-skanzen of three folk compounds unique to the Őrség. Built around a central courtyard, the houses have large overhangs which allowed neighbours to chat when it rained – a frequent occurrence in this very wet area. The **Calvinist church** in the village centre has murals from the 16th century. The museum is open from 10 am to 6 pm Tuesday to Sunday from April to October (100/50Ft).

Places to Stay & Eat
The cheapest accommodation in Őriszentpéter is at the simple *Őrségi* inn (*☎ 428 046, Városszer 57*), a tourist hostel with eight rooms and a camping ground (open June to August) just around the corner from the bus station. Doubles are 2400Ft with washbasin (2800Ft with shower), and it costs 600/500/400Ft per adult/child/tent to camp. The manager can also book you a *private room* or accommodation at one of the *peasant houses* in Szalafő, from 1500Ft per person. During off-hours you can find her at Kovácsszer 16 (*☎ 428 044*).

The *Domino* (*☎ 428 115, fax 444 048, Siskaszer 5*), a five-room motel about 300m down the road opposite the turn for Szalafő, charges 1500Ft per person or 4500Ft to 5000Ft for a small holiday house.

The *Bognár* (*Kovácsszer 96*), Őriszentpéter's only real restaurant, is about 500m up the hill, south of the bus station. The *Pitvar Presszó* (*Városszer 101*) in the centre of the village serves snacks and drinks.

Getting There & Away
Őriszentpéter and Szalafő can be reached by bus six times a day from Körmend and from Zalaegerszeg via Zalalövő. Other destinations include Kőszeg (one or two buses a day), Szentgotthárd (four), Sopron (one) and Lenti (three). Some six daily buses leave Őriszentpéter for Szalafő.

ZALAEGERSZEG
☎ 92• postcode 8900 • pop 62,200
Zala (as the locals gratefully call their city with the long name) is an oil town, and the Zala fields to the south have contributed enormously to this county seat's development since the 1930s, bringing with it such modern eyesores as the ever-present TV tower and an expensive sport centre.

However, the other part of Zalaegerszeg's name speaks of a very different world: *éger* are the moisture-loving alder trees of the Göcsej Hills to the west, an area that gets the most rainfall and has some of the worst soil in all of Hungary. Lying side by side, the city's two open-air museums (one devoted to oil, the other to traditional village life) illustrate all too well the dichotomy that is Zalaegerszeg.

Orientation & Information
The bus station is a few minutes' walk east of Széchenyi tér on Balatoni út. The train station is about 1.5km south at the end of Zrínyi Miklós utca on Bajcsy-Zsilinszky tér.

The rather frenetic Tourinform office (☎/fax 316 160, ✉ zalaegerszeg@tourinform .hu) at Kossuth Lajos utca 17-19 which is open from 9 am to 5 pm weekdays and till noon on Saturday. All the big agencies are represented in Zalaegerszeg as well, including

WESTERN TRANSDANUBIA

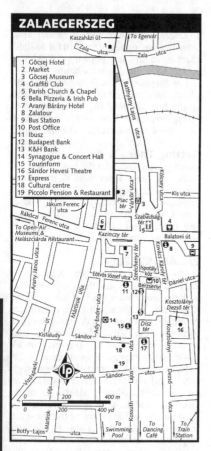

ZALAEGERSZEG

1 Göcsej Hotel
2 Market
3 Göcsej Museum
4 Graffiti Club
5 Parish Church & Chapel
6 Bella Pizzeria & Irish Pub
7 Arany Bárány Hotel
8 Zalatour
9 Bus Station
10 Post Office
11 Ibusz
12 Budapest Bank
13 K&H Bank
14 Synagogue & Concert Hall
15 Tourinform
16 Sándor Hevesi Theatre
17 Express
18 Cultural centre
19 Piccolo Pension & Restaurant

Zalatour (☎ 311 443, fax 311 469) at Kovács Károly tér 1, Express (☎ 314 144) at Dísz tér 3 and Ibusz (☎ 311 458, fax 326 655) at Eötvös utca 6-10. All are open from 8 or 9 am to 5 or 5.30 pm on weekdays and till noon on Saturday.

There's a Budapest Bank branch at Kossuth Lajos utca 2 and a K&H bank a bit farther south on Dísz tér. The main post office is at Ispotály köz 1.

Things to See & Do

The rose-coloured **synagogue** (1904) at Ady Endre utca 14, with its enormous Torah-shaped organ and stained-glass rose windows, now serves as a concert hall and gallery. On Szabadság tér there's an interesting baroque **parish church** (plébániatemplom), built in 1760 near the ruins of a 15th-century chapel, with lovely frescoes by the Austrian painter Johannes Cymbal.

Zalaegerszeg is best known for its museums. The **Göcsej Museum** at Batthyány Lajos utca 2, north of Szabadság tér, is divided into two parts. The first examines the work of painter-sculptor Zsigmond Kisfaludi Strobl, who moved away from portraits and busts of Somerset Maugham, the Duke of Kent and other social-set personalities of the 1920s and 1930s to socialist themes after the war. He also designed the striking *Independence* statue atop Gellért Hill in Budapest – for Admiral Miklós Horthy's son during WWII. After the war, when heroic monuments were in short supply, Kisfaludi Strobl passed it off as a memorial to the Soviets. He very much deserves his nickname, the 'Side-Stepper'. The next section of the museum concerns local history and folk art and is very well presented; the Roman finds from nearby Zalalövő are especially interesting, but labelled only in Hungarian. The museum is open from 10 am to 6 pm Tuesday to Sunday from April to October and to 4 pm the rest of the year.

The **Göcsej Village Museum** (Göcseji Falumúzeum), at Falumúzeum utca 2, defined by a backwater of the Zala River off Ola utca, north-west of the centre, is the oldest skanzen in Hungary and it shows; of the three dozen structures, a good one-third are shut tight or rotting into oblivion. Still, the museum offers a realistic view of a Göcsej traditional village 100 years ago, with its unique U-shaped farmhouses that lead to a central courtyard (kerített házak), pálinka stills and smokehouses. The five carved and painted house facades date from the late 19th century. The museum is open from 10 am to 6 pm Tuesday to Sunday from April to October. The open-air **Hungarian Oil Industry Museum** (Magyar Olajipari Múzeum), which keeps the same hours, is a few steps to the west.

The indoor and outdoor pools and sauna at Mártírok útja 78 are open from 1 to 6.30 pm on Monday, from 5.30 am to 6.30 pm Tuesday to Friday and from 9 am to 6.30 pm at the weekend.

Places to Stay

Ask Zalatour about *private rooms* for 3000Ft per double. They can also book you into old *peasant houses* that accommodate between three and five people in the Göcsej Hills south-west of Zalaegerszeg (6000Ft for two), but you'll have to be travelling under your own steam to get there.

Zalatour also runs the *Várkastély* hostel (☎ 364 015, *Vár utca*) at the romantic 18th-century 'Castle Palace' in Egervár, 10km north of Zalaegerszeg. A bed in its six dormitory rooms is about 1250Ft.

The 22-room *Göcsej* hotel (☎ 311 580, *fax 311 469, Kaszaházi utca 2*) is not very conveniently located and no bargain at 4400Ft for a double. The eight-room *Piccolo* pension (☎ 312 775, fax 320 100, Petőfi Sándor utca 16), on a quiet street off Kossuth Lajos utca, charges 4500Ft for doubles.

The 48-room *Arany Bárány* hotel (☎ 314 100, fax 320 347, Széchenyi tér 1) has both a new and an old wing (1898) and singles/doubles for 6800/8200Ft.

Places to Eat

A decent place for a meal in Zalaegerszeg is the homey restaurant at the *Piccolo* pension (see Places to Stay). The *Bella Pizzeria & Irish Pub* – yes, you are reading that right – (*Kazinczy tér 11*) makes for a nice change from gulyás and stays open till midnight. If you're looking for lunch near the Village and Oil museums, you couldn't do better than at the *Halászcsárda* fish restaurant (*Rákóczi utca 47*), with garden seating in summer.

Zalaegerszeg's lively *fruit & vegetable market* is on Piac tér west of Szabadság tér.

Entertainment

The *County Cultural Centre* (☎ 314 580, *Kisfaludy Sándor utca 7-10*) is a good source for what's on in Zalaegerszeg. Check the listings in the freebie weekly *Zalai Est* for clubs, theatre, parties and sporting events. The *Sándor Hevesi Theatre* (☎ 314 405, Kosztolányi Dezső tér 1) is well known for its drama and musical productions (though they will be in Hungarian). The city's symphony orchestra may be playing here or at the *concert hall* (hangverseny terem) in the former synagogue.

Two popular clubs are the *Graffiti Club* (*Balatoni út 2a*) at the Balaton hotel open till 5 am at the weekend and the *Dancing Café* (*Zrínyi Miklós utca 6*) open 9 pm to 5 am Wednesday to Saturday.

Getting There & Away

More than a dozen buses a day head for Egervár, Keszthely and Lenti. Other destinations include Balatonfüred (six buses a day), Budapest (six), Győr (five), Kaposvár (four), Körmend (eight), Nagykanizsa (eight), Pécs (six), Sárvár (four), Sopron (two), Sümeg (six or seven), Székesfehérvár (three), Szombathely (six to eight), Tapolca (five) and Veszprém (four).

Zalaegerszeg was bypassed during railway construction in the 19th century; today few places of any interest are serviced by trains from here. Up to four trains a day leave for Szombathely, but generally you'll have to change at Zalaszentiván. For Budapest you'll have to change at Celldömölk.

Getting Around

Bus Nos 1a and 1y run from the train station to Széchenyi tér and then west along Rákóczi utca and Ola utca to the open-air museums. To reach the Göcsej hotel, take bus No 3 or 3y.

You can order a local taxi on ☎ 333 666 or ☎ 336 699.

Central Transdanubia (includes Lake Balaton)

Hungary may not have majestic mountains or ocean beaches but it does have Lake Balaton, the largest freshwater body of water in Europe outside Scandinavia. This oblong lake is 78km long, 15km across at its widest point and covers an area of almost 600 sq km.

Lake Balaton (Balaton-tó), 'Hungary's inland sea', is bounded by hills to the north, gentle slopes to the south and its surface seems to change colour with the seasons and the time of day. The lake has been eulogised in songs, poems and paintings for centuries, and the surrounding region produces some of Hungary's best wines.

But Balaton is not everyone's cup of tea. The resorts (especially those on the south side) can be overrun in summer. The lake is shallow, averaging about 3m in depth, and on the southern shore you'll paddle for a kilometre before the water gets above your waist. The water is silty and alkaline – almost oily – and not very refreshing, averaging 25° to 27°C in summer and 26°C in winter. Then there are reed beds, especially on the western and north-western shores, which suggest a swampy marsh. Indeed, the lake's name comes from the Slavic root word *blatna*, which means just that.

Lake Balaton lies in (and dominates) Central Transdanubia (Közép-Dunántúl), about 100km from Budapest. It is fed by about 40 canals and streams, but its main source is the Zala River to the south-west. The lake's only outflow is the Sió Canal, which connects it at Siófok with the Danube River east of Szekszárd.

History

The area around Lake Balaton was settled as early as the Iron Age, and the Romans, who called the lake Pelso, built a fort at Valcum (now Fenékpuszta), south of Keszthely, in the 2nd century AD. Throughout the Great Migrations, Lake Balaton was a reliable

HIGHLIGHTS

- Castle Hill in Veszprém and its wonderful architecture
- Tihany's Abbey Church
- The Festetics Palace at Keszthely
- A meal or a drink at the Kisfaludy House restaurant overlooking Lake Balaton at Badacsony
- A dip in the Gyógy-tó (Thermal Lake) at Hévíz
- Franz Anton Maulbertsch's wonderful frescoes at the Church of the Ascension in Sümeg

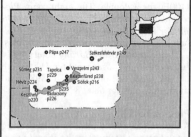

source of water, fish, reeds for thatch and ice in winter. The early Magyars found the lake a natural defence line, and many churches, monasteries and villages were built in the vicinity. In the 16th century the lake served as the divide between the Turks, who occupied the southern shore, and the Habsburgs to the north-west, but before the Ottomans were pushed back they had already crossed the lake and razed many of the towns and border castles in the northern hills. Croats, Germans and Slovaks resettled the area in the 18th century, and the subsequent building booms gave towns like Sümeg, Veszprém and Keszthely their baroque appearance.

Balatonfüred and Hévíz developed early as resorts for the wealthy, but it wasn't until the late 19th century that landowners, their vines destroyed by phylloxera lice, began building summer homes to rent out to the burgeoning middle classes. The arrival of the southern railway in 1861 and the northern line in 1909 increased the tourist influx, and by the 1920s resorts on both shores welcomed some 50,000 holiday-makers each summer. Just before the outbreak of WWII, that number had increased fourfold. After the war, the communist government expropriated private villas and built new holiday homes for trade unions. In recent years, many of these have been turned into hotels, greatly increasing the accommodation options.

Orientation

The two shores of Lake Balaton are as different as chalk and cheese. The southern coast is essentially one long resort: from Siófok to Fonyód, there are high-rise hotels, concrete embankments to prevent flooding, and minuscule grassy 'beaches' packed with sunbathers in summer. Here the water is at its shallowest and safest for children, and the beaches are not reedy as they often are on the northern shore.

Things change dramatically as you round the bend from Keszthely, a pretty town hugging the westernmost end of the lake, to the northern shore. The north has many more historical towns and sights, mountain trails and better wine. The resorts at Badacsony, Tihany and Balatonfüred have more grace and atmosphere and are far less commercial than, say, Siófok or Balatonboglár to the south.

Activities

The main pursuits for visitors at Lake Balaton – apart from swimming, of course – are boating and fishing. Motorboats running on fuel are banned entirely, so 'boating' here means sailing, rowing and windsurfing. Fishing is good – the indigenous *fogas* (pike-perch) and the young version, *süllő*, being the prized catch – and edible *harcsa* (catfish) and *ponty* (carp) are in abundance.

You can get a fishing licence from Siotour in Siófok (see Information in that section) or from the national angling association, Mohosz (☎ 1-319 1443), XII Korompai utca 17, Budapest. One of the big events of the year at the lake is the Cross-Balaton Swimming Race (Balatonátúszó verseny) from Révfülöp to Balatonboglár in late July.

If you can get into the swing of it, the lake is a good place to meet people as it is one of the few places where Hungarians really do let their hair (and most everything else) down. Bear in mind, though, that during the low season (roughly late October to early April) virtually all the hotels, restaurants, museums and recreational facilities here shut down.

Getting There & Away

Trains to Lake Balaton usually leave from Budapest-Déli train station and buses from the station at Erzsébet tér. If you're travelling north or south from the lake to towns in Western or Southern Transdanubia, buses are usually preferable to trains.

Getting Around

Railway service on both the northern and southern sides of the lake is fairly frequent. A better way to see the lake up close, though, is on a Mahart Balaton ferry (☎ 84-310 050, ✉ mahart@mail.matav.hu), based at Krúdy sétány 2 in Siófok. Check out its Web site at www.balatel.hu/mahart. Ferries operate on the Siófok-Balatonfüred-Tihany route and the one between Fonyód and Badacsony up to four times a day in April/May and September/October, with much more frequent sailings from June to August. From late May to early September, ferries ply the lake from Balatonkenese to Keszthely. There are also car ferries crossing the lake between Tihanyi-rév and Szántódi-rév (from early March to late November), and between Badacsony and Fonyód (from April to late October). There are no passenger services on the lake in winter.

Fares are cheap. Adults pay 300Ft for distances of one to 10km, 500Ft for 11 to 20km, 580Ft for 21 to 40km and 640Ft for

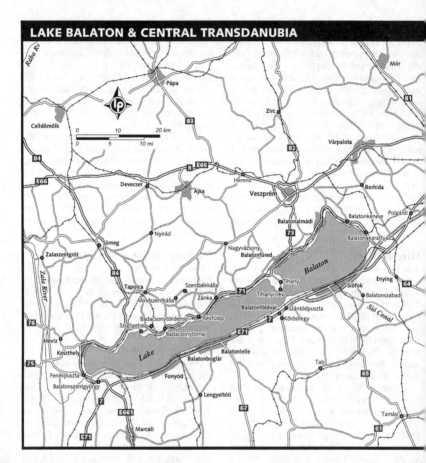

LAKE BALATON & CENTRAL TRANSDANUBIA

41 to 70km. Children pay half-price, and return fares are slightly less than double the one-way fare. It costs 250/350Ft to transport a bicycle one way/round trip. The car ferries charge 160/160/320/640Ft per person/bicycle/motorcycle/car.

SIÓFOK

☎ 84 • postcode 8600 • pop 22,600

Siófok, 106km south-west of Budapest, typifies the resorts of the southern shore: it's loud, brash and crowded. The dedicated pursuits here are eating, drinking, sunbathing, swimming and sleeping – and whatever comes in between. It is the largest of the lake's resorts and is always jammed at the height of summer.

Siófok didn't start out this way. In the 19th century it was every bit as elegant as Balatonfüred, and the lovely villas on Batthyány Lajos utca near Jókai Park and the lakeside promenade recall those days. But late in the 20th century, after the southern railway line had reached Siófok, more and more people began to holiday here. Today many of the villas have been converted to hotels or offices, and the promenade, with its mock gas lamps, has been

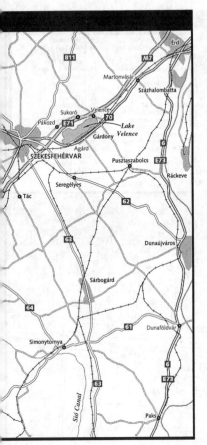

the west is the lake-draining Sió Canal, which runs south-east to the Danube.

Szabadság tér, the centre of Siófok, is to the east of the canal and about 500m south-east of the ferry pier. The bus station and *fin-de-siècle* train station are on Váradi Adolf tér just off Fő utca, the main drag.

Information

Tourinform (☎ 315 355, fax 310 117, ✉ siofok@tourinform.hu) has an office at the base of the old water tower (víztorony) on Szabadság tér (open from 8 am to 8 pm Monday to Saturday and till noon on Sunday from June to August and from 9 am to 4 pm weekdays only the rest of the year). Check out its Web site at www.siofok.com. Commercial agencies include Siotour (☎ 310 900, fax 310 009), Szabadság tér 6, and Ibusz (☎ 311 066, fax 311 481) at Fő utca 174. Generally they're open from 8 am to 4 pm Monday to Friday, but they also stay open as late as 8 pm weekdays and are open on Saturday morning in summer.

There's an OTP bank branch with a currency-exchange machine opposite the bus station at Fő utca 188, but you'll find exchange offices all over town. The main post office is just across Széchenyi utca at Fő utca 186.

Things to See

There's not a whole lot to see of cultural or historical importance in a place where the baser instincts tend to rule. The **Mineral Museum** (Ásványmúzeum), Kálmán Imre utca 10, is no different from similar exhibits that have sprung up all over Hungary and there's an **Ocean Aquarium** (Tengeri Akvárium) along the canal at Somogyi utca 4.

The **lock system** of the canal, which had been partly built by the Romans in 292 AD and used extensively by the Turks in the 16th and 17th centuries, can be seen from Krúdy sétány, the walkway near the ferry pier, or Baross Bridge to the south. Nearby is the headquarters of the Hungarian navy. The tower on the western tip of the canal entrance is the **weather observatory** of the National Meteorological Service (Országos Meteorológiai Szolgálat). Believe it or not,

paved. Tourism on a mass scale is now the business of Siófok and since 1997 it has been allowed to call itself 'Hungary's summer capital'.

Orientation

Greater Siófok stretches for some 17km, as far as the resort of Balatonvilágos to the east (once reserved exclusively for communist honchos) and Balatonszéplak to the west. The dividing line between the so-called Gold Coast (Aranypart) in the east, where most of the big hotels are, and the less-developed Silver Coast (Ezüstpart) to

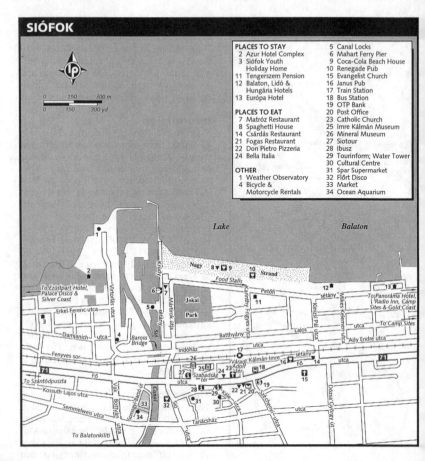

SIÓFOK

PLACES TO STAY
2 Azur Hotel Complex
3 Siófok Youth
  Holiday Home
11 Tengerszem Pension
12 Balaton, Lidó &
  Hungária Hotels
13 Európa Hotel

PLACES TO EAT
7 Matróz Restaurant
8 Spaghetti House
14 Csárdás Restaurant
21 Fogas Restaurant
22 Don Pietro Pizzeria
24 Bella Italia

OTHER
1 Weather Observatory
4 Bicycle &
  Motorcycle Rentals

5 Canal Locks
6 Mahart Ferry Pier
9 Coca-Cola Beach House
10 Renegade Pub
15 Evangelist Church
16 Janus Pub
17 Train Station
18 Bus Station
19 OTP Bank
20 Post Office
23 Catholic Church
25 Imre Kálmán Museum
26 Mineral Museum
27 Siotour
28 Ibusz
29 Tourinform; Water Tower
30 Cultural Centre
31 Spar Supermarket
32 Flört Disco
33 Market
34 Ocean Aquarium

Balaton can actually get quite rough when the wind picks up, and there's a system of warning signals.

The wooden **water tower** on Szabadság tér dates from 1912. If you walk north on narrow Hock János köz, you'll reach the **Imre Kálmán Museum** at Kálmán Imre sétány 5. It is devoted to the life and works of the composer of popular operettas who was born in Siófok in 1882. East of Szabadság tér in Oulu Park, Hungary's maverick architect Imre Makovecz strikes again with his winged and 'masked' **Evangelist church** (Evangélikus templom), which bears a strong resemblance to an Indonesian *garuda*, or mythical bird.

Activities

Nagy Strand, Siófok's 'Big Beach' is east of the observatory and just north of Petőfi sétány and open to the public. There are many more 'managed' swimming areas along the Gold and Silver Coasts. Entry generally costs 200/100Ft for the day or 1200/720Ft per week.

There are rowing boats and sailing boats for rent at various locations along the lake, including the Nagy Strand. You are able to hire bicycles and motorcycles from the Móló stand (☎ 314 692) on the corner of Vitorlás utca and Horgony utca on the canal's western bank from 10 am to 7 pm daily from mid-May to mid-September. Bicycles cost 400/2200Ft per hour/day, motorcycles 1200/4500Ft.

Places to Stay

Siófok is one of the few places on the lake where you might have trouble finding accommodation in high season. Siófok gets some 100,000 visitors in late July and August and all but closes down between late October and early April.

Camping There are some two dozen camping grounds along the Balaton's southern shore, and Siófok has eight, most with bungalows, open from May to September. *Aranypart Camping* (☎ 352 519, Szent László utca 183-185), 4km east of the centre in Balatonszabadi, has its own beach; if you're coming from Budapest by train, get off at the Szabadi-fürdő station, one stop before Siófok. *Ifjúság Camping* (☎ 352 851, Pusztatorony tér 1) is in Sóstó, 7km east of Siófok between tiny 'Salt Lake' and Lake Balaton. The correct train station for this camp site is Balatonszabadi-Sóstó. Prices for the four-person bungalows vary widely, from lows of DM39 at the Ifjúság and DM59 at the Aranypart in May to a whopping DM109 and DM139 respectively in most of July and August. The Ifjúság site also has small wooden two-person bungalows available late May to mid-September for between DM9 and DM19. It will pay to check these prices with one of the agencies before setting out.

For those who like to camp *au naturel*, there's a nudist site at Balatonakarattya at the north-eastern end of the lake about 12km east of Siófok. *Piroska* (☎ 481 084, Aligai út 15), is open from mid-May to chilly early September and has bungalows. It is within easy walking distance of the Balatonakarattya train station, which is on the line running along the lake's northern shore.

Hostels From June to August, a hostel with multi-bed rooms (1000Ft to 1400Ft in doubles or quads) operates in the *Siófok Youth Holiday Home* (*Siófoki Ifjúsági Üdülő;* ☎ 310 131, Erkel Ferenc utca 48) on the Silver Coast. The huge *Ezüstpart* hotel (see Hotels) on Liszt Ferenc sétány also has hostel rooms available from mid-May to mid-October costing between 700Ft and 2300Ft, depending on the room size and whether it has facilities.

Private Rooms The agencies can find you a double private room for DM20 to DM25 and an apartment for four to six people for DM80 to DM100. Singles are rare and those staying only one or two nights are generally unwelcome; if you want to do it alone, check for '*Zimmer frei*' signs along Erkel Ferenc utca on the Silver Coast and Petőfi sétány and Beszédes József sétány on the Gold Coast.

Pension One of the more unusual places to stay in Siófok is the *Tengerszem* pension (☎/fax 310 146, Karinthy Frigyes utca 4) just south of the Nagy Strand. Singles/doubles are 4000/6000Ft and it is open May to August.

Hotels The Pannonia chain has four hotels (fax 313 6304, ✉ balaton@pannoniahotels .hu) with more than 560 rooms collectively along Petőfi sétány – Nos 9 to 17 – and also a narrow beach at the start of the Gold Coast: the *Balaton* (☎ 310 655); *Lidó* (☎ 310 633); *Hungária* (☎ 310 677); and the *Európa* (☎ 313 411). All except the Balaton are three-star and each has about 130 rooms. Singles at the Európa, the most expensive of the four and open mid-April to mid-October, are DM58 to DM98, doubles DM66 to DM116, depending on the season. At the others (open from May/June to August/September) they range from DM42 to DM75 for a single and DM56 to DM96 for a double.

A better deal can be had at the former trade-union holiday homes farther east. The 56-room *Radio Inn Siófok* (☎ 311 634, fax 313 832, Beszédes József sétány 77) has doubles with bath for 5500Ft to 7000Ft, depending on the season. The 154-room *Panoráma* (☎/fax 311 637, Beszédes József *sétány 80)* charges from DM41 to DM52 for singles and DM57 to DM83 for doubles.

Though it's not in the nicest part of Siófok, the *Ázur* hotel complex *(☎ 312 419, fax 312 105, Vitorlás utca 11)* on the western side of the canal mouth is friendly and reasonably priced. It has over 400 rooms in four buildings; singles are DM29 to DM40 and doubles DM60 to DM82, depending on the season. The main building (No 4) is the nicest one.

The enormous *Ezüstpart* hotel *(☎ 350 622, fax 350 358, ✉ reserve@balaton .huguest.hu, Liszt Ferenc sétány 2-4)* counts more than 800 rooms in five different buildings. Rooms (of which there are three categories) cost from DM30/38 for singles/doubles in the low season and from DM80/100 in August. Most rooms are available from mid-April to mid-October only.

Places to Eat

There are a number of *food stalls* by the Nagy Strand along Petőfi sétány. *Bella Italia (Szabadság tér 1)* and the cellar *Don Pietro* restaurant *(Fő utca 178)* serve pizza, pasta and other Italian dishes. The *Spaghetti House* on the Nagy Strand is popular with students in summer.

The *Matróz* bar-restaurant *(Krúdy sétány)*, with outside tables facing the canal's lock system and moored boats, is convenient to the ferry. *Csárdás (Fő utca 105)* near Kinizsi Pál utca is a reliable place in an old townhouse open till 11 pm. Most Siófokers say that *Fogas (Fő utca 184)* next to the post office is the best fish restaurant in town.

There's an excellent covered *market (Somogyi utca 2)* along the Sió Canal, just north of the aquarium.

Entertainment

Concerts, dance performances and plays are staged at the *South Balaton Cultural Centre (☎ 311 855, Fő tér 2)*, Siófok's main cultural venue. Organ recitals can be enjoyed in the *Catholic church* on Váradi Adolf tér.

The regional white wine in these parts comes from Balatonboglár and is usually light and not very distinctive (though the Chardonnay isn't bad). Decent places for a quiet drink include the pub at the *Janus* hotel *(Fő utca 93-95)*.

Two popular dancing venues are the *Flőrt* disco *(Sió utca 4)*, open till 6 am daily in season, and the huge *Palace* disco *(Deák Ferenc utca 2)* on the Silver Coast, which is accessible by a free bus from outside Tourinform every day in summer at 9 pm from May to mid-September. More informal – and livelier for that – is the *Coca-Cola Beach House* on the Nagy Strand, with free concerts on Wednesday and Saturday nights in high season. Everyone then moves on to the *Renegade* pub a short distance to the east for drinking and bopping.

Getting There & Away

Bus Buses serve a lot of destinations from Siófok, but compared with the excellent train connections, they're not very frequent. The exceptions are Kaposvár and Nagyberény with hourly departures. Other destinations include: Budapest (seven a day), Gyula (one a day), Győr (one), Harkány (one), Hévíz and Keszthely (two), Kecskemét (two), Pécs (three), Szeged (three), Szekszárd (five), Tapolca (one), Tatabánya (one), Veszprém (eight) and Zalaegerszeg (three). A bus bound for Hamburg departs at 7.45 pm on Wednesday, Friday and Sunday and one for Rotterdam at 7 pm daily from mid-June to early September.

Train The main railway line running through Siófok carries trains to Székesfehérvár and Budapest-Déli and to the other resorts on the lake's southern shore and Nagykanizsa up to 20 times a day in each direction. Two trains a day from Budapest to Zagreb and one to Venice stop at Siófok. Local trains run south from Siófok to Kaposvár four times a day.

Boat From late March to October, four ferries a day link Siófok with Balatonfüred, three of which carry on to Tihany. Up to eight ferries follow the same route in July and August.

Getting Around

From the stations, bus No 1 is good for the Silver Coast, No 2 for the Gold Coast, Nos 4 and 14 for Balatonkiliti and Nos 5 and 6 for Balatonszéplak.

For a local taxi, ring ☎ 312 240 or 312 222.

KESZTHELY

☎ 83 • postcode 8360 • pop 22,000

Keszthely, at the western end of Lake Balaton about 70km from Balatonfüred, is the only town on the lake not entirely dependent on tourism. As a result, Keszthely does not have that melancholy, ghost-town feel to it that Siófok does in the low season.

The Romans built a fort at Valcum (now Fenékpuszta) 5km to the south, and their road north to the colonies at Sopron and Szombathely is today's Kossuth Lajos utca. The town's fortified monastery and church on Fő tér were strong enough to repel the Turks in the 16th century.

In the middle of the 18th century, Keszthely and its surrounds (including Hévíz) came into the possession of the Festetics family, progressives and reformers very much in the tradition of the Széchenyis. In fact, Count György Festetics (1755-1819), who founded Europe's first agricultural college, the Georgikon, here in 1797, was an uncle of István Széchenyi.

Today, Keszthely is a pleasant town of grand houses, trees, cafes and enough to see and do to hold you for a spell. It has a unique view of both the northern and southern shores of Lake Balaton, and the large student population contributes to the town's nightlife.

Orientation

The centre of town is Fő tér, from where Kossuth Lajos utca, lined with colourful old houses, runs to the north (pedestrian only) and south. The bus and train stations are opposite one another near the lake at the end of Mártírok útja. From the stations, follow Mártírok útja up the hill, then turn north into Kossuth Lajos utca to reach the centre. The ferry docks at a stone pier within sight of the Hullám hotel. From here, follow the path past the hotel. Erzsébet királyné utca, which flanks Helikon Park, leads to Fő tér.

Information

Tourinform (☎/fax 314 144) at Kossuth Lajos utca 28 is an excellent source of information on Keszthely and the entire Balaton area. It is open from 9 am to 5 pm weekdays and to 1 pm at the weekend from April to October and from 8 am to 4 pm weekdays and 9 am to 1 pm on Saturday the rest of the year. Other agencies on Kossuth Lajos utca include Keszthely Tourist (☎ 314 288) at No 25 and Zalatour (☎ 312 560) at No 1; Ibusz (☎ 314 320) is at Erzsébet királyné utca 2. These three are open till 4 or 5 pm weekdays and sometimes till noon or 1 pm on Saturday.

There's a huge OTP bank facing the park south of the Catholic church and a Budapest Bank at Pethő Ferenc utca 1. The main post office is at Kossuth Lajous utca 46-48.

Things to See

The **Festetics Palace** (Festetics kastély; 1745), in the large 'English garden' at Kastély utca 1, contains 100 rooms in two sprawling wings. The 19th-century north wing houses a music school, city library and conference centre; the **Helikon Palace Museum** (Helikon Kastélymúzeum) and the palace's greatest treasure, the **Helikon Library** (Helikon Könyvtar), are in the baroque south wing. The entrance fee is an outrageous 1000/600Ft for adults/students though Hungarians pay only 300/160Ft. A one-hour tour in one of four languages costs 2000Ft.

The museum's rooms (about a dozen in all, each in a different colour scheme) are full of portraits, bric-a-brac and furniture, much of it brought from England by one Mary Hamilton, a duchess who married one of the Festetics men in the 1860s. The library is renowned for its 90,000-volume collection, but just as impressive is the golden oak shelving and furniture carved by local craftsman János Kerbl in 1801. Also worth noting are the Louis XIV Salon with its stunning marquetry, the rococo Music Room and the private chapel (1804). The museum is open from 9 am to 6 pm Tuesday to Sunday in July and August, to 5 pm in June and from 10 am to 5 pm the rest of the year.

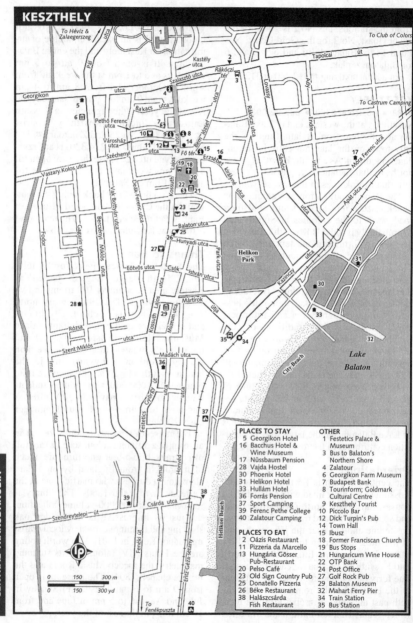

KESZTHELY

To Hévíz &
Zalaegerszeg

To Club of Colors

Kastély utca

Szalasztó utca

Rákóczi tér

Tapolcai út

Georgikon utca

To Castrum Camping

Bakacs utca

Pethő Ferenc utca

Városház utca

Széchenyi utca

Vaszary Kolos utca

Fő tér

Erzsébet királyné utca

Móra Ferenc utca

Balaton utca

Hunyadi utca

Helikon Park

Eötvös utca

Csók István utca

Mártírok útja

Madách utca

Lake Balaton

City Beach

Helikon Beach

Szendreytelepi út

Feneki út

Ebíz Géza Sétány

Csárda utca

To Fenékpuszta

0   150   300 m
0   150   300 yd

PLACES TO STAY
5 Georgikon Hotel
16 Bacchus Hotel &
   Wine Museum
17 Nüssbaum Pension
28 Vajda Hostel
30 Phoenix Hotel
31 Helikon Hotel
33 Hullám Hotel
36 Forrás Pension
37 Sport Camping
39 Ferenc Pethe College
40 Zalatour Camping

PLACES TO EAT
2 Oázis Restaurant
11 Pizzeria da Marcello
13 Hungária Gösser
   Pub-Restaurant
20 Pelso Café
23 Old Sign Country Pub
25 Donatello Pizzeria
26 Béke Restaurant
38 Halászcsárda
   Fish Restaurant

OTHER
1 Festetics Palace &
   Museum
3 Bus to Balaton's
   Northern Shore
4 Zalatour
6 Georgikon Farm Museum
7 Budapest Bank
8 Tourinform; Goldmark
   Cultural Centre
9 Keszthely Tourist
10 Piccolo Bar
12 Dick Turpin's Pub
14 Town Hall
15 Ibusz
18 Former Franciscan Church
19 Bus Stops
21 Hungaricum Wine House
22 OTP Bank
24 Post Office
27 Golf Rock Pub
29 Balaton Museum
32 Mahart Ferry Pier
34 Train Station
35 Bus Station

The **Georgikon Farm Museum** (Georgikon Majormúzeum) at Bercsényi Miklós utca 65 is housed in several early 19th-century buildings of what was the Georgikon's experimental farm. It contains exhibits on the history of the college and the later Pannon Agricultural University (now a few blocks to the south-east on the corner of Széchenyi utca and Deák Ferenc utca), viniculture in the Balaton region and traditional farm trades such as those performed by wagon builders, wheelwrights, coopers and blacksmiths. The museum is open from 10 am to 5 pm Monday to Saturday and to 6 pm on Sunday from April to October (60/20Ft).

Fő tér is a colourful square with some lovely buildings, including the late baroque **Town Hall** on the northern side, the **Trinity Column** (1770) in the centre and the former **Franciscan church** (Ferences templom) in the park to the south. The church was originally built in the late 14th century for Franciscan monks in the Gothic style, but many alterations were made in subsequent centuries, including the addition of the steeple in 1898. The Gothic rose window above the porch remains, though, as do some faded 15th-century frescoes in the sanctuary and on the southern wall. Count György and other Festetics family members are buried in the crypt below.

The **Balaton Museum** at Múzeum utca 2 (corner of Mártírok útja & Kossuth Lajos utca) was purpose-built in 1928 and contains much on the Roman fort at Valcum and traditional life around Lake Balaton. But most interesting is the history of navigation on the lake and the photographs of summer frolickers at the start of the 20th century. The museum is open from 10 am to 6 pm Tuesday to Sunday from May to October and to 5 pm the rest of the year (150/75Ft).

There's a bird-ringing camp run by the Hungarian Ornithological Society (MME) with very knowledgeable staff in Fenékpuszta near the delta of the Zala River south of Keszthely. It's just one stop on the train heading for Balatonszentgyörgy; if you're driving, the exit is at the 111 km stone on route No 71.

Activities

Keszthely has two beaches: City Beach (Városi Strand), close to the ferry pier, and reedy Helikon Beach farther south. There's a windsurfing school at City Beach in summer and another one at Vonyarcvas-hegy Strand across the bay in Gyenesdias.

There are several horse-riding schools north-east of Keszthely in Sömögye-dűlő, including Musztáng (☎ 312 289) and János (☎ 314 533).

Wine tasting is available at the Hungaricum Wine House (Hungaricum Borház) near the OTP bank at Helikon utca 4 (10 am to 6 pm daily; 100Ft) and the lovely Bacchus Wine Museum (Bacchus Bor Múzeum) at Erzsébet királyné utca 18 (10 am to 10 pm daily; 250Ft).

Special Events

The biggest annual cultural event in Keszthely is the Balaton Festival held throughout May. Balaton Autumn (Balatoni Ősz), a festival Keszthely shares with Hévíz and other nearby towns, takes place in September.

Places to Stay

Camping There are three camping grounds near the lake, two of which have bungalows and are open from May to September. As you leave the train station, head south across the tracks and you'll soon reach *Sport Camping* (☎ 313 777, *Csárda utca*). However, wedged between the railway tracks and a road, it's noisy and not very clean. Carry on south for 20 minutes to *Zalatour Camping* (☎ 312 782, *Ernszt Géza sétány*), a much bigger place with large bungalows for four people from DM50 to DM70 and smaller holiday houses for DM18 to DM24. There are tennis courts, and the site has access to Helikon Beach. *Castrum Camping* (☎ 312 120), north of the stations at Móra Ferenc utca 48, has its own beach but no bungalows and is really for caravans. It is open from April to October.

Hostels In July and August you can stay in the student dormitory at *Ferenc Pethe College* (☎ 311 290, *Festetics György út 5*) for

1480Ft per person. From mid-June to August, the János Vajda College becomes the **Vajda Hostel** (☎ *311 361, Gagarin utca 4*).

Private Rooms Private rooms are available from Ibusz, Zalatour and Keszthely Tourist for about 2000Ft to 2500Ft per person. Ask around, though, as prices vary.

If you're only staying one night, some of the agencies levy heavy surcharges, making it worthwhile to forgo their services and go directly to houses with *szoba kiadó* or *Zimmer frei* signs outside, where you may be able to bargain with the owners. There are lots along Móra Ferenc utca.

Pension Close to the lake, the 35-room **Forrás** (☎ *311 418, fax 314 617, Római út 1*) has singles/doubles with washbasin for 1800/3100Ft to 3500Ft. Singles with shower or bath cost 3000Ft to 3500Ft, doubles 4900Ft to 5500Ft, depending on the season. The **Nüssbaum** (☎/fax *314 365, Móra Ferenc utca 15*) is a comfortable pension in a quiet, leafy residential area close to the lake. Doubles are DM50 to DM80, depending on the season.

Hotels Housed in one of the agricultural college's original buildings, the **Georgikon** apartment hotel (☎ *312 363, fax 315 730, Georgikon utca 20*) has 14 suites with cooking facilities and all the mod cons. Singles/doubles with bath are 5000/7500Ft; there's a huge family suite for five people for 17,000Ft. One drawback is that the hotel backs onto busy route No 71.

The attractive, 26-room **Bacchus** hotel (☎/fax *314 097*, 🖲 *bacchush@matav.hu, Erzsébet királyné utca 18*) is the new kid on the block where wine reigns supreme (see Activities). Singles cost DM50 to DM75, doubles DM65 to DM100, depending on the season.

Three expensive hotels on the lake are among the most attractive and best equipped resort facilities in Hungary. The most charming is the renovated 50-room **Hullám** (☎ *312 644, fax 315 338, Balaton-part 1*), straight up from the ferry pier and built in 1892. Singles are from DM64 to DM100, doubles from DM84 to DM120. The 73-room **Phoenix** (☎ *312 630, fax 314 225, Balaton-part 3*), in the park behind the Hullám, has more of a woodsy feel to it and is much cheaper, but mosquitoes might be a problem. Singles are from DM38 to DM85, doubles DM48 to DM79, depending on the season. These two hotels are open from April to October.

The **Helikon** (☎ *311 330, fax 315 403,* 🖲 *dhhelikon@mail.matav.hu, Balaton-part 5*), by far the biggest hotel in Keszthely with 232 rooms and open all year, is a few minutes' walk north-east through the park. The Helikon has its own island for swimming, an indoor swimming and sports centre with covered clay tennis courts and anything else you could imagine. Singles are DM54 to DM124, doubles DM86 to DM164, depending on the season.

Places to Eat

The **Pizzeria da Marcello** (*Városház utca 4*), in a cellar with rustic furniture, serves made-to-order pizzas and salads till 10 pm. Another option is **Donatello Pizza** (*Balaton utca 1a*) open daily till 11 pm. The **Oázis** (*Rákóczi tér 3*), a 'reform' restaurant east of Festetics Palace, serves vegetarian dishes such as felafel, salads and pickles (100Ft for 180g) from 11 am to 4 pm Monday to Saturday. The **Old Sign Country Pub** (*Kossuth Lajos utca 44*) is another one of those Western-themed places offering chilli con carne and steak which Hungarians seem to have fallen in love with.

The **Hungária Gösser** pub-restaurant (*Kossuth Lajos utca 35*), in a historical building with stained-glass windows at the corner of Fő tér, has pizza, German and Hungarian dishes and a salad bar. The **Béke** (*Kossuth Lajos utca 50*) has a reasonable menu including several fish dishes, an attractive outside seating area and a decent cafe. A new place worthy of a splurge is the restaurant at the **Bacchus** hotel (see Places to Stay).

The **Pelso Cafe**, in a two-level modern tower-like structure in the park just south of the Catholic church, is a wonderful place to sit over cake and coffee and watch the world go by below you. It's open till 9 or 10 pm and even later in season.

Entertainment

On Sunday at 8.30 pm from July to mid-August, you can see Hungarian folk dancing in the courtyard of the *Károly Goldmark Cultural Centre (☎ 314 286, Kossuth Lajos utca 28)* next door to Tourinform. Concerts are often held in the Music Room of *Festetics Palace* in summer.

Dick Turpin's Pub (Városház utca 2) has great music while the *Piccolo (Városház utca 9)* is a small pub with Czech beer that attracts friendly students and soldiers (Keszthely is a garrison town). The *Golf Rock Pub (Kossuth Lajos utca 95)* attracts a young crowd and is open till late. One of the more popular dancing venues is the *Club of Colors (Tapolcai út)*, north-east of the centre.

Getting There & Away

Bus The only important destinations with more than 10 daily departures from Keszthely are Hévíz, Tapolca, Veszprém and Zalaegerszeg; there are about six to Nagykanizsa and Sümeg. Other towns served by bus include Badacsony (two buses a day), Baja (one), Budapest (six), Győr (two), Nagyvázsony (one), Pápa (three), Pécs (three), Székesfehérvár (six) and Szombathely (two). Some of these buses – including those to Hévíz, Zalaegerszeg, Nagykanizsa and Sümeg – can be boarded at the bus stops in front of the Catholic church on Fő tér.

For buses to the lake's northern shore (Badacsony, Nagyvázsony and Tapolca), you can catch the bus along Tapolcai út.

Train Keszthely is on a branch line linking Tapolca and Balatonszentgyörgy, from where up to 10 daily trains continue along the southern shore to Székesfehérvár and Budapest-Keleti or Budapest-Déli. To reach Szombathely or towns along Lake Balaton's northern shore by train, you must change at Tapolca and sometimes at Celldömölk too, but the connections are quick. For Pécs take a train to Kaposvár, then change to a bus.

From late June to late August, MÁV Nostalgia (☎ 1-317 1665), based at Belgrád rakpart 26 in Budapest, runs a vintage steam train (*nosztalgiavonat*) from Keszthely to Badacsonytomaj and Tapolca at 9.50 am from Tuesday to Sunday. Verify this service and schedule with MÁV Nostalgia by phone or via its Web site at www.miwo.hu/old_trains before making plans.

Getting Around

Bus Nos 1 and 2 run from the train and bus stations to the Catholic church on Fő tér, but unless there's one waiting on your arrival, it's just as easy to walk.

You can order a taxi on ☎ 333 666 or ☎ 312 222.

HÉVÍZ

☎ 83 • postcode 8380 • pop 4250

If you enjoy visiting spas and taking the waters, you'll love Hévíz, site of Europe's largest thermal lake (Gyógy-tó). The people of this town some 7km north-west of Keszthely have made use of the warm mineral water for centuries, first in a tannery in the Middle Ages and later for curative purposes. The lake was first developed as a private resort by Count György Festetics of Keszthely in 1795.

Orientation & Information

The centre of Hévíz is really Parkerdő, the large 'Park Wood', and its thermal lake. The bus station can be found on Deák tér a few steps from one of two main entrances to the lake; the small commercial centre lies to the west of the station. Kossuth Lajos utca, where most of the big hotels are located, forms the western boundary of the Parkerdő.

There are two tourist agencies north-west of the bus station on Rákóczi utca: Hévíz Tourist (☎ 341 348) at No 2 and Zalatour (☎ 341 048) at No 8. The first is open from 8.30 am to 5.30 pm weekdays and from 9 am to 1 pm on Saturday; the second opens and shuts a half-hour earlier on weekdays and is open from 9 am to 1 pm on Saturday.

OTP has a branch near the bus station at Erzsébet királynő utca 7. The post office is at Kossuth Lajos utca 4.

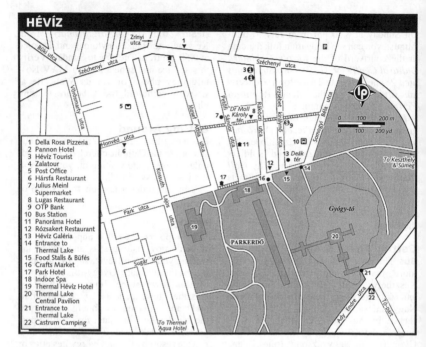

HÉVÍZ

1 Della Rosa Pizzeria
2 Pannon Hotel
3 Hévíz Tourist
4 Zalatour
5 Post Office
6 Hársfa Restaurant
7 Julius Meinl
   Supermarket
8 Lugas Restaurant
9 OTP Bank
10 Bus Station
11 Panoráma Hotel
12 Rózsakert Restaurant
13 Hévíz Galéria
14 Entrance to
   Thermal Lake
15 Food Stalls & Büfés
16 Crafts Market
17 Park Hotel
18 Indoor Spa
19 Thermal Hévíz Hotel
20 Thermal Lake
   Central Pavilion
21 Entrance to
   Thermal Lake
22 Castrum Camping

Thermal Lake

The **gyógy-tó** is an astonishing sight: a surface of almost five hectares in the Parkerdő, covered for most of the year in pink and white lotuses. The source is a spring spouting from a crater some 40m below ground that disgorges up to 80 million litres of warm water a day, renewing itself every 48 hours or so. The surface temperature averages 33°C and never drops below 26°C in winter, allowing bathing throughout the year while there's ice on the fir trees of the Parkerdő.

A covered bridge leads to the lake's *fin-de-siècle* central pavilion, from where catwalks and piers fan out. You can swim protected beneath these or make your way to the small rafts and 'anchors' farther out. There's a couple of piers along the shore for sunbathing as well.

The lake is open in summer from 8.30 am to 5 pm and in winter from 9 am to 4.30 pm. Entry costs 460Ft for three hours or 920Ft for the whole day; a *carnet* of 10 three-hour tickets is 4300Ft. The indoor spa at the entrance to the park is open year round from 7 am to 4 pm (400/200Ft).

Places to Stay

Castrum Camping (☎ *343 198, Tó-part*), at the lake's southern end, is the most central of Hévíz's several sites and stays open all year. It costs 560/840/560Ft per tent/adult/child in high season (mid-April to mid-October) and has no bungalows.

Zalatour and Hévíz Tourist can find you a double room for 4000Ft, though things could be tight in summer. You'll see a lot of 'Zimmer frei' and 'szoba kiadó' signs on Kossuth Lajos utca and Zrínyi utca, where you can make your own deals directly.

The 46-room ***Pannon*** (☎ *340 482, fax 340 481, Széchenyi utca 23*), housed in a former trade-union holiday home and with an attractive garden, has singles/doubles with bath for 3500/7000Ft. The 13-storey

Panoráma hotel (☎ *341 074, fax 340 485,* ☻ *reserve@hotelpanorama.hunguest.hu, Petőfi Sándor utca 9*), with 208 rooms in two buildings, is more expensive: singles are DM48 to DM62, doubles DM68 to DM88, depending on the season.

The 30-room **Park** (☎ *341 190, fax 341 193, Petőfi Sándor utca 26*), in elegant Kató Villa (1927), is the loveliest hotel in Hévíz and just a few steps up from the Parkerdő. The Park's singles are DM62 to DM98, doubles DM83 to DM125, depending on the season. Hotel guests can use the indoor and outdoor pools, sauna, solarium, gym and tennis courts at the nearby **Thermal Hévíz** (☎ *341 180, fax 340 666,* ☻ *dhtheviz@mail.matav.hu, Kossuth Lajos utca 9-11*), with 210 rooms costing DM92 to DM178 for a single and DM152 to DM250 for a double, depending on the room and the season. Its sister hotel located to the south, the 229-room **Thermal Aqua** (☎ *341 090, fax 340 970,* ☻ *dhtaqua@mail.matav.hu, Kossuth Lajos utca 13-15*) charges DM82 to DM149 for a single, DM136 to DM216 for a double.

Places to Eat
The best place for a quick bite is Deák tér south of the bus station, which has *food stalls* and *büfés* selling *lángos*, sausages, fish and hamburgers. The *Della Rosa* pizzeria *(Széchenyi utca)* at the northern end of József Attila utca, has pizzas for 500Ft to 600Ft and is open till 10 pm.

For a proper Hungarian meal, try the *Rózsakert (Rákóczi utca 3)*, with a large beer garden near the bus station; the *Lugas (Dr Moll Károly tér)*, which has a terrace with tables on the steps down to Rákóczi utca; or the *Hársfa (Honvéd utca 13)*, a restaurant and wine bar on a quiet leafy street just up from Kossuth Lajos utca.

Getting There & Away
Hévíz isn't on a railway line, but buses travel east to Keszthely almost every half-hour from stand No 3. There are at least a dozen daily departures to Sümeg and Zalaegerszeg and there are half as many to Badacsony, Balatonfüred, Nagykanizsa and

Veszprém. Other destinations include: Baja (one departure daily), Budapest (five), Győr (three), Kaposvár (three), Kecskemét (one), Pápa (seven), Pécs (two), Sopron (three), Székesfehérvár (five), Szekszárd (one) and Szombathely (six).

BADACSONY
☎ 87
Four towns make up the Badacsony region: Badacsonylábdihegy, Badacsonyörs, Badacsonytördemic and Badacsonytomaj. But when Hungarians say Badacsony, they usually mean the little resort at the Badacsony train station, near the ferry pier south-west of Badacsonytomaj (pop 2550).

Badacsony has been thrice-blessed. Not only does it have the lake for swimming and the mountains for wonderful walks and hikes, but it has produced wine – lots of it – since the Middle Ages. Badacsony was one of the last places on Balaton's northern shore to be developed and has more of a country feel to it than most other resorts here. Only Tihany vies for supremacy in the beauty stakes (both places are 'landscape protection reserves'), and you might stop here for a day or two to relax.

Orientation
Route No 71, the main road along the lake's northern shore, runs through Badacsony as Balatoni út; this is where the bus will let you off. The ferry pier is on the east side of this road; almost everything else is west. Above the village, several pensions and houses with private accommodation ring the base of the hill on Római út, which debouches into Balatoni út at Badacsonytomaj, a few kilometres to the north-east. Szegedi Róza utca branches off to the north from Római út through the vineyards to the Kisfaludy House restaurant and the base of the hill.

Information
Tourinform has an office (☎/fax 472 023, ☻ badacsonytomaj@ tourinform.hu, Római út 55) inconveniently located at the József Egry Cultural Centre in Badacsonytomaj. It is open – in theory – from 9 am to 6 pm

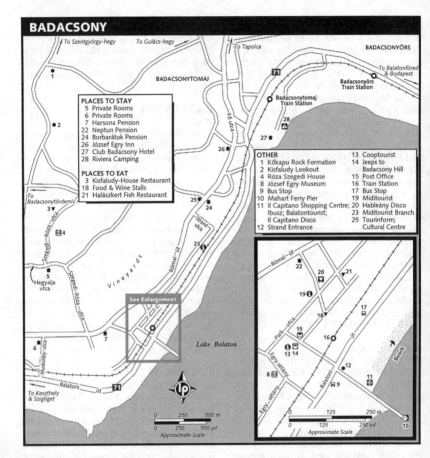

BADACSONY

PLACES TO STAY
5 Private Rooms
6 Private Rooms
7 Harsona Pension
22 Neptun Pension
24 Borbarátok Pension
26 József Egry Inn
27 Club Badacsony Hotel
28 Riviera Camping

PLACES TO EAT
3 Kisfaludy-House Restaurant
18 Food & Wine Stalls
21 Halászkert Fish Restaurant

OTHER
1 Kókapu Rock Formation
2 Kisfaludy Lookout
4 Róza Szegedi House
8 József Egry Museum
9 Bus Stop
10 Mahart Ferry Pier
11 Il Capitano Shopping Centre;
   Ibusz; Balatontourist;
   Il Capitano Disco
12 Strand Entrance
13 Cooptourist
14 Jeeps to
   Badacsony Hill
15 Post Office
16 Train Station
17 Bus Stop
19 Miditourist
20 Hableány Disco
23 Miditourist Branch
25 Tourinform;
   Cultural Centre

weekdays and to 1 pm at the weekend from June to August and from 8 am to 4 pm weekdays only the rest of the year. Miditourist (☎ 431 117) is in the centre of the village at Park utca 6, and Cooptourist (☎ 431 134) is hidden behind some food stalls nearby at Egry sétány 1. Balatontourist (☎ 431 249) is in the Il Capitano shopping centre below Balatoni út near the ferry pier, as is Ibusz (☎ 431 047). Most of these agencies are open only in the high season from May to September or October weekdays from 8.30 or 9 am to 5 or 6 pm and on Saturday morning till noon or 1 pm.

At other times, check with Miditourist's branch at Park utca 53 (☎ 431 028).

You can change money at the post office (Park utca 3), opposite the line of 4WDs that transport passengers up to Badacsony Hill.

Things to See & Do

The **József Egry Museum** at Egry sétány 12 in town is devoted to the Balaton region's leading painter (1883-1951) and is open from 10 am to 6 pm Tuesday to Sunday from May to October (100/50Ft).

The dramatic slopes and vineyards above the centre are sprinkled with little wine-press houses and 'folk baroque' cottages. One of these is the **Róza Szegedi House** (1790), which belonged to the actress wife of the poet Sándor Kisfaludy from Sümeg. It contains a literary museum.

The flat-topped forested massif overlooking the lake is just the place to escape the tipsy herds. If you'd like to get a running start on your hike, catch one of the open 4WDs marked 'Badacsony-hegyi járat', which depart from opposite the post office between May and September from 9 am to 7 or 8 pm whenever at least six paying passengers climb aboard (500/800Ft one way/round trip). The driver will drop you off at the Kisfaludy House restaurant, a press house (1798) once belonging to the Kisfaludy family where a large map outlining the marked trails is posted by the car park. Or you might arm yourself in advance with a copy of Cartographia's *A Balaton* 1:40,000 topographical map (No 41; 400Ft).

Several paths lead to lookouts – at 437m **Kisfaludy Lookout** (Kisfaludy kilátó) is the highest – and to neighbouring hills like **Gulács-hegy** (393m) and **Szentgyörgy-hegy** (415m) to the north. The landscape includes abandoned quarries and large basalt towers that resemble organ pipes; of these, **Kőkapu** (Stone Gate) is the most dramatic. Several of the trails take you past **Rózsakő** (Rose Rock). A 100-year-old plaque explains an unusual tradition: 'If a lad and a lass sit here together with their backs to the lake, they will be married in a year.' Good luck – or regrets (as the case may be).

The postage-stamp-size **beach** (strand); 200/100Ft) is reedy and not among the best on the lake; you would do better to head a few kilometres north-east to Badacsony-tomaj or Badacsonyörs for a swim.

Places to Stay

Camping The closest camping ground is *Riviera Camping* (☎ 471 321) at the water's edge next to the Club Badacsony hotel in Badacsonytomaj. It's a casual place and has bungalows, but be sure to bring mosquito repellent. The season here is from mid-May to September.

Hostels The *József Egry* inn (☎/fax 471 057, Római út 1) in Badacsonytomaj has budget accommodation in rooms with one to five beds for between 1700 and 600Ft per person. It is open April to October. The *Neptun* pension (see Pensions section for details) has rooms with two to four beds and shared showers for between DM12 and DM15.

Private Rooms Miditourist has a particularly good list of private rooms for the entire Badacsony area. Balatontourist charges from 5000Ft for a double, depending on the season, while Cooptourist's cheapest accommodation for two is a small holiday home for 6000Ft. The private house near the wine-bottling plant at Muskotály utca 4-6 has a few cheap doubles for short stays. A house at Szegedi Róza utca 83 (☎ 431 192) has fantastic views of the lake and is within easy walking distance of the trails up to Badacsony Hill. Doubles are 4500Ft to 5000Ft.

Pensions There are several small pensions among the vineyards on the road above the railway line, a 10-minute walk from the station, including the 12-room *Harsona* (☎/fax 431 379, ✉ harsona@elender.hu, Római út 190) and the 16-room *Neptun* (☎/fax 431 293, ✉ borbaratok@elender.hu, Római út 156). The latter, open April to December, charges DM40 to DM45 for a double, depending on the season. Its sister pension in Badacsonytomaj, the friendly *Borbarátok* (☎/fax 471 597, ✉ borbaratok@elender.hu, Római út 78) has a dozen modern, very comfortable rooms available for the same price during the same period.

Hotel The 54-room *Club Badacsony* hotel (☎ 471 040, fax 471 059, Balatoni út 14), on the shore in Badacsonytomaj with a sauna and its own beach, is the biggest and most expensive place in the area, with doubles from DM80 to DM130, depending on the season. It is open from April to October.

Places to Eat

There are *food stalls* with picnic tables dispensing sausage, fish soup, lángos and gyros as well as *wine stalls* (35Ft a glass, 350Ft to

400Ft a litre) between the train station and Park utca. The *Halászkert (Park utca 5)* is crowded and touristy, but the fish dishes are excellent. *Pizzeria Il Capitano* is in the shopping centre by the ferry pier. The bar and restaurant at the *Borbarátok* (see Pensions) is very lively; this is the place to try a glass of Badacsony's premier white wines, Kéknyelű (Blue Stalk) or Szürkebarát (Pinot Gris).

The best place for a meal or a drink in Badacsony is the al fresco terrace at the *Kisfaludy House (Szegedi Róza utca 87)*, perched on the hill overlooking the vineyards and the lake. To the west is Szigliget Bay, the loveliest on the lake, and directly across to the south lie what Hungarians call the two 'breasts' of Fonyód: the Sípos and Sándor hills. Kisfaludy House, open daily till midnight from April to November, is relatively expensive.

Entertainment
The *József Egry Cultural Centre (☎ 331 169, Római út 55)* is opposite the Borbarátok pension. *Il Capitano* is a big nightclub and disco in the shopping centre by the beach that heaves in summer. The *Hableány* restaurant *(Park utca 12)* sometimes has a weekend disco during the season.

Getting There & Away
Three buses a day head for Balatonfüred and Székesfehérvár. Other destinations include: Budapest (one trip daily), Hévíz (one to two), Keszthely (one), Nagykanizsa (one), Révfülöp (three), Tapolca (two), Várpalota (one), Veszprém (one) and Zalaegerszeg (four). Badacsony is on the rail line linking all the towns on Lake Balaton's northern shore with Budapest-Déli and Tapolca. To get to Keszthely you must change at Tapolca, but there's often an immediate connection.

Passenger and car between Badacsony and Fonyód run at least four times a day from April to late October; they are much more frequent in summer. In Fonyód you can get a connection to Southern Transdanubia by taking a train direct to Kaposvár.

A boat ride to Badacsony from Siófok or Balatonfüred is the best way to get the feel of Lake Balaton. Boats operate in July and August from June to early September. Ferries also travel to Keszthely more frequently at this time.

TAPOLCA
☎ 87 • postcode 8300 • pop 18,000
This pleasant town has a particularly fine setting wedged between the Balaton Highlands and the Southern Bakony Hills some 14km north-east of Badacsony. To the south-west lies the Káli Basin and such picturesque towns as Mindszentkálla and Szenbékkálla, with Romanesque church ruins, gentle landscapes and bountiful vineyards.

Tapolca has always been an important crossroads; under the Romans both the road between Rome and Aquincum and the one linking Savaria (Szombathely) and Arrabona (Győr) passed through here. The Romans were followed by the Avars and, in turn, by the early Slavs, who called the area Topulcha, from the Slavic root word for 'hot springs'. Tapolca's original source of wealth was wine – a legacy of the Romans – but the town only really appeared on the map when the Bakony bauxite mining company set up its headquarters here.

Orientation & Information
Tapolca's main thoroughfare is Deák Ferenc utca, which runs west from Hősök tere, where the bus station is located, to Fő tér, just north of Mill Lake. The train station is on Dózsa György út, about 1200m south-west of the centre.

Tourinform (☎/fax 323 415, ❷ tapolca@ tourinform.hu) is just south of the bus station at Deák Ferenc utca 20. It opens from 9 am to 4.45 pm on weekdays and to 11.45 am on Saturday. Balatontourist (☎ 311 179), in the Postaudvar shopping centre at No 7 of the same street, is open from 8 am to 3.30 pm weekdays and 9 to 11.30 am on Saturday. There's an OTP branch at Fő tér 2. The post office is opposite Tourinform at Deák Ferenc utca 19.

Mill Lake
Mill Lake (Malom-tó), which is just south of Fő tér (reach it through the gateway at No 8 or by walking south along Arany

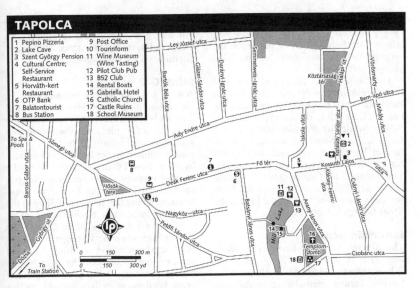

TAPOLCA

1 Pepino Pizzeria	9 Post Office
2 Lake Cave	10 Tourinform
3 Szent György Pension	11 Wine Museum
4 Cultural Centre;	(Wine Tasting)
Self-Service	12 Pilot Club Pub
Restaurant	13 B52 Club
5 Horváth-kert	14 Rental Boats
Restaurant	15 Gabriella Hotel
6 OTP Bank	16 Catholic Church
7 Balatontourist	17 Castle Ruins
8 Bus Station	18 School Museum

János utca), is divided in two by a small footbridge: to the north is the **Big Lake** (Nagy-tó) and to the south the **Little Lake** (Kis-tó). Created in the 18th century to power a water mill, the lake has been artificially fed since the nearby bauxite mine lowered the level of the karst water. But it remains a picturesque area, with pastel-coloured houses reflecting in the water of the Big Lake, a church and a museum near the Little Lake choked with water lilies and the mill house (now the Gabriella hotel) in the centre, its blades turning slowly.

The **Catholic church** on Templom-domb just east of the lake has a Gothic sanctuary but the rest of the church is 18th-century baroque. The ruins of Tapolca's **medieval castle**, destroyed during the Turkish occupation, can be seen to the south-west. Nearby at Templom-domb 15 is the small **School Museum** (Iskola Múzeum) open from 9 am to 4 pm Tuesday to Sunday from mid-April to mid-October and the same hours on weekdays the rest of the year (60/30Ft).

Lake Cave

Tapolca's second big attraction, the Lake Cave (Tavasbarlang), is a short distance to the north-east at Kisfaludy utca 3. You can visit about 100m of the cave and even row a boat (300Ft) on a small underground pond, which has only recently returned since mining stopped here in 1990. The cave is open from 10 am to 6 pm daily from June to August and to 5 pm Tuesday to Sunday in April/May and September/October (160/80Ft).

Activities

Boats are available for hire on the Big Lake from 10 am to 6 pm daily (except when raining; 100Ft). There's a thermal spa and open-air swimming pool north-west of the centre on Sümegi út open weekdays from 10 am to 8 pm and from 9 am at the weekend from May to September. You can sample various Bakony wines at the Wine Museum (Bormúzeum) at the northern end of the Big Lake from noon to 5 pm weekdays.

Places to Stay & Eat

Accommodation in Tapolca is limited to one pension and one hotel. The *Szent György* (☎ *413 809, Kisfaludy utca 1*) is an attractive and well-run pension next to the Lake Cave with singles/doubles for

5800/6500Ft. The 14-room *Gabriella* hotel (☎ *412 642, fax 511 077,* ✆ *mludasz@mail .elender.hu, Batsányi tér 7),* housed in the original mill in the centre of the lake, charges 6500/9600Ft.

The cheapest place for a meal is the *self-service restaurant* at the cultural centre (see Entertainment). *Pepinó (Kisfaludy utca 9),* near the Lake Cave, has decent pizzas (from 500Ft), while the *Horváth-kert (Kossuth Lajos utca 4)* around the corner, is an up-market Hungarian restaurant, with mains for 780Ft to 900Ft and courtyard seating. The setting of the *Gabriella* hotel's restaurant is delightful, with tables on the footbridge in warm weather, but the food at the *Szent György* is much better.

Entertainment

The *Bauxite Cultural Centre (Kisfaludy utca 2)* is in a 1970s building called the White House (Fehér-ház) built onto the town's former neo-Gothic synagogue (1863); walk around to the west side facing Iskola utca for a better look. There are a couple of interesting places for a drink along Tópart on the northern end of the Malom-tó, including the *Pilot Pub.* Behind the Pilot and up the stairs is the popular *B52* club *(Arany János utca 3)* open to 5 am at the weekend.

Getting There & Away

Bus Tapolca is an important transport hub with buses departing at least hourly for Keszthely, Nagyvázsony, Sümeg and Veszprém. Other important destinations include: Balatonfüred (two buses a day), Badacsonytomaj (five to six), Budapest (four), Győr (two), Hévíz (eight), Kaposvár (one), Nagykanizsa (two), Pápa (five), Sárvár (one), Sopron (one), Szombathely (two) and Székesfehérvár (two).

Train Tapolca is also the main terminus for the rail line linking most of the towns along Lake Balaton's northern shore with Székesfehérvár and Budapest. Another line heads for Balatonszentgyörgy, from where up to 10 daily trains continue along the southern shore to Székesfehérvár and

Budapest-Keleti or Budapest-Déli. A third rail line goes north-west to Sümeg and Celldömölk, from where three daily trains continue on to Szombathely.

SÜMEG
☎ 87 • postcode 8330 • pop 6800

This small town, some 19km north-west of Tapolca between the Bakony and Keszthely Hills, has a few pleasant surprises. Sümeg was on the map as early as the 13th century, when an important border fortress was built by King Béla IV in the aftermath of the Mongol invasion. The castle was strengthened several times during the next three centuries, repelling the Turks but falling to the Habsburg forces, who torched it in 1713.

Sümeg's golden age came later in the 18th century when the all-powerful bishops of Veszprém took up residence here and commissioned some of the town's fine baroque buildings. Sümeg declined in later years, but those glory days live on in its fine architecture.

Orientation & Information

Kossuth Lajos utca is the main street running north-south through Sümeg. The bus station is on Béke tér, a continuation of Kossuth Lajos utca south of the town centre. The train station is a 10-minute walk northwest, at the end of Darnay Kálmán utca.

Tourinform (☎/fax 352 481, ✆ sumeg@ tourinform.hu) has an office in the former Kisfaludy hotel at Kossuth Lajos utca 13 and can provide information about Sümeg, the Balaton and Central Transdanubia. It is open from 9 am to 5 pm weekdays and to 1 pm on Saturday from May to mid-October and from 7.30 am to 3.30 pm weekdays only the rest of the year.

There's an OTP bank and currency-exchange machine in a renovated town-house at Kossuth Lajos utca 17. The post office is at Kossuth Lajos utca 1, opposite the bus station.

Sümeg Castle

This imposing castle sits on a 270m cone of limestone above the town – a rare substance in this region of basalt. You can reach it by

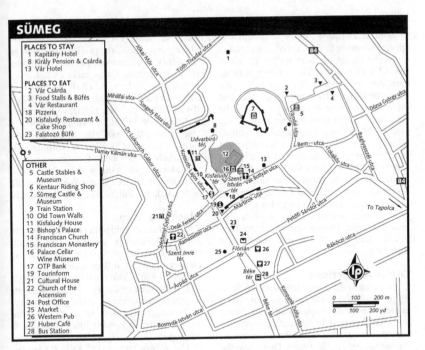

SÜMEG

PLACES TO STAY
1 Kapitány Hotel
8 Király Pension & Csárda
13 Vár Hotel

PLACES TO EAT
2 Vár Csárda
3 Food Stalls & Büfés
4 Vár Restaurant
18 Pizzeria
20 Kisfaludy Restaurant &
Cake Shop
23 Falatozó Büfé

OTHER
5 Castle Stables &
Museum
6 Kentaur Riding Shop
7 Sümeg Castle &
Museum
9 Train Station
10 Old Town Walls
11 Kisfaludy House
13 Bishop's Palace
14 Franciscan Church
15 Franciscan Monastery
16 Palace Cellar
Wine Museum
17 OTP Bank
19 Tourinform
21 Cultural House
22 Church of the
Ascension
24 Post Office
25 Market
26 Western Pub
27 Huber Café
28 Bus Station

climbing Vak Bottyán utca, which is lined with lovely baroque *kúriák* (mansions), from Szent István tér and then following Vároldal utca past the **Castle Stables** (Váristálló) at No 5, which house both horseflesh and a rather specialised museum dealing with saddles, harnesses and the Redetzky Hussar Regiment. The castle is also accessible from the north-east via route No 84.

Sümeg Castle fell into ruin after the Austrians abandoned it early in the 18th century, but was restored in the 1960s. Today it is the largest and best preserved castle in Transdanubia and well worth the climb for the views east to the Bakony Hills and south to the Keszthely Hills. There's a small **Castle Museum** (Vármúzeum) of weapons, armour and castle furnishings in the 13th-century **Old Tower** (Öregtorony), pony rides and archery in the castle courtyard for children, a snack bar and a wine cellar. You can still see bits of the old town walls below the castle at the northern end of Kossuth Lajos utca

(Nos 13 to 33). A 16th-century tower is now the living room of the house at No 31. The castle is open from 8 am to 8 pm daily from April to September and from 8 am to 4 pm the rest of the year.

Church of the Ascension

The castle may dominate the town, but for many people it is not Sümeg's most important sight. For them that distinction is reserved for the Church of the Ascension on Szent Imre tér, west of Kossuth Lajos utca and just off Deák Ferenc utca. You would never know it from the outside; architecturally, the building (1756) is unexceptional. But step inside and marvel at what has been called the 'Sistine Chapel of the rococo'.

That's perhaps an overstatement, but it's true that Franz Anton Maulbertsch's frescoes (1757-58) are the most beautiful baroque ones in Hungary and by far the prolific painter's best work. The frescoes, whose subjects are taken from the Old and

CENTRAL TRANSDANUBIA

New Testaments, are brilliant expressions of light and shadow, but you should pay special attention to the Crucifixion scene in *Golgotha* on the northern wall in the nave, the *Adoration of the Three Kings* with its caricature of a Moor opposite across the aisle, the *Gate of Hell* under the organ loft on the western side under the porch, and the altarpiece of Christ ascending airily to the clouds. Maulbertsch managed to include himself in a couple of his works, most clearly among the shepherds in the first fresco on the southern wall (he's the one holding the round cheeses and hamming it up for the audience). The commissioner of the frescoes, Márton Padányi Bíró, bishop of Veszprém, is shown on the western wall near the organ. Drop a coin in the machine to illuminate the frescoes and view them at their best.

Other Attractions

The Church of the Ascension steals the limelight from the 17th-century **Franciscan church** (Ferences templom) at Szent István tér, which has modern frescoes, a beautifully carved baroque altar, and a Pietà that has attracted pilgrims for 300 years. Don't miss the ornate pulpit with the eerie dismembered hand grasping a crucifix. The baroque **Franciscan monastery** (Ferences kolostor, 1657) is next door at Szent István tér 9.

The former **Bishop's Palace** (Püspöki palota) at No 8-10 of the same square was a grand residence when completed in 1755. It is now in an advanced state of decay, but you can still admire the two Atlases holding up the balcony at the entrance, and the copper rain spouts in the shape of sea monsters. **Kisfaludy House** (Kisfaludy szülőháza) at Kisfaludy tér 3 is the birthplace of Sándor Kisfaludy (1772-1844), the Romantic 'poet of the Balaton'. Together with a history of his life and work, the museum (open 10 am to 6 pm Tuesday to Sunday from March to October, from 8 am to 4 pm weekdays only the rest of the year) contains further exhibits on Sümeg Castle and the area's geology. Outside along a wall is the **Sümeg Pantheon** of local sons and daughters who made good.

Activities

There is some excellent hiking east of Sümeg into the Bakony Hills (known as 'Hungary's Sherwood Forest'), but get yourself a copy of Cartographia's *Bakonyhegység – déli rész* (Bakony Hills – Southern Part) 1:40,000 map (No 3; 400Ft). If you want to go horse riding, visit the Castle Stables (☎ 352 367), Vároldal 5. There's also information available at the Kentaur riding shop (☎ 351 836) at Vároldal 10, open daily from 9 am to 6 pm.

You can taste wine at the Palota Pince Bormúzeum (Palace Cellar Wine Museum) at the Bishop's Palace from 1 to 6 pm daily.

Places to Stay

Tourinform can help with *private rooms* for about 1500Ft per person; the Szabó family (☎ 351 099) has rooms for that price including breakfast at Bem utca 9.

The 29-room *Vár* hotel (☎ 352 414, fax 352 352, Vak Bottyán utca 2), a spruced-up former hostel, is a very central place to stay, with singles/doubles without bath for 1400/2800Ft and 4000/5000Ft for those with one.

The *Király* (☎/fax 352 605, Udvarbíró tér 5) is a seven-room, family-run pension in an old farmhouse behind the Kisfaludy Memorial House on Szent István tér. Doubles with showers at this cosy, flower-bedecked place are DM40. There's a sauna, fitness room, wine cellar and csárda here.

The 44-room *Kapitány* hotel (☎ 352 598, fax 351 101, ✉ hot@elender.hu, Tóth Tivadar utca 19), a modern, well-designed hotel north of the castle, has a swimming pool, sauna, tennis court, horses for rent and a wine cellar. Singles/doubles are 7600/8800Ft.

Places to Eat

The access road to the castle from route No 84 is lined with *snack stands* and *büfés*. South of the castle, *Falatozó* (Kossuth Lajos utca 7), a cheap stand-up büfé at a butcher's, is open 7 am to 5 pm weekdays and till noon on Saturday. The *Pizzéria* (Szent István tér 1) has pizza, Hungarian dishes and a salad bar.

The restaurant at the former *Kisfaludy* hotel *(Kossuth Lajos utca 13)* remains open and is one of the few places in the centre of town where you can have a sit-down meal. It's open to 11 pm daily. Up by the castle on the eastern side, the *Vár* restaurant specialises in game. Closer to the castle, the new *Vár Csárda* is touristy with Gypsy music and lots of Germans but it's very pleasant sitting under the walnut trees in full view of the hilltop fortress in warmer weather (mains 600Ft to 900Ft). The *cukrászda* at the Kisfaludy restaurant is popular for ice cream and cakes.

The *fruit & vegetable market* is on Árpád utca, just west of Kossuth Lajos utca.

Entertainment
Kisfaludy Cultural House (☎ 352 332, Széchenyi György utca 9-11), near the Church of the Ascension, will let you know what's on in Sümeg. Popular watering holes include the *Huber Cafe (Béke tér 8)* and the divey *Western Pub (Petőfi Sándor utca 1)*, with split-log tables and Marlboro Country music.

Getting There & Away
Hourly buses leave Sümeg each day for Hévíz, Keszthely, Tapolca and Veszprém; departures to Pápa and Zalaegerszeg are also frequent. Other destinations include Budapest (four buses daily), Győr (five), Kaposvár (one), Nagykanizsa (four), Sopron (three), Pécs (one), Szombathely (four) and, on the border with Slovenia, Lenti (two).

Sümeg is on the railway line linking Tapolca and Celldömölk, from where three daily trains continue on to Szombathely. For Budapest and other points to the east and west along the northern shore of Lake Balaton, change at Tapolca.

NAGYVÁZSONY
☎ 88 • postcode 8281 • pop 1750
When you grow tired of the Balaton hubbub, take an easy excursion north to Nagyvázsony, a sleepy little market town in the southern Bakony Hills. The drive from Badacsony via Tapolca or from Tihany,

15km to the south-east, takes you through some of the prettiest countryside in Central Transdanubia, and the town has an important 15th-century castle.

Orientation & Information
The three bus stops and an OTP bank branch (no ATM) are in the centre of town on Kinizsi utca. Opposite at Kinizsi utca 59 is the post office.

Vázsonykő Castle
This castle, on a gentle slope north of the tiny town centre at the end of Vár utca, was begun early in the 15th century by the Vezsenyi family, but was presented to Pál Kinizsi by King Matthias Corvinus in 1462 in gratitude for the brave general's military successes against the Turks. It became an important border fortress during the occupation and was used as a prison in the 1700s.

The castle is essentially a rectangle with a horseshoe-shaped barbican. The 30m, six-storey keep is reached via a bridge over the dry moat. A large crack runs from the top of the tower to the bottom, but it must be secure enough: the upper rooms contain the **Kinizsi Castle Museum** (Kinizsi Vármúzeum). Part of General Kinizsi's red-marble sarcophagus sits in the centre of the restored chapel, and there's a collection of archaeological finds in the crypt. The castle is open from 9 am to 6 pm daily from April to October (400/250Ft).

Other Attractions
The **Post Office Museum** (Postmúzeum) is just south of the castle at Temető utca 3. Nagyvázsony was an important stop along the post road between Budapest and Graz in the 19th century, and horses were changed here. The museum is a lot more interesting than it sounds, particularly the section on the history of the telephone in Hungary beginning with the installation of the first switchboard in Budapest in 1890. It's open from 10 am to 6 pm Tuesday to Sunday and to 2 pm the rest of the year. Opposite is an 18th-century **Evangelist church** with a freestanding belfry.

Nearby at Bercsényi utca 21 is a small **Open-Air Folk Museum** (Szabadtéri Néprajzi Múzeum) at a farmhouse dating from 1825. It was once the home of a coppersmith, and his workshop remains. It is open from 10 am to 6 pm daily from May to October. The **Church of St Stephen** (Szent István templom), on Rákóczi utca, was built by Kinizsi in 1481 on the site of an earlier chapel. Most of the interior, including the richly carved main altar, is baroque.

Places to Stay

The *Kinizsi* hostel (*☎/fax 264 318, Vár utca 9*), with six eight-bed rooms opposite the castle, is the cheapest place in Nagyvázsony but opens from May to mid-October only. Otherwise try the seven-room *Vázsonykő* pension (*☎ 264 344, fax 264 707, Sörház utca 2*). Doubles are DM40. The flashier *Malomkő* pension (*☎/fax 364 165, Kinizsi utca 47-49*) in the town centre and open all year, charges about the same.

The *Kastély* hotel (*☎/fax 264 109, ✉ ibusz@mail.matav.hu, Kossuth Lajos utca 16*) north-east of the centre is a new building with 16 rooms accommodating guests for an expensive DM120 in doubles. It is next to the old Kastély hotel that is undergoing extensive renovations, an 18th-century mansion on six hectares of parkland that once belonged to the aristocratic Zichy family.

Places to Eat

The thatched *Vár Csárda* (*Temető utca 5*) overlooking the castle is open in summer only. Try the good home cooking at the *Vázsonykő* pension at other times or the csárda at the *Kastély* hotel open till 11 pm daily. In the centre the *Napsugár* (*Kinizsi utca 86*) is OK for pizza. The cukrászda at the *Malomkő* pension has good cakes.

Getting There & Away

Some 12 buses a day link Nagyvázsony and Veszprém, 23km to the north-east, and eight run to Tapolca to the south-west. You can also reach Balatonfüred via Tótvázsony and Keszthely (two or three buses a day), Ajka (six), Budapest (one) and there is one bus to Zalaegerszeg via Sümeg.

TIHANY
☎ 87 • postcode 8237 • pop 1500

The place with the greatest historical significance on Lake Balaton is Tihany, 11km south-west of Balatonfüred. Tihany village is on a peninsula of the same name that juts 5km into the Balaton, almost linking the lake's two shores. The entire peninsula is a nature reserve of hills and marshy meadows; it has an isolated, almost wild, feel to it that is unknown around the rest of the lake. The village, on a hill top on the eastern side of the peninsula, is one of the most charming in the Balaton region.

There was a Roman settlement in the area, but Tihany only appeared on the map in 1055, when King Andrew I (ruled 1046-60), a son of King Stephen's great nemesis, Vászoly, founded a Benedictine monastery here. The *Deed of Foundation* of the Abbey of Tihany, now in the archives of the Benedictine abbey at Pannonhalma, south of Győr, is one of the earliest known documents bearing any Hungarian words – some 50 place names within a mostly Latin text. It's a linguistic treasure in a country where the vernacular in its written form was spurned – particularly in education – in favour of the more 'cultured' Latin and German until the 19th century.

In 1267 a fortress was built around the church and was able to keep the Turks at bay when they arrived 300 years later. But the castle was demolished by Habsburg forces in 1702, and all you'll see today are ruins.

Tihany Peninsula is a popular recreational area with beaches on its eastern and western coasts and a big resort complex on its southern tip. The waters of the so-called Tihany Well off the southern end of the peninsula are the deepest – and coldest – in the lake, reaching an unprecedented 12m in some parts.

Orientation

Tihany village, perched on an 80m-high plateau along the peninsula's eastern coast, is accessible by two roads when you turn south off route No 71. The Inner Harbour (Belső kikötő), where ferries to/from

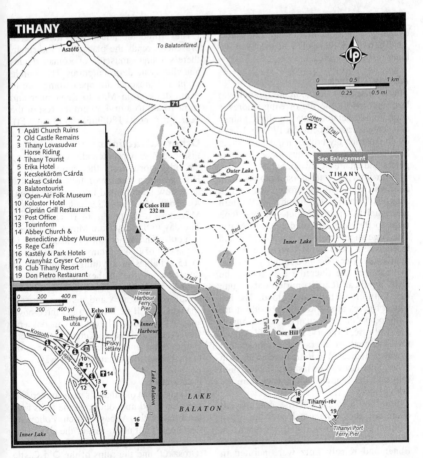

TIHANY

1 Apáti Church Ruins
2 Old Castle Remains
3 Tihany Lovasudvar
   Horse Riding
4 Tihany Tourist
5 Erika Hotel
6 Kecskeköröm Csárda
7 Kakas Csárda
8 Balatontourist
9 Open-Air Folk Museum
10 Kolostor Hotel
11 Ciprián Grill Restaurant
12 Post Office
13 Tourinform
14 Abbey Church &
   Benedictine Abbey Museum
15 Rege Café
16 Kastély & Park Hotels
17 Aranyház Geyser Cones
18 Club Tihany Resort
19 Don Pietro Restaurant

Balatonfüred and Siófok dock, is below
the village. Tihanyi-rév (Tihany Port), to
the south-west at the tip of the peninsula,
is Tihany's recreational area. From here,
car ferries run to Szántódi-rév and passenger ferries to Balatonföldvár.

Two inland basins on the peninsula are
fed by rain and ground water: the Inner
Lake (Belső-tó), almost in the centre of the
peninsula and visible from the village, and
the Outer Lake (Külső-tó) to the north-
west, which has almost completely dried
up and is now a tangle of reeds. Both
attract bird life.

Information

The bus from Balatonfüred stops on Kossuth
Lajos utca below the Abbey Church. Tourinform (☎ 448 804), Kossuth Lajos utca 20,
is open from 9 am to 6 pm weekdays and to
1 pm at the weekend from June to August and
from 9 am to 3 pm weekdays only the rest of
the year. Tihany Tourist (☎ 448 481, fax 448
804), open from 9 am to 6 pm daily from
April to October, is at Kossuth Lajos utca 11.
Balatontourist (☎ 448 519) has an office at
Kossuth Lajos utca 12 (corner of Visszhang
utca) and is open from 8.30 am to 4.30 pm
weekdays and to 1 pm on Saturday in season.

The post office, which has an ATM and exchange bureau, is at Kossuth Lajos utca 37. There's another ATM at the Club Tihany resort, Rév utca 3.

Abbey Church

This twin-spired, ochre-coloured church was built in 1754 on the site of King Andrew's church and contains fantastic altars, pulpits and screens carved between 1753 and 1779 by an Austrian lay brother named Sebastian Stuhlhof. They are baroque-rococo masterpieces and all are richly symbolic.

With your back to the sumptuous main altar (the saint with the broken chalice and snake is Benedict, the founder of Western monasticism) and the Abbot's Throne, look right to the side altar dedicated to Mary. The large angel kneeling on the right is said to represent Stuhlhof's fiancee, a fisherman's daughter who died in her youth. On the Altar of the Sacred Heart across the aisle, a pelican (Christ) nurtures its young (the faithful) with its own blood. The besotted figures atop the pulpit beside it are four doctors of the Roman Catholic Church: Sts Ambrose, Gregory, Jerome and Augustine. The next two altars on the right and left sides are dedicated to Benedict and his twin sister, Scholastica; the last pair, a baptismal font and the Lourdes Altar, date from the 20th century.

Stuhlhof also carved the magnificent choir rail above the porch and the organ with all the cherubs. The frescoes on the ceilings by Bertalan Székely, Lajos Deák-Ébner and Károly Lotz were painted in 1889, when the church was restored.

The remains of King Andrew lie under a limestone sarcophagus in the Romanesque **crypt**. The spiral sword-like cross on the cover is similar to ones used by 11th-century Hungarian kings.

The **Benedictine Abbey Museum** (Bencés Ápátsági Múzeum) next door in the former Benedictine monastery, which is entered to the right of the main altar in the Abbey Church, contains exhibits related to Lake Balaton, liturgical vestments, a library of manuscripts and a bedroom where the deposed Habsburg Emperor Charles IV and his wife Zita spent a week in October 1921. ('They filled the house with their sacred presence,' reads the plaque.) In the cellar, there's a small museum of Roman statues and ghastly modern sculptures. The church, crypt and museum are open from 9 am to 6 pm daily from May to September and from 10 am to 3 or 4.30 pm the rest of the year. Entry costs 180/90Ft (family: 450Ft).

Other Attractions

Pisky sétány, a promenade running along the ridge north from the church to Echo Hill, passes a cluster of folk houses that have now been turned into a small **Open-Air Folk Museum** (Szabadtéri Néprajzi Múzeum). It is open from 10 am to 6 pm Tuesday to Sunday from May to October.

You'll find **Echo Hill** (Visszhang-hegy) at the end of Pisky sétány. At one time, up to 15 syllables of anything shouted in the direction of the Abbey Church would bounce back but, alas, because of more building in the area and perhaps climatic changes, you'll be lucky to get three nowadays. From Echo Hill you can descend Garay utca and Váralja utca to the Inner Harbour and a small beach, or continue on to the hiking trails that pass this way.

Activities

Walking is one of Tihany's main attractions; there's a good map outlining the trails near the front of the Abbey Church. Following the Green Trail north-east of the church for an hour will bring you to the **Russian Well** (Oroszkút) and the ruins of the **Old Castle** (Óvár), where Russian Orthodox monks brought to Tihany by Andrew hollowed out cells in the soft basalt walls.

The 232m **Csúcs Hill**, with panoramic views of Lake Balaton, is about two hours west of the church via the Red Trail. From here you can join up with the Yellow Trail originating in Tihanyi-rév, which will lead you north to the 13th-century **Apáti Church ruins** (Ápáti templomrom) and route No 71. The Blue Trail takes you south to the **Inner Lake** and **Aranyház**, a series of geyser cones formed by warm-water springs and resembling (somewhat) a 'Golden House'.

Horses are available for hire at the Tihany Lovasudvar (☎ 438 747), just north of the Inner Lake at Kiserdőtelepi utca 10 daily from 9 am to 6 pm year round.

Places to Stay

Accommodation is limited and expensive in Tihany; you should consider making it a day trip from Balatonfüred by bus, which takes only 20 minutes. Also, most of the hotels and restaurants listed in this section are closed between mid-October or November and March or April.

Tihany Tourist has private rooms for 3000Ft to 4000Ft per double in the low season and 4000Ft to 5000Ft in the high season. Many houses along Kossuth Lajos utca and on the little streets north of the Abbey Church have 'Zimmer frei' signs.

The *Kolostor* (☎ 448 408, Kossuth Lajos utca 14) is a seven-room hotel above a popular restaurant with doubles for 6000Ft. A couple of rooms with low ceilings under the eaves cost only 4000Ft. The swish, 15-room *Erika* hotel (☎ 448 644, fax 448 646, Batthyány utca 6) charges from DM80 to DM100 per double with bath and all the mod cons. It has a small swimming pool.

On the Inner Harbour, the *Kastély & Park* hotels (☎ 448 611, fax 448 409, Fürdőtelepi út 1) have 25 rooms in a former Habsburg summer mansion (the Kastély) and 44 more in an ugly modern wing (the Park). Singles in the Kastély with bath and balcony are priced from DM70 to DM120, doubles are DM90 to DM140; the Park rooms are DM60 to DM90 for singles, DM80 to DM110 for doubles. The hotels have a five-hectare garden and their own beach.

The *Club Tihany* (☎ 538 500, fax 448 083, @ clubtihany@mail.matav.hu, Rév utca 3), just up from the car-ferry pier at Tihanyi-rév, is a 13-hectare resort with 160 bungalows and a 330-room hotel – and every sporting, munching and quaffing possibility imaginable. Bungalows for two start at DM70 in the low season and reach as high as DM240 from early July to late August. Singles with lake view and balcony in the high-rise hotel are DM60 to DM140, doubles DM80 to DM170.

Places to Eat

The *Rege Cafe (Kossuth Lajos utca 22)* in the former monastery stables next to the church and museum serves light meals and cakes and offers a panoramic view from its terrace. You would do better to eat at the atmospheric *Kecskeköröm Csárda (Kossuth Lajos utca 19)*, a few hundred metres northwest on the main road, or at the *Kakas Csárda (Batthyány utca 1)* in a rambling basalt house almost opposite. The restaurant at the *Kolostor* hotel (see Places to Stay) has German-Hungarian pub grub and makes its own beer on the premises. The *Ciprián Grill* next door is another decent choice. In Tihanyi-rév, the *Don Pietro (Rév utca 4)* next to the ferry pier is reliable.

Getting There & Away

Buses cover the 11km from Balatonfüred's train station to and from Tihany about 20 times a day. The bus stops at both ferry landings before climbing to Tihany village.

The Balaton passenger ferries from Siófok, Balatonfüred and elsewhere stop at Tihany from April to late October. Catch them at the pier below the abbey or at Tihanyi-rév. From early March to late November the car ferry takes 10 minutes to cross the narrow stretch of water between Tihanyi-rév and Szántódi-rév every 40 minutes to an hour.

BALATONFÜRED

☎ 87 • postcode 8230 • pop 13,500

Balatonfüred is the oldest and most popular resort on the northern shore of Lake Balaton. It has none of the frenzy or brashness of Siófok, partly because of its aristocratic origins and partly because the thermal waters of its world-famous heart hospital attract a much older crowd.

The thermal water here, rich in carbonic acid, had been used as a cure for stomach ailments for centuries, but its other curative properties were only discovered by scientific analysis in the late 18th century. Balatonfüred was immediately declared a spa with its own chief physician in residence.

Balatonfüred's golden age was in the 19th century, especially the first half, when political and cultural leaders of the Reform

BALATONFÜRED

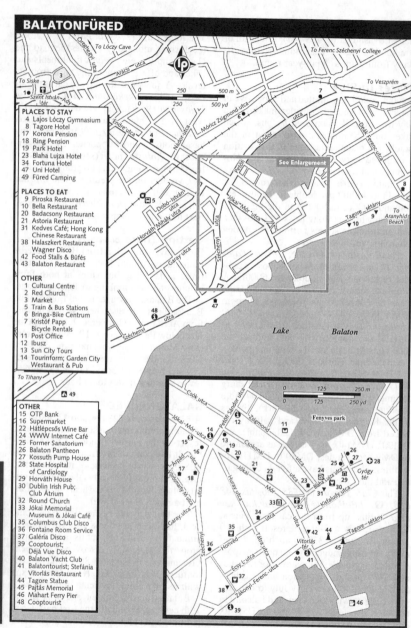

To Lóczy Cave
To Siske
Oreghegyi utca
Arácsi utca
To Ferenc Széchenyi College
To Veszprém
Szent István Ady tér
Móricz Zsigmond utca
Endre utca
Nádor utca
Petőfi Sándor
See Enlargement
Dobó-István utca
Jókai-Mór utca
Horváth Mihály utca
Garay utca
Széchenyi utca
Tagore-sétány
To Aranyhíd Beach
Deák Ferenc utca
Széchenyi utca
To Tihany
To Tihany

PLACES TO STAY
4 Lajos Lóczy Gymnasium
8 Tagore Hotel
17 Korona Pension
18 Ring Pension
19 Park Hotel
23 Blaha Lujza Hotel
34 Fortuna Hotel
47 Uni Hotel
49 Füred Camping

PLACES TO EAT
9 Piroska Restaurant
10 Bella Restaurant
20 Badacsony Restaurant
21 Astoria Restaurant
31 Kedves Café; Hong Kong
   Chinese Restaurant
38 Halaszkert Restaurant;
   Wagner Disco
42 Food Stalls & Büfés
43 Balaton Restaurant

OTHER
1 Cultural Centre
2 Red Church
3 Market
5 Train & Bus Stations
6 Bringa-Bike Centrum
7 Kristóf Papp
   Bicycle Rentals
11 Post Office
12 Ibusz
13 Sun City Tours
14 Tourinform; Garden City
   Westaurant & Pub

OTHER
15 OTP Bank
16 Supermarket
22 Hátlépcsős Wine Bar
24 WWW Internet Café
25 Former Sanatorium
26 Balaton Pantheon
27 Kossuth Pump House
28 State Hospital
   of Cardiology
29 Horváth House
30 Dublin Irish Pub;
   Club Átrium
32 Round Church
33 Jókai Memorial
   Museum & Jókai Café
35 Columbus Club Disco
36 Fontaine Room Service
37 Galéria Disco
39 Cooptourist;
   Déjà Vue Disco
40 Balaton Yacht Club
41 Balatontourist; Stefánia
   Vitorlás Restaurant
44 Tagore Statue
45 Pajtás Memorial
46 Mahart Ferry Pier
48 Cooptourist

Lake   Balaton

Csók utca
Jókai-Mór utca
Árpád utca
Vörösmarty Mihály
Garay utca
Honvéd
Écsy L utca
Széchenyi
Zákonyi Ferenc utca
Petőfi Sándor utca
Zsigmond
Csokonai
Huray utca
Jókai
Mór
Tátra utca
Kisfaludy utca
Tagore-sétány
Fenyes park
Gyógy tér
Vitorlás tér

Era (roughly 1825-48) gathered here in summer. The town became a writers' colony of sorts. Balatonfüred was also the site chosen by István Széchenyi to launch the lake's first steamship in 1846.

By 1900, Balatonfüred was a popular place for increasingly wealthy middle-class families to escape the city's heat. Wives would base themselves here all summer along with their children while husbands would board the 'bull trains' in Budapest at the weekend. The splendid promenade and a large wooden bath were built on the lake to accommodate the increasing crowds.

Orientation

Balatonfüred has two distinct districts: the lakeside resort area and the commercial centre in the older part of town around Szent István tér to the north-west. Almost everything to see and do is down by the water.

The train and bus stations are on Dobó István utca, about a kilometre north-west of Vitorlás tér, where the ferry pier is located. The quickest way to get to the lake from either is to walk east on Horváth Mihály utca and then south on Jókai Mór utca.

Information

The helpful Tourinform office (☎ 342 237, fax 340 556, ✉ balatonfured@tourinform .hu) at Petőfi Sándor utca 8 is open from 9 am to 7 pm Monday to Saturday and to 1 pm on Sunday from June to August. In March, April and October the hours are 9 am to 4 pm weekdays and to 1 pm on Saturday. During the rest of the year the hours are 9 am to 2 pm weekdays only.

Balatontourist (☎ 342 822) is at Tagore sétány 1. It is open from 9 am to 5 pm and, in summer, also on Saturday to 5 pm and Sunday to 1 pm. Ibusz (☎ 342 028, fax 342 251) is at Petőfi Sándor utca 4a. There's a branch of Cooptourist (☎ 343 027) for booking private rooms at Baricska telep 1 along Széchenyi utca.

There's an OTP bank branch next to the large supermarket at Jókai Mór utca 15. The post office is at Zsigmond utca 14. The WWW Internet Cafe at Blaha Lujza utca 6 is open from 4 pm to 8 pm daily.

Things to See

The **Jókai Memorial Museum** (Jókai Emlék-múzeum) is housed in the summer villa of the prolific writer Jókai Mór at Honvéd utca 1 just north of Vitorlás tér. In his study here, Jókai churned out many of his 200 novels under the stern gaze of his wife, the actress Róza Laborfalvi. The museum is open from 10 am to 6 pm Tuesday to Sunday from April to October (120/60Ft). Across the street at Blaha Lujza utca 1 is the tiny neoclassical **Round Church** (Kerek templom) completed in 1846. The *Crucifixion* (1891) by János Vaszary above the altar on the western wall is the only thing notable inside.

If you walk down Blaha Lujza utca you'll pass the villa (now a hotel) at No 4 where the 19th-century actress-singer Lujza Blaha summered from 1893 to 1916. A short distance farther is Gyógy tér, the heart of the spa. In the centre of this leafy square, **Kossuth Pump House** (1853) dispenses slightly sulphuric, but drinkable, thermal water. This is as close as you'll get to the hot spring. Although Balatonfüred is a major spa, the mineral baths are reserved for patients.

The late baroque **Horváth House** at Gyógy tér 3, for many years a hotel, was the site of the first Anna Ball in 1825. The ball has since become the big event in Balatonfüred and every July is held in the former **Sanatorium** (1802) opposite, now the Árkád Hotel.

Nearby is the **Balaton Pantheon**, with memorial plaques from those who took the cure at the hospital. The Bengali poet Rabindranath Tagore was one of them. A bust of this Nobel Prize-winning man of letters stands on Tagore sétány before a lime tree that he planted in 1926 to mark his recovery from illness after treatment here. Diagonally opposite and closer to the lake, there's a bizarre new memorial of a hand stretching out of the water in memory of those who drowned in the lake when a boat called the *Pajtás* sank in 1954.

On the eastern side of Gyógy tér at No 2 is the sprawling, 600-bed **State Hospital of Cardiology** (Országos Szívkórház), which put Balatonfüred on the map.

CENTRAL TRANSDANUBIA

Activities

Balatonfüred has three public beaches open from 8.30 or 9 am to 6 or 7 pm daily from mid-May to mid-September and costing 200/120Ft per day and 1200/720Ft a week. The best beach is Kisfaludy Strand along Aranyhíd sétány to the east of Tagore sétány. You can rent boats at Füred Camping as well as the Balaton Yacht Club (BYC; ☎ 343 955), Zákonyi Ferenc utca 2. From the ferry pier there are one-hour lake cruises (☎ 343 955 for information) in summer at 11 am and 2, 4 and 6 pm daily (500/350Ft) and 2½-hour cruises at 10 am on Wednesday, Friday and Sunday (1350/800Ft).

The Roland Garros Tennis Centre (mobile ☎ 06-30 9577 634), with clay courts, instruction and equipment for hire next to the Margaréta hotel west of the centre at Széchenyi utca 27 is open in summer from 6 am to 11 pm.

You can rent bicycles from several places in Balatonfüred, including Kristóf Papp (☎ 343 937) at Petőfi Sándor utca 62b and the Bringa-Bike Centrum (☎ 481 077) at Nádor utca 37. Rental costs from 800Ft per hour.

Consider walking or cycling to **Lóczy Cave** (Lóczy-barlang), north of the old town centre on Öreghegyi utca. It is the largest cave in the Balaton region and accessible from Szent István tér. Just walk east a couple of minutes on Arácsi utca past the excellent **market** and then north on Öreghegyi utca. The cave is open from 9 am to 5 pm Tuesday to Sunday from May to September. There's also good hiking in the three hills with the names Tamás (Thomas), Sándor (Alexander) and Péter (Peter) to the north-east.

Places to Stay

Camping There's only one camping ground at Balatonfüred, but it can accommodate 3500 people. *Füred Camping* (☎ 343 823, Széchenyi utca 24) is beside the Marina hotel on the lake, about 1.5km south-east of the train station. Four-person bungalows here start at DM95 from mid-June to August, DM70 from May to mid-June and in early September, and DM45 in April and from mid-September to mid-October. Camping (April to October) for three people with a tent or caravan costs from DM20 to DM30. To get a bungalow you have to arrive during reception office hours (8 am to 1 pm and 3 to 7 pm daily).

Private Rooms & Hostels As elsewhere around Lake Balaton, private room prices are rather inflated. The staff at Balatontourist and Cooptourist have them for 4000Ft to 5000Ft for a double. Another good place for booking rooms is Sun City Tours (☎/fax 481 798) at Csokonai utca 1 opposite Tourinform. Fontaine Room Service (☎ 343 673) at Honvéd utca 11 claims to be open 24 hours. There are lots of houses with rooms for rent on the streets north of Kisfaludy Beach.

The *Lajos Lóczy Gymnasium* (☎ 343 428, Bartók Beutca 4) near the stations and the far-flung *Ferenc Széchenyi College* (☎ 343 844, Hősök tere), 3km to the north-east of the resort, usually have accommodation in summer and charge 1250Ft for a bed in dormitory rooms in summer.

Pensions The 12-room *Ring* pension (☎/fax 342 884, Petőfi Sándor utca 6a) is so named because the owner was a champion boxer and not a jeweller. Neat, clean singles with shared bath cost DM30 to DM45, doubles DM50 to DM90. The nearby *Korona* (☎/fax 343 278, Vörösmarty Mihály utca 4), with 20 rooms, costs DM55/75 for singles/doubles.

Hotels The most central place in town is the cosy 19-room *Blaha Lujza* hotel (☎/fax 343 700, Blaha Lujza utca 4), erstwhile summer home (1893-1916) of the much loved 19th-century actress-singer. It was being extensively renovated as we went to press but may have reopened by now.

Once a retreat for burnt-out school teachers, the upmarket *Fortuna* (☎ 343 037, fax 343 859, Huray utca 6) has 34 rooms and charges from 5000Ft to 8000Ft for doubles with bath.

The run-down *Tagore* hotel (☎ 343 173, fax 342 603, Deák Ferenc utca 56), with 36 rooms by Kisfaludy Beach, charges DM31 to DM49 for singles and DM46 to DM90 for doubles, depending on the season.

Of the dozen or so high-rise hotels lining the lake in Balatonfüred, one of the best (and cheapest) is the 45-room *Uni* (☎ *341 822, fax 343 085,* ✉ *hoteluin@elender.hu, Széchenyi utca 10)*, with singles from 3340Ft to 8640Ft and doubles from 4310Ft to 10,300Ft, depending on the season. One of the poshest places in town is the old-world 32-room *Park* hotel (☎ *343 203, fax 342 005, Jókai Mór utca 24)*. Singles are DM47 to DM84, doubles DM60 to DM100.

Places to Eat

The *food stalls* on the north-eastern side of Vitorlás tér are great for something fast and cheap, especially the large pieces of fried carp and catfish sold by weight. The nearby *Stefánia Vitorlás* restaurant *(Tagore sétány 1)*, with its central location, is expensive and touristy; walk west on Zákonyi Ferenc utca to the *Halászkert* at No 3, which serves some of the best *korhely halászlé* (drunkard's fish soup) in Hungary. The once low-rent *Balaton* (*Kisfaludy utca 5)* facing the lake has got a face-lift and is now a cool, leafy oasis amidst all the hubbub.

The eastern end of Tagore sétány is now a strip of pleasant bars and terraced restaurants including the *Bella*, with good pizzas (450Ft to 660Ft), Hungarian staples and the wonderful Panorama terrace facing the lake, and the *Piroska* restaurant, very popular with local residents.

Jókai Mór utca is another good hunting ground for restaurants. The *Badacsony* (*Jókai Mór utca 26)* has a menu in nine different languages and has oddities like ostrich Nairobi-style. The opulent *Astoria* restaurant in a restored 19th-century villa next door at No 28 is for the very well-heeled indeed.

The *Kedves (Blaha Lujza utca 7)* is a cafe where Lujza Blaha herself took cha. There's a Chinese restaurant upstairs called the *Hong Kong* open daily till midnight.

Entertainment

The *cultural centre* (☎ *481 187, Kossuth Lajos utca 3)* near Szent István tér can tell you what's on.

The *Jókai (Jókai Mór utca 29)* is a fun coffee house and bar sacrilegiously located in the back of the Jókai Museum and open till 2 am.

To sample one of Balatonfüred's famous Rieslings, visit the *Hátlépcsős* wine bar *(Back Steps; Jókai Mór utca 30)*. If you prefer a beer, carry on north to the big *City Pub* at the Garden City Westaurant *(Petőfi Sándor utca 2)* or the popular *Dublin Irish Pub (Blaha Lujza utca 9)*.

There are clubs all over town in summer, including two side by side on Zákonyi Ferenc utca: the *Wagner* at the Halászkert restaurant and the *Galéria*. The *Déjà Vue* disco is on the opposite side of Zákonyi Ferenc utca. Other hot spots are the *Columbus Club (Honvéd utca 7)* and the *Club Átrium* at the Dublin Irish pub on Blaha Lujza utca.

Getting There & Away

Bus Buses for Tihany and Veszprém leave continually throughout the day. Other daily departures are to Budapest (four), Esztergom (one), Győr (five to seven), Hévíz (seven), Kecskemét (one), Nagykanizsa (one), Sopron (two), Székesfehérvár (two), Tata (one), Tatabánya (two) and Zalaegerszeg (five).

Train Frequent express and local trains travel north-east to Székesfehérvár and Budapest-Déli and south-west to Tapolca and lakeside towns as far as Badacsony.

Boat From April to late October, Mahart ferries a day link Balatonfüred with Siófok and Tihany.

Up to 10 ferries a day serve the same ports from late May to mid-September; one ferry just before 9 am goes on to various ports, terminating at Badacsony.

Getting Around

You can reach Vitorlás tér and the lake from the train and bus stations on bus Nos 1, 1a and 2; bus No 1 continues on to the camp site.

Local taxis can be ordered by calling ☎ 482 000 or ☎ 444 444.

VESZPRÉM

☎ 88 • postcode 8200 • pop 63,800

Spreading over five hills between the northern and southern ranges of the Bakony Hills, Veszprém has one of the most dramatic locations in Central Transdanubia. The walled castle district, atop a plateau, is a living museum of baroque art and architecture. Though not as rich as, say, Sopron in sights or historical buildings, Veszprém's buildings are generally in better condition. It's a delight to stroll through the windy Castle Hill district's single street, admiring the embarrassment of fine churches. As the townspeople say, 'Either the wind is blowing or the bells are ringing in Veszprém.'

The Romans did not settle in what is now Veszprém but 8km to the south-east at Balácapuszta, where important archaeological finds have been made. Prince Géza, King Stephen's father, founded a bishopric in Veszprém late in the 10th century, and the city grew as a religious, administrative and educational centre (the university was established in the 13th century). It also became a favourite residence of Hungary's queens.

The castle at Veszprém was blown up by the Habsburgs in 1702, and it lost most of its medieval buildings during the Rákóczi independence war shortly thereafter. But this cleared the way for Veszprém's golden age, when the city's bishops, rich landlords all, built most of what you see today. The church's iron grip on Veszprém prevented it from developing commercially, however, and it was bypassed by the main railway line in the 19th century.

Orientation

The bus station is on Piac tér, a few minutes' walk north-east from Kossuth Lajos utca, a pedestrian street of shops and travel agencies. If you turn north at the end of Kossuth Lajos utca at Szabadság tér, and walk along Rákóczi utca you'll soon reach the entrance to Castle Hill (Vár-hegy) at Óváros tér.

The train station is 3km north of the bus station at the end of Jutasi út.

Information

Tourinform (☎/fax 404 548, ✉ veszprem@ tourinform.hu) at Rákóczi utca 3 is open from 9 am to 6 pm weekdays and to 1 pm on Saturday from June to August and from 9 am to 5 pm weekdays only the rest of the year. Balatontourist (☎ 429 630) at Kossuth Lajos utca 21, between the bus station and the castle, can provide information and a map; Ibusz (☎ 426 492) is across the road at Kossuth Lajos utca 10. These last two are open from 8.30 or 9 am to 4.30 or 5 pm weekdays and in summer on Saturday to noon.

You can change money at the OTP bank branch at Óváros tér 25; there's a much bigger branch with a currency-exchange machine at the corner of Brusznyai utca and Mártírok útja. The post office is at Kossuth Lajos utca 19.

Óváros tér

You should begin any tour of Veszprém in Óváros tér, the medieval market place. Of the many fine 18th-century buildings here, the most interesting is the late baroque **Pósa House** (1793) with an iron balcony at No 3, now a bank. The buildings at Nos 7 and 9 are the former **customs house** and the **town hall**.

Overlooking the square to the north-west is the **firewatch tower** (tűztorony). Like the one in Sopron, it is an architectural hybrid of Gothic, baroque and neoclassical styles. The chimes heard on the hour throughout Veszprém emanate from here, and you can climb to the top for excellent views of the rocky hill and the Bakony Hills. The entrance to the tower is at Vár utca 17 (open 10 am to 6 pm daily from mid-April to mid-October; 100Ft).

Castle Hill

As you begin to ascend Castle Hill and its sole street, Vár utca, you'll pass through **Heroes' Gate** (Hősök kapuja), an entrance built in 1936 from the stones of a 15th-century castle gate.

The extremely rich **Piarist church** (Piarista templom) at Vár utca 12 was built in 1836 in the neoclassical style. The red marble **altar stone** (1467) diagonally opposite outside the parish office at No 27 is

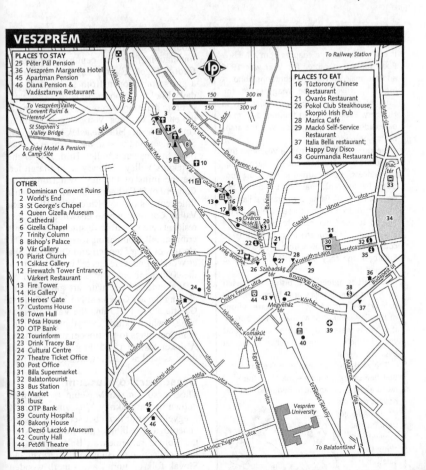

VESZPRÉM

PLACES TO STAY
25 Péter Pál Pension
36 Veszprém Margaréta Hotel
45 Apartman Pension
46 Diana Pension &
   Vadásztanya Restaurant

PLACES TO EAT
16 Tűztorony Chinese
   Restaurant
21 Óváros Restaurant
26 Pokol Club Steakhouse;
   Skorpió Irish Pub
28 Marica Café
29 Mackó Self-Service
   Restaurant
37 Italia Bella restaurant;
   Happy Day Disco
43 Gourmandia Restaurant

OTHER
1 Dominican Convent Ruins
2 World's End
3 St George's Chapel
4 Queen Gizella Museum
5 Cathedral
6 Gizella Chapel
7 Trinity Column
8 Bishop's Palace
9 Vár Gallery
10 Piarist Church
11 Csikász Gallery
12 Firewatch Tower Entrance;
   Várkert Restaurant
13 Fire Tower
14 Kis Gallery
15 Heroes' Gate
17 Customs House
18 Town Hall
19 Pósa House
20 OTP Bank
22 Tourinform
23 Drink Tracey Bar
24 Cultural Centre
27 Theatre Ticket Office
30 Post Office
31 Billa Supermarket
32 Balatontourist
33 Bus Station
34 Market
35 Ibusz
38 OTP Bank
39 County Hospital
40 Bakony House
41 Dezső Laczkó Museum
42 County Hall
44 Petőfi Theatre

the oldest piece of Renaissance stonework in Hungary.

The U-shaped **Bishop's Palace** (Püspöki palota), at Vár utca 16, is where the queen's residence stood in the Middle Ages. It faces Szentháromság tér, named for the **Trinity Column** (1751) in the centre. The palace, designed by Jakab Fellner of Tata in the mid-18th century, is, sadly, no longer open to the public.

Next to the Bishop's Palace at Vár utca 18 is the early-Gothic **Gizella Chapel** (Gizella-kápolna), named after the wife of King Stephen, who was crowned near here

early in the 11th century. The chapel was discovered when the Bishop's Palace was being built in the mid-18th century. Inside the chapel are Byzantine-influenced 13th-century frescoes of the Apostles. The **Queen Gizella Museum** of religious art is opposite at Vár utca 35. Both are open from 9 am to 5 pm daily from May to October and cost 20Ft and 100Ft respectively.

Parts of the **cathedral** (székesegyház), which is dedicated to St Michael and the site of the first bishop's palace, date from the beginning of the 11th century, but the cathedral has been rebuilt many times since

Reach Out & Touch

It could have been a chapter from a Mills & Boon for the macabre. The year was 1996 and the millecentenary celebrations honouring the arrival of the Magyars in the Carpathian Basin in 896 were under way in Hungary. People were in the mood to mark dates and one of those people was the archbishop of Veszprém.

He knew that it had been in Veszprém that the future king, Stephen, and Gizella, a Bavarian princess, were married in 996. Just suppose, he thought, that the bishop of the Bavarian city of Passau, where Gizella's remains had been resting these nine centuries, agreed to send her hand to Hungary. The Holy Dexter, St Stephen's revered right hand, could be brought down from the Basilica in Budapest and they could... Well, the mind boggled.

All parties agreed (the bishop of Passau even threw in Gizella's arm bone) and the date was set. On 4 May, in the square in front of the Cathedral of St Michael, in Veszprém, the hands were laid together and – 1000 years to the day – coyly touched in marital bliss once again.

The world did not change as we know it that fine spring morning – the No 2 tram raced along the Danube in Budapest; Mr Kovács dished out steaming *lángos* from his stall somewhere along Lake Balaton; schoolchildren in Sárospatak recited their *ábécé*. But all true Magyars knew, deep in their hearts, that all was right with the world.

TONY FANKHAUSER

then. The early Gothic crypt is original, though. Beside the cathedral, the octagonal foundation of the 13th-century **Chapel of St George** (Szent György kápolna) sits under a glass dome (open from 10 am to 5 pm daily May to October; 20Ft).

From the rampart known as **World's End** at the end of Vár utca, you can gaze north to craggy Benedict Hill (Benedek-hegy) and the Séd Stream and west to the concrete viaduct (now St Stephen's Valley Bridge) over the Betekints Valley. Below you, in Margit tér, are the ruins of the medieval **Dominican Convent of St Catherine** and to the west what little remains of the 11th-century **Veszprém Valley Convent**, whose erstwhile cloistered residents are said to have stitched Stephen's crimson silk coronation robe in 1031. The **statues of King Stephen and Queen Gizella** at World's End were erected in 1938 to mark the 900th anniversary of Stephen's death.

Vár utca is lined with **art galleries**, including the **Kis Galéria** at No 3, the **Csikász Galéria** at No 15-17 and the **Vár Galéria** at No 21, which exhibit everything from religious paintings to postmodernist sculpture. A ticket costing 150/50Ft gets you into all three as well as the firewatch tower.

Dezső Laczkó Museum

The Dezső Laczkó Museum (sometimes known as the Bakony Museum), south of Megyeház tér at Erzsébet sétány 1, has archaeological exhibits (the emphasis is on the Roman settlement at Balácapuszta), a large collection of Hungarian, German and Slovak folk costumes and superb wooden carvings, including objects made by the famed outlaws of the Bakony Hills in the 18th and 19th centuries. Next to the main museum is **Bakony House** (Bakonyi ház), a copy of an 18th-century thatched peasant dwelling in the village of Öcs, south-west of Veszprém. It has the usual three rooms found in Hungarian peasant homes, and in the *kamra* the complete workshop of a flask maker has been set up. Both are open from 10 am to 6 pm Tuesday to Sunday from mid-March and mid-October and to 2 pm the rest of the year. Entry costs 120/60Ft and 60/30Ft.

Petőfi Theatre

Take a peek inside this theatre at Óváry Ferenc utca 2 even if you're not attending a performance. It's a pink, grey and burgundy gem of Hungarian Art Nouveau architecture and decoration designed by István Medgyaszay in 1908. It's also important structurally; it was the first building in Hungary to be made entirely of reinforced concrete. The large round stained-glass window entitled *The Magic of Folk Art* by Sándor Nagy is exceptional.

Places to Stay

The small *Erdei Camping* (☎ 326 751, *Kittenberger utca 14*) north-west of town near the zoo is open from mid-April to mid-October. There's a pension and motel nearby (see Pensions later in this section).

Ibusz and Balatontourist can help with private rooms (2000Ft per person) and flats (from 6000Ft).

The *Erdei* motel (☎ 326 751, *Kittenberger utca 14*) at the camping site is one of the cheapest places to stay in Veszprém, with rooms with shared shower for 1500Ft per person. It's open between mid-April and mid-October. The smaller *Erdei* pension (☎ 425 458) next door at No 12 is much more expensive.

There are two pensions in attractive villas on József Attila utca south-west of the centre: the *Apartman* (☎ 420 097, *fax 420 711*) at No 25 with 18 rooms and the 10-room *Diana* (☎ *fax 427 897*) across the street at No 22. Expect to pay from 6000Ft for a double. The *Péter Pál* (☎/fax 328 091, *Dózsa György utca 3*) is a fine 12-room pension with a lovely garden perched above a busy street. Singles/doubles/triples are 4000/5400/6600Ft.

The 74-room *Vezsprém Margaréta* hotel (☎ 424 876, *fax 424 076, Budapest út 6*) is the most central, though being on a very busy thoroughfare it's not a particularly nice place to stay. Singles/doubles are 7900/8500Ft.

Places to Eat

The cheapest place in town for a bite is the self-service *Mackó* (*Kossuth Lajos utca 6*),

which serves up little pizzas, salads and cakes in the Cserhát shopping complex. It's open daily to between 5.30 and 7.30 pm. The *Gourmandia* (*Megyeház tér 2*) is seriously misnamed, but it's central. It's open to 9 pm (3.30 pm on Sunday) and most mains are around 600Ft. The *Italia Bella* (*Budapest út 7*) does decent pizza and pasta.

There are very few places to eat on Castle Hill, but the *Tüztorony* Chinese restaurant (*Vár utca 1*) between the firewatch tower and Heroes' Gate is a friendly place open daily to 10.30 pm and the *Várkert* (*Vár utca 17*) has a three-course set menu for 890Ft. Restaurants around Szabadság tér include the *Óváros* (*Szabadság tér 14*) in a lovely baroque building with outside seating on various levels and, a short distance to the west, the *Pokol Club* steak restaurant (*Virág Benedek utca 1*).

The *Vadásztanya* restaurant at the Diana pension gets rave reviews from local people and readers. If you've got wheels, there's a wonderful 18th-century csárda called the *Betyár* (Outlaw) at Nemesvámos about 4km south-west of Veszprém. It's on the road to Nagyvázsony and Tapolca.

The *Marica* cafe (*Kossuth Lajos utca 5*) near Szabadság tér is a decent place for cakes and a popular student hang-out.

The large *covered market* is on Piac tér south of the bus station.

Entertainment

The *Veszprém Cultural Centre* (☎ 429 111, *Dózsa György utca 2*) is where the city's symphony orchestra is based. The magnificent *Petőfi Theatre* (☎ 424 235) stages both plays and concerts; tickets are available from the box office (☎ 422 440) at Szabadság tér 7 between 9 am and 1 pm and 2 and 5 pm weekdays. Concerts are often held in July and August in front of the *Bishop's Palace* in Szentháromság tér, which is said to have perfect acoustics, and from time to time at the *Piarist church*.

In the same building, the *Skorpió Irish Pub* and the *Pokol Club* (*Virág Benedek utca 1*) are good places for a pint or to kick up your heels. They're open till 2 am (4 am on Friday and Saturday). Opposite is the

Drink Tracey (Virág Benedek utca 4), which attracts a *very* young crowd. Another popular club with an unfortunate name is the *Happy Day Disco (Budapest út 7)* opposite the Veszprém Margaréta hotel and open Friday to Sunday till 4 am.

Getting There & Away

Bus Connections are excellent from Veszprém, with hourly departures to Budapest (both five express buses and many more via Székesfehérvár), Herend, Tapolca, Pápa, Nagyvázsony, Keszthely via Balatonfüred and Tapolca. Other important destinations include Esztergom (three buses daily), Győr (up to 12), Kaposvár (two), Kecskemét (two or three), Nagykanizsa (three), Pécs (two), Siófok (nine) Sopron (three), Sümeg (six), Szeged (three or four), Székesfehérvár (eight), Szekszárd (three), Szombathely (three) and Zalaegerszeg (five).

Train Three railway lines meet at Veszprém. The first connects Veszprém with Szombathely and Budapest-Déli station via Székesfehérvár (up to eight a day in each direction). The second line carries up to six daily trains north to Pannonhalma and Győr, where you can transfer for Vienna. The third, south-east to Lepsény, links Veszprém with the railway lines on the northern and southern shores of Lake Balaton.

Getting Around

Bus Nos 1, 2 and 9 run from the train and bus stations to Szabadság tér. Bus Nos 1 and 2, which you can also board outside the Veszprém Margaréta hotel, also go to the zoo and Erdei camp site, pension and motel.

For a local taxi, ring ☎ 444 444.

AROUND VESZPRÉM
Herend

☎ 88 • postcode 8440 • pop 3200

The porcelain factory at Herend, 13km west of Veszprém, has been producing Hungary's finest hand-painted chinaware for over a century and a half. There's not a lot to see in this dusty one-horse village, and prices at the outlet don't seem any cheaper than elsewhere in Hungary, but the **Porcelain Museum**

(Porcelánmúzeum), displaying the most prized pieces, is definitely worth a trip. It's at Kossuth Lajos utca 140, a five-minute walk north-east from the bus station, and is open from 8.30 am to 4 pm daily from May to October, from 10 am to 3 pm weekdays the rest of the year (200/50Ft). Labels are in four languages including English, which makes it easy to follow the developments and changes in patterns and tastes (see boxed text 'Herend Porcelain').

Across from the museum is a new shopping mall with the expensive china for sale; the shop at Kossuth Lajos utca 147 sells antique pieces. Should you feel hungry, the *Lila Akác* restaurant *(Kossuth Lajos utca 122)*, west of the museum and across Vasút utca, can oblige and the nearby *Eszkimó* pub *(Kossuth Lajos utca 130)* will slake

Herend Porcelain

A terracotta factory set up at Herend in 1826 began producing porcelain 13 years later under Mór Farkasházi Fischer of Tata in Western Transdanubia.

Initially it specialised in copying and replacing the nobles' broken chinaware settings imported from Asia, and you'll see some pretty kooky 19th-century interpretations of Japanese art and Chinese faces on display in the museum here. But the factory soon began producing its own patterns; many, like the Rothschild bird and *petites roses*, were inspired by Meissen and Sèvres designs from Germany and France. The Victoria pattern of butterflies and wild flowers of the Bakony was designed for Queen Victoria after she admired a display of Herend pieces at the Great Exhibition in London in 1851.

To avoid bankruptcy in the 1870s, the Herend factory began mass production; tastes ran from kitschy pastoral and hunting scenes to the ever-popular animal sculptures with the distinctive scale-like triangle patterns. In 1992, the factory was purchased from the state by its 1500 workers and became one of the first companies in Hungary privatised through an employee stock-ownership plan.

your thirst on a hot day. There's an MKB branch a short distance east of the museum along Kossuth Lajos utca.

Getting There & Away You can reach Herend by bus from Veszprém at least every 30 minutes; other destinations include Sümeg (three) and Balatonfüred (two). Five local trains run through Herend every day on their way to Ajka. Change there for Szombathely.

PÁPA

☎ 89 • postcode 8500 • pop 33,800

This attractive town some 50km north-west of Veszprém has been called the 'Athens of Transdanubia' largely because of its Calvinist school. It was attended by such literary greats as the poet Sándor Petőfi and the novelist Mór Jókai in the 19th century. Religious tolerance has been a hallmark of Pápa for centuries.

Protestantism gained ground swiftly in the area in the 16th century and the first Hungarian translation of the Heidelberg Catechism was published here in 1577. During the late Middle Ages, Pápa was the third-most important Protestant stronghold in Transdanubia after Sopron and Sárvár.

Pápa flourished after liberation from the Turks, with Bishop Károly Esterházy, whose family effectively owned the town from 1648 to after WWII, overseeing the construction of many of its fine baroque buildings. His brother Ferenc encouraged trade by allowing Jews to settle in Pápa. They ran the pottery, broad cloth and paper-making industries and by the end of the 19th century, Pápa had one of the largest Jewish populations in Hungary. But the railways – and large-scale industrialisation – passed Pápa by, allowing it to retain much of its lovely architecture.

Orientation & Information

Pápa's main drags are Fő tér and Fő utca, which run south-east from Kastély-park to Március 15 tér. Pedestrian Kossuth Lajos utca runs southward from the large parish church on Fő tér. The bus station is on Szabadság utca, a short distance east of the church. The train station is in Béke tér,

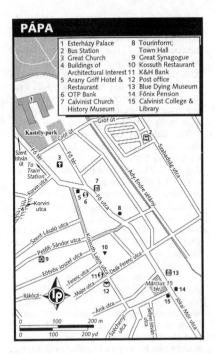

PÁPA

1 Esterházy Palace
2 Bus Station
3 Great Church
4 Buildings of Architectural Interest
5 Arany Griff Hotel & Restaurant
6 OTP Bank
7 Calvinist Church History Museum
8 Tourinform; Town Hall
9 Great Synagogue
10 Kossuth Restaurant
11 K&H Bank
12 Post office
13 Blue Dying Museum
14 Fónix Pension
15 Calvinist College & Library

north of the centre at the end of Esterházy Károly utca.

Tourinform (☎/fax 311 535, ❷ papa@tourinform.hu, Fő tér 12) in the town hall (városház) is open from 8 am to 4 pm weekdays and from 9 am till noon on Saturday from June to August and weekdays only the rest of the year. There's an OTP branch at Fő tér 5 and a K&H branch at Kossuth Lajos utca 27. The main post office is opposite at No 27 of the same street.

Things to See

The enormous U-shaped yellow building at the entrance to Kastély-park is the former **Esterházy Palace** (Esterházy kastély) built in 1784 on the foundations of an older castle. Russian soldiers were billeted here until as late as 1990. The palace contains a museum that has been undergoing renovations forever, a music school and a library.

South of the palace on Fő tér is the Catholic **Great Church** (Nagytemplom) built by Jacob Fellner in 1786 and dedicated to St Stephen. It contains wonderful frescoes (1781-82) of St Stephen's life and martyrdom by Franz Anton Maulbertsch (the same artist who did the frescoes in Sümeg) and Hubert Mauer. The spooky remains of the Roman martyr St Martialis are preserved in a see-through coffin below the altar in the Virgin's Chapel to the left.

The **Calvinist Church History Museum** (Református Egyhátörténeti Múzeum) at Fő tér 6 (open 9 am to 5 pm Tuesday to Sunday from May to October; 80/50Ft) may not sound like a crowd-pleaser but it puts Protestantism and the role of the Calvinist College (Reformátis Kollégium), farther south at Március 15 tér, in perspective. The latter has a library containing 75,000 valuable tomes, which can be visited from 8 am to 4 pm weekdays and 9 am to 5 pm at the weekend from May to October.

Arguably the most popular museum in Pápa is the **Blue Dyeing Museum** (Kékfestő Múzeum) at Március 15 tér 12, which showcases a method of colouring cotton fabric deep blue that was a famous Pápa export throughout Hungary. The museum is housed in a factory that closed in 1956, but the machines remain in perfect working conditions, demonstrations are sometimes held and there's an interesting display of samples and old photographs. The museum is open from 9 am to 5 pm Tuesday to Sunday from May to September and till 4 pm the rest of the year (200/100Ft).

The streets running west off Kossuth Lajos utca are particularly rich architecturally, especially Korvin utca; check out the Gothic, baroque and rococo gems at Nos 4, 9, 7 & 13 on Korvin utca. To the south at Petőfi Sándor utca 24-26, the **Great Synagogue** (Nagy Zsinagóga), a romantic structure built in 1846 with some 100,000 bricks donated by the Esterházy family, barely stands.

Places to Stay

The none-too-salubrious *Főnix* pension *(☎ 342 361, fax 313 344, Jókai Mór utca)*, with five rooms just south of the Blue Dyeing Museum, has doubles for around 3500Ft, but ask for a room in the back away from noisy Jókai Mór utca. The 25-room *Arany Griff (☎ 312 000, fax 312 005, Fő tér 15)* is across from the Great Church and as central as you'll find. Singles cost DM44 to DM55, doubles DM64 to DM83, depending on the season.

Places to eat are also scarce though the restaurant at the back of the *Arany Griff* and its cukrászda with outside seating out front in the warmer months have been recommended. The *Kossuth* restaurant *(Kossuth Lajos utca 22)* in a quiet courtyard in the Kossuth Udvar shopping mall is an option.

Getting There & Away

Bus Bus service to/from Pápa is excellent with hourly departures to Ajka, Győr and Veszprém. Other important destinations include: Balatonfüred (two buses a day), Budapest (three), Kaposvár (one), Keszthely (nine), Nagykanizsa (three), Sárvár (four), Sopron (four), Sümeg (10), Szeged (one to two), Szombathely (three), Tapolca (seven) and Zalaegerszeg (three).

International destinations include Vienna at 6.55 am on Monday, Thursday and Friday and two other Austrian cities: Eisenstadt (Kismárton) at 7.45 am on Tuesday and Oberwart (Felsőőrr) at 7.45 am on Thursday,

Train Pápa is on the rail line linking Győr with Celldömölk, from where you can carry on to Szombathely up to seven times a day. The only other place you can reach by rail from Pápa is Csorna, which is on the main line between Győr and Sopron.

SZÉKESFEHÉRVÁR
☎ 22 • postcode 8000 • pop 109,000
Székesfehérvár may look like just another big city off the M7 between Budapest and Lake Balaton, 35km to the south-west, but this city (German: Stuhlweissenburg) is traditionally known as the place where the Magyar chieftain Árpád first set up camp, making this the oldest town in Hungary.

Although Székesfehérvár is not on Lake Balaton, everyone travelling between Budapest and the lake passes this way.

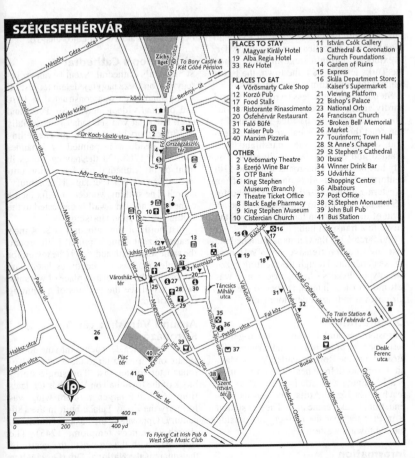

SZÉKESFEHÉRVÁR

PLACES TO STAY
1 Magyar Király Hotel
19 Alba Regia Hotel
33 Rév Hotel

PLACES TO EAT
4 Vörösmarty Cake Shop
12 Korzó Pub
17 Food Stalls
18 Ristorante Rinascimento
20 Ősfehérvár Restaurant
31 Faló Büfé
32 Kaiser Pub
40 Marxim Pizzeria

OTHER
2 Vörösmarty Theatre
3 Ezerjó Wine Bar
5 OTP Bank
6 King Stephen
  Museum (Branch)
7 Theatre Ticket Office
8 Black Eagle Pharmacy
9 King Stephen Museum
10 Cistercian Church
11 István Csók Gallery
13 Cathedral & Coronation
   Church Foundations
14 Garden of Ruins
15 Express
16 Skála Department Store;
   Kaiser's Supermarket
21 Viewing Platform
22 Bishop's Palace
23 National Orb
24 Franciscan Church
25 'Broken Bell' Memorial
26 Market
27 Tourinform; Town Hall
28 St Anne's Chapel
29 St Stephen's Cathedral
30 Ibusz
34 Winner Drink Bar
35 Udvárház
   Shopping Centre
36 Albatours
37 Post Office
38 St Stephen Monument
39 John Bull Pub
41 Bus Station

Székesfehérvár can also be seen as a day trip from Budapest. Close to the city is Velence, a much smaller and more subdued lake than the Balaton.

History

As early as the 1st century, the Romans had a settlement at Gorsium near Tác, 17km to the south (see Around Székesfehérvár). When Árpád arrived late in the 9th century, the surrounding marshes and the Sárvíz River offered protection – the same reason Prince Géza built his castle here less than 100 years later. But it was Géza's son,

Stephen, who raised the status of Székesfehérvár by building a fortified basilica in what he called Alba Regia. Hungary's kings (and some of its queens) would be crowned and buried here for the next 500 years. In fact, the city's seemingly unpronounceable name ('SAYK-esh-fehair-vahr') means 'Seat of the White Castle', as it was the royal capital and white was the king's colour.

With Visegrád, Esztergom and Buda, Székesfehérvár served as an alternative royal capital for centuries, and it was here in 1222 that King Andrew II was forced by his *servientes* (mercenaries) to sign the

Golden Bull, an early bill of rights. The Turks captured Székesfehérvár in 1543 and used Stephen's basilica to store gunpowder. It exploded during a siege in 1601; when the Turks left in 1688, the town, the basilica and the royal tombs were in ruins.

Stephen – much less Árpád – would hardly recognise today's Székesfehérvár. The stones from his basilica were used to construct the Bishop's Palace in 1801; several decades later, the marshland was drained and the Sárvíz was diverted. The city had been at a crossroads since the 11th century, when crusaders on a budget from Western Europe passed through Székesfehérvár on their way to the Adriatic. The arrival of the railway in the 1860s turned the city into a transport hub.

In March 1945 the Germans launched the last big counteroffensive of WWII near Székesfehérvár. Though the fighting razed the city's outskirts (the historic centre was left more or less intact), it opened the way for postwar industrial development.

Orientation

Városház tér and Koronázó tér together form the core of the old town. Pedestrian Fő utca – what the Romans called Vicus Magnus – runs north from here. The train station is a 15-minute walk south-east in Béke tér; reach it via József Attila utca and its continuation, Deák Ferenc utca. The bus station is in Piac tér near the market, just outside the old town's western wall.

Information

Tourinform (☎/fax 312 818, @ fejer-m@tourinform.hu) has an office in the town hall at Városház tér 1 and is open from 9 am to 4.30 pm weekdays only. Other agencies in town include Albatours (☎ 312 494) at Kossuth Lajos utca 14a; Ibusz (☎ 329 393), south of Koronázó tér at Vasvári Pál utca 3; and Express (☎ 312 510), a few minutes' walk to the north-east at Rákóczi utca 4. All are open from 8 or 8.30 am to 4 or 5 pm on weekdays only.

There's an OTP bank branch at Fő utca 6 and a foreign currency exchange machine in the entrance to the Udvárház shopping centre at Kossuth Lajos utca 14. The main post office is nearby at Kossuth Lajos utca 16.

St Stephen's Cathedral

St Stephen's Cathedral (Szent István székesegyház) on Géza nagyfejedelem tér just off Arany János utca was constructed in 1470 and originally dedicated to Sts Peter and Paul, but what you see today is essentially an 18th-century baroque church. The ceiling frescoes inside were painted by Johannes Cymbal in 1768. On the paving stones in front of the cathedral are foundation outlines of an earlier (perhaps 10th-century) church. The striking wooden crucifix on the cathedral's northern wall is dedicated to the victims of the 1956 Uprising.

Just north of the cathedral is **St Anne's Chapel** (Szent Anna kápolna) built around the same time, with additions (the tower, for example) made some centuries later. The Turks used the chapel as a place of worship; you can still see the remains of a painting from that era.

Around Városház tér & Koronázó tér

Arany János utca debouches into the double square of Városház tér to the west and Koronázó tér to the east. The single-storey block of the **town hall** on Városház tér dates from 1690; the larger northern wing was formerly the Zichy Palace built in the 18th century. Opposite is the austere **Franciscan church** (Ferences templom; 1745). The stone ball with the crown in the centre of the square is the **National Orb** (Országalma – 'national apple' in Hungarian) dedicated to King Stephen. The monument that looks like a broken bell (1995) lying on its side is dedicated to the victims of WWII.

The most imposing building on Koronázó tér is the Zopf-style **Bishop's Palace** (Püspöki palota) built with the rubble from the medieval basilica and royal burial chapels. They stood to the east, in what is now the **Garden of Ruins** (Romkert). The site is particularly sacred to Hungarians – some three dozen of their kings and queens were crowned and 15 buried here. The doleful-looking white-marble sarcophagus in the chamber to the right as you enter the main gate is thought to contain the remains of Géza, Stephen or his young son, Prince Imre. Decorative stonework from the basilica and royal tombs lines the walls of the loggia, and in the garden are the foundations of the cathedral and the Coronation Church. Excavation of the site continues. The Garden of Ruins is open from 9 am to 5 pm Tuesday to Sunday from April to October (100/50Ft), but you get to see most of it from the street or the viewing platform to the west on Koronázó tér.

Around Fő utca

Lying to the north of the town centre, the **Black Eagle** (Fekete Sas) at Fő utca 5 is a pharmacy set up by the Jesuits in 1758, with beautiful rococo furnishings. A few steps to the west, off Oskola utca, in the bizarre cultural centre at Bartók Béla tér 1, the **István Csók Gallery** has a good collection of 19th and 20th-century Hungarian art (open from 10 am to 7 pm weekdays, till 6 pm at the weekend; 100/50Ft).

The **King Stephen Museum** (István Király Múzeum) at Fő utca 6 has a large collection of Roman pottery (some of it from Gorsium), an interesting folk-carving display and an exhibit covering 1000 years of Székesfehérvár history. The museum branch at Országzászló tér 3 has temporary exhibits.

Both are open from 10 am to 6 pm Tuesday to Sunday from May to September and to 2 pm the rest of the year. (100/50Ft).

Places to Stay

Express may know about accommodation in college dormitories in July and August. Private rooms are available from Ibusz and Albatours.

The **Két Góbé** (☎ 329 578, fax 327 578, Gugásvölgyi út 4) is a 23-room pension north-east of the city centre. Facing busy route No 8, it's noisy, but the price is right: from 4500Ft for a double.

The 63-room **Rév** hotel (☎ 314 441, fax 327 061, József Attila utca 42) is a workers' residence-cum-hotel. Here you pay 2700Ft for a spartan but clean room with washbasin. Showers and toilets are down the hall.

If you're feeling flush, the 150-year-old **Magyar Király** hotel (☎ 311 262, fax 327 788, Fő utca 10) has 57 rooms at 9000Ft single or double. The **Alba Regia** (☎ 313 484, fax 316 292, ✉ albaregia@eravishotels.hu, Rákóczi utca 1), a stone's throw from the Garden of Ruins, is a modern, multistorey hotel with 104 rooms and expensive outlets. Singles/doubles are 9300/11,000Ft.

If you fancy staying in a stately home, the Zichy family's country manor house (1821) at Seregélyes, some 16km south-east of Székesfehérvár, now houses the **Taurus Kastély** hotel (☎ 447 030, fax 447 032, Kastély utca 1) with 36 well-appointed rooms, a frescoed dining hall, tennis court, pool and sauna on 22 hectares of parkland. Doubles are 9900Ft, enormous suites from 12,800Ft.

Places to Eat

The **Faló Büfé** (Távírda utca 19) south-east of the Alba Regia hotel is a cheap place to eat. There are a bunch of decent *food stalls* (Kégi György utca) in the square in front of the Skála department store.

The **Korzó** pub (Fő utca 2) is a decent place for lunch or dinner and closes at 10 pm. Also good (and surprisingly cheap, with mains for 400Ft to 600Ft) is the **Ósfehérvár** restaurant (Táncsics Mihály utca 1), opposite the Garden of Ruins. The **Ristorante Rinascimento** (Távírda utca 15) in the small Ferenc shopping mall claims to have 'real Italian food' and is open daily till midnight. The **Kaiser** pub (Távírda utca 14) is a good place for a cheap pizza (320Ft to 490Ft). There's a branch of Marxim (Megyház köz), the Budapest pizzeria chain with pizzas called Gulag, brÁVO and the like, just north of the bus station.

The popular **Vörösmarty** cake shop (Fő utca 6) is open daily till 9 pm.

Entertainment

You can buy tickets to cultural performances at the **Vörösmarty Theatre** (Fő utca 8), next to the Magyar Király hotel, from the box office (☎ 314 591) in the courtyard at Fő utca 3. It's open weekdays from 9 am to 5.30 pm.

CENTRAL TRANSDANUBIA

The wine to try in these parts is Ezerjó ('a thousand good things') from Mór, 27km to the north-west in Central Transdanubia's Vértes Hills. It's an acidic, greenish-white tipple that is light and fairly pleasant. You'll find it at the *Ezerjó (Országzászló tér 2)*, a *borozó* opposite the King Stephen Museum branch.

The *Kaiser* pub on Távírda utca is always a good place for a drink (it has a couple of pool tables in an adjoining room) as is the *Winner Drink Bar (Budai út 14)*, a student hang-out not far from the Rév hotel. The *John Bull* chain *(Petőfi utca 14)* has another one of its cookie-cutter pubs east of the bus station.

The *Bahnhof Fehérvár (Takaródó utca)* east of the train station revs (and raves) up at the weekend. Another popular place is the *West Side Music Club* at the *Flying Cat Irish Pub (Vörösmarty tér)* south-east of the bus station.

Getting There & Away

Bus Buses depart for Budapest, Veszprém and the vineyards near Mór at least once every 30 minutes, and you can reach Lake Velence towns like Pákozd, Sukoró, Velence and Gárdony (via Agárd) frequently throughout the day.

Other destinations from Székesfehérvár include Baja (two buses daily), Balatonfüred (six), Esztergom (two), Győr (seven or eight), Hévíz (two or three), Kalocsa (two), Kecskemét (two), Kaposvár (two), Keszthely (four), Pápa (two), Pécs (two to four), Siófok (seven), Sopron (two), Sümeg (five), Szeged (five), Szekszárd (five), Tapolca (four), Tata (four) and Zalaegerszeg (two).

Train Székesfehérvár is an important rail junction, and you can reach most destinations in Transdanubia from here. One line splits at Szabadbattyán some 10km to the south, leading to Lake Balaton's northern shore and Tapolca on one side of the lake and to the southern shore and Nagykanizsa on the other.

Trains every half-hour link Székesfehérvár with Budapest-Déli; another seven a day run to Szombathely via Veszprém. A local train runs north six to eight times a day to Mór and Komárom, where you cross over to Slovakia.

Getting Around

Bus No 26a will take you from the bus station to Bory Castle. Local taxis can be ordered on ☎ 222 222 or 343 343.

Southern Transdanubia

Southern Transdanubia (Dél-Dunántúl) is bordered by the Danube to the east, the Dráva River and Croatia to the south and west, and Lake Balaton to the north. It is generally flatter than Western and Central Transdanubia, with the Mecsek and Villány Hills rising in isolation from the plain, milder and considerably wetter.

Although there are some large towns here, Southern Transdanubia is not nearly as built-up or industrial as the rest of Transdanubia. In general, it is thickly settled with villages, mostly small in population. Agriculture is still the mainstay – from the fruit orchards of the Zselic region south of Kaposvár and the almonds of Pécs to the wines of Szekszárd and the Villány-Siklós region.

Southern Transdanubia was settled by the Celts and then the Romans, who built important towns at Alisca (Szekszárd) and Sophianae (Pécs) and introduced grape-growing. The north-south trade route passed through here, and many of the settlements prospered during the Middle Ages.

The region was a focal point of the Turkish occupation. The battle that led to the Ottoman domination of Hungary for more than a century and a half was fought at Mohács in 1526, and one of the most heroic stands taken by the Hungarians against the invaders took place at Szigetvár some 40 years later. Pécs was an important political and cultural centre under the Turks.

Late in the 17th century, the abandoned towns of Southern Transdanubia were resettled by Swabian Germans and Southern Slavs, and after WWII ethnic Hungarians came from Slovakia and Bukovina in Romania as did Saxon Germans. They left a mark that can still be seen and felt today in local architecture, food and certain traditions.

This part of Transdanubia has a lot to offer travellers – from the art museums of Pécs and the castles of Siklós and Szigetvár to the thermal spas of Harkány and Zalakaros. Driving through the countryside is like stepping back in time: whitewashed

HIGHLIGHTS

- The Zsolnay and Csontváry museums and the old synagogue in Pécs
- The wines of Villány and the wine cellars of Villánykövesd
- A ride on the narrow-gauge train through the Gemenc Forest in the Sárköz region
- The Castle Museum's collection of gloves, fans and umbrellas at Siklós
- A performance at Kaposvár's splendid Gergely Csiky Theatre
- The outdoor folk village museum at Szenna

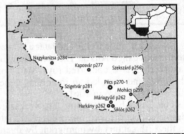

farmhouses with thatched roofs and long colonnaded porticoes decorated with floral patterns and plaster work haven't changed in centuries.

SZEKSZÁRD
☎74 • postcode 7100 • pop 38,800

Szekszárd lies south of the Sió River, which links Lake Balaton with the Danube, among seven of the Szekszárd Hills. It is the capital of Tolna County and the centre of the Sárköz folk region, but more than anything else Szekszárd is the gateway to Southern Transdanubia. In fact, you can actually see the region start in the town's main square (Garay tér), where the Great Plain, having crossed the Danube, rises slowly, transforming into the Szekszárd Hills.

SOUTHERN TRANSDANUBIA

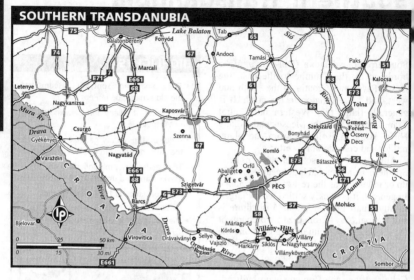

Szekszárd was a Celtic and later a Roman settlement called Alisca. The sixth Hungarian king, Béla I, conferred royal status on the town and founded an important Benedictine abbey here in 1061.

The Turkish occupation left Szekszárd desolated, but the area was repopulated late in the 17th century by immigrant Swabians from Germany, and the economy was revitalised in the next century by wheat cultivation and viticulture. For more information on Szekszárd's fabulous reds, see the Wines of Hungary special section in the Facts for the Visitor chapter.

Orientation & Information

The bus and train stations are opposite one another on Pollack Mihály utca. From here, follow pedestrian Bajcsy-Zsilinszky utca west through the park to the city centre. Garay tér ascends to the old castle district, today's Béla tér. Munkácsy Mihály utca runs south-west from Béla tér to Kálvária utca and Calvary Hill.

The helpful Tolna Tourist office (☎ 312 144), Széchenyi utca 38, is open from 8 am to 4.30 pm Monday to Thursday, to 4 pm on Friday and till noon on Saturday. Ibusz

(☎ 319 822), Széchenyi utca 20, keeps the same hours.

There's an OTP bank at Mártírok tere 5-7 and a K&H bank at Széchenyi utca 34. The main post office is at Széchenyi utca 11-13.

Things to See

You can get a good overview of Szekszárd by following Kálvária utca from outside the Alisca hotel and up the grassy steps to 205m **Calvary Hill** (Kálvária-hegy). The hill's name recalls the crucifixion scene and chapel erected here by grief-stricken parents who had lost their child in the 18th century (still remembered thanks to a famous poem by Mihály Babits, a native son of Szekszárd). The Danube and the Great Plain are visible to the east, the Sárköz region beyond the hills to the south, the Szekszárd Hills to the west and, on a clear day, you can just see the nuclear power station at Paks, 30km to the north.

The little village – the so-called Upper Town (Felsőváros) – in the valley to the north-west is full of vineyards and private cellars. Walk along Remete utca to **Remete Chapel** (Remeta kápolna; 1778) at the end, an important pilgrimage site, and return via Bethlen Gábor utca to the north of Szekszárd Stream.

The neoclassical **County Hall** (vármegyeháza) in Béla tér, designed by Mihály Pollack in 1828, sits on the site of Béla's abbey and an earlier Christian chapel; you can see the excavated foundations in the central courtyard. On the upper floor of the building, there is the **Franz Liszt Exhibition** and across the hall the **Eszter Mattioni Gallery**, whose works in striking mosaics of marble, glass and mother-of-pearl invoke peasant themes with a twist. Both are open 9 am to 5 pm Tuesday to Saturday from April to October, till 3 pm the rest of the year (80Ft). The square's baroque yellow **Inner City Catholic Church** (Belvárosi templom; 1805) is the largest single-nave church in Hungary.

The **Mór Wosinszky Museum** at Mártírok tere 26 was purpose-built in 1895 and is now named after a local priest and archaeologist who discovered the remains of a Neolithic culture at the town of Lengyel to the northwest. The finds, artefacts left by various peoples who passed through the Danube Basin ahead of the Magyars, are among the best anywhere (don't miss the fine Celtic and Avar jewellery), as is the large folk collection of Serbian, Swabian and Sárköz artefacts. Three period rooms – that of a well-to-do Sárköz farming family and their coveted spotted-poplar furniture, another from the estate of the aristocratic Apponyi family of Lengyel, and a poor gooseherd's hut – illustrate very clearly the different economic brackets that existed side by side in the region a century ago. Also interesting are the exhibits relating to the silk factory that was started in Szekszárd in the 19th century with Italian help.

The Moorish flourishes of the **House of Arts** (Művészetek Háza), behind the museum at Mártírok tere 28, reveal its former life as a synagogue. It is now used as a gallery and concert hall and opens from 10 am to 6 pm Tuesday to Friday. Four of its original iron pillars have been brought outside and enclosed in an arch, suggesting the tablets of the 10 Commandments, and

there's a striking 'tree of life' monument a short distance south to 'Szekszárd's heroes and victims of WWII'.

Franz Liszt performed several times at the pink neo-Gothic **Augusz House**, Széchenyi utca 36-40; today it houses a music school and Tolna Tourist.

Szekszárd produced two of Hungary's most celebrated poets: Mihály Babits (1883-1941) and the lesser-known János Garay. The **Mihály Babits' Birthplace** (szülőháza), Babits Mihály utca 13, has been turned into a memorial museum. Although the poet's avant-garde, deeply philosophical verse may be obscure, even in Hungarian, it's a good chance to see how a middle-class family lived in 19th-century provincial Hungary. It's open 9 am to 5 pm Tuesday to Sunday from April to October and till 3 pm Tuesday to Saturday the rest of the year.

Activities

The covered thermal baths and outdoor pools (200/110Ft) are near the train and bus stations at Toldi utca 6. The pools are open from 9 am to 6 pm daily from May to August, the baths weekdays from 6 am to 8 pm (from 2 pm on Monday) all year.

The **Zöldfa pension** (☎ 311 911) at Siótorok-Árvízkapu 1, some 16km southeast of Szekszárd, has horses for hire but the real centre for horse riding in these parts is **Sütvény** (☎ 439 133), a riding hotel some 50km to the north-west, at Felszabadulás utca 42 in Dalmand.

Unlike the wine-producing towns of Eger, Tokaj and even little Villány, Szekszárd has few places in which to sample the local vintage. The best venue is the Aliscavin outlet on Garay tér, opposite the Szász pub (see Entertainment), with some of Szekszárd's best wines for tasting and for sale. It's open from 10 am to 6 pm weekdays, from 8 am to 2 pm on Saturday and from 8 am till noon on Sunday.

Special Events

Among the big events staged annually in Szekszárd are the Alisca Wine Days (Alisca Bor Napok) in mid-June, choral

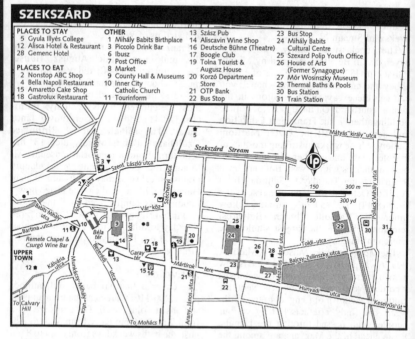

SZEKSZÁRD

PLACES TO STAY
5 Gyula Illyés College
12 Alisca Hotel & Restaurant
28 Gemenc Hotel

PLACES TO EAT
2 Nonstop ABC Shop
4 Bella Napoli Restaurant
15 Amaretto Cake Shop
18 Gastrolux Restaurant

OTHER
1 Mihály Babits Birthplace
3 Piccolo Drink Bar
6 Ibusz
7 Post Office
8 Market
9 County Hall & Museums
10 Inner City
    Catholic Church
11 Tourinform

13 Szász Pub
14 Aliscavin Wine Shop
16 Deutsche Bühne (Theatre)
17 Boogie Club
19 Tolna Tourist &
    Augusz House
20 Korzó Department
    Store
21 OTP Bank
22 Bus Stop

23 Bus Stop
24 Mihály Babits
    Cultural Centre
25 Szexard Polip Youth Office
26 House of Arts
    (Former Synagogue)
27 Mór Wosinszky Museum
29 Thermal Baths & Pools
30 Bus Station
31 Train Station

gatherings in May and September, the Danube Folklore Festival (Dunai Folklórfesztivál, jointly sponsored with Kalocsa and Baja in July, and the Szekszárd Vintage Festival (Szekszárdi Szüreti Fesztivál) in late September.

Places to Stay

There are usually dormitory rooms available in July and August for 1000Ft per person at the **Gyula Illyés College** (☎ 412 133, Mátyás király utca 3) north of the centre, and Tolna Tourist has **private rooms** for 1200Ft to 1600Ft per person.

The 19-room **Alisca** hotel (☎ 312 228, fax 311 242, Kálvária utca 1) has singles/doubles with bath for 6100/8200Ft. It's a pleasant place up in the hills, with almost a country feel to it.

The 91-room **Gemenc** hotel (☎ 311 722, fax 311 335, Mészáros Lázár utca 1), in an ugly but centrally located block house, has all the usual outlets – restaurant, coffee

shop, nightclub, etc. Singles are DM40 to DM60, doubles DM50 to DM80, depending on the season. There is also a floor of basic rooms with three beds costing DM30 (or DM10 per person).

Places to Eat

The **Gastrolux** pub-restaurant (Garay tér) is a dreary place but central and open till midnight. The **Bella Napoli** (Szent László utca), in a small shopping centre north-west of Garay tér, is decent for pasta and pizzas and stays open to 10.30 or 11 pm Monday to Saturday. The restaurant at the **Alisca** hotel has a lovely outside terrace open in the warmer months, with views of the city. Try the ice cream at the **Amaretto** cake shop (Garay tér 6); it's the best in town.

Food supplies can be bought from a large **market** in Piac tér along Vár köz just down the steps from Béla tér. The **ABC** shop (Flórián utca 4) north of Béla tér is open round the clock.

Entertainment

The modern *Mihály Babits Cultural Centre* (☎ *316 722, Mártírok tere 10*) has information about concerts and other cultural events taking place in the county hall courtyard, the New City Church (Újváros templom) on Pázmány tér and the House of Arts. For alternative culture, contact the 'Szexard' Polip youth office (☎ 315 022) in the same building, to the rear, open from 1 to 6 pm Monday to Saturday.

For a quiet drink, choose the *Piccolo Drink Bar (Fürdőház utca 3)* or, better yet, the more central *Szász (Garay tér 20)*, the 'Saxon' pub just a few metres west of the Romantic-style Deutsche Bühne (Német Színház in Hungarian), Garay tér 4, a German theatre dating from the early 20th century and still staging performances. The most central place for an evening out is *Boogie Club (Garay tér)*, which is next door to the Gastrolux restaurant and open from 8 pm to 4 am Thursday to Saturday.

Getting There & Away

Bus There are between nine and a dozen daily departures to Budapest, Baja, Dombóvár, Paks and Pécs, and at least six buses leave every day for Decs, Tamási, Siófok, Mohács and Harkány (via Pécs). From Szekszárd you can also reach Székesfehérvár (five buses a day), Kecskemét (two or three), Balatonfüred (two), Kaposvár (two), Szeged (three), Győr (two) and Veszprém (four). Some of these buses can be boarded on Mártírok tere south of the cultural centre.

Buses bound for Keselyűs (between four and five daily) will drop you off near the Gemenc Excursion Centre in Bárányfok.

Train Only a couple of direct trains leave Budapest-Déli station every day for Szekszárd. Otherwise, take the Pécs-bound train from the same station and change at Sárbogárd. To travel east (eg to Baja), west (to Kaposvár) or south (to Pécs), you must change trains at Bátaszék, 20km to the south. Őcsény and Decs, 4km and 8km to the south respectively, are on the train line to Bátaszék.

Getting Around

Bus No 1 goes from the stations through the centre of town to Béla tér and then on to the Upper Town as far as Remete Chapel. Local taxis can be ordered on ☎ 316 033 or ☎ 411 111.

AROUND SZEKSZÁRD
Gemenc Forest

The Gemenc, an 18,000-hectare flood forest of poplars, willows, oxbow lakes and dikes 12km east of Szekszárd, is now part of the Danube-Drava National Park. Until engineers removed some 60 curves in the Danube in the mid-19th century, the Gemenc would flood to such a degree that the women of the Sárköz region would come to the market in Szekszárd by boat. Under the old regime, it was the favourite hunting ground of former Communist leaders, who came here to shoot its famous red deer.

Today the backwaters, lakes and ponds beyond the earthen dams, which were built by wealthy landowners to protect their farms, offer sanctuary to red deer, boar, black storks, herons and woodpeckers. Hunting is restricted to certain areas, and you can visit the forest all year, but not on foot.

The main entrance is at the **Gemenc Excursion Centre** (☎ 312 552) in Bárányfok, about halfway down Keselyűsi út between Szekszárd and the forest. It's open from 10 am to 5 pm, daily. Keselyűsi út was once the longest stretch of covered highway in the Austro-Hungarian Empire, and in the late 19th century mulberry trees were planted along it to feed the worms at the silk factory in Szekszárd.

A **narrow-gauge train**, which once carried wood out of the Gemenc, is a fun – but difficult – way to go; all in all, it's probably easier to organise a tour of the forest through Tolna Tourist in Szekszárd (see Orientation and Information in that section). The train runs from Bárányfok to Pörböly, some 30km to the south (see the Around Baja section in the Great Plain chapter), once a day at 3.35 pm from May to October; two others – at 10.30 am and 1.30 pm – go only as far as the Gemenc

Delta (19km) before turning around. The abridged trip in itself is worthwhile, weaving and looping around the Danube's remaining bends, but make sure you double-check the times with Tolna Tourist in Szekszárd or with the train station at Pörböly (☎ 491 483) before you set out.

Near the centre, an ornate wooden hall, built without nails for Archduke Franz Ferdinand to house his hunting trophies in the late 19th century, until recently contained the Trophy Museum. But it has now been closed, awaiting its next incarnation. The hall was exhibited at the 1896 Millenary Exhibition in Budapest and is now in its fourth location – most recently reassembled from Mártírok tere in Szekszárd by Polish labourers who – this is *not* a Polish joke – used nails. The *Trófea* is a csárda-style restaurant near the entrance to the centre and opens daily till 10 pm. See the Szekszárd Getting There & Away section for information on transport.

Sárköz Region

The folkloric region of Sárköz, consisting of five towns south-east of Szekszárd between route No 56 and the Danube, is the centre of folk weaving in Hungary. **Öcsény** is the largest town, but for the visitor the most interesting is **Decs**, with its high-walled cottages, late Gothic Calvinist church and folk houses.

The Sárköz became a very rich area after flooding was brought under control in the mid-19th century. In a bid to protect their wealth and land, most families limited themselves to having one child and, judging from the displays at the **Regional Museum** (Tájmúzeum), in a peasant house at Kossuth utca 34-36 in Decs, they spent a lot of their money on lavish interior decoration and some of the most ornate (and Balkan-looking) embroidered folk clothing in Hungary. The house was built in 1836 of earth and woven twigs so that when the floods came only the mud had to be replaced; check out the ingenious porcelain 'stove with eyes' (concave circles) to radiate more heat. The museum is open from 9 am to 4 pm Tuesday to Sunday.

Traditions Alive!

The isolation of areas like the Sárköz region near Szekszárd and the Ormánság region south of Szigetvár – places 'somewhere behind the back of God', as the Hungarians call them – helped preserve folk customs and crafts not found elsewhere in Hungary.

In the Sárköz, be on the lookout for local pottery decorated with birds, the distinctive black and red striped woven fabric so common that it was once used as mosquito netting in this bug-infested region and the unique *írókázás fazékok*, 'inscribed pots' usually made as wedding gifts.

In the Ormánság, shepherds have always been famed for the everyday items they'd carve from horn or wood, including crooks, pocket mirror frames and shaving kits. The oaken trousseau chests made to hold the distinctive Ormánság bride's brocaded skirts and 'butterfly' head-dresses, and decorated with geometrical shapes are unique and superior to the 'tulip chests' (*tulipán láda*) found in prosperous peasant houses elsewhere in Hungary.

The *Görönd Presszó*, on the museum grounds, which serves drinks, sandwiches and snacks, closes at 10 pm. The church nearby has inscriptions dating from 1516. In August mock Sárköz-style weddings are staged at the Village House (Faluház; ☎ 495 040 for information) on Ady Endre utca. See the Szekszárd Getting There & Away section for information on transport.

MOHÁCS

☎ 69 • postcode 7700 • pop 20,300

The defeat of the Hungarian army by the Turks here on 29 August 1526 was a watershed in the nation's history. With it came partition and foreign domination that would last almost five centuries. It is not hyperbole to say that the effects of the battle at Mohács can still be felt in Hungary today.

Mohács is a sleepy little port on the Danube that wakes up only during the annual Busójárás festival, which is a pre-Lenten free-for-all late in February or March. The town is also a convenient gateway to Croatia and beaches of the Adriatic, with the border crossing at Udvar some 12km to the south.

Orientation & Information

The centre of Mohács lies on the west bank of the Danube; residential New Mohács (Újmohács) is on the opposite side. Szabadság utca, the main street, runs west from the river, beginning and ending with large war memorials in decay.

The bus station is on Rákóczi utca, south of leafy Deák tér. Catch trains about 1.5km north of the city centre near the Strandfürdő at the end of Bajcsy-Zsilinszky utca.

Mecsek Tours (☎/fax 511 024) at the Csele hotel, Szent Mihály tér 6-7, is open from 8 am to 4.30 pm on weekdays only. Ibusz (☎/fax 311 531), Szabadság utca 4-6, keeps the same hours.

You'll find an OTP bank branch at Jókai Mór utca 1 and a K&H bank at Szabadság utca 23, at the corner with Rákóczi utca.

The post office is in the southern wing of the Moorish Town Hall at Széchenyi tér 2.

Mohács Historical Memorial Site

The Mohács Historical Memorial Site (Mohácsi Történelmi Emlékhely), west of route No 56 at Sátorhely (literally 'encampment') about 6km south-west of Mohács, was opened in 1976 to mark the 450th anniversary of the battle. It's a fitting memorial to the dead: over 100 carved wooden markers in the shape of bows, arrows, lances and heads lean this way and that over a common grave that was only discovered in the early 1970s. Above the entrance, a carved sign proclaims: 'Here began the deterioration of a strong Hungary.' The memorial site is open from 9 am to 5 pm Tuesday to Sunday from April to October (200/120Ft).

Dorottya Kanizsai Museum

This museum, named after the heroic noblewoman from Siklós who presided over the

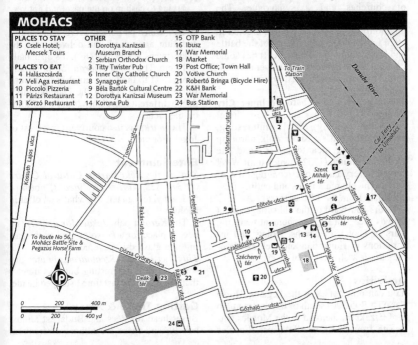

MOHÁCS

PLACES TO STAY	OTHER	15 OTP Bank
5 Csele Hotel;	1 Dorottya Kanizsai	16 Ibusz
Mecsek Tours	Museum Branch	17 War Memorial
	2 Serbian Orthodox Church	18 Market
PLACES TO EAT	3 Titty Twister Pub	19 Post Office; Town Hall
4 Halászcsárda	6 Inner City Catholic Church	20 Votive Church
7 Veli Aga restaurant	8 Synagogue	21 Robertó Bringa (Bicycle Hire)
10 Piccolo Pizzeria	9 Béla Bartók Cultural Centre	22 K&H Bank
11 Párizs Restaurant	12 Dorottya Kanizsai Museum	23 War Memorial
13 Korzó Restaurant	14 Korona Pub	24 Bus Station

burial of the dead after the battle at Mohács, has two branches. Both are open from 10 am to 5 pm Tuesday to Saturday from April to October and from 10 am to 4 pm on the same days the rest of the year (40/20Ft).

The smaller branch at Szerb utca 2 next to the Serbian Orthodox church is devoted entirely to the 1526 battle and is a well balanced exhibit, with both the Turks and the Hungarians getting the chance to tell their side of the story. The museum's other branch, next to the town hall at Városház utca 1, has a large collection of costumes worn by the Sokác, Slovenes, Serbs, Croats, Bosnians and Swabians who repopulated this devastated area in the 17th century. The distinctive (and, to some, ugly) grey-black pottery of Mohács and the various devil's or ram's-head masks worn at the Busójárás carnival are also on display.

Other Attractions

The city's other sights amount to a handful of churches and a synagogue. The Byzantine-style **Votive Church** (Fogadalmi templom) on Széchenyi tér was erected in 1926 for the 400th anniversary of the battle and looks not unlike a mosque. It has some contemporary frescoes of the event and inspired modern stained-glass windows in its large dome.

The pulpit in the baroque **Inner City Church** (1776) near the Csele hotel on Szent Mihály tér is interesting, and from here it's a short walk north up Szentháromság utca to No 33 and the **Orthodox church** (1732), which until WWI served a very large local congregation of Serbs. The church's icons and ceiling frescoes date from the 18th century.

In the courtyard of the old **synagogue** at Eötvös utca 1, a large monument featuring stars of David, menorahs, tablets and inscriptions in Hungarian and Hebrew, honours the Jewish victims of fascism.

Activities

You can rent horses at the Pegazus Horse Farm (☎ 305 500) south of the centre at No 2 of Eszéki út, the road to the Mohács battle site, from mid-June till August. Bicycles

are available for hire from a shop called Robertó Bringa, Szabadság utca 21.

Places to Stay

See Mecsek Tours or Ibusz about *private rooms* or head for the only hotel in town: the modern, 49-room *Csele* (☎ 511 825, fax 511 023, Szent Mihály tér 6-7) fronting the Danube. Singles here are 3900Ft to 5900Ft and doubles 5400Ft to 8600Ft, depending on the season and the view. All rooms have a bath; choose one of the riverside ones with a balcony on the 2nd floor.

Places to Eat

The *Párizs* (Szabadság utca 20) is an ordinary Hungarian restaurant that stands out only for its night-time music. The *Korzó* (Szabadság utca 11), with outside seating on a pedestrians-only street, is a much better choice. The *Piccolo* (Szabadság utca 24) in a small courtyard is an upbeat, friendly pizzeria open till 11 pm.

Trying to cash in on the past (and not very successfully) is the *Veli Aga* (Szentháromság utca 7), which purports to serve 'real Turkish and Hungarian food' but delivers only the latter (mains: 600Ft to 700Ft). It's open daily to 11 pm. The *Halászcsárda* (Szent Mihály tér 5) next to the Csele hotel has a beautiful terrace overlooking the Danube and a dozen different fish dishes (600Ft to 700Ft) on the menu.

The *market* is in a courtyard just west of Jókai Mór utca.

Entertainment

Staff at the *Béla Bartók Cultural Centre* (☎ 311 828, Vörösmarty utca 3) north of Széchenyi tér can tell you what's on offer in Mohács.

The *Korona* pub (Jókai Mór utca 2) is a decent place for a *korso* or two, with seating in a glassed-in pavement pavilion. The *Titty Twister* pub (Szentháromság utca 30) sounded, well, interesting but was quieter than the grave the last time I stepped inside.

Getting There & Away

Buses head for Pécs and Budapest almost hourly, and there are almost as frequent departures to Villány, Siklós, the spa at Harkány and Bátaszék. Other destinations include: Baja (up to 12 buses a day), Békéscsaba (one), Kaposvár (one), Kalocsa (one at the weekend), Kecskemét via Baja (two), Szeged (seven), Szekszárd (six) and Székesfehérvár (one).

Mohács is linked by rail with Villány and Pécs (up to eight departures a day), but to get anywhere else, the bus is the best – indeed, often the only – option.

Getting Around

Buses headed for any of the following towns will let you off at the Mohács battle site: Nagynyárád, Majs, Lippó, Bezedek and Magyarbóly. A year-round car ferry links Szent Mihály tér south of the Csele hotel with residential New Mohács – and the start of the Great Plain – across the Danube to the east. The trip takes only a few minutes.

Local taxis can be ordered on ☎ 303 303 or 300 900.

SIKLÓS

☎ 72 • postcode 7800 • pop 10,600
Until very recently, the medieval fortress in Siklós, Hungary's southernmost town, was the longest continuously inhabited castle in the country. But Siklós hardly needs superlatives to delight. Protected from the north, east and west by the Villány Hills, Siklós has been making wine (mostly whites) since the Romans settled here at a place they called Seres. Siklós is also close to Villány (in competition with Szekszárd for producing Hungary's best red wines) and the spa centre at Harkány. Today the town is a favourite destination for shoppers south of the border, and you'll see almost as much Croatian as you will Hungarian.

Orientation & Information

The town centre of Siklós runs from the bus station on Szent István tér along Felszabadulás utca to Kossuth tér. Siklós Castle stands watch over the town from the hill to the west. The main train station is north-east of Kossuth tér at the end of Táncsics Mihály utca. The town's other train station, Siklósi-szőlők, north-west of the centre on the road to Máriagyűd, is more convenient to the bus station.

Siklos can claim the dubious distinction of being one of the few towns in Hungary without a tourist information office; wait till you get to Harkány or rely on the kindness of the staff at the Castle Museum. There's also an OTP bank branch at Felszabadulás utca 60-62 and a K&H bank at No 46-48 of the same street. The post office, with pretty folkloric motifs in front, is at Flórián tér 1.

Siklós Castle

Though the original foundations of Siklós Castle date from the mid-13th century, what you see when you look up from the town is an 18th-century baroque palace girdled by 15th-century walls and bastions. The castle has changed hands many times since it was built by the Siklósi family. Its most famous occupant was the reformer Count Kázmér Batthyány (1807-54), among the first of the nobility to free his serfs. He joined the independence struggle of 1848 and was named foreign minister by Lajos Kossuth at Debrecen.

Walk to the castle either from Kossuth tér via Batthyány Kázmér utca or up Váralja from Szent István tér near the bus station. The drawbridge leads to the entrance at the **barbican**, which is topped with loopholes and a circular lookout. You can also explore the castle and enjoy some fine views of the Villány Hills from along the promenade linking the four mostly derelict towers.

The three-storey palace in the central courtyard housed a hotel and a hostel in three of its wings until 1993; the **Castle Museum** (Vármúzeum) is in the south wing. To the right as you enter the main door is an unusual exhibit devoted to the manufacture and changing styles of gloves, fans and umbrellas since the Middle Ages, with much emphasis on the Hamerli and Hunor factories at Pécs, which produced some of Europe's finest kid gloves in the 19th century. The **cellar** contains barely recognisable stone fragments from Roman, Gothic and Renaissance times. Most of the 1st floor is

SIKLÓS, MÁRIAGYŰD & HARKÁNY

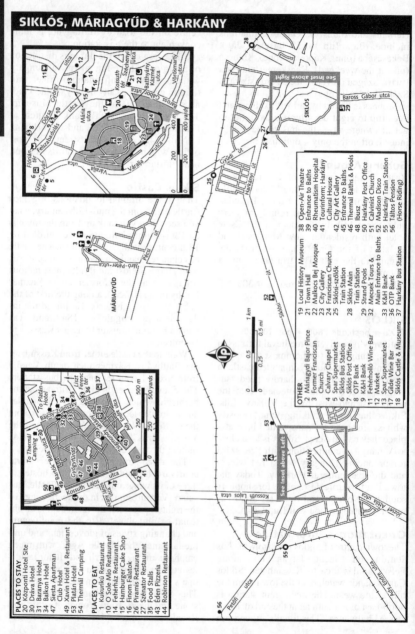

PLACES TO STAY
20 Központi Hotel Site
30 Dráva Hotel
31 Baranya Hotel
34 Balkon Hotel
47 Siesta Apartman
   Club Hotel
49 Xavin Hotel & Restaurant
53 Platán Hotel
54 Thermál Camping

PLACES TO EAT
1 Kukurikú Restaurant
10 O Sole Mio Restaurant
14 Fehérház Restaurant
15 Hamburger Cake Shop
16 Finom Falatok
26 Piramis Restaurant
27 Szénator Restaurant
35 Food Stalls
43 Éden Pizzeria
44 Robinson Restaurant

OTHER
2 Máriagydi Bajor Pince
3 Former Franciscan
   Church
4 Calvary Chapel
5 Spar Supermarket
6 Siklós Bus Station
7 Siklós Post Office
8 OTP Bank
9 K&H Bank
11 Fehérholló Wine Bar
12 Market
13 Spar Supermarket
17 Glide Wine Bar
18 Siklós Castle & Museums
19 Local History Museum
21 Town Hall
22 Malkocs Bej Mosque
23 City Gallery
24 Franciscan Church
25 Siklósi-szőlők
   Train Station
28 Siklós Main
   Train Station
29 Strand Pools
32 Mecsek Tours &
   Main Entrance to Baths
33 K&H Bank
36 OTP Bank
37 Harkány Bus Station
38 Open-Air Theatre
39 Entrance to Baths
40 Rheumatism Hospital
41 Tourinform; Harkány
   Cultural House
42 City Art Gallery
45 Entrance to Baths
46 Thermal Baths & Pools
48 Ibusz
50 Harkány Post Office
51 Calvinist Church
52 Madison Disco
55 Harkány Train Station
56 Táltos Pension
   (Horse Riding)

now a modern art gallery, but don't miss the wonderful **Sigismund Hall** (Zsigmond-terem) with its Renaissance fireplace and star-vaulted, enclosed balcony.

To the right of the museum entrance, two doors lead to the dark and spooky **cells** – a real dungeon if ever there was one. The walls are several metres thick, and up to five grilles on the window slits discouraged would-be escapers. Woodcuts on the walls of the upper dungeon explain how various torture devices were put to use. After this, the Gothic **chapel** is a vision of heaven itself, with its brilliant arched windows behind the altar, web vaulting on the ceiling and 15th-century frescoed niches.

The castle and its exhibits are open from 9 am to 6 pm Tuesday to Sunday from mid-April to mid-October and to 4 pm the rest of the year (90/60Ft).

Other Attractions

The **Franciscan church** south of the castle, but still within its walls, on Vajda János tér is 15th-century Gothic, but you'd hardly know it from the outside. The Franciscan cloister at No 4 is now the **City Gallery** (Városi Galéria), with revolving exhibits, mostly dealing with ceramics (open 10 am to 4 pm daily, 50/25Ft). At No 6 of the same square, the small **Local History Museum** (Helytörténeti Múzeum) contains exhibits on the history of Siklós, folk art and agriculture. It is open from 10 am to 4 pm Tuesday to Sunday from mid-April to mid-October (40/20Ft).

If you walk down Batthyány Kázmér utca past the little statue of the heroic Dorottya Kanizsai (see the Mohács section), you'll come to the 16th-century **Malkocs Bej Mosque** (Malkocs bej dzsámija) at Kossuth tér 15. Now beautifully restored, the mosque houses temporary exhibits (open 9 am to 5 pm Tuesday to Sunday from mid-April to mid-October, 40/20Ft).

The busy **market**, with everything from knock-off jeans and trainers to čevapčiči (spicy Balkan meatballs) is south of Dózsa György utca behind the Spar supermarket on Mária utca.

Activities

The pools at the Strandfürdő at Baross Gábor utca 2 are open from 10 am to 6 pm early June to August.

Places to Stay & Eat

With the Központi hotel on Kossuth Lajos tér undergoing extensive renovations, Siklos can also boast being one of the few towns in the country with no real hotel, though you will see quite a few houses advertising *private rooms* along Harkány út north-west of the centre. Otherwise, make Siklós a side trip from Harkány, 6km to the west, or book a private room through one of the agencies there.

Places for a quick bite include the stand-up *Finom Falatok* (Felszabadulás utca 16), open from 8 am to 4 pm weekdays and till 1 pm on Saturday, and *O Sole Mio* (Dósza György utca 2d), in a courtyard that also can be accessed from Felszabadulás utca 44, with pizzas and simple pastas. For something close to the bus and train stations, try the *Szénator* (Felszabadulás utca 65a), a small place with pleasant service that stays open till 10 pm, or the nearby *Piramis* pub-restaurant (Felszabadulás utca 69), which stays open till 10 pm Monday to Thursday and till midnight Friday and Saturday. The *Fehérház* restaurant is across the road from the market.

The *Hamburger* cake shop (Felszabadulás utca 22) serves delicious sweet things, despite its savoury name.

Entertainment

You should really save the wine tasting for Villány and the cellars at Villánykövesd, but if you want to sample a glass here, try the little *borozó* (wine bar) in the castle courtyard, the divey *Gilde* (Felszabadulás utca 7) near Kossuth tér open till midnight, or the *Fehérholló* (Szabadság utca 7), north of the market which stays open till 10 pm.

The *Madison*, halfway between Siklós and Harkány, about 3km west of Siklós, is a more popular disco.

Getting There & Away

Generally you won't wait more than 30 minutes for buses to Pécs or Harkány (via

Máriagyűd); hourly buses leave for Máriagyűd and Villány. For Mohács, count on between four and nine buses a day. Other destinations include Budapest and Székesfehérvár (one bus each daily), Szigetvár (one to three), Szekszárd (three or four) and Sellye (up to four).

Trains link Siklós with Villány (change here for Mohács or Pécs), Máriagyűd, Harkány, Sellye and Barcs. But trains are infrequent, and only four of them run the full line.

AROUND SIKLÓS
Máriagyűd
☎ 72 • postcode 7818

The erstwhile **Franciscan church** in this village at the foot of 408m-high Mt Tenkes, north-west of Siklós, has been a place of pilgrimage for 800 years, and you can make your own by walking (or hopping on a Máriagyűd or Harkány-bound bus) for about 3km along Gyűdi út and Pécs út and turning north on Járó Péter utca when the church's two towers come into view. The chance to sample some of Siklós' white wines here is also an attraction.

Máriagyűd was on the old trade route between Pécs and Eszék (now Osijek in Croatia), and a church has stood here since the mid-12th century. Today's church is a large 18th-century affair with modern frescoes on the ceiling, baroque painted altars, some beautifully carved pews and the main object of devotion: Mary and the Christ Child in gold and silver over the main altar. The most interesting time to visit is on Sunday or on a *búcsú* (a patron's festival – the Virgin Mary has lots of them) when merchants set up their stalls beside the church (see boxed text 'Farewell to All That'). Mass is conducted in Hungarian in the church, but at the outdoor altar on the hill above it, just as many people attend German-language services, often with accompanying oompah band music. Large Stations of the Cross in Zsolnay porcelain line the way to the Zopf-style Calvary Chapel (Kálvária kápolna), a short distance up Mt Tenkes.

There are a couple of places to sample wine in Máriagyűd, including the *Máriagyűdi Bajor Pince* in an old cellar in the square just below the church, as well as the *Kukurikú* restaurant (that's 'cock-a-doodle-doo' in Hungarian) in an old rectory. From here, you can start a 6km hike up and around Mt Tenkes.

HARKÁNY
☎ 72 • postcode 7815 • pop 3350

It's a wonder that no statue stands in honour of János Pogány in this spa town 6km west of Siklós and 26km south of Pécs. He was the poor peasant from Máriagyűd who cured himself of swollen joints early in the 19th century by soaking in a hot spring he had discovered here. The Batthyány family recognised the potential almost immediately, erecting bathing huts in 1824 near the 62°C spring, which has the richest sulphuric content in Hungary.

Of course, all that means crowds (well over 100,000 Hungarian, Croatian and Yugoslavian visitors in the high season), lángos and gyro stalls in spades and an all-pervasive stench of rotten eggs. But you might like it. People come to Harkány to socialise, and the town is on the western edge of the Villány-Siklós region, so there is plenty of wine about.

Orientation

Harkány is essentially the Gyógyfürdő, a 12-hectare green square filled with pools, fountains and walkways, and bordered by hotels and holiday homes of every description. The four streets defining the thermal complex are Bartók Béla utca to the north, Ady Endre to the south, Bajcsy-Zsilinszky utca (with most of the hotels) on the east, and Kossuth Lajos utca, with several restaurants, on the west. The bus station is on Bajcsy-Zsilinszky utca at the south-east corner of the park. The train station is to the north-west on Petőfi utca, which branches off from Kossuth Lajos utca.

Information

Tourinform (☎ 479 624, fax 479 989, @ harkany@tourinform.hu) has an office at the Harkány Cultural House, Kossuth Lajos utca 2, and is open 9 am to 7 pm Monday to

Saturday from mid-June to September and 9 am to 4 pm weekdays the rest of the year. The City Art Gallery is next door. Mecsek Tours (☎ 580 815, fax 479 045) is at the main entrance to the baths at Bajcsy-Zsilinszky utca 4, north of the bus station, while Ibusz (☎/fax 480 425068) is at Kossuth Lajos utca 40. These two offices are open from 9 am to 4 or 5 pm weekdays and till noon on Saturday in summer and from 9 am to 4 pm weekdays only the rest of the year.

K&H bank has a bureau de change at the main entrance to the spa; there's an OTP bank branch just north of the bus station on Bajcsy-Zsilinszky utca. The post office is at Kossuth Lajos utca 57.

Thermal Spa

The main entrance to the **thermal baths** (gyógyfürdő) and **outside pools**, which are meant to cure just about everything, is on Bajcsy-Zsilinszky utca. The baths complex is open from 9 am to 11 pm mid-June to August; during the rest of the year it keeps office hours – 9 am to 5 pm. The pools are open from 9 am to 7 pm daily (to 11 pm Friday to Sunday from mid-June to August). Services range from drinking cures and mud massage to the enticing 'wine foam bath', but it's a treat just to swim in the 38°C outdoor pool, especially in cool weather. Entrance to the pools costs 400/250Ft (250/150Ft after 2 pm) for adults/children and 1000/550Ft for the thermal baths.

Activities

You can ride horses or hire a coach at the Táltos pension (☎ 480 228) north-west of the centre at Széchenyi tér 30d, off Petőfi utca. Thermál Camping hires out bicycles from 8 am to 7 pm daily in summer.

Places to Stay

Camping Along with tent sites, *Thermál Camping* (☎ 580 814, Bajcsy-Zsilinszky utca 6), has a 20-room motel (DM20 to DM22 per double), a hotel with 26 rooms (DM31 to DM36) and two dozen bungalows with two double rooms and kitchen from DM48 to DM65. All are open between mid-April and mid-October.

Private Rooms Both Mecsek Tours and Ibusz have private rooms for about 2000Ft per person, but for a one-night stay you may be better off going to a hotel or investigating the possibilities yourself by strolling east on Bartók Béla utca, where *Zimmer frei* signs proliferate. A two/four-room apartment in one of the former holiday homes lining that street cost from DM30/60.

Hotels Harkány has an incredible array of hotels and pensions to suit all budgets though some have recently been renovated, including the *Baranya* hotel (☎ 480 245, fax 480 160, Bajcsy-Zsilinszky utca 5), which now occupies three buildings with a total of 80 rooms opposite the baths entrance. Singles/doubles are 4290/8580Ft.

The 71-room *Dráva* (☎ 580 810, fax 580 813, Bartók Béla utca 1), with 71 rooms in two buildings, is in a pretty park just short of the camp site. Doubles are DM50 to DM70, depending on the month and whether you've chosen building B or the superior building A. The 60-room *Platán* (☎/fax 480 411, Bartók Béla utca 15) is in two former trade union holiday houses to the east. Singles are 5330Ft to 6500Ft, doubles 7900Ft to 9360Ft, depending on the building.

The 49-room *Balkon* (☎ 480 049, fax 480 443, Bajcsy-Zsilinszky utca 2) is housed in an Art Deco sanatorium once used by Communist Party honchos. It has a certain charm and lovely grounds, but the clientele is composed almost entirely of pensioners on health cures. Singles/doubles are 3550/4440Ft or 5740Ft for a room for two with balcony.

The fanciest places to stay are on the west side of the spa park, including the 79-room *Siesta Apartman Club* (☎ 480 611, fax 480 302, ✉ schhotel@mail.matav.hu, Kossuth Lajos utca 17), with singles/doubles for DM60/80, and the pension-like *Xavin* (☎/fax 479 399, Kossuth Lajos utca 43) with singles/doubles for DM40/60.

Places to Eat

You're not going to starve or die of thirst in this town of sausage stands and wine kiosks, but if you want to sit down while eating, try the island-themed *Robinson (Kossuth Lajos utca 7)*, with pizza and other dishes. *Éden (Kossuth Lajos utca 12)*, in a beautiful pink Eclectic building across the street, serves pizzas till 11 pm from Tuesday to Sunday. The *Xavin* hotel (see Places to Stay) has a lovely silver-service restaurant.

For South Slav-style grills like čevapčiči and pleskavici, try the grill on the terrace of the renovated older building of the *Baranya* hotel.

Entertainment
The *Harkány Cultural House (Harkányi Művelődési Ház; ☎ 480 459, Kossuth Lajos utca 2a)* can tell you what's on but don't expect too much in the way of high-brow entertainment here.

Getting There & Away
Bus While buses depart once or twice an hour for Siklós and Pécs, other destinations are not so well served, with only one bus a day to Baja (June to September only), Kecskemét, Kalocsa (on Sunday), Sellye (weekdays), Veszprém, Szeged (June to August) and Székesfehérvár. Other destinations include Budapest (one bus a day), Szekszárd (one), Szigetvár and Máriagyűd (one or two each) and Mohács (up to three).

In summer, buses to Stuttgart via Munich leave Harkány on Thursday at 1.30 pm and arrive in the German city at 6.30 am on Friday. Buses also go to Frankfurt via Nuremberg at 1.30 pm on Sunday, arriving there at 8 am on Monday.

Train By rail from Harkány, you can reach Sellye and Barcs to the west (four to five a day) and Siklós and Villány to the east (six). Change at Villány for Mohács or Pécs.

Getting Around
For a local taxi, ring ☎ 480 435.

VILLÁNY
☎ 72 • postcode 7773 • pop 2900
Some 13km north-east of Siklós and dominated by cone-shaped Mt Szársomlyó (422m) to the west, Villány is a village of vineyards, vines and grapes. It was the site

in 1687 of what has become known as the 'second battle of Mohács', a ferocious confrontation in which the Turks got their comeuppance and were driven southward by the Hungarians and slaughtered in the Dráva marshes. Serbs and Swabians moved in after the Turkish occupation and viticulture resumed. Today, Villány is one of Hungary's principal producers of wine. For more information, see the Wines of Hungary special section in the Facts for the Visitor chapter.

You might consider visiting Villány (German: Wieland) during the September harvest, when the town is a beehive of activity: human chains pass buckets of almost black grapes from trucks to big machines that chew off the vines, reduce the fruit to a soggy mass and pump the must – the unfermented grape juice – into enormous casks.

Orientation & Information
Villány is essentially just one main street, Baross Gábor utca, and the bus stops in the centre of the village near the ABC supermarket and the town hall. The train station is about 1200m to the north on Ady Endre fasor, en route to Villánykövesd.

There's an OTP bank at Baross Gábor utca 27, and the post office is at No 35 of the same street next to the Oportó restaurant.

Wine Museum & Wine Tasting
The Wine Museum (Bormúzeum), housed in a 200-year-old tithe cellar at Bem József utca 8, has a collection of 19th-century wine-producing equipment, such as barrels, presses and hand corkers. Downstairs in the sand-covered cellars, Villány's celebrated wines age in enormous casks, and vintage bottles dating from 1895 to 1971 are kept in safes. It's open 9 am to 5 pm Tuesday to Sunday. There's a small shop at the entrance selling Villány and Siklós wines, some of them vintage and among the best labels available in Hungary. You can sample wines at the museum (650Ft to 1300Ft per person) and in many of the family cellars that line Baross Gábor utca, including Pólya at No 58, Költő at No 71, Szende at No 87 and Fritsch at No 97.

But the best place for tasting is in the cellars cut into the loess soil at **Villánykövesd** (German: Growisch), about 3.5km northwest of town along the road to Pécs. Cellars line the main street (Petőfi út) and the narrow lane (Pincesor) above it. Along the former, try the deep Polgár cellar at No 51 or the Nádrai & Tiffán one at No 56. On Pincesor, No 14-15 is the cellar of master vintner Imre Tiffán while Neumann is at No 18 and Blum at No 5. The cellars keep difficult hours, so it's a hit-or-miss proposition. For advice on what to try, see the Wines of Hungary special section in the Facts for the Visitor chapter.

Places to Stay & Eat

There are plenty of signs advertising *private rooms* in Villány, but don't miss the chance to stay at the eight-room *Gere* pension (*☎/fax 492 195, Diófás tér 4*), with doubles for 4800Ft to 6000Ft. They have more rooms in another location some 300m south at Fáy András utca 17. Should they be full, the six-room *Júlia* pension (*☎ 492 710, Baross Gábor utca 41*) is just down the road and charges 5600Ft for a double. If you really want to stay in the centre of the wine area, consider the 15-room *Cabernet* (*☎ 493 200, fax 493 222, Petőfi utca 29*) in Villánykövesd with rooms from 6720Ft to 8400Ft.

The *Oportó (Baross Gábor utca 33)* is a large, pleasant restaurant with a terrace near the town centre and close to where the bus lets you off. The intimate little restaurant at the *Julia* pension serves some of the best veal pörkölt in Hungary. Villány also has a simple *pizzeria (Baross Gábor utca 71a)* open daily till 11 pm.

The *Fülemüle Csárda (Nightingale Inn; Ady Endre fasor)*, a couple of hundred metres past the train station, is a good place to stop for a bite on your way to/from Villánykövesd.

Getting There & Away

There are infrequent buses to Pécs, Siklós, Harkány, Budapest, Mohács and Villánykövesd (five on weekdays, two on Saturday), but for most destinations, you must go to Siklós first. Trains run east to Mohács, west to Siklós and Harkány and north to Pécs.

ORMÁNSÁG REGION

About 30km west of Harkány, this plain was prone to flooding by the nearby Dráva River for centuries. That and the area's isolation is reflected in its unusual architecture, folk ways and distinct dialect. Couples in the Ormánság usually limited themselves to having just one child since, under the land-tenure system here, peasants were not allowed to enlarge their holdings. That's not the only reason why the area's 'footed' *talpás házak* are so small: these 'soled' houses were built on rollers so that they could be dragged to dry land in the event of flooding.

Sellye

☎ 73 • postcode 7960 • pop 3200

In Sellye, the 'capital' of the Ormánság region, a representative footed house of mortar, lime and a wooden frame sits behind the **Géza Kiss Ormánság Museum** located at Köztársaság tér 6. (Mátyás király utca, the main drag, is south-west of the bus station, and the train station is to the south-east on Vasút utca.) The house has the typical three rooms and some big differences: the parlour was actually lived in; the front room was a 'smoke kitchen' without a chimney; and to keep mosquitoes at bay, what few windows the house had were kept very small. The museum's rich collection contains Ormánság costumes and artefacts. The museum is open from 10 am to 4 pm Tuesday to Sunday from April to October and to 2 pm the rest of the year (50/30Ft).

There's an **arboretum** with rare trees and plants surrounding the Draskovich family mansion (now a school) behind the museum.

Other Ormánság Villages

The Calvinist church at **Drávaiványi**, with a colourful panelled ceiling and choir loft dating from the late 18th century, is 5km south-west of Sellye and can be reached by bus. **Vajszló**, another Ormánság village 11km south-east of Sellye with several footed houses, is on the same train line as

Sellye. Buses travel eastward from Vajszló to **Kórós**, whose folk-decorated Calvinist church (1795) is among the most beautiful in the region.

Getting There & Away

Harkány is the easiest starting point for any excursion into the Ormánság, but the area is also accessible by public transport from Szigetvár – in fact, it is actually closer to that city. However, the infrequent milk-run buses from Szigetvár take almost two hours to cover 25km (admittedly passing through some very attractive little villages), and if you catch the train, you must change at Szentlörinc. The train from Harkány to Vajszló and Sellye (five a day) involves no change and takes only an hour to 70 minutes. See Getting There & Away in the Harkány section for more information.

PÉCS

☎ 72 • postcode 7600 • pop 170,000

Blessed with a mild climate, an illustrious past and a number of fine museums and monuments, Pécs is one of the most pleasant cities to visit in Hungary. For those reasons and more, many travellers put it second to Budapest on their 'must-see' list.

Lying equidistant from the Danube to the east and the Dráva to the south on a plain sheltered from northern winds by the Mecsek Hills, Pécs enjoys an extended summer and is ideal for viticulture, fruit and nut growing, especially almonds. But for the visitor, the capital of Baranya County is more than anything else a 'town of art', beating Szentendre on the Danube Bend hands down.

History

The Romans may have settled in Pécs for the region's weather, fertile soil and abundant water, but more likely they were sold by the protection offered by the Mecsek Hills. They called their settlement Sophianae, and it quickly grew into the commercial and administrative centre of Lower Pannonia. The Romans brought Christianity with them, and reminders of it can be seen in the early clover-shaped chapels unearthed at several locations here.

Pécs' importance grew in the Middle Ages, when it was known as Quinque Ecclesiae after its five churches (it is still called Fünfkirchen in German). King Stephen founded a bishopric here in 1009, and the town was a major stop along the trade route to Byzantium. Pécs developed as an intellectual and humanist centre with the founding of a university – Hungary's first – in 1367. The 15th-century bishop Janus Pannonius, who wrote some of Europe's most celebrated Renaissance poetry in Latin, was based in Pécs.

The city was fortified with walls after the Mongol invasion of the early 13th century, but they were in such poor condition three centuries later that the Turks took the city with virtually no resistance in 1543. The Turks moved the local populace outside the walls and turned Pécs into their own administrative and cultural centre. When they were expelled almost 150 years later, Pécs was virtually abandoned, but still standing were monumental souvenirs that now count as the most important Turkish structures in the nation. The resumption of wine production by German and Bohemian immigrants and the discovery of coal in the 18th century spurred Pécs' development. The manufacture of luxury goods (gloves, Zsolnay porcelain, Pannonvin sparkling wine, Angster organs) as well as the exploitation of nearby uranium mines came later.

Orientation

The oval-shaped inner town, virtually all of it now pedestrians-only, has as its heart Széchenyi tér, where a dozen streets converge. One of these is Király utca, a promenade of restored shops, pubs and restaurants to the east. To the north-west lies Pécs' other important square, Dóm tér. Here you'll find the cathedral, several early Christian chapels and Káptalan utca, the 'street of museums'.

Pécs' train station is in Indóház tér – follow Jókai Mór utca north to reach the inner town. The bus station is close to the big market on Zólyom utca. Walk north along Bajcsy-Zsilinszky utca and Irgalmasok utcája to the centre.

Information

The helpful, knowledgeable staff at Tourinform (☎ 213 315, fax 212 632, ✉ baranya-m@tourinform.hu), Széchenyi tér 9, have copious amounts of information on Pécs and Baranya County. The office is open from 8 am to 5.30 pm weekdays and 9 am to 2 pm at the weekend from March to October and 8 am to 4 pm weekdays only the rest of the year. Mecsek Tours (☎ 212 044), Széchenyi tér 1, is another excellent source of information and is open from 9 am to 5 pm weekdays, to 1 pm on Saturday all year. Ibusz (☎ 212 157, fax 211 011), Apáca utca 1, is open from 9 am to 5 pm (4 pm on Fridays) weekdays only.

The main OTP bank is on Rákóczi út, and there's a branch on Kiraly utca and another ATM at the Pécs Cultural Centre, Széchenyi tér 1. M&M Exchange at Király utca 16 offers a decent rate and opens from 8 am to 3 pm and 3.30 to 10 pm Monday to Saturday and from noon to 8 pm on Sunday.

The main post office is at Jókai Mór utca 10, in a beautiful Art Nouveau building dating from 1904 (note the angels in relief writing, mailing and delivering the post). The Corvina Art Bookshop, in the Artists House (Művészetek Háza) at Széchenyi tér 7-8, has an excellent selection of English-language books.

Many of Pécs' museums (especially those on Káptalan utca) and other sites are open from 10 am to 6 pm Tuesday to Sunday from April to October and till 4 pm on the same days during the rest of the year and cost 120Ft to 200Ft for adults and 60Ft to 100Ft for students and seniors to enter. Opening times and admission fees are included later in the chapter only when they differ from these.

Széchenyi tér

This lovely square of mostly baroque buildings backed by the Mecsek Hills is where you should start a walking tour of Pécs. Dominating the square – indeed, the very symbol of the city – is the former Pasha Gazi Kassim Mosque. Today it's the Inner Town Parish Church (Belvárosi plébánia-templom) but more commonly known as the **Mosque Church**. It is the largest building still standing in Hungary from the time of Turkish occupation.

The square mosque with a green copper dome was built with the stones of the ruined medieval church of St Bertalan in the mid-16th century; after the expulsion of the Turks, the Catholic Church repossessed it. The northern semicircular part was added in the 20th century. The Islamic elements on the south side are easy to spot: windows with distinctive Turkish ogee arches; the prayer niche (*mihrab*) carved into the interior southeast wall; faded verses from the Koran to the south-west; lovely geometric frescoes on the corners. The mosque's minaret was pulled down in 1753 and replaced with a tower. The Mosque Church can be visited from 10 am to 4 pm Monday to Saturday and 11.30 am to 4 pm on Sunday from mid-April to mid-October. During the rest of the year the hours are 10 am till noon from Monday to Saturday, 11.30 am to 2 pm on Sunday.

The **Janus Pannonius Archaeology Museum** (Janus Pannonius Régészeti Múzeum), behind the Mosque Church at Széchenyi tér 12 in the 17th-century home of a janissary commander, traces the history of Baranya County up to the time of Árpád and contains many examples of Roman stonework from Pannonia, a model of St Bertalan's Church and medieval porcelain. It's open 10 am to 4 pm Tuesday to Sunday from April to October, to 2 pm the rest of the year (120/60Ft).

The **Trinity Column** in the lower part of Széchenyi tér is the third one to grace the spot and dates from 1908. The **porcelain Zsolnay Fountain** with a lustrous glaze, to the south-east in front of the rather gloomy **Church of the Good Samaritan**, was donated to the city by the Zsolnay factory in 1892.

Kossuth tér

This square south-east of Széchenyi tér has two important buildings: the Eclectic **town hall** (1891) to the north and the restored **synagogue** to the east. The synagogue (open from 9 am till noon and 12.30 to 4 pm Sunday to Friday from May to October, 40/30Ft) was built in the Romantic style in

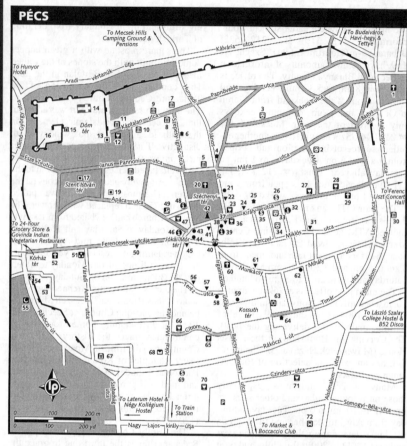

PÉCS

1869. Fact sheets in a dozen languages are available. Shortly after the fascist Hungarian government established a ghetto in Pécs in May 1944 most of the city's 3000 Jews were deported to the Nazi death camps.

Around Dóm tér

The foundations of the four-towered **Basilica of St Peter** – or simply the cathedral (*székesegyház*) – on Dóm tér date back to the 11th century and the side chapels are from the 1300s. But most of what you see today of the neo-Romanesque structure is the result of renovations carried out in 1881.

The basilica is very ornate inside; the elevated central altar is a reproduction of a medieval one. The most interesting parts of the basilica are the four chapels under the towers and the crypt, the oldest part of the structure. The **Chapel of Mary** on the north-west side and the **Chapel of the Sacred Heart** to the north-east contain works by the 19th-century painters Bertalan Székely and Károly Lotz. The **Mór Chapel** to the south-east has more works by Székely as well as magnificent pews. The **Corpus Christi Chapel** on the south-west side (enter from the outside) boasts a 16th-century red marble

PÉCS

PLACES TO STAY		9	Modern Hungarian Art	40	Zsolnay Fountain
4	Főnix Hotel;		Gallery	42	Trinity Column
	Cellárium Restaurant	10	Endre Nemes Museum;	43	House of Artists;
6	Centrum Motel		*Utca* Exhibit		Corvina Art Bookshop
25	Palatinus	11	Ferenc Martyn Museum	44	Zsolnay Porcelain Outlet
53	Pátria	12	Kioszk Cafe	46	Ibusz
64	Diana	13	Jug Mausoleum	47	Nothing But the Blues Club
		14	Basilica of St Peter	48	Tourinform
PLACES TO EAT		15	Bishop's Palace	49	Lajos Nagy Swimming Pool;
22	Mecsek Cake Shop	16	Barbican		Fontana Café
24	Dóm	17	Tomb Chapel	51	Pasha Memi Baths (Ruins)
31	Ali Baba	18	Csontváry Museum	52	Franciscan Church
37	Planet Pécs	19	Roman Tomb Site	54	OTP Bank
41	Virág Cake Shop	20	Mosque Church	55	Hassan Jakovali Mosque
45	Nonstop Shop	21	Former Nádor Hotel	58	Blazek Leather Shop
50	Hellas Taverna	23	Royal Café	59	Town Hall
56	Tex-Mex Café	26	OTP Bank	60	Church of the
57	Aranykacsa	27	Arizona Ranch Pub		Good Samaritan
61	Vörös Sárkány	28	Liceum Pub	62	Lenau House
		29	Church of St Stephen	63	Synagogue
OTHER		30	City History Museum	65	Dani Wine Bar
1	St Augustine Church	32	Theatre Ticket Office	66	Rundó Pub
2	Bóbita Puppet Theatre	33	Pécs National Theatre	67	Ethnography Museum
3	Croatian Theatre	34	Chamber Theatre	68	Main Post Office
5	Janus Pannonius	35	M&M Exchange	69	OTP Bank
	Archaeology Museum	36	John Bull Pub	70	Pécs Youth House &
7	Zsolnay Porcelain	38	Pécs Cultural Centre;		Billentyű Club
	Museum		ATM	71	Fair Play Disco
8	Vasarely Museum	39	Mecsek Tours	72	Bus Station

tabernacle, one of the finest examples of Renaissance stonework in the country. The basilica is open from 9 am to 5 pm weekdays, 9 am to 2 pm on Saturday and 1 to 5 pm on Sunday from April to October. During the rest of the year opening hours are 10 am to 4 pm Monday to Saturday and 1 to 4 pm on Sunday (220/110Ft).

The **Bishop's Palace** (Püspöki palota; 1770) to the south-west is not generally open to the public, but have a look at the curious **statue of Franz Liszt** (Imre Varga, 1983) peering over from a balcony. On the southern side of the baroque Ecclesiastical Archives (Egyházi levéltár) is the entrance to the **Jug Mausoleum** (Korsós sírkamra), a 4th-century Roman tomb whose name comes from a painting of a large drinking vessel with vines found here. The **early Christian tomb chapel** (Ókeresztény sírkápolna), across Janus Pannonius utca in Szent István tér, dates from about 350 AD and has frescoes of Adam and Eve, and

Daniel in the lion's den. There's another later **Roman tomb site** containing 110 graves a little farther south at Apáca utca 14.

The **Csontváry Museum**, Janus Pannonius utca 11, exhibits the major works of Kosztka Tivadar Csontváry (1853-1919), a unique symbolist painter whose tragic life is sometimes compared with that of Vincent van Gogh, who was born in the same year. Many of Csontváry's oversized canvases are masterpieces, especially *Storm on the Great Hortobágy* (1903), *Solitary Cedar* (1907) and *Baalbeck*, an artistic search for a larger identity through religious and historical themes.

To the west and north of Dóm tér is a long stretch of the **old city wall** that enclosed an area far too large to defend properly. The circular **barbican**, Esze Tomás utca 2, the only stone bastion to survive in Pécs, dates from the late 15th century and was restored in the 1970s. You can stroll along the catwalk running just below the loopholes.

Káptalan utca

Káptalan utca, running east from Dóm tér to Hunyadi János út, contains half a dozen art museums, all of them in listed buildings.

The **Ferenc Martyn Museum** at Káptalan utca 6 displays works by the Pécs-born painter and sculptor (1899-1986) and sponsors special exhibits of local interest. The house at No 5 is devoted to paintings by the surrealist **Endre Nemes** (1908-85) and the sculptures of **Amerigo Tot** (1909-84). In a separate pavilion behind it is Erzsébet Schaár's *Utca* (Street), a complete artistic environment in which the sculptor set her whole life in stone. The **Modern Hungarian Art Gallery** (Modern Magyar Képtár) at No 4 is the best place for an overview of art in Hungary from between 1850 till today. For work up to 1950 pay special attention to the works of Simon Hollósy, József Rippl-Rónai and Ödön Márffy. For more abstract and constructionist art, watch out for the names András Mengyár, Tamás Hencze, Béla Uitz and Gábor Dienes. The **Péter Székely Gallery** behind the museum has large stone and wood sculptures.

The two most interesting museums are at the eastern end of the street: the **Vasarely Museum** at No 3 and the **Zsolnay Porcelain Museum** at No 2. Victor Vasarely was the father of Op Art and, although some of the works on exhibit by him and his disciples are dated, most are evocative, very tactile and just plain fun. To my mind, the most striking of Vasarely's works here is *Vega-Sakk* (1969), a red, blue and orange weaving of an orb that grows into a distended belly as you stare at it.

The Zsolnay porcelain factory was established in Pécs in 1853 and was at the forefront of art and design in Europe for more than half a century. Many of its majolica tiles were used to decorate buildings throughout the country and contributed to establishing a new pan-Hungarian style of architecture. Zsolnay's darkest period came when the postwar communist government turned it into a plant for making ceramic electrical insulators. It's producing art again (in very limited quantities), but contemporary Zsolnay can't hold a candle to the chinoiserie pieces from the late 19th century and the later Art Nouveau and Art Deco designs done in the lustrous eosin glaze. The museum, housed in a residence dating from the Middle Ages, was the home of the Zsolnay family and contains many of their furnishings and personal effects.

Other Attractions

South-west of the inner town and opposite the Pátria hotel at Rákóczi út 2 is the **Pasha Hassan Jakovali Mosque** (Jakováli Hasszán Pasa dzsámija), wedged between a trade school and a hospital. The 16th-century mosque – complete with minaret – is the most intact of any Turkish structure in Hungary and contains a small museum of Ottoman *objets d'art*. It's open from 10 am to 6 pm Thursday to Tuesday from April to September (120/60Ft). The **Ethnography Museum** (Néprajzi Múzeum), to the south-east at Rákóczi út 15, examines ethnic Hungarian, German and South Slav folk art in the region (120/60Ft).

One of Pécs' most enjoyable pedestrian streets, Ferencesek utcája (lots of funky clothes and jewellery shops, restaurants and cafes) runs east from Rákóczi út to Széchenyi tér, and then Király utca also becomes pedestrian. You'll pass the ruins of the 16th-century **Pasha Memi Baths** (Ferencesek utcája 35), three beautiful old churches and, on Király utca, the neo-rococo **Pécs National Theatre**. Just beyond the **Church of St Stephen** (1741), Király utca 44a, turn south (right) on to Felsőmalom utca 9, where you'll find the excellent **City History Museum** (Várostörténeti Múzeum, 120/60Ft).

The suburb of Budaiváros to the northeast of the town centre is where most Hungarians settled after the Turks banned them from living within the city walls. The centre of this community was the **All Saints' Church** just off Tettye utca. Originally built in the 12th century and reconstructed in Gothic style 200 years later, it was the only Christian church allowed in Pécs during the occupation and was shared by three sects – who fought bitterly for every square centimetre. It was the Turks who had to keep the peace among the Christians.

To the north-east up on a hill is **Havihegy Chapel**, built in 1691 by the faithful after the town was spared the plague. The church is an important city landmark and offers wonderful views of the inner town and the narrow streets and old houses of the Tettye Valley.

You can get a taste of the Mecsek Hills by walking north-east from the centre of Pécs to Tettye and the **Garden of Ruins** (Romkert) – what's left of a bishop's summer residence built early in the 16th century and later used by Turkish dervishes as a monastery. To the north-west, up Fenyves sor and past the **zoo** (*állatkert*; open from 9 am to 6 pm daily April to October), a winding road leads to **Misina Peak** (535m) and a **TV tower**, an impressive 194m structure with a viewing platform and cafe-bar. It is open from 9 am to 9 pm Sunday to Thursday and to 10 pm on Friday and Saturday in summer and until 7 or 8 pm the rest of the year (200/180/150Ft). But these are just the foothills; from here, trails lead to the lovely towns of **Orfű** and **Abaliget**, on a plateau 15 and 20km to the north-west respectively, and to Southern Transdanubia's highest peak, **Mt Zengő** (682m). See the following Mecsek Hills section for more details.

The Sunday **flea market** at Vásártér, about 3km south-west of the inner town on Megyeri út, attracts people from the countryside, especially on the first Sunday of the month.

Activities

The outdoor Lajos Nagy swimming pool, up a few steps from Cisztercei köz, off Apáca utca, is open in summer from 9 am to 7 pm (300/250Ft, 250/200Ft after 2 pm); there's a great little cafe called the Fontana attached. The Koncz Tennis Team (☎ 326 860) based at the Makár Tanya motel (☎ 224 400), west of the inner town at Középmakár dűlő 4, has tennis and squash courts and gives lessons from 7 am to dusk.

Special Events

Among the big annual events in this party town are: the International Music Festival (Nemzetközi Zenei Fesztivál) in late June;

the Pannonian Summer (Pannon Nyár) arts festival from mid-July to mid-August; Pécs Days (Pécs Napok) in September, a 10-day festival of dance and music with a couple of alcohol-related events thrown in for good measure; and the International Folklore Festival (Nemzetközi Folklórfesztivál) in October.

Places to Stay

Camping Along with tent and campervan sites, *Mandulás Camping* (☎ 315 981, Ángyán János utca 2), up in the Mecsek Hills near the zoo, has 28 *bungalows* with shared shower from DM35, a *motel* and a 20-room *hotel* with doubles (including bath) from DM45.

Hostels & Private Rooms In July and August, the *Négy Kollégium* at Janus Pannonius University (☎ 251 203, Szántó Kovács János utca 1c) to the west of the centre and the *László Szalay College* (☎ 324 473, Universitas út 2) to the east, accommodate travellers in dormitory rooms with two to four beds for 700Ft to 1300Ft.

Mecsek Tours and Ibusz, which has a better list, can arrange *private rooms* from 1500Ft per person; apartments range from 4000Ft to 6000Ft.

Pensions As in Budapest, most of the pensions in Pécs are sprinkled in the surrounding hills and rather difficult to get to without your own transport. The 12-room *Toboz* (☎/fax 210 631, Fenyves sor 5), on a tree-lined street just south of the zoo, charges from 6000Ft for a double. Nearby, the *Avar* (☎ 321 924, fax 316 584, Fenyves sor 2), with seven cramped rooms, is cheaper but a distant second choice. One of the few central places is the six-room *Centrum* motel (☎ 311 707, Szepesy Ignác utca 4), which is more like a B&B than a motel, with rooms from 3800Ft.

Hotels A central yet affordable place is the 16-room *Főnix* (☎ 311 680, fax 324 113, Hunyadi János út 2), a stone's throw from the Mosque Church. Singles/doubles with shared shower cost 3990/5890Ft, a double with shower is 6690Ft. Another great option in the inner town is the *Diana* (*☎/fax 333 373, Tímár utca 4a*), an eight room *kishotel* (small hotel – almost a pension), just south of the synagogue, with rooms from 3800Ft.

An excellent (though far-flung) place to stay is the enormous *Laterum* hotel (*☎ 254 963, fax 252 131, Hajnóczy utca 37-39*), with 133 rooms on the far west side of town. Prices range from 1500Ft to 3500Ft per head, depending on whether you sleep in a dorm room, a room with shared bath or a single or double with private bath, and there's an inexpensive self-service restaurant just off the hotel lobby.

The *Hunyor* (*☎ 512 640, fax 512 643, ✉ mthuny@mail.matav.hu, Jurisics Miklós utca 16*) is in the Mecsek foothills and a bit out of the way but has excellent views of the city and almost a resort feel. There's a pleasant restaurant attached and all 50 rooms have TVs, telephones and baths. Singles/doubles are DM55/110.

Farther still into 'them thar' hills and near the TV tower is the *Kikelet* hotel (*☎ 512 900, fax 512 901, Károlyi Mihály utca 1*) in a couple of erstwhile trade-union holiday houses. Its 40 rooms without/with bath are 5800/6500Ft for a double. South of the Kikelet, the 19-room *Fenyves Panoráma* hotel (*☎/fax 315 996, Szőlő utca 64*) charges 6200Ft for a double and, as its name suggests, has a great views.

Pécs' old-world hotel, the 94-room *Palatinus* (*☎ 233 022, fax 232 261, ✉ palatinuspatria@mail.matav.hu, Király utca 5*), has been 'under renovation' as long as I can remember. It is swamped by tour groups and is way overpriced at DM110 to DM121 for a single and DM120 to DM130 for a double, depending on the season. Palatinus' wicked (but somewhat cheaper) stepsister, the *Pátria* (*☎ 213 322, fax 212 820, ✉ palatinuspatria@mail.matav.hu, Rákóczi út 3*), is in an ugly 113-room block (singles/doubles from DM90/100 to DM112/120).

Places to Eat
The *Ali Baba* (*Perczel Mór utca 23*) is a small takeaway place with Middle Eastern specialities like gyros and felafel. For a cheap and filling Chinese meal, graze at the *Vörös Sárkány* (*Red Dragon; Munkácsy Mihály utca 9*), with lunchtime specials for 350Ft. It's open from 11 am to 7 pm weekdays, to 5 pm on Saturday. *Govinda* (*Hungária utca 3*) is a branch of the Krishna vegetarian chain open to 8 pm from Monday to Saturday. *Planet Pécs* (*Király utca 2*) is a central, and very groovy, place for a pizza.

The *Hellas Taverna* (*Ferencesek utcája 9*) has Greek dishes like dolmades, pastitsio and moussaka along with the requisite gyros. The *Tex-Mex Cafe* (*Teréz utca 10*), one of my favourites in Pécs, is an attractive cellar restaurant with tacos and enchiladas for 780Ft, fajitas for 1100Ft. The *Cellárium* (*Hunyadi Jánis út 2*) just below the Főnix hotel is a reliable choice for a meal and is close to the centre.

Two excellent bets for a somewhat upscale meal are the *Aranykacsa* (*Teréz utca 4*), south of Széchenyi tér, which has a salad bar, and the *Dóm* (*Király utca 3*), a small loft restaurant in a courtyard with wonderful *fin-de-siècle* paintings and stained-glass windows (open till 11 pm).

There's an ongoing debate in Pécs over which *cukrászda* serves better cakes and ice cream: the *Mecsek* (*Széchenyi tér 16*) near the old Nádor hotel or the *Virág* (*Irgalmasok utcája*). I vote the latter.

There are *24-hour grocery stores* at Jókai utca 1 in the centre and at Hungária utca 18 west of Kórház tér. Pécs' *fruit & vegetable market* is near the bus station on Zólyom utca.

Entertainment
The *House of Artists* (*☎ 315 388, Széchenyi tér 7-8*), open noon to 5 pm on weekdays, advertises its many cultural programs outside, including classical music concerts. For tickets visit the *Pécs Cultural Centre* (*☎ 336 622, Széchenyi tér 1*). These are the places to ask about classical music concerts. Other musical venues include the *Ferenc Liszt Concert Hall*, east of the town centre at Király utca 83 and *Lenau House* (*Munkácsy Mihály utca 8*).

Pécs is also renowned for its opera company and the Sophianae Ballet. If you're told that tickets to the *Pécs National Theatre (Király utca)* are sold out, try for a cancellation at the box office an hour before the performance. Advance tickets can be purchased from the theatre office (☎ 310 539) at Király utca 18.

Other stages are the *Chamber Theatre* next door to the National Theatre, the *Croatian Theatre (Anna utca 17)* and the *Bóbita Puppet Theatre (Mária utca 18)*.

Pécs is a big university town and that is reflected in the city's nightlife. Some of Pécs' most popular discos and music clubs include: *Boccaccio (Bajcsy-Zsilinszky utca 45)*; the *Fair Play Disco (Czindery utca 6)*; the *Billentyű* at the Pécs Youth House *(Pécs Ifjúsági Ház; Nagy Lajos király útja 13)*; and the *B52 Disco (Universitas út 35)*.

There are pubs and bars almost the entire length of Király utca, many of them with outside tables in summer. The *Royal Cafe* at No 1, the *John Bull* at No 2, the *Arizona Ranch* at No 29 and the *Liceum* in the courtyard at No 35 are all good bets. The *Nothing but the Blues* pub *(Apáca utca 1)* has live music some nights.

There's a nice little wine bar called *Dani* in a courtyard called Colonia Passage along Citrom utca south of Széchenyi tér. The wine to try here is the white Cirfandli, a speciality of the Mecsek Hills. A nearby pub called *Rundó (Citrom utca 16)* attracts a motley crowd.

While visiting the cathedral or the museums along Káptalan utca, stop in for a drink or a coffee at the *Kioszk* in the little park between Káptalan utca and Janus Pannonius utca. It's probably the only chance you'll ever have to drink in what was once a baptistry.

The weekly freebie *Pécsi Est* is a great source for information on what's on in Pécs and surrounding towns.

Shopping

Pécs has been renowned for its leatherwork since Turkish times, and you can pick up a few bargains in several shops around the city; try one called Blázek at Teréz utca 1. There's a Zsolnay porcelain outlet at Jókai tér 2.

Getting There & Away

Bus Departures are frequent (once or even twice an hour) to Siklós, Mohács, Harkány, Kaposvár, Vajszló, Szigetvár and Szekszárd. You can also reach Budapest on five buses a day, Békéscsaba (one), Győr (two), Hévíz (two), Kecskemét (two), Sellye (four to six), Siófok (three or four), Székesfehérvár (four to five), Sopron (one), Szeged (seven), Veszprém (two or three), Villány (one to two) and Zalaegerszeg (four to five).

There are hourly buses in summer to Abaliget and Orfű in the Mecsek Hills, but only seven to 10 in winter.

Buses run between three and four times a day between Barcs and Zagreb. There are also three buses a day (11.50 am, 4.30 and 4.35 pm) from Pécs to Osijek in Croatia.

Train Up to 10 trains a day connect Pécs with Budapest-Déli station. You can reach Nagykanizsa and other points north-west via a rather circuitous but scenic 148km line along the Dráva River. From Nagykanizsa, a couple of trains a day continue on to Szombathely. One early morning express (5.40 am) follows this route from Pécs all the way to Szombathely.

Getting Around

To get to the Hunyor hotel, take bus No 32 from the train station or from opposite the Mosque Church. Bus Nos 34 and 35 run direct to the Kikelet and Fenyves hotels from the train station. Bus No 34 goes on to the camping ground, while bus No 35 continues to the TV tower. For the Laterum hotel, take bus No 2 or 4 from the train station or the market near the bus station to the end of the line at Uránváros. Bus Nos 3 and 50 from the train station are good for the flea market on Vásártér. You can order a local taxi on ☎ 222 222, ☎ 233 333 or ☎ 333 333.

MECSEK HILLS

Buses from Pécs reach most towns in the Mecsek Hills, but if you plan to do a lot of hiking, get a copy of Cartographia's 1:40,000 *A Mecsek* map (No 15; 400Ft) before setting out.

Orfű

☎ 72 • postcode 7677 • pop 580

The most accessible of the Mecsek resorts and the one with the most recreational facilities is Orfű, a series of settlements on four artificial lakes where you can swim, row, canoe and fish. There's a riding school called Eldorádó at Petőfi utca 3 in nearby Tekeres. From Széchenyi tér you can walk south along tiny Lake Orfű to the **Mill Museum** (Malommúzeum), a series of old pump houses open from 10 am to 6 pm daily from May to September and to 4 pm Tuesday to Friday only the rest of the year (80/65Ft).

Places to Stay & Eat *Panoráma Camping* (☎ 378 434, *Dollár utca 1*), above the large public beach in the lake's southwestern corner and open mid-April to mid-October, has basic *hostel* accommodation for 750Ft per person and *bungalows* from 3300Ft. There are dinghies, sailboards and bicycles for rent. Other places to stay in Orfű include the four-room *Vaskakas* pension (☎ 498 219, *Mecsekárosi utca 29*) on the lake's eastern shore with doubles for 4000Ft and the eight-room *Molnár* pension (☎ 498 363, *Széchenyi tér 18a*). The *Muskátli (Széchenyi tér)*, close to the latter, is a pleasant little restaurant.

Abaliget

☎ 72 • postcode 7678 • pop 630

Abaliget, 3km north-west of Orfű and accessible by bus or on foot via a trail up and over the hill behind Panoráma Camping, is quieter but not as attractive. There are lots of *private rooms* for rent along Kossuth Lajos utca, the main street, but the only standard accommodation in town is at *Barlang Camping* (☎ 498 730) on the town's tiny lake and near the 450m **Abaliget Cave**, (open from 8 am to 6 pm daily from mid-May to mid-October, (200/120Ft).

The site also has a nine-room *motel* (1800Ft for two), a 14-room *hotel* (doubles for 3600Ft) and *bungalows* for up to four people for 3000Ft. There's a small horse-riding school here as well.

KAPOSVÁR

☎ 82 • postcode 7400 • pop 71,800

Somogy County is usually associated with the Balaton and rightly so: it controls the entire money-spinning southern shore of the lake from Siófok to Balatonberény. Kaposvár, the county seat some 55km to the south, does not generally spring to mind.

It's not an unattractive city, it must be said, situated in the Zselic foothills along the valley of the Kapos River. But don't come to 'Kapos Castle' looking for a fortress like the one at Siklós or Szigetvár; the Turks and then the Habsburgs dispatched that long ago. In fact, so heavy and constant was the fighting here over the centuries that few buildings date from before 1900. Instead, visit Kaposvár for its art (the city is associated with three great painters: the postimpressionists József Rippl-Rónai and János Vaszary, as well as Aurél Bernáth) and theatre, among the best in provincial Hungary.

The village of Taszár, 8km to the east, became the site of NATO's first operating military base in the former Eastern bloc. The base opened in December 1995 as the main logistical centre for troops and supplies funnelling into the US-run northern zone of the peacekeeping operation in Bosnia. With Hungary now a full member of the organisation, the base remains in operation but you won't see many of the 2000 American GIs garrisoned here – there are strict limits on their fraternising with the locals.

Orientation & Information

The train and bus stations are a block apart south of the city centre, on Budai Nagy Antal utca just south-east of Petőfi Sándor tér. From here, walk up Teleki utca to Kossuth tér and Fő utca, a lovely pedestrian street where most of the action is.

For information about Kaposvár and surrounds, see Tourinform (☎/fax 320 404, ✉ kapos@tourinform.hu) at Fő utca 8. It is open from 9.30 am to 5.30 pm on weekdays and to 1.30 pm Saturday June to August, from 9 am to 5 pm on weekdays and till noon on Saturday the rest of the year. Siotour (☎ 320 537, fax 312 459), in the same

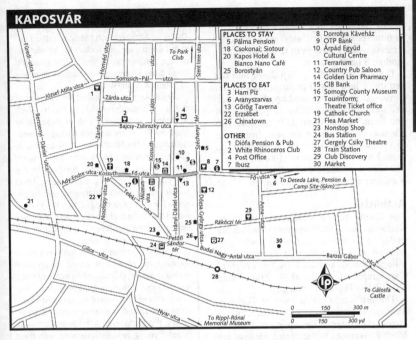

KAPOSVÁR

PLACES TO STAY
5 Pálma Pension
18 Csokonai; Siotour
20 Kapos Hotel &
   Bianco Nano Café
25 Borostyán

PLACES TO EAT
3 Ham Piz
6 Aranyszarvas
13 Görög Taverna
22 Erzsébet
26 Chinatown

OTHER
1 Diófa Pension & Pub
2 White Rhinoceros Club
4 Post Office
7 Ibusz

8 Dorrotya Kávéház
9 OTP Bank
10 Árpád Együd
   Cultural Centre
11 Terrarium
12 Country Pub Saloon
14 Golden Lion Pharmacy
15 CIB Bank
16 Somogy County Museum
17 Tourinform;
   Theatre Ticket office
19 Catholic Church
21 Flea Market
23 Nonstop Shop
24 Bus Station
27 Gergely Csiky Theatre
28 Train Station
29 Club Discovery
30 Market

building as the Csokonai hotel at Fő utca 1, is open from 8 am to 4.30 pm on weekdays. Ibusz (☎/fax 315 477) is at Fő utca 37-39.

OTP's main branch (with several ATMs) is at Széchenyi tér 2, and there's a CIB bank at Kossuth Lajos utca 4. The main post office is at Bajcsy-Zsilinszky utca 15, west of Széchenyi tér.

Things to See

The **Somogy County Museum** (Somogy Megyei Múzeum), in the former county hall (1820) at Fő utca 10, contains a large ethnographical collection and a gallery of contemporary art on the ground floor. Works by Vaszary and Bernáth are on the 1st floor and a more extensive collection of paintings by Ödön Márffy, Gyula Rudnay and Béla Kádár is on the 2nd floor.

The folk collection is noteworthy for its wood and horn carvings (at which the swineherds of Somogy County excelled), examples of famous indigo-dyed cotton fabrics (kékfestő), an exhibition on the county's infamous outlaws (including the paprika-tempered 'Horseshoe Steve'), and costumes of the Croatian minority, who dressed and decorated their houses in white fabric during mourning periods as the Chinese do. The museum was being renovated when I last visited but is usually open from 10 am to 4 pm Tuesday to Sunday from April to October and till 3 pm the rest of the year (80/50Ft).

József Rippl-Rónai (1861-1927), Kaposvár's most celebrated – and arguably Hungary's best – painter, was born at Fő 19, above the lovely **Golden Lion Pharmacy** (Aranyoroszlán patika; 1774), now a museum. Most of his work is exhibited in the **Rippl-Rónai Memorial Museum** (Rippl-Rónai Emlékmúzeum), a graceful 19th-century villa at Róma-hegy 88, about 3km south-east of the city centre. It is open from 10 am to 6 pm Tuesday to Sunday from April to October and till 4 pm the rest of the year (100/80Ft).

The cream and lemon-coloured Secessionist **Gergely Csiky Theatre** (1911), with its hundreds of arched windows at Rákóczi tér 2, is worth a look even if you are not attending a performance.

If you can handle it, step down into the **Terrarium** in a humid cellar at Fő utca 31. Cobras, caymans, boas and a python as thick as a stevedore's forearm are all there to greet you from 9 am to 6 pm daily from May to August and, the rest of the year, from 9 am to 5 pm weekdays, till noon on Saturday and from 2 to 5 pm on Sunday (100/80Ft).

There's a small daily **flea market** at Vásárteri út, west of the bus station.

Activities

The Zselic region (Zselicség) south of Kaposvár, some 9000 hectares of which are under a nature-conservation order, is webbed with trails for easy hikes through villages, forests and low hills. Get a copy of Cartographia's 1:60,000 *A Zselic* map (No 17; 400Ft) before you go.

The artificial Deseda Lake at Toponár, 8km north-east of the city centre, offers swimming, other water sports and tennis. More convenient to the centre, though, are the outdoor pools (open 9 am to 7 pm daily from mid-May to August) and the thermal baths (9 am to 7 pm Tuesday to Sunday the rest of the year).

Places to Stay

Deseda Camping (☎ *312 020*) in Toponár does not have bungalows, but travellers armed with a tent can take bus No 8 or the train headed for Siófok and get off at the second stop. It's open from mid-June to September. The ***Deseda*** pension (☎ *310 344*) here is open from April to October.

Siotour and Ibusz can book you a ***private room*** for 1200Ft to 1400Ft for a single (difficult to find, as always) and 2000Ft to 2500Ft for a double. The homely *Pálma* pension (☎/*fax 420 227, Széchenyi tér 6*), which has six comfortable rooms, charges 5900Ft for a double and has a great cake and ice-cream shop below it. A similarly priced option is the *Diófa* pension (☎/*fax 312 154, József Attila utca 24*).

Farewell to All That

The word *búcsú* (church patronal festival) derives from the ancient Turkish for 'absolution' or 'the forgiveness of sins'. From medieval times it has taken on the additional meaning of 'pilgrimage' in Hungarian.

Búcsúk were usually linked with an icon or statue in a particular church, such as the Black Madonnas at Andocs, north of Kaposvár in Southern Transdanubia, and Máriapócs, near Nyírbátor in the North-East. They could also honour the name of a church's patron saint. People would march, often for days, to the holy place carrying banners and singing. Local people would accommodate and feed the pilgrims for little or nothing. Often the faithful would spend the night in the church itself, believing that the absolution – or the cure – was more likely to occur in sleep.

Over the centuries búcsúk took on a more secular tone. Merchants would set up their stalls around the church, selling not only relics and religious articles but clothing, food and drinks as well. Showmen, buskers and musicians entertained the crowds and, in some places, there was even a 'bride market' with hopeful young women appearing with their full dowries. While the old and infirm congregated in the church to touch and venerate the holy picture or statue, the young remained outside for the entertainment.

As it happens, búcsú has yet another meaning in Hungarian: 'farewell'. Thus the Búcsú Fesztivál (Goodbye Festival) in Budapest every June marking the departure of the last Soviet soldier from Hungarian soil in 1991 has a double meaning: it is both a raging party paying homage to hedonism and a 'goodbye' to the last of the much despised occupiers.

Kaposvár has a pair of interesting hotels. The *Csokonai* (☎ *312 011, fax 312 459,* **e** *siotour@mail.datanet.hu, Fő utca 1*) is a 21-room inn in an 18th-century house. Singles/doubles with shared shower are DM20/35, doubles with shower and toilet are DM45. The upmarket *Borostyán* (☎ *320*

735, fax 310 123, Rákóczi tér 3), a nine-room Art Nouveau extravaganza, is one of provincial Hungary's most interesting cara-vanserais. Singles are 4900Ft to 5700Ft, doubles 6900Ft to 9200Ft, depending on the room size.

The 79-room *Kapos* hotel *(☎/fax 316 022, Ady Endre utca 2)* is an unattractive, modern affair but friendly and very cen-trally located. Singles range from 5400Ft to 7400Ft, doubles from 6900Ft to 8900Ft, de-pending on the room category.

If you want to do some horse riding, con-sider the 46-room *Gálosfa Castle* hotel *(☎/fax 370 801, Dózsa György utca 1)* at Gálosfa in the Red Apple Hills, some 20km south-east of Kaposvár. Tennis, fishing, sauna, horses – it has the works. Singles are 3200Ft, doubles range in price from 3800Ft to 4400Ft.

Places to Eat

For pizza, pasta and simple Hungarian fare, try the *Erzsébet (Noszlopy Gáspár utca 6)* in a gorgeous old blue house, open daily till midnight. The coffee shop *Bianco Nano* at the Kapos hotel has pizza as well as a salad bar and stays open daily to 11 pm (10 pm on Sunday). The studenty *Ham Piz (Bajcsy-Zsilinszky utca 13)* next to the post office serves the two fast foods of choice in Hun-gary these days to 11 pm daily.

Görög Taverna (Fő utca 14), at the cor-ner of Irányi Dániel utca, serves passable Greek-ish food daily until midnight. The food at the *Chinatown (Budai Nagy Antal utca 9)*, with its entrance on Dózsa György utca opposite the Gergely Csiky Theatre, is almost American-Chinese; indeed, members of the US Army Europe National Support Element Operation Joint Guard (a mouthful in itself) based at Taszár awarded China-town a 'scroll of appreciation' in 1998. Main dishes are 600Ft to 750Ft; there are lunchtime set menus for 380Ft and 480Ft.

Aranyszarvas (Golden Deer; Fő utca 46) is a typical, middle-range Hungarian restau-rant with game specialities. The restaurant at the *Csokonai* has seating both in a charming courtyard and a rather cramped cellar. One of the fanciest places in town is

the dining room at the *Borostyán* (open daily except Sunday to 11 pm).

There's a *24-hour shop (Budai Nagy Antal utca)* across from the bus station, The *fruit & vegetable market* is east of Rákóczi tér just north of Baross Gábor utca.

Entertainment

For information on things cultural on offer in Kaposvár, visit the *Árpád Együd Cul-tural Centre (☎ 319 845, Csokonai utca 1)*.

Aside from being a masterpiece of Art Nouveau (or Secessionist) architecture, the wedding cake *Gergely Csiky Theatre (☎ 320 833, Rákóczi tér 2)* has a great repu-tation and was at the forefront of Hungarian artistic innovation in the 1970s. The book-ing office (☎ 311 113) is at Tourinform, Fő utca 8, and is open from 8.30 am to 5 pm weekdays and till noon on Saturday.

Kaposvár is known for its choral groups, and concerts are given in venues around the city, including the *Catholic church* on Kos-suth tér.

Dorottya Kávéház (Széchenyi tér 8) at Dorottya House, where most of the action in playwright Mihály Csokonai Vitéz's comic epic *Dorottya* (1804) takes place, is a good spot for a beer, as is the *Diófa* pub *(Zárda utca 39)* north of Kossuth tér. An-other place is the *County Pub Saloon (Dózsa György utca 3)*, yet another Wild West-themed Hungarian bar.

If you're looking for something a bit more frisky, head for the *Fehér Orrszarvú (White Rhinoceros; Bajcsy-Zsilinszky utca 1c)* with a 'nostalgia' (read oldies) disco Friday and Saturday till 4 am in a big old dusky pink house north-east of Kossuth tér. Two other popular venues are *Club Dis-covery (Rákóczi tér 9-11)* with 'two rooms, two styles every Saturday' and *Park (Sent Imre utca 29)*, with the same deal on Friday.

For up-to-date entertainment, check the listings in the freebie weekly *Kapos Est*.

Getting There & Away

Bus Between six and nine daily buses link Kaposvár with Barcs, Pécs, Siófok and Gálosfa. Other destinations include: Baja (one bus a day), Budapest (two), Győr (two),

Hévíz (two), the thermal spa at Igal (two to seven), Mohács (two), Nagykanizsa (three to four), Sopron (one), Szeged (one), Szekszárd (two), Szenna (three from stop No 11), Szigetvár (three), Szombathely (two) and Tapolca (one).

Train You can reach Kaposvár by train from both the eastern (Siófok) and western (Fonyód) ends of Lake Balaton's southern shore. Another line links Kaposvár with Budapest (via Dombóvár) to the north-east three times a day and, to the west, with Gyékényes, from where international trains depart for Zagreb (three a day).

Getting Around
Bus No 8 terminates near the lake and the camp site in Toponár. For the Rippl-Rónai Memorial Museum in Róma-hegy, take bus No 15.

Local taxis are available on ☎ 313 333 or ☎ 555 555.

SZIGETVÁR
☎ 73 • postcode 7900 • pop 11,350
Szigetvár, 33km west of Pécs and 40km south of Kaposvár, was a Celtic settlement and then a Roman one called Limosa before the Magyar conquest. The strategic importance of the town was recognised early on, and in 1420 a fortress was built on a small island – Szigetvár means 'island castle' – in the marshy areas of the Almás River. But Szigetvár would be indistinguishable today from other Southern Transdanubian towns had the events of September 1566 not taken place (see boxed text 'Big Sally of Szigetvár').

Today you can visit what remains of the town's celebrated castle, and there are a handful of Turkish-era monuments to gawk at. The opening of the Park of Turkish-Hungarian Friendship, north of the city, as well as a Turkish Consulate on Zrínyi tér has helped to cement the friendly ties between the two former enemies.

Orientation & Information
The bus and train stations are close to one another a short distance south of the town

centre at the end of Rákóczi utca. To reach the centre follow this road north into lovely Zrínyi tér. Vár utca on the northern side of the square leads to the castle.

Mecsek Tours (☎ 413 388, fax 312 817), open from 8.30 am to 4 pm on weekdays, is just off the lobby of the Oroszlán hotel at Zrínyi tér 2. There's a branch of OTP at Vár utca 4, and the main post office is at József Attila utca 27-31.

Zrínyi Castle
Our hero Miklós Zrínyi would probably not recognise the four-cornered castle he so valiantly fought to save more than 400 years ago. The Turks strengthened the bastions and added buildings; the Hungarians rebuilt it again in the 18th century. Today there are only a few elements of historical interest left: walls from 3m to 6m thick linked by the four bastions; the **Baroque Tower** crowning the southern wall; the 16th-century **Sultan Suleiman Mosque** (Szulejmán pasa dzsámija) with a truncated minaret; and a summer mansion built by Count Andrássy in 1930, which now houses the **Castle Museum** (Vármúzeum).

Naturally, the museum's exhibits focus on the siege and its key players. Zrínyi's praises are sung throughout, there's a detailed account of how Suleiman built a bridge over the Dráva in 16 days to attack Szigetvár, and the miniatures of Hungarian soldiers being captured, chopped up and burned are still quite horrifying. Sebestyén Tinódi, the beloved 16th-century poet and wandering minstrel who was born in Szigetvár, also rates an altar of worship. The mosque next door, completed in the year of the siege, contains an art gallery; the arches, prayer niches and Arabic inscriptions on the walls are worth a look. The castle museum is open from 9 am to 6 pm Tuesday to Sunday from May to September and from 9 am to 3 pm in April and October (120/100Ft).

Other Attractions
The tiny **Local History Collection** (Helytörténeti Gyűtemény), Vár utca 1, is a hotchpotch of folk carvings, embroidery and

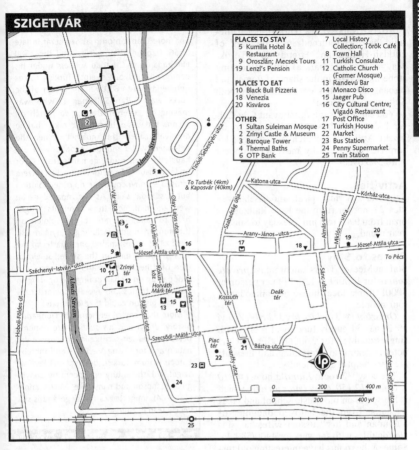

SZIGETVÁR

PLACES TO STAY
5 Kumilla Hotel & Restaurant
9 Oroszlán; Mecsek Tours
19 Lenzl's Pension

PLACES TO EAT
10 Black Bull Pizzeria
18 Venezia
20 Kisváros

OTHER
1 Sultan Suleiman Mosque
2 Zrínyi Castle & Museum
3 Baroque Tower
4 Thermal Baths
6 OTP Bank
7 Local History Collection; Török Café
8 Town Hall
11 Turkish Consulate
12 Catholic Church (Former Mosque)
13 Randevú Bar
14 Monaco Disco
15 Jaeger Pub
16 City Cultural Centre; Vigadó Restaurant
17 Post Office
21 Turkish House
22 Market
23 Bus Station
24 Penny Supermarket
25 Train Station

valuables from local churches, but it displays a great collection of 18th and 19th-century shop signs as well as locks and keys from the castle. It's open 9 am to 4 pm Tuesday to Saturday (30/15Ft).

The ogee-arched (called 'donkey's back' arches in Hungarian) windows and hexagonal roof of the baroque **Catholic church** at Zrínyi tér 9 are the only exterior signs that this was once the Pasha Ali Mosque, built in 1589. The altarpiece of the Crucifixion and the muted ceiling frescoes depicting the deaths of Zrínyi and Suleiman were painted by István Dorffmeister in 1789.

The 16th-century **Turkish House** (Törökház) near the bus station at Bástya utca 3, was a caravansery during the occupation and contains an exhibit of Turkish miniatures. It is open from 10 am to noon and 2 to 4 pm daily from May to September (30Ft).

The Catholic church at Turbékpuszta, about 4km north-east of Szigetvár, was originally built as a **tomb for Suleiman**. But according to local tradition, only the sultan's heart lies within; his son and successor, Selim II, had the body exhumed and returned to Turkey.

Some 3km north of Szigetvár on route No 67 to Kaposvár, a Turkish-era battlefield has been turned into the **Park of Turkish-Hungarian Friendship** (Török-Magyar barátság parkja) with interesting stone memorials in the shape of domes and turbans and statues commemorating both Suleiman and Zrínyi.

You can't miss the flamboyant **City Cultural Centre** (Városi Művelődési Ház) on József Attila utca, which was designed – surprise, surprise – by maverick architect Imre Makovecz.

Activities
Szigetvár's thermal spa at Tinódi Sebestyén utca 23, not far from the Kumilla hotel, is open from 9 am to 6 pm Tuesday to Sunday year round.

Places to Stay
Staff at Mecsek Tours can organise *private rooms* for 1000Ft to 12000Ft per person or 4000Ft for a local house accommodating four people.

Oroszlán (☎ 310 116, fax 312 817, Zrínyi tér 2) has 34 purely functional rooms with singles/doubles for 3600/4500Ft, but the hotel is central to everything and the staff are very helpful and friendly.

The cosy, 32-room *Kumilla* hotel *(☎ 310 150, fax 312 150, Olay Lajos utca 6)*, which is housed in an old music school and takes its name from the beloved daughter of Suleiman and his Russian wife, has singles/doubles with showers for 4900/5800Ft. Some of the rooms have interesting old furniture. Another option is the attractive *Lenzl's* pension *(☎ 413 045, József Attila utca 63)*, with singles/doubles for 3000/6000Ft.

If you're more interested in recreation than sightseeing and don't mind staying out of town, the 28-room *Domolos Castle* hotel *(☎ 311 250, fax 311 222)* in Domolospuszta near Zsibót, about 6km north-east of Szigetvár, is housed in a 19th-century mansion designed by Mihály Pollack and set on a small lake. There's horse riding as well as a sauna, tennis courts and fishing. Doubles are 6000Ft.

Big Sally of Szigetvár

For more than a month at Szigetvár in late 1566, Captain Miklós Zrínyi and the 2500 Hungarian and Croatian soldiers under his command held out against Turkish forces numbering up to 80,000. The leader of the Turks was Sultan Suleiman I, who was making his seventh attempt to march on Vienna and was determined to take what he derisively called 'this molehill'. When the defenders' water and food supplies were exhausted – and reinforcements from Győr under Habsburg Emperor Maximilian II were refused – Zrínyi could see no other solution but a suicidal sally. As the moated castle went up in flames, the opponents fought hand to hand, and most of the soldiers on the Hungarian side, including Zrínyi himself, were killed. An estimated one-quarter of the Turkish forces died in the siege; Suleiman died of a heart attack and his corpse was propped up on a chair during the fighting to inspire his troops and avoid a power struggle until his son could take command.

More than any other heroes in Hungarian history, Zrínyi and his soldiers are remembered for their self-sacrifice in the cause of the nation and for saving Vienna – and thereby Europe – from Turkish domination. *Peril at Sziget*, a 17th-century epic poem by Zrínyi's great-grandson and namesake, Miklós Zrínyi (1662-64), immortalises the siege and is still widely read in Hungary.

Places to Eat
There are a lot of food stalls at the *market (Piac tér)* near the bus station. The *Kisváros (József Attila utca 77)* serves basic Hungarian dishes in pleasant surroundings while, to the west, the *Venezia (József Attila utca 41)* serves decent pizzas daily till 11 pm. A more central place for similar fare is the *Black Bull Pizzeria (Széchenyi tér 2)*, next to the Turkish Consulate.

The *Vigadó* in the cultural centre on József Attila utca is a good place for lunch or dinner and is open daily to 10 pm. The restaurant at the *Kumilla* hotel is quiet but pleasant, especially on the terrace in warm weather.

The coffee shop *Török* at the Local History Collection, Vár utca 1, is a central place to take the weight off your feet.

Entertainment

A couple of watering holes on Horváth Márk tér, a small square linking Zrínyi tér with Zárda utca, are worth a look. *Randevú* attracts a more mature crowd, *Jaeger* is younger and has outside tables. *Monaco* disco *(Zárda utca 3)* is just behind the latter.

Getting There & Away

Bus Between nine and 12 buses a day depart Szigetvár for Pécs, while three to six run to Kaposvár. Otherwise, there are three or four daily departures to Barcs, one to Hévíz, one or two to Mohács, one to Szentlőrinc, one to Veszprém, three or four to Zalaegerszeg and two or three to Nagykanizsa and Siklós. From Barcs, on the border with Croatia 32km to the southwest, three or four buses head for Zagreb each day.

Sellye and the Ormánság folk region are accessible from Szigetvár, but there is only one excruciatingly slow bus at 12.40 pm on weekdays and at 12.20 pm on Saturday. By train, you must travel east for 15km and change at Szentlőrinc.

Train Szigetvár is on a rail line linking Pécs and Nagykanizsa. The 84km stretch from Barcs to Nagykanizsa follows the course of the Dráva River and is very scenic, especially around Vízvár and Bélavár. If you're trying to leave Hungary from here, get off at Murakeresztúr (two stops before Nagykanizsa), through which trains pass en route to Zagreb, Ljubljana, Trieste and Venice.

NAGYKANIZSA

☎ 93 • postcode 8800 • pop 54,000

Lying on a canal linking the Zala River to the north with the Mura River on the Croatian border, Nagykanizsa hosted a succession of settlers, including Celts, Romans, Avars and Slavs, before the arrival of the Magyars. Early in the 14th century, King Charles Robert ceded the area to the Kanizsay family, who built a castle in the marshes of the canal west of what is now the town centre. The castle was fortified after the fall of Szigetvár in 1566 but, despite the heroics of one Captain György Thury, it too was taken by the Turks and remained an important district seat for 90 years. Development didn't really begin until a few centuries later with the construction of the Budapest-Adriatic rail line through the town and the discovery of the Zala oil fields to the west.

Nagykanizsa is not especially noted for its sights (nothing remains of the castle that was blown to smithereens by the Habsburgs in the 18th century); the town is almost totally focused on drilling for oil, making light bulbs and furniture, and brewing beer. But if you think of it as a convenient stepping stone, you'll literally be on the right track. From Nagykanizsa you can easily reach Western Transdanubia, both shores of Lake Balaton, Italy, Slovenia, Croatia and the beaches of the Adriatic.

Orientation & Information

The train station is south of the city centre on Ady Endre utca. To reach the centre walk north along this road for about 1200m, and you'll be on Fő út, the main street. The bus station is in the centre to the west of Erzsébet tér.

Zalatour (☎ 311 185), Fő út 13, is open from 8 am to 4.30 pm on weekdays and till 11.30 am on Saturday. OTP bank has a branch at Deák Ferenc tér 15 on the corner of Sugár út and another one at Ady Endre utca 6. The main post office is at Ady Endre utca 10.

Things to See

The **György Thury Museum** at Fő út 5 has a surprisingly interesting standing exhibit called 'The Forest and the People in Zala'; absolutely nothing connected with wood, the woods and forestry is overlooked – from antique saws and charcoal-burning equipment to household utensils made of bark and exquisite hunting knives and rifles. The contemporary illustrations of Kanizsa Castle are fascinating, especially the idealised Turkish

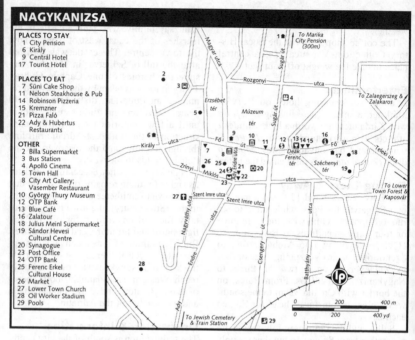

NAGYKANIZSA

PLACES TO STAY
1 City Pension
6 Király
9 Centrál Hotel
17 Tourist Hotel

PLACES TO EAT
7 Süni Cake Shop
11 Nelson Steakhouse & Pub
14 Robinson Pizzeria
15 Kremzner
21 Pizza Faló
22 Ady & Hubertus
      Restaurants

OTHER
2 Billa Supermarket
3 Bus Station
4 Apolló Cinema
5 Town Hall
8 City Art Gallery;
      Vasember Restaurant
10 György Thury Museum
12 OTP Bank
13 Blue Café
16 Zalatour
18 Julius Meinl Supermarket
19 Sándor Hevesi
      Cultural Centre
20 Synagogue
23 Post Office
24 OTP Bank
25 Ferenc Erkel
      Cultural House
26 Market
27 Lower Town Church
28 Oil Worker Stadium
29 Pools

one from 1664 showing 14 minarets within the castle walls. The museum is open from 10 am to 6 pm Wednesday to Sunday (80Ft).

The **City Art Gallery** (Városi Képtár) is in the 18th-century Iron Man House (Vasemberház) at Erzsébet tér 1, named after the suit of armour on the facade that once advertised an ironmonger's shop. The gallery (enter from Ady Endre utca) exhibits small sculptures and other work by local artists from 10 am to 2 pm on Wednesday and Thursday and from 2 to 6 pm Friday to Sunday.

The neoclassical **synagogue**, built in 1810 in a courtyard behind Fő út 6 (once a Jewish school), is in appalling condition, though it is occasionally used for concerts and lectures. Outside the western entrance a cenotaph remembers the 2700 Jews who were rounded up here in late April 1944 and deported to the death camps at Auschwitz. The synagogue can be visited from 2 to 6 pm from Tuesday to Saturday (free).

At the corner of Szent Imre utca and Nagyváthy utca, the Franciscan **Lower Town Church** (Alsóvárosi templom), begun in 1702 but not completed for 100 years, has some ornate stucco work and a rococo pulpit, but you can't miss the holy-water font, carved from the burial stone of the Turkish general Pasha Mustafa.

Even if you're not going to see a film, have a look at the **Apolló Cinema** (formerly the Municipal Theatre), Sugár út 5, in a small garden south of Rozgonyi utca. It's a unique example of Art Nouveau and Hungarian folk architecture designed by István Medgyaszay in 1926.

Activities

The so-called Lower Town Forest (Alsóvárosi erdő), 6km east of the town centre, has a large rowing lake with boats available in summer.

There are outdoor pools (open 9.30 am to 6.30 pm daily June to mid-September) and an indoor one (6 am to 6 pm weekdays, from

2 pm on Monday and from 9 am at the weekend) in the Kiskert, south of the centre at Csengery út 49. But if you want to take the (thermal) waters, you'll have to go to the spa at Zalakaros, 18km to the north-east near the Little Balaton (Kis-Balaton). The Zalakaros spring, which gushes out of the ground at an incredible 92°C, was discovered by workers drilling for oil in the early 1960s.

Places to Stay

Zalatour can organise *private rooms* for about 1500Ft per person. The hostel-like *Tourist* hotel (☎ 312 340, Fő út 24) has 37 rooms with singles/doubles/triples costing 1500/2240/3360Ft.

The *Király* (☎ 325 489, cnr Király utca & Kalmár utca), a pleasant nine-room pension on the 1st floor of a small shopping and office complex, has singles/doubles/triples for 4500/7000/8500Ft. The *City* pension (☎ 311 969, fax 318 800, ✉ touring@mail .matav.hu, Sugár út 26) has only four rooms but its sister-pension, the *Marika City* (☎ 318 800, fax 320 194, Sugár út 45), a couple of hundred metres north, has another seven more.

The 36-room *Centrál* hotel (☎ 314 000, fax 310 111, Erzsébet tér 23), built in 1912, has recently been given a fairly major face-lift with an eye to cornering the business travel market, making it a rather expensive place to stay: singles/doubles with bath and all the mod cons are 9000/13,000Ft.

Places to Eat

There are a number of cheap places on Ady Endre utca, including *Pizza Faló* at No 3, *Ady* at No 5 and *Hubertus* at No 7. The *Vasember* restaurant in the Iron Man House (cnr Ady Endre utca & Erzsébet tér) has pizza as well as Hungarian main courses for about 600Ft and stays open till 10 pm.

For more upmarket options, try any one of a string of restaurants along Fő utca and Deák tér. The *Nelson* (Fő utca 7) is a pub-restaurant with a great steak menu (850Ft to 1200Ft) while the *Robinson* (Deák tér 9) is a fashionable pizzeria popular with Nagykanizsa's young bloods and open till

late. The *Kremzner* (Deák Ferenc tér 11) is a clean, modern place with a Germanic twist.

For cakes and ice cream try the *Süni* (Erzsébet tér 2).

Entertainment

The *Sándor Hevesi Cultural Centre* (☎ 311 464, Széchenyi tér 5-9) should be able to tell you what's on in Nagykanizsa. It and the *Ferenc Erkel Cultural House* (☎ 313 040, Ady Endre utca 8) behind the post office host weekend discos.

The local Kanizsai beer flows as freely throughout the year as it does at the Kanizsai Days festival and there are a lot of decent pubs and bars, including the *Nelson* (see Places to Eat). But my favourite new place is the *Blue Cafe* (Deák tér) with a cool glass brick bar and neon lighting. You could easily be in Miami.

Getting There & Away

There's a bus running every 30 minutes to the Zalakaros spa and also hourly ones to Zalaegerszeg and Keszthely. Otherwise, there are between five daily departures to Budapest, two to Sopron, one to Szeged, three to Pápa, seven to Kaposvár, eight to Balatonmagyaród on the Little Balaton, five to Pécs and eight to Szombathely.

From Nagykanizsa, some seven daily trains go north to Szombathely and other points in Western Transdanubia including Sopron, and at least two head south for Zagreb, Ljubljana, Trieste and Venice. Trains run direct to Budapest-Déli and Budapest-Keleti and the southern shore resorts, but if you're headed for the western or northern sides (such as Keszthely or Balatonfüred), you must change at Balatonszentgyörgy.

Getting Around

Nagykanizsa is an easy walking city, but you may prefer to wait and ride. From the train station, bus No 18 goes to the bus station and city centre. Bus No 17b terminates near the rowing lake in the Lower Town Forest, or you can take the Budapest-bound local train and get off at the first stop (Nagyrécse).

Local taxis are available on ☎ 312 000 or ☎ 312 222.

Great Plain

The Great Plain (Nagyalföld) is Hungary's 'Midwest', an enormous prairie that stretches for hundreds of kilometres east and south-east of Budapest. It covers nearly half of the nation's territory – some 45,000 sq km – but only about one-third of all Hungarians live here.

After Budapest and Lake Balaton, no area is so well known outside Hungary as the Great Plain. Like Australians and their Outback, many Hungarians tend to view the Great Plain romantically as a region of hardy shepherds fighting the wind and the snow in winter and trying not to go stir-crazy in summer as the notorious *délibáb* (mirages) rise off the baking soil, leading them, their mop-like *puli* dogs and flocks astray. This mythology of the Great Plain can be credited to 19th-century paintings like *Storm on the Puszta* and *The Woebegone Highwayman* by Mihály Munkácsy, and the nationalist poet Sándor Petőfi, who described the Plain as 'My world and home... The Alföld, the open sea'.

But that's just a part of the story of the Great Plain; like the USA's Midwest, it defies such an easy categorisation. Grassland abounds in the east but much of the south is given over to agriculture, and there's industry in the centre. The graceful architecture of Szeged and Kecskemét, the recreational areas along the Tisza River, the spas of the Hajdúság region, the paprika fields around Kalocsa – all are as much a part of the Great Plain as the whip-cracking *csikós* (cowboy).

Five hundred years ago the region was not a steppe but forestland – and at the constant mercy of the flooding Tisza and Danube Rivers. The Turks chopped down most of the trees, destroying the protective cover and releasing the topsoil to the winds; villagers fled north or to the market and *khas* (towns under the sultan's jurisdiction). The region had become the *puszta* (meaning 'deserted' or 'uninhabited'), and it was the home to shepherds, fisherfolk, runaway

HIGHLIGHTS

- Kecskemét's wonderful Art Nouveau and Secessionist architecture and Museum of Naive Artists

- The Ferenc Móra Museum, Art Nouveau synagogue and *szegedi halászlé* (spicy fish soup) of Szeged

- Bird-watching and horse riding in the Hortobágy region

- Debrecen's colourful flea market

- The horse show at Bugac in Kiskunság National Park

- The incredibly rich Cathedral Treasury in Kalocsa

serfs and outlaws. The regulation of the rivers in the 19th century dried up the marshes and allowed for methodical irrigation, paving the way for intensive agriculture, particularly on the Southern Plain.

Hungarians generally divide the Great Plain in two: the area 'between the Danube and the Tisza Rivers', stretching from the foothills of the Northern Uplands to the border with Yugoslavia, and the land 'beyond the Tisza' (Tiszántúl) from below Hungary's North-East region to Romania. But this does not really reflect the lay of the land, the routes that travellers usually take or, frankly, what's of interest. Instead, it can be divided into the Central Plain, the Eastern Plain and the Southern Plain.

Central Plain

The Central Plain, stretching eastward from the capital and including Szolnok, Jászberény and the Tisza River, is the smallest of the Great Plain's divisions. Though it offers the least of the three areas to travellers, there are still some attractions: the spas and resorts on Lake Tisza attract visitors by the busload every year. But the Central Plain (Közép-Alföld) is usually crossed without a second glance en route to 'richer' areas.

Though it had been a crossroads since Neolithic times, the Central Plain only came into its own after the Mongol invasion of the early 13th century, which left it almost completely depopulated. In a bid to strengthen his position, King Béla IV (ruled 1235-70) settled the area with Jász, or Jazygians, an obscure pastoral people of Persian origin whose name still appears in towns throughout the region, and Kun (or Cumans) from western Siberia, known for their equestrian skills.

The area suffered under the Turks and during the independence wars of the 18th and 19th centuries. But Transylvanian salt and timber from the Carpathians had brought commerce to the region and, with the construction of the Budapest-Szolnok railway line (1847) and river drainage, industry developed.

SZOLNOK
☎ 56 • postcode 5000 • pop 78,300
A 'deed of gift' issued by King Géza I makes mention of what was then called Zounok as early as 1075, and it has remained the most important settlement in the Central Plain since that time. Szolnok has had its own share of troubles; it was laid to waste more than a dozen times over the centuries. The last disaster came in 1944, when Allied bombing all but flattened the city and the retreating German troops blew up the bridge over the Tisza. The appearance of present-day Szolnok dates from after WWII, but a few old monuments, the city's thermal spas and the Tisza (a river Daniel

Defoe once described as 'three parts water and two parts fish') give it a calm, almost laid-back feel.

Orientation
Szolnok is situated on the confluence of the Tisza and the narrow Zagyva Rivers. Its main street, Kossuth Lajos út, runs roughly west-east a few blocks north of the Tisza. Across the Tisza Bridge (Tisza híd), rebuilt in 1963, is the city's recreational area, Tisza-liget (Tisza Park), with a camp site and other accommodation as well as swimming pools. A backwater of the Tisza (Alcsi-Holt-Tisza) lies south-east of the park.

The city's busy train station is on Jubileumi tér, a couple of kilometres west of the city centre at the end of Baross Gábor út (the continuation of Kossuth Lajos út). The bus station is a few minutes' walk north of Kossuth Lajos út.

Information
Tourinform (☎ 424 803, fax 341 441, ✉ szolnok-m@tourinform.hu) is at Ságvári körút 4, around the corner from the bus station. It's open from 8 am to 5 pm weekdays and 9 am till noon at the weekend from May to September. The rest of the year it is open from 8 am to 4 pm weekdays only. Ibusz (☎ 423 602, fax 420 039), farther south at Szapáry utca 24, is open from 8 am to 5 pm on weekdays.

There's an OTP bank at Szapáry utca 31 and an MKB bank on the corner of Baross Gábor út and Sütő utca. The main post office is at Baross Gábor út 14.

Things to See
Like so many fortresses on the Great Plain, Szolnok Castle was blown to bits by the Habsburgs in 1710, and the rubble was later used to rebuild the city centre. What little is left of the castle ruins – just a bit of wall – can be seen near Gutenberg tér across the Zagyva River. Gutenberg tér is also the site of Hungary's most famous artists' colony (művésztelep), founded in 1902 and once counting among its members the realist painters Adolf Fényes, István Nagy and László Mednyánszky. Fronting the Zagyva

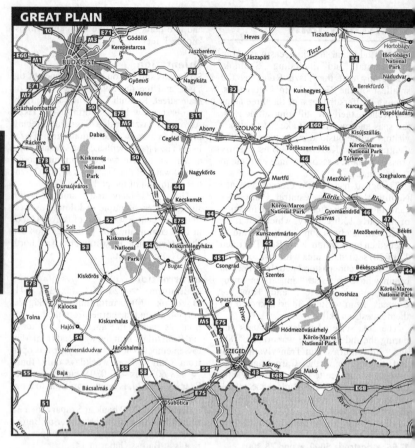

GREAT PLAIN

north-east of Szabadság tér is the **Tabán district** with the last remaining peasant houses in Szolnok.

The **János Damjanich Museum** at Kossuth tér 4, long under renovation, is now divided into three sections: archaeological finds from the Bronze Age and Roman times (100/50Ft); an extensive ethnographical collection (100/50Ft); and exhibits relating to Szolnok's history, especially the artists' colony (50/25Ft). It is open from 9 am to 5 pm Tuesday to Sunday from May to October and from 10 am to 4 pm the rest of the year. Damjanich, a great hero during

the siege of Szolnok in 1849, was one of the Martyrs of Arad – 13 generals executed by the Austrians there later that year (see The 1848-49 War of Independence & the Dual Monarchy in the History section of the Facts about the Country chapter).

The **Szolnok Gallery** at Templom utca 2, which keeps the same hours as the museum (100/50Ft), shows works by contemporary artists, but they're disappointing for this artsy town. The primary reason for visiting the gallery is to see the building itself – a Romantic-style **synagogue** designed by Lipót Baumhorn in 1898. (Baumhorn also

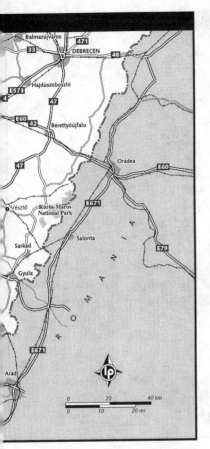

Tisza Park thermal pools across the river on Tiszaligeti sétány are open from 8 am to 6 pm daily from June to August. There's a small rowing lake behind.

, Closer to town, west of Tisza Bridge at Damjanich utca 3, the Damjanich complex has an indoor and outdoor thermal pool (from May to September) and a large sunbathing area. The more serious thermal baths, those at the Tisza hotel, are mock Turkish with a bit of Art Deco thrown in and are a great place to laze away an afternoon.

Places to Stay
Camping *Tiszaligeti Camping* (☎ 424 403, *Tiszaligeti sétány 34*), on the island south of the centre, is open from May to mid-October and charges 450/400/500Ft per adult/tent/caravan. There's also a 40-room *motel* open year round with singles/doubles for 3000/4000Ft or dormitory accommodation in rooms with up to three beds for 1000Ft per person.

Private Rooms & Hostel Ibusz can get you a private room for 2000Ft to 2500Ft for a double and 4000Ft to 4500Ft for an apartment.

The *Tourist Centre* (*Turistikai Központ;* ☎ 424 705), while not very conveniently located at the western end of Tisza Park, is a good deal. A former Young Pioneer holiday camp, the centre has triples (2850Ft), quads (3000Ft) and dormitory accommodation in bungalows for about 800Ft per person. The eight little cottages with six beds (650Ft per person) are available May to mid-September only.

Hotels Also in Tisza Park, the bare-bones *Sport* hotel (☎/fax 411 704, *Tiszaligeti sétány 10*) has singles/doubles/triples for 2000/3200/4200Ft. Breakfast is an extra 300Ft per person. Closer to Tisza Bridge at the entrance to the park, the *Touring* hotel (☎ 379 805, fax 376 003, *Tiszaligeti sétány*) has 35 rooms charging 5500Ft to 6100Ft for singles and 8000Ft to 8600Ft for doubles, all with shower or bath.

On the opposite bank and closer to the centre of town, the *Student* hotel (☎ 421 688,

did the glorious temples in Szeged and Gyöngyös.) West of the gallery at No 8 is the baroque **Franciscan church & monastery** (Ferences templom és kolostor) completed in 1757 – the city's oldest buildings.

Architecture buffs should walk up Szapáry utca from the Szolnok Gallery to No 19 for a look at a fine example of a **Hungarian Art Nouveau building**. Today it houses a few small businesses.

Activities
Szolnok is a spa town and has several places where you can 'take the waters'. The

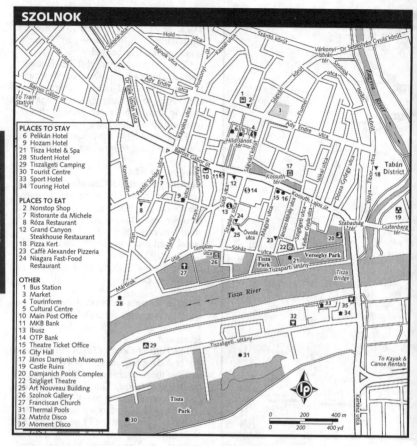

SZOLNOK

PLACES TO STAY
6 Pelikán Hotel
9 Hozam Hotel
21 Tisza Hotel & Spa
28 Student Hotel
29 Tiszaligeti Camping
30 Tourist Centre
33 Sport Hotel
34 Touring Hotel

PLACES TO EAT
2 Nonstop Shop
7 Ristorante da Michele
8 Róza Restaurant
12 Grand Canyon
    Steakhouse Restaurant
18 Pizza Kert
23 Caffè Alexander Pizzeria
24 Niagara Fast-Food
    Restaurant

OTHER
1 Bus Station
3 Market
4 Tourinform
5 Cultural Centre
10 Main Post Office
11 MKB Bank
13 Ibusz
14 OTP Bank
15 Theatre Ticket Office
16 City Hall
17 János Damjanich Museum
19 Castle Ruins
20 Damjanich Pools Complex
22 Szigliget Theatre
25 Art Nouveau Building
26 Szolnok Gallery
27 Franciscan Church
31 Thermal Pools
32 Matróz Disco
35 Moment Disco

fax 426 719, Mártírok útja 8-14) has 22 rooms with showers, available all year, at 2500Ft to 3000Ft for doubles, 3500Ft to 4000Ft for triples. From late June to late August, another 160 beds become available. This is the best place to stay in Szolnok if you're looking for company; the small bar is a congenial meeting spot.

Also on the river's right bank, the ***Tisza*** (*☎/fax 421 520, Verseghy park 2*) is Szolnok's old world hotel built in 1928 over a thermal spring. It has 33 rooms, an attached spa, a decent pub and restaurant and loads of atmosphere. Singles are DM59 to DM63, doubles are DM88 to DM93, depending on the season and the room. Room Nos 108 to 111 overlook the garden and river; the rooms on the 3rd floor with dormer windows are the cheapest.

The ***Pelikán*** hotel (*☎ 423 855, fax 340 203, Jászkürt utca 1*), in the centre, is a good example of what happened to Hungarian hotel design in the 1960s and 70s. It's a big cement block sitting on a podium with 96 rooms, an indifferent restaurant and bar, billiard club and casino. Singles/doubles are DM50/80. The new kid on the block is the very flash – and expensive – 11-room

Hozam hotel *(☎ 510 530, fax 420 778, Mária utca 25)* on a quiet residential street in the centre. Singles/doubles are DM117/156 and there's a sauna, Jacuzzi, a lovely restaurant and a chi-chi club.

Places to Eat

Niagara (Szapáry utca 23) is a fast-food place with a salad bar open to 10 pm (midnight at the weekend). For pizza, a popular place is the *Caffè Alexander (Táncsics Mihály utca 15)* near the Szigliget Theatre. It's open till midnight (to 1 am on Friday and Saturday). Or try the *Pizza Kert (Pólya Tibor utca 35)* in the Tabán district.

The *Róza (Konstantin utca 36)* is a bit out of the way but serves Hungarian dishes that are better than average. An agreeable choice is the upscale *Ristorante da Michele (Petőfi Sándor utca 6)* nearby. It has decent pastas and salads among other things, is largely nonsmoking and stays open till midnight seven days a week. The *Grand Canyon Steak House (Baross Gábor út 6)* is for carnivores who like live music (Wednesday, Friday and Saturday evenings).

The garden of the *restaurant* at the Tisza hotel (see Places to Stay, earlier in this section) is the most pleasant spot in town for a meal on a warm summer night, watching the crowds stroll along the river walk.

There's a *nonstop shop* by the bus station on Ady Endre utca.

Entertainment

The *City Cultural Centre (☎ 344 133, Hild János tér 1)* across from the Pelikán hotel can tell you whether there are concerts on at the *Franciscan church* or whether Szolnok's celebrated symphony orchestra or Béla Bartók Chamber Choir are performing.

The *Szigliget Theatre (Szigligeti színház; Sóház utca)*, across from the Tisza hotel and one of the most attractive theatres in provincial Hungary, was at the forefront of drama in Hungary in the 1970s and 80s and was the first in Eastern Europe to stage *Dr Zhivago* (1988), which was pretty daring at the time. Tickets are available at the box office (☎ 422 902), Kossuth tér 17-23, from 9 am to 7 pm weekdays.

The *Moment* disco next to the Touring hotel and the *Matróz (Tiszaligeti sétány 7)* rage till the wee hours on Wednesday, Friday and Saturday. For up-to-date entertainment, check the listings in the freebie weekly *Szolnoki Est.*

Getting There & Away

There are up to 15 daily buses to Jászberény, nine to Kecskemét, at least a dozen to Kunszentmárton, seven to Szeged, six to Gyöngyös, five to Eger, six to Tiszafüred and two to Karcag.

Szolnok has excellent rail service; you can travel to/from Budapest, Debrecen, Nyíregyháza, Békéscsaba, Warsaw, Bucharest and dozens of points in between without changing. (For Miskolc, change at Hatvan; Hódmezővásárhely is where you transfer for Szeged.)

Between April and October you may be able to link up with one of the charter boats making the 90km run south to Csongrád. Check with Tourinform.

Getting Around

From the train station, bus No 6, 7 or 8 will take you to Kossuth tér. If heading for the Tourist Centre or other accommodation in Tisza Park, take bus No 15. For a local taxi, dial ☎ 344 111.

JÁSZBERÉNY

☎ 57 • postcode 5100 • pop 29,400

Jászberény was the main political, administrative and economic centre of the Jász (Jazygian) settlements as early as the 13th century but developed slowly as the group began to die out.

The town's biggest draw has always been the Lehel Horn, which was the symbol of power of the Jazygian chiefs for centuries. Nowadays, say 'Lehel' and most Hungarians will think of the country's largest manufacturer of household appliances, located several kilometres west of the city.

Orientation & Information

Jászberény's main street is actually a long 'square' (Lehel vezér tér), which runs almost

GREAT PLAIN

parallel to the narrow 'city branch' of the Zagyva River. The bus station is a couple of blocks to the west across the Zagyva on Petőfi tér. The train station is 1.5km south-west at the end of Rákóczi út.

Tourinform (☎ 406 439, fax 412 163, ✉ jaszbereny@tourinform.hu) has an office in the Deryné Cultural Centre at Lehel vezér tér 33. It is open from 8 am to 5 pm weekends and, from mid-June to mid-September, till noon on Saturday. Ibusz (☎ 412 143, fax 412 820) is to the south-west at Szövetkezet utca 7a.

There's an OTP bank at Lehel vezér tér 28. The main post office is to the north on the same street at No 8.

Things to See & Do

The **Jász Museum**, housed in what was once the Jazygian military headquarters at Táncsics Mihály utca 5, runs the gamut of Jász culture and life – from costumes and woodcarving to language. But all aisles lead to the **Lehel Horn**, an 8th-century Byzantine work carved in ivory. Legend has it that a Magyar leader called Lehel (or Lél) fell captive during the Battle of Augsburg against the united German armies in 955 AD and, just before he was executed, killed the king by striking him on the head with the horn. The alleged murder weapon, richly carved with birds, battle scenes and anatomically correct satyrs, doesn't seem to have suffered any serious damage from the blow to the royal noggin.

The museum also spotlights local sons and daughters who made good, including the watercolourist András Sáros and the 19th-century actress Róza Széppataki Déryné. You've seen Mrs Déry before, though you may not know it. She is forever immortalised in that irritating Herend porcelain figurine you see in antique shops everywhere in Hungary of a woman in a wide organza skirt playing her *lant* (lute) and kissing the air. The Jász Museum is open from 9 am to 5 pm Tuesday to Sunday (50/30Ft).

Have a look at the fading ceiling frescoes inside the Roman Catholic **parish church** (plébániatemplom) at Szentháromság tér 4; the nave was designed in 1774 by András Mayerhoffer and József Jung, two masters of baroque architecture.

The **thermal spa** at Hatvani út 5 is open from 9 am to 6 pm Tuesday to Sunday year round. The **outdoor pools** there are open the same times, daily from May to mid-September (210/120Ft).

Places to Stay

Ibusz can arrange *private rooms* from a list of about 40.

The *Kakukkfészek* pension (☎ 412 345, Táncsics Mihály utca 8), with nine triple rooms costing 1200Ft per person, is convenient to the museum and town centre. The nine-room *Sólyom* pension (☎ 401 267, Sólyom út 8), is nicer but is about 800m north-east of the centre up Ady Endre utca, and charges 4000Ft for a double.

The signless, 26-room *Touring* hotel (☎ 412 051, fax 414 353, Serház utca 3), near the tiny Zagyva River branch, is a clean and central place but overpriced at 6900Ft for a double.

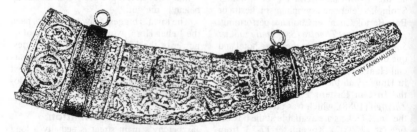

The Lehel Horn at the Jász Museum in Jászberény

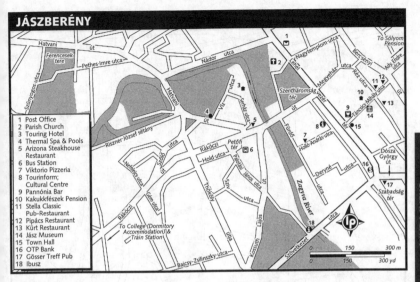

JÁSZBERÉNY

1 Post Office
2 Parish Church
3 Touring Hotel
4 Thermal Spa & Pools
5 Arizona Steakhouse
  Restaurant
6 Bus Station
7 Viktorio Pizzeria
8 Tourinform;
  Cultural Centre
9 Pannónia Bar
10 Kakukkfészek Pension
11 Stella Classic
  Pub-Restaurant
12 Pipács Restaurant
13 Kürt Restaurant
14 Jász Museum
15 Town Hall
16 OTP Bank
17 Gösser Treff Pub
18 Ibusz

GREAT PLAIN

Places to Eat

Táncsics Mihály utca near the Jász Museum is your best hunting ground. The *Pipács* at No 10 is a traditional Hungarian restaurant while the *Stella Classic* pub-restaurant *(cnr of Táncsics Mihály utca & Réz utca)*, nearby, has a much more interesting menu. The *Kürt (Mészáros Lázár utca)*, a few steps to the south is a pretty garden restaurant.

The *Gösser Treff (Dózsa György út)* has pub-style food in relatively upmarket surrounds and shuts at midnight during the week and at 2 am on Friday and Saturday. The *Viktorio Pizzeria (Holló András utca)* around the corner from the cultural centre keeps the same hours. Close to the bus station, the *Arizona Steakhouse (cnr of Rákóczi út & Serház utca)* is a popular place with Jászberény's young bloods.

Entertainment

The *Déryné Cultural Centre (☎ 412 163, Lehel vezér tér 33)* is your best source of information. There's a disco here from 11 pm on Tuesday and Saturday.

The *Pannónia* bar *(Táncsics Mihály utca 4)* is a disco till 5 am on Thursday, Friday and Saturday.

Getting There & Away

Frequent bus departures include those to Budapest (15 a day), Gyöngyös (10), Szolnok and Hatvan (10 each) and Kecskemét (seven). There are also daily buses to Szeged and Miskolc (three each); Tiszafüred, Eger and , Mátraháza (two each); and Baja, Kalocsa and Karcag (one each).

Jászberény lies approximately halfway between Hatvan and Szolnok on the railway line. These two cities are on Hungary's two main trunks, and virtually all main cities in the east are accessible from one or the other. Both Hatvan and Szolnok have direct links to Budapest.

Getting Around

Bus Nos 2 and 4 connect the train station and bus terminus, from where you can walk to the centre of town.

TISZAFÜRED

☎ 59 • postcode 5350 • pop 14,300

Tiszafüred was a rather sleepy town on the Tisza River until the early 1980s when the river was dammed and a reservoir opened up more than 125 sq km of lakes to holiday-makers. While hardly the 'Lake Balaton of

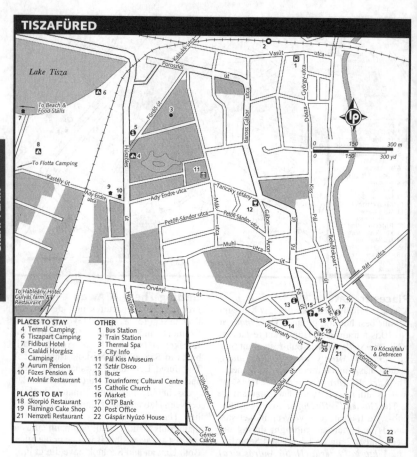

TISZAFÜRED

Lake Tisza

PLACES TO STAY
4 Termál Camping
6 Tiszapart Camping
7 Fidibus Hotel
8 Családi Horgász Camping
9 Aurum Pension
10 Füzes Pension & Molnár Restaurant

PLACES TO EAT
18 Skorpió Restaurant
19 Flamingo Cake Shop
21 Nemzeti Restaurant

OTHER
1 Bus Station
2 Train Station
3 Thermal Spa
5 City Info
11 Pál Kiss Museum
12 Sztár Disco
13 Ibusz
14 Tourinform; Cultural Centre
15 Catholic Church
16 Market
17 OTP Bank
20 Post Office
22 Gáspár Nyúzó House

---

the Great Plain' as the tourist brochures say (it's about one-fifth the size and has none of the facilities or life of its big sister in Central Transdanubia), Lake Tisza (Tisza-tó) and its primary resort, Tiszafüred, offer swimmers and boating enthusiasts a break before continuing on to the Hortobágy region, 30km to the east, and Debrecen, or Eger and the Northern Uplands. The lake can get very crowded in the high season.

Orientation & Information

Tiszafüred lies at the north-east end of Lake Tisza (Tisza-tó). From the bus and train stations opposite one another on Vasút utca, walk 10 or 15 minutes west and then south-west to the beach and camp sites. To reach the centre of town, follow Baross Gábor utca and then Fő út south for about a kilometre.

Tourinform has an office (☎/fax 353 000, ✉ tiszafured@tourinform.hu) in the cultural centre at Örvényi út 6. It's open from 8 am to 7 pm weekdays and to 4 pm at the weekend from May to September and from 8 am to 4 pm weekdays only, the rest of the year. Another excellent source of information and closer to the lake is City Info (☎/fax

351 552) at Fürdő út 21 open, in season, from 9 am till noon and 2.30 to 6 pm weekdays, 10 am to 1 pm on Saturday and 9 am till noon on Sunday. Ibusz (☎/fax 351 253) has an office at Fő út 30.

There's an OTP bank behind Fő út at Piac út 3. The post office is at Fő út 14.

Things to See

Tiszafüred is essentially a resort town, but there are a couple of interesting sights. The **Pál Kiss Museum** is in a beautiful old manor house (1840) south of the city's thermal baths at Tariczky sétány 6. Most of the collection is given over to the everyday lives of Tisza fisherfolk and the work of local potters. The museum is open from 10 am till noon and 1 to 6 pm from Tuesday to Sunday (60Ft).

The area south of Szőlősi út is chock full of traditional houses with thatched roofs and orderly little flower and vegetable gardens – a nice respite from the hubbub of the beach. One of them, the **Gáspár Nyúzó House** (Nyúzó Gáspár Fazekas Tájház) at Malom utca 12, is a former potter's residence and contains antique potting wheels, drying racks, furniture and plates in the light primary colours, and patterns of stars, and birds and flowers unique to the region. The house is open from 10 am to 4 pm Tuesday to Sunday from May to October (20Ft).

Activities

Tiszafüred's thermal spa, at the northern end of town on Poroszlói út, has four openair pools open from 7.30 am to 7 pm from May to September (180/150Ft), as well as a sauna and a wide range of medical services available from 8 am to 7 pm from midMarch to mid-November.

Both the Horgász camp site and City Info (see Orientation & Information, earlier in this section) rent bicycles and mountain bikes for 900Ft a day. At the latter, daily prices decrease the longer you keep the bike (eg, five days cost 500Ft a day). You can rent canoes/kayaks/motorboats from the Hableány hotel (see Places to Eat, later in this section) as well as Flotta Camping for 1200/1200/2800Ft a day. If you prefer to let

someone else do the driving while on the water, contact City Info or the Fidibus boat hotel moored by the public beach for information about boat tours (from 6300Ft for four people).

There's horse riding available (1800Ft to 2500Ft per hour) at the Gulyás farm (☎ 351 814) in Tiszaörvény near the Hableány hotel.

Places to Stay

There are eight camping grounds in and around Tiszafüred, open from as early as April and as late as October. The four-star *Termál Camping* (☎ 352 911, Húszöles út 2), unattractively located on a busy road south-west of the thermal spa, has bungalows for four people (5900Ft to 7400Ft) and clay tennis courts. Camping costs from 530Ft to 630Ft per person and 430Ft to 500Ft per tent, depending on the season.

The lakeside *Családi Horgász Camping* (☎ 351 220, Holt-Tisza part) has snack stalls, a restaurant, recreational facilities (including tennis) and holiday homes accommodating two/three people for 2900/3600Ft with shared showers. The public beach is a short distance to the north. *Tiszapart* (☎ 351 132), a few minutes east along the shore and past the reed beds, is for visitors with tents and caravans only. *Flotta Camping* (☎ 352 424, Holt-Tisza part), to the south-west, is suitable only for those with their own transport. Bungalows for four people here cost around 3000Ft.

Ibusz has *private rooms* available for 1500Ft to 2000Ft per person. The 10-room *Fidibus* hotel (☎ 351 818), on a ship moored near the public beach (szabad strand), charges from 3200Ft for a double and is open from April to October.

South of the camp sites, the friendly *Füzes* (☎/fax 353 772, Húszöles út 31b) is a comfortable 10-room pension with doubles for 4480Ft. All the rooms have showers and TVs, and there's a popular restaurant and busy local bar in the cellar. The flashier *Aurum* pension (☎ 351 338, Ady Endre utca 29) almost next door is more expensive, with doubles/quads for 5200/9000Ft.

GREAT PLAIN

Places to Eat

There are plenty of *food stalls* (gyros, pizza, lángos, etc) at the public beach and the camp sites. The *Nemzeti* restaurant *(Fő út 8)* is a newly renovated place just beyond the central Piac tér, open late only in summer with Gypsy music. A better choice would be a table on the breezy terrace of the *Molnár* restaurant at the Füzes pension (see Places to Stay) or the *Skorpió (Piac út)* in the small shopping arcade near the market.

According to local people, the best restaurant in the Tiszafüred area is at the *Hableány* hotel, but you'll need to have your own wheels: it's at Hunyadi utca 2 in Tiszaörvény, about 4km to the south-west. Another good choice is the *Gémes* csárda *(Húszöles út 80a)*, but it too is a ways out.

The *Flamingo (Fő út)*, a combination 'cukrászda and bronzárium' opposite the start of Szőlősi út, does some excellent baking (well, of cakes – we don't know about the quality of the tanning).

Entertainment

The open-air bar on top of the *Fidibusz* 'boatel' is a great place for a sundowner and the pub in the basement of the *Aurum* pension is a popular local meeting place. The *Sztár* disco *(cnr of Tariczky sétány & Gábor Áron út)* is open from 9 pm to 5 am at weekends.

Getting There & Away

Some 10 buses a day link Tiszafüred with Abádszalók, another popular lake resort to the south. Other destinations served daily include Budapest (four buses a day), Szolnok (three to five), Karcag (two to four), Eger (six to eight), Szeged and Jászberény (two each), Miskolc and Debrecen (at least three each) and Hajdúszoboszló (one to three).

Tiszafüred is on the railway line linking Karcag (the transfer point from Szolnok and once the seat of the Kun chiefs) and Füzesabony, from where you can carry on to Eger or Miskolc. The train going east towards Debrecen passes through the Hortobágy region.

Eastern Plain

The Eastern Plain (Kelet-Alföld) includes Debrecen, the towns of the Hajdúság region, and the Hortobágy, the birthplace of the puszta legend. This part of the Great Plain was important for centuries as it was on the Salt Road – the route taken by traders in that precious commodity, from Transylvania via the Tisza River and across the Eastern Plain by bullock cart to the wealthy city of Debrecen. When the trees were chopped down and the river was regulated, the water in the soil evaporated, turning the region into a vast, saline grassland suitable only for grazing. The myth of the lonely *pásztor* (shepherd) in billowy trousers, the wayside csárdas, and Gypsy violinists was born – to be kept alive in literature, fine art and the imagination of the Hungarian people.

DEBRECEN

☎ 52 • postcode 4000 • pop 212,200

Debrecen is Hungary's second-largest city, and its name has been synonymous with wealth and conservatism since the 16th century. That may not be immediately apparent on Piac utca on a Saturday night as you collide with drunks and kids on in-line skates, but you don't have to go far to find either.

The area around Debrecen had been settled since the earliest times, and when the Magyars arrived late in the 9th century they found a colony of Slovaks here who called the region Dobre Zliem for its 'good soil'. Debrecen's wealth, based on salt, the fur trade and cattle-raising, grew steadily through the Middle Ages and increased during the Turkish occupation; the city kept all sides happy by paying tribute to the Ottomans, the Habsburgs and Transylvanian princes at the same time.

Most of the large estates on the Eastern Plain were owned by Debrecen's independent-minded burghers, who had converted to Protestantism in the mid-16th century. These *čivis* (from the Latin for 'citizen') lived in the city while the peasants raised horses and cattle in the Hortobágy. *Hajdúk* (from *hajt*, 'to drive') – landless peasants who would later play an important role in the wars with the Habsburgs as Heyduck mercenaries (see boxed text 'The Heyducks') – drove the animals on the hoof westward to markets as far as France.

Debrecen played a pivotal role in the 1848-49 War of Independence and, late in the 19th century and early in the 20th, it experienced a major building boom. Today it is the capital of Hajdú-Bihar County and an important university city.

Orientation

Debrecen is an easy city to negotiate. A ring road, built on the city's original earthen walls, encloses the Belváros (Inner Town). This is bisected by Piac utca, which runs northward from the train station at Petőfi tér to Kálvin tér, site of the Great Church and Debrecen's centre. With the exception of Nagyerdei Park, the recreational 'Big Forest Park' some 3km farther north, almost all of Debrecen's attractions are within easy walking distance of Kálvin tér.

The Heyducks

The Hajdúság region was settled in the 15th century predominantly by the *hajdúk* (English: Heyducks or Haiduks), a community of Magyar and Slav drovers and brigands turned mercenaries and renowned both for their skill in battle and their bisexuality. When the Heyducks helped István Bocskai (1557-1606), prince of Transylvania, rout the Habsburg forces at Álmosd, south-east of Debrecen, in 1604, they were raised to the rank of nobility, and some 10,000 were granted land – as much to keep the ferocious, randy brigands in check as to reward them.

The Heyducks built towns with walled fortresses around the region. Many of the streets in today's Hajdú towns trace the concentric circles of these walls, the outermost forming ring roads. The Hajdúság continued as a special administrative district until 1876, when it was incorporated into Hajdú-Bihar County and the Heyducks privileges were terminated.

The bus station is on Külső-Vásártér, the 'outer marketplace' at the western end of Széchenyi utca.

Information

The helpful Tourinform office (☎ 412 250, fax 314 139, @ debrecen@tourinform.hu) is in the town hall at Piac utca 20. It is open from 8 am to 8 pm daily from June to August, from 9 am to 5 pm weekdays only the rest of the year. Hajdútourist (☎ 415 588) is at Kálvin tér 2a at the entrance to the Udvarház shopping mall across from the Great Church while Ibusz (☎ 415 555, fax 410 756) is near the Little Church at Révész tér 2. Those offices are open 8 am to 5 pm weekdays and till noon or 12.30 pm on Saturday.

There's an OTP bank on Hatvan utca, opposite the main post office, which is at No 5-9. You'll find other ATMs at Piac utca 16 and No 45 of the same street. The Csokonai Bookshop, Piac utca 45, has a good foreign language and map selection.

Things to See

The yellow neoclassical **Great Church**, built in 1821 on Kálvin tér, has become so synonymous with Debrecen that mirages of its twin clock towers were reportedly seen on the Great Plain early in the last century. Accommodating some 3000 people, the Nagytemplom is Hungary's largest Protestant church, and it was here that Lajos Kossuth read the Declaration of Independence from Austria on 14 April 1849. Don't miss the magnificent organ in the loft behind the pulpit. The church is open from 9 am to 4 pm weekdays, till noon on Saturday and from 11 am to 4 pm on Sunday (40/20Ft).

North of the church at Kálvin tér 16 stands the **Reformed College** (Református Kollégium; 1816), the site of a prestigious secondary school and theological college since the Middle Ages. Downstairs, there are exhibits on religious art and sacred objects (including a 17th-century chalice made from a coconut) and on the school's history; go up to visit the 650,000-volume **library** and the **oratory**, where the breakaway National Assembly met in 1849 and Hungary's postwar provisional government was declared in

GREAT PLAIN

GREAT PLAIN

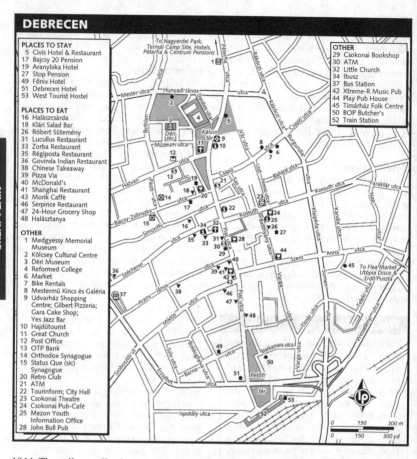

DEBRECEN

PLACES TO STAY
5 Civis Hotel & Restaurant
17 Bajcsy 20 Pension
19 Aranybika Hotel
27 Stop Pension
49 Főnix Hotel
51 Debrecen Hotel
53 West Tourist Hostel

PLACES TO EAT
16 Halászcsárda
18 Klári Salad Bar
26 Róbert Sütemény
31 Lucullus Restaurant
33 Zorba Restaurant
35 Régiposta Restaurant
36 Govinda Indian Restaurant
39 Chinese Takeaway
39 Pizza Via
40 McDonald's
41 Shanghai Restaurant
43 Morik Caffè
46 Serpince Restaurant
47 24-Hour Grocery Shop
48 Halásztanya

OTHER
1 Medgyessy Memorial Museum
2 Kölcsey Cultural Centre
3 Déri Museum
4 Reformed College
6 Market
7 Bike Rentals
8 Mestermű Kincs és Galéria
9 Udvarház Shopping Centre; Gilbert Pizzeria; Gara Cake Shop; Yes Jazz Bar
10 Hajdútourist
11 Great Church
12 Post Office
13 OTP Bank
14 Orthodox Synagogue
15 Status Que (sic) Synagogue
20 Retro Club
21 ATM
22 Tourinform; City Hall
23 Csokonai Theatre
24 Csokonai Pub-Café
25 Mezon Youth Information Office
28 John Bull Pub

OTHER
29 Csokonai Bookshop
30 ATM
32 Little Church
34 Ibusz
37 Bus Station
42 Xtreme-R Music Pub
44 Play Pub House
45 Tímárház Folk Centre
50 BOP Butcher's
52 Train Station

1944. The college collections are open from 9 am to 5 pm Tuesday to Saturday and to 1 pm on Sunday (60/40Ft).

Folklore exhibits at the **Déri Museum**, a short walk west of the Reformed College at Déri tér 1, offer excellent insights into life on the puszta and among the bourgeois citizens of Debrecen up to the 19th century. Mihály Munkácsy's mythical interpretations of the Hortobágy and his *Christ's Passion* take pride of place in a separate art gallery. The museum's entrance is flanked by four superb bronzes by sculptor Ferenc Medgyessy, a local boy who merits his own

Medgyessy Memorial Museum in an old burgher house at Péterfia utca 28. The Déri Museum is open from 10 am to 6pm Tuesday to Sunday from April to October and to 4 pm the rest of the year (300/150Ft).

Just walking along Piac utca and down some of the side streets, with their array of neoclassical, baroque and Art Nouveau buildings, is a treat. Kossuth utca and its continuation, Széchenyi utca, where the baroque Calvinist **Little Church** (Kistemplom; 1726) stands with its bastion-like tower, is especially interesting. The **Status Que Conservative Synagogue** (1909) on

Kápolnási utca just south of Bajcsy-Zsilinszky utca is worth a look if the caretaker will let you in. The derelict **Orthodox synagogue** is nearby at Pászti utca 6.

Tímárház is a folk-craft centre and workshop at Nagy Gál István utca 6, where embroiderers, basket weavers, carvers and so on do their stuff in rotation from 10 am to 6 pm Tuesday to Friday and to 2 pm on Saturday.

Definitely worth the trip is the colourful **flea market** near the large sports complex on Vágóhíd utca, served by bus Nos 30, 30a, 9 & 15 from the train station. In the morning it attracts a motley group of Ukrainians, Poles, Romanians, Roma and Hungarians from Transylvania who hawk everything from used shoes to caviar. A fascinating **horse market** is usually held there on Friday morning.

Activities

The city's Nagyerdei Park offers boating and walks along leafy trails, but the main attraction here is the **thermal bath**, a complex offering a half-dozen indoor and open-air pools of brownish mineral and fresh water, sauna and every type of therapy imaginable. The indoor spa is open 8 am to 4 pm weekdays from May to August and from 6 am to 7 pm the rest of the year. The outdoor pools are open from 9 am to 7 pm daily from May to September.

If you want to see more of the great outdoors, head for the **Erdőpuszta** (Puszta Forest), a protected area of pine and acacia forests, lakes and trails a few kilometres to the east and south-east of Debrecen. **Bánk**, the centre, has a splendid arboretum (Fancsika utca 93a) and there are boats for rent on Vekeri Lake (Vekeri-tó).

You can rent bikes from the bicycle shop at Csapó utca 19 in Debrecen for 400Ft a day from 9 am to 5 pm weekdays and to 1 pm on Saturday.

Special Events

Annual events to watch out for include the Hajdúság Carnival (Hajdúsági Fasang) in February, the Spring Festival (Tavaszi Fesztivál) of performing arts and Jazz Days (Dzsessznapok) in March and the famous

Flower Carnival (Virágkarnevál) held on 20 August.

Places to Stay

Camping Of the three camp sites in Debrecen, the best is the **Termál** (☎ 412 456, Nagyerdei körút 102), north-east of Nagyerdei Park. Tents are available for rent, and bungalows accommodating four people start at 7000Ft. The site is open from May to September.

Private Rooms & Hostels Hajdútourist and Ibusz can arrange *private rooms* for 2000Ft per person and apartments for four people from 4500Ft. With so many universities and colleges in town, there's plenty of *dormitory accommodation* in summer (and sometimes at the weekend, year round), costing well under 1000Ft per person. Tourinform can provide you with a list. The *West* tourist hostel (☎ 420 891, Wesselényi utca 4) is a tourist hostel near the train station with accommodation in rooms with three or four beds starting at 1000Ft per person.

Pensions The *Péterfia* pension (☎/fax 423 582, Péterfia utca 37b), with 18 rooms in a charming row house, charges from 3500Ft for a double. Next door, the 20-room *Centrum* (☎ 416 193, fax 442 843, Péterfia utca 37a) is flashier and more expensive: from 4500Ft to 5000Ft for singles, 5500Ft to 7000Ft for doubles, depending on whether you're in the old or newer wing.

A more central place is the 14-room *Stop* (☎ 420 301, Batthyány utca 18), a friendly place in a courtyard off a pedestrians-only street with doubles for 3900Ft. Another central, though dingier, option is the *Bajcsy 20* pension (☎ 343 321, fax 368 968, Bajcsy-Zsilinszky utca 20). Doubles start at 4500Ft.

Hotels Opposite the train station and popular with Russian and Ukrainian 'beesneesmen', the 85-room *Debrecen* hotel (☎ 410 111, fax 419 672, Petőfi tér 9) charges 2500Ft for a double room with shower on the hall and 3800Ft for a room with shower. It's pretty run-down and noisy. A better choice would be the *Főnix* (☎ 413 355, *fax 413 054, Barna utca 17)* with 52 rooms on a relatively quiet side street north-west of Petőfi tér. Doubles with shower are 5640Ft, while singles/doubles with shared shower cost 1920/3440Ft.

The *Nagyerdő* (☎ *410 588, fax 319 739, Pallagi út 5)* is a huge, 106-room spa hotel in the park with singles/doubles for 9300/12,800Ft. The *Termál* (☎ *411 888, fax 311 730,* @ *dbgyogy@datanet.hu, Nagyerdei park 1)* has 96 rooms, with singles/doubles from 17,500/19,500Ft (entry to the baths included).

The landmark Art Nouveau *Aranybika* (☎ *416 777, fax 421 834,* @ *civisrt@mail.datanet.hu, Piac utca 11-15)* with 227 very different rooms is still the place to stay in Debrecen, despite the advent of the flashier *Cívis* (☎/*fax 418 522,* @ *civhot@mail.datanet.hu, Kálvin tér 4)* a few years back. Singles at the Aranybika range from DM68 to DM132 and doubles from DM89 to DM166, depending on whether you stay in the charming old wing or garish new building. Singles at the Cívis are 7250Ft to 9950Ft and doubles 8900Ft to 12,350Ft.

Places to Eat

Debreceners flock to the *Serpince a Flaskához (Miklós utca 4)*, a cellar restaurant with excellent regional specialities including stuffed cabbage, which originated in Debrecen. Walk through the wood-shingled 'bottle' (flaska) and down the stairs. You'll have to line up for the pizza and pasta at *Gilbert* pizzeria *(Kálvin tér)* in the Udvarház shopping mall. I prefer the surrounds of the modern and very stylish *Pizza Via (Arany János utca 2)* open daily till 11 pm.

The *Halászcsárda (Simonffy utca 4)* serves basic, inexpensive fish dishes until 10 pm daily. A more upmarket – and expensive – choice for similar fare is the upbeat *Halásztanya (Piac utca 70-74)*. Romantics will enjoy the *Régiposta (Széchenyi utca 6)*, a 17th-century inn with Gypsy music.

For Asian try either the *Chinese takeaway (Arany János utca 28)*, a short distance east of the bus station and open to 10 pm, or the sit-down *Shanghai (Piac utca 57)* down a small alley just south of McDonald's and open to 11 pm. Vegetarians are catered for at the *Klári Salátabár (Bajcsy-Zsilinszky utca)*, open weekdays from 9 am to 6 pm, and at *Govinda (cnr of Széchenyi utca & Szepességi utca)*, a meat-less Indian place near the bus station. The *Zorba (Révész tér)* near the Little church serves gyros, shiskebabs, etc, daily to 10 pm.

A restaurant that gets top marks from local people for a night out is the *Lucullus* cellar restaurant *(Piac utca 41)*, with mains from 690Ft to 1250Ft (open daily to 11 pm).

The *Gara (Kálvin tér)* in the Udvarház mall gets my vote for having the best cakes and ice cream (made with real fruit) outside Budapest. It's open daily from 9 am to 6 pm. Two other good choices are *Róbert Sütemény (Batthyány utca 6)*, open to 6 pm weekdays and 2 pm on Saturday, and the *Morik Caffè (cnr Piac utca & Miklós utca)*, a place for serious coffee drinkers where the waitresses wear blue frocks and frilly white bonnets.

There's a *24-hour shop (Piac utca 75)* within walking distance of the train station. The covered *fruit & vegetable market (Csapó utca)* is open daily.

Entertainment

Debrecen prides itself on its cultural life; check with staff at the delightful *Csokonai Theatre* (☎ *417 811, Kossuth utca 10)* or the *Kölcsey Cultural Centre* (☎ *413 977, Hunyadi János utca 1-3)* behind the Déri Museum, for event schedules. Concerts are sometimes held in the in the *Bartók Hall* (Bartók terem) of the Aranybika hotel or at the *Great Church*. The Mezon youth information office (☎ *415 498)*, Batthyány utca 2b, can fill you in on the popular music scene (open 10 am to 6 pm weekdays and to 1 pm on Saturday) or check the listings in the weekly entertainment freebie *Debreceni Est*.

A pub-cafe attracting a young crowd is the *Csokonai (Kossuth utca 21)*; the *John Bull (Piac utca 28)* is another link in the popular chain. The outside tables at the *Play Pub House (Batthyány utca 24-26)* on a pedestrians-only street are very pleasant in the warm weather.

The *Yes Jazz Bar* (*Kálvin tér 8*) has live blues and jazz sets most nights. The *Xtreme-R Music Pub* (*Piac utca 57b*) in the Amfora Udvar shopping centre near McDonald's has music – canned and live – daily to 2 am. Popular clubs include the *Retro Club* (*Bajcsy-Zsilinszky utca*) next to the Klári Salátabár is open from 9 pm to 3 am; the *Vigadó Dance Club* in Nagyerdei Park; and the popular *Utópia* (*Vágohíd utca*) south-east of the centre.

Shopping

You can't leave the city without buying – or at least trying – some of the famous Debrecen sausage available at butcher shops (eg, on Kossuth utca) and grocery stores everywhere, including BOP near the train station on Iparkamara utca.

There's a lovely antique-cum-curio shop called Mestermü Kincs és Galéria at Csapó utca 22. Buy me something.

Getting There & Away

From Debrecen you can catch a direct bus to any of the following destinations: Bánk (five a day); Békéscsaba (10 or 11); Berettyóújfalu (hourly); Eger (five); Gyöngyös (two); Gyula (five to seven); Hajdúböszörmény (half-hourly); Hajdúnánás (10 to 12); Hajdúszoboszló (half-hourly); Hódmezővásárhely and Szeged (three); Kecskemét (one); Mátészalka (two); Miskolc (hourly); Nádudvar (12); Nyírbátor and Nyíregyháza (three each); Sátoraljaújhely (two); Szarvas (two); and Tokaj (two).

Foreign destinations served by bus include Košice (Kassa) in Slovakia at 7 am Monday to Thursday and, in Romania, Baia Mare (Nagybánya) at 5.30 am on Friday and Oradea (Nagyvárad) at 6.30 am on Tuesday and Thursday and at 5 am and 4 pm on Saturday.

Debrecen is served by some two dozen trains a day from Budapest-Nyugati (and sometimes Keleti) via Szolnok, including five 2½-hour expresses. Cities to the north and north-west – Nyíregyháza, Tokaj and Miskolc – can be reached most effectively by train. For Eger, take the train to Füzesabony and change. For points south, use the bus or a bus/train combination.

Daily international departures from Debrecen reach Košice in Slovakia; Kraków and Warsaw in Poland; Satu Mare and Baia Mare in Romania; Lvov in Ukraine; and Moscow.

Getting Around

Tram No 1 – the only line in town – is ideal both for transport and sightseeing. From the train station, it runs north along Piac utca to Kálvin tér and then carries on to Nagyerdei Park, where it loops around for the same trip southward.

Most other city transport can be caught at the southern end of Petőfi tér. Bus Nos 12 and 19 and the No 2 trolley bus link the train and bus stations. Ticket inspectors are a regular sight in Debrecen, and riding 'black' – particularly on the buses to the flea market – is risky (see Things to See). They show no mercy: you'll be fined on the spot.

For a local taxi, ring ☎ 444 444 or ☎ 455 555.

HORTOBÁGY

☎ 52 • postcode 4071 • pop 1700

This village, some 40km west of Debrecen, is the centre of the Hortobágy region, once celebrated for its sturdy cowboys, inns and Gypsy bands. But you'll want to come here to explore the 75,000-hectare Hortobágy National Park and wildlife preserve – home to hundreds of birds as well as plant species that are usually found only by the sea.

It's true that the Hortobágy has been milked by the Hungarian tourism industry for everything it's worth, and the stage-managed horse shows, costumed *csikósok* and tacky gewgaws on sale are all over the top. Still, dark clouds appearing out of nowhere to cover a blazing sun and the possibility of spotting a mirage may have you dreaming of a different Hortobágy – the mythical one that only ever existed in paintings, poems and the imaginations of the people.

Orientation & Information

Buses – as few as there are – stop on the main road (route No 33) near the village

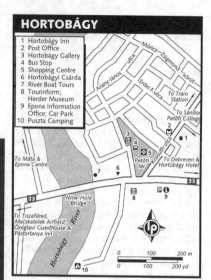

HORTOBÁGY

1 Hortobágy Inn
2 Post Office
3 Hortobágy Gallery
4 Bus Stop
5 Shopping Centre
6 Hortobágyi Csárda
7 River Boat Tours
8 Tourinform;
   Herder Museum
9 Epona Information
   Office; Car Park
10 Puszta Camping

centre or on Petőfi tér near the new shopping centre; the train station is to the northeast at the end of Kossuth utca. Tourinform (☎/fax 369 119, ✉ hortobagy@tourinform .hu) has an office in the Herder Museum at Petőfi tér 1 and is open from 9 am to 5 pm daily from June to August and from 8 am to 4 pm weekdays only for most of the other seasons except in November and December when the hours are 8 am to 2 pm. The post office, where you can change money, is opposite the Hortobágy inn at Kossuth utca 2.

Hortobágy National Park

With its varied terrain and water sources, the park offers some of the best birdwatching in Europe. Indeed, some 344 species (of the continent's estimated 410) have been spotted here in the past 20 years, including many types of grebes, herons, egrets, spoonbills, storks, kites, shrikes, warblers and eagles. The great bustard, one of the world's largest birds, standing a metre high and weighing in at 20kg, has its own reserve with limited access to two-legged mammals (see 'The Birds of Hungary' special section in the Facts about the Country chapter).

Visitor passes (800Ft for a day), available from Tourinform, allow entry to three restricted areas of the park. To see the best parts of the park, though – the closed areas north of route No 33 and the saline swamplands south of it – you must have a guide and travel by horse, carriage or special 4WD. Contact Tourinform or Aquila Nature Tours (☎/fax 456 744 or ☎/fax 386 348, ✉ aquila@elender.hu), PO Box 8, H-4015 Debrecen, a private travel agency with specialised birdwatching and nature tours. The price is 1500Ft per hour plus 20Ft per kilometre. Week-long tours including accommodation cost about US$600 per person.

The national park office offers a two hour coach tour of the park through Tourinform (1600Ft). Buses leave from the car park in front of the Herder Museum for the starting points at the 79km and 86km stones on route No 33 at approximately 11 am, noon, 2 and 4 pm every day from April to October. Epona does a similar tour for the same price.

Other Attractions

The **Nine-Hole Bridge** (Kilence lyukú híd; 1833) spanning the marshy Hortobágy River is the longest stone bridge (and certainly the most sketched, painted and photographed bridge) in Hungary. Just before it, at Petőfi tér 2, stands the **Hortobágyi Csárda**, one of the original eating houses (1781) used by salt traders on their way from the Tisza River to Debrecen. The going was rough along the muddy trails, and bullock carts could only cover about 12km a day. That's why you'll still find inns spaced at those intervals today at, for example, Látókép, Nagyhegyes and Hortobágy. The inns provided itinerant Roma fiddlers with employment, though they did not originally live in this part of Hungary. Gypsy music and csárdas have been synonymous ever since.

The **Hortobágy Gallery**, just behind the restaurant, has a potpourri of art styles and media with a Hortobágy theme, some of them saccharine-sweet, others quite evocative. Check the big skies in some of the works by László Holló or Arthur Tölgyessy and see if they don't match the real one. The gallery is open from 9 am to 5 pm Tuesday to Sunday from April to October and to 4 pm the rest of the year (100/50Ft).

The **Herder Museum** (Pásztormúzeum), housed in an 18th-century carriage house across from the csárda at Petőfi tér 1, has good exhibits on how riders, cowherds, shepherds and swineherds fed and clothed themselves and played their music. Spare some time for a close look at the finely embroidered jackets and elaborate long capes (szűr) they wore. The Herder Museum is open daily from 9 am to 6 pm daily from April to October (200/100Ft).

Máta, about 2km north of Hortobágy village, is the centre of the Hortobágy horse industry, and the mighty Nonius is bred here. State-owned until the early 1990s, the horses, carriages, herds of grey Hungarian cattle and the *racka* sheep with their corkscrew-like horns have been taken over by a German-Hungarian riding and hotel company called Epona. But even if you don't ride and aren't interested in staged 'rodeos', it's worth a walk over for a look at the stables, the horses and the fine old carriages.

Activities
Horse Riding At Máta, the Epona Riding Village (☎ 369 020) offers any number of horse-related activities: riding and roping displays by the csikósok, with a two-hour tour of the puszta by carriage (1600Ft) to see the cattle, sheep and perhaps something a little wilder; horse riding (2300Ft); and lessons in riding (1800Ft per hour) and carriage-driving (6000Ft). Epona has an information booth in the car park near the Herder Museum.

Other Activities From mid-May to September, there are hourly motorboat tours along the Hortobágy River between 9 am and 8 pm. The one-hour tour costs 700/350Ft for adults/children.

A company called Poszméh Air (☎ 369 105) offers sightseeing flights of the region from 10 am to 6 pm from April to November. Prices vary considerably but expect to pay between 6000Ft and 15,000Ft for

flights lasting five to 12 minutes over the Hortobágy or farther afield on the puszta. Planes take off from the airfield at Macskatelek, about 3km west of the village at the 70km stone.

Special Events
The area is busiest in late June/early July when Máta hosts the International Equestrian Days (Nemzetközi lovasnapok) and during the Hortobágy Bridge Fair (Hortobágyi hídi vásár) on 19-20 August, an attempt to recreate the old 'outlaw' fairs held here in the last century.

Places to Stay
Puszta Camping (☎ 369 300), about 300m south of the Herder Museum, has a bungalow (4000Ft for two) and tents available from May to October. Camping costs 315Ft to 380Ft per person and per tent and 640Ft to 760Ft for a caravan, depending on the season. It even has a tiny thermal pool. A less convenient site is *Róna Camping* (☎ 369 071) at the Hortobágy hotel in Borsós, 2km to the east. The *Sándor Petőfi College* (☎ 369 128, József Attila utca 1) has four-bed dormitory rooms available in summer for less than 1000Ft per person. Tourinform can organise *private rooms* for 1500Ft to 2000Ft per person, or try the houses at Kossuth utca 23, Czinege János utca 2 and 21 or Arany János utca 14 and 17.

The most central place is the 10-room *Hortobágy* inn (☎ 369 137, Kossuth utca 1), which has singles/doubles/triples for 2000/3400/4000Ft with showers in the hall. It's a basic but pleasant place with friendly staff. If there's no room at the inn, check the *Hortobágy* hotel (☎/fax 369 071), an attractive enough place with a central garden and 20 rooms in an old building and a newer concrete shoebox in Borsós. It's open April to October and doubles cost 5000Ft.

Two other possibilities are a bit far out, but each has its own attractions. The nine-room *Öregtavi* guesthouse (☎/fax 369 119), by the Hortobágyi halastó (Hortobágy Fish Pond) 7km north-west of the village, is an excellent spot for some informal birdwatching. It charges about 5000Ft for a double. The *Pástortanya* inn (☎ 369 127) is a traditional Hortobágy-style farmhouse with five rooms about 5km to the west.

The *Epona* resort hotel (☎ 369 020, fax 369 027, ✆ epona@mail.datanet.hu) in Máta, with its 58 deluxe rooms, 20 individual houses (complete with private stables), swimming pool, fitness centre and two restaurants, is a world apart. The prices are out of this world too: DM120/170 or DM130/190 for singles/ doubles, depending on the season. A suite is DM210 and a separate house accommodating four to six people is DM220.

Places to Eat
It's touristy and a little pricey, but you've got to have a meal at the *Hortobágyi Csárda*, Hungary's most celebrated roadside inn. Order a duck dish, relax to the Gypsy standards and admire the Hortobágy kitsch taking up every square centimetre of wall space. And check your change on departure.

There ain't much else around. The *Hortobágy* inn has a small, rather rough restaurant and the *Csárda* and the *Hajdú* restaurants at the Epona are open late. The *Nyerges* near the paddocks and stables is pleasant for a drink – if the wind is in your favour.

Getting There & Away
Four daily buses between Debrecen (via Hajdúszoboszló) and Eger stop in Petőfi tér. Hortobágy is on the railway line linking Debrecen and Füzesabony and is served by between eight and 10 trains a day, with the last train leaving for Debrecen about 8.15 pm. Trains headed for Füzesabony (last one at 8.20 pm) also stop at the Hortobágyi halastó station near the Öregtavi guesthouse and Tiszafüred.

HAJDÚSÁG REGION
The Hajdúság region is a loess (silt) area of the Eastern Plain west of Debrecen that was settled by the Heyducks, a medieval community of drovers and outlaws turned mercenaries and renowned for their skill in battle (see boxed text 'The Heyducks' under Debrecen, earlier in this chapter).

The Hajdúság continued as a special administrative district until the late 19th century but lost its importance after that. Today it is one of the most sparsely populated areas of Hungary – dusty and forlorn but evocative.

Hajdúszoboszló
☎ 52 • postcode 4200 • pop 23,800
Hajdúszoboszló, 20km south-west of Debrecen, was a typical Hajdúság town until 1925, when springs were discovered during drilling for oil and natural gas. Today, with its huge spa complex, park, pools, grassy 'beaches' and other recreational facilities, it is Hungary's Coney Island, Blackpool and Bondi Beach all rolled into one – for better or for worse.

It may indeed be the 'poor man's Balaton', as one holiday-maker described it, but Hajdúszoboszló has its serious side too. A large percentage of the hundreds of thousands of visitors who flock here every year are in search of a cure from its therapeutic waters.

Orientation Almost everything you'll want or need can be found on the broad street (route No 4) running through town and changing names four times: Debreceni útfél, Szilfákalja út, Hősök tere and Dózsa György utca. The thermal baths and park, lumped together as the Holiday Area (Üdülőterület), occupy the north-eastern portion of Hajdúszoboszló. Hősök tere – the town centre – lies to the south-west.

The bus station is on Fürdő utca, just north of Debreceni útfél. The train station lies about 3km south on Déli sor. Reach Hősök tere by walking north-west along Rákóczi utca. To get to the Holiday Area, follow Rákóczi utca north for three blocks and then head north-east on Hőforrás utca.

Information The Tourinform office (☎/fax 361 612, ✆ hajduszoboszlo@ tourinform.hu) is in the cultural centre building at Szilfákalja út 2. It is open from 9 am to 5 pm weekdays (to 4 pm September to May) and till noon on Saturday. Hajdútourist (☎ 362 966, fax 361 440) is at József Attila utca 2, just up from the spa's main entrance. It's open from 8.30 am to

5.30 pm and, in summer, on Saturday and from 8.30 am till noon on Sunday. Cooptourist (☎/fax 362 041) is around the corner at Szilfákalja út 44b next to the post office branch. The main post office is at Kálvin tér 1. There's a large OTP bank next to the ABC supermarket at Szilfákalja út 10 and another ATM on Hősök tere.

Things to See & Do The main attraction in Hajdúszoboszló is the **thermal baths** complex of a dozen mineral and freshwater pools, saunas, solarium and treatment centre. With the exception of the summer-only outdoor pools, the centre is open every day from 8 am to 6 pm. Admission costs 360Ft to 400Ft for adults and 220Ft to 300Ft for children. There are weekly, two-week and three-week passes and entry is cheaper after 4 pm. You can rent rowing boats for 600Ft per hour.

Near the **Calvinist church** (1717) on Hősök tere is a 20m stretch of wall and a small tower – all that remains of a 15th-century Gothic **fortress** destroyed by the Turks in 1660. Across Hősök tere a statue of István Bocskai stands not so proud – a pint-sized prince out of all proportion to his snorting stallion and great deeds.

Down Bocskai utca, past the 18th-century baroque **Catholic church** at No 6, where Pope John Paul II prayed as Karol Wojtyla, bishop of Kraków, in the early 1970s, is the **Bocskai Museum** (Bocskai utca 12), a temple to the memory of Prince István and his Heyduck helpers. Among the saddles, pistols and swords hangs Bocskai's banner, the standard of the Heyduck cavalry, picturing the prince doing battle with a leopard (which mysteriously changes into a lion in later versions). There are also exhibits of the city's cultural achievements and of the development of the thermal baths, with some curious Art Deco spa posters and medical instruments that could have come from a medieval dungeon. It's open from 9 am to 1 pm and 2 to 6 pm Tuesday to Sunday from May to September and to 5 pm the rest of the year.

A lovely thatched cottage at Ady Endre utca 2 houses the **István Fazekas Pottery House** (Fazekas István Fazekasház), featuring the distinctive black pottery produced by the Fazekas family in neighbouring Nádudvar (see the following section). But unless you're in Hajdúszoboszló on a Monday between 8 am and 4 pm, you'll miss it.

You can rent motor scooters (1000/1700Ft per half-hour/hour) from the stand on the corner of Gábor Aron utca and Mátyás király sétány opposite the Al Hambra Eastern Bar, in season.

There's a striking new monument called *Forest of Bells* a short distance to the west along Mátyás király sétány honouring the dead of wars throughout Hungarian history.

Special Events The main event here is the Szoboszló Summer (Szoboszlói Nyár) festival in mid-July.

Places to Stay The choice of accommodation in this tourist-oriented town is enormous, and prices vary according to the season.

Hajdútourist Camping (☎ 362 427, Debreceni útfél 6) in the park along the noisy motorway to Debrecen has cabins accommodating four people for 4000Ft to 5900Ft as well as hotel rooms (3000Ft to 4500Ft) available from mid-April to mid-October. There's another camping ground – *Thermal Camping (☎ 365 991, Böszörményi út 35a)* – north-east of the thermal spa area open from mid-March to October.

Virtually every third household in Hajdúszoboszló lets out *private rooms* in the high season, and 'szoba kiadó' signs sprout like mushrooms after a rain along the city's quiet backstreets, especially Wesselényi utca, Bessenyei utca and Jókai sor, south of route No 4. If you're not into DIY, have Hajdútourist make the arrangements for you from about 1200Ft per person. Apartments from Cooptourist start at about 7500Ft.

The 47-room *Gambrinus* hotel (☎ 362 054, József Attila utca 3), opposite Hajdútourist, is one of the dumpiest hotels in Hungary but if you're on a really tight budget, the price is right with doubles 3000Ft with shower, 2000Ft without. A better deal overall, though, if you value your health is at the *Hortobágy (☎ 362 357, fax 365 639,*

GREAT PLAIN

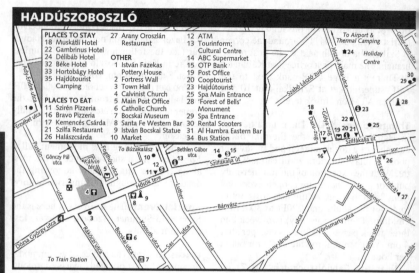

HAJDÚSZOBOSZLÓ

PLACES TO STAY
18 Muskátli Hotel
22 Gambrinus Hotel
24 Délibáb Hotel
32 Béke Hotel
33 Hortobágy Hotel
35 Hajdútourist Camping

PLACES TO EAT
11 Szirén Pizzeria
16 Bravo Pizzeria
17 Kemencés Csárda
21 Szilfa Restaurant
26 Halászcsárda

27 Arany Oroszlán Restaurant

OTHER
1 István Fazekas Pottery House
2 Fortress Wall
3 Town Hall
4 Calvinist Church
5 Main Post Office
6 Catholic Church
7 Bocskai Museum
8 Santa Fe Western Bar
9 István Bocskai Statue
10 Market

12 ATM
13 Tourinform; Cultural Centre
14 ABC Supermarket
15 OTP Bank
19 Post Office
20 Cooptourist
23 Hajdútourist
25 Spa Main Entrance
28 'Forest of Bells' Monument
29 Spa Entrance
30 Rental Scooters
31 Al Hambra Eastern Bar
34 Bus Station

Mátyás király sétány 3), a complex of four guesthouses near the baths with doubles for 5400Ft.

Among the best small hotels is the **Muskátli** (☎ 363 744, Daru zug 5a). It has 33 large and small rooms with singles for 6800Ft to 7600Ft and doubles 8800Ft to 9300Ft, a swimming pool, a thermal bath and a pleasant restaurant with outside seating in front.

Of the larger spa hotels (many of which offer one and two-week 'cure' packages), the 252-room **Délibáb** (☎ 360 366, fax 362 059, ✉ hdelibab@debrece.com, József Attila utca 4) has singles from DM55 and doubles from DM76 in its cheapest wing and the price drops after three days. Prices at the **Béke** (☎ 361 411, fax 362 748, ✉ reserve@ hotelbeke.huguest.hu, Mátyás király sétány 10), with 191 rooms in the park to the east of the thermal baths, are higher: singles are DM56 to DM78 and doubles DM94 to DM130.

Places to Eat There are plenty of sausage, lángos and ice-cream **stalls** along Szilfákalja út and in the park. For pizza try the Szabadság hotel's **Bravo** (Szilfákalja

út 51), which also has very good salads, or **Szirén** (Hösök tere 13).

The **Szilfa** (József Attila utca 1) is a pleasant eatery with a covered terrace on the corner of Szilfákalja út and less touristy than the flashier **Kemencés** (Szilfákalja út 40a), a csárda-like place a few paces to the east (mains from about 600Ft). Across busy Szilfákalja út, the tarted-up **Halászcsárda** (Jókai sor 12) serves expensive fish dishes till midnight daily. The **Arany Oroszlán** (Golden Lion; Bessenyei utca 14) is a quiet, relaxing place on a leafy residential street.

Entertainment The **City Cultural Centre** (☎ 361 031, Szilfákalja út 2) can offer advice on what's on in Hajdúszoboszló, including organ and choral concerts in the Calvinist church.

After a long day soaking in steamy brown mineral water, the al fresco **Al Hambra Eastern Bar** (Mátyás király sétány 8) is a suitable place to rehydrate. Save the **Santa Fe Western Bar** (cnr of Hösök tere & Kossuth utca) for later on.

Getting There & Away Buses from Hajdúszoboszló depart for Miskolc five times a

day and for Eger (via Hortobágy) and Szeged once each daily. There's direct service twice a day to Hortobágy and an extra one at 7.30 am added on from mid-June to September. International destinations served by bus include Oradea (Thursday at 6 am) and Baia Mare (Friday at 5 am) in Romania and, in Slovakia, Košiče (Tuesday at 6.20 am).

Trains headed for Szolnok and Budapest from the Debrecen stop at Hajdúszoboszló a couple of times an hour throughout the day.

Nádudvar
☎ 54 • postcode 4181 • pop 8700
This town, 18km west of Hajdúszoboszló and easily reached by one of up to nine daily Debrecen-Hajdúszoboszló buses, is the centre of the black-pottery cottage industry.

From the bus station on Kossuth Lajos tér (the post office is on the south side), turn left onto Fő utca and walk 800m in a westerly direction past the neoclassical **Catholic church**, graves of Soviet soldiers killed in WWII, and a huge modern cultural centre, to No 152, where Ferenc Fazekas maintains his **pottery workshop**. The potter's clay, rich in iron, is gathered and stored for a year before it is turned on a wheel into

vases, jugs, pitchers and candlesticks, then decorated, smoked in a kiln and polished, giving the objects their lovely and quite distinctive black glossy appearance. Ferenc is usually on hand to give visitors a demonstration, and his wares are available in the small shop next door. There is also a small **museum** containing 18th-century pottery made by the Fazekas family and an old foot-operated potter's wheel. Do not confuse this workshop with the touristy Fazekasház almost opposite at Fő utca 159.

The old *Csillag* restaurant *(Kossuth Lajos tér)* serves decent Hungarian dishes, and the *Korona Presszó (Fő utca 128)* is fine for snacks and drinks.

Southern Plain

The Southern Plain spans the lower regions of the Danube and Tisza Rivers and contains many of the most interesting towns and cities on the Great Plain. Even so, at times the plain seems even more endless here, with large farms and the occasional *tanya* (homestead) breaking the monotony. The Southern Plain (Dél-Alföld) was even less protected than the rest of the region, and its destruction by the Turks was complete. With little precipitation and frequent drought, the area is the hottest part of the Great Plain and, summer lasts well into October.

KECSKEMÉT
☎ 76 • postcode 6000 • pop 102,500
Lying halfway between the Danube and the Tisza Rivers in the heart of the Southern Plain, Kecskemét is ringed with vineyards and orchards that don't seem to stop at the limits of this 'garden city'. Colourful architecture, fine museums, apricot groves and the region's excellent *barackpálinka* (apricot brandy) beckon, and the Kiskunság National Park, the puszta of the Southern Plain, is right at the back door.

History has been kind to Kecskemét, now the capital of Hungary's largest county (Bács-Kiskun). While other towns on the Ottoman-occupied Great Plain were administered by the dreaded *spahis*, who had to

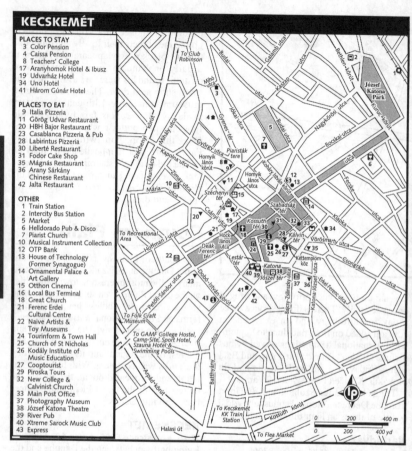

KECSKEMÉT

PLACES TO STAY
3 Color Pension
4 Caissa Pension
8 Teachers' College
17 Aranyhomok Hotel & Ibusz
19 Udvarház Hotel
34 Uno Hotel
41 Három Gúnár Hotel

PLACES TO EAT
9 Italia Pizzeria
11 Görög Udvar Restaurant
20 HBH Bajor Restaurant
23 Casablanca Pizzeria & Pub
28 Labirintus Pizzeria
30 Liberté Restaurant
31 Fodor Cake Shop
35 Mágnás Restaurant
36 Arany Sárkány
    Chinese Restaurant
42 Jalta Restaurant

OTHER
1 Train Station
2 Intercity Bus Station
5 Market
6 Helldorado Pub & Disco
7 Piarist Church
10 Musical Instrument Collection
12 OTP Bank
13 House of Technology
    (Former Synagogue)
14 Ornamental Palace &
    Art Gallery
15 Otthon Cinema
16 Local Bus Terminal
18 Great Church
21 Ferenc Erdei
    Cultural Centre
22 Naive Artists &
    Toy Museums
24 Tourinform & Town Hall
25 Church of St Nicholas
26 Kodály Institute of
    Music Education
27 Cooptourist
29 Piroska Tours
32 New College &
    Calvinist Church
33 Main Post Office
37 Photography Museum
38 József Katona Theatre
39 River Pub
40 Xtreme Sarock Music Club
43 Express

pay their own way and took what they wanted when they wanted it, Kecskemét – like Szeged farther south – was a *khas* town, under the direct rule and protection of the sultan. In the 19th century the peasants in the region planted vineyards and orchards to bind the poor, sandy soil. When phylloxera struck in 1880, devastating vineyards throughout Hungary, Kecskemét's vines proved immune: apparently the dreaded lice didn't like the sand. Today the region is responsible for one-third of Hungary's total wine output, though it must be said that this thin, rather undistinguished 'sand wine' is

not the best. It's also a major producer of *foie gras*, and the large goose farms – some of them with tens of thousands of the cranky creatures – have increased the Plain's fox population substantially.

Kecskemét's agricultural wealth was used wisely – it was able to redeem all its debts in cash in 1832 – and today the city can boast some of the most spectacular architecture in the country. Art Nouveau and the so-called Historical Eclectic (or Hungarian Romantic) style predominate, giving the city a turn-of-the-20th century feel. It also was – and still is – an important cultural centre: an artists' colony was established here in 1912, and the composer Zoltán Kodály chose Kecskemét as the site for his world-famous Institute of Music Education. Two other local boys who made good include László Kelemen, who formed Hungary's first provincial travelling theatre here late in the 18th century, and József Katona (1791-1830), the father of modern Hungarian drama.

Orientation

Kecskemét is a city of multiple squares that run into one another without warning and can be a little confusing at first. The bus and main train stations are opposite one another near József Katona Park. A 10-minute walk south-west along Nagykőrösi utca will bring you to the first of the squares, Szabadság tér. The city's other train station, Kecskemét KK, from where narrow-gauge trains head for Bugac, is on Halasi út, which is the southern continuation of Batthyány utca.

Information

Tourinform (☎/fax 481 065, 📧 Kecskemet@ tourinform.hu) is on the north-east side of the town hall at Kossuth tér 1. It is open from 8 am to 6 pm weekdays and from 9 am to 1 pm at the weekend from June to August and from 8 am to 5 pm weekdays and from 9 am to 1 pm on Saturday the rest of the year. Other agencies include: Ibusz (☎ 486 955, fax 480 557) in the Aranyhomok hotel at Kossuth tér 3; Express (☎ 329 236), out of the way at Dobó István körút 11; and Cooptourist (☎ 481 472, fax 481 694), Kéttemplom köz 9-11.

OTP bank has a branch at Szabadság tér 5 next to the former synagogue. The main post office is at Kálvin tér 10-12.

Things to See

Kecskemét is chock-a-block with museums (most cost 150/50Ft and are open from 10 am to 5 pm unless noted otherwise), churches and other interesting buildings.

Around Kossuth tér On the eastern side of Kossuth tér is the **Franciscan Church of St Nicholas** (Szent Miklós ferences templom),

dating in parts from the late 13th century; the **Zoltán Kodály Institute of Music Education** (Kodály Zoltán Zenepedagógiai Intézet) occupies the baroque monastery behind it to the east at Kéttemplom köz 1. But the main building in the square is the sandypink **town hall** (városháza), a lovely late 19th-century building designed by Ödön Lechner, who mixed Art Nouveau/ Secessionist with folkloric elements to produce a uniquely Hungarian style. Another beautiful example of this style is the restored **Otthon Cinema** (Kossuth tér 4), on the corner of pedestrian Hornyik János utca. The town hall's carillon chimes out strains of works by Ferenc Erkel, Kodály, Mozart, Handel and Beethoven several times during the day, and groups are allowed into the spectacular **Council Chamber** (☎ 483 683 for information). The floral ceilings and the frescoes of Hungarian heroes and historical scenes were painted by Bertalan Székely, who tended to romanticise the past. Just outside and hidden by a rhododendron bush, the **József Katona Memorial** marks the spot where the young and much loved playwright dropped dead of a heart attack in 1830.

You can't miss the tall tower of the Catholic **Great Church** (Nagytemplom; 1806) just north of the town hall. The big tablets on the front honour (from left to right) a mounted regiment of Hussars that served in WWI; citizens who died in the 1848-49 War of Independence; and the Kecskemét victims of WWII.

Szabadság tér Walking north-east into Szabadság tér, you'll pass the 17th-century **Calvinist church** and the **Calvinist New College** (Református újkollégium; 1912), a later version of the Hungarian Romantic style that looks like a Transylvanian castle and is now a music school. Two other buildings in the square are among the city's finest. The Art Nouveau **Ornamental Palace** (Cifrapalota), dating from 1902 and covered in multicoloured majolica tiles, now contains the **Kecskemét Gallery** (Kecskeméti Képtár), Rákóczi utca 1. Don't go in so much for the art; climb the steps to the aptly named **Decorative Hall** (Díszterem) to see the amazing stucco peacock, bizarre windows and more tiles. The **House of Technology** (Technika Háza; 1871), the Moorish structure across Rákóczi utca at No 2, was once a synagogue. Today it is used for conferences and exhibitions.

Museums The **Hungarian Museum of Naive Artists** (Magyar Naiv Müvészek Múzeuma), arguably the city's most interesting museum and one of the few of its kind in Europe, is in the Stork House (1730), surrounded by a high white wall at Gáspár András utca 11 just off Petőfi Sándor utca. Lots of predictable themes here, but the warmth and craft of Rozália Albert Juhászné's work, the drug-like visions of Dezső Mokry-Mészáros and the paintings of András Süli (Hungary's answer to Henri Rousseau) will hold your attention. There's a gallery in the cellar where you can purchase original paintings almost as good as those on display upstairs.

The **Toy Museum** (Szoénusz Játékmúzeum) next door has a small collection of 19th and early 20th-century dolls, wooden trains, board games and so on, dumped haphazardly in glass cases. But the museum spends most of its time and money on organising events and classes for kids. Much is made of Ernő Rubik, the Hungarian inventor of that infuriating Rubik cube from the 1970s.

The granddaddy of all museums in Kecskemét – the **Hungarian Folk Craft Museum** (Magyar Népi IsparmÜvészet Múzeuma) – is farther south-west at Serfőző utca 19a, a block in from Dózsa György út. Some 10 rooms of an old farm complex are crammed with embroidery, woodcarving, furniture, agricultural tools and textiles, so don't try to see everything.

The **Hungarian Photography Museum** (Magyar Fotográfiai Múzeum), housed in an Art Deco Orthodox synagogue at Katona József tér 12, is not very impressive but it is the only such collection in the country. It's open Wednesday to Sunday from 10 am to 5 pm.

The **Leskowsky Musical Instrument Collection** (Leskowsky Hangszergyüjtemény),

at Zimay László utca 6a, traces the development of music-making over the centuries and has a decent collection of instruments from five continents. It is open from 9 am to 5 pm Monday to Saturday.

Market Kecskemét's lively **flea market** is south-east of the city on Kulső Szegedi út.

Activities
Kecskemét has an abundance of thermal water, and in summer the four Szék-tó pools on Izsáki út, the continuation of Dózsa György út, or the lake in Leisure Time Park (Szabadidőpark) just north of them are a treat. There's a large indoor swimming pool at Izsáki út 1 open from 6 am to 9 pm daily throughout the year.

Special Events
Special events in Kecskemét include both the Bohém Ragtime & Jazz Festival and the cultural Spring Festival (Tavaszi Fesztivál) in March and the Kecskemét Animated Film Festival (Kesckeméti Animációs Filmfesztivál) and the Kodály International Music Festival (Kodály Nemzetközi Zenei Fesztivál) in June. The Hirős Week Festival (Hirős Hét Fesztivál) pays homage to the richness of Kecskemét agricultural produce, notably the golden *sárgabarack* (apricot).

Places to Stay
Camping *Autós Camping (☎ 329 398, Csabay Géza körút 5)*, on the south-western side of Kecskemét, is nearly 5km from the train station and crammed with German and Dutch tourists in caravans. If you must, the site also has bungalows for two for about 4500Ft and bicycles for rent. It is open from mid-April to mid-October.

Hostels & Private Rooms About three blocks from the camping ground, the *GAMF Ságvári College (☎ 321 916, @ koll@gamf.hu, Izsáki út 10)* has accommodation in a four-bed room for 1000Ft per person and singles/doubles are available. Officially it's only open from mid-June to August, but you can sometimes get a bed in other months. In summer you can also find accommodation in the *Teachers' College* (☎ *486 186, Piaristák tere 4)* right in the centre of town for 1200Ft per head in triple rooms.

Ibusz charges from 1500Ft to 2000Ft per person for a *private room* (probably in one of the high rises on Dobó István körút). Cooptourist is about the same but usually has only doubles.

Farm Accommodation If you want a quiet break, have your own transport and can stay put in one place for a minimum of three nights, a farmhouse stay is a great option. The area outside Kecskemét is called the *tanya világ,* or 'farm world', and is very picturesque, with isolated thatch-roofed farmhouses and distinctive sweep-pole wells (*gémeskút*) set amid orchards and mustard fields. Village Tourism (Falusi Turizmus; ☎/fax 486 230) at Csongrádi utca 25 has lists of houses for rent throughout the county, but many are within a 30km radius of Kecskemét at Bugac, in the Helvécia vineyards to the south-west, and at Lajosmizse, a horse-riding centre to the north-west.

Pensions & Hotels *Color (☎/fax 483 246, Jókai utca 26)* is a small pension with eight rooms at 3800Ft for a double. The 11-room *Caissa (☎ 481 685, Gyenes tér 18)* has doubles for 4900Ft and larger rooms for up to five people are also available. Caissa's location is excellent so it's always worth a try.

The *Aranyhomok (☎ 486 286, fax 481 195, Kossuth tér 3)* is the city's largest and ugliest hotel, with 111 rooms and a slew of outlets. Singles/doubles with bath are DM87/93. The newer *Udvarház (☎ 413 912, fax 413 914, Csányi utca 1-3),* tucked away in a courtyard with 17 rooms, charges 9100Ft for a double while the modern, 25-room *Uno (☎ 480 046, fax 476 697,* 🖂 *hoteluno@mail.datanet.hu, Benuczky Ferenc utca 4)* east of the centre charges from 6600Ft.

For something smaller and far more charming, try the friendly *Három Gúnár (☎ 483 611, fax 481 253, Batthyány utca 1-7),* a small hotel with some nonsmoking rooms formed by cobbling four old townhouses together. Its 46 smallish rooms (the best are Nos 306 to 308) cost 6900Ft to 7500Ft for singles and 8400Ft to 9400Ft for doubles. The hotel has a so-so restaurant and a popular bar called the President Club with pool tables and pizza, open till 2 am daily.

Farther afield, the dumpy but clean *Sport* hotel (☎/fax 323 090, Izsáki út 15a) has 30 cramped double rooms for 4200Ft. The 38-room *Szauna (☎ 481 859, fax 326 633, Csabay Géza körút 3)* is a vast, modern place in a quiet location next to the thermal spa. Doubles start at 7300Ft, and it has a restaurant, a gym and, naturally enough, a sauna.

Places to Eat

The pizza at the *Italia (Hornyik János körút 4)* is acceptable, but you can opt instead for gyros (600Ft), souvlaki (700Ft) and moussaka (720Ft) by crossing the street to the classy *Görög Udvar* restaurant (*Greek Court; Széchenyi tér 9).* The *Casablanca (Dobó István körút 1)* is a popular student hangout with decent pizza and a large terrace overlooking Deák Ferenc tér. The *Labirintus (Kéttemplom köz 2)* is a cellar restaurant with pizza and pastas. The *Arany Sárkány (Golden Dragon; Erkel Ferenc utca 1a)* is a Chinese place south-east of Katona József tér.

For well-prepared Germano-Hungarian food, try the *HBH Bajor (Csányi utca 4)* in a sheltered courtyard behind the cultural centre. A better choice for similar food is the upmarket *Magnás* cellar restaurant (*Csongrádi utca 2).* The *Jalta (Batthyány utca 2),* opposite the Három Gúnár hotel, is a rather homely wine cellar with a menu in English and German (mains: 550Ft to 650Ft). Its speciality is grilled South Slav dishes. If you wanted to splurge, you couldn't do better than the *Liberté (Szabadság tér 2)* in a historical building east of the Great Church. The best ice cream and cakes in Kecskemét are at *Fodor* in the same building.

Kecskemét's large *market (Jókai utca),* with both a covered and an open section, is located north of Szabadság tér behind the Piarist church.

GREAT PLAIN

Entertainment

Kecskemét is a city of music and theatre; you'd be crazy not to see at least one performance here. Head first for the *Ferenc Erdei Cultural Centre* (☎ 484 594, *Deák Ferenc tér 1*), which sponsors some events and is a good source of information. The 19th-century *József Katona Theatre* (☎ 483 283, *Katona József tér 5*) stages dramatic works as well as operettas and concerts by the Kecskemét Symphony Orchestra; the ticket office there (☎ 481 064) is open Tuesday to Friday from 10 am to 1 pm and 3 to 6 pm.

Kecskemét has a plethora of Wild West-themed pubs, including the convivial *River Pub* (*Lestár tér 1*) west of the József Katona Theatre. The *Helldorado* (*Rákóczi utca 15*) is a popular pub and club open till midnight (to 3 am on Saturday). *Club Robinson* (*Akadémia körút 2*) is a large, popular disco open much later on Wednesday to Sunday. Another great venue is the *Xtreme Sarock Music Club* (*Kisfaludy utca 4*) open to 2 am Monday to Saturday.

Pick up a free copy of *Kecskeméti Est* for more information on clubs, films, events and parties.

Getting There & Away

Bus It's not surprising, given its central location, that Kecskemét is well served by buses, with frequent departures for the most far-flung destinations. There are twice-hourly buses to Kiskunfélegyháza, hourly ones to Budapest, buses every couple of hours to Szeged and two a day to Pécs. Other destinations include Baja (three buses a day), Békéscsaba (three), Eger (one), Gyula (2) and Szolnok (six).

Train Kecskemét is on the railway line linking Budapest-Nyugati with Szeged, from where trains cross the border to Subotica and Belgrade. To get to Debrecen and other towns on the Eastern Plain, you must change at Cegléd. A very slow narrow-gauge train leaves Kecskemét KK train station south of the city centre five times a day for Kiskőrös. Transfer there for Kalocsa. Kecskemét KK is also the station from which trains leave for Bugac (see the following section).

Getting Around

Bus Nos 1, 5 and 11 link the bus and train stations with the local bus terminus behind the Aranyhomok hotel. From Kecskemét KK station, catch the No 2 or 13 to the centre. For the pools, hotels and camp site on Csabay Géza körút, bus Nos 1, 11 and 22 are good. The No 12 goes past the flea market.

Local taxis can be ordered on ☎ 481 481 or ☎ 484 848.

KISKUNSÁG NATIONAL PARK
☎ 76

Kiskunság National Park consists of half a dozen 'islands' of land totalling more than 48,000 sq hectares. Much of the park's alkaline ponds, dunes and grassy 'deserts' are off-limits to casual visitors, but you can get a close look at this environmentally fragile area – and see the famous horse herds go through their paces to boot – at **Bugac** on a sandy steppe 30km south-west of Kecskemét.

The easiest but most pricey way to see the sights of Bugac is to join a tour in Kecskemét with Bugac Tours (☎ 372 688, fax 481 643), Szabadság tér 5a, or Piroska Tours (☎ 328 636, fax 328 863), nearby at Szabadság tér 2. For between 4000Ft and 6500Ft, they'll bus you to the park, take you by carriage past costumed shepherds and carefully 'planted' racka sheep and grey cattle to the horse show and, depending on which tour you've chosen, serve you lunch at a touristy csárda.

But if you've had enough of geriatric Germans, take the 10.52 am narrow-gauge train from Kecskemét KK station – not the main train station in Kecskemét (see Orientation in the Kecskemét section). Make sure you get off at the Bugac felső station (31km; 1¼ hours) and *not* the Bugacpuszta or Bugac train stations, which come before it.

From the Bugac felső station, walk north for 15 minutes to the Bugaci Karikás Csárda and the park entrance (900/300Ft). There you can board a horse-driven carriage for 1800Ft or walk another 1.5km along the sandy track to the **Herder Museum** (Pásztormúzeum), a circular structure designed to look like a horse-driven dry mill that is filled with stuffed fauna and pressed flora of the Kiskunság, as well as branding irons, carved wooden pipes, embroidered fur coats and a tobacco pouch made from a gnarled old ram's scrotum. It's open from 10 am to 3 pm Tuesday to Sunday from April to October.

There will still be a few minutes to inspect the stables before the **horse show** at 1 pm (the time can vary slightly so ask at the park entrance). Outside, you may come across a couple of noble Nonius steeds being made to perform tricks that most dogs would be disinclined to do (sit, play dead, roll over). The real reason for coming, though, is to see the horseherds crack their whips, race one another bareback and ride 'five-in-hand', a breathtaking performance in which one csikós gallops five horses around the field at full speed while standing on the backs of the last two.

Bugaci Karikás Csárda, with its gulyás and folk-music ensemble (starters/mains from 400/600Ft), can be a lot more fun than first appears, and they have horses for riding (1300Ft per hour) and a *camp site (☎ 372 522)* accommodating 60 people (500Ft per person). Bugac Tours, with a branch office at the park entrance, has rustic *cottages* for rent nearby for DM60 for two people.

If you miss the 3.11 pm train back to Kecskemét, you can entertain yourself with birdwatching or drinking apricot pálinka under the trees at the csárda until the next (and last) train leaves at 6.14 pm. Otherwise catch one of four buses back to Kecskemét from the main highway (route No 54). You can also reach Kiskunfélegyháza, 18km to the east, from where buses depart more regularly for Kecskemét.

KALOCSA
☎ 78 • postcode 6300 • pop 18,300

It is doubtful that Pál Tomori, the 16th-century archbishop of Kalocsa and military commander at the fateful battle of Mohács, would recognise his town today. When he last saw it before galloping off to fight the Turks, Kalocsa was a Gothic town on the Danube with a magnificent 14th-century cathedral.

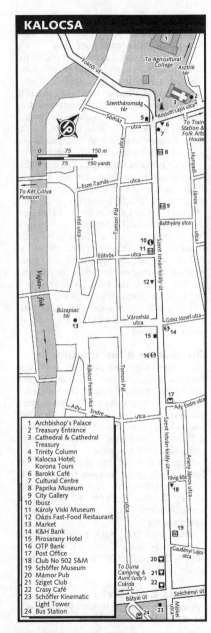

KALOCSA

1 Archbishop's Palace
2 Treasury Entrance
3 Cathedral & Cathedral Treasury
4 Trinity Column
5 Kalocsa Hotel; Korona Tours
6 Barokk Café
7 Cultural Centre
8 Paprika Museum
9 City Gallery
10 Ibusz
11 Károly Viski Museum
12 Oázis Fast-Food Restaurant
13 Market
14 K&H Bank
15 Pirosarany Hotel
16 OTP Bank
17 Post Office
18 Club No 502 S&M
19 Schöffer Museum
20 Mámor Pub
21 Sziget Club
22 Crasy Café
23 Schöffer Kinematic Light Tower
24 Bus Station

GREAT PLAIN

Today an 18th-century baroque church stands in its place and the river is 6km to the west, the result of 19th-century regulation.

With Esztergom, Kalocsa was one of the two episcopal seats founded by King Stephen in 1009 from the country's 10 dioceses. The town had its heyday in the 15th century when, fortified and surrounded by swamps and the river, it could be easily protected. But Kalocsa was burned to the ground during the Turkish occupation and was not rebuilt until the 18th century.

While never as significant as Esztergom, Kalocsa played an important role after the 1956 Uprising. For 15 years, while the ultra-conservative József Mindszenty, archbishop of Esztergom and thus primate of Hungary, took refuge in the US Embassy in Budapest (see boxed text 'Cardinal Mindszenty' in the Danube Bend chapter), the prelate of Kalocsa was forced to play a juggling game with the government to ensure the church's position – and, indeed, existence – in a nominally atheistic communist state.

Today Kalocsa is a quiet town, as celebrated for its paprika and folk art as for its turbulent history.

Orientation & Information

The streets of Kalocsa fan out from Szentháromság tér, site of Kalocsa Cathedral and the Archbishop's Palace. The bus station lies at the southern end of the main avenue, tree-lined Szent István király út. The train station is to the north-east on Mártírok tere, a 20-minute walk from Szentháromság tér along Kossuth Lajos utca.

Ibusz (☎ 462 102, fax 461 601) at Szent István király út 23, is open from 8 am to 4 pm weekdays only and there's another agency, Korona Tours (☎ 462 186), in the Kalocsa hotel (room No 16) at Szentháromság tér 4.

There's an OTP bank branch at Szent István király út 43-45 and a K&H bank at No 28. The post office is at Szent István király út 44.

Kalocsa Cathedral

Almost everything of interest in Kalocsa is on or near Szent István király út, beginning at Szentháromság tér, where the **Trinity Column** (1786) is corroding into sand. Kalocsa Cathedral, the fourth church to stand on the site, was completed in 1754 by András Mayerhoffer and is a baroque masterpiece, with a dazzling pink and gold interior full of stucco, reliefs and tracery. Some believe that the sepulchre in the crypt is that of the first archbishop of Kalocsa, Asztrik, who brought King Stephen the gift of a crown from Pope Sylvester II, thereby legitimising the Christian convert's control over Hungary. A new plaque on the south side outside memorialises this event. Franz Liszt was the first one to play the cathedral's magnificent 3560-pipe organ.

The **Cathedral Treasury** (Főszékesegyházi kincstár) in the back of the cathedral up a set of winding steps (open from 9 am to 5 pm Tuesday to Sunday from May to October) is a trove of gold and bejewelled objects and vestments. In case you were wondering, the large bust of St Stephen was cast for the millenary exhibition in 1896 and contains 48kg of silver and 2kg of gold. Among the other valuable objects is a 16th-century reliquary of St Anne and a gold and crystal baroque monstrance.

Archbishop's Palace

The Great Hall and the chapel of the Archbishop's Palace (Érseki palota; 1766), Szentháromság tér 1, contain magnificent **frescoes** by Franz Anton Maulbertsch, but you won't get to see these unless there's a concert on. The **Episcopal Library** (Érsekikönyvtár), however, is open to visitors in groups of less than 10 from 9 am till noon and 2 to 5 pm on Monday, Wednesday and Saturday from April to October. The library contains more than 100,000 volumes, including 13th-century codices, a Bible belonging to Martin Luther and annotated in the reformer's hand, illuminated manuscripts, and verses cut into palm fronds from what is now Sri Lanka.

Museums

The **Károly Viski Museum** at Szent István király út 25 is as rich in folklore and art as the Palóc Museum in Balassagyarmat in the

Northern Uplands but is also more heterogeneous, highlighting the life and ways of the Swabian (Sváb), Slovak (Tót), Serbian (Rác) and Hungarian peoples of the area. It's surprising to see how plain the interiors of peasant houses were early in the 19th century and what rainbows they became 50 years later as wealth increased: walls, furniture, doors – virtually nothing was left undecorated by the famous 'painting women' of Kalocsa. Yet at a marriage the wedding party wore black while the guests were dressed in clothes gaily embroidered (a craft at which the women of Kalocsa also excel). The museum also has a large collection of coins dating from Roman times to today and is open from 9 am to 5 pm Tuesday to Sunday. The **City Gallery** (Városi Képtár) is diagonally opposite at Szent István király út 12-14.

Along with Szeged, Kalocsa is the largest producer of paprika, the 'red gold' (*piros arany*) so important in Hungarian cuisine (see boxed text 'Hungary's Red Gold' later in this section). You can learn a lot more than you need to know about its development, production and beneficial qualities at the **Paprika Museum** (Szent István király út 6), which is set up like the inside of a barn used for drying the pods in long garlands. If you happen to be in Kalocsa in September, get out to any of the nearby villages to see the green fields transformed into red carpets. The museum is open from 11 am to 5 pm Tuesday to Sunday from April to October.

Other places to see examples of wall and furniture painting include the **House of Folk Arts** (Népmüvészeti tájház) at Tompa Mihály utca 5-7 (open mid-April to mid-October) and **Juca néni csárdája** (Aunt Judy's Csárda), a touristy restaurant near the Danube 6km south-west of Kalocsa. Some people find today's flower and paprika motifs twee and even garish; compare the new work with that in the museums and see what you think.

An exhibition of the futuristic work of the Paris-based artist Nicholas Schöffer, who was born in Kalocsa in 1912, can be seen at the **Schöffer Collection** at Szent

Hungary's Red Gold

Paprika, the 'red gold' (*piros arany*) so essential in many Hungarian dishes, is cultivated primarily around Szeged and Kalocsa. About 10,000 tonnes of the spice are produced annually, 55% of which is exported. Hungarians themselves consume about 0.5kg of the spice per capita every year.

Opinions vary on how and when the *Capsicum annum* plant first arrived in Hungary – from India via Turkey and the Balkans or from the New World – but mention of it is made in documents dating from the 16th century.

There are many types of fresh or dried paprika available in Hungarian markets and shops, including the rose, apple and royal varieties. But as a ground spice it is most commonly sold as *csipős* or *erős* (hot or strong) paprika and *édes* (sweet) paprika.

Capsicum annum is richer in vitamin C than citrus fruits, and it was during experimentation with the plant that Dr Albert Szent-Györgyi of Szeged first isolated the vitamin. He was awarded the Nobel Prize for medicine in 1937.

István király út 76, open 9 am to noon and 2 to 5 pm Tuesday to Sunday. If you can't be bothered, have a look at his 'kinematic light tower' *Chronos 8* (1982) near the bus station – a Meccano-set creation of steel beams and spinning, reflecting mirrors that is supposed to portend the art of the new century. *Jó Istenem*, let's hope not.

Special Events
The Danube Folklore Festival (Dunai Folklórfesztivál) is jointly sponsored with Szekszárd and Baja and held in July. Kalocsa Paprika Days (Kalocsia Paprikanapok) in September celebrate the harvest of the town's 'red gold'.

Places to Stay
Duna Camping (☎ 462 534, *Meszesi út*), about 5km south-west of town, operates between June and August only and has bungalows. Ibusz has *private rooms* in Kalocsa, and vicinity, for about 1500Ft per person.

GREAT PLAIN

The 22-room dusky pink *Pirosarany* hotel (☎ 462 220, fax 462 621, Szent István király utca 37) is an odd place – half hotel, half office building – with double rooms for 5000/3300Ft with/without shower. The *Két Gólya* inn (☎/fax 462 259, Móra Ferenc utca 8), across the little Vajas stream, charges from 4500Ft for its eight basic doubles.

The *Kalocsa* hotel (☎/fax 461 244, ✉ beta@mail.externet.hu, Szentháromság tér 4), housed in beautifully restored episcopal offices built in 1780, has 31 rooms in a main building and a courtyard annexe. Rooms are 5700/8000/10,300Ft.

Places to Eat

For something fast (pizza, gyros, burgers), try the simple *Oázis* (Szent István király út 31). The oddly-named *Club No 502 S&M* (Szent István király út 64) has basic main courses for 310Ft to 590Ft. The *Kalocsa* hotel has a somewhat pricey restaurant, where – I feel compelled to say – I ate the worst meal I have ever had in Hungary.

If you happen to be heading for the Danube ferry crossing over to Gerjen southwest of Kalocsa or staying at the camping ground, the *Juca néni csárdája* (see the Museums section) is in the vicinity.

Kalocsa's *market* on Búzapiac tér has a lot more than just grain.

Entertainment

The *Kalocsa Cultural & Youth Centre* (☎ 462 200, Szent István király út 2-4) is housed in an 18th-century baroque seminary; inquire about any concerts scheduled in the *Great Hall* (Nagy Terem) of the Archbishop's Palace or the *cathedral*. The *Barokk* cafe in the same building and facing Szentháromság tér attracts the town's many students.

Several popular bars – this is a garrison town – can be found along Szent István király út in the direction of the bus station, including the *Crasy Cafe* at No 89, the *Sziget Club* at No 87, the *Mámor* pub in a small house behind No 85, and the *Club No 502 S&M* at No 64. All except the first have outside seating in the warmer months. The most popular dancing venue in area is the *Fekete Horgony*

(Black Anchor), 4km west of Kalocsa and open till very late at the weekend.

Getting There & Away

There are very frequent buses to/from Budapest, Baja (mostly via Hajós) and Solt, a horse-breeding centre with many riding and carriage-driving opportunities. There are also buses to Kiskunhalas (five to seven daily), Szeged (five or six), Székesfehérvár (five to seven), Nagykőrös (two to four) and Eger (one). You can catch a daily bus to Arad in Romania at 5.40 am.

Kalocsa is at the end of a rail spur to Kiskőrös, the birthplace of Hungary's greatest poet, Sándor Petőfi (1823-49); there are six departures a day. From Kiskőrös you can make connections to Budapest and over the border to Subotica and Belgrade. A very slow (2¼-hour) narrow-gauge train links Kiskőrös with the smaller of Kecskemét's two train stations, Kecskemét KK, five times day.

BAJA

☎ 79 • postcode 6500 • pop 38,600

On the Danube about 45km south of Kalocsa, Baja was a fortified town during the Turkish occupation but suffered greatly and had to be repopulated with Germans and Serbians in the 18th century. Today it is an important commercial centre and river port, but it is perhaps best known as a holiday and sports centre – the perfect place to relax for a spell before heading on.

Baja has one of the loveliest locations of any town on the Southern Plain. One of its main squares (Szentháromság tér) gives on to a branch of the Danube, and just across are two recreational islands with beaches and flood-bank forests. The bridge across the river to the north is an important one. There's only one other crossing between here and Budapest (at Dunaföldvár, 78km to the north), and the Baja Bridge serves as a gateway to Transdanubia.

Orientation & Information

Vörösmarty utca and pedestrians-only Eötvös utca link Baja's three main squares: Vörösmarty tér, Szent Imre tér and Szentháromság

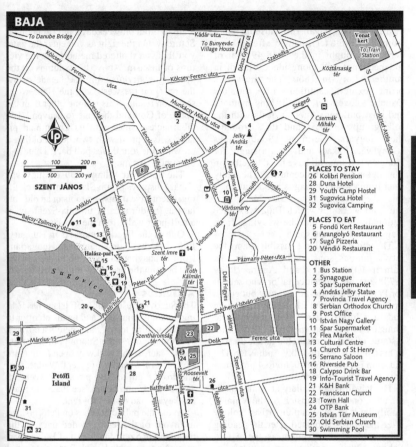

BAJA

SZENT JÁNOS

0   100   200 m
0   100   200 yd

Sugovica

Petőfi Island

PLACES TO STAY
26 Kolibri Pension
28 Duna Hotel
29 Youth Camp Hostel
31 Sugovica Hotel
32 Sugovica Camping

PLACES TO EAT
5 Fondü Kert Restaurant
6 Arangolyó Restaurant
17 Sugó Pizzéria
20 Véndió Restaurant

OTHER
1 Bus Station
2 Synagogue
3 Spar Supermarket
4 András Jelky Statue
7 Provincia Travel Agency
8 Serbian Orthodox Church
9 Post Office
10 István Nagy Gallery
11 Spar Supermarket
12 Flea Market
13 Cultural Centre
14 Church of St Henry
15 Serrano Saloon
16 Riverside Pub
18 Calypso Drink Bar
19 Info-Tourist Travel Agency
21 K&H Bank
22 Franciscan Church
23 Town Hall
24 OTP Bank
25 István Türr Museum
27 Old Serbian Church
30 Swimming Pool

tér. The last one lies on the Kamarás-Duna
(or Sugovica as it is known locally), a branch
of the Danube River that cuts Petőfi and
Nagy Pandúr Islands off from the mainland
before emptying into the main river down-
stream. The bus station is on Csermák Mihály
tér north-east of the centre; the train station is
a few minutes to the north across Vonat kert
(Train Garden).

None of the big agencies have offices in
Baja any longer; try your luck at Info-Tourist
(☎ 427 533, fax 422 970) on Halász-part
(open 9 am to 4 pm weekdays) or Provincia
(☎ 428 534) at Kossuth Lajos utca 11.

There's a K&H bank branch and currency exchange machine at Szentháromság
tér 10 and an OTP bank on the corner of
Szentháromság tér and Deák Ferenc utca.
The post office is at Oroszlán utca 5.

Things to See

The enormous **Szentháromság tér**, a
colourful square of baroque and neoclassical buildings marred only by the
multitude of parked cars, is dominated on
the east side by the city's renovated **town
hall** and its 'widow's walk' looking out
towards the Danube.

South of the town hall at Deák Ferenc utca 1 stands the **István Türr Museum** (enter from Roosevelt tér), named after a local hero who fought in the 1848-49 War of Independence and alongside Garibaldi in southern Italy in 1860. The museum's prime exhibit, entitled 'Life on the Danube', covers wildlife, fishing methods and boat building. Another deals with the folk groups of Baja and its surrounds: the Magyars, Germans, South Slavs (Bunyevác, Sokac) and – surprisingly for Hungary – Roma; all have lived together in this region for several centuries. The rarely seen Roma woodcarving is good, but don't miss the exquisite South Slav black lace, the gold work for which Baja was once nationally famous, and the weavings from Nagybaracska to the south.

The museum couldn't possibly ignore the city's famous sons, including Türr, the painter István Nagy and András Jelky (1738-83), an apprentice tailor who set out for Paris in the mid-18th century but ended up wandering around China, Japan, Ceylon and Java for 10 years before returning to Hungary to write his memoirs. You'll find a statue of this unusual Hungarian dressed in his Chinese best on Jelky András tér. The museum is open from 10 am to 4 pm Tuesday to Sunday (80/40Ft).

The **István Nagy Gallery** at Arany János utca 1 – once the mansion of the Vojnich family built in 1820 and an artists' colony after the war – is named after the leading painter of what is known as the Alföld School. Other members are featured, including Gyula Rudnay, as well as 'outsiders' like the cubist Béla Kádár and sculptor Ferenc Medgyessy. The gallery is open from 10 am to 4 pm on Tuesday, Thursday and Friday only (80/40Ft).

Buildings of architectural note include the **Franciscan church** (Ferences templom; 1728) behind the town hall on Bartók Béla utca, which has a fantastic baroque organ; and the late baroque **Serbian Orthodox church** in a quiet square at Táncsics Mihály utca 21. The iconostasis is definitely worth a detour.

But the neoclassical **synagogue** (1845) at Munkácsy Mihály utca 7-9 beats them both.

Now a public library, it can be visited from 9 am to 6 pm on weekdays and till noon on Saturday. On the right as you enter the gate, you'll pass a sheltered memorial to the victims of fascism. Above the columns on the synagogue's tympanum (the facade below the roof) on the west side, the Hebrew inscription reads: 'This is none other than the house of God and the gate to heaven.' The tabernacle inside, with its Corinthian pilasters, is topped with two lions holding a crown while four doves pull back a blue and burgundy curtain.

The **Bunyevác Village House** (Bunyevác tájház) displays South Slav furniture, clothing, decorative items and tools in an old cottage at Pandúr utca 51 in Baja-Szentistván, a half-hour walk from the city centre.

One of the liveliest **markets** in Hungary, full of Serbs, Romanians and Hungarians from Transylvania, is north of Árpád tér just beyond the bridge over to Petőfi Island.

Activities

The Sugovica resort on Petőfi Island has fishing, boating, mini-golf and tennis on offer to anyone willing to pay, and there's a covered swimming pool – the Sports Pool (Sportuszoda) – across the walkway open from 6 am to 7.30 pm weekdays (except Wednesday) and from 8 am to 7.30 pm at the weekend. The Youth Camp hostel (see Places to Stay) has kayaks and canoes for rent.

Avoid the public beaches on Petőfi Island in favour of the less crowded ones on the mainland in Szent János east of Halász-part or on Nagy Pandúr Island. But be prepared to swim to the latter or face a long walk to the southern suburb of Homokváros, across the bridge to Nagy Pandúr Island and then north to the beach.

Places to Stay

The *Youth Camp* hostel (*Ifjúsági Tábor, ☎324 022, Petőfi-sziget 5*), in a block at the northern end of Petőfi Island, has a total of 53 rooms, 37 of which are open all year. Singles/triples, with shower, in the pension cost 2800/3700Ft; accommodation in rooms with four to eight beds in the main building costs 1100Ft per head. The pavilion, which has 16 rooms with four to six beds each, is open from May to September only. Accommodation here costs 900Ft per person.

Bungalows at nearby *Sugovica Camping* (☎ *321 755*) to the south are expensive, but they are in a relatively attractive camp site. There are 19 in all, with doubles costing from 2900Ft to 6800Ft, according to the season. The two most 'remote' ones are those designated R9 and R10, though they're not directly on the water.

The five rooms at the *Kolibri* pension (☎ *321 628, Batthyány utca 18*) are small but cheap enough at 3000Ft for doubles with shared shower. The pension is just south-east of Szentháromság tér.

The 50-room *Duna* hotel (☎ *323 224, fax 324 844, Szentháromság tér 6*) has had a coat of green paint slapped on it, but that's done nothing to spoil the atmosphere of this wonderfully tired old place. Hard by the Danube (many rooms have river views), the hotel has singles with shower for 3600Ft and doubles with/without for 4000/3000Ft. If there are four of you (or money is no problem), stay in No 118, a two-room suite with bath and a beautiful roof terrace overlooking the river. Other good rooms to ask for are Nos 110, 111, 238, 239 and 246.

The 34-room *Sugovica* (☎ *321 755, fax 323 155*) on Petőfi Island is Baja's most expensive hotel, with singles from 6800Ft, doubles from 7800Ft. All rooms have bathroom, TV, minibar and a balcony looking onto the park or river. There's even a private mooring and winching for guests arriving by boat.

Places to Eat

Neither the *Duna* hotel's restaurant nor pub (open till midnight) is very agreeable, but the terrace cafe out the front on the square is a great place to sit in warmer months. For outside seating, though, nothing beats the *Véndió* restaurant, a few minutes across the bridge at the northern end of Petőfi Island. *Sugó Pizzeria*, across the river in Halász-part, is another great spot when the weather is fine (pizzas from 350/550Ft small/large).

The *Fondü Kert* (*Kossuth Lajos utca 19*), which used to trade in melted cheese, has now switched to standard (though well-prepared) Hungarian dishes. An inexpensive place beside the bus station is the *Aranygolyó (Csermák Mihály tér 9)*, but it closes at weekends.

Entertainment

The *József Attila Cultural Centre* (☎ *324 229, Árpád tér 1*) is your source for information about what's going on in Baja. Ask about concerts in the old Serbian church (now a music school and hall) on Batthyány utca.

There's a stretch of lively pubs and bars facing the water at Halász-part, including the *Calypso Drink Bar*, the *Riverside Pub* and the *Serrano Saloon*.

Getting There & Away

Bus Buses to Kalocsa, Szeged and Mohács depart at least once an hour; there are seven to 10 daily departures to Szekszárd, Pécs, Kecskemét and Budapest as well. Other destinations include: Békéscsaba and Csongrád (two each), Hévíz (one), Jászberény (one), Kaposvár (two), Orosháza (two), Szolnok (one), Veszprém (two) and Zalaegerszeg (one). International buses depart for Arad in Romania on Friday at 5.40 am and Sunday at 6 am and for Subotica and Sombor in Yugoslavia on Friday at 7.20 am.

Train The rail line here links Bátaszék and Kiskunhalas; you must change at the former for Budapest, Szekszárd, Pécs and other points in Southern Transdanubia. From Kiskunhalas, it's impossible to get anywhere of importance without at least another change (the one exception is the fast train to Budapest).

AROUND BAJA
Gemenc Forest

From May to October, a narrow-gauge train runs from Pörböly, 13km west of Baja, along some stunning hairpin turns of the Danube to the protected Gemenc Forest near Szekszárd. The reserve is incredibly beautiful and a rich hunting ground. From the terminus at Bárányfok, you can carry on to Szekszárd and other points in Southern Transdanubia.

The best way to schedule such a trip is to take the 7.02 am train from Baja to Pörböly, from where you'll catch the little train at 7.50 am to Bárányfok (30km, 1¼ hours). From here there are four or five buses to Szekszárd. Two other trains from Pörböly – at 9.30 am and 1 pm go only as far as the Gemenc Delta before turning around. The trains do not always run to schedule; check times and dates at the Baja train station or ring the United Forest Railways office (ÁEV; ☎ 74-491 483), Bajai út 100, in Pörböly before you set out. You wouldn't want to be marooned in the Gemenc with a lot of crazy hunters running wild.

For more information on the Gemenc Forest, see the Around Szekszárd section in the Southern Transdanubia chapter.

SZEGED
☎ 62 • postcode 6700 • pop 175,500

Szeged – a corruption of the Hungarian word *sziget*, or 'island' – is the largest and most important city on the Southern Plain and lies just west of where the Tisza and Maros Rivers converge. In fact, some would argue that, in terms of culture and sophistication, Szeged (German: Segedin) beats Debrecen hands down as the 'capital' of the Great Plain as a whole.

Remnants of the Körös culture suggest that these goddess-worshipping people lived in the Szeged area 4000 or 5000 years ago, and one of the earliest Magyar settlements in Hungary was at Ópusztaszer to the north. By the 13th century, the city was an important trading centre, helped along by the royal monopoly it held on the salt being shipped in via the Maros River from Transylvania. Under the Turks, Szeged was afforded some protection since the sultan's estates lay in the area, and it continued to prosper in the 18th and 19th centuries as a free royal town.

But disaster struck in March 1879, when the Tisza swelled its banks and almost wiped the city off the map. All but 300 houses were destroyed, and Szeged, under the direction of engineer Lajos Tisza, was rebuilt with foreign assistance between 1880 and 1883. As a result, the city has an architectural uniformity unknown in most other Hungarian cities, and the leafy, broad avenues that ring the city in an almost perfect circle were named after the European cities that helped bring Szeged back to life. (The Moscow and Odessa sections appeared after the war for political reasons and the latter has since been changed to Temesvári körút in honour of Timişoara, where the Romanian revolution of 1989 began.)

Since WWII, Szeged has been an important university town – students marched here in 1956 before their classmates in Budapest did – and a cultural centre. Theatre, opera and all types of classical and popular music performances abound, culminating in the Szeged Open-Air Festival in summer. But the city is just as famed for its edibles: Szeged paprika, which mates so wonderfully with fish from the Tisza River in *szegedi halászlé* (spicy fish soup), and Pick, Hungary's finest salami. Its other claim to fame is the unusual Szeged accent in Hungarian (eg 'e' is pronounced as 'ö'), which sounds strange in a country with so few dialectical differences.

Orientation
The Tisza River, joined by the Maros, flows west and then turns abruptly south through the centre of Szeged, splitting the city in two as cleanly as the Danube bisects Budapest. But comparison of the two cities and their rivers stops there. The Tisza is a rather undignified muddy channel here, and the other side of Szeged is not the city's throbbing commercial heart as Pest is to Budapest but a large park given over to sunbathing, swimming and other hedonistic pursuits.

Szeged's many squares and inner and outer ring roads make the city confusing for some, but virtually every square in the city has a large signpost with detailed plans and a legend in several languages. The main train station is south of the city centre on Indóház tér; tram No 1 connects the station with the town. The bus station, to the west of the centre on Mars tér, is within easy walking distance via pedestrians-only Mikszáth Kálmán utca.

The Mosque Church in Pécs is an important reminder of the Turkish occupation.

The lustruous glaze of Zsolnay Fountain, Pécs.

Restored shopfronts liven up the heart of Pécs.

Enter Siklós Castle's' 18th-century baroque palace via a drawbridge and through the barbican.

Szeged's town hall sits gracefully under plane trees in Szechenyi ter.

GREAT PLAIN

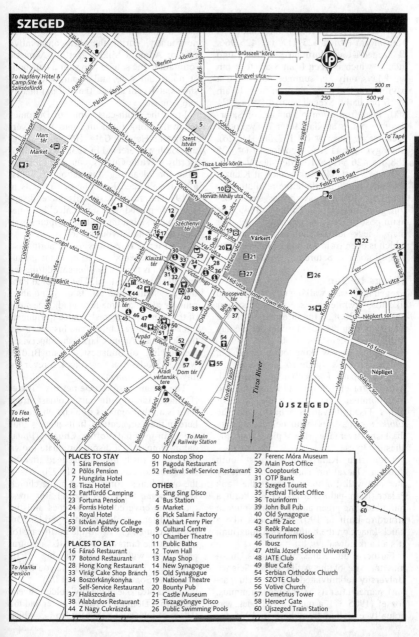

SZEGED

PLACES TO STAY	50 Nonstop Shop	27 Ferenc Móra Museum
1 Sára Pension	51 Pagoda Restaurant	29 Main Post Office
2 Pölös Pension	52 Festival Self-Service Restaurant	30 Cooptourist
7 Hungária Hotel		31 OTP Bank
18 Tisza Hotel	**OTHER**	32 Szeged Tourist
22 Partfürdő Camping	3 Sing Sing Disco	35 Festival Ticket Office
23 Fortuna Pension	4 Bus Station	36 Tourinform
24 Forrás Hotel	5 Market	39 John Bull Pub
41 Royal Hotel	6 Pick Salami Factory	42 Caffè Zacc
53 István Apáthy College	8 Mahart Ferry Pier	43 Reök Palace
59 Loránd Eötvös College	9 Cultural Centre	45 Tourinform Kiosk
	10 Chamber Theatre	46 Ibusz
PLACES TO EAT	11 Public Baths	47 Attila József Science University
16 Fáraó Restaurant	12 Town Hall	48 JATE Club
17 Botond Restaurant	13 Map Shop	49 Blue Café
28 Hong Kong Restaurant	14 New Synagogue	54 Serbian Orthodox Church
33 Virág Cake Shop Branch	15 Old Synagogue	55 SZOTE Club
34 Boszorkánykonyha	19 National Theatre	56 Votive Church
Self-Service Restaurant	20 Bounty Pub	57 Demetrius Tower
37 Halászcsárda	21 Castle Museum	58 Heroes' Gate
38 Alabárdos Restaurant	25 Tiszagyöngye Disco	60 Újszeged Train Station
44 Z Nagy Cukrászda	26 Public Swimming Pools	

Information

The best source of tourist information is Tourinform (☎/fax 425 711, fax 425 966, ✉ szeged@tourinform.hu), Victor Hugo utca 1, which is open from 8 am to 4 pm weekdays only. In summer they have a pavilion on Dugonics tér open from 10 am to 10 pm daily. Szeged Tourist (☎/fax 321 800), open from 9 am to 5 pm and on Saturday to 1 pm, is at Klauzál tér 7. Two other agencies are Ibusz (☎ 471 177, fax 311 626), Somogyi utca 11, and Cooptourist (☎ 425 158, fax 426 541) at Kis Menyhért utca 2.

There's an OTP bank branch at Klauzál tér 2, the building where the revolutionary hero Lajos Kossuth gave his last speech before going into exile in Turkey in 1849. The main post office is at Széchenyi tér 1. For maps check out the shop at Attila utca 9, which is open from 9 am to 5 pm weekdays and till noon on Saturday.

Things to See

Szeged is an easy walking city but if you'd like to sit while you see the sights, tour buses (☎ 420 428 for information) leave Klauzál tér on the hour throughout the day in July and August (600/350Ft).

Begin an easy walking tour of Szeged in Széchenyi tér, a square so large it almost feels like a park. The neobaroque **town hall**, with its graceful tower and colourful tiled roof, dominates the square, while statues of Lajos Tisza, István Széchenyi and the *kubikosok* (navvies) who helped regulate the Tisza River take pride of place under the chestnut trees.

Pedestrian Kárász utca leads south through Klauzál tér. Turn west on Kölcsey utca and walk for about 100m to the **Reök Palace** (Reök-palota) at Tisza Lajos körút, a mind-blowing green and lilac Art Nouveau structure built in 1907 that looks like a knick-knack on the bottom of an aquarium. It's a bank nowadays.

Farther south, Kárász utca meets Dugonics tér, site of the **Attila József Science University** (abbreviated JATE in Hungarian), named after its most famous alumnus. József (1905-37), a much loved poet, was actually expelled from here in 1924 for writing the verse 'I have no father and I have no mother/I have no God and I have no country' during the ultra-conservative rule of Admiral Miklós Horthy. A **music fountain** in the square plays for a half-hour at noon and 4.30 and 8 pm, with extra shows at 10 am and 7.30 and 9 pm in July and August.

From the south-east corner of Dugonics tér, walk along Jókai utca into Aradi vértanúk tere. **Heroes' Gate** (Hősök kapuja) to the south was erected in 1936 in honour of Horthy's White Guards, who were responsible for 'cleansing' the nation of 'Reds' after the ill-fated Republic of Councils in 1919. The fascistic murals have disappeared (replaced with some 'nice' but amateurish ones), but the brutish sculptures will send a chill down your spine.

Dóm tér, a few paces to the north-east, contains Szeged's most important monuments and is the centre of events during the annual summer festival. The **National Pantheon** – statues and reliefs of 80 notables running along an arcade around three sides of the square – is a crash course in Hungarian art, literature, culture and history. Even the Scotsman Adam Clark, who supervised the building of Budapest's Chain Bridge, wins accolades, but you'll look forever for any sign of a woman.

The Romanesque **Demetrius Tower** (Dömötör-torony), the city's oldest structure, is all that remains of a church erected here in the 12th century. In its place stands the twin-towered **Votive Church** (Fogadalmi templom), a disproportionate brown brick monstrosity that was pledged after the flood but not completed until 1930. About the only things worth seeing in the church are the organ, with more than 11,500 pipes, the dome covered with frescoes and the choir. Instead, peek inside the **Serbian Orthodox church** (1778) to the north-east for a look at the fantastic iconostasis: a central gold 'tree' with 60 icons hanging off its 'branches'. It costs 100/80Ft and you'll find the key at Somogyi utca 3 (flat I/5).

Oskola utca, one of the city's oldest streets, leads from Dóm tér to Roosevelt tér and the Palace of Education (1896) at No 1-3, which now houses the **Ferenc Móra Museum** (open 10 am to 3 pm Tuesday and to 5 pm Wednesday to Sunday; 100/50Ft). The museum's strength lies in its collection of folk art from Csongrád County, bearing intelligent descriptions in several languages. That, and the unique exhibit of 7th-century Avar finds done up to look like a clan yurt, put this light years ahead of most other museums in Hungary. The park north of Roosevelt tér – Várkert – contains ruins of what was Szeged Castle. It served as a prison in the 18th century before being pulled down after the flood. The casemates now contain the very informative **Castle Museum** (Vármúzeum).

For many people, Szeged's most compelling sight is the Hungarian Art Nouveau **New Synagogue** (Új zsinagóga), Gutenberg utca 13, which was designed by Lipót Baumhorn in 1903. It is the most beautiful Jewish house of worship in Hungary and still very much in use. If the grace and enormity of the exterior don't impress you, the blue and gold interior will. The cupola, decorated with stars and flowers (representing Infinity and Faith), appears to float skyward, and the tabernacle of carved acacia wood and metal fittings is a masterpiece. The synagogue is open from 9 am to 6 pm Sunday to Friday from April to September and to 2 pm the rest of the year (150/60Ft). There are a few other buildings of interest in this area, the former Jewish quarter, including the neoclassical **Old Synagogue** (Ózsinagóga; 1843) at Hajnóczy utca 12. The remains of another old **synagogue** (now a private house) can be seen at Nádor utca 3.

If you'd like to know more about the making of Szeged's famed salami – from hoof to shrink-wrap – the **Pick Salami Factory** (Pick Szalámigyár) at Maros utca 21 ('since 1869') can oblige, but you must call in advance on ☎ 421 814 to arrange a time.

The **flea market** is near Vám tér at the start of Szabadkai út south-west of the centre.

Activities

Across the Tisza River, the parkland of Újszeged (New Szeged) has swimming pools and a thermal spa (300/250Ft, 200Ft after 4 pm) on Partfürdő utca, as well as

beaches along the river. But the best place for swimming is in the suburb of Sziksósfürdő, about 10km to the west of town at Kiskundorozsma. Along with a conventional strand, swimming pool and rowing boats, this thermal 'Soda Salt Lake' also has a nudist beach open 10 am to 6 pm weekdays and from 8 am at the weekend May to September.

Special Events

The Szeged Open-Air Festival (Szegedi Szabadtéri Játékok) unfolds on Dóm tér with the two towers of the Votive Church as a backdrop from mid-July to late August. The outdoor theatre here seats some 6000 people. Main events include an opera, an operetta, a play, folk dancing, classical music, ballet and a rock opera. Festival tickets and information are available from the ticket office (☎ 471 466) at Deák Ferenc utca 28-30 (open weekdays from 10 am to 5 pm and, in July and August, to 1 pm at the weekend). But Szeged isn't all highbrow; others might prefer the annual International Trucker Country Meeting (Nemzetközi Kamionos Country Találkoz') in mid-July when lorries gather.

Places to Stay

Camping Szeged has five camping grounds, most of which operate between May and September/October and have bungalows. *Partfürdő* (☎ 430 843, Középkikötő sor), in New Szeged along the river opposite the city centre, charges 450Ft per person and per tent, and there are 40 hotel rooms at 2200/3200Ft per double without/with shower. Guests have free use of the swimming and thermal pools nearby.

A second (and much less attractive) site, convenient to the city, is *Napfény Camping* (☎ 421 800, fax 467 579, ✉ hotelnapfeny@ mail.tiszanet.hu, Dorozsmai út 4), across a large bridge near the western terminus of tram No 1. Bungalows for three/four are 5900/8000Ft.

There are a couple of camping grounds by Sziksósfürdő in Kiskundorozsma, including *Sziksós Camping* (☎ 463 050) and *Naturista Camping* (☎ 463 988), an *au naturel* site by the lake's beach.

Hostels & Private Rooms Plenty of student dormitories in Szeged open their doors to travellers in July and August, including *István Apáthy College* (☎ 420 488, Eötvös utca 4) next to the Votive Church and *Loránd Eötvös College* (☎ 310 641, Tisza Lajos körút 103). They generally cost 800/600Ft for adults/students in basic dormitories and 1500Ft per person with rooms with facilities.

Your best bets for a *private room* are Ibusz and Szeged Tourist, which charge 2000Ft to 2500Ft per person; flats are from 4000Ft.

Pensions If you arrive by bus you'll be within walking distance of the five-room *Sára* pension (☎ 498 206, Zákány utca 13), where singles/doubles are 3500/4500Ft. If it's full there's the larger *Pölös* pension (☎ 498 208, Pacsirta utca 17a) just opposite. Most of the other pensions are over in New Szeged, including the seven-room *Fortuna* (☎ 431 907, Pécskai utca 8). Doubles here are 5900Ft.

Hotels The fine old *Tisza* hotel (☎/fax 478 278, ✉ tiszo@zenon.eunet.hu, Wesselényi utca 6), just off Széchenyi tér, has been given a partial overhaul (and an extra star) but some rooms still remain relatively good value: singles/doubles with shared facilities are 3800/6200Ft, with shower 5000/7100Ft and with bath 7400/8500Ft. It's a lovely place, with large, bright and airy rooms and a free private garage.

The *Napfény* hotel (see Camping) has both a motel (open May to September) and a year-round hotel with a total of 160 rooms. Basic doubles at the former are 2400Ft; at the latter singles/doubles/triples with shower are 6200/7800/8900Ft.

The most central of Szeged's upmarket hotels is the *Royal* (☎ 475 275, fax 312 123, Kölcsey utca 1-3), with 96 rooms in renovated old and new wings. Singles/doubles with bath are DM92/108.

The biggest hotels in town are the boxy, 114-room *Hungária* (☎ 480 580, fax 322 457, ✉ hungaria@tiszanet.hu, Maros utca 1) near a noisy stretch of road but with good views of the river (singles/doubles from 8900/10,680Ft), and the *Forrás* spa hotel (☎ 430 130, fax 430 866, ✉ forras@ zenon.hu, Szent-Györgyi Albert utca 16-24) with 177 rooms in New Szeged. Singles/doubles here are DM102/116, though the ones in the attic are cheaper.

Places to Eat

The *Boszorkánykonyha* (Híd utca 8), just off Széchenyi tér, is an unappetising, but very cheap, self-service place. Better to try the *Festival* (Oskola utca 5), a similar place opposite the Votive Church, which also has cheap Chinese dishes. It's open from 10 am to 6 pm daily.

The *Botond* (Széchenyi tér 13) serves better-than-average Hungarian food with pleasant outside seating in summer. Another possibility is the pharaonic *Fáraó* cellar restaurant (Nagy Jenő utca 1) just around the corner.

The *Pagoda* (Zrínyi utca 5) serves mock Chinese food amid faded vermilion, but it does have a nonsmoking room. For better Chinese, though, head for the *Hong Kong* (Deák Ferenc utca 24) with noodle and rice dishes for 200Ft to 500Ft and more substantial mains for 500Ft to 800Ft. It's open daily to 11.30 pm or midnight.

The *Halászcsárda* (Roosevelt tér 14) is a Szeged institution and serves up *szegedi halászlé* by the cauldron.

Szeged's 'silver-service' eatery is the *Alabárdos* (Oskola utca 13), where overattentive waiters fawn over German tourists who have come to see Segedin.

For cakes, coffee and ice cream, check out the *Virág* (Klauzál tér 1), which has tables inside and on the square and museumquality Herend coffee machines. The Virág outlet opposite at No 8 is for stand-up service and takeaway. Another great old-style cukrászda is *Z Nagy* (Somogyi utca 2).

Szeged has two big *fruit & vegetable markets*, one on Mars tér, site of the notorious Star Prison for political prisoners early in the 1950s, and the other north-west of Széchenyi tér on Szent István tér. There's a *nonstop shop* at Zrínyi utca 1 and another at Márs tér 17.

Entertainment

Your best sources of entertainment information in this culturally active city are Tourinform or the *Gyula Juhász Cultural Centre* (☎ 425 248, Vörösmarty utca 5). The *Szeged National Theatre (Szegedi Nemzeti Színház; ☎ 479 279, Deák Ferenc utca 12-14)*, built in 1886, has always been the centre of cultural life in Szeged and usually stages operas and ballet. For plays, go to the *Chamber Theatre (Kamara Színház; Horváth Mihály utca 3)*. The ticket office (☎ 476 555) at Kárász utca 15, is open from 10 am to 5 pm weekdays, till noon on Saturday.

There's a vast array of bars, clubs and other night spots in this student town, especially around Dugonics tér; the *Blue Cafe (Toldy utca 2)* and *Caffè Zacc (Kölcsey utca 11)* opposite McDonald's are always worth a look. The *Bounty Pub (Stefánia utca 4)* behind the Tisza hotel is a large bar with live entertainment at the weekend. There's a *John Bull Pub (Oroszla'utca 6)* west of Klauzál tér.

The *JATE Club (Toldy utca 7)* is the best place to meet students on their own turf; there's a disco here on Thursday, Friday and Saturday to 4 or 5 am. Another university place, the *SZOTE Club (Dom tér 13)*, has its own following. The huge *Tiszagyöngye* disco *(Közép-kikötő sor)* in New Szeged is open till 4 am on Wednesday and Saturday. The *Sing Sing Disco* , on the corner of Mars tér and Dr Baross József utca, occupies a huge pavilion near the bus station. It's open the same nights.

For more information about venues and events check the free weekly entertainment guides *Szegedi Mozaik* and *Szegedi Est*.

Getting There & Away

Bus Bus service is very good from Szeged, with frequent departures to Békéscsaba, Csongrád, Ópusztaszer, Makó and Hódmezővásárhely. Other destinations include Budapest's Népstadion (seven buses daily), Debrecen (three), Eger (two), Gyöngyös (two), Győr (two), Gyula (five), Kecskemét (10 to 12), Mohács (five), Pécs (six), Siófok (two), Székesfehérvár (five), Tiszafüred (two) and Veszprém (three). Buses

also cross the Romanian border for Arad daily at 6.30 am with extra ones on Thursday at 11.15 am, Friday at 7.40 am, Saturday at 10.10 am and Sunday at 8.10 am. There are buses to Timişoara on Thursday and Friday at 6.30 am and on Saturday at 10.10 am.

Train Szeged is on a main railway line to Budapest-Nyugati. Another line connects the city with Hódmezővásárhely and Békéscsaba, where you can change trains for Gyula or Romania. Southbound local trains leave Szeged for Subotica in Yugoslavia twice a day at 6.35 am and 4.20 pm.

Getting Around

The No 1 tram from the train station will take you north to Széchenyi tér. It turns west on Kossuth Lajos sugárút and goes as far as Izabella Bridge, where it turns around. Alight there for the Napfény hotel, motel and camp site.

You can get closer to the Napfény on bus No 78, which stops directly opposite the complex on Kossuth Lajos sugárút. Get off just after you cross the bridge over the railway tracks. The correct bus to Szentmihály and the flea market is the No 76; you can also take tram No 4. For Sziksósfürdő, take bus 7f from the main bus station.

Local taxis can be ordered on ☎ 444 888 or ☎ 488 488.

ÓPUSZTASZER

☎ 62 • postcode 6767 • pop 2200

About 28km north of Szeged, the **Ópusztaszer National Historical Memorial Park** (Ópusztaszeri Nemzeti Történeti Emlékpark) in Ópusztaszer commemorates the single most important event in Hungarian history: the *honfoglalás*, or 'conquest', of the Carpathian Basin by the Magyars in 896.

Contrary to what many people think (Hungarians included), the park does not mark the spot where Árpád, mounted on his white charger, first entered 'Hungary'. That was actually the Munkács Valley, Hungarian territory until after WWI and now Ukrainian territory. But according to the 12th-century chronicler known as

Anonymous, it was at this place called Szer that Árpád and the six clan chieftains, who had sworn a blood oath of fidelity to him, held their first assembly, and so it was decided that a **Millennium Monument** would be erected here in 1896. (Scholars had actually determined the date of the conquest to be between 893 and 895, but the government was not ready to mark the 1000-year anniversary until 1896.)

Situated atop a slight rise in the Great Plain about a kilometre from the Szeged road, the park is an attractive though sombre place. Besides the neoclassical monument with Árpád taking pride of place, there are ruins of an 11th-century **Romanesque church** and **monastery** still being excavated, and an excellent **open-air museum** (skanzen) with a farmhouse, windmills, an old post office, a schoolhouse and cottages moved from villages around south-east Hungary. In one, the home of a rather prosperous and smug onion grower from Makó, a sampler admonishes potential gossips: 'Neighbour lady, away you go/If it's gossip you want to know' (or words to that effect).

To the west of the park beside the little lake, a museum reminiscent of a Magyar chieftain's tent houses a huge **panorama painting** entitled *The Arrival of the Hungarians*. Completed by Árpád Feszty for the millenary exhibition in Budapest in 1896, the enormous work, which measures 15m x 120m, was badly damaged during WWII and was restored by a Polish team in time for the 1100th anniversary of the conquest in 1996.

The park is open from 9 am to 7 pm daily from April to September and to 5 pm Tuesday to Sunday the rest of the year. Admission costs 400Ft for just the park and 800/600Ft for adults/students and children to view the panorama painting as well.

Szeri Camping (☎ 275 123, Árpád liget 111) has 14 bungalows (from about 3000Ft for a double with shared shower; open mid-April to mid-October), and you can go horse riding across the street for 800Ft an hour. The *Szeri Csárda* next door serves a decent *gulyás*.

HÓDMEZŐVÁSÁRHELY
☎ 62 • postcode 6800 • pop 51,200

Sitting on the dried-up bed of what was once Lake Hód, some 25km north-east of Szeged, the city of 'Hód Meadow Marketplace' was no more than a collection of disparate communities until the Turkish invasions, when much of the population was dispersed and the town's centre razed. The peasants of Hódmezővásárhely returned to subsistence farming in the 17th century, but the abolition of serfdom in the mid-19th century, without the redistribution of land, only increased their isolation and helped bring about an agrarian revolt led by János Kovács Szántó in 1894, an event the townspeople are justly proud of – and which the communist regime trumpeted for decades.

Folk art, particularly pottery, has a rich tradition in Hódmezővásárhely; some 400 independent artisans working here in the mid-1800s made it the largest pottery centre in Hungary. Today you won't see much more pottery outside the town's museums than you would elsewhere, but the influence of the dynamic artists' colony here is felt well beyond Kohán György utca – from the galleries and Autumn Weeks art festival to the ceramic and bronze street signs by eminent artists.

Orientation & Information

The bus station is just off Andrássy utca on Bocskai utca, about a 10-minute walk east from Kossuth tér, the city centre. There are two train stations in town: the main one and Hódmezővásárhelyi-Népkert. The first is east of the city centre at the end of Mérleg utca, the second south-west at the end of Ady Endre utca.

The Tourinform office (☎/fax 248 292, ✉ hodmezovasarhely@tourinform.hu) is at Kossuth tér 6 and is open from 8 am to 5 pm weekdays (to 4 pm on Friday). Szeged Tourist (☎ 341 432) is housed in an old granary next to the Old Church at Szőnyi utca 1. It is open from 9 am to 5 pm weekdays and, in summer, till noon on Saturday.

OTP bank has a branch at Andrássy utca 1 (corner of Kossuth tér). The main post office is on the north-west corner of Kossuth tér at Hódi Pál utca 2.

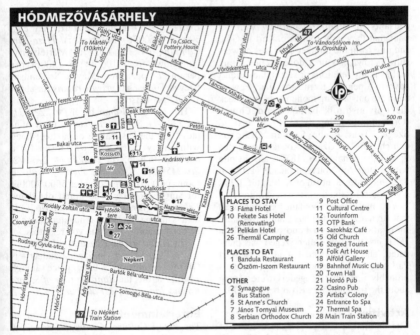

HÓDMEZŐVÁSÁRHELY

PLACES TO STAY	
3	Fáma Hotel
10	Fekete Sas Hotel (Renovating)
25	Pelikán Hotel
26	Thermál Camping

PLACES TO EAT	
1	Bandula Restaurant
6	Őszöm-Iszom Restaurant

OTHER	
2	Synagogue
4	Bus Station
5	St Anne's Church
7	János Tornyai Museum
8	Serbian Orthodox Church
9	Post Office
11	Cultural Centre
12	Tourinform
13	OTP Bank
14	Sarokház Café
15	Old Church
16	Szeged Tourist
17	Folk Art House
18	Alföld Gallery
19	Bahnhof Music Club
20	Town Hall
21	Hordó Pub
22	Casino Pub
23	Artists' Colony
24	Entrance to Spa
27	Thermal Spa
28	Main Train Station

GREAT PLAIN

Things to See

Museums & Galleries The **János Tornyai Museum** at Szántó Kovács János utca 16-18, named after a leading member of the Alföld School of *al fresco* painting, displays some early archaeological finds, but its *raison d'être* is to show off the folk art of Hódmezővásárhely – the painted furniture, 'hairy' embroidery done with yarn-like thread, and pottery unique to the region. The collection of jugs, pitchers and plates, most of them made as wedding gifts, is the finest of all and represents the many types once made here and named after city districts, including Csúcs (white and blue), Tabán (brown) and Újváros (yellow and green). The museum is open from 10 am to 6 pm Tuesday to Sunday (100/50Ft).

More pottery is on display at the **Csúcs Pottery House**, (Csúcsi Fazekasház) once the home of master potter Sándor Vékony, at Rákóczi utca 101 (open from 1 to 5 pm Tuesday to Sunday), and at the **Folk Art House** (Népmüvészeti tájház), two old thatched farmhouses standing self-consciously in the middle of a housing estate at Árpád utca 21 and open 9 am till noon and 3 to 6 pm Tuesday to Sunday. Enter from Kaszap utca.

Outsiders are not allowed into the **artists' colony** (művésztelep) at Kohán György utca 2, founded in the early part of this century, but you can view selected members' work at the **Alföld Gallery**, across from Szeged Tourist in a neoclassical former Calvinist school at Kossuth tér 8. Naturally the Alföld School dominates; you might go a little crazy looking at horses and sweep wells and cowboys on the Great Plain in every season through the eyes of Tornyai, István Nagy and József Koszta, but there are other things to enjoy such as the work of Menyhért Tóth and the impressionist János Vaszary. The gallery is open Tuesday from 10 am to 3 pm, and to 5 pm Wednesday to Sunday.

Other Attractions It was said that the peasants of Hódmezővásárhely were so poor that they only found comfort in God. Judging from the number of places of worship in town (about a dozen representing half as many religions or sects), they didn't have two pennies to rub together. Few of them are outstanding monuments, but check the Calvinist folk baroque **Old Church** (Ótemplom) dating from 1724 next to Szeged Tourist; the **Serbian Orthodox church** (1792) at Szántó Kovács János utca 9; and the **synagogue** (1857), an old pile with a later Art Nouveau facade (1906) at Szeremlei utca 3, north of Kálvin tér. It has a wonderful stained-glass rose window.

You may wonder about the long stone wall that stretches from the bus station westward for almost 4km. It's a **flood barrier** built in 1881, just two years after Szeged was inundated. The Hód-tó Canal south of Népkert Park may not look very threatening, but that's probably just what Szegeders were saying about the tranquil Tisza River before 1879.

Activities

The thermal spa in the Népkert, south of Kossuth tér on Ady Endre utca, has hot and cold pools open from 8 am to 8 pm daily, but Mártély, about 10km to the north-west on a backwater of the Tisza, is the city's real recreational centre, with boating, fishing and swimming available.

The Vándorsólyom inn (☎ 341 900), about 4km north-east of the city on route No 47 (Kutasi út) en route to Orosháza, has horses for cross-country riding and carriage driving. See Places to Stay & Eat for more information.

Special Events

If you're in the area in October and the first half of November, check the dates for the Autumn Weeks (Őszi Hetek), a nationally attended arts festival. The city's other big festival – antipodeans take note – is the Sheep Fair (Juhászverseny) in April.

Places to Stay & Eat

There are a handful of rather uncomfortable (but convenient) bungalows for two people at *Thermál Camping* (☎ 245 033, Ady Endre utca 1) in the Népkert; they cost 3000Ft (3500Ft with shower). *Tisza-part Camping* (☎ 228 057) in Mártély has bungalows from 1000Ft to 1200Ft per person. It's open from May to September. Szeged Tourist has *private rooms* for about 1500Ft per person.

The 15-room *Fáma* hotel (☎ 222 231, fax 222 344, Szeremlei utca 7), a few minutes from the bus station on a street lined with cherry trees, charges 5500Ft for a double with bath. The *Pelikán* (☎ 245 072, fax 245 855, Ady Endre utca 1), with 20 rooms next to the spa, charges 5500/7000Ft for singles/doubles. The grand old dame *Fekete Sas* (Black Eagle) hotel on Hódi Pál utca is at long last being renovated and may be open again by the time you read this.

The *Öszöm-Iszom* (Szent Antal utca 8) – that's 'I Eat-I Drink' in Szeged dialect – is OK for a quick meal. A better place (though a bit far out) is the *Bandula* (cnr of Szántó Kovács János utca & Pálffy utca).

Entertainment

The *Petőfi Cultural Centre* (☎ 341 750, Szántó Kovács János utca 7) can advise you on what's on in town.

The *Sarokház* cafe, on the corner of Andrássy utca and Szönyi utca, is the best place for people-watching in Hódmezővásárhely. Near the town hall building, the *Hordó* pub, on the corner of Városház utca and Hősök tere, is fine for a glass as is the *Casino Pub* (Hősök tere) next door. The *Bahnhof Music Club* (Kossuth tér 1), which you enter from Hősök tere, is the bopping-est venue in town.

Getting There & Away

Buses to Szeged, Békéscsaba, Makó, Szentes, Csongrád and the resort area of Mártély are very frequent; there is a minimum of three daily departures to Szolnok, Jászberény, Budapest, Orosháza and Szeghalom. One or two buses a day head for Baja, Parádfürdő, Tiszafüred, Miskolc, Debrecen, Hajdúszoboszló, Gyöngyös and Pécs.

Two railway lines pass through Hódmezővásárhely, and all trains serve both train stations, which are 2km apart. The more important of the two lines connects Szeged with Békéscsaba. The smaller line links Makó, Hungary's onion capital and the birthplace of Joseph Pulitzer, with Szolnok.

CSONGRÁD

☎ 63 • postcode 6640 • pop 20,200

The 13th century did not treat the town of Csongrád (from the Slavic name Černigrad, meaning 'black castle') very well. Once the royal capital of Csongrád County, the town and its fortress were so badly damaged when the Mongols overran it that Béla IV transferred the seat to Szeged in 1247.

Csongrád never really recovered from the invasion, and development was slow; until the 1920s it was not even a town. As a result, the Öregvár (Old Castle) district to the east looks pretty much the way it did in the 17th century: a quiet fishing village of thatched cottages and narrow streets on the bank of the Tisza.

Orientation & Information

Csongrád lies on the left bank of the Tisza, close to where it is joined by the Körös River, some 58km north of Szeged. A backwater (Holt-Tisza) south of town is used for recreation. The bus station is on Hunyadi tér, five minutes from the main street, Fő utca. The train station lies to the south-west at the end of Vasút utca.

Tourinform (☎/fax 481 008, ✉ csongrad@tourinform.hu) at Fő utca 16 is usually open from 8 am to 5 pm weekdays and till noon on Saturday but in July and August it moves to a kiosk outside the cultural centre and opens from 8 am to 8 pm daily. You can also get information at the Erzsébet hotel when Tourinform is closed. Szeged Tourist (☎ 483 069, fax 483 232) at Fő utca 14 is open from 9 am to 5 pm on weekdays.

There's an OTP bank branch next to the cultural centre at Szentháromság tér 8. The main post office is north-east of the bus station at Dózsa György tér 1.

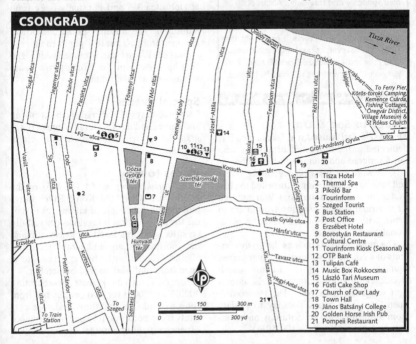

CSONGRÁD

To Ferry Pier, Körös-toroki Camping, Kemence Csárda, Fishing Cottages, Öregvár District, Village Museum & St Rókus Church

1 Tisza Hotel
2 Thermal Spa
3 Pikoló Bar
4 Tourinform
5 Szeged Tourist
6 Bus Station
7 Post Office
8 Erzsébet Hotel
9 Borostyán Restaurant
10 Cultural Centre
11 Tourinform Kiosk (Seasonal)
12 OTP Bank
13 Tulipán Café
14 Music Box Rokkocsma
15 László Tari Museum
16 Füsti Cake Shop
17 Church of Our Lady
18 Town Hall
19 János Batsányi College
20 Golden Horse Irish Pub
21 Pompeii Restaurant

0   150   300 m
0   150   300 yd

To Train Station

To Szeged

GREAT PLAIN

A Dubious Distinction

Hungary has Europe's highest rate of suicide – 38.6 per 100,000 people – and more people take their own lives in Csongrád County on the Southern Plain than any other place in the country.

Psychologists are still out to lunch on why Hungary should have such a high incidence of suicide. Some say that Hungarians' inclination to gloom leads to the ultimate act of despair (see Society & Conduct in the Facts about the Country chapter). Others link it to a phenomenon not uncommon late in the 19th century. As the Hungarian aristocracy withered away, the *kisnemesség* (lower nobility), some of them no better off than the local peasantry, would do themselves in to 'save their name and honour'. As a result, suicide was – and is – not looked upon dishonourably in Hungary, victims may be buried in hallowed ground and the euphemistic sentence used in obituaries is: 'Kovács János/Erzsébet died suddenly and tragically'. About 60% of suicides are by hanging.

And, who, you may ask, comes next in the suicide sweepstakes? Believe it or not, it's the Finns, the Magyars' closest linguistic cousins, who rank second with 26.6 per 100,000. Forget genes; apparently we're all tied by tongues.

Things to See & Do

The **László Tari Museum** at Iskola utca 2 is dedicated to the thousands of navvies who left Csongrád and vicinity in the 19th century to work on projects regulating rivers and building canals. Some travelled to sites as far away as Istanbul and Warsaw and were virtual slaves, working from 5 am to 8 pm with meatless meals and the occasional 'smoke' break.

The museum also contains the grisly contents of a couple of 8th-century Avar graves found in nearby Felgyő and some superb woodcarving (roof frames, lintels, doors) by Csongrád's fisherfolk. The museum is open from 1 to 5 pm Tuesday to Friday, from 9 am till noon on Saturday and from 9am to 5 pm on Sunday (100/50Ft).

Walking eastward from the museum to the Öregvár district, you'll pass the baroque **Church of Our Lady** (Nagyboldogasszony temploma; 1769) and the beautiful Secessionist **János Batsányi College** on Kossuth tér. A bit farther on is **St Rókus Church**, built in 1722 on the site of a Turkish mosque.

The cobblestone streets of the protected **Öregvár** district begin at a little roundabout three blocks east of the church. Most of the district is made up of private homes or holiday houses, but the **Village Museum** (Tájház) at Gyökér utca 1 is open to all from 1 to 5 pm Wednesday to Sunday from May to September and gives a good idea of how the simple fisherfolk and navvies of Csongrád lived until not so long ago. It's housed in two old cottages connected by a long thatched roof and contains period furniture, household items and lots of fish nets and traps.

The **thermal spa**, fed by a spring with water that reaches 46°C, is in a large park at Dob utca 3-5 and is usually open from 7 am to 7 pm daily (to 10 pm Thursday to Saturday). The **outdoor pools** and strand are open from 10 am to 7 pm in summer.

Szeged Tourist can arrange fishing and boating trips from the Körös-toroki camp site as well as bike rentals.

Special Events

Csongrád Days (Csongrádi Napok) of fun and games and the Csongrád Vintage (Csográdi Szüret) wine festival are both held in August.

Places to Stay

Körös-toroki Camping (☎ *481 185*), on the beach near where the Körös River flows into the Tisza a couple of kilometres east of the town centre, has bungalows (mercifully on stilts – the area floods in heavy rain and the mosquitoes are unbearable) costing 1000Ft (4000Ft with shower). The site is open from mid-May to mid-September.

Szeged Tourist has *private rooms* costing 3000Ft to 4000Ft for two people, but from June to mid-October they'll almost certainly try to book you into one of their more expensive *fishing cottages* in the Öregvár district. If you're feeling flush, this is the most atmospheric place to stay (available May to September). Prices for these 200-year-old houses, some of which have kitchens and living rooms, start at about 6500Ft, with the average about 9000Ft. The nicest ones are at Öregvár 49, 57b and 58.

The *Erzsébet* (☎ *483 960, fax 483 631, Fő utca 3*) is an old 13-room hotel minutes from the bus station, with singles/doubles/triples with shower for 3600/4800/7200Ft; doubles without bath are from 3600Ft. To the west, the modern 15-room *Tisza* hotel (☎/*fax 483 594, Fő utca 23*) charges 7500/9400Ft for a single/double with shower.

Places to Eat

The *Tulipán (Szentháromság tér 2-6)* is a simple cafe-restaurant in the centre of Csongrád; the *Pompeii (Kis Tisza utca 6)* is a bit out of the way but it serves decent pizza and South Slav specialities in a renovated old house.

The *Borostyán (Jókai Mór utca 1)* is a comfortable modern eatery in a courtyard, off the main drag, with Hungarian and Serb main courses for 500Ft to 700Ft. The obvious choice in the Öregvár district for a meal is the *Kemence (Öregvár 54)*, an attractive csárda in an old cottage. There are no fish dishes on the menu – surprising in a fishing town – but whatever you have, try a glass of Csongrádi Kadarka, the spicy, ruby-red local wine.

For something sweet, the *Füsti* cake shop *(Fő utca 3)* on the corner with Iskola utca is a good choice.

Entertainment

The *Kossuth Cultural Centre* (☎ *483 414, Szentháromság tér 8)* can tell you what might be on in Csongrád.

The *Pikoló (Fő utca 13)* is a poky little neighbourhood pub but central, opposite Tourinform. There will surely be more exciting things going on at the *Music Box (József Attila utca 3)*, a *rokkocsma* (ie rock pub) just north of Kossuth tér.

The *Golden Horse Irish Pub (Gróf Andrássy Gyula utca 17a)* is farther east on the way to the Öregvár.

Getting There & Away

Bus From Csongrád buses run to Baja (two daily), Békéscsaba (three), Budapest (eight or nine), Eger (two), Gyula (two), Hódmezővásárhely and Kecskemét (10 to 12 each), Kiskunfélegyháza (every half-hour), Lajosmizse (three), Orosháza (seven), Szentes (every 15 minutes) and Szolnok (four). The 10 or 11 daily buses to Szeged go via Ópusztaszer.

There's a daily departure for Arad in Romania at 5.30 am and another one at 7.05 am from Monday to Thursday.

Train Csongrád is on the 80km secondary railway line linking Szentes to the east with Kiskunfélegyháza to the west. But you can't get very far from either of those places; buses are always a faster, more frequent option.

BÉKÉSCSABA
☎ 66 • postcode 5600 • pop 67,100

When most Hungarians hear mention of Békéscsaba, they usually think of two very disparate things: fatty sausage and bloody riots. Csabai, a sausage not dissimilar to Portuguese *chorizo* is manufactured here, and Békéscsaba was the centre of the Vihar Sarok, the 'Stormy Corner' where violent riots broke out among day labourers and harvesters in 1890. Ironically, the city is now the capital of Békés – 'Peaceful' – County.

Békéscsaba was an important fortified settlement as early as the 14th century, but it was razed and its population scattered under Turkish rule. Early in the 18th century, a Habsburg emissary named János György Harruckern invited Rhinelanders and Slovaks to resettle the area, and it soon became a Lutheran stronghold. The influence of the Slovaks in particular can be felt to this day – in the city's bilingual street signs and the Slovak-language schools and social clubs, among other things.

Development began to reach Békéscsaba in the 19th century when the railway passed through the city (1858). In 1906, in response to the earlier agrarian movements, András Áchim founded his radical Peasants' Party here, an important political force

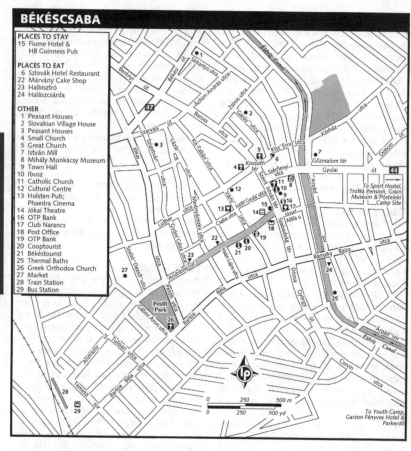

BÉKÉSCSABA

PLACES TO STAY
15 Fiume Hotel &
   HB Guinness Pub

PLACES TO EAT
6 Szlovák Hotel Restaurant
22 Márvány Cake Shop
23 Halbisztró
24 Halászcsárda

OTHER
1 Peasant Houses
2 Slovakian Village House
3 Peasant Houses
4 Small Church
5 Great Church
7 István Mill
8 Mihály Munkácsy Museum
9 Town Hall
10 Ibusz
11 Catholic Church
12 Cultural Centre
13 Holsten Pub;
   Phaedra Cinema
14 Jókai Theatre
16 OTP Bank
17 Club Narancs
18 Post Office
19 OTP Bank
20 Cooptourist
21 Békéstourist
25 Thermal Baths
26 Greek Orthodox Church
27 Market
28 Train Station
29 Bus Station

in Hungary for many years. By 1950, Békéscsaba had surpassed nearby Gyula in importance and the county seat was moved here – something for which Gyula has yet to forgive her sister city.

Relying essentially on agriculture (wheat, rice, cattle) and food-processing, Békés County has been in the economic doldrums for some time, with high unemployment and a falling population. That may not sound like much of an incentive to visit Békéscsaba, but it is a pleasant, friendly place to tarry on the way to the spas at Gyula or perhaps to Romania.

Orientation & Information

Békéscsaba's train and bus stations stand side by side at the south-western end of Andrássy út, the main drag. A long stretch of this street, from Petőfi utca and Jókai utca to Szent István tér, is a pedestrian walkway, and just beyond it lies the Élővíz-csatorna, the 'Living Water Canal' that links Békéscsaba with Békés to the north, Gyula to the east, and the Körös River. To the east of the canal lies the Parkerdő, the city's cool and leafy playground.

The staff at Békéstourist (☎ 323 448) at Andrássy út 10 are well informed and helpful. The office is open from 8 am to 4 pm on weekdays (to 3.30 pm on Friday). Cooptourist (☎/fax 326 545), Andrássy út 6, keeps the same hours while Ibusz (☎/fax 325 554), next to the town hall at Szent István tér 9, opens from 8 am to 5 pm weekdays and till noon on Saturday.

There are OTP banks at Szent István tér 3 and Andrássy út 4. The main post office is at Szabadság tér 1-3 opposite the Fiume hotel.

Things to See & Do

The **Mihály Munkácsy Museum** at Széchenyi utca 9 has exhibits devoted to the wildlife and ecology of the Great Plain as well as to the folk culture of the region, but it's essentially a temple to the painter Munkácsy (1844-1900). Some may find his depictions of the Great Plain and its denizens a little sugar-coated, but as a chronicler of that place and time (real or imagined) he is unsurpassed in Hungarian fine art. An ethnographic exhibit traces the history of the Romanian, Slovak, German and Hungarian ethnic groups of the region. Don't miss the fine Slovak embroidery and the Hungarian painted furniture. The museum is open from 10 am to 6 pm Tuesday to Sunday (100/50Ft).

Present or future farmers would no doubt be interested in the **Grain Museum** (Gabonamúzeum), at Gyulai út 65, housed in several old thatched barns and crammed with traditional tools and implements (open from 10 am to 5 pm Tuesday to Sunday; 100/50Ft). The bladeless 19th-century windmill nearby is one of the best examples surviving in Hungary.

The **Slovakian Village House** (Szlovák tájház), at Garay utca 21, is a wonderful Slovakian farmhouse built in 1865 and full of folk furniture and ornamentation. It is open from 10 am till noon and 2 to 6 pm Tuesday to Sunday. A lot of other typical peasant houses can be found in the neighbourhood, especially on Szigetvári utca and Sárkantyú utca.

Don't miss the 19th-century **István Mill** (István Malom), a grey-brick colossus from the early 20th century on Gőzmalom tér, best viewed from the small canal bridge near the Mihály Munkácsy Museum. It was the first steam mill built in Hungary and is still in operation. It contains museum-quality flour sifters and shakers.

The Lutheran **Great Church** (Nagytemplom; 1824) and the 18th-century **Small Church** (Kistemplom) facing each other across Kossuth tér attest to the city's deeply rooted Protestantism. The baroque **Greek Orthodox church** (1838), Bartók Béla utca 51-53, could easily be mistaken for yet another Lutheran church from the outside.

The splendid **town hall** (városháza), with a facade (1873) designed by the overworked Budapest architect Miklós Ybl, is at Szent István tér 7. Walk east on József Attila utca to the canal and Árpád sor, which is lined with busts of Hungarian literary, artistic and musical greats and some wonderful late 19th-century mansions.

The **Árpád thermal baths** (open 6 am to 6 or 7 pm daily) and indoor and outdoor **swimming pools** are near the Halászcsárda restaurant at Árpád sor 2.

Places to Stay

The *János Arany College* (☎/fax 459 366, Lencsési út 136) in the Youth Camp (Ifjúsági-tábor) near the Parkerdő has dormitory rooms available from late June to August. The agencies in Békéscsaba can book you a ***private room*** from 1500Ft per person.

The 14 rooms of the *Sport* hostel (☎ 449 449, Gyulai út) ring the upper floors of a large stadium north-west of the Parkerdő. Doubles are 3600Ft to 4000Ft, depending on the floor and the room, and all rooms have showers and TV. Sporting events and concerts are held in the huge auditorium across from the rooms, so don't expect much sleep if a rock band or a basketball game is on. Still, you couldn't ask for better seats. There's a raucous used-car market outside on Sunday.

The *Troféa* (☎/fax 441 038, Gyulai út 61), next to the Grain Museum, is a 10-room pension with singles/doubles for 4500/5000Ft some 3.5km east of the centre. The 26-room *Garzon Fényves* hotel (☎ 457 377, fax 456 126) in the Ifjúsági-tábor is a cool and leafy oasis but not very convenient to the centre unless you have your own wheels. Doubles are 5900Ft.

Békéscsaba's premier hotel and one of the nicest in Hungary is the restored *Fiume* (☎ *443 243, fax 441 116, Szent István tér 2*), which bears the old name of the Adriatic port of Rijeka (now Croatia). The 39-room hotel has a top-class restaurant and a popular pub-restaurant. Singles are 6400Ft, doubles 8500Ft.

Places to Eat

The cheap stand-up *Halbisztró (Andrássy út 31)* serves several varieties of fish and is open from 8 am to 5 pm on weekdays (to 2 pm on Monday) and to 1 pm on Saturday. Another inexpensive option is the restaurant at the *Szlovák* hotel *(Kossuth tér 10)*, which serves hearty Slovak and Hungarian specialities till 10 pm.

The *HB Guinness Pub* at the Fiume hotel serves some of the best food in town in clean, bright surroundings. But on a warm evening, all that meat won't do. Cross the canal and head for the *Halászcsárda* fish restaurant *(Árpád sor 1)* near the spa.

You can satisfy your sweet tooth at the *Márvány* cake shop *(Andrássy út 21)*. It has outside seating on a pretty square with a fountain and stays open till 10 pm daily.

There's a big food *market (Szabó Dezső utca)* just north of Andrássy út open on Wednesday and Saturday.

Entertainment

The beautifully restored *Jókai Theatre* (☎ *441 527, Andrássy út 1*) built in 1875 and the *Great Church* are the main cultural venues in Békéscsaba. Ask the staff at Békéstourist or the *County Cultural Centre (☎ 442 122, Luther utca 16)* for dates and times. Check the listings in *Békés Est*, a weekly entertainment guide distributed for free.

The *Holsten Pub (Irány utca 10)* next door to the vintage Phaedra movie house is a popular place for pool and pints till midnight daily. But the best place out is the *Club Narancs (Szent István tér 1)*, a meeting place for students in a cellar with vaulted ceilings, cold beer and live or canned music opposite the Fiume hotel. It's

open to 11 pm Monday to Wednesday and becomes the *Rock Est Club* (open to 4 am) from Thursday to Saturday.

Getting There & Away

For points north like Debrecen, take one of a dozen daily buses. Buses leave for Gyula and Békés every half-hour and for Szarvas once an hour. Some 10 buses a day go to Szeged and two to Budapest. Other destinations and their daily departure frequencies include Baja (two), Berettyóújfalu (12), Eger (two), Hajdúszoboszló (one), Hódmezővásárhely (10), Karcag (one), Kecskemét (seven), Miskolc (one), Pécs (one), Szeghalom (12), Szolnok (one) and Vésztő (five to eight – direct, via Gyula or via Mezőberény).

A dozen daily trains – most of them expresses – link Békéscsaba with Szolnok and Budapest-Keleti. Trains are frequent (up to 16 a day) to Gyula, and about half of them continue on to Vésztő. Up to 11 trains a day depart Békéscsaba for Szeged. As many as five international trains leave Békéscsaba daily for Bucharest via Arad and Braşov.

Getting Around

From the bus and train stations you can reach Szent István tér via Andrássy út in about 20 minutes or wait for bus No 5 to Szabadság tér. Bus Nos 9 and 19 pass through the same square on their way past the stadium, Grain Museum, Troféa pension and Parkerdő.

You can order a taxi on ☎ 444 222 or ☎ 444 555.

VÉSZTŐ

☎ 66 • postcode 5530 • pop 7800

The **Vésztő-Mágor National Historical Monument** (Vésztő-Mágor Történelmi Emlékhely), 4km north-west of Vésztő, contains two burial mounds of a type found throughout Hungary and as far east as Korea. Such mounds are not all that rare on the Great Plain, but these are particularly rich in archaeological finds. The first is a veritable layer cake of cult and everyday objects, shrines and graves dating from the 4th century BC onward. The second contains the 10th-century **Csolt monastery** and church. The site is open from 9 am to 6 pm daily from May to September, from 10 am to 4 pm in April and October (100/50Ft). It is in the centre of the patchwork 46,000-hectare **Körös-Maros National Park**, which is very rich in aquatic vegetation and wildlife. For information contact the park directorate (☎ 313 855, fax 611 658) at PO Box 72, Anna-liget, H-5541 Szarvas.

Vésztő is 36km north of Gyula (served by up to a dozen buses a day) and roughly the same distance north-east of Békéscsaba, from where between five to eight buses depart for Vésztő. From the village you can walk for 4km to the site or catch one of five daily buses bound for Szeghalom, which will drop you off just outside. Seven trains a day leave Békéscsaba for Vésztő, but be warned that they follow a circuitous route by way of Gyula and take 1½ hours to cover just 64km.

SZARVAS
☎ 66 • postcode 5540 • pop 19,000
Szarvas is a pretty, very green town 45km north-west of Békéscsaba on a backwater of the Körös River (Holt-Körös). Szarvas was a market town that also suffered decimation

under the Turks; Slovaks came here in large numbers late in the 18th century. But the best thing that ever happened to Szarvas was the arrival of Sámuel Tessedik, a Lutheran minister and pioneering scientist who established one of Europe's first agricultural institutes here in 1770.

Szarvas' big draws are water sports on the Holt-Körös, and the town's arboretum, easily the best in Hungary.

Orientation & Information
Szabadság út, the main street, bisects the town and leads westward to the Holt-Körös and the arboretum. On either side of Szabadság út are dozens of small squares organised in chessboard-like fashion by Tessedik that are full of flower gardens and even small orchards.

The train station is in the eastern part of town at the end of Vasút utca, while the bus station is in the centre on Szabadság út at the corner with Bocskai István utca.

Tourinform (☎/fax 311 140, @ szarvas@tourinform.hu) has an office in the cultural centre at Kossuth tér 3 and is open from 8 am to 5 pm weekdays and, from June to August, from 10 am to 3 pm at the weekend.

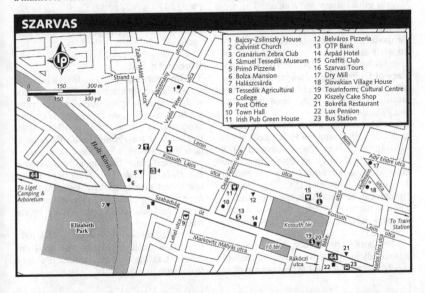

SZARVAS

1 Bajcsy-Zsilinszky House	12 Belváros Pizzeria
2 Calvinist Church	13 OTP Bank
3 Granárium Zebra Club	14 Árpád Hotel
4 Sámuel Tessedik Museum	15 Graffiti Club
5 Primó Pizzeria	16 Szarvas Tours
6 Bolza Mansion	17 Dry Mill
7 Halászcsárda	18 Slovakian Village House
8 Tessedik Agricultural	19 Tourinform; Cultural Centre
College	20 Kiszely Cake Shop
9 Post Office	21 Bokréta Restaurant
10 Town Hall	22 Lux Pension
11 Irish Pub Green House	23 Bus Station

Szarvas Tours (☎/fax 313 627), a commercial travel agency at Kossuth Lajos utca 60, is open from 8 am till noon and 1 to 5 pm weekdays only.

OTP has a bank branch west of the Árpád hotel on Szabadság út while the main post office is on the other side of the street at Szabadság út 9.

Things to See & Do

The **Szarvas Arboretum**, with some 30,000 individual plants not native to the Great Plain, is Hungary's finest. On 85 hectares it contains some 1100 species of rare trees, bushes and grasses, including mammoth pine, ginkgo, swamp cedar, Spanish pine and pampas grass. Boats can be rented at the river pier in the arboretum (in season). The arboretum, some 2km north-west of the centre across the Holt-Körös, is open from 8 am to 6 or 7 pm from mid-March to October and to 3 pm the rest of the year (180/130Ft).

The **Sámuel Tessedik Museum** at Vajda Péter utca 1 has some interesting Neolithic exhibits from the goddess-worshipping Körös culture taken from burial mounds on the Great Plain, and much on Slovakian and Magyar ethnic dress and folk art. The section devoted to Tessedik and his work in making Szarvas bloom is interesting but unfortunately only in Hungarian. It's open from 10 am till noon and 12.30 to 4 pm Tuesday to Sunday (150/50Ft). The **birthplace of Endre Bajcsy-Zsilinszky**, the resistance leader murdered by Hungarian fascists in 1944, is on the same street four blocks to the north.

The neoclassical **Bolza Mansion** (Bolzakastély; 1810) facing the Holt-Körös at Szabadság út 2 was the homestead of a land-owning family of that name who founded the arboretum. Today it is part of the Tessedik Agricultural College but the grounds can be visited. On the steps leading down to the river stands a statue of Romulus and Remus, revealing the Bolza's Roman origins.

The horse-driven **dry mill** (szárazmalom), dating from the early 19th century at Ady Endre utca 1, is the best preserved in

Hungary. It was still operating until the 1920s and is 100% original. Ask the guide to explain how the two horses actually got into the mill to work and how the miller was paid his tithe of anything ground here. The mill is open from 1 to 5 pm Tuesday to Sunday from April to October.

The **Slovakian Village House** (Szlovák tájház) nearby at Hoffmann utca 1 has three rooms filled with hand-woven textiles and articles from everyday life. It's open from 1 to 4 pm on Saturday and 10 am till noon on Sunday from May to September only (100/50Ft).

Places to Stay

Liget Camping (☎/fax 311 954), which also has an 11-room pension, is across the river just beyond Erzsébet-liget (Elizabeth Park) on route No 44. The *Tessedik Agricultural College* (☎ 313 311, Szabadság út 1-3) has dormitory rooms available in summer. Szarvas Tours can organise *private rooms*

A stone's throw from the bus station, the *Lux* pension (☎ 313 417, fax 312 754, Szabadság út 35) charges 4000Ft for doubles with bath. The old world *Árpád* hotel (☎ 312 120, fax 311 564, Szabadság út 32), with 20 rooms in a partly renovated 19th-century mansion, charges 5000/7000Ft for singles/doubles.

Places to Eat

The *Bokréta* (Szabadság út 38) is a basic little restaurant convenient to the bus station with Hungarian specialities. For pizza, try the *Belváros* (Kossuth Lajos utca 21), which is open to 11 pm weekdays and 1 am at the weekend, or the *Primó* (Vajda Péter utca) near the museum, which has a salad bar.

The best place for a meal in Szarvas is the *Halászcsárda* fish restaurant in the north-east corner of Elizabeth Park just over the bridge west of town. It's open till 11 pm and has tables on a terrace by the river.

The *Kiszely* (cnr of Szabadság út & Béke utca) is a great cukrászda next to Tourinform and the cultural centre. It's open from 9 am to 9 pm daily.

Entertainment

The *Péter Vajda Cultural Centre* (☎ *311 181, Kossuth tér 3*) should have updates on what might be on in Szarvas. Szarvas has a couple of excellent music clubs with live acts most weekends: the *Graffiti Club* (*Kossuth Lajos utca 50*) and the *Granárium Zebra Club* (*Kossuth Lajos utca 2*) in a splendid old townhouse. The *Irish Pub Green House* (*Kossuth Lajos utca 25*) is a sprawling place open till late daily.

Getting There & Away

Szarvas can be reached by bus from Békéscsaba (at least hourly), Debrecen (two a day), Gyula (three), Kecskemét (10 to 12), Miskolc (two), Orosháza (six), Szentes (six), Szolnok (one) and Tiszafüred (two).

Szarvas is on the train line linking Mezőhegyes and Orosháza with Mezőtúr and has services seven times a day. From Békéscsaba, it's faster to take an express train to Mezőtúr and change for Szarvas there.

GYULA

☎ 66 • postcode 5700 • pop 34,300

A town of spas with the last remaining medieval brick castle on the Great Plain, Gyula is a wonderful place to recharge your batteries before crossing the border into Romania just 4km to the east.

A fortress was built at Gyula (the name comes from the title given to tribal military commanders among the ancient Magyars) in the 14th century, but it was seized by the Turks and held until 1695. Like Békéscsaba, Gyula came into the hands of the Harruckern family after the aborted Rákóczi independence war of 1703-11. They settled Germans and other groups in different sections of Gyula, and the names have been retained to this day: Big and Little Romanian Town (Nagy Románváros, Kis Románváros), German Town (Németváros) and Hungarian Town (Magyarváros).

Gyula refused to allow the Arad-bound railway to cross through the town in 1858 – a development welcomed by Békéscsaba, 20km to the west. As a result, Gyula was stuck at the end of a spur and developed at a much slower pace. In 1950 the county

seat was moved from here (after 500 years, Gyulans like to point out) to its sister city. Gyula is still seething and a strong rivalry persists between the two: from who should be allocated more county money to whose football team and sausage is better (for the latter, my vote goes to the leaner, spicier Gyulai).

But for better or worse, Gyula's spas, summer theatre in the castle and proximity to Romania attract far more visitors than Békéscsaba's scant offerings. And if we're counting local boys who made good, Gyula wins hands down. The composer Ferenc Erkel and the artists Mihály Munkácsy and György Kohán were all born here, and Gyula is the ancestral town of the 16th-century German painter Albrecht Dürer.

Orientation

Gyula is actually two towns: the commercial centre on Városház utca to the west and the Várfürdő (Castle Bath) in a large park to the east. The areas are within easy walking distance of each other. The Élővíz Canal runs east-west through the centre of Gyula, from a branch of the Körös River to Békéscsaba and beyond.

Gyula's bus station is south of Kossuth Lajos tér on Vásárhelyi Pál utca. Walk north through the park to the square and over the canal bridge to reach the town centre. The train station is at the northern end of Béke sugárút.

Information

Your best source of information is Tourinform in a gallery (☎/fax 463 421, 📧 bekesm@tourinform.hu) at Kossuth Lajos utca 7. It is open from 9 am to 7 pm weekdays and to 1 pm at the weekend from June to August, and from 9 am to 5 pm weekdays only the rest of the year. Gyulatourist (☎ 463 026), Eszperantó tér 1, is open from 8 am to 5 pm weekdays and from 9 am till noon on Saturday. Ibusz (☎/fax 463 084), which keeps the same hours, is at Harruckern tér 10, south of the Inner City Church.

There's an OTP bank branch at Hét vezér utca 2-6, west of Városház utca. The main post office is at Petőfi tér 1.

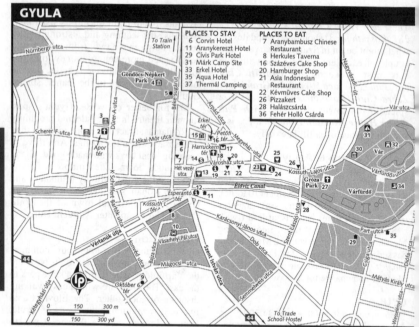

GYULA

PLACES TO STAY
6 Corvin Hotel
11 Aranykereszt Hotel
29 Cívis Park Hotel
31 Márk Camp Site
33 Erkel Hotel
35 Aqua Hotel
37 Thermál Camping

PLACES TO EAT
7 Aranybambusz Chinese
   Restaurant
8 Herkules Taverna
16 Százéves Cake Shop
20 Hamburger Shop
21 Asia Indonesian
   Restaurant
22 Kévműves Cake Shop
26 Pizzakert
28 Halászcsárda
36 Fehér Holló Csárda

Things to See

Gothic **Gyula Castle**, overlooking a picturesque moat near the baths, was originally built in the mid-15th century but has been expanded and renovated many times over the centuries, most recently late in the 1950s. In the vaulted former chapel is a small **museum** tracing the history of the castle and city; it's usually open 9 am to 5 or 6 pm Tuesday to Sunday but may still be 'resting'. The squat 16th-century **Rondella** tower houses a cafe and wine bar with a delightful terrace in summer.

The **György Kohán Museum**, in Göndöcs-Népkert, a park at Béke sugárút 35, is Gyula's most important art museum with more than 3000 paintings and graphics bequeathed to the city by the artist upon his death in 1966. The large canvases of horses and women in dark blues and greens and the relentless summer sun of the Great Plain are quite striking and well worth a look. It's open 9 am to 5 pm Tuesday to Sunday (100/50Ft)

The baroque **Inner City Church** (Belvárosi templom; 1777) on Harruckern tér has some interesting contemporary ceiling frescoes highlighting events in Hungarian and world history – including an astronaut in space! The Zopf **Romanian Orthodox church** (1812) to the east in Gróza Park has a beautiful iconostasis (you can get the key from the house just south of the church entrance), but for contemporary icons at their kitschy best, no place can compare with the **Mary Museum** at Apor tér 11, open from 9 am to noon and 12.30 to 3 pm Monday to Saturday and Sunday afternoon from March to November, and from 9 am till noon Tuesday to Sunday the rest of the year. You've never seen the Virgin in so many guises. On the same square at No 7 stands the **birthplace of Ferenc Erkel**, who composed operas and the music for the Hungarian national anthem.

The **Ferenc Erkel Museum** at Kossuth Lajos utca 17 has a **Dürer Room** devoted to the Ajtóssy family (whose name is derived

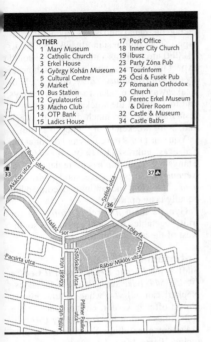

OTHER
1 Mary Museum
2 Catholic Church
3 Erkel House
4 György Kohán Museum
5 Cultural Centre
9 Market
10 Bus Station
12 Gyulatourist
13 Macho Club
14 OTP Bank
15 Ladics House

17 Post Office
18 Inner City Church
19 Ibusz
23 Party Zóna Pub
24 Tourinform
25 Ócsi & Fusek Pub
27 Romanian Orthodox
   Church
30 Ferenc Erkel Museum
   & Dürer Room
32 Castle & Museum
34 Castle Baths

Activities

The Castle Baths (Várfürdő) are in the 30-hectare castle Garden (Várkert) east of the city centre and count a total of 20 pools. The nine pools inside the spa are open all year from 8 am to 7 pm; the 11 outdoor ones can be used from 8 am to 8 pm May to September. Entrance costs 500/300Ft or 250Ft after 2 pm.

Special Events

The biggest event of the year is the Gyula Theatre Festival (Gyulai Várszínház Fesztivál), with performances in the castle courtyard from July to mid-August. There's an All-Hungarian Folkdance Festival (Minden Magyarok Néptáncfesztivája) in mid-August.

Places to Stay

Camping Of Gyula's three camp sites, *Márk* (☎ 463 380, Vár utca 5) is the friendliest and most central, but it's tiny and only for caravans and tents; there are no bungalows. The charge is 2000Ft to 2200Ft per site and it's open year round. *Thermál Camping* (☎ 463 704, Szélső utca 16) has a huge camping ground that is also open year round.

from the Hungarian word for 'door'). They emigrated from Gyula to Germany in the 15th century and changed their name to Dürer (from the German word for 'door', *Tür*).

An interesting – and, for Hungary, very unusual – museum is **Ladics House**, Jókai Mór utca 4, the perfectly preserved and beautifully furnished mid-19th century residence of a prosperous bourgeois family. Guided tours (in Hungarian only) start every half-hour or so and offer an excellent look into what life was like in a Hungarian market town. Ladics House is open from 9 am to 5 pm Tuesday to Sunday (100/50Ft).

Next door, the **Százéves** cake shop and museum facing Erkel tér is both a visual and culinary delight. Established in about 1840 (no doubt Mrs Ladics bought her *petits-fours* here), the Regency-blue interior is filled with Biedermeier furniture and mirrors in gilt frames. It is one of the most beautiful cukrászdák in Hungary, and is open daily from 10 am to 10 pm.

Private Rooms & Hostels Gyulatourist and Ibusz can book you a private room from 1500Ft to 2000Ft per person or an entire apartment with kitchen and living room from 5500Ft. you'll see lots of signs advertising rooms along Szent László utca and, east of the spa, Tiborc utca and Diófa utca. The *girl's trade school* (☎ 463 822, Szent István utca 69) turns into a 102-bed hostel from mid-June to August with dormitory accommodation for under 1000Ft.

Hotels The most charming hotel in Gyula is the *Aranykereszt* (☎/fax 463 197, Eszperantó tér 2) alongside the canal. Its 20 rooms all have telephones, TVs and minibars, and there's a popular restaurant and a bar with two tenpin bowling lanes. Singles are 3000Ft to 4000Ft and doubles 3500Ft to 4500Ft, depending on the season. More central but less interesting is the 22-room *Corvin* hotel (☎ 362 044, fax 362 158, Jókai utca 9-11) with doubles from 4500Ft to 6500Ft.

GREAT PLAIN

There are plenty of hotels in or around the Várfürdő, most of them sprawling, modern affairs with the requisite outlets and satellite TVs. Room rates vary widely depending on the season, but generally the most expensive times are from June to September and over the Christmas and New Year holidays.

The cheapest is the 60-room *Aqua* (☎/fax 463 146, Part utca 7c), a former trade union holiday house on a quiet bank of the canal with singles/doubles without facilities for 1000/2000Ft and ones with bath for 1800/3400Ft. A short distance to the east, the 56-room *Cívis Park* (☎ 463 711, fax 463 124, ✉ civisrt@mail.datanet.hu, Part utca 15) has doubles for 6600Ft, a small swimming pool, solarium and sauna. The 61-room *Agro* (☎ 463 522, fax 463 478, Part utca 5), which has lovely gardens at the back, charges 6900Ft for its doubles.

The closest hotel to the spa – in fact, it is connected by a corridor – is the sprawling *Erkel* (☎/fax 463 555, Várkert 1), with almost 400 rooms. Depending on the season and whether you're in the old or new wing, singles/doubles start at 3000/4800Ft or 6600/10,100Ft between late May and August.

Places to Eat

The *Pizzakert* (Kossuth Lajos utca 16) is a popular pizzeria and pasta restaurant in a back courtyard in the centre of Gyula. The *Hamburger Shop* (Városház utca), a take-away place with burgers and salads, is open to 11 pm weekdays and 1 am at the weekend.

If you're staying near the castle and baths, the *Fehér Holló* (Tiborc utca 49) is a good choice for csárda-style Hungarian meals. It is open daily till midnight. The *Halászcsárda* (cnr of Part utca & Szent László utca) next to the Agro hotel and facing the canal offers the usual fishy dishes in pleasant surroundings. The colourful *Herkules Taverna* (Kossuth tér 3) near the bus station serves Greek specialities till midnight daily.

Gyula maintains its hold on a restaurant superlative: it has the only Indonesian eatery in all of Hungary (including Budapest). If you crave a fix of gado-gado, lumpia and satay, head straight for the *Asia* (Városház utca 15), which has outside seating in a garden courtyard (in summer) facing the canal and stays open till midnight. The Indonesian dishes (850Ft to 1100Ft) are, well, as authentic as you could expect in south-east Hungary. For Chinese, try the *Aranybambusz* (Béke sugár út), both a takeaway place open to 9 pm weekdays and to 11 pm at the weekend and a proper restaurant open for lunch during the week and, at the weekend, for dinner to 11 pm.

You can't miss the cakes and decor at the *Százéves* cukrászda (Erkel tér 1); the Things to See section has more details. The *Kévműves* (Artisan) cake shop (Városház utca 21) is a less enchantingly decorated but equally tasty option.

Gyula's main *market* (Október 6) for fruit, vegetables and other produce is south-west of the bus station.

Entertainment

Staff at the *Ferenc Erkel Cultural Centre* (☎ 463 544, Béke sugárút 35) in Göndöcs-Népkert can tell you what cultural events are on offer in Gyula. Organ concerts are sometimes held at the *Inner City Church*.

Decent pubs along Kossuth Lajos utca include *Party Zóna* at No 3 and the *Őcsi & Fusek*, with a great back courtyard, at No 6. The unfortunately named *Macho* (Városház utca 1) is a very popular club open daily to 4 am (6 am on Friday and Saturday).

Getting There & Away

With Gyula lying on an unimportant rail spur, buses are the preferred mode of transport. There are dozens each day departing for Békéscsaba and up to a half-dozen go to Debrecen. Other destinations include Budapest (one a day), Eger (one), Kecskemét (three), Miskolc (one), Szeged (five), Szeghalom via Vésztő (five or six) and Vésztő direct (six).

Some 15 trains a day run west on line 128, Gyula's link to the Békéscsaba-Szolnok-Budapest rail line. Travelling north on this poky line will get you to Vésztő, Szeghalom and eventually to Püspökladány, where you can change trains for Debrecen. The only international train from Gyula leaves for the Romanian town of Salonta three times per day.

Northern Uplands

The Northern Uplands (Északi Felföld) make up Hungary's mountainous region – foothills of the mighty Carpathians that roll eastward from the Danube Bend almost as far as Ukraine, some 300km away. By anyone's standards, these mountains don't amount to much: the highest peak – Kékes in the Mátra Range – 'soars' to just over 1000m. But in a country as flat as Hungary, these hills are important for environmental and recreational reasons.

The Northern Uplands include five or six ranges of hills – depending on how you count. From west to east they are: the Börzsöny, home to many of Hungary's Slovak ethnic community and best reached from Vác (see the Danube Bend chapter); the Cserhát; the Mátra; the Bükk; the Aggtelek (an adjunct of the eastern Cserhát region); and the Zemplén.

Generally, these hilly regions are forested, though a large part of the lower hills are under cultivation (mostly grapes). Castles and ruins abound, and the last vestiges of traditional folk life can be found here, especially among the Palóc people of the Cserhát Hills and the Mátyó of Mezőkövesd just south of the Bükk. The ranges are peppered with resorts and camping grounds, and it is a region famed for its wine. Two of Hungary's best-known tipples – sweet amber Tokaj and ruby-red Bikavér (Bull's Blood) from Eger – are produced here.

But the Northern Uplands are not always so idyllic. Here too are industrial Miskolc, once a socialist 'iron city that works' and now the centre of the country's widest rust belt, the polluted Sajó Valley and the depressed towns of Nógrád County.

Cserhát Hills

The Cserhát Hills are a rather unimpressive entry to the Northern Uplands. None of them reaches higher than 650m, and much

HIGHLIGHTS

- The rich collection of folk art at the Palóc Museum in Balassagyarmat
- The unusual Buddhist stupa in Sándor Kőrösi Csoma Memorial Park at Tar
- Just about everything in Eger: its castle, architecture and wine
- Hollókő's restored castle and living folk traditions
- Riding the narrow-gauge railway from Miskolc through the Bükk Hills to Lillafüred
- Wine tasting in Tokaj

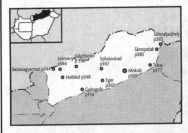

of the area is cultivated and densely populated, obviating any serious hiking. But people don't visit the Cserhát for the hills; instead they come for folk culture, particularly that of the Palóc people (see the boxed text 'The Good Palóc People').

BALASSAGYARMAT
☎ 35 • postcode 2660 • pop 18,100
As the centre of the Cserhát region, Balassagyarmat bills itself as the 'capital of the Palóc' and, while other places may look more folksy, the town's excellent Palóc Museum gives it the leading edge. Lying just south of the Ipoly River and the Slovakian border, Balassagyarmat suffered more than most towns in the region during the Turkish occupation. Its castle was reduced

NORTHERN UPLANDS

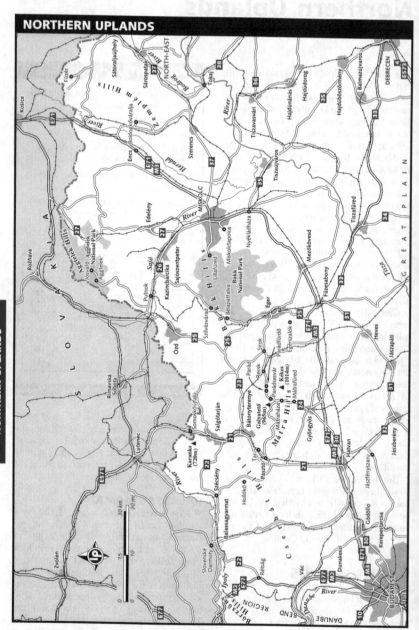

NORTHERN UPLANDS

to rubble and its houses were abandoned for decades. It regained stature late in the 18th century as the main seat of Nógrád County, but even that honour was taken away after WWII in favour of the 'new town' of Salgótarján. Today Balassagyarmat's few baroque and neoclassical buildings and the odd monument don't pull in the crowds. It's the town's link with Palóc culture that beckons.

Orientation & Information

The train station is some 650m south of the town centre at the end of Bajcsy-Zsilinszky utca. The bus station is behind the town hall on Köztársaság tér, which splits Rákóczi fejedelem útja, the main drag, in two.

You can try Ibusz (☎ 301 949) at Rákóczi fejedelem útja 61 for information but, while it can book you a private room, it is really geared up more for Hungarians travelling abroad. The office is open weekdays from 8 am to 4 pm and Saturday till noon. The staff at the City Gallery (Városi Képtár; ☎ 300 186) at Köztársaság tér 5 opposite the former county hall are helpful. It is open from 10 am till noon and 1 to 5 pm Tuesday to Sunday.

OTP bank has a branch at Rákóczi fejedelem útja 44 and there's a Budapest Bank branch at No 31. The post office can be found at Rákóczi fejedelem útja 24.

Palóc Museum

The Palóc Museum, in Palóc Park just west of Bajcsy-Zsilinszky utca, was purpose-built in 1914 to house Hungary's richest collection of Palóc artefacts and is a must for anyone planning to visit traditional villages in the Cserhát Hills.

The standing exhibit 'From Cradle to Grave' on the 1st floor takes you through the important stages in the life of the Palóc people and includes pottery, superb carvings, mock-ups of a birth scene, a classroom and a wedding. There are also votive objects used for the all-important *búcsú*, or church patronal festivals (see boxed text 'Farewell to All That' under Máriagyűd in the Southern Transdanubia chapter). But the Palóc women's agility with the needle – from the

distinctive floral embroidery in blues and reds to the almost microscopic white-on-white stitching – leaves everything else in the dust.

An open-air museum (open May to September), including an 18th-century **Palóc house** and stable, stands in the garden behind the main museum. The museum is open from 10 am to 4 pm Tuesday to Sunday from May to September and the same time Tuesday to Saturday the rest of the year (160/80Ft).

Other Attractions

The **City Gallery** at Köztársaság tér 5 is devoted to contemporary Nógrád painters, sculptors and graphic artists and is worth a look around. The **Local History Collection**, in an 18th-century noble's house at Rákóczi fejedelem útja 107, honours more locals, including the artist Endre Horváth, who lived in the house and designed some of the forint notes still in circulation. It's open 8 am to noon and 1 to 5 pm Tuesday to Sunday.

The imposing, neoclassical **old county hall** (1834) at Köztársaság tér 6 and, two blocks further north-east, the 18th-century

---

The Good Palóc People

The Palóc are a distinct Hungarian group living in the fertile hills and valleys of the Cserhát range of hills. Ethnologists are still debating whether they were a separate people who later mixed with the Magyars (their name means Cuman in several Slavic languages, suggesting they came from western Siberia) or just a Hungarian ethnic group which, through isolation and Slovakian influence, developed their own ways. What's certain is that the Palóc continue to speak a distinct dialect of Hungarian (unusual in a country where language differences are virtually nonexistent) and, until recently, were able to cling to their traditional folk dress, particularly in such towns as Hollókő, Buják, Rimóc and Őrhalom. Today they are considered the guardians of living folk traditions in Hungary.

BALASSAGYARMAT

SLOVAKIA

1 Local History Collection
2 Cultural Centre
3 Caffè Orchidea
4 Market
5 Ibusz
6 OTP Bank
7 Former Serbian Orthodox Church & Art Gallery
8 Balassa Restaurant
9 Post Office
10 Catholic Church
11 Bus Station
12 Budapest Bank
13 Town Hall
14 Old County Hall
15 City Gallery
16 Club Pension & Pub
17 Palóc Museum
18 Orchidea Cake Shop
19 Szalézi College

Catholic church with its rococo altar, are worth a look. The tiny **Serbian Orthodox church** on Szerb utca (enter via Rákóczi fejedelem útja 30) now contains a gallery of paintings by local artist Olga Bajusová and is open 2 to 6 pm from Tuesday to Sunday (free).

Places to Stay & Eat

There's a small *camping ground* (☎ 300 404, Kővári út 13) on the main road leading west out of town. The *Szalézi College* (☎ 301 765, Ady Endre utca 1/a) has 180 dormitory beds available from mid-June to late August and maybe at weekends, but the only year-round option in Balassagyarmat proper is the 15-room *Club* pension (☎/fax 301 824, Teleki László utca 14) with doubles for 6700Ft. The *Sztár Motel* (☎/fax 301 152, Kővári út 12) is near the camp site to the west of town.

For food, there are plenty of stand-up places and *food stalls* at the market on

Thököly utca. The *Balassa* is a cheap (set menus from 350Ft) sit-down restaurant at Rákóczi fejedelem útja 32-36, and the *pub* at the Club pension serves food as well as suds, with main courses from 640Ft to 1300Ft. For drinks and light meals, try the *Caffè Orchidea (Rákóczi fejedelem útja 48)*. Opposite Palóc Park, the *Orchidea Cukrászda (Bajcsy-Zsilinszky utca 12)* has excellent ice cream and cakes.

Entertainment

See the people at the modern *Imre Madách Cultural Centre* (☎ 300 622, Rákóczi fejedelem útja 50) for what's on in Balassagyarmat.

Getting There & Away

At least 12 buses a day link Budapest's Népstadion station with Balassagyarmat via Vác and Rétság. There are two buses a day to Hatvan, one each to Gyöngyös and Pászto, and plenty to Salgótarján via Litke or Endrefalva. Some five buses a day go to Szécsény, the place to change for Hollókő. There's a weekday bus at 6.20 pm to Lučenec in Slovakia.

Balassagyarmat can be reached throughout the day via a snaking train line from Vác. The trip takes almost two hours to cover 70km; the bus will cut that time in half. If coming from Budapest or the east by train, change at Aszód.

There's an international border crossing into Slovakia a short distance north of Balassagyarmat at Slovenské Darmoty.

SZÉCSÉNY
☎ 32 • postcode 3170 • pop 6600

Some 18km east of Balassagyarmat in the picturesque Ipoly Valley bordering Slovakia, Szécsény is usually given a miss by travellers headed for its tiny but much better known neighbour to the south, Hollókő. But while Hollókő's draw is folklore, Szécsény's is history. In 1705, in a camp behind where Forgách Manor now stands, the ruling Diet made Ferenc Rákóczi II of Transylvania the prince of Hungary and the commander in chief of the *kuruc* forces fighting for independence from the Austrians.

Orientation & Information
The train station is 1.5km north of the town centre on the road to Litke. Buses stop along Király utca east of the firewatch tower on Fő tér.

Tourinform (☎ 370 777, fax 370 170, ✉ szecseny@tourinform.hu), Rákóczi út 90/b, is open 8 am to 4 pm on weekdays only from September to May and from 9 am to 5 pm weekdays and 10 am to 6 pm on Saturday from June to August. You'll find an OTP bank branch near the town hall at Rákóczi út 86. The post office is at Dugonics utca 1, which leads south from Fő tér.

Forgách Manor
Forgách Manor, an imposing manor house at the end of Ady Endre utca, was built around 1760 from the remains of a medieval border fortress. In the mid-19th century it passed into the hands of the aristocratic Forgách family, who made further additions, and

today it houses a motley assortment of exhibits as the Ferenc Kubinyi Museum.

On the ground floor there's a small pharmaceutical exhibit as well as a few rooms done up much the way the Forgách family would have liked to see them. Upstairs, beyond the Stone Age bones and chips, the reconstructed Neolithic house and the Bronze Age jewellery, is a ghastly hunting exhibit with any number of 'useful' items (napkin rings, cups, pistol butts, umbrella handles) carved and whittled from the carcasses of our furred and feathered friends.

Only a little less frightening is the Bastion Museum (Bástya Múzeum) located in the north-east tower, from where part of the original 16th-century castle wall can be seen to the west and south. The exhibits include an all-too-complete collection of torture implements: racks, yokes, stocks and a flogging bench.

Those of a nervous disposition will seek refuge in the Sándor Kőrösi Csoma Memorial House in the manor's gate house. Kőrösi Csoma (1784-1842) was a Hungarian Franciscan monk who travelled to Tibet and wrote the first Tibetan-English dictionary. The Dalai Lama paid homage to him by visiting Hungary on the 150th anniversary of his death in 1992 and dedicating a Buddhist stupa and memorial park in his memory at Tar, south of Salgótarján (see that section later in this chapter). The Ferenc Kubinyi Museum is open 10 am to 4 pm Wednesday to Sunday from May to September and the same hours Tuesday to Saturday the rest of the year (160/80Ft).

Franciscan Church & Monastery
Parts of the Gothic church at Haynald Lajos utca 7-9 date from the 14th century and the monastery (kolostor) has now been returned to the church and restored to its former glory after years of neglect. In the sanctuary (the oldest section), a guide will point out the 500-year-old carvings of saints, flowers and fruits in the vaulted ceiling (the carvings on the pillars were destroyed by the Turks when they occupied Szécsény in 1552) You can also see where Muslims carved out a *mihrab*, or prayer niche, in the

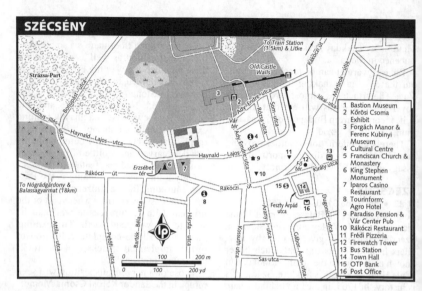

SZÉCSÉNY

1 Bastion Museum
2 Kőrösi Csoma Exhibit
3 Forgách Manor & Ferenc Kubinyi Museum
4 Cultural Centre
5 Franciscan Church & Monastery
6 King Stephen Monument
7 Iparos Casino Restaurant
8 Tourinform; Agro Hotel
9 Paradiso Pension & Vár Center Pub
10 Rákóczi Restaurant
11 Frédi Pizzeria
12 Firewatch Tower
13 Bus Station
14 Town Hall
15 OTP Bank
16 Post Office

south wall. In the nave, the baroque main and side altars are actually wood, though they're disguised as marble, and the richly carved pulpit is from the 18th century.

In the baroque monastery (dating from the 17th century, though with parts of the 14th-century church incorporated into it), you'll see the monks' cells and, depending on what's open, the library, dining hall, Gothic oratory overlooking the church's interior, and/or the Rákóczi Room, where the newly appointed prince and military commander met with his war cabinet in 1705. Tours of the church and monastery depart at 10 and 11 am and 2, 3 and 4 pm Tuesday to Saturday and at 3 and 4 pm on Sunday (50/25Ft).

Other Attractions

You may think you're seeing things but, yes, the early 18th-century **firewatch tower** (tűztorony) dominating Fő tér is leaning (by 3°), a result of shelling and bombing in 1944. There are plans to open an exhibition on local history here.

A **monument to King Stephen** in Erzsébet tér near the Franciscan church bears a strange and plaintive inscription: 'Where are

you King Stephen? The Hungarian people yearn for you.' It grabs your heart somehow.

The Keresztvölgy-Puszta Horse Farm (☎ 370 081, Ifjúság út 2) in Őrhalom, 7.5km west of Szécsny on route No 22, offers cross-country riding and excursions.

Places to Stay & Eat

The hostel-like **Agro** hotel (☎ 370 382, fax 370 936, Rákóczi út 90/b), in the same building as Tourinform, has doubles/quads in 10 rooms where a bed costs 1500/1300Ft per person. The only other option in town is the **Paradiso** (☎/fax 370 427, Ady Endre utca 14), a comfortable 17-room pension in the former servants' quarters of Forgách Manor. Singles/doubles with shower are 4000/6500Ft.

The **Rákóczi** restaurant (Rákóczi út 95), south of the castle, serves up the usual sludge till 10 pm (1 am at the weekend); the **Iparos Casino** (Erzsébet tér 3) is a similar place with better and even cheaper food (mains: 675Ft to 985Ft) open to 10 pm (8 pm on Sunday). For something more upbeat, try the **Frédi** (Rákóczi út 85), a decent pizzeria (340Ft to 600Ft) with a wood-burning oven. The restaurant at the **Paradiso** pension is quite good, serves local specialities and has outside seating in a lovely courtyard with a fountain.

Entertainment

The staff at the *cultural centre* (☎ *370 860, Ady Endre utca 12*) may have information on what's on in Szécsény (notice the curious dragons on either side of the sloping roof). There's a pub called the *Vár Center* in the cellar below the Paradiso pension; the Saturday night disco here draws boppers from throughout the Cserhát region.

Getting There & Away

Some 10 buses depart for Hollókő on weekdays, with between seven and eight leaving at the weekend. You shouldn't have to wait more than a half-hour for buses to Balassagyarmat or Salgótarján (with a possible change for the latter at Litke or Nográdmegyer). There are between seven and nine daily buses to Budapest and three to five to Pászto.

Szécsény is on a minor railway line linking it with Balassagyarmat and Aszód to the west and south-west and Ipolytarnóc to the north on the Slovakian border, where you can board trains for Lučenec. To get to Vác from Szécsény by train, you must change at Balassagyarmat.

HOLLÓKŐ

☎ 32 • postcode 3176 • pop 470

People either love Hollókő or hate it. To some, the two-street village nestling in a valley 16km south-east of Szécsény is Hungary's most beautiful and deserves kudos for holding on to its traditional architecture and some old customs. Others see it as a staged tourist trap run by Budapest entrepreneurs with paid 'performers'. Unesco agreed with the former view in 1987 when it put Hollókő on its World Heritage List of cultural sites – the first village in the world to receive such protection. What sets Hollókő (Raven Rock) apart is its restored 13th-century castle and the architecture of the so-called Old Village (Ófalu), where some 55 houses and outbuildings have been listed as historic monuments.

Most of what you see is, strictly speaking, not original. The village has burned to the ground many times since the 13th century (most recently in 1909), but the villagers have always rebuilt their houses exactly to plan with wattle and daub – interwoven twigs plastered with clay and water.

Women in traditional Palóc dress – wide red-and-blue pleated and embroidered skirts, ornate headpieces – are very thin on the ground these days. Still, on Sunday mornings, important feast days like Easter and Assumption Day (15 August) or during a wedding, you may get lucky and catch some traditional costumes.

Orientation & Information

Don't be disappointed as you ascend the hill into Hollókő: on your right is Újfalu (New Village), dating back to the middle of the 20th century and of no particular interest. The bus stops on Dózsa György utca at the top of Kossuth Lajos utca; from there walk down the hill to the Old Village.

There's an information office called the Foundation for Hollókő (Hollókőért Közalapítvány; ☎ 379 043, fax 379 266) at Kossuth Lajos utca 68 or you might try ID-KER (☎ 379 273), an outfit based in the Pajtakert (Barnyard) shop and gallery at No 46 of the same street. Both are open from 9 am to 3 or 4 pm daily from April to September but on weekdays only the rest of the year. You can change money at the post office at Kossuth Lajos utca 72.

Things to See

The village's wonderful **folk architecture** is its main attraction. Stroll along the two cobblestone streets, past the whitewashed houses with carved wooden gables and porches and red-shingled roofs. Wine is stored in the small cellars that open onto the streets.

The little wooden **village church** is on the corner where Petőfi utca, the Old Village's 'other' street, branches off from Kossuth Lajos utca. Built as a granary in the 16th century and sanctified in 1889, it is a fairly austere affair both inside and out.

Several small museums in traditional houses line Kossuth Lajos utca. The first is the **Postal Museum** at No 80 (open from 10 am to 5 pm daily from April to October;

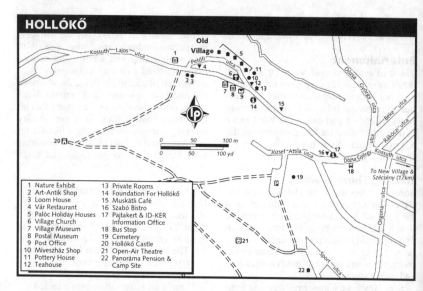

HOLLÓKŐ

1 Nature Exhibit	13 Private Rooms
2 Art-Antik Shop	14 Foundation For Hollókő
3 Loom House	15 Muskátli Café
4 Vár Restaurant	16 Szabó Bistro
5 Palóc Holiday Houses	17 Pajtakert & ID-KER
6 Village Church	Information Office
7 Village Museum	18 Bus Stop
8 Postal Museum	19 Cemetery
9 Post Office	20 Hollókő Castle
10 Míveszház Shop	21 Open-Air Theatre
11 Pottery House	22 Panoráma Pension &
12 Teahouse	Camp Site

50/30Ft). The **Village Museum** (Falu-múzeum) next door at No 82 (open from 10 am to 4 pm Wednesday to Sunday from April to September, from 10 am to 2 pm on Thursday, noon to 2 pm on Friday and 10 am to 4 pm at the weekend the rest of the year; 60/30Ft) is the usual three-room Hungarian setup (kitchen, fancy parlour, workroom) with folk pottery, painted furniture, embroidered pillows and an interestingly carved wine press dated 1872 in the back yard. A standing **nature exhibition** called 'Landscape and the People' (Táj es a Nép) at Kossuth Lajos utca 99 (open from 9 am to 5 pm Tuesday and Thursday to Sunday from April to October, from 10 am to 3 pm on the same days the rest of the year; 120/90Ft) deals with the flora, fauna and human inhabitants of the Eastern Cserhát Landscape Protection Reserve, part of which surrounds the village.

Hollókő Castle The castle on Szárhegy (Stalk Hill) can be reached by following the trail up the hill across from the nature exhibit or from the bus stop by walking up to József Attila utca and then following the west-bound trail from the car park. At

365m, the castle has a commanding view of the surrounding hills. To the south-east is Purga (575m), one of the highest 'peaks' in this part of the Cserhát, and to the north is the Ipoly Valley.

The castle was built at the end of the 13th century and strengthened 200 years later. It was captured by the Turks and not liberated until 1683 by the Polish king John III Sobieski (ruled 1674-96). It was partially destroyed after the War of Independence early in the 18th century but is, in fact, one of northern Hungary's most intact fortresses. A small museum contains cooking implements, ornamental tiles, jewellery and other items unearthed during restoration work, carried out over three decades and completed for the millecentenary celebrations in 1996.

The views from the top of the pentagonal keep are stunning. The castle is open from 10 am to 6 pm daily year round but may shut down in the dead of winter.

Activities

Both the Foundation for Hollókő and ID-KER (see Orientation & Information) can organise touristy folk-craft lessons, such as weaving, woodcarving, pottery and egg painting. There are some gentle walks into the hills and valleys to the west of the castle. *A Cserhát*, the 1:60,000 Cserhát map (No 8; 400Ft) from Cartographia, will help you plan your route, but is not absolutely necessary.

Special Events

Hollókő marks its calendar red for the annual Easter Festival (Húsvéti Fesztivál) in late March or April, the Palóc Folklore Festival (Palóci Folklórfesztivál) held at the open-air stage in August and the Castle Days (Várnapok), a touristy medieval tournament at and around the castle on 20 August.

Places to Stay

There's a *camping ground* at the Panoráma complex (see information later in this section) costing 450/400/100Ft per person/tent or caravan/car. *Private rooms* are available directly at Kossuth Lajos utca 77 (from 1500Ft per person), and the Foundation for Hollókő and ID-KER can arrange accommodation at one of the 10 *Palóc holiday houses* along Petőfi utca (though you should book well ahead in the high season). Prices start at about 3500Ft for a double. House E at Petőfi utca 20, set back from the road in its own garden, is among the quietest and most isolated.

There's a rather obtrusive holiday complex offering a less-than-warm welcome called *Panoráma (π/fax 379 048, Orgona utca 31)* perched on the hill top off Sport utca south of the village. It has a nine-room pension with doubles/quads for 3500/4800Ft and five bungalows in its camping site with four beds (4200Ft).

Places to Eat

One of the few places to eat in Hollókő is the *Vár (Kossuth Lajos utca 95)*, but remember that this is still very much an early-to-bed, early-to-rise farming community: it closes at 8 pm. The *Muskátli (Kossuth Lajos utca 61)*, a coffee shop that serves meals as well, is open to 6 pm from Wednesday to Friday, to 8 pm on Saturday and to 5 pm on Sunday. The little *Teaház (Teahouse; Petőfi utca 4)* in the Múveszház (Art House) beside the

church has a small wine bar in the cellar. The local hang-out for all ages is the *Szabó Kocsma (Kossuth Lajos utca 48)*, a little bistro near the bus stop.

Shopping

Szövőház (Loom House) at Kossuth Lajos utca 94 is a good place for finding handwoven and embroidered goods; it's interesting to watch the women demonstrate how their enormous loom works. Míveszház, Petőfi utca 6, has an excellent selection of Palóc folk dress and costumes while the jewellery at Art-Antik, Kossuth Lajos utca 96, mixes contemporary and traditional designs. Fazekasház (Pottery House) behind the Teaház on Petőfi utca has hand-thrown vases, jugs, candlesticks and decorative items. I love the decorated honey cakes (*mézeskalács*) for sale at the Pajtakert, Kossuth Lajos utca 46.

Getting There & Away

Szécsény is the gateway to Hollókő, with some buses heading there twice an hour Monday to Saturday and 10 leaving on Sunday. You can also catch one of about seven weekday buses (six on Saturday, four on Sunday) to Salgótarján via Pászto.

SALGÓTARJÁN

☎ 32 • postcode 3100 • pop 47,800

After an idyllic day in Hollókő or any of the rural villages of the Cserhát, arriving in this modern city 25km east of Szécsény is like stepping into a cold shower. Ravaged by fire in 1821 and by serious flooding 70 years later, Salgótarján can boast almost no buildings that predate this century. And that's apparent as soon as you step off the train: row after row of concrete blocks and towers wall the city in from the picturesque Medves Hills.

Those hills have been exploited for their coal since the 19th century, and it is on this that Salgótarján's success is based. As in Miskolc, the communists found the coal miners and steelworkers here sympathetic to their cause and were supported both during the Republic of Councils and after the war (though this did not stop the dreaded

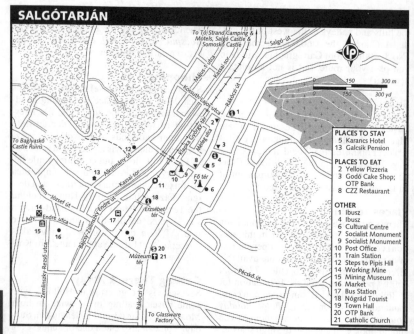

SALGÓTARJÁN

To Tó-Strand, Camping &
Motels, Salgó Castle &
Somoskő Castle

Salgó-út

To Baglyaskő
Castle Ruins

To Bagyaskő

PLACES TO STAY
5 Karancs Hotel
13 Galcsik Pension

PLACES TO EAT
2 Yellow Pizzeria
3 Godó Cake Shop;
  OTP Bank
8 CZZ Restaurant

OTHER
1 Ibusz
4 Ibusz
6 Cultural Centre
7 Socialist Monument
9 Socialist Monument
10 Post Office
11 Train Station
12 Steps to Pipis Hill
14 Working Mine
15 Mining Museum
16 Market
17 Bus Station
18 Nógrád Tourist
19 Town Hall
20 OTP Bank
21 Catholic Church

Fő tér
Erzsébet tér
Múzeum tér

To Glassware
Factory

To Pécskő út

ÁVH secret police from shooting down over 100 people here during the 1956 Uprising). For its support, Salgótarján was made the county seat in 1950 and rebuilt throughout the 1960s.

Except to see Salgó and Somoskő castles, and perhaps to hike in the Karancs Hills to the north-west (see the Around Salgótarján section), few travellers make their way here. Perhaps for that reason and the large, friendly student population – almost a dozen colleges and trade schools are located here – the city is worth a stopover.

Orientation & Information

Because it has virtually swallowed the village of Somoskőújfalu some 10km to the north, Salgótarján feels like a large city. The train and bus stations are a short distance apart to the west of the city centre.

Nógrád Tourist (☎ 316 940) is on the first level of the shopping arcade at Erzsébet tér 5 and open from 8 am to 5 pm on weekdays,

till noon on Saturday. Ibusz (☎ 421 200, fax 421 300), Rákóczi út 10, keeps similar weekday hours but closes at 3 pm on Friday.

There's an OTP bank branch at Rákóczi út 12 next to the Godó cake shop and another below the Catholic church at Rákóczi út 22. The main post office's address is Fő tér 1 but it is closer to the end of Klapka György tér.

Things to See

The **Mining Museum** (Bányászati Múzeum), the city's only real sight, is on Zemlinszky Rezső utca 1, a short walk south-west of the train and bus stations. Filled with geological maps and samples, old uniforms and a statue of St Barbara, the patroness of miners, standing proudly next to old communist banners calling for the nationalisation of the mines, the museum's style is somewhat outdated and is not particularly interesting. But across the street an actual mine continues to be 'worked' by performers in unrealistically clean overalls, and you can wander through the pits. You almost get a feel for life below the surface as the signs wish you *Jó szerencsét!* ('Good luck!'), what miners traditionally say to one another when they enter the pit. The museum is open from 9 am to 3 pm Tuesday to Sunday from April to September, from 10 am to 2 pm on the same days during the rest of the year (160/80Ft).

The production of glassware has been an important industry in Salgótarján since at least the start of the 20th century and – should you be ready for more industrial tourism – you can visit the ST Glassware Factory (ST Öblösüveggyár; ☎ 410 433) at Huta utca 1, about 700m south of the centre along Rákóczi út. It is open from 9 am to 1 pm on weekdays.

A set of steps west of the train station off Alkotmány út lead up to Pipis Hill (Pipishegy; 341m), which offers great views of the city and surrounding hills. To the southwest at Kőváralja lies the rubble of Baglyaskő Castle, built on an extinct volcano in the early 14th century.

Salgótarján is one of the few cities in Hungary which still have socialist-style monuments prominently displayed (Budapest has put its collection in the 'zoo' that is Statue Park) and both are in Fő tér. One to the west of the square depicts a supporter of Béla Kun's 1919 Republic of Councils running with a rifle in hand; the other, to the east in front of the cultural centre, shows a couple of socialist youths looking rather guilty as they set doves free.

Special Events

The big annual event in Salgótarján is the acclaimed International Dixieland Festival, hosted by the home-grown Benkó and Molnár Dixieland bands. The cultural centre (see Entertainment) will have information.

Places to Stay

Tó-Strand Camping (☎ 430 168, Kempingtelep út), about 5km north-east of the centre of town just off the road to Somoskő, charges 250/300/500Ft per person/tent/caravan. There are also two year-round

motels with a total of 19 rooms; a double with one shower shared by two rooms costs 2200Ft. Doubles in a nonheated *motel* and *bungalows* are available from April to September for 1400Ft. There's a boating lake, tennis courts and a pool nearby. You can reach the camping site on bus No 6 from Rákóczi út.

For *private rooms* in one of the city's many high-rises, contact Ibusz; Nógrád Tourist usually deals with longer-term accommodation.

One of the better deals around is at the 32-room *Galcsik* pension (☎ 316 524, Alkotmány út 2) near the bus station. Singles/doubles with shower in this well-maintained pension are 1880/2180Ft while those with bath are 2680/3680Ft.

The *Karancs* hotel (☎ 410 088, fax 414 994, Fő tér 6) has 48 very ordinary rooms as well as a bar, restaurant and nightclub. Singles/doubles are DM59/69.

Places to Eat

The *Yellow* pizzeria (*corner of Rákóczi út & Kossuth Lajos út*) is a decent choice for a cheap (if unexceptional) meal, as is the tiny *CZZ* restaurant (*Fő tér 1*) opposite the Karancs hotel. Mains at the latter, which closes at 9 pm, are 380Ft to 460Ft. For much better food, though, head for the restaurant at the *Galcsik* pension, which stays open to 10.30 or 11 pm daily. The best cake shop in town is the *Godó* (*Rákóczi út 12*) just north of the Karancs hotel.

Entertainment

The *Attila József Cultural Centre* (☎ 310 503, Fő tér 5) is Salgótarján's highbrow cultural venue, but it'll be able to help you with information on more down-to-earth forms of amusement.

Getting There & Away

Buses leave Salgótarján very frequently for Balassagyarmat and Szécsény via Litke or Nógrádmegyer. You can also get to Budapest (half-hourly departures, some via route No M3), Pászto (half-hourly), Eger (12 departures Monday to Saturday, three on Sunday), Miskolc (two departures daily), Hatvan

NORTHERN UPLANDS

(three), Hollókő (five), Gyöngyös (five) and Parádfürdő (two) in the Mátra Hills.

A train line links Salgótarján with Hatvan and the main Budapest-Miskolc trunk to the south and, to the north, Somoskőújfalu and, in Slovakia, Lučenec.

AROUND SALGÓTARJÁN
Salgó & Somoskő Castles

Salgó Castle, 8km north-east of the city centre, was built atop a basalt cone some 625m up in the Medves Hills in the 13th century. After Buda Castle fell to the Turks in 1541, Salgó served as an important border fortress, but it too was taken 23 years later and fell into ruin after the Turks abandoned it in the late 16th century. The castle is remembered best for the visit made by Sándor Petőfi in 1845, which inspired him to write one of his best loved poems, *Salgó*. Today you can just make out the inner courtyard, tower and bastion from the ruins, but views of Somoskő and Slovakia are excellent from this peaceful spot. The castle is open 9 am to 5 pm Tuesday to Sunday (60Ft).

To visit the interior of **Somoskő Castle**, which is now in Slovakian territory, you must cross the border at Somoskőújfalu and follow a path east on foot for about 3km to the castle. But most people will be content with what they can see from the Hungarian side. Somoskő, built in the 14th century from basalt blocks, was able to hold off the Turkish onslaught longer than Salgó Castle, not falling until 1576.

Somoskő Castle is much larger and more interesting than the Salgó fortress, and the Slovakians have restored much of it, with conical wooden roofs now topping two of the bastions. If you do visit it from the Slovakian side, you can walk around the inner castle, the remains of the palace and even into the casemates if the entrance isn't blocked. Make sure you have a look at the basalt formations north-east of the castle; they are lava flows that have frozen into enormous 'organ pipes'.

The adventurous with time on their hands might want to follow the marked trail westward from Somoskőújfalu along the Slovakian border for 4km to 720m **Mt Karancs**;

you can see the High Tatras from the lookout tower atop what is known locally as the 'Palóc Olympus'. Just make sure you have a copy of Cartographia's 1:60,000 *A Karancs, a Medves és a Heves-Borsodi-dombsá* (No 11; 400Ft), the map that covers these hills, which form, a continuation of the Cserhát from Salgótarján east to Ózd.

To get to Salgó Castle, catch bus No 11/b anywhere along Rákóczi út to the Eresztvény recreational area. From here the castle is up the hill to the south-west. An easier way to reach it, though, is to stay on the same bus to the terminus in Salgóbánya, the city's old mining district, and follow the path to the west. Bus No 11/a also goes to Eresztvény and then heads for Somoskő.

Buddhist Stupa

Travelling along route No 21 toward Pászto, some 22km south of Salgótarján, you might think you've driven through a black hole and arrived in South-East Asia. There, on a hillside to the north of the village of Tar, is a full-sized Buddhist stupa, its little chimes sounding and coloured pendants fluttering in the gentle breeze. It is part of **Sándor Kőrösi Csoma Memorial Park**, consecrated in 1992 by the Dalai Lama in memory of the early 19th-century Hungarian Franciscan monk who became a Hungarian Bodhisattva (Buddhist saint). The stupa, with a revolving prayer wheel containing sacred texts, has become something of a local tourist attraction. The Karma Ratna Dargye Ling Buddhist society (☎ 32-470 206, mobile ☎ 06-209 443 860) runs a gift shop and snack bar here (complete with non-vegetarian pizza) open 9 am to 6 pm Tuesday to Friday and to 7 pm at the weekend. The society also organises weekend retreats and meditation courses costing about 3500Ft, including room and board. The train between Hatvan and Salgótarján stops in Tar a couple of kilometres south of the stupa.

Mátra Hills

The Mátra Hills, which boast Hungary's highest peaks, are the most developed and

Kecskemét's colourful Art Nouveau Town Hall.

Eger's cathedral from a side street in the Old Town.

Szilvásvárad's narrow-gauge railway takes you past the streams and forests of Szalajka Valley.

Hollókő Castle holds a commanding position atop Stalk Hill in the Northern Uplands.

Hollókő's little wooden church.

The ribbed vault of Nyírbátor's bell tower.

easily accessible of all the hills in the Northern Uplands. Indeed, at only 80km from the capital, the region is very popular with Budapesters looking for fresh air and a bit of greenery. With all the accommodation and recreational options – from hiking and picking wild mushrooms in the autumn to hunting and skiing in winter – there's enough here to satisfy all tastes.

The Mátra Hills can be reached from other cities like Eger and Pászto, but Gyöngyös is its real springboard. It is also the centre of the Mátraalja wine-growing region, noted for its whites. While its rieslings, Leányka and sweet muscatel have all been praised, the Mátra's great contribution to the world of wine is Hárslevelű ('linden leaf'), a greenish-tinted white wine that is spicy and slightly sweet at the same time.

GYÖNGYÖS
☎ 37 • postcode 3200 • pop 36,500
A colourful small city at the base of the Mátra Hills, Gyöngyös (from the Hungarian word meaning 'pearl') has been an important trading centre since Turkish times and later became known for its textiles. Today, people come here to see the city's churches (the largest Gothic church in Hungary is here), visit its rich medieval library or to have a glass or two of wine before heading for the hills.

Orientation & Information
The bus station is on Koháry út, a 10-minute walk east of Fő tér, the main square. The main train station is on Vasút utca, near the eastern end of Kossuth Lajos utca. The Előre station, from where the narrow-gauge trains depart (see the Activities section), is at the start of Dobó István utca.

The Tourinform office (☎/fax 311 155, ✉ gyongyos@tourinform.hu), at Fő tér 10, is open from 8.30 am to 5 pm weekdays and till noon on Saturday from June to September (7.30 am to 4 pm Monday to Thursday and to 1.30 pm Friday the rest of the year). Ibusz (☎ 311 861, fax 311 807), Kossuth Lajos utca 6, is open 8 am to 5 pm weekdays as is Mátratourist (☎ 311 565) at Hanisz Imre tér 2.

You'll find a large OTP bank branch at Fő tér 1 near Mátratourist; there's a Budapest Bank at the southern end of the square at No 19, but its ATM is around the corner on Móricz Zsigmond utca. The main post office is at Páter Kiss Szaléz utca 9-11 on the corner of Mátyás király utca.

Things to See
The **Mátra Museum**, housed in an old manor house in Orczy Garden at Kossuth Lajos utca 14, contains exhibits on the history of Gyöngyös, with much emphasis on Benevár, a 14th-century castle north-east of Mátrafüred and now in ruins, and the natural history of the Mátra region, including a reassembled 'baby' mammoth. City lore has it that the wrought-iron railings enclosing the garden were made from gun barrels taken during the Napoleonic Wars. Downstairs is the **Mikroárium**, an aquarium-terrarium full of snakes, lizards and tropical fish from around the world. The museum is open from 9 am to 5 pm Tuesday to Sunday from March to October and 10 am to 2 pm on the same days the rest of the year. Entry costs 200/100Ft; the Mikroárium is an extra 80/60Ft.

St Bartholomew's Church (Szent Bertalan templom) is on the east side of Hanisz Imre tér, just a few blocks west of the museum on Kossuth Lajos utca. It was built in the 14th century and is the largest Gothic church in Hungary. You'd hardly know it, though, with the baroque restoration (including a curious upper-storey gallery inside) that was carried out 400 years later. The attractive little baroque building behind the church at Szent Bertalan utca 11 was once a Jesuit school (1752) and now serves as a music academy. The so-called House of the Holy Crown (Szent Korona-ház) at Szent Bertalan utca 3, which served as a safe house for the Crown of St Stephen during the Napoleonic Wars, contains the city's **Ecclesiastical Treasury** (Egyházi Kincstár), one of the richest collections of liturgical objects in the country. It is open Tuesday to Sunday from 9 am till noon and 2 to 5 pm (50/30Ft).

The **Franciscan church** at Barátok tere 1 was built around the same time as St

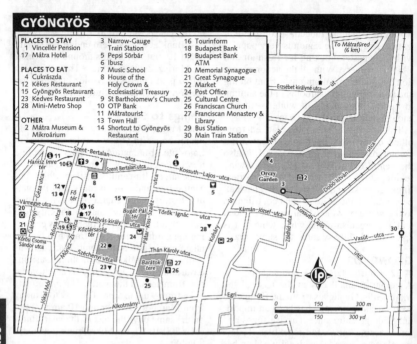

GYÖNGYÖS

PLACES TO STAY	3 Narrow-Gauge	16 Tourinform
1 Vincellér Pension	Train Station	18 Budapest Bank
17 Mátra Hotel	5 Pepsi Sörbár	19 Budapest Bank
	6 Ibusz	ATM
PLACES TO EAT	7 Music School	20 Memorial Synagogue
4 Cukrászda	8 House of the	21 Great Synagogue
12 Kékes Restaurant	Holy Crown &	22 Market
15 Gyöngyös Restaurant	Ecclesiastical Treasury	24 Post Office
23 Kedves Restaurant	9 St Bartholomew's Church	25 Cultural Centre
28 Mini-Metro Shop	10 OTP Bank	26 Franciscan Church
	11 Mátratourist	27 Franciscan Monastery &
OTHER	13 Town Hall	Library
2 Mátra Museum &	14 Shortcut to Gyöngyös	29 Bus Station
Mikroárium	Restaurant	30 Main Train Station

Bartholomew's, but it too has undergone some major changes, with the frescoes and baroque tower added in the 18th century. The church's most celebrated occupant – well, second-most to the faithful – is János Vak ('the Blind') Bottyán, a heroic commander who served under Ferenc Rákóczi II during the War of Independence. The former monastery (1730), which is attached to the church, contains the **Hungarian Franciscan Memorial Library** (Magyar Ferencesek Műemlék Könytára), the only historical archive in Hungary to have survived the Turkish occupation intact. Among its 14,000 volumes are 210 incunabula, some of the most valuable in the nation. The library is open from 2 to 4 pm Tuesday to Friday and from 10 am to 1 pm on Saturday (20Ft).

Gyöngyös was home to a relatively large Jewish community from the 15th century to WWII, and two splendid synagogues bear witness to history. The older of the two, the neoclassical **Memorial Synagogue** built in 1816, is on Vármegye tér facing Gyöngyös Stream and now houses the city's TV studios. The **Great Synagogue**, just south of the Memorial Synagogue on the corner of Gárdonyi Géza utca and Kőrösi Csoma Sándor utca, was designed by Lipót Baumhorn in 1930, two decades after he completed his masterpiece in Szeged. It is now a warehouse.

Activities

Two narrow-gauge trains (☎ 312 447 for information) depart from Előre station just beyond the Mátra Museum. One heads 7km north-east for Mátrafüred – the most enjoyable way of entering the Mátra Hills. The other goes to Lajosháza, 11km north of Gyöngyös. This trip offers no real destination, except a place to begin hiking – perhaps east along the Nagy-völgy (Big Valley) past a series of water catchments or north as far as Galyatető, at 965m Hungary's second-highest peak. On the way back from Mátrafüred, get off at Farkas-mály-Borpincék, where there's a row of wine cellars offering the local vintage. To return, wait for the train (last one at 5.25 or 6.35 pm, depending on the season) or jump onto a bus coming down route No 24, but it's an easy 4km walk (or crawl) back to Gyöngyös.

Be advised that the Lajosháza train runs only on Saturday, Sunday and holidays from May to September (maximum six trains a day) with extra ones on Wednesday and Friday from mid-June to August. Up to 10 trains daily make the run to Mátrafüred from April to October. During the rest of the year, count on about six or seven trains on weekdays and up to 10 at the weekend.

Special Events
The big event in Gyöngyös is the Mátra Vintage Festival (Mátrai Szüreti Fesztivál) held around 20 August, with most of the action taking place on Fő tér.

Places to Stay
The closest *camping ground* is at Sástó, 3km north of Mátrafüred (see that section). Ibusz and Mátratourist can book you a *private room* in Gyöngyös or the Mátra Hills from between 1000 and 2000Ft per person.

The 15-room *Vincellér (π/fax 311 691, Erzsébet királyné út 22)*, north-east of the centre, is an attractive though relatively expensive pension with singles/doubles/triples for 4500/6500/8500Ft. The *Mátra (π 313 063, fax 312 057, **O** inn-side@mail.matav .hu, Mátyás király utca 2)* facing Fő tér, is the city's only hotel and some of the public areas have at last got a much-needed facelift though the 40 guestrooms look pretty much as they always did. Singles/doubles cost DM57/70.

Places to Eat
One of the cheapest places in town for a meal is the *Kedves (Széchenyi utca 9)* near the large *covered market* on Köztársaság tér south-west of Fő tér. But it keeps early hours: from 6 am to 2 pm on Monday and Saturday, to 6 pm Tuesday to Friday and to 11 am on Sunday.

My favourite restaurant here is the *Gyöngyös (Bugát Pál tér 2)*, which can be reached from Fő tér via a narrow alley next to Tourinform. It serves excellent regional specialities (from 350Ft for starters, 1000Ft for mains) and wine in a 'neo-rustic' environment. The *Kékes (Fő tér 7)* has a lovely terrace on the square and a few vegetarian dishes but closes at 10.30 pm.

The nameless *cukrászda* in Orczy Garden at the start of Mátrai út has excellent cakes and ice cream and is open from 9 or 10 am to 6 pm Wednesday to Monday.

The *Mini-Metro* shop *(Koháry út 9)* opposite the bus station is not a nonstop but stays open till 2 am daily.

Entertainment
The *Mátra Cultural Centre (π 312 281, Barátok tere 3)*, a 'Finnish functionalist-style building' we're told, with huge stained-glass windows, is where Gyöngyös entertains itself.

There are a number of popular night spots around town, including the *Pepsi Sörbár (Kossuth Lajos utca 23)*, which turns into a popular club at the weekend.

Getting There & Around
Bus You won't wait for more than 20 minutes for buses to Budapest, Eger, Hatvan, Mátrafüred and Mátraháza. There are about a dozen buses a day to destinations farther into the Mátra like Parád and Parádfürdő, 10 buses to Recsk and five to Sirok. You can also catch buses to Jászberény (12 daily), Szolnok (six), Salgótarján (five), Kecskemét (five), Miskolc (three) and Hajdúszoboszló (two) and Tiszafüred (three).

Train Gyöngyös is on a dead-end spur some 13km from the Vámosgyörk stop on the main Budapest-Miskolc line. A dozen trains a day connect the city with Vámosgyörk.

Taxi You can order a taxi on 302 222 or 313 300.

GYÖNGYÖS TO EGER
Route No 24 wends its way through the Mátra Hills north of Gyöngyös and then cuts

eastward; if you're under your own steam, it's a great way to get to Eger (60km) via some of the prettiest scenery in the Northern Uplands. Buses to Mátrafüred, Mátraháza, Parád and Parádfürdő are frequent, but the best approach is by the narrow-gauge train that terminates in Mátrafüred.

Mátrafüred
☎ 37 • postcode 3232

Mátrafüred is a pleasant little resort at a height of 340m. Though there is a small **Palóc collection** of dolls and folk craft on exhibit in the centre just south of the narrow-gauge train station (open 9 am to 4.30 pm Monday to Saturday) on Parádi utca, the many easy walks in the area is the main attraction. Make sure you have a copy of Cartographia's 1:40,000 *A Mátra* map (No 14; 400Ft) before setting out.

From Mátrafüred, a trail leading northeast passes the ruins of **Benevár Castle** after a kilometre or so and continues for another 10km up to **Mt Kékes**, Hungary's highest peak (1014m). Another trail heading northwest joins the main road at Sástó, 3km away, and then carries on up through the hills for another 6km to Mátraháza.

You can change money at the post office at Béke utca 5.

Places to Stay & Eat There are lots of signs advertising *private rooms* along Béke utca, which runs west off Parádi utca (route No 24).

The main hotel in Mátrafüred is the *Avar* *(☎ 320 400, fax 320 134, Parádi utca 24)*, a 114-room monstrosity opposite the narrow-gauge train station. It has a heated indoor swimming pool, sauna and a gym and rents bicycles. Singles are DM60 to DM70 and doubles DM80 to DM90, depending on the season and whether you're in a 'new' (renovated) or old room. The 12-room *Diana (☎ 320 136, fax 323 022, Turista utca 1)* just off Béke utca charges 2500/5000/7000Ft for basic but comfortable singles/doubles/triples.

There are plenty of *food stalls* and the like opposite the train station; the *Benevár (Parádi utca 13)* next to the Avar hotel is an

attractive csárda open till 11 pm. The *Feketerigó (Avar utca 2)* is a cheaper option, with main courses averaging about 600Ft.

Sástó
☎ 37 • postcode 3232

Sástó Camping (☎/fax 374 025, ✉ matrat@ mail.matav.hu) at Sástó is the highest camping ground in Hungary (520m) and certainly one of the most attractive. Centred around a small lake with rowing boats, fishing and a 54m-high lookout tower, the camp site complex (open from mid-April to mid-October) offers a wide range of accommodation – from 2nd-class *bungalows* for two/three people (1600/2400Ft) and a double without bath in the 28-room *motel* (2400Ft) to a *cottage* on the lake for three/four people with bath, fridge and TV (4500/5200Ft). *Snack bars* abound, and there is a *restaurant* and small *grocery shop* here.

Mátraháza
☎ 37 • postcode 3233

Mátraháza, with **Kékestető**, the country's centre for winter sport nearby, is built on a slight incline 715m above sea level and about 5km from Sástó. This is an attractive spot to base yourself for short walks in the immediate area or more adventurous hiking farther afield. The post office is at the start of the road to Kékestető there's an ATM at the bus station along the main road through the village.

Places to Stay & Eat Along route No 24 to Mátraháza from Sástó, you'll pass two big resort hotels. The 128-room *Bérc* *(☎ 374 102, fax 374 095)* has a large indoor swimming pool, health facilities, 10-pin bowling and tennis courts. Doubles with bath are 6500Ft to 7400Ft, depending on the room and the season (make sure you get an upper-floor room with a balcony looking out onto the Kékes Hills). The more attractive *Ózon (☎ 374 004, fax 374 039, ✉ reserve@ hotelozon.hunguest.hu)*, with 59 rooms (many with balconies) in a quiet park, is a tranquil place with all the mod cons. Singles are 3600Ft to 4700Ft in the old ('classic') building and 6300Ft to 8200Ft in the new ('business') one, with doubles 4300Ft to 5500Ft and 7000Ft to 9000Ft.

In Mátraháza village, the old *Pagoda* hotel *(☎ 374 013 or 374 022, ✉ reserve@ hotelpagoda.hunguest.hu)* has dozens of differently styled rooms in four buildings spread out over a large garden. Prices vary, but expect to pay 3300/5600Ft for singles/doubles with bath. Some eight small rooms, with washbasin only, at the top of building B are 1750Ft per person.

There are plenty of *snack bars* and the like at the main car park in the centre of Mátraháza; the modern (and nameless) *vendéglő* at the start of the road to Kékestető has decent food and a lovely outside seating pavilion. The *Presszó* restaurant in building A of the Pagoda hotel holds no surprises, but it's cheap.

Kékestető

☎ 37 • postcode 3221

Next to the Pagoda hotel in Mátraháza, you'll see the end of a ski trail that runs down from Kékestető and Mt Kékes. In the absence of a lift, skiers wanting another go hop on the bus, which continuously covers the 4km to the top. The nine-storey **TV tower** at the top is open to view-seekers; the old tower in front of it now houses the 17-room *Hegycsúcs* hotel (*☎/fax 367 086*) with a sauna and a gym and singles/doubles for 2500/5000Ft. Choose one of the two rooms on the 7th floor (No 13 is a twin, No 14 a double), and you'll be sleeping at the highest point in Hungary.

The 14-room *Édosz* holiday house (*☎ 367 044, fax 367 086*) on the road down toward Mátraháza has much more basic accommodation available at half the price.

Parádsasvár

☎ 36 • postcode 3242 • pop 540

The road divides about 3km from Mátraháza, heading north-west to Mt Galyatető and north to Parádsasvár, where Hungary's most effective – and smelliest – *gyógyvíz* (medicinal drinking water) is bottled. Stop for a glass if you can stand the stench of this sulphuric brew. The glass factory nearby pro-

duces high-quality Parád crystal; prices at the retail outlet (☎ 364 051), Rákóczi utca 46-48, are slightly cheaper at the outlet here than in Budapest (open 9 am to 3 pm weekdays, to 1 pm at the weekend).

Parádsasvár can now boast having one of provincial Hungary's most beautiful (and expensive) hotels: the 57-room *Sasvár* castle hotel (*☎ 444 444, fax 544 010, Kossuth Lajos utca 1)* in a restored Renaissance-style manor built in 1882 by Miklós Ybl, who was responsible for the State Opera House in Budapest and many other fine buildings. It has every mod con you could possibly wish for and is surrounded by 2.5 hectares of parkland. Singles are DM224 to DM256, doubles DM293 to DM324, depending on the season.

Parád & Parádfürdő

☎ 36 • postcodes 3240 & 3244

• pop 2350

Parád and Parádfürdő run into one another and nowadays effectively make up one long town. You can't miss the **Coach Museum** (Kocsimúzeum), housed in the red marble Cifra (Ornamental) stables of Count Károlyi at Kossuth Lajos utca 217 and one of the most interesting small museums in Hungary. (For the record, the word 'coach' comes from Kocs, a small village in Transdanubia where these lighter horse-drawn vehicles were first used in place of the more cumbersome wagons.) Inspect the interiors of the diplomatic and state coaches, which are richly decorated with silk brocade; the closed coach used by 19th-century philanderers on the go; and the bridles containing as much as 5kg of silver. The museum is open 9 am to 5 pm daily from April to October and 10 am to 4 pm the rest of the year (150/100Ft).

The Palócland Merrymaking Festival (Palócföldi Vigasságok) is a week-long folk and cultural festival held in Parádfürdő in mid-July.

Recsk & Sirok

☎ 36 • postcodes 3245 & 3332

• pop 3200 & 2370

The road continues on for 2km to Recsk, a place that lives on in infamy as the site of

NORTHERN UPLANDS

Hungary's most brutal forced-labour camp (1950-53) in the early days of communism. A monument at the quarry (kőbánya) about 5km north of the village honours those who died here. Sirok, 8km to the east, is effectively the last town in the Mátra Hills. The ruins of an early 14th-century castle perched on a mountain top provide superb views of the Mátra and Bükk Hills and the mountains of Slovakia. *Vár Camping* (☎ *361 558, Dobó István utca 30*) lies at the foot of the castle ruins.

Bükk Hills

The Bükk Hills, which take their name from the many 'beech trees' growing here, are a green lung buffering Eger and the industrial city of Miskolc. Although much of the area has been exploited for its ore for the ironworks of Miskolc and other towns of the scarred Sajó Valley to the east, a large tract – almost 42,000 hectares – is a national park. The Bükk teems with wildlife, and there are some 800 caves in the mountains. The Bükk National Park Directorate (☎ 36-411 581, fax 412 791) is in Eger at Sánc utca 6.

The Bükk Plateau, a 20-sq-km limestone area rising to heights of between 800m and 900m, is particularly attractive. Following the winding road by car or bike (permission for this may be required) or a series of trails on foot from Szilvásvárad down to Lillafüred or Miskolc (springboards for the eastern Bükk) is an unforgettable experience.

EGER

☎ 36 • postcode 3300 • pop 62,000

Everyone loves Eger, and it's immediately apparent why: beautifully preserved baroque architecture gives the town a relaxed, almost Mediterranean feel; it is the home of the celebrated Egri Bikavér (Eger Bull's Blood) wine known the world over; and it is flanked by two of the Northern Uplands' most beautiful ranges of hills. Hungarians visit Eger for those reasons and more, for it was here that their forebears fended off the Turks for the first time during the 170 years of occupation in 1552 (see boxed text 'The Siege of Eger').

The Turks came back to Eger in 1596 and this time captured the city, turning it into a provincial capital and erecting several mosques and other buildings until they were driven out at the end of the 17th century. All that remains of this architectural legacy is a lonely little minaret pointing its long finger towards the heavens in indignation.

Eger played a central role in Ferenc Rákóczi II's attempt to overthrow the Habsburgs early in the 18th century, and it was then that a large part of the castle was razed by the Austrians. Having enjoyed the status of an episcopate since the time of King Stephen, Eger flourished in the 18th and 19th centuries, when the city acquired most of its wonderful baroque architecture.

Eger (Erlau in German) lies in the Eger Valley between the Bükk and Mátra Hills. While it is not as convenient a springboard as Miskolc and Gyöngyös for these ranges, both are accessible from here via Szilvásvárad – yet another reason for visiting this pretty, friendly area.

The Siege of Eger

The story of the Turks' attempt to take Eger Castle is the stuff of legend. Under the command of István Dobó, a mixed bag of 2000 soldiers held out against more than 100,000 Turks for a month in 1552. As every Hungarian kid in short trousers can tell you, the women of Eger played a crucial role in the battle, pouring boiling oil and pitch on the invaders from the ramparts.

Also significant was Eger's wine, if we're to believe the tale. Dobó, it seems, sustained his soldiers with the ruby-red vintage. When they fought on with increased vigour – and stained beards – rumours began to circulate among the Turks that the defenders were gaining strength by drinking the blood of bulls. Egri Bikavér – Bull's Blood – was born.

Géza Gárdonyi's *Eclipse of the Crescent Moon* (1901), which describes the siege and is required reading in some Hungarian schools, can be found in bookshops throughout the land.

Orientation

Dobó István tér, the centre of Eger, is just a few minutes on foot to the east from the renovated bus station on Barkóczy utca. To reach the centre from the main train station on Vasút utca, walk north along Deák Ferenc utca and then pedestrian Széchenyi István utca. The Egervár train station, which serves Szilvásvárad and other points north, is a five-minute walk north of the castle.

Information

Tourinform (☎ 321 807, fax 321 304, ✉ eger@tourinform.hu), next to the Minorite church at Dobó István tér 2, can supply all the brochures you care to carry and several of the staff speak English better than you or I. It is open from 9 am to 6 pm weekdays and 10 am to 1 pm on Saturday and Sunday from June to August and 9 am to 5 pm weekdays and Saturday 10 am to noon the rest of the year. Tourinform sells a museum card for 500/250Ft valid for a week that allows entry to all the exhibitions in the castle area as well as four city museums.

Egertourist (☎ 411 724), Bajcsy-Zsilinszky utca 9, is open 9 am to 5 pm weekdays; Cooptourist (☎ 311 998, fax 320 333), Dobó István tér 3, keeps the same hours weekdays and opens Saturday to 1 pm, as does Ibusz (☎ 311 451, fax 312 652) at Széchenyi utca 9. Express (☎ 427 865) at No 28 of the same street is open 9 am to 5 pm Monday to Thursday, to 4 pm Friday.

There's an OTP bank branch at Széchenyi utca 2, and the main post office is at No 20-22 of the same street.

Eger Castle

The best overview of the city can be had by climbing up the cobblestone lane from Dózsa György tér to the castle, erected in the 13th century following the Mongol invasion. It's open from 9 am to 5, 6 or 7 pm (depending on the season) Tuesday to Sunday, though you can visit the castle casemates from 8 am to 8 pm in summer (earlier in winter) seven days a week. Much of the castle is of modern construction, but you can still see the foundations of 12th-century St John's Cathedral, which was destroyed by the Turks.

The István Dobó Museum inside the 14th-century Bishop's Palace has models of how the cathedral looked in its prime, as well as furnishings (tapestries, porcelain etc). On the ground floor, a statue of Dobó takes pride of place in Heroes' Hall. The 19th-century building on the north-western side of the courtyard houses the Eger Art Gallery, with portraits of leading contemporary Hungarians and several works by Mihály Munkácsy. Tours to the casemates built after the siege leave from outside the ticket office and are included in the entry fee.

A ticket to see everything in the castle area costs 300/150Ft; if you just want to walk around the grounds without entering anything, it's 100/50Ft. On Monday, when only the casemates are open, the charge is 250/120Ft.

Eszterházy tér

Back in town, begin a walking tour of the city at Eger Cathedral (1836), a neoclassical monolith designed by József Hild, the same architect who later worked on the cathedral at Esztergom. Despite the cathedral's size and ornate altars, the interior is surprisingly light and airy. If you're lucky, you'll chance upon someone playing the baroque organ. Northeast of the cathedral in the Archbishop's Palace (Éseki palota), Széchenyi utca 5, is the Ecclesiastical Collection (Egyházi Gyűtemény) open 9 am to 4 pm weekdays (and on Saturday in May and June).

Directly across from the cathedral on Eszterházy tér is the sprawling Zopf-style Lyceum, named after Károly Eszterházy, a bishop of Eger and one of the school's founders. The ceiling fresco (1778) in the library on the 1st floor of the south wing is a trompe l'oeil masterpiece depicting the Counter-Reformation's Council of Trent (1545-63) and a lightning bolt setting 'heretical' manuscripts ablaze. The library contains hundreds of priceless manuscripts and codices, some of which are on display. The observatory on the 6th floor of the east wing contains 18th-century astronomical equipment; climb three more floors up to the observation deck for a great view of the city and surrounding vineyards.

NORTHERN UPLANDS

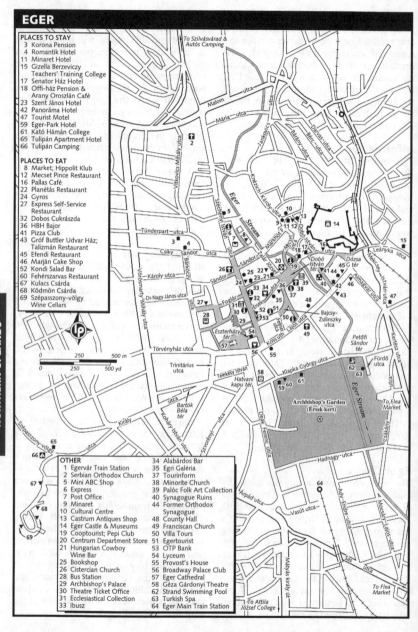

EGER

PLACES TO STAY
3 Korona Pension
4 Romantik Hotel
11 Minaret Hotel
15 Gizella Berzeviczy
   Teachers' Training College
17 Senator Ház Hotel
18 Offi-ház Pension &
   Arany Oroszlán Café
23 Szent János Hotel
42 Panoráma Hotel
47 Tourist Motel
59 Eger-Park Hotel
61 Kató Hámán College
65 Tulipán Apartment Hotel
66 Tulipán Camping

PLACES TO EAT
8 Market; Hippolit Klub
12 Mecset Pince Restaurant
16 Pallas Café
22 Planétás Restaurant
24 Gyros
27 Express Self-Service
   Restaurant
32 Dobos Cukrászda
36 HBH Bajor
41 Pizza Club
43 Gróf Buttler Udvar Ház;
   Talizmán Restaurant
45 Efendi Restaurant
46 Marján Cake Shop
52 Kondi Salad Bar
60 Fehérszarvas Restaurant
67 Kulacs Csárda
69 Ködmön Csárda
69 Szépasszony-völgy
   Wine Cellars

OTHER
1 Egervár Train Station
2 Serbian Orthodox Church
5 Mini ABC Shop
6 Express
7 Post Office
9 Minaret
10 Cultural Centre
13 Castrum Antiques Shop
14 Eger Castle & Museums
19 Cooptourist; Pepi Club
20 Centrum Department Store
21 Hungarian Cowboy
   Wine Bar
25 Bookshop
26 Cistercian Church
28 Bus Station
29 Archbishop's Palace
30 Theatre Ticket Office
31 Ecclesiastical Collection
33 Ibusz
34 Alabárdos Bar
35 Egri Galéria
37 Tourinform
38 Minorite Church
39 Palóc Folk Art Collection
40 Synagogue Ruins
44 Former Orthodox
   Synagogue
48 County Hall
49 Franciscan Church
50 Villa Tours
51 Egertourist
53 OTP Bank
54 Lyceum
55 Provost's House
56 Broadway Palace Club
57 Eger Cathedral
58 Géza Gárdonyi Theatre
62 Strand Swimming Pool
63 Turkish Spa
64 Eger Main Train Station

NORTHERN UPLANDS

The Lyceum's museums are open from 9.30 am to 3 pm Tuesday to Sunday from mid-April to September and 9.30 am to 1 pm Tuesday to Friday and till noon at the weekend the rest of the year. Tickets (330/100Ft) are available from the desk to the left as you enter from Eszterházy tér. The Lyceum's frescoed **chapel** and **ceremonial hall** can be visited only by appointment.

Other Attractions

Walk north along Széchenyi utca to No 15 and the **Cistercian church** (1743). The theatrical baroque altar sculpture of St Francis Borgia in gilt and white stucco is well worth a look. The **Serbian Orthodox church** (Ráctemplom) and its enormous iconostasis of gold leaf and braid is farther north; enter from Széchenyi utca 59. It is open from 10 am to 4 pm Tuesday to Sunday.

Retrace your steps along Széchenyi utca for 200m and turn east onto Knézich Károly utca to the **minaret**, 40m high and now topped with a cross. Non-claustrophobes will brave the 100 narrow spiral steps to reach the top from 10 am to 6 pm daily from April to October. Mecset utca south of the minaret leads to central Dobó István tér, site of the town's market in medieval times.

On the southern side of the square stands the **Minorite church** (1773), one of the most beautiful baroque buildings in the world. The altarpiece of the Virgin Mary and St Anthony (the church's patron) is by Johann Kracker, the Bohemian painter who also did the fire-and-brimstone ceiling fresco in the Lyceum library. Statues of István Dobó and the Hungarians routing the Turks fill the square, and in the former monastery at Dobó István tér 6 there's a collection of **Palóc folk art** (open 9 am to 5 pm Tuesday to Sunday from April to October; 60/30Ft).

From Dobó István tér, cross the little Eger Stream back to Dózsa György tér and turn west onto Kossuth Lajos utca, a fine, tree-lined street with dozens of architectural gems. At No 17 stands the former **Orthodox synagogue**, built in 1893 and now backing onto a shopping mall. (An older neoclassical synagogue dating from 1845 and now in drastic ruins is around the corner at Dr Hibay Károly utca 7.) You'll pass several baroque and Eclectic buildings, including the **county hall** at No 9 with a wrought-iron grid above the main door of Faith, Hope and Charity by Henrik Fazola, a Rhinelander who settled in Eger in the mid-18th century. Walk down the passageway, and you'll see two more of his magnificent works: baroque wrought-iron gates decorated on both sides that have taken over from the minaret as the symbol of Eger. The gate on the right shows the seal of Heves County and has a comical figure on its handle. The more graceful gate on the left is decorated with grapes. The **Franciscan church** at No 14 was completed in 1755 on the site of a mosque. The wrought-iron balcony and window grids of the rococo **Provost's House** (open 10 am to 6 pm weekdays) at No 4 were also done by Fazola.

Eger's big **flea market** is to the south-east of the city centre at the end of Kertész utca; reach it on bus No 5.

Wine Tasting

You can sample Eger's famous wines at many places around town, including the **Borkóstoló a Magyar Csikóshoz** – a local wine bar on Dobó István tér with a mouthful of a name that just means 'Wine Tasting at the Sign of the Hungarian Cowboy'. You can also sample wines from around Hungary in the István Cellar below the Korona pension (see Places to Stay). But why bother drinking here when you can do the same in the wine cellars of the evocatively named **Valley of the Beautiful Women** (Szépasszony-völgy) so close by? The best time to visit the valley is the late afternoon on a warm day.

From the western end of Eger Cathedral, walk south on Trinitárius utca to Bartók Béla tér and then west along Király utca to Szépasszony-völgy utca. Veer to the left as you descend the hill past the camping ground and into the valley, and you'll see dozens of cellars – some with musicians, some with outside tables, others locked up tight as their owners party elsewhere. This is the place to sample Bull's Blood – one of very few reds produced in Eger – or any of the whites: Leányka, Olaszrizling and Hárslevelű from Debrő.

The choice of wine cellars can be a bit daunting and their characters can change so walk around and have a look yourself. Nos 11, 16 & 17 are always popular; for schmalzy Gypsy music, No 42 is the one. But if you're interested in good wine, visit cellars 5, 13, 18, 23, 31 & 32. Be careful though; those 1dl glasses (about 40Ft) go down easily. Hours are erratic, but a few cellars are sure to be open till the early evening.

Other Activities

The Archbishop's Garden (Érsek kert), once the private reserve of papal princes, has open-air swimming pools (open from 6 am to 7 pm weekdays and from 8 am at the weekend May to September; 280/170Ft) and covered ones (9 am to 7 pm daily October to April). Enter from Petőfi tér 2. The thermal baths (women: noon to 6 pm Wednesday and Friday; men: same hours Tuesday and Thursday and 10 am to 2 pm Saturday; 160Ft) dating from Turkish times are at Fürdő utca 1-3.

Bicycles can be rented from Mountain Bike Rentals (mobile ☎ 429 957) at Sólyom utca 28, or from Autós Caraván Camping (see Accommodation). Horse-riding enthusiasts should head for the Egedhegy Lipizzaner Horse Farm (☎ 312 804) in Vécsey-völgy, north-east of the centre, from May to September. Riding costs 1800Ft per hour. The bus to Noszvaj (*not* Novaj) goes past the farm.

Organised Tours

Tours of Eger lasting about three hours leave from Tourinform at 10.30 am on Tuesday, Thursday and Saturday from mid-May to mid-September. The cost is 1500Ft per person.

Special Events

Annual events include the Agria International Folkdance Festival (Agria Nemzetközi Néptáncfesztivál) in June, the Border Fortress Historical Tournament (Végvári Történelmi Játékok) at the castle in July, Baroque Weeks (Barokk Hetek) in late July/early August and Vintage Days in Eger (Szüreti Napok Egerben) in mid-September

Places to Stay

Camping *Tulipán Camping* (☎/fax 410 580, Szépasszony-völgy utca 7), has two-bed *caravans* (2180Ft) and four-bed *bungalows* (6500Ft) with shared bath, as well as five-bed bungalows with private bath, kitchen and TV (7200Ft). Camping costs 400Ft per person and per tent. Guests at the site (open April to September) can use the pool at the Tulipán Apartment hotel (see Hotels) on the hill above the camping ground.

Autós Caraván Camping (☎ 410 558, @ egertour@mail.agria.hu, Rákóczi út 79), 4km north of Eger (turn left at the Shell station), is only of interest to people with cars. Camping costs 450/350 per person/tent and there's a 40-room *motel* and 16 *bungalows*. It is open from mid-April to mid-October.

Hostels The 300-bed *Gizella Berzeviczy Teachers' Training College* (☎ 520 430, @ davidi@gemini.ektf.hu, Leányka utca 2) east of the castle has two and four-bed dormitory rooms with washbasins (800Ft per person) and doubles with showers (1900Ft) available from July to early September. Other summer hostels include the 135-bed *Kató Hámán College* (☎ 413 661, Klapka utca 12) from 600Ft to 950Ft per person and the 300-bed *Attila József College* (☎ 410 571, Mátyás király út 62) with rooms from 700Ft to 1000Ft.

Private Rooms Egertourist and Ibusz can organise private rooms for 1300Ft to 2200Ft per person. Villa Tours (☎ 410 215), Jókai utca 3, has them for 1500Ft to 3500Ft. If you arrive after the tourist offices are closed, try for a room at Almagyar utca 7 or No 19, along Mekcsey István utca south of the castle or on Knézich Károly utca near the minaret.

Pensions & Hotels The cheapest place in town is the run-down *Tourist* (☎ 429 014, @ egertour@mail.agria.hu, Mekcsey István utca 2), a 'motel' south of the castle with 50 rooms in two buildings. It has singles/doubles with shared bath for 1800/2800Ft and doubles with private bath for 5200Ft.

The *Korona* pension (☎ *313 670, fax 310 261,* ✆ *koronaho@mail.agria.hu, Tündérpart utca 5),* on a quiet side street off Csíky Sándor utca, has 40 doubles from DM62 to DM94, depending on the season. It also has a 'wine museum' in its 200-year-old wine cellar called István Pince where you can sample wines from Hungary's 22 wine-producing regions from 10 am to 10 pm daily. A wonderful alternative nearby is the very friendly, very cosy 12-room *Romantik* hotel (☎ *310 456, fax 321 543, Csíky Sándor utca 26),* with singles/doubles for DM80/95 and a suite for DM110.

The 38-room *Minaret* (☎ *410 233, fax 410 473, Knézich Károly utca 4)* is a family-run hotel offering singles/doubles with shower for DM60/77, but there always seem to be noisy groups checking in or out when I visit. Instead, opt for the *Szent János* (☎ *410 409, fax 312 164, Szent János utca 3),* a somewhat antiseptic 10-room new place hewn out of a baroque townhouse with singles for DM55 to DM85 and doubles DM85 to DM110, depending on the season.

The *Tulipán Apartment* hotel (☎ *410 580, Szépasszony-völgy utca 7)* above the camping ground in Szépasszony-völgy has self-catering rooms for 3500Ft to 7000Ft, depending on the size and the amenities. There is also a nine-room *hotel* with doubles for about 5200Ft.

If you want to splurge on accommodation in Hungary, save it for Eger and choose the *Senator Ház* (☎/fax *320 466, Dobó István tér 11),* a delightful 18th-century inn with 11 rooms in Eger's main square that many – including me – consider to be the best small hotel in provincial Hungary. Singles are DM40 to DM70 and doubles are DM60 to DM95, depending on the season. *Off Ház* (☎ *311 005, fax 311 330,* ✆ *offihaz@ mail.matav.hu, Dobó István tér 5),* a 'hotel' consisting of five cramped rooms above the Arany Oroszlán restaurant, is central but a very, very distant second choice to the Senator Ház. It charges an outrageous DM100 for a double.

The *Eger-Park* (☎ *413 233, fax 413 114,* ✆ *hotelpark@mail.matav.hu, Szálloda utca 1-3),* with an ugly modern wing (Eger) and an old-world one (Park – enter from Klapka György utca 8), has a total of 204 rooms, but make sure you get one of the Park's three dozen – preferably looking out onto the Archbishop's Garden. The hotels have all the facilities you'd expect at three-star prices: swimming pool, sauna, gym, bowling alley and three restaurants. Singles are DM65 to DM86, doubles DM96 to DM110.

Eger's flashiest new hotel is the four-star *Panoráma* (☎ *412 886, fax 410 136,* ✆ *panhotel@lelender.hu, Dr Hibay Károly utca 2),* whose 38 rooms occupy what was once the Unicornis hotel, favourite of budget travellers. Singles are DM70 to DM99 and doubles DM85 to DM120, depending on the season.

Places to Eat

Surprisingly, Eger is not overly endowed with restaurants. The *Express* (*Pyrker tér 4)* just north of the bus station, is a large cheap self-service restaurant open daily till 8 pm. The *Planétás* (*Zalár József utca 5-7)* near Dobó István tér has good, reasonably priced food (mains 300Ft to 600Ft).

Two more inexpensive places for a decent meal on Széchenyi utca are *Gyros* (*Széchenyi utca 10),* with Greek salads (385Ft), tsatsiki (350Ft) and moussaka (590Ft), and the *Kondi* salad bar (*Széchenyi utca 2).* The former is open daily till 10 pm; the latter closes at 7 pm (5 pm on Saturday, 1 pm on Sunday). The *Pizza Club* (*Fazolka Henrik utca 1),* south of the castle and open daily till 10 or 11 pm, can be recommended for its pizzas (500Ft to 720Ft).

The *HBH Bajor* (*Bajcsy-Zsilinszky utca 19)* serves reliable Hungarian-Germanic food in a bright, clean environment. I was saddened to see that one of my favourite Hungarian eateries in Eger, the Talizmán wine-cellar restaurant, had metamorphosed into the *Efendi* (*Kossuth Lajos utca 19),* an uninspired place with one of the funniest menus in memory but have since learned that it will reopen almost opposite in the renovated Gróf Buttler Udvár Ház. The **Mecset Pince** *(Harangöntő utca 5)* near the minaret serves solid Hungarian food and there's outside seating in the courtyard in summer.

The **Fehérszarvas Vadásztanya** *(Klapka György utca)* near the Park hotel is Eger's silver-service restaurant. But the 'White Deer Hunters' Farm', with its game specialities (1250Ft to 1950Ft) and exposed kitchen, is really a place to enjoy in autumn and winter. In summer, dine at the open-air restaurant on the Park hotel's back terrace.

There are a couple of csárdas amidst the wine cellars (see the previous Wine Tasting section) in Szépasszony-völgy, including the vine-covered **Kulacs** (open Tuesday to Sunday till 11 pm) and the much bigger (and expensive) **Ködmön**.

For something sweet, try the **Marján** cake shop *(Kossuth Lajos utca 28)* south of Dózsa György tér. Other options include the **Pallas** *(Dobó István utca 20)*, a coffee shop in a small courtyard with a fountain, and the **Dobos** *(Széchenyi utca 6)*.

The **Mini ABC** *(Széchenyi utca 38)* is open 24 hours seven days a week. The covered **fruit & vegetable market** *(Katona István tér)* is by the little Eger Stream. It's open 6 am to 6 pm weekdays, till 1 pm on Saturday and 10 am on Sunday

Entertainment

The **County Cultural Centre** *(☎ 410 673, Knézich Károly utca 8)* across from the minaret, or the city's **ticket office** *(☎ 312 660, Széchenyi utca 3)*, open 9 am to 4.30 pm weekdays, can tell you what concerts and plays are on in Eger. Venues are the rebuilt **Géza Gárdonyi Theatre**, the **Lyceum**, and **Eger Cathedral**. From mid-May to mid-October there are half-hour organ concerts at 11.30 am daily from Monday to Saturday and at 12.45 pm on Sunday in the cathedral.

Dobó István tér has wine bars and cafes with outside seating in summer, including the **Pepi Club** at No 3, the **Arany Oroszlán** at No 5 and the **Minorita** at No 7. A pleasant bar called the **Alabárdos** *(Érsek utca 7)* stays open till midnight. Beneath the cathedral

steps on Eszterházy tér, a bizarre, cave-like place called the **Broadway Palace** rages Thursday to Saturday from 9 pm to 6 am. Another place is the **Hippolit Klub** *(Katona István tér 2)* near the market, which boasts a disco 'free of house and techno' on Friday and Saturday.

Shopping

The Egri Galéria at Érsek utca 8 has lovely jewellery, fine art, pottery and other collectibles for sale. One of the best places to look for antiques in Eger is Castrum Antivitás at Harangöntő utca 2.

Getting There & Away

Bus Bus services are good, with buses every 30 to 40 minutes to Felsőtárkány in the Bükk, Gyöngyös, Mezőkövesd, Noszvaj, Szilvásvárad and Bélapátfalva. Other destinations include: Aggtelek and Jósvafő (one bus daily), Békéscsaba (two buses daily), Budapest (hourly via route No 3), Hatvan (eight), Kecskemét (three), Debrecen (five), Miskolc (10) and Szeged (two). Remember that the bus to Miskolc only goes through the Bükk via Felsőtárkány on Sunday at 7 and 11.25 am. On other days it follows the boring route No 3 via Mezőkövesd.

Train Eger is on a minor railway linking Putnok and Füzesabony; you usually have to change at the latter for Budapest, Miskolc or Debrecen. There are up to five direct trains a day to and from Budapest-Keleti.

Getting Around

From the main train station, bus No 11, 12 or 14 will drop you off at the bus station or town centre. For the flea market at the end of Kertész utca, take bus No 5 or 5/a.

You can order a taxi on ☎ 411 411 or ☎ 411 222.

AROUND EGER
Egerszalók
☎ 36 • postcode 3394 • pop 1700

The open-air hot spring *(hőforrás)* at Egerszalók, 8km to the south-west, makes an excellent day trip from Eger. It's quite a sight: cascades of *very* hot water running down from what look like steaming icebergs but what are in fact mounds of salt and other mineral deposits. Above the main pool in the hills to the right is a naturist area (follow the *nudizmus terület* signs) with a small pond shaded by apple trees. The hot spring's opening hours are almost round-the-clock: 7 am to 5 am. Entry costs 150/80Ft per person/car till 6 pm and 170/100Ft after that. The bus to Kerecsend via Demjén will drop you off a couple of hundred metres north of the entrance.

Mezőkövesd

☎ 49 • postcode 3400 • pop 18,000

Those interested in Hungarian peasant life and its traditions will want to make the easy trip to Mezőkövesd, about 18km south-east of Eger. Mezőkövesd is the centre of the Mátyó, a Magyar people famous for their fine embroidery and other folk art.

From the Mezőkövesd bus station on Rákóczi utca, walk south for 50m and then east along Mátyás király út – Borsod Tourist (☎ 412 614), open 9 am to 5 pm Monday to Thursday, till 2 pm Friday, is at No 155 – to the **Mátyó Museum** in the cultural centre at Szent László tér 20. The displays explain the regional differences and historical development of Mátyó needlework: from white-on-white stitching and patterns of blue and red roses to the metallic fringe that was banned in the early 1920s because the high cost was ruining some families. The museum is open 9 am till noon and 1 to 4 pm Tuesday to Sunday (200/100Ft). Across Szent László tér is the **Catholic church** with an overwrought romantic fresco of a Mátyó wedding (1961) above the arch in the east transept.

From Hősök tere a short distance southwest of Szent László tér, enter any of the small streets running southward to find a completely different world: thatched and whitewashed cottages with old women outside stitching the distinctive Mátyó rose patterns in the sun. Interesting lanes (*köz*) to stroll along are Patkó köz, Kökény köz and Mogyoró köz, but the centre of activity is really Kis Jankó Bori utca, named after

Hungary's own 'Grandma Moses' who lived and stitched her famous '100 roses' patterns here for almost 80 years. Bori's 200-year-old three-room cottage at No 24 is now a **folk museum** filled with needlework and brightly painted furniture and open 10 am till noon and 1 to 5 pm from Tuesday to Sunday. Other houses on the street that you can visit and watch the women at work are Nos 1, 7 (the folk-art cooperative and *táncpajta* or 'dance barn'), 9, 12 and 32 – though the house numbers are a bit jumbled or missing altogether. Most of the work is for sale directly from the embroiderers, or you can buy it at the folk-art shop on the south-west corner of Szent László tér (open weekdays from 8 am to 4 pm) or a shop called Gerti at Mátyás király út 80.

With Eger so close, there's no point in staying overnight in Mezőkövesd. But if you miss the last bus or you want to catch an early-morning one to Miskolc, try the 10-room *Ost* hotel (☎/fax 411 405, Széchenyi utca 12) south-west of the bus station, which has doubles with shower for 4000Ft, or the similarly priced *Ádám* hotel (☎ 431 100, Nyárfa utca 1), south-east of the station, which has five rooms. For something to eat, try the *Hungária* restaurant and cafe (corner of Mátyás király út & Mátyás utca) opposite the church or the *Pizzeria Nero* (Eötvös utca 9), south of Hősök tere.

There's an OTP bank at Mátyás király út 149 near Borsod Tourist and the post office is at Mátyás király út 87 just south of the bus station. Buses run to and from Eger and Miskolc every 30 to 40 minutes. Other destinations accessible from Mezőkövesd include Budapest (two to three buses a day), Debrecen (two), Gyöngyös (up to four), Nyíregyháza (three), Szeged (two) and Tisztafüred (six).

SZILVÁSVÁRAD

☎ 36 • postcode 3348 • pop 1900

The western Bükk region is most easily approached from Szilvásvárad, some 28km north of Eger. The private domain of the profascist Count Palavicini (he razed an entire village in south-east Hungary in the

1920s when his tenants were acting up) until after WWII, Szilvásvárad is an easy day trip from Eger. It is an ideal base for hiking into the Szalajka Valley and is the centre of horse breeding in Hungary, with some 250 prize Lipizzaners in local stables (see boxed text 'The Magnificent White Stallions'). It is also the place to ride on one of Hungary's most delightful narrow-gauge trains.

Orientation & Information

Get off the train at the first of Szilvásvárad's two stations, Szilvásvárad-Szalajkavölgy, and walk along Egri út north-east for about 10 minutes to the centre of town. The town's main station is 3km to the north. The bus from Eger will drop you off at several stops in the centre of town.

There are no major tourist offices in Szilvásvárad, but those in Eger can provide you with whatever information you need as well as sell you Cartographia's three 1:40,000 maps of the Bükk region for 400Ft each: *A Bükk-fennsík* (Bükk Plateau; No 33); *A Bükk – északi rész* (Bükk – northern section; No 29) and *A Bükk – déli rész* (Bükk – southern section; No 30).

An OTP bank branch (no ATM) at Egri út 30/a changes money. The post office is a bit farther north at No 12.

Things to See & Do

Some people come to Szilvásvárad just to ride the **narrow-gauge railway** into the Szalajka Valley. The open-air, three-car train leaves seven times a day from May to September (nine times a day on weekends), with three departures daily in April and October (four at the weekend). The station is south of the open racecourse at Szalajka-völgy 6.

The little train chugs along for 5km, passing well-stocked trout ponds, streams and bubbling little waterfalls before reaching the terminus at **Szalajka-Fátyolvízesés**. From there, you can also walk for 10 minutes to **Istállóskő Cave**, where Stone Age pottery shards were discovered in 1912, or climb 958m **Mt Istállóskő**, the highest peak in the Bükk. To return to Szilvásvárad, either stay on the train for the return trip or walk back for

The Magnificent White Stallions

Lipizzaners, the celebrated white horses bred originally for the imperial Spanish Riding School in Vienna under the Habsburgs, are considered to be the finest riding horses in the world – the *haute école* of dressage horses. And with all the trouble that's put into breeding and training them, it's not surprising. They are very intelligent, sociable animals, quite robust and graceful.

Lipizzaners are bred for riding and show at Lipica in Slovenia; at Piber, north-east of Graz in Austria, for the Spanish Riding School still; and in the US state of Illinois. The Lipizzaners at Szilvásvárad, on the other hand, are also raised as carriage horses. As a result they are bigger and stronger.

Breeding, as they say, is paramount. Some six families with 16 ancestors (including Spanish, Arabian and Berber breeds) can be traced back to the early 18th century, and their pedigrees read like those of medieval royalty. When you walk around the stables at the stud farm you'll see charts on each horse's stall with complicated figures, dates and names like 'Maestoso', 'Neapolitano' and 'Pluto'. It's all to do with the horse's lineage.

A fully mature Lipizzaner measures about 15 hands (that's about 153cm) and weighs between 500kg and 600kg. They have long backs, short, thick necks, silky manes and expressive eyes. They live for 25 to 30 years and are particularly resistant to disease. But, like most horses, they are somewhat short-sighted (near-sighted) and they will nuzzle you out of curiosity if you approach them while they graze.

Surprisingly, Lipizzaners are not born white but grey, bay or even chestnut. The celebrated 'imperial white' does not come about until they are between five and 10 years old, when their hair loses its pigment. Think of it as part of the old nag's ageing process. Their skin remains grey, however, so when they are ridden hard and sweat, they become mottled and aren't so attractive.

1½ hours along well-trodden, shady paths, taking in the sights along the way. The **Forestry Museum** (Erdészeti Múzeum) deals with everything the forest contains or surrenders: timber, game, plant life etc. It is open from 8.30 am to 4.30 pm Tuesday to Sunday from May to September. In April and October the hours are 8.30 am to 3 or 4 pm; during the rest of the year the hours are 9 am to 2.30 pm weekdays only. There's also an **Open-Air Forest Museum** (Szabadtéri Erdei Múzeum) with more interesting exhibits, including a 16th-century water-powered saw and bellows once used by charcoal burners.

In Szilvásvárad, both the covered and the open **racecourses** put on Lipizzaner parades and coach races (150/100Ft) at weekends throughout the summer, but times are not fixed. You may find someone at the ticket office, or check the notice board nearby.

You'll learn more about these intelligent horses, and just how the stud ended up here after starting out in Lipica (now Slovenia) in the 16th century, by visiting the **Horse Museum** (Lovas Múzeum) in an 18th-century stable, which you enter at Park utca 8 (open 9 am till noon and 1 to 5 pm Tuesday to Sunday from April to October and at the same times at the weekend only the rest of the year; 80/50). The **Lipizzaner Stud** (Lipicai Ménes) at the top of Fenyves utca can also be visited from 8.30 am till noon and 2 to 4 pm Tuesday to Sunday (80/50Ft). They also rent horses (1700/3500Ft per hour in the paddock/farther afield) and offer coach rides (from 3000/5000Ft for a two/four-horse coach seating three people).

The Protestant **Round Church** (Kerektemplom; 1841), with its Doric columns and dramatic dome, looks to some like a provincial attempt to duplicate Eger Cathedral. It's off Aradi vértanúk útja across the stream from Miskolci út. At Miskolci út 58, displays in a 17th-century farmhouse called **Orbán House** are devoted to the flora, fauna and geology of the Bükk National Park. It is open from 9 am till noon and 1 to 5 pm Tuesday to Sunday from May to October (100/50Ft).

You can hire a bicycle from Eger-based Mountain Bike Rentals (☎ 429 957) near the entrance to the park. The charge is

SZILVÁSVÁRAD

To Main Railway Station
To Miskolc
Jókai utca
Miskolci út
Aradi vértanúk útja

1 Round Church
2 Orbán House
3 Szilvás Kastély Hotel
4 Horse Museum
5 Lipizzaner Stud
6 Post Office
7 Lipicai Hotel
8 Bus Stop
9 OTP Bank
10 Bus Stop

Park utca
Fenyves utca
Egri út

11 Car Park
12 Ticket Office
13 Covered Racecourse
14 Büfé
15 Open Racecourse
16 Lovas Restaurant
17 Mountain Bike Rentals
18 Food Stands & Büfés
19 Park Entrance
20 Narrow-Gauge Train Station
21 Hegyi Camping
22 Bus Stop
23 Bus Stop

To Szalajka Valley
Szalajka-völgy
To Eger & Szilvásvárad-Szalajkavölgy Train Station

0   150   300 m
0   150   300 yd

NORTHERN UPLANDS

500/1500Ft per hour/day. Regular push bikes available from the Szilvás Kastély hotel (see Places to Stay) cost 250/1100Ft.

Special Events
The National Horse Festival (Nemzeti Lovas Fesztivál) takes place in late July while the International Carriage Driving Competition is held in early September.

Places to Stay
Hegyi Camping (☎ 355 207, Egri út 36/a), a stone's throw from the Szilvásvárad-Szalajkavölgy train station and is open

mid-April to mid-October, has small *holiday houses* for two for 3000Ft. Camping costs 400Ft to 550Ft per tent and 500Ft per person. If you're in search of a *private room*, look around you; there are *szoba kiadó* signs everywhere.

The 29-room *Lipicai* hotel (☎ *355 100, fax 355 200, Egri út 12-14*) offers very basic accommodation in a blockhouse-like building for 3900/4900Ft for doubles/triples. The 41-room *Szilvás Kastély* hotel (☎ *355 211, fax 355 324, @ reserve@ hotelszilvas.hunguest.hu, Park utca 6*), just beyond the Horse Museum in the former Palavicini mansion, is the most interesting place to stay in Szilvásvárad. Prices can vary greatly from season to season and whether or not your room has a bath, a shower and/or a WC, but you can expect to pay from 4800Ft to 6200Ft for a single, 5500Ft to 6600Ft for a double. The hotel also has motel-style accommodation in *bungalows* for two people in the back for 3600Ft and rents out bikes (see Things to See & Do).

Places to Eat

Food stalls and small *büfés* line Szalajka-völgy, the road leading to the park entrance. The nearby *Lovas* restaurant has a pleasant covered back terrace and is open to 10 pm.

Getting There & Away

Buses to/from Eger are very frequent and, though they stop at Mónosbél and Bélapátfalva, they're faster than the train. Buses also go to Ózd (about two departures an hour on weekdays, hourly at the weekend), Budapest (three to four buses a day), Aggtelek (one), Mezőkövesd (one on weekdays), Miskolc (one), Gyöngyös (up to four), Mátraháza (one) and Putnok (three).

Up to eight trains a day link Eger with Szilvásvárad. If heading for Szilvásvárad from the centre of Eger, board the train at the Egervár station, north of the castle on Gárdonyi Géza utca. Five of these trains carry on to Putnok, from where you can enter Slovakia via Bánréve or head southeast for Miskolc.

MISKOLC

☎ 46 • postcode 3500 • pop 196,500

Hungary's third-largest city and traditionally its most important industrial centre, Miskolc is a difficult child to love. It is a sprawling metropolis ringed by refineries and factories (many now abandoned) and cardboard-quality housing blocks. A relatively affluent mining and steel-making town under the old regime, Miskolc was hit harder than most by the collapse of heavy industry in Hungary in the early 1990s.

So why come to this, the 'capital of the rust belt'? For one thing, its location at the foot of the Bükk Hills makes it an ideal place to start a trek or walk into the national park. The thermal waters of nearby Miskolctapolca are among the most effective in Hungary, and the western suburb of Diósgyőr boasts a well-preserved castle. And Miskolc proper has put on a new face, with central Széchenyi István út now pedestrianised and many of the buildings lining it either renovated or freshly painted.

Orientation

Miskolc is a long, narrow city stretching east to west from the unlovely Sajó Valley to the foothills of the Bükk. The main drag, Széchenyi István út, is lined with some interesting old buildings; those around the so-called Dark Gate (Sötétkapu), an 18th-century vaulted passageway, are especially colourful. Almost everything of interest in central Miskolc is on or near this street.

The main train station (Tiszai pályaudvar) lies to the south-east on Kandó Kálmán tér, a 15-minute tram ride from the centre. The bus station is on Búza tér, a short distance north-east of Széchenyi út.

Information

Tourinform's main branch (☎/fax 348 921, @ bordod-m@tourinform.hu) is in the International Trade Centre at Mindszent tér 1 but the branch in the centre (☎ 350 425, fax 350 439), Széchenyi út 2, is much more convenient and open from 9 am to 5 pm weekdays and, from May to September, 9 am to 4 pm on Saturday and 10 am to 2 pm on Sunday as well. Other agencies on

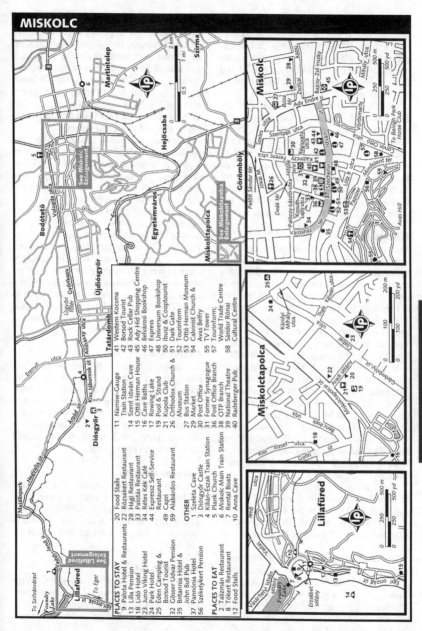

MISKOLC

NORTHERN UPLANDS

PLACES TO STAY
9 Palota Hotel & Restaurants
13 Illa Pension
18 Lidó Hotel
23 Juno Viking Hotel
24 Park Hotel
25 Eden Camping & Borsod Tourist
32 Gösser Udvar Pension
35 Britannia Hotel &
John Bull Pub
37 Pannónia Hotel
56 Székelykert Pension

PLACES TO EAT
2 Talizmán Restaurant
8 Tököt Restaurant
12 Food Stalls

20 Food Stalls
22 Rózsakert Restaurant
28 Hági Restaurant
33 Palotás Restaurant
34 Rétes Kék Café
44 Expressz Self-Service Restaurant
49 Capri
59 Alabárdos Restaurant

OTHER
1 Szeleta Cave
3 Diósgyőr Castle
4 Kilián-Észak Train Station
6 Miskolc Main Train Station
7 Rental Boats
10 Anna Cave

11 Narrow-Gauge Train Station
14 Szent István Cave
15 Ottó Herman House
16 Cave Baths
17 Rowing Lake
19 Pool & Strand
21 Kupola Club
26 Orthodox Church & Museum
27 Bus Station
29 Market
30 Post Office
31 Former Synagogue
36 Post Office Branch
38 OTP Branch
39 National Theatre
40 Radeberger Pub

41 Western Kocsma
42 Borsod Tourist
43 Rock Cellar Pub
45 Ady Híd Shopping Centre
46 Belvárosi Bookshop
47 Express
48 Universum Bookshop
50 Ibusz & Cooptourist
51 Dark Gate
52 Tourinform
53 Ottó Herman Museum
54 Calvinist Church & Avas Belfry
55 TV Tower
57 Tourinform; World Trade Centre
58 Sándor Rónai Cultural Centre

Széchenyi út include Borsod Tourist (☎ 350 666) at No 35; Cooptourist (☎ 328 812) at No 14; Ibusz (☎ 324 090) at No 18; and Express (☎ 349 400) at No 56. All agencies are open from 8 or 9 am to between 4.30 and 6 pm on weekdays and – usually in summer only – till noon or 1 pm on Saturday.

OTP has a branch at Széchenyi út 15. The main post office is at Kazinczy utca 16 on the eastern side of Hősök tere, but a more convenient branch can be found upstairs at Széchenyi út 3-9. The Belvárosi bookshop at Széchenyi út 64 stocks some foreign-language publications and maps, including the Bükk and Zemplén maps from Cartographia. Universum at No 34 of the same street is another good bookshop.

Things to See

Two houses of worship attest to the large communities of Greeks and Jews who once called Miskolc their home. The **Orthodox church**, a splendid late-baroque structure at Deák tér 7, has an iconostasis (1793) which is 16m high with almost 100 icons. A guide will escort you from the **Orthodox Ecclesiastical Museum** (open from 10 am to 6 pm Tuesday to Saturday from May to September, till 4 pm the rest of the year; 100/60Ft) near the main gate. Make sure the guide points out the Black Madonna of Kazan, presented to the church by Catherine the Great, and the jewel-encrusted Mt Athos Cross brought to Miskolc by Greek settlers late in the 18th century. To the south-east at Kazinczy utca 7 stands the large and crumbling **Orthodox synagogue**, designed by Ludwig Förster, the architect of Budapest's Great Synagogue.

The Calvinist **Plank Church** (Deszkatemplom), built in 1938, is a Transylvanian-style wooden church in the cemetery north of Petőfi tér. It is currently under renovation after having been torched by arsonists in 1996.

The **Ottó Herman Museum**, at Papszer 1 south of the centre, has one of Hungary's richest collections of Neolithic finds (many from the Bükk), a good ethnographical collection and a fine art exhibit. It is open from 10 am to 4 pm Tuesday to Sunday

(200/100Ft). From here, take a stroll up leafy **Avas Hill**; the best approach is via Mélyvölgy utca, off Papszer, or Földes Ferenc utca, off Mindszent tér. Veer to the right along the narrow lane past some of the more than 800 wine cellars cut into the limestone. The **TV tower** at the top of the hill provides some superb views of the Bükk and, on a very clear day, even the Carpathians beyond the ugly housing blocks and industrial wasteland.

In a cemetery below the hill is the large Gothic **Avas Calvinist Church** (1410), with a painted wooden interior. The bell tower standing away from the church dates from the late 16th century. The key is in the parish office at Papszer 14.

A must-see but a bit of a journey from the centre is the four-towered **Diósgyőr Castle** on Vár utca in a suburb of that name some 7km west of the centre. Begun in the 13th century, the castle was heavily damaged early in the 18th century and was only restored – very insensitively in some parts – in the 1950s. It is open from 9 or 10 am to 6 pm Tuesday to Sunday from April to November, and guided tours leave at 15 and 45 minutes past the hour (300/150Ft).

Activities

The Balogh Park Horse Club (☎ 412 527) has horses for riding and runs a riding school at Görgey utca 12 south of Mindszent tér. Farther afield, there's a horse-riding school at the Sárga Csikó hotel (☎/fax 368 471) in Görömböly, south of the city on route No 3 (Pesti út). Take bus No 4 from the bus station.

Special Events

A number of special events and festivals are held at Diósgyőr Castle in summer including the Diósgyőr Castle Games (Diósgyőri Várjátékok) and the celebrated open-air Kaláka festival of folk music in mid-July.

Places to Stay

In July and August, the *Bolyai College* (☎ 565 111, Egyetem utca 17) at the university in Egyetemváros has hundreds of dormitory beds available for about 1000Ft per person. There are up to 25 available during the rest of the year. *Private rooms* for two people from Ibusz or Borsod Tourist cost 2500Ft to 3000Ft, but they'll probably be in one of the housing projects ringing the city.

The seven-room *Gösser Udvar* pension (*☎/fax 344 425, Déryné utca 7*) is not worth the 5000Ft it charges for a double, but it's central and one of a very few accommodation options. Its sister pension, the seven-room *Székelykert* (*☎/fax 411 222, Földes Ferenc utca 4*) below Avas Hill charges the same. The *Britannia hotel* (*☎/fax 351 066, Hunyadi utca 3*), a new kid in old clothes above the John Bull pub (see Entertainment) has eight rooms that cost 7900/9500Ft for a single/double.

Miskolc's No 1 hotel is the *Pannónia* (*☎ 329 811, fax 329 877, Kossuth Lajos utca 2*) very much in the centre. It has a restaurant, brasserie, a popular pizzeria, 34 ordinary rooms and is very overpriced at 9700/12,950 for a single/double.

Places to Eat

Among the cheapest places for a meal (about 300Ft) in Miskolc is the *Expressz* self-service restaurant (*Széchenyi út 107*).

The terrace at the *Pannónia* hotel's pub-restaurant is a pleasant place for an evening meal in summer. A much cheaper place is the nearby *Palotás* (*Kossuth Lajos utca 1*), but it's gloomy inside. Near the bus station, the shocking-pink *Hági* restaurant (*Zsolcai kapu 5*), with mains 350Ft to 500Ft, is an island haven in a sea of trashy pubs and video game parlours. The *John Bull* pub below the Britannia hotel (see Places to Stay) has three-course set lunches for 600Ft between 11 am and 5 pm.

Some say that the *Alabárdos* (*Kis Avas Elsősor 5*) is Miskolc's best restaurant, but it's really just a tarted-up Hungarian restaurant serving the same old things as far as I can tell. Go instead to the restaurant at the *Székelykert* pension (see Places to stay), which has Transylvanian specialities, dishes rarely encountered at restaurants in Hungary.

In Diósgyőr, the *Talizmán* (*Vár utca 14*) can be recommended for its menu and

pleasant location on a chestnut tree-lined pedestrian street just up from Diósgyőr Castle.

The *Capri* (*Széchenyi út 16*) is a decent enough cukrászda, but the best place for pastries in town is the unappetisingly named *Rétes Kék* cafe (*Blue Strudel; Városház tér*).

There is a large *produce market* (*Zsolcai kapu*) near Búza tér.

Entertainment

Plays and other performances are staged at the *National Theatre* (*☎ 344 711, Déryné utca 1*), where the beloved 19th-century actress Róza Széppataki Déryné walked the floorboards, and at the *Sándor Rónai Cultural Centre* (*☎ 342 485, Mindszent tér 3*). There are regular organ concerts at the baroque *Minorite church* (*Hősök tere*) built in 1734 and at the *Avas Calvinist Church*.

The *Radeberger* pub (*Déryné utca 8*) is popular among Miskolc students and a good place to meet people as is the *Western Kocsma* (*Kazinczy utca 1*). The *Rock Cellar Pub* (*Széchenyi utca 59*) is another likely choice and open till midnight Monday to Thursday, till 2 am Friday and Saturday.

Getting There & Away

Bus Some two dozen buses a day leave for Debrecen. If you're heading south, it is best to take the bus, though departures are infrequent (eg, there's only one bus daily to Békéscsaba and Gyula and two to Kecskemét). There are about 10 buses a day to Eger, but if you're travelling on a Sunday, be sure to take the one at 6.25 am or 3.15 pm. These buses follow the scenic route through the Bükk Hills via Felsőtárkány, which is an excellent starting point for more mountain walks.

Train Miskolc is served by hourly trains which depart from Budapest-Keleti, and some 15 depart for Nyíregyháza via Tokaj. Up to five of these trains carry on to Debrecen, but generally you'll have to change at Nyíregyháza. About a dozen trains leave Miskolc each day for Sárospatak and Sátoraljaújhely.

Daily international trains from Miskolc include those departing for Košice in Slovakia (four) and Kraków and Warsaw in Poland (two). For Oradea and Cluj-Napoca in Romania, you'll have to change at Püspökladány. For Lvov, Kiev and Moscow, change at Nyíregyháza or Debrecen.

Getting Around

Tram Nos 1 and 2 begin at the train station and travel the length of the city, including along Széchenyi út, before turning around in Diósgyőr. You can also reach Diósgyőr on the No 1 bus. To get to Miskolctapolca, board bus No 2 at Búza tér; bus No 12 is good for the university.

You can order a taxi by ringing ☎ 333 444.

AROUND MISKOLC
Miskolctapolca
☎ 46 • postcode 3519

The curative waters of the thermal spa in this south-western recreational suburb, past the university about 7km from Miskolc's city centre, have been attracting bathers since the Middle Ages, though the gimmicky **Cave Bath** (Barlangfürdő), Pazár István sétány 1, with its 'mildly radioactive waters' and thrashing shower at the end, are relatively new arrivals (1959). It is open from 9 am to 1 pm and 1.30 to 7 pm daily from April to September and from 9 am to 1 pm and 2 to 6 pm Tuesday to Sunday the rest of the year. Admission costs 460/580/400/800Ft in the morning/afternoon/after 4 pm/all day for adults and 250/300/250/680 for children. The pretty **park strand** in the centre of town has outside pools and a giant slide open from 9 am to 7 pm May to September (200/130Ft, 150/90Ft after 5 pm).

Éden Camping (☎/fax 368 917, Károlyi Mihály utca 1) has **bungalows** accommodating four people for 6000Ft to 8000Ft; it costs 600Ft to 700/500 per tent/person. The camping site is open from May to mid-October. Borsod Tourist (☎/fax 368 917), which has an office at Éden Camping, can book you a *private room* for 1500Ft per person, though there are signs offering them at private houses everywhere, eg, Görömbölyi út 15.

The 66-room *Park* hotel (☎ *360 811, fax 369 931, Csabai utca 35)* near the camping ground has basic rooms for 3800Ft and ones with facilities for 8000Ft. The 54-room *Lídó (☎/fax 369 800, Kiss József utca 4)*, relatively far from the action and in an unattractive bunker-like building, is even cheaper.

The top hotel here is the 96-room *Juno Viking (☎ 364 133, fax 360 420, Csabai utca 2-4)*, a modern glass-and-concrete structure with tennis courts and a well-equipped gym. Singles are DM45 to DM49 and doubles are DM56 to DM59, depending on the season.

The *Rózsakert* restaurant *(Aradi sétány)* is a decent place for a sit-down meal. The *Kupola* disco *(Aradi sétány)* above the entrance to the strand is a popular spot after dark.

Bus No 2 serves Miskolctapolca from Búza tér in Miskolc.

Lillafüred
☎ 46 • postcode 3517

At 320m above sea level, Lillafüred lies at the junction of two valleys formed by the Garadna and Szinva streams, 12km west of Miskolc. Lillafüred has been a resort since the early part of this century and 'sights' as such are few. But it is a pleasant break from Miskolc and the springboard for walks and hikes into the eastern Bükk Hills.

Some people travel to Lillafüred just to take the **narrow-gauge train** from Miskolc. It's one of the most enjoyable little train trips in Hungary and, as you loop through the forest, you can almost reach out and touch the beech and chestnut trees.

Caves There are three limestone caves in Lillafüred: **Anna Cave** (also known as Petőfi Cave) near the Palota hotel; **Szent István Cave** about 500m up the mountain road leading to Eger; and **Szeleta Cave** above the village on the road to Miskolc. The first two can be visited on one-hour guided tours from 9 am to 4 pm Tuesday to Sunday from mid-May to mid-October and till 4 pm the rest of the year (200/140Ft). Szent István has stalagmites, stalactites, sinkholes and large chambers, while Anna Cave has fossils: leaves, branches – even entire trees.

Hiking A number of beautiful walks can be undertaken from the terminuses of the two lines of the narrow-gauge train at **Garadna** and **Taksalápa**, but accommodation is sparse in these parts and hikers had better be prepared to camp rough if they miss the train. Be sure to have a copy of the northern Bükk map (No 29) from Cartographia and carry extra water.

There are *holiday houses* in Szentlélek (☎ *370 656*) and Bánkút (☎ *390 182*), west and south-west of Garadna, where you can spend the night before setting off for **Mt Bálvány** (956m). From Bánkút there are a number of excellent walks south to **Nagymező** and east to **Nagy Csipkés** (869m).

Hollóstető, 6km south of Lillafüred, is another good base for hikes and has a *camping ground* and the 11-room *Hollóstető* inn (☎ *390 163*). About 45 minutes to the east is Bükkszentkereszt, another quiet resort with excellent walks and both the 23-room *Bükk* inn (☎ *390 165, Őz utca 5*) and the 25-room *Gabona* hotel (☎/fax *390 115, Táncsics út 3*). Bükkszentlászló is about 1½ hours to the north. From here you can catch a bus back to Miskolc.

Boating Foundry Lake (Hámori-tó), named after the proto-blast furnace set up here by a German in the early 19th century to exploit the area's iron ore, offers fishing and boating (rowing boats 100/50Ft per half-hour for adults/children, paddle boats 400Ft per half-hour) on its jade-coloured water.

Places to Stay & Eat Apart from the options mentioned in the Hiking section, there are places to stay in Lillafüred itself. The town is dominated by the *Palota* (☎ *331 411*, fax *379 273*, @ reserve@hotelpalota .hungust.hu, *Erzsébet sétány 1*), an odd mock-Gothic structure that's a hotel again after a 40-year stint as a trade-union holiday home. Like it or not, the Palota has been synonymous with the town since 1930 when the 'haves' of Hungarian society would descend upon it for a summer of wining, dining and

dancing. Rates vary according to the season but singles are DM117 to DM158, doubles are DM129 to DM179. The hotel has two well-appointed restaurants, including the posh *Mátyás*, with stained-glass windows and enormous fireplace.

The *Lilla* pension (☎/fax *379 299*, *Erzsébet sétány 7*), in a park behind the Palota, has five doubles without bath for 4000Ft. Its tidy little restaurant with outside seating under the pines is a nice change from the grandeur of the Palota, and the staff are friendly.

There are several *food stalls* serving lángos and sausage near the narrow-gauge train station. The *Falatozó* bistro serves cheap, decent meals and has picnic tables. The *Tókert* restaurant next to the Palota overlooks the lake and has set lunches for 500Ft to 600Ft.

Getting There & Away You can reach Lillafüred by bus or the narrow-gauge train; if you're returning to Miskolc, take the bus up and the little train back. Bus No 1 from Miskolc terminates at Majális Park. Transfer here to bus No 5 or 15, which leaves every half-hour or so for Lillafüred. The No 15 continues on to Garadna, Ómassa, Szentlélek and Bánkút. Bus No 68 runs every half-hour between Újgyőri főtér on Andrássy utca west of Miskolc's centre and Bükkszentlászló.

Kilián-Észak train station, from where the little narrow-gauge train for Lillafüred departs, is off Kiss tábornok út in western Miskolc, almost in Diósgyőr. There are only a couple of weekday departures between October and the middle of April (twice that number in summer) and between six and eight at the weekend, so check the schedules carefully or call ☎ *370 663* for information. From Lillafüred, the train carries on another 6km to Garadna.

Another line of the narrow gauge branches off at Papírgyár – the paper factory that polluted the Szinva Stream – and covers the 20km between Kilián-Észak station and Taksalápa. The frequency of this underutilised line is now just one departure at the weekend between May and September (8.45 am out, 6 pm back).

Aggtelek Karst Region

If you thought the caves at Lillafüred were kid's stuff, head 60km north to Aggtelek National Park, a hilly karst region encompassing just under 20,000 hectares. The Baradla-Domica caves network is the largest stalactite system in Europe, with 25km of passageways (7km of them in Slovakia), and was declared a dual-nation Unesco World Heritage Site in 1995. The array of red and black stalactite drip stones, stalagmite pyramids and enormous chambers is astonishing and a must-see.

In the summer, a tour of the cave sections usually includes a short organ recital in the Concert Chamber and, if the water is high enough, a boat ride on the 'Styx', an underground stream. The lighting is quite effective, and you won't have difficulty recognising the odd formations of dragons, tortoises, xylophones and the like, which your guide will point out.

AGGTELEK
☎ 48 • postcode 3759 • pop 650

There are three entrances to the Baradla Cave system – at Aggtelek village; at Jósvafő, 6km to the east; and at Vörös-tó (Red Lake), just before Jósvafő. The entrance to what is called Jaský Na Domica (Domica Cave) in Slovak is across the border, a couple of kilometres to the north-west in Slovakia. Guided tours of the Baradla Cave system depart from these four points, but the most popular short and long tours can be joined at the Aggtelek entrance, where you should start.

Orientation & Information
In Aggtelek, the staff at the Naturinform office (☎ 343 029), Baradla oldal 1, at the small museum near the cave ticket office can supply you with information and sell you a copy of *Aggteleki-karszt és környéke* (Aggtelek Karst & Surrounds) map (No 1; 400Ft), an excellent 1:40,000 hiking map from Cartographia. For more detailed information, contact the Aggtelek National Park Directorate (☎/fax 350 006, ✆ info.anp@ mail.matav.hu), Tengerszem oldal 1, 3758 Jósvafő.

The post office in Aggtelek (Kossuth utca 37-39 has an ATM. You can change money at the Cseppkő hotel (see Places to Stay).

Baradla Cave
The cave is open all year – from 8 am to 6 pm from April to September (last tour: 5 pm) and to 4 pm the rest of the year (last tour: 3 pm). Tours depart even with one participant. Students with an international ID pay 50% of the admission fee and children under six go free.

Tours lasting about one hour (1km; 600Ft) start at the Aggtelek entrance at 10 am, 1 and 3 pm with an additional tour at 5 pm from April to September. A one-hour tour (450Ft) that covers 1.5km of a different section is also available from the Jósvafő entrance near the Tengerszem hotel, Tengerszem oldal 2, at noon and 5 pm from April to September and at 10 am and 3 pm the rest of the year.

A two-hour 'middle tour' of the Jósvafő section (2.5km; 750Ft) departs at 9 am and 1 and 2.50 pm in high season and at noon the rest of the year from the Vörös-tó entrance and ends at the one in Jósvafő. You can also buy a reduced-price ticket that combines the Aggtelek short and the Jósvafő middle tours over two days (3.5km; 1000Ft). A bus (six or seven a day) will take you from just outside the Cseppkő hotel in Aggtelek to the Jósvafő entrance via Vörös-tó. The temperature at this level is usually about 10°C with humidity over 95%, so be sure to bring a sweater along.

Serious spelunkers will be tempted by the two five-hour tours (3200Ft and 4000Ft) that each take in different 7km sections of the cave and must be booked in advance through the park directorate one month in advance. Participants should wear boots and helmets and dress warmly; they will be issued battery-powered torches. You must seek special permission from the directorate to explore the Béke and Szabadság caves to the south-east.

A small **museum** near the Aggtelek entrance to the cave has exhibits dealing with the flora and fauna of the karst caves and surrounding countryside.

Other Activities

You can join up with some excellent hiking trails above the Naturinform office in - Aggtelek, affording superb views of the rolling hills and valleys. A relatively easy 1½-hour walk along the blue trail will take you from Aggtelek to Jósvafő. There's a 20km bicycle route linking Aggtelek and Szögliget to the north-east. The Hucul Stud (Hucul Ménes) in Jósvafő has horses for hire (800Ft per hour) and offers hour-long carriage and, in winter, sledge (sleigh) rides for 1500Ft.

The park directorate organises a number of programs, including two and three-hour guided walks in Aggtelek and Jósvafő (400Ft each) as well as a number of themed tours of the national park lasting three to six hours – from ecology (600Ft to 1200Ft) to zoology and botany (1500Ft to 3000Ft).

Special Events

Main events in Aggtelek and vicinity are the International Choir Festival (Nemzetközi Kórustalálkozó) in Baradla Cave in late June, the Baradla Cultural Days (Baradla Művészeti Napok) in late July and the Autumn Festival (Őszi Fesztivál) in late September. Mountaineering Days (Hegymászó Találkozó) in late August attract climbers from all over Hungary.

Places to Stay & Eat

Baradla Camping (☎ 343 073, Baradla oldal 1), where you can pitch a tent (500Ft plus another 500Ft per person) or rent a four-person bungalow for 800Ft to 850Ft per person, is next to the Aggtelek cave entrance. Accommodation in the attached *hostel (☎ same)*, with rooms of between two and four beds, costs 1200Ft per person (1050Ft for adults). The camping site is open from mid-April to mid-October, the hostel year round.

The 70-room *Cseppkő (☎ 343 075, fax 343 026, Gyömrői út 2)*, on a scenic hill above the entrance to the cave, is the only hotel in Aggtelek and has a restaurant, bar, terrace with splendid views, tennis court and sauna/solarium. Doubles are about 6000Ft.

If you intend to join cave tours at both the Aggtelek and Jósvafő entrances, you may consider staying at the renovated, 22-room *Tengerszem* hotel *(☎ 350 006, fax 350 098, Tengerszem oldal 2)* in Jósvafő, which has singles/doubles/triples with shower for 4000/6000/7500Ft. '

There are a number of *food stalls* in the car park near the cave entrance in Aggtelek as well as the *Szikla-kert* (Rock Garden) restaurant at the entrance itself.

Getting There & Away

Direct buses link Aggtelek with Budapest and Miskolc as well as Eger and Gyöngyös. They leave for Budapest Népstadion twice daily at 5.30 am and 3.55 pm (with an additional bus at 4.20 pm Friday to Sunday) and for Miskolc twice a day at 3.50 and 5 pm.

Aggtelek can also be reached from Miskolc (1½ hours) on between five and seven trains a day – you want the one heading for Tornanádaska. The Jósvafő-Aggtelek train station is some 14km east of Jósvafő (and 20km from Aggtelek village); a local bus meets each of the trains to take you to either town.

Zemplén Hills

The Zemplén region is not uniform. On the southern and eastern slopes are the market towns and vineyards of the Tokaj-Hegyalja region. The wine trade attracted Greek, Serbian, Slovak, Polish, Russian and German merchants, and their influence can be felt in the area's architecture, culture and wine to this day. The northern Zemplén on the border with Slovakia is the nation's 'wildest' region and is full of castle ruins and dusty one-horse towns.

BOLDOGKŐVÁRALJA

☎ 46 • postcode 3885 • pop 1150

The train linking Szerencs (on the main Budapest-Miskolc-Nyíregyháza trunk line) with Hidasnémeti, near the Slovakian border, stops at more than a dozen wine-producing towns as it wends its way some 50km up the picturesque Hernád Valley. Some of the towns, such as Tállya and Gönc, are interesting in themselves, while others serve as starting points for forays into the southern Zemplén Hills. But not one combines the two so well as Boldogkőváralja, a charming village with an important castle.

Orientation

Heading north from Szerencs, make sure you sit on the right-hand side of the train to see Boldogkőváralja's dramatic castle as it comes into view. The train stops on the other side of the highway about some 2.5km west of the castle. You can follow the surfaced road to the left or climb any of the steep trails up from the village to reach the castle's main entrance.

Boldogkő Castle

Perched atop a basalt mountain, 'Happy Rock' Castle commands a splendid 360° view of the southern Zemplén Hills, the Hernád Valley and nearby vineyards. Originally built in the 13th century, the castle was strengthened 200 years later but gradually fell into ruin after the kuruc revolt late in the 17th century.

There's a tiny **museum** here with exhibits explaining who was who and what was what and lots of medieval weapons, but walking through the uneven courtyard up onto the ramparts and looking out over the surrounding countryside in the late afternoon is much more satisfying. It's easy to see how the swashbuckling lyric poet Bálint Balassi (1554-94) came to love this place and produced some of his finest work here. The castle is open from 9 am to 6 pm mid-April to mid-October (150/100Ft).

Regional History Museum

This little exhibit at Kossuth Lajos utca 32 has some interesting items devoted to Balassi and local sons and daughters who made it good overseas (one set up the first Hungarian-language newspaper in the USA), as well as a display of folk dress and a fully

equipped smithy regional history. It is open from 10 am to 4 pm on Friday, Saturday and Sunday from May to October (70/50Ft).

Hiking

Marked trails lead from the castle's northern side to **Regéc**, about 15km to the northeast via Arka and Mogyoróska, skirting mountains and 14th-century castle ruins along the way. From here you can either retrace your steps to Boldogkőváralja or follow the road westward to the Fony train stop (six trains a day in each direction) about 10km away.

The hardy and/or prepared may want to carry on another 8km north to **Gönc**, a pretty town where the special barrels used to age Tokaj wine have been made for centuries. Gönc is on the main train line back to Szerencs. Depending on which way you're hiking, make sure you're armed with the north (No 22) or south (No 23) section of the *Zempléni-hegység* (Zemplén Hills) 1:40,000 map (400Ft each).

Places to Stay & Eat

The *Tekerjes* inn (☎ 387 732, fax 387 742, *Kossuth Lajos utca 41*) has eight very basic rooms that cost a rock-bottom 540Ft per person, but it's open from mid-April to October only. Another option is the old *Parasztház (Peasant House; ☎ 387 730)*, a traditional little farmhouse for rent (May to mid-October) near the history museum at Kossuth Lajos utca 75. The house at Major utca 4 nearby has *private rooms*.

Aside from the restaurant at the *Tekerjes*, the only other place for a sit-down meal is the *Bodókő (Kossuth Lajos utca)* near the road to the castle. The *Alagút Büfé* in the castle has the usual basic snacks. A cukrászda called *Pözsi Néni (Kossuth Lajos utca 15)* near the village centre has cakes and ice cream.

Getting There & Away

Boldogkőváralja is on the train line connecting Szerencs with Hidasnémeti, and six trains per day in each direction stop at the town. Only one of these is direct; the rest require a change (no wait) at Abaújszántó.

TOKAJ

☎ 47 • postcode 3910 • pop 5350

The wines of Tokaj, a picturesque little town of vineyards and nesting storks in the south-eastern corner of the Zemplén region, have been celebrated for centuries. Tokaj is, in fact, just one of 28 towns and villages of the Tokaj-Hegyalja, a 6600-hectare vine-growing region that produces wine along the southern and eastern edges of the Zemplén Hills. For more information on Tokaj wines, see the Wines of Hungary special section in the Facts for the Visitor chapter.

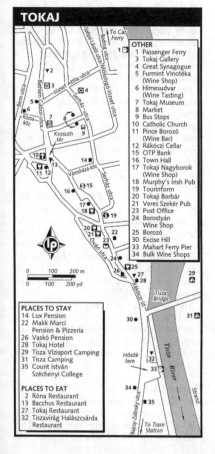

TOKAJ

OTHER
1 Passenger Ferry
3 Tokaj Gallery
4 Great Synagogue
5 Furmint Vinotéka (Wine Shop)
6 Hímesudvar (Wine Tasting)
7 Tokaj Museum
8 Market
9 Bus Stops
10 Catholic Church
11 Pince Borozó (Wine Bar)
12 Rákóczi Cellar
15 OTP Bank
16 Town Hall
17 Tokaji Nagyborok (Wine Shop)
18 Murphy's Irish Pub
19 Tourinform
20 Tokaji Borbár
21 Veres Szekér Pub
23 Post Office
24 Borostyán Wine Shop
25 Borozó
30 Excise Hill
33 Mahart Ferry Pier
34 Bulk Wine Shops

PLACES TO STAY
14 Lux Pension
22 Makk Marci Pension & Pizzeria
26 Vaskó Pension
28 Tokaj Hotel
29 Tisza Vízisport Camping
31 Tisza Camping
35 Count István Széchenyi College

PLACES TO EAT
2 Róna Restaurant
13 Bacchus Restaurant
27 Tokaj Restaurant
32 Tiszavirág Halászcsárda Restaurant

Orientation & Information

Tokaj's centre lies west of where the Bodrog and Tisza Rivers meet. The train station is south of the town centre at the end of Baross Gábor utca; you can wait for a bus, but it's only a 15-minute walk north along Baross Gábor utca and Bajcsy-Zsilinszky utca to the main thoroughfare, Rákóczi út. Intercity buses arrive and depart from along Serház utca east of Kossuth tér. The main stop is in front of house No 30.

The helpful Tourinform office (☎ 353 390, fax 352 323, ℮ tokaj@tourinform.hu), Serház utca 1, is open from 9 am to 5 pm on weekdays and till 1 pm on Saturday. The OTP bank branch is at Rákóczi út 35, the main post office at No 24 of the same street.

Things to See

The **Tokaj Museum**, in the 18th-century Greek Trading House (Görög Kereskedő Haza) at Bethlen Gábor utca 7, leaves nothing unsaid about the history of Tokaj, the Tokaj-Hegyalja region and the production of its wines.

Particularly interesting are the exhibits showing French, Italian, American and South African attempts to duplicate Tokaj wine; the Alsatian variety is said to be closest to the real thing.

There's also a superb collection of liturgical art, including icons, medieval crucifixes and triptychs and Judaica from the Great Synagogue. The museum is open from 9 am to 5 pm Tuesday to Sunday from May to November (200/100Ft).

Just up the road, in an 18th-century Greek Orthodox church at Bethlen Gábor utca 15, the **Tokaj Gallery** exhibits works by local artists; the carved wooden pulpit is the best thing inside. It is open from 10 am to 4 pm Tuesday to Sunday from April to September (free).

Behind the gallery on Serház utca, the 19th-century **Great Synagogue**, which was used as a German barracks during WWII, is once again boarded up and falling into ruin after a partial renovation in 1992. There's a large **Orthodox Jewish cemetery** in Bodrogkeresztúr, 6km north-west of Tokaj.

NORTHERN UPLANDS

Wine Tasting

The **Rákóczi Cellar** at Kossuth tér 15, a 600-year-old cellar where bottles of wine mature in long corridors (one measures 28m by 10m), has tastings of six Tokaj wines (1200Ft per person) from 10 am to 7 or 8 pm daily from April to October. Local people say the best commercial place to taste Tokaj wines is the **Hímesudvar**, a wine cellar and shop at Bem utca 2. There are also private cellars (*pincék*) throughout town that offer a more relaxed atmosphere, including those at Rákóczi út 2, 6 & 8; Óvári utca 36, 40 & 54; and Bem József utca 2. Don't be intimidated if the cellars appear locked up tight; just ring the bell and someone will appear.

Start with 100 mL glasses; you may swallow more than you think. If you're serious, the correct order of sampling Tokaj wines is: Furmint, dry Szamorodni, sweet Szamorodni and then the Aszú wines – from three to five or four to six puttonyos.

If you prefer your wine ladled in decilitre measures the **Pince Borozó** around the corner from the Rákóczi Cellar can oblige daily from 9 am to 7 pm as can the very ordinary little *borozó* at Rákóczi út 7.

You can see traditional *kádárok* (coopers) still at work at Rákóczi út 18 and 30 and at József Attila utca 12 near the Great Synagogue.

Other Activities

In summer, water tours of the Bodrog and Tisza Rivers are available from the Mahart ferry pier at Hősök tere near the Tiszavirág Halászcsárda restaurant. Contact the Unió Foundation (☎/fax 352 927), Bodrogkresztúri út 5, about canoe and kayak rentals. You could also just cross over the Tisza Bridge to the grassy riverfront beach for a lazy afternoon of sunning and swimming in the river.

Kopasz-hegy (Bald Mountain) and its TV tower west of the town centre offer a stunning panorama of Tokaj and the surrounding vineyards, but the less ambitious will be content with the easy climb up Fináncdomb (Excise Hill) on Rákóczi út opposite Tisza Bridge.

Special Events

The Tokaj Wine Festival (Tokaji Borfesztivál), held in early August, attracts oenophiles from far and wide as do the Vintage Days (Szüreti Napok) in early October.

Places to Stay

Tisza Camping (☎ 352 012, *Tisza-part*), across the river and just south of the bridge, has *bungalows* for 1200Ft per person. It also has its own restaurant, boat rentals and beach. *Tisza Vízisport Camping* (☎ 352 645), on the northern side of the bridge, has similar accommodation for 1000Ft per person and rents kayaks and canoes. Both are open April to September or October, but be warned: they can be plagued by mosquitoes. The *Count István Széchenyi College* (☎ 352 555, *Bajcsy-Zsilinszky utca 15-17*) has at least a few beds in dormitory rooms available throughout the year for 850Ft per person.

Private rooms (1500Ft per person) are available from Tourinform and directly throughout Tokaj: just watch out for the signs along Óvári utca (Nos 6, 46 & 48), Bem József utca and Bethlen Gábor utca (Nos 10, 20, 20/a & 49). Rooms on offer along Hegyalja utca (eg, No 23) are convenient to the train station and are surrounded by vineyards.

The three-room *Vaskó* pension (☎ 352 107, Rákóczi út 12) is as central as you can get and has doubles for 4400Ft. The *Makk Marci* pension (☎ 352 336, fax 353 088, Liget köz 1), has seven rooms, all with shower, that cost the same. The friendly *Lux* pension (☎ 352 145, fax 352 533, Serház utca 14) is a little more expensive, with doubles at 4750Ft.

The only hotel in Tokaj is the 42-room *Tokaj* (☎ 352 344, fax 352 759, Rákóczi út 5), where the two rivers meet. Doubles with bath are 5950Ft though a row of badly ventilated rooms with showers on the 4th floor cost less.

Places to Eat

The *Tiszavirág Halászcsárda* (*Bajcsy-Zsilinszky utca*) serves decent fish soup and a lot of scaly things from the Tisza. The pizzeria at the *Makk Marci* is open till

10 pm and is a friendly place for a quick bite. For something more Hungarian try the simple *Bacchus (Kossuth tér 17)* under the lindens in the town centre (mains 350Ft to 650Ft).

The *Tokaj* restaurant *(Rákóczi út 3)*, part of the Tokaj hotel, is a pleasant enough place – if somewhat pricey (fish dishes from 680Ft to 1550Ft). If you sit on the terrace be sure to have plenty of insect repellent handy. *Róna (Bethlen Gábor utca 19)* has a varied menu of fish dishes (500Ft to 950Ft) and is open to 9 pm.

Entertainment

Should you get tired of all that wine, there are a couple of pubs to turn your head – or lips – to beer, including the *Veres Szekér (Rákóczi út 30-32)*, a congenial pub in a little courtyard open daily till 2 am, and (it had to happen) *Murphy's Ír Söröző (Rákóczi út 42)*, the first 'Irish pub' in the Zemplén.

There's a *fruit & vegetable market (Szépessi köz)* just east of the Tokaj Museum.

Shopping

Wine, wine and more wine – from a 10L plastic jug of new Furmint to a bottle of six-puttony Aszú – is available in shops and cellars throughout Tokaj. Buy bulk wines (160Ft to 200Ft a litre) along Bajcsy-Zsilinszky utca and at the Tokaji Borbár at Rákóczi út 36. Just make sure it's corked tightly if pulled from a cellar cask. For a better choice of bottled wines, try the shop at the Rákóczi Pince at Kossuth tér 15, the Tokaji Nagyborok shop at Rákóczi tér 44, the Borostyán wine shop at Rákóczi út 11 or the Furmint Vinotéka, with both folk art and wine for sale, at Bethlen Gábor utca 14.

Getting There & Away

Seven buses a day go to Szerencs, the chocolate capital of Hungary, but it's just as easy to get there by train. Up to 14 trains a day connect Tokaj with Miskolc and Nyíregyháza; change at the latter for Debrecen. To travel north to Sárospatak and Sátoraljaújhely, take the Miskolc-bound train and change at Mezőzombor.

SÁROSPATAK
☎ 47 • postcode 3950 • pop 15,000

While not the gateway to the northern Zemplén that it may appear to be on the map, the town of 'Muddy Stream' is renowned for its college and castle, the finest example of a Renaissance fort extant in Hungary. Sárospatak is also a convenient stop en route to Slovakia.

Sárospatak has played a much greater role in Hungarian history than its diminutive size would suggest. A wealthy, wine-producing free royal town since the early 15th century, it soon became a centre of Calvinist power and scholarship and 200 years later was the focal point for Hungarian resistance to the Habsburgs. The alumni of its Calvinist college, which helped earn Sárospatak the nickname the 'Athens of Hungary', read like a who's who of Hungarian literary and political history and include the patriot Lajos Kossuth, the poet Mihály Csokonai Vitéz and the novelist Géza Gárdonyi.

Orientation & Information

Sárospatak is a compact city lying on the snaking Bodrog River and its attractive backwaters. The bus and train stations are cheek-by-jowl at the end of Táncsics Mihály utca, north-west of the city centre. Walk east through shady Iskola Park to join up with Rákóczi út, the main thoroughfare.

Tourinform (☎ 315 316, fax 315 317, @ sarospatak@tourinform.hu), in the Sárospatak Cultural Centre at Eötvös utca 6, is open from 8 am to 4 pm weekdays and may keep Saturday morning hours in summer. Ibusz (☎/fax 311 244), Rákóczi út 29, opens from 8 am to 4 pm weekdays (till 6 pm in summer and on Saturday till noon). There's an OTP bank branch at Eötvös utca 3; the main post office is at Rákóczi út 45, near Béla király tér.

Rákóczi Castle

This castle, which you may recognise from the verso of the 500Ft note, should be your first port of call; enter the Várkert (Castle Garden) by crossing over the dry moat at the southern end of Rákóczi út or from

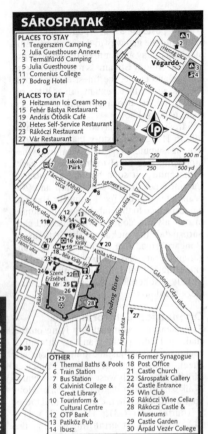

SÁROSPATAK

PLACES TO STAY
1 Tengerszem Camping
2 Julia Guesthouse Annexe
3 Termálfürdő Camping
5 Julia Guesthouse
11 Comenius College
17 Bodrog Hotel

PLACES TO EAT
9 Heitzmann Ice Cream Shop
15 Fehér Bástya Restaurant
19 András Ötödik Café
20 Hetes Self-Service Restaurant
23 Rákóczi Restaurant
27 Vár Restaurant

OTHER
4 Thermal Baths & Pools
6 Train Station
7 Bus Station
8 Calvinist College & Great Library
10 Tourinform & Cultural Centre
12 OTP Bank
13 Patikköz Pub
14 Ibusz
16 Former Synagogue
18 Post Office
21 Castle Church
22 Sárospatak Gallery
24 Castle Entrance
25 Win Club
26 Rákóczi Wine Cellar
28 Rákóczi Castle & Museums
29 Castle Garden
30 Árpád Vezér College

Szent Erzsébet utca. Although the oldest part of the castle, the renovated five-storey **Red Tower**, dates from the late 15th century, the Renaissance **palace** was built in the following century and later enlarged by its most famous owners, the Rákóczis of Transylvania. They held it until 1711 when Ferenc Rákóczi II's aborted independence war against the Habsburgs drove him into exile in Turkey and put the castle in the hands of Austrian aristocrats.

Today the Renaissance wings of the palace and the 19th-century additions contain the **Rákóczi Museum** devoted to the uprising and

the castle's later occupants, with bedrooms and dining halls overflowing with period furniture, tapestries, porcelain and glass. Of special interest is the small, five-windowed bay room on the 1st floor near the Knights' Hall with its stucco rose in the middle of a vaulted ceiling. It was here that nobles put their names *sub rosa* (literally 'under the rose' in Latin) to the kuruc uprising against the Habsburg emperor in 1670. The expression, which means 'in secret', is thought to have originated here. You should also look out for the **Fireplace Hall** with its superb Renaissance hearth, and, outside in the courtyard, the so-called **Lorántffy Gallery**, a 17th-century loggia linking the east palace wing with the Red Tower. It's straight out of *Romeo and Juliet*.

The casemates of the Italian Bastion (Olászbástya) contain a small **Wax Museum** focusing on Hungarian royalty and an exhibit in the cellars of the east wing is devoted to the history of wine and wine-making in the surrounding Tokaj-Hegyalja region.

The castle is open from 10 am to 6 pm Tuesday to Sunday from April to October and till 5 pm the rest of the year (300/150Ft).

Other Attractions

The **Castle Church** (Vártemplom) north of the castle on Szent Erzsébet utca, is one of Hungary's largest Gothic hall churches (those within castle walls) and has flip-flopped from serving Catholics to Protestants and back many times since the 14th century. The enormous baroque altar was moved here from the Carmelite church in Buda Castle late in the 18th century; the 200-year-old organ from Kassa (now Košice in Slovakia) is still used for concerts throughout the year. The statue by Imre Varga outside the church depicts the much revered St Elizabeth, a 13th-century queen of Hungary who was born in Sárospatak, riding side-saddle, and her husband Louis IV on foot. The church can be visited from 9 am to 5 pm Tuesday and Saturday and from noon to 4 pm on Sunday (50/20Ft).

To the south-west of the church on Szent Erzsébet utca is the **Sárospatak Gallery**, which displays the work of the sculptor János Andrássy Kurta along with some temporary exhibits. It is open from 10 am to 4 pm Tuesday to Sunday.

The history of the celebrated **Calvinist College**, at Rákóczi út 1, is told in words and displays at the **Comenius Memorial Museum** in the last of the college's original buildings, an 18th-century physics classroom. The collection is named after János Amos Comenius, a Moravian humanist who organised the education system here late in the 17th century and wrote the world's first illustrated textbook for children, *Orbis Pictus* (World in Pictures). Many of the college's illustrious pupils are quoted at some point during the exhibit, including the novelist Zsigmond Móricz who recalled his 'dog-difficult days at the Patak College'.

The main reason for visiting the college, though, is its 75,000-volume **Great Library** in the main building, a long oval-shaped hall with a gallery and a trompe l'oeil ceiling simulating the inside of a cupola. The college is open from 9 am to 5 pm Monday to Saturday, 9 am to 1 pm on Sunday. Guided tours of the library leave on the hour. Tickets are available from room No 6 on the ground floor.

The former **synagogue** at Rákóczi út 43, near the post office, is now a furniture store. Almost all of the 1200 Jews living in Sárospatak before the war died in Nazi concentration camps.

Sárospatak counts a number of buildings designed by the 'organic' architect Imre Makovecz, including the cultural centre on Eötvös utca, the Hild Udvar shopping complex on Béla Király tér and the cathedral-like Árpád Vezér College on Arany János utca. Some people think they're beginning to look pretty dated.

Wine Tasting

The **Rákóczi Wine Cellar**, just south of the Sárospatak Gallery at Szent Erzsébet utca 26 and originally built in 1684, offers wine tastings from 8 am to 6 pm weekdays and 10 am to 8 pm at the weekend from May to September and from 8 am to 4 pm weekdays the rest of the year. They take place in groups on the hour and cost 400/600/770/1000/1200Ft for one/three/four/five/six wines.

Other Activities

The thermal baths and pools in the Végardó recreational complex about 2km north-east of the centre are open 10 am to 6 pm daily from May to September. Entry costs 200/120Ft; after 2 pm it's 50Ft cheaper.

Special Events

Saint Elizabeth Days (Szent Erzsébet Napok) is a popular weekend festival in late May in the castle and castle quarter. Sárospatak hosts some of the events of the Zemplén Arts Days (Zempléni Művészeti Napok) in late August along with Sátoraljaújhely, Serencs and Füzér.

Places to Stay

Termálfürdő Camping (☎ 311 510, Határ utca 2/b), near the thermal spa in Végardó, charges 500/750Ft for a tent/caravan and adults/children pay 650/400Ft each. *Bungalows* for four cost 4800Ft. It's open May to September. *Tengerszem Camping* (☎ 312 744, Herceg utca 2), a much nicer site opposite the baths, charges 500/750/150 per tent/caravan/car. Its 10 *bungalows* for two/four people cost 3800/5200Ft (open April to October).

Dormitory rooms are available in summer at the cultural centre's *Youth Camp* (*Ifjúsági Tábor;* ☎ 311 811, Eötvös utca 6) for 550Ft per person. Accommodation at the *Comenius College* (☎ 312 211, Eötvös utca 5-7) is a lot more expensive – 3400/4500 for doubles/quads – but much more comfortable. Tourinform and Ibusz can organise *private rooms* for 1500Ft and 2000Ft per person.

The *Júlia* (☎/fax 312 871, Határ utca 6) is a comfortable, friendly guesthouse but a bit far from whatever action Sárospatak has to offer. Doubles are 3500Ft. If they're full, they may put you up in their annexe at Herceg utca 5, which has two large *apartments* costing 4000Ft.

The *Bodrog* (☎ 311 744, fax 311 527, Rákóczi út 58) is a charmless, four-storey block with 49 rooms in the centre of town. It charges 5400Ft to 7900Ft for singles and 6000Ft to 8600Ft for doubles. All rooms have shower or bath and air-conditioning, and there's a big restaurant and a beer bar.

Places to Eat

The **Hetes** *(Kossuth Lajos utca 57)* is a cheap, self-service restaurant open 10 am to 3 pm on weekdays.

The **Fehér Bástya** *(Rákóczi út 39)* is an intimate little Hungarian restaurant with mains for 420Ft to 850Ft, but an even better central choice is the **Rákóczi** restaurant *(Szent Erzsébet utca 4)*, which has tables both in a cellar and, in warmer months, a back courtyard. Main courses average around 650Ft.

The **Vár** *(Árpád utca 35)*, across the Bodrog and opposite the castle, remains my favourite restaurant in Sárospatak. Try one of its specialities (most mains under 1000Ft, fish dishes around 1500Ft) like *harcsagulyás* (catfish goulash) with pasta and *túrós* (curds) – better than it sounds.

The **Heitzmann** ice-cream shop *(Rákóczi út 16/a)* has lickers lining up all day (open 9 am to 5 pm Tuesday to Sunday). Try *András Ötödik (Béla király tér 3)* for cakes.

Entertainment

The staff at the anthropomorphic-looking *Sárospatak Cultural Centre* (☎ *311 811, Eötvös utca 6)*, designed by Imre Makovecz in 1983, will fill you in on what's on in town. Be sure to ask about organ concerts at the **Castle Church** or **castle courtyard**.

Popular places after dark in Sárospatak are the **Win Club** *(Szent Erzsébet utca 22)* and the **Patiköz** pub *(Patika köz 5)*, open till 11 pm nightly.

Getting There & Away

Bus Most of the southern Zemplén region is not easily accessible by bus from Sárospatak, though there is one bus a day to the pretty village of Erdőbénye, from where you can connect to Baskó and Boldogkőváralja. Other destinations include Debrecen (two daily buses), Kisvárda (one), Miskolc (one or two), Nyíregyháza (two), Sátoraljaújhely (hourly) and Tokaj (two). Buses to Debrecen, Nyíregyháza and Miskolc can be boarded just outside the Bodrog department store on Rákóczi út; catch the bus to Sátoraljaújhely on the other side of the street.

Train To explore the southern Zemplén, you'd do better to take one of six daily trains up the Hernád Valley from Szerencs and use one of the towns along that line such as Abaújkér, Boldogkőváralja or Korlát-Vizsoly as your base. For the northern Zemplén, take a train or bus (hourly) to Sátoraljaújhely.

Up to 10 daily trains connect Sárospatak and Sátoraljaújhely with Miskolc, and a couple of those continue on to Slovenské Nové Mesto in Slovakia, from where you can board a train to Košice. If you are coming from Debrecen, Nyíregyháza or Tokaj, change trains at Mezőzombor.

Getting Around

Hourly buses link the bus and train stations and the Bodrog shopping centre on Rákóczi út with the Végardó recreational centre to the north. You can order a taxi on ☎ 311 744.

SÁTORALJAÚJHELY

☎ 47 • postcode 3980 • pop 19,000

Sátoraljaújhely, 12km north of Sárospatak, fell into the hands of the Rákóczi family in the 17th century (they lived on Kazinczy utca) and, like the family's base, Sárospatak, the city played an important role in the struggle for independence from Austria. It was not the last time the city would be a battleground. In 1919, fighting took place in the nearby hills and ravines between communist partisans and Slovaks, and once again in the closing days of WWII.

Today Sátoraljaújhely (roughly translated as 'tent camp new place' and pronounced 'shah-toor-all-ya-oy-hay') is a quiet frontier town surrounded by forests and vineyards and dominated by 514m Magas-hegy (Tall Mountain). Though definitely not worth a visit in itself, Sátoraljaújhely is a good base for trekking into the northern Zemplén Hills and for crossing the border into Slovakia.

Orientation & Information

The bus and train stations sit side by side a kilometre south of the city centre. From there, follow Fasor utca north to Kossuth Lajos utca, past the overgrown Jewish cemetery

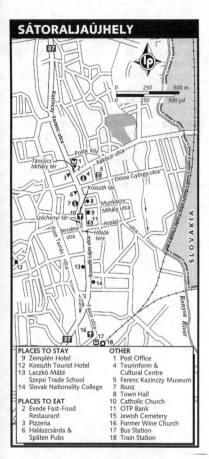

SÁTORALJAÚJHELY

PLACES TO STAY	OTHER
9 Zemplén Hotel	1 Post Office
12 Kossuth Tourist Hotel	4 Tourinform &
13 Laczkó Máté	Cultural Centre
Szepsi Trade School	5 Ferenc Kazinczy Museum
14 Slovak Nationality College	7 Ibusz
	8 Town Hall
PLACES TO EAT	10 Catholic Church
2 Evede Fast-Food	11 OTP Bank
Restaurant	15 Jewish Cemetery
3 Pizzeria	16 Former Wine Church
6 Halászcsárda &	17 Bus Station
Späten Pubs	18 Train Station

an OTP bank branch at Széchenyi tér 13. For the post office, go to Kazinczy utca 10.

Things to See

The decrepit neo-Gothic former **Wine Church** (Bortemplom), with seals of the Tokaj-Hegyalja towns in Zsolnay porcelain decorating its sides, greets you upon arrival at the bus or train station. Don't expect much from this Frankenstein's castle; it's now just used to store wine in cellars below.

The baroque **Catholic church** (1792) at Széchenyi tér 10, with its stark interior, is not very interesting in itself, though it was here that the teachings of Martin Luther were first read aloud in public in Hungary. The same can be said for the **town hall** at Kossuth tér 5, but it too is remembered for a momentous event. In 1830, then-lawyer Lajos Kossuth gave his first public speech from the balcony looking down onto the square.

The **Ferenc Kazinczy Museum** at Dózsa György utca 11, covers the history of the city, with emphasis on the Rákóczi family, as well as the natural history of the Zemplén region. The museum is named after the 19th-century language reformer and patriot who did much of his research at the Zemplén Archives (today's town hall) from 1815 to 1831, It is open 8 am to 4 pm Monday to Saturday (200/100Ft).

Places to Stay & Eat

Accommodation is available in summer at two colleges south of the centre: the *Laczkó Máté Szepsi Trade School* (☎ 322 244, Kossuth Lajos utca 26) for 850Ft per person and at the *Slovak Nationality College* (☎ 322 568, Kossuth Lajos utca 31) almost opposite for 600Ft. Tourinform and Ibusz can organise *private rooms* for 1200Ft and 1500Ft respectively. The 22-room *Kossuth Tourist Hotel* (☎ 370 550, fax 370 059, Török utca 1) is a very basic affair and a bit far out but cheap.

The 30-room *Zemplén* hotel (☎ 322 255, fax 322 522, Széchenyi tér 5-7), is an unattractive block sitting atop a supermarket, but as central as you'll find here. Singles/doubles start at 3000/4000Ft; a larger 'suite' is 500Ft more.

and Hősök tere, and continue until you reach Széchenyi tér. Two more squares follow – Kossuth tér and Táncsics Mihály tér – and then Kazinczy utca. Slovakia comes next.

A Tourinform office (☎/fax 321 458, ✉ satoraljaujhely@tourinform.hu) shares a building with the Lajos Kossuth Cultural Centre in a courtyard at Táncsics Mihály tér 3. It is open from 8.30 am to 5 pm Monday to Friday and from 8 am to noon on Saturday May to September, weekdays only the rest of the year. Ibusz (☎/fax 321 757), Kossuth tér 26, is open from 7.30 am to 4.30 pm on weekdays, till noon on Saturday. There's

For something quick try the little no-name *pizzeria (Kazinczy utca 1)*, open daily till 9 pm. The *Evede* fast-food restaurant *(Kazinczy utca 8)* serves burgers and 'real gyros' Monday to Saturday till 8 pm. The *Halászcsárda* and the *Späten*, sitting side by side at Kossuth tér 10, offer fish dishes and Hungarian pub grub – in that order – for under 500Ft.

Getting There & Away

There are frequent buses to the towns and villages of the northern Zemplén Hills, including four on weekdays (two at the weekend) to Füzér, up to 10 on weekdays (four at the weekend) to Hollóháza, one to Telkibánya and one to Hidasnémeti, from where you can pick up trains north to the Slovakian city of Košice, south to Miskolc, or to Szerencs and the towns along the western edge of the Zemplén.

Some 10 trains a day link Sátoraljaújhely with Sárospatak and Miskolc; two of them cross the border with Slovakia at Slovenské Nové Mesto, where you can catch a train to Košice. If you are approaching Sátoraljaújhely from the south or east (Debrecen, say, or Nyíregyháza or Tokaj), you must change at Mezőzombor.

North-East

On the map, Hungary's north-east corner may appear to be a coextension of the Northern Uplands or even the Great Plain. But it is so different physically, culturally and historically from both of those regions that most consider it a separate area. Essentially North-East Hungary encompasses just one county (Szabolcs-Szatmár-Bereg) and is bordered by Slovakia, Ukraine and Romania.

The North-East is neither mountainous nor flat but a region of ridges and gentle hills formed by sand blown up from the Tisza River basin. Apart from the industries based in and around the county seat of Nyíregyháza, the area is almost entirely given over to agriculture – apples are the most important crop – with occasional stands of silver poplars and birch trees.

Until the regulation of the Tisza in the 19th century, large parts of the North-East would often be flooded and cut off from other areas by swampland. This helped to protect the area from the devastation suffered elsewhere during the Turkish occupation; as a result, the North-East has always been more densely populated than the Great Plain. Isolation also saved the region's distinctive wooden churches and other traditional architecture from oblivion.

But isolation has worked against the North-East and hindered development. Szabolcs-Szatmár-Bereg was hard hit by the recession of the 1990s and the stagnant economies of Ukraine, Romania and, to a lesser extent, Slovakia have contributed little to overall development. However, recent investments from outside Hungary, notably Germany and the USA, could change all that in the near future.

Before WWII, the North-East was home to most of the Jews in Hungary living outside Budapest, and their erstwhile presence can be seen everywhere in the region's dilapidated synagogues and untended cemeteries. Today a large percentage of the country's Roma (see boxed text 'The Roma') live here.

HIGHLIGHTS

- The Gothic Calvinist church and bell tower, and the carved wooden altars at the Minorite church in Nyírbátor

- The enormous iconostasis at the Greek Catholic cathedral in Máriapócs

- Szatmárcseke's ancient cemetery with its intriguing boat-shaped grave markers

- The narrow-gauge train trip from Dombrád to Nyíregyháza

- The folk baroque painted wooden ceiling at Tákos' Calvinist church

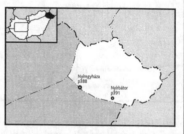

The North-East's remoteness and cultural diversity make it an interesting area to visit. If you want to see real Hungarian village life – replete with dirt roads, horse-drawn carts laden with hay, thatched roofs and ancient churches – this is the place to come.

Nyírség Region

Two rivers – the Szamos and the serpentine Tisza – carve the North-East up into three distinct areas. The largest of these is the Nyírség, the 'birch region' of grassy steppes and hills that lies between Nyíregyháza and the historical town of Nyírbátor. Until just a century ago, the life of the people here was shaped by the Tisza floods and the swamps that remained year round. A cyanide spill in

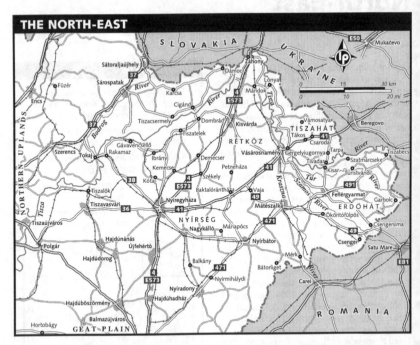

early 2000 has effected the ecology of this river. See boxed text 'Cyanide Spill' in Facts about Hungary chapter.

NYÍREGYHÁZA
☎ 42 • postcode 4400 • pop 114,000

Nyíregyháza (roughly 'birch church'), the commercial and administrative centre of the Nyírség, is not a particularly historical town. It was the private domain for many centuries of the princes of Transylvania and was resettled by Slovaks from Szarvas on the southern Great Plain in the 18th century. But with its well-tended squares and gardens and some beautifully restored buildings, Nyíregyháza is not a bad place to spend some time. It is also an excellent springboard for other North-East towns as well as northern Romania and Ukraine.

Orientation

Nyíregyháza's centre is made up of a handful of interconnecting squares, including Országzászló tér, Kálvin tér, Kossuth tér and Hősök tere, and is surrounded by both an inner and an outer ring road. Streets running north lead to Sóstófürdő, the city's sprawling 600-hectare recreational area of woods, parkland, the little Salt Lake (Sóstó) and a large spa complex.

The main train station is on Állomás tér, about 1.5km south-west of the centre at the end of Arany János utca. The bus station is just north of the train station on Petőfi tér, at the western end of Széchenyi utca.

Information

The helpful staff at Tourinform (☎ 310 430, fax 312 606, ✉ szabolcs-m@tourinform .hu), Országzászló tér 6, will supply as much information as you can carry and/or absorb about the city and the region. It is open from 8 am to 6 pm on weekdays and 9 am to 5 pm on Saturday from May to September and from 9 am to 5 pm weekdays only the rest of the year. Ibusz (☎ 312 695) in the same block is open from 8 am to 5 pm weekdays, till noon on Saturday. Express (☎ 311 650), Arany János utca 2, may help with basic information and student accommodation. Tourinform has a seasonal branch (☎ 411 193) in the Water Tower (Víztorony) in Sóstófürdő (open 9 am to 5 pm daily from mid-May to mid-September only).

OTP bank has a branch at Dózsa György utca 2; the main post office is at Bethlen Gábor utca 4 south of the town hall. You'll find a small but quite good map shop called Nyír-Karta at Kálvin tér 14.

Things to See

There are a variety of houses of worship in the inner city, including the late baroque **Evangelist church** (1786) at Luther tér 14 and, dominating Kossuth tér at No 14, the neo-Romanesque **Catholic cathedral** (1904), with arabesque pastel-coloured tiles inside. The **Greek Catholic church** (1895) at Bethlen Gábor utca 5 contains a rich **liturgical collection** of vestments and plate. It is open 8 am to 4 pm weekdays, till noon on Saturday (free). The magnificent **synagogue** at Síp utca 6, which still functions as a house of worship, can be visited Monday to Thursday from 8 am to 4 pm.

A lot of the architecture in the centre is worth more than a casual glance; if you can, visit the Eclectic **county hall** (1892) with its splendid Ceremonial Hall (Nagy Terem) on Hősök tere, the blue and white Art Nouveau building housing a bank and offices on Országzászló tér, or the restored **Korona hotel** on Dózsa György utca. **Benczúr Gyula tér** is another treasure trove of Art Nouveau and Secessionist architecture. A more recent must-see is the bizarre **cultural centre** (1981) on Szabadság tér, a wobbly-looking, bridge-like structure inspired by 'the principles of Japanese metabolism', we're told.

The enormous **András Jósa Museum** at Benczúr Gyula tér 21 has exhibits devoted to Nyíregyháza's history since the Middle Ages (open from 9 am to 4 pm Tuesday to Saturday, till 2 pm on Sunday; 100/60Ft) while the **Gyula Benczúr Gallery** at Dózsa György utca 3 is a paean in stone to the eponymous Romantic epic painter who was

born here. It contains exhibits of fine and applied arts and is open from 9.30 am to 5.30 pm Tuesday to Friday, 10 am to 1 pm on Saturday. Entry is 100/50Ft.

Nyíregyháza's most interesting sight, however, is the open-air **Sóstó Museum Village** (Sóstói Múzeumfalu) at Tölgyes utca 1 in Sóstófürdő, open from 9 am to 5 or 6 pm Tuesday to Sunday from April to October (130/50Ft). Though not as big as the skanzen at Szentendre, its reconstructed three-room cottages, school, draw wells and general store offer an easy introduction to the architecture and way of life in the various regions of Szabolcs-Szatmár-Bereg. All the nationalities that make up this ethnically diverse region are represented, including the Tirpák, Slovakians who lived in isolated 'bush farms' known as *bokor tanyák*. The new **zoo** (*állatpark*) a short distance to the south-east is open 9 am to 7 pm daily (250/200/180Ft for adults/students/children).

The **fruit & vegetable market** on Búza tér is one of the more colourful in provincial Hungary, but the **Nagybani flea market** on Tokaji út, the north-west extension of Rákóczi út, is even more vibrant, attracting a motley crowd of Hungarians, Romanians, Poles, Ukrainians and Roma selling the usual diamonds-to-rust mixture of goods.

Activities

The Park Baths (Parkfürdő) in Sóstófürdő, 5km north of the city centre, is just the place to while away a hot summer's afternoon, with a half-dozen large pools of fresh and thermal water, a sauna, solarium and so on. It's open from 9 am to 7 pm daily from early June to August (265/175Ft). The Lake Baths (Tófürdő) have the same opening hours but a longer season: mid-May to early September. A more central, less crowded option is the Julia Fürdő, an indoor thermal spa with three pools at Malom utca 16 (open 10 am to 7 pm weekdays and 9 am to 8 pm at the weekend).

The Sóstó Riding Club (☎ 475 202) next to the open-air Museum Village on Tölgyes utca rents horses (1800Ft per hour). Another excellent place for riding is the Szil-Ko Stud

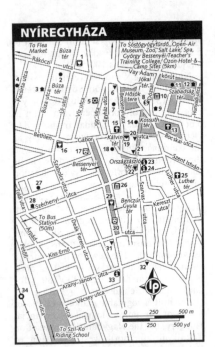

NYÍREGYHÁZA

PLACES TO STAY
3 Senátor Pension
9 Korona Hotel; John Bull Pub; X Café
12 Európa Hotel
28 Ilona Zrínyi College

PLACES TO EAT
6 HBH Bajor Pub-Restaurant
20 City Grill
21 Gösser Restaurant
22 Omni Café
31 Mozzarella Pizzeria
32 Shuang He

OTHER
1 Unicum Pub
2 Fruit & Vegetable Market
4 Fehér Narancs Jazz Venue
5 Synagogue
7 County Hall
8 OTP Bank; Zucchini Salad Bar;
10 Gyula Benczúr Gallery
11 Cultural Centre; Open Doors Club
13 Catholic Church
14 Town Hall
15 Greek Catholic Church & Liturgical Collection
16 Bahnhof Music Club
17 Zsigmond Móricz Theatre
18 Nyír-Karta Map Shop
19 Post Office
23 Ibusz
24 Tourinform
25 Evangelist Church
26 András Jósa Museum
27 Julia Baths
29 Summer Beer Garden
30 City Open-Air Theatre
33 Express
34 Train Station

& Riding School (☎/fax 342 085, @ lovi@
szabolcs.net) south-west of the centre at
Bem József utca 22-23.

Places to Stay

There are several camping grounds in
Sóstófürdő (250Ft to 400Ft per person,
350Ft to 400Ft per tent), including:
Fenyves (☎ 409 344, Sóstói út 72), which
also has hostel accommodation for about
600Ft per person in four to six-bed cabins;
Paradise (☎ 402 011, Sóstói út 76); and
Igrice (☎ 479 705, Blaha Lujza sétány 8).
Accommodation in the Igrice's bungalows
costs from 2100Ft.

Tourinform and Express can advise on
dormitory rooms at local colleges in summer. If the agencies are closed, go directly
to the *György Bessenyei Teachers' Training College* (☎ 402 488, Sóstói út 31b) or
the *Ilona Zrínyi College* (☎ 315 618,
Széchenyi utca 35-39); both charge about
900Ft per person. The *tourist hotel* at the

Paradise camping ground has dormitory accommodation (1120Ft to 1770Ft) available
from mid-April to mid-October.

Private rooms available through Ibusz
and Tourinform in Sóstófürdő (not the office in the centre) cost 1500Ft to 2000Ft per
person.

The *Senátor* (☎ 311 796, Búza tér 11), a
15-room pension opposite the lively produce
market, is in desperate need of an upgrade
but remains a bargain: doubles with shower
are 3900Ft, singles/doubles with washbasin
only are 2000/2600Ft. The *Ózon* (☎ 402 001,
Csaló köz 2), a former communist summer

retreat near Sóstófürdő, has 26 modern doubles from 5500Ft.

The *Európa* (☎ *403 676, fax 405 030, Hunyadi utca 2)*, a nondescript new 60-room hotel facing the busy outer ring road, charges 5000/5500Ft for singles/doubles. For a splurge stay at the lovingly restored *Korona* (☎ *409 300, fax 409 339, Dózsa György utca 1-3)*, which first opened its doors in 1895. It has 35 rooms scattered along seemingly endless corridors. Singles/doubles with all the mod cons are 7000/7900Ft.

Places to Eat

The *City Grill* (*Bethlen Gábor utca 2)*, next to the main post office, is fine for a cheap, fast meal. Vegetarians should head for the *Zucchini Salad Bar* (*Hősök tere 15)*, accessible from the small courtyard at Dózsa György utca 2.

For more comfortable surroundings, try the *HBH Bajor* (*Hősök tere 6)*, a decent choice for some well-prepared Hungarian dishes in a lovely square. The *Gösser* (*Országzászló tér 10)*, a similar but more cramped spot, also has pizzas and pasta dishes from 450Ft – though for the latter you might want to venture farther south to *Mozzarella Pizzéria* (*Kiss Ernő utca 10)*.

The *Shuang He* (*Szarvas utca 56)* serves Chinese food like none I've ever seen or tasted before, but if you need a fix of noodles or rice it's due east of the train station (mains: 500Ft to 600Ft).

For a cup of coffee or tea and something sweet, try the lovely *Omni* (*Széchenyi utca 1)*, a posh *kávészalon* (cafe) facing Országzászló tér and open daily from 7 am to 11 pm.

Entertainment

Check with the staff at the *Zsigmond Móricz Theatre* (☎ *311 333, Bessenyei tér 13)* or the *Mihály Váci Cultural Centre* (☎ *411 822, Szabadság tér 9)* for current listings. And if there's a concert on at the *Evangelist church* (*Luther tér)*, jump at the chance. The theatre ticket office (☎ 310 360) at Tourinform, Országzászló tér 6, is open from 9 am to 5 pm on weekdays. In

The Roma

The origins of the Gypsies (Hungarian: *cigány*), who call themselves the Roma (singular Rom) and speak Romany, a language closely related to several still spoken in northern India, remain a mystery. It is generally accepted, however, that they began migrating to Persia from India sometime in the 10th century and had reached the Balkans by the 14th century. They have been in Hungary for at least 500 years, and their numbers today are estimated at anywhere between 150,000 and a quarter of a million people.

Though traditionally a travelling people, in modern times the Roma have by and large settled down in Hungary and worked as smiths and tinkers, livestock and horse traders and as musicians (see Music & Dance under Arts in the Facts about the Country chapter). As a group, however, they are chronically underemployed and have been the hardest hit by economic recession. Statistically, Roma families are twice the size of *gadje*, or 'non-Roma' ones.

Unsettled people have always been persecuted in one form or another by those who stay put and Hungarian Roma are no exception. They are widely despised and remain the scapegoats for everything that goes wrong in certain parts of the country, from the rise in petty theft and prostitution to the loss of jobs. Though their rights are inscribed in the 1989 constitution along with other ethnic minorities, their housing ranks among the worst in the nation, police are regularly accused of harassing them and, more than any other group, they fear a revival of right-wing nationalism. You will probably be shocked at what even educated, cosmopolitan Hungarians say about Roma and their way of life.

summer, Benczúr Gyula tér is the site of the *City Open-Air Theatre* (Városi Szabadtéri Színpad) and attached outdoor *beer garden*.

The *John Bull* pub-restaurant (*Dózsa György utca 1-3)* at the bottom of the Korona hotel is a little bit of ersatz England in north-eastern Hungary. For a bit more local colour, try the *Unicum (Búza tér 2)* opposite the market. The *Fehér Narancs (White Orange; Pacsirta utca 20)* west of Búza utca remains a popular venue for jazz and opens to 2 am during the week and 4 am at the weekend.

The most popular clubs in town are the *Bahnhof Music (Bethlen Gábor utca 24)*, the *X Cafe* below the John Bull pub and the always heaving *Open Doors* at the cultural centre.

Getting There & Away

Generally, buses serve towns near Nyíregyháza or those not on a railway line – and there are up to four departures an hour to Nagykálló. Other destinations include Debrecen (three buses a day), Eger (two), Fehérgyarmat (four to seven), Gyöngyös (one), Hajdúnánás (three), Kisvárda (four to six), Máriapócs (eight), Mátészalka (eight), Miskolc (three), Nyírbátor (up to 12) and Vásárosnamény (six). International destinations include Užgorod in Ukraine at 2 and 3 pm daily and Satu Mare in Romania at 7.30 pm on Tuesday and Saturday.

A half-dozen daily express trains link Nyíregyháza with Debrecen and Budapest-Nyugati, but you can count on at least one normal train an hour to Debrecen and up to a dozen a day to Miskolc. Up to eight trains depart Nyíregyháza each day for Vásárosnamény and seven head for Mátészalka, stopping at Nagykálló, Máriapócs and Nyírbátor en route. The Tisza express train en route to Lvov, Kiev and Moscow also stops here every day just before 8 pm; the Partium crossing the Ukrainian border to Csop, departs at 9.46 am.

Getting Around

Almost everything in the city – with the exception of Sóstófürdő – can be easily reached on foot. Take bus No 7 or 8 from the train or bus stations to reach the centre of town; the latter then carries on to Sóstófürdő. For the flea market, catch bus No 1 or 1a; the former carries on to the airport, the latter terminates at the market.

You can order a taxi on ☎ 444 444 or ☎ 313 313.

AROUND NYÍREGYHÁZA
Nagykálló
☎ 42 • postcode 4320 • pop 10,000

This dusty town 14km south-east of Nyíregyháza boasts some important listed buildings in its central square (Szabadság tér) – a baroque **Calvinist church** on the south side with a free-standing Gothic bell tower originally built in the 15th century, and the splendid former **county hall** to the north-east at No 13, which was built in the Zopf style in 1749 and later turned into a notorious insane asylum.

But most visitors to Nagykálló are Orthodox Jewish pilgrims who come to pay their respects at the **tomb of Isaac Taub Eizik,** especially on the anniversary of his death (February/March). Known as the 'Wonder Rabbi of Kálló', he was an 18th-century philosopher who advocated a more humanistic approach to prayer and study. You can visit his small tomb in the old Jewish cemetery on Nagybalkányi út, less than a kilometre due south of Szabadság tér, but you must seek the key from the house at Bessenyei út 15 (☎ 262 947 or mobile ☎ 06-209 214 800).

The *Belvárosi Eszpresszó (Kossuth Lajos utca)* to the north-east of the square has sandwiches and the *Tamás Ételbár* on the same street to the west is both a snack bar and a cake shop. In late June, Nagykálló hosts the popular Téka Tábor, a nine-day folk festival 'camp' held in a bizarre structure designed by Imre Makovecz at Harangodi-tó, some 2km north of town. For information contact the Rákóczi Cultural Centre (☎ 263 141) at Báthory utca 1.

Up to seven trains a day linking Nyíregyháza and Mátészalka stop at Nagykálló. A bus meets each incoming train and goes as far as Szabadság tér. You can also reach Nagykálló by bus throughout the day from Nyíregyháza. Many of these carry on to Máriapócs and Nyírbátor on weekdays but only four do at the weekend.

NYÍRBÁTOR
☎ 42 • postcode 4300 • pop 13,850

Nyírbátor, 38km south-east of Nyíregyháza in the centre of the lovely Nyírség region, is

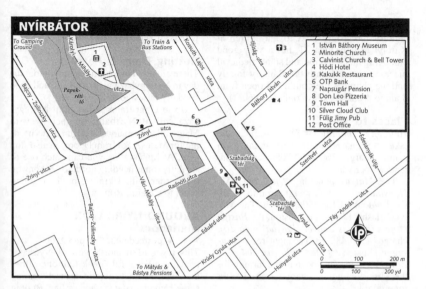

NYÍRBÁTOR

1 István Báthory Museum
2 Minorite Church
3 Calvinist Church & Bell Tower
4 Hódi Hotel
5 Kakukk Restaurant
6 OTP Bank
7 Napsugár Pension
8 Don Leo Pizzeria
9 Town Hall
10 Silver Cloud Club
11 Fülig Jimy Pub
12 Post Office

well worth a visit – however fleeting. It contains two Gothic churches built in the latter part of the 15th century by István Báthory, the ruthless Transylvanian prince whose family is synonymous with the town. As the Báthory family's economic and political influence grew from the 15th to 17th century, so did that of Nyírbátor.

Orientation & Information
Nyírbátor is compact, and everything of interest can be easily reached on foot. The train and bus stations are in the northern part of town on Ady Endre utca less than a kilometre from the centre (Szabadság tér) via Kossuth Lajos utca.

There's an OTP bank across the road from Szabadság tér at Zrínyi utca 1. The main post office is on the south-west side of Szabadság tér.

Things to See
The **Calvinist church**, on a small hill just off Báthory István utca, is one of the most beautiful Gothic churches in Hungary. The ribbed vault of the nave is a masterpiece, and the long lancet windows flood the stark white interior with light. István Báthory's

remains lie in a marble tomb at the back of the church; the family's coat of arms embellished with wyverns (dragon-like creatures) is on top. The 17th-century wooden **bell tower**, standing apart from the church (as was once required of Calvinists in this overwhelmingly Catholic country) has a Gothic roof with four little turrets. You can climb the 20m to the top 'at your own risk'. The pastor, who lives in the modern house just behind the church to the west, holds the massive medieval keys to the church and tower. Visiting hours are 8 am to noon and 2.30 to 4 pm (on Sunday from 10 am to noon and 3 to 4 pm).

The **Minorite church** on Károlyi Mihály utca is another Báthory contribution. Originally late Gothic, it was ravaged by the Turks in 1587 and rebuilt in the baroque style 130 years later. Five spectacular altars carved in Prešov (now eastern Slovakia) in the mid-18th century fill the nave and chancel. The most interesting is the first on the left, the **Krucsay Altar of the Passion** (1737), with its diverse portraits of fear, longing, devotion and faith. The church is open from 9 am to 5 pm weekdays, till 7 pm on Saturday and from 8 am to 6 pm on Sunday.

NORTH-EAST

The **István Báthory Museum**, in the 18th-century monastery next to the church at Károlyi Mihály utca 21, has a very good ethnographic collection and some medieval pieces connected with the Báthory family and the churches they built. It's open from 8 am to 4 pm weekdays only (100/60Ft).

Places to Stay

Holdfény Camping (☎ 281 494), near the lake at Széna rét north-west of the town centre, charges 200/500/800Ft per person/tent/camper van.

The **Mátyás** pension (☎/fax 281 657, Hunyadi utca 8) has eight rooms, with singles/doubles for 3500/3800Ft. The Mátyás' flashy 17-room extension, the **Bástya** (☎/fax same as above, Hunyadi utca 10), charges 4200/4800Ft. The eight-room **Napsugár** pension (☎ 283 878, fax 284 491, Zrínyi utca 15), just beyond the turning for the Minorite church, charges from 3800Ft for a double.

The attractive **Hódi** hotel (☎ 283 556, fax 281 012, Báthory István utca 12) is in a small courtyard east of Szabadság tér. Its 11 rooms have all the features of a top-class place, and there's a small swimming pool, sauna, restaurant and bar. Singles/doubles are 6900/7900Ft (7900/9500Ft with air conditioning).

Places to Eat

A popular place for a light meal is **Don Leo Pizzeria** (Bajcsy-Zsilinszky utca 62) a couple of hundred metres beyond Napsugár pension. **Kakukk** (Szabadság tér 21) is the only real restaurant in the centre. Its well-prepared daily menu is very reasonable (main courses 450Ft to 850Ft), but it closes at 10 pm. The Mátyás pension has a csárda-style restaurant called the **Trófea** serving fish and – ever popular in these parts – game.

Entertainment

Organ concerts and recitals can be heard throughout the year at the **Calvinist church**.

The **Silver Cloud** club (Szabadság tér 7) at the end of the big, sand-coloured town hall with the clock tower, is open till midnight on weekdays and at weekends till late.

The **Fülig Jimy** pub next door is popular with Nyírbátor's young bloods.

Getting There & Away

There are regular departures throughout the day to Nyíregyháza via Nagykálló and up to six daily buses go to Máriapócs.

Up to eight trains a day from Nyíregyháza call at Nyírbátor on their way to Mátészalka; as many as a dozen trains heading for Mátészalka from Debrecen also stop here. At Mátészalka, you can catch one of six daily trains heading north for Záhony on the border with Ukraine, or three going south to Carei in Romania.

AROUND NYÍRBÁTOR
Máriapócs
☎ 42 • postcode 4326 • pop 2200

This town 12km north-west of Nyírbátor contains a beautiful **Greek Catholic cathedral**, with an ornate gold iconostasis soaring some 15m up to the vaulted ceiling. Built in the middle of the 18th century on the site of a small wooden church, the cathedral has been an important pilgrimage site from at least 1696 when the **Black Madonna** icon, which now takes pride of place above the altar on the north side of the church, first shed tears (she wept again in 1715 and 1905). In fact, this is not the original icon but a 19th-century copy; the real one is now in St Stephen's Cathedral in Vienna. The church is open from 7 am to 6 pm weekdays and till 7 pm at the weekend.

Buses from Nagykálló, Nyírbátor and Nyíregyháza (between two and eight buses a day) will drop you off by the church. All the trains between Nyírbátor and Nyíregyháza stop at the Máriapócs train station, which is 4km south of the town centre. Buses make the run between the centre and the station, but they are not very reliable. Should you need to spend the night, the cathedral has a 22-room **guesthouse** (☎ 385 528, Kossuth tér 17).

Otherwise the six-room **Fekete Bárány** inn (☎ 385 722, Állomás tér) is opposite the train station on the road linking Nyírbátor and Nagykálló and charges from about 3500Ft for a double.

Tiszahát & Erdőhát Regions

The most traditional parts of the county lie east and south of the Tisza River and are commonly referred to by their geographical locations: 'behind the Tisza' (Tiszahát) and 'behind the woods' (Erdőhát) of Transylvania. Because of these regions' isolation, folk traditions have lived on. Some of the finest examples of Hungarian popular architecture and interior church painting can be found here. It is also the site of Hungary's most unusual cemetery.

With its rolling hills, ever-present Tisza and the soft silver-green of the poplar trees, the area is among the prettiest in Hungary. Unfortunately, it is also one of the most difficult to get around and, without your own transport, you should be prepared for long waits to connect between small towns. Distances are generally not great, though.

For those of you not under your own steam, the best idea is to take the train or bus from Nyíregyháza or Nyírbátor to Vásárosnamény and use that town as your springboard. Or, better still, go on a tour organised by Air-Mediterrán (☎/fax 42-314 303, ✉ mail@airmed.hu) at Szarvas utca 5-7 in Nyíregyháza; no-one knows this part of the country better than they do. See Organised Tours in the Getting Around chapter for details.

Things to See & Do

Vásárosnamény Vásárosnamény is today a sleepy town of just over 9000 people, but it was once an important trading post on the lucrative Salt Road from the forests of Transylvania via the Tisza River and then across the Great Plain to Debrecen. Though it won't hold your interest for long, the **Bereg Museum**, at Rákóczi utca 13, has a small, though interesting, collection of local embroidery, weaving and painted Easter eggs– a popular local art form. Keep an eye open for the famous Bereg cross-stitching, a blend of many different styles. The museum is open from 8.30 am to 4.30 pm Tuesday to Friday and till 4 pm at the weekend from March to October. During the rest of the year it opens weekdays only. Entry 100/50Ft.

Tákos The 18th-century wattle-and-daub **Calvinist church** in this village (pop 460), 8km north-east of Vásárosnamény on route No 41, has a spectacularly painted coffered ceiling of blue and red flowers, a floor of beaten earth and an ornately carved 'folk baroque' pulpit sitting on a large millstone. Outside the church, which villagers call the 'barefoot Notre Dame of Hungary', stands a perfectly preserved **bell tower** (1767). The keeper of the keys lives in a house just north of the church at Bajcsy-Zsilinszky utca 40; if you're driving, sound the horn three times and she'll soon arrive at the church to let you in.

Csaroda A **Romanesque church** dating from the 13th century stands on Kossuth utca in this village (pop 680), some 3km east of Tákos. The church is thought to have been founded by King Stephen himself, following his plan to have at least one church for every 10 villages in his domain. The church is a wonderful hybrid of a place with both Western and Eastern-style frescoes (some from the 14th century) as well as some fairly crude folk murals dated 9 July 1647. On the short walk from the car park or bus stop, you'll pass two wooden **bell towers** of much more recent vintage. The key to the church is at Kossuth Lajos utca 15.

Tarpa Some 6km farther east on route No 41 will take you to the turn-off for Fehérgyarmat. Another 10km to the south is Tarpa, a town of 2500 people boasting one of Hungary's last examples of a horse-driven **dry mill** (szárazmalom). The mill, with a distinctive conical roof, went through many incarnations – as a bar, a cinema and dance hall – before its renovation in the late 1970s. It is at Árpád utca 36. Nearby is a decorated **Calvinist church** and a small **provincial house** (tájház), Kossuth utca 21, open to visitors.

Szatmárcseke To get to this village, site of a cemetery with intriguing boat-shaped **grave markers** (kopjafák), travel another 5km south to Tivadar and the Tisza River. After crossing the river, turn east and carry on another 7km north-east to Szatmárcseke. The 600 carved wooden markers in the cemetery are unique in Hungary, and the notches and grooves cut into them represent a complicated language all of their own: it details marital status, social position, age, etc. One of the few stone markers in the cemetery is that of native son Ferenc Kölcsey (1790-1838), who wrote the words to *Himnusz*, the Hungarian national anthem.

Túristvándi There is a wonderfully restored 18th-century **water mill** (vízimalom) at Malom utca 1 on a small tributary of the Tisza at Túristvándi, 4km due south of Szatmárcseke. It is open daily from 8 am to 4 pm (50Ft).

Places to Stay

The *Tiszavirág* camp site (☎ 45-470 076) is across the Tisza River from Vásárosnamény in Gergelyiugornya, and there's a hotel in Vásárosnamény itself called the *Marianna Center* (☎ 45-470 401, fax 470 434, Szabadság tér 19), with double rooms from 3900Ft.

In Mátészalka, the *Szatmár* hotel (☎ 44-311 429, fax 310 428, Hősök tere 8) has rooms from 4200Ft.

In Csaroda, the *Kúria* (☎ 45-311 202, József Attila utca 67), an old manor house functioning as an inn, has four three-bedded rooms costing 2000Ft to 3000Ft. In Tarpa, the *Riviera* pension (☎ 313 032, Árpád utca 24) near the dry mill has doubles for 4000Ft.

In Tivadar, *Katica Camping* (☎ 44-363 859, Petőfi utca 11) and its sister camp site *Diós Camping* (☎ same as above, Tiszapart) charge 300Ft to 325Ft per person and 250Ft to 270Ft for a tent site. Both are open from June to August.

In Szatmárcseke, the 14-room *Kölcsey* inn (☎ 44-432 108, Honvéd utca 6) is a run-down old place on a quiet, leafy street. It's dirt cheap (doubles from 1600Ft) but it closes in winter. You'll see quite a few houses along the main street in Szatmárcseke with *szoba kiadó* or *Zimmer frei* signs outside.

In Túristvándi, the *Vízimalon* pension (☎ 44-434 075, Malom utca 3), next to the old water mill, charges 1000Ft per person for a bed in one of its eight rooms.

Getting There & Away

The ideal way to visit this part of Hungary is by car or bicycle. If neither is an option, you can visit most of the places mentioned here by bus from Vásárosnamény, Mátészalka or Fehérgyarmat. But departures are infrequent, averaging only two or three a day. Check return schedules from your destination carefully before setting out.

From Nyíregyháza, there are eight daily trains leaving for Vásárosnamény, and seven for Mátészalka via Nagykálló, Máriapócs and Nyírbátor. You can reach Fehérgyarmat via two direct trains a day or travel to Mátészalka and change there on three others.

Rétköz Region

The Rétköz area north-east of Nyíregyháza lies somewhat lower than the rest of North-East Hungary and was particularly prone to flooding. Agriculture was possible only on the larger of the islands in this mosquito-infested swampland, and the isolation spurred the development of strong clan ties and a wealth of folk tales and myths. That's all in the past now, and you won't see any more evidence of it than the once celebrated Rétköz homespun cloth. But you might get lucky...

KISVÁRDA
☎ 45 • postcode 4600 • pop 18,300
Kisvárda, 45km north-east of Nyíregyháza and the centre of the Rétköz region, was an important stronghold during the Turkish invasions, and the remains of its fortress can still be seen. It's only 23km north from here to Ukraine and, if you're continuing onward, it's a much nicer place to spend the night than the border town of Záhony.

Orientation & Information

Kisvárda's bus and train stations lie just over 2km south-west of Flórián tér, the town centre. Local buses await arriving trains, but it's an easy, straightforward walk north along tree-lined Bocskai utca, Rákóczi Ferenc utca and Szent László utca to town. The last stretch of Szent László utca is particularly colourful. Some buses also go as far as Flórián tér, and there's a schedule posted outside the Volán office at Flórián tér 2.

You'll find an OTP bank at the corner of Mártírok útja and Szent László utca. The main post office is at Somogyi Rezső utca 4.

Things to See & Do

Flórián tér offers the usual Gothic-cum-baroque **Catholic church** painted lime green and a late-19th-century dusky pink **Calvinist church** sitting uncomfortably close by. Far more interesting is the Zopf-style **town library** that takes pride of place on the square.

A short distance to the east of the square at Csillag utca 5 is the **Rétköz Museum**. Housed in a disused synagogue built in 1900, the building itself is as interesting as the exhibits, with its geometric ceiling patterns, blue and yellow stained glass and wrought-iron gates in the shape of menorahs. Lots of 'typical' Rétköz village rooms and workshops (a smithy, loom, etc) are set up on the ground floor of the museum, but the 1st floor has some interesting art. Just inside the west entrance is a memorial tablet with over 1000 names of Jewish citizens of Kisvárda who died in Auschwitz. The museum is open from 9 am till noon and 1 to 4.30 pm Tuesday to Sunday from April to October (50/30Ft).

The ruins of **Kisvárda Castle** are about 10 minutes on foot north-west of Flórián tér at the end of Vár utca. Though part of one wall dates from the 15th century, most of the castle has been heavily restored. The courtyard is used as an open-air theatre in summer.

The **Várfürdő** beside the castle ruins on Városmajor utca is a small complex of freshwater and thermal pools, with sauna and sunbathing areas. It's open from 9 am to 7 pm daily from May to September.

Places to Stay

The 29-room **Vár** hotel (☎ 421 578, fax 421 539, Városmajor utca 43), a rundown holiday house beside the castle ruins and baths, has very basic accommodation for 1500Ft per person. A bit farther to the north-east is the equally basic **Stíl** pension (☎ 410 791, fax 421 100, Városmajor utca 60). It charges 1000Ft per person for a bed in one of its seven rooms.

A more central choice is the **Bástya** hotel (☎/fax 421 100, Krucsay Márton utca 2) in a 'turret' on the 1st floor of a modern shopping arcade. Its 18 double rooms cost 3000/2800Ft with/without shower.

Places to Eat

The **Várda** (Szent László utca 16), behind the hideous modern town hall, is a dreary place to have a meal, but it's central, inexpensive and open till 10 pm Monday to Saturday. A better choice would be the **Amadeus** cellar restaurant (Szent László utca 27) a bit farther south. **Fekete Nyolcás** (Black Eight Ball; Mártírok útja 3) is a pizzeria open till midnight (2 am on Friday and Saturday). A more recent arrival is **Opál** (Csillag utca 33), a pub-restaurant a couple of hundred metres east of the Rétköz Museum. Mains average about 700Ft.

The cukrászda with the best cakes and ice cream in town is the **Poncsák** (Mártírok útja 2) open daily till 8 pm though the **Sarok** (Szent László utca 2) is a bit more central.

Entertainment

Plays are sometimes put on at the **Castle Stage** (Várszínpad) at the castle in summer; check with the staff at the modern **cultural centre** (☎ 405 238, Flórián tér 20), which also contains the small **Castle Theatre** (Várszínház).

The **Belvárosi Kávézó** (Szent László utca 22) is more a pub than a coffee shop but a place keeping much later hours is the **Fortuna Club** bar (Csillag utca), opposite the Rétköz Museum.

Getting There & Away

Only a few destinations are accessible by bus, including Dombrád (up to 12 a day), Nyíregyháza (two) and Vásárosnamény (five).

The town is on the railway line connecting Nyíregyháza with Záhony, and

you have a choice of 15 trains a day, six of which originate in Budapest. The two daily express trains headed for Ukraine and Russia – the *Partium* and the *Tisza* – also stop in Kisvárda before crossing the border at Záhony.

Language

Hungarian (Magyar) belongs to the Finno-Ugric language group and is related – only distantly – to Finnish (with five million speakers), Estonian (one million) and about a dozen other minority languages with far fewer speakers in Russia and western Siberia. It's not an Indo-European language, meaning that English is actually closer to French, Russian and Hindi in vocabulary and structure than it is to Hungarian. As a result you'll come across very few familiar words – with the exception of things like *disco* or *hello* (the slangy way young Hungarians say 'goodbye').

There are also a fair number of misleading homophones (words with the same sound but different meanings) in Hungarian: *test* is not a quiz but 'body'; *fog* is 'tooth'; *comb* is 'thigh'; and *part* is 'shore'. *Ifjúság*, pronounced (very roughly) 'if you shag', means 'youth'; *sajt* (pronounced 'shite'), as in every visiting Briton's favourite *sajtburger*, means 'cheese'.

For more Hungarian words and phrases than there is space for here, get a copy of Lonely Planet's *Eastern* or *Central Europe* phrasebook.

Pronunciation

Hungarian is not difficult to pronounce – though it may look strange with all those accents. Unlike English, Hungarian is a 'one-for-one' language: the pronunciation of each vowel and consonant is almost always consistent. Stress falls on the first syllable (no exceptions), making the language sound a bit staccato to untrained ears.

Consonants

Consonants in Hungarian are pronounced more or less as in English; the exceptions are listed below. Double consonants (**ll, tt, dd**) are not pronounced as one letter as in English, but lengthened so you can almost hear them as separate sounds. Also, what are called consonant clusters (**cs, zs, gy, sz**)

are separate letters in Hungarian and appear that way in the telephone directory and alphabetical listings. For example, the word *cukor* (sugar) appears in the dictionary before *csak* (only).

c	as the 'ts' in 'hats'
cs	as the 'ch' in 'church'
gy	as the 'j' in 'jury' with your tongue pressed against the roof of your mouth
j	as the 'y' in 'yes'
ly	also as the 'y' in 'yes' but with a slight 'l' sound
ny	as the 'ni' in 'onion'
r	pronounced with the tip of your tongue; a slightly trilled 'r' as found in Spanish or Scottish
s	as the 'sh' in 'shop'
sz	as the 's' in 'salt'
ty	as the 'tu' in 'tube' in British English
w	as the 'v' in 'vat' (used in foreign words only)
zs	as the 's' in 'pleasure'

Vowels

Vowels are quite tricky, and the difference between an **a**, **e** or **o** with and without an accent mark is great. *Hát* means 'back' while *hat* means 'six'; *kérek* means 'I want' while *kerek* means 'round'. Try to imagine a Briton with a standard 'TV' accent or an American from Boston pronouncing the following sounds:

a	as the 'o' in hot
á	as the 'a' in 'father' or 'shah'
e	as the 'e' in 'set'
é	as the 'e' as in 'they' (without the 'y' sound)
i	similar to the 'i' in 'hit'
í	as the 'i' in 'police'
o	as the 'o' in 'open'
ó	a longer version of **o** above
ö	as the 'o' in 'worse' (without any 'r' sound)
ő	a longer version of **ö** above

LANGUAGE

u	as the 'u' in 'pull'
ú	as the 'oo' in 'food'
ü	a tough one; similar to the 'u' in 'flute' or as in German *fünf*
ű	even tougher; a longer, breathier version of ü above

Polite & Informal Forms

As in many other languages, verbs in Hungarian have polite and informal form in the singular and plural. The polite address (marked as 'pol' in this guide) is used with strangers, older people, officials and service staff. The informal address (marked as 'inf') is reserved for friends, pets, children and sometimes foreigners, but is used much more frequently and sooner than it is in, say, French. Almost all young people use it among themselves – even with strangers. In the following phrases, the polite 'you' (*Ön* and *Önök*) is given except for situations where you might wish to establish a more personal relationship.

Basics

Yes	*Igen*
No	*Nem*
Maybe	*Talán*
Please	*Kérem.* (asking for something)
	Tessék. (offering/inviting)
Thank you (very much)	*Köszönöm (szépen)* *Köszi* (inf)
You're welcome	*Szívesen*
Excuse me	*Legyen szíves* (for attention)
	Bocsánat (eg, to get past someone)
I'm sorry	*Sajnálom/Elnézést*

Greetings & Civilities

Hello.	*Jó napot kívánok.* (pol)
Hi.	*Szia* or *szervusz.* (inf)
Goodbye	*Viszontlátásra* (pol)
	Szia/Szervusz (inf)
Good day	*Jó napot* (most common greeting)
Good morning.	*Jó reggelt*
Good evening.	*Jó estét*

Small Talk

How are you?	*Hogy van?* (pol)
	Hogy vagy? (inf)
I'm fine, thanks.	*Köszönöm, jól.*
What's your name?	*Hogy hívják?* (pol)
	Mi a neved? (inf)
My name is ...	*A nevem ...*
I'm a ... tourist/ student.	*Turista/diák.*
Are you married?	*Ön férjezett?* (to a woman)
	Ön nős? (to a man)
Do you like Hungary?	*Tetszik önnek Magyarország?*
I like it very much.	*Nagyon tetszik.*
Where are you from?	*Honnan jön?*

I'm ...	*... vagyok.*
American	*Amerikai*
British	*brit*
Australian	*ausztrál*
Canadian	*kanadai*
a New Zealander	*új-zélandi*

How old are you?	*Hány éves vagy?* (inf)
	Hány éves? (pol)
I'm 25 years old.	*Húszonöt éves vagyok.*
Just a minute.	*Egy pillanat.*
May I?	*Lehet?* (general permission)
	Szabad? (eg, asking for a chair)
It's all right.	*Rendben van.*
No problem.	*Nem baj.*

Language Difficulties

Do you speak...?	*Beszél ...?*
English	*angolul*
French	*franciául*
German	*németül*
Italian	*olaszul*

Does anyone here speak English?	*Van itt valaki, aki angolul beszél?*
I understand.	*Értem.*
I don't understand.	*Nem értem.*
I don't speak Hungarian.	*Nem beszélek magyarul.*
How do you say ... in Hungarian?	*Hogy mondják magyarul ...?*

Please write it down.	Kérem, írja le.
Would you please show me (on the map)?	Meg tudná nekem mutatni (a térképen)?

Getting Around

What time does ... leave/arrive?	Mikor indul/ érkezik ...?
the bus	az autóbusz
the tram	a villamos
the train	a vonat
the boat/ferry	a hajó/komp
the plane	a repülőgép
The train is ...	A vonat ...
delayed	késik
on time	pontosan érkezik
early	korábban érkezik
cancelled	nem jár
How long does the trip take?	Mennyi ideig tart az út?
Do I need to change trains?	Át kell szállnom?
You must change trains.	Át kell szállni.
You must change platforms.	Másik vágányhoz kell menni.
I want to go to ...	... akarok menni.
Esztergom	Esztergomba
Debrecen	Debrecenbe
Pécs	Pécsre
I want to book a seat to Prague.	Szeretnék helyet foglalni Prágába.
train station	vasútállomás/ pályaudvar
bus station	autóbuszállomás
platform	vágány
ticket	jegy
one-way ticket	egy útra/csak oda
return ticket	oda-vissza/retúrjegy
ticket office	jegyiroda/pénztár
timetable	menetrend
left-luggage	csomagmegőrző
I'd like to hire a car.	Autót szeretnék bérelni.

Signs

Vészkijárat	Emergency Exit
Bejárat	Entrance
Kijárat	Exit
Meleg	Hot
Hideg	Cold
Információ	Information
Tilos Belépni	No Entry
Tilos A Dohányzás	No Smoking
Nyitva	Open
Zárva	Closed
Tilos	Prohibited
Foglalt	Reserved
WC/Toalett	Toilets
Férfiak	Men (toilet)
Nők	Women (toilet)

I'd like to hire a ...	... szeretnék kölcsönözni.
bicycle	kerékpárt
motorcycle	motorkerékpárt
horse	lovat
I'd like to hire a guide.	Szeretnék kérni egy idegenvezetőt.
I have a visa/ permit.	Nekem van vízum/ engedélyem.

Directions

How do I get to ...?	Hogy jutok ...?
Where is ...?	Hol van ...?
Is it near/far?	Közel/messze van?
What ... is this?	Ez melyik ...?
street/road	utca/út
street number	házszám
city district	kerület
town	város
village	falu/község
(Go) straight ahead.	(Menyen) egyenesen előre.
(Turn) left.	(Forduljon) balra.
(Turn) right.	(Forduljon) jobbra.
at the traffic lights	a közlekedési lámpánál
next/second/third corner	következő/második/ harmadik saroknál
up/down	fent/lent
behind/in front	mögött/előtt

opposite	szemben
here/there	itt/ott/
everywhere	mindenhol
north	észak
south	dél
east	kelet
west	nyugat

Around Town

Where is ...?	Hol van ...?
a bank	bank
an exchange office	pénzváltó
the city centre	a város központ or a centrum
the ... embassy	a ... nagykövetség
the hospital	a kórház
the market	a piac
the police station	a rendőrkapitányság
the post office	a posta
a public toilet	nyilvános WC
a restaurant	étterem
the telephone centre	a telefonközpont
tourist information office	idegenforgalmi iroda

beach	strand
bridge	híd
castle	vár
cathedral	székesegyház
church	templom
synagogue	zsinagóga
island	sziget
lake	tó
(main) square	(fő) tér
market	piac
mosque	mecset
palace	palota
mansion	kastély
ruins	rom or romok
tower	torony

Accommodation

I'm looking for ...	... keresem.
a guesthouse	fogadót
a campground	campinget/ kempinget
the youth hostel	az ifjúsági szállót
a hotel	szállodát

the manager	a főnököt
the owner	a tulajdonost
rooms available	szoba kiadó
Do you have a ... available?	Van szabad ...?
bed	ágyuk
cheap room	olcsó szobájuk
single room	egyágyas szobájuk
double room	kétágyas szobájuk

What is the address?	Mi a cím?

Do you have ...?	Van ...?
a clean sheet	tiszta lepedő
hot water	meleg víz
a key	kulcs
a shower	zuhany

for one/two nights	egy/két éjszakára
How much is it per night/ per person?	Mennyibe kerül éjszakánként/ személyenként?
Is service included?	A kiszolgálás benne van?
May I see the room?	Megnézhetem a szobát?
Where is the toilet/ bathroom?	Hol van a WC/ fürdőszoba?
It is very dirty/ noisy/expensive.	Ez nagyon piskos/ zajos/drága.
I'm/We're leaving.	El megyek/ El megyünk.

Shopping

How much is it?	Mennyibe kerül?
I'd like to buy this.	Szeretném megvenni ezt.
It's too expensive for me.	Ez túl drága nekem.
Can I look at it?	Megnézhetem?
I'm just looking.	Csak nézegetek.

I'm looking for...	Keresem ...
chemist/pharmacy	a patikát
clothing	ruhát
souvenirs	emléktárgyat

Time & Dates

When?	Mikor?
At what time?	Hány órakor?
What time is it?	Hány óra?

Emergencies

Help!	Segítség!
It's an emergency!	Sürgős!
There's been an accident!	Baleset történt!
Call a doctor!	Hívjon egy orvost!
Call an ambulance!	Hívja a mentőket!
Call the police!	Hívja a rendőrséget!
I've been raped.	Megerőszakoltak.
I've been robbed!	Kiraboltak!
I'm lost.	Eltévedtem.
Go away!	Menjen el!
Where are the toilets?	Hol van a WC?

It's ... o'clock.	... óra van.
1.15	negyed kettő ('one-quarter of two')
1.30	fél kettő ('half of two')
1.45	háromnegyed kettő ('three-quarters of two')
in the morning	reggel
in the evening	este
noon	dél
midnight	éjfél
today	ma
tonight	ma este
tomorrow	holnap
day after tomorrow	holnapután
yesterday	tegnap
all day	egész nap
every day	minden nap
Monday	hétfő
Tuesday	kedd
Wednesday	szerda
Thursday	csütörtök
Friday	péntek
Saturday	szombat
Sunday	vasárnap
January	január
February	február
March	március
April	április
May	május
June	június
July	július
August	augusztus
September	szeptember
October	október
November	november
December	december

Numbers

0	nulla
1	egy
2	kettő (két before noun)
3	három
4	négy
5	öt
6	hat
7	hét
8	nyolc
9	kilenc
10	tíz
11	tizenegy
12	tizenkettő
13	tizenhárom
14	tizennégy
15	tizenöt
16	tizenhat
17	tizenhét
18	tizennyolc
19	tizenkilenc
20	húsz
21	huszonegy
22	huszonkettő
30	harminc
40	negyven
50	ötven
60	hatvan
70	hetven
80	nyolcvan
90	kilencven
100	száz
101	százegy
110	száztíz
1000	ezer

1 million	egy millió

Health

I'm ...	... vagyok.
diabetic	cukorbeteg
epileptic	epilepsziás
asthmatic	asztmás
I'm allergic to ...	... allergiás vagyok
penicillin	penicillinre
antibiotics	antibiotikumra

I've got diarrhoea.	*Hasmenésem van.*
I feel nauseous.	*Hányingerem van.*
antiseptic	*fertőzésgátló*
aspirin	*aszpirin*
condoms	*óvszer* or *gumi*
contraceptive	*fogamzásgátló*
medicine	*orvosság*
suntan lotion	*napozókrém*
sunblock cream	*fényvédőkrém*
tampons	*tampon*

FOOD

restaurant	*étterem* or *vendéglő*
food stall	*laci konyha* or *pecsenyesütő*
grocery store/ delicatessen	*élelmiszer csemege*
market	*piac*
breakfast	*reggeli*
lunch	*ebéd*
dinner/supper	*vacsora*
the menu	*az étlap*
set (daily) menu	*napi menü*

At the Restaurant

I'm hungry.	*Éhes vagyok.*
I'm thirsty.	*Szomjas vagyok.*
The menu, please.	*Az étlapot, kérem.*
I'd like the set menu, please.	*Mai menüt kérnék.*
Is service included in the bill?	*Az ár tartalmazza a kiszolgálást?*
I'm a vegetarian.	*Vegetáriánus vagyok.*
I'd like some ...	*Kérnék ...*
Another ... please.	*Még (egy) ... kérek szépen.*
The bill, please.	*A számlát, kérem* or *Fizetek.*

bread	*kenyér*
chicken	*csirke*
coffee	*kávé*
eggs	*tojás*
fish	*hal*
food	*étel*
fruit	*gyümölcs*
fruit juice	*gyümölcslé*
meat	*hús*
milk	*tej*
mineral water	*ásvány víz*
pepper	*bors*

pork	*disznóhús*
salt	*só*
soup	*leves*
sugar	*cukor*
tea	*tea*
vegetables	*zöldség*
water	*víz*
wine	*bor*
hot/cold	*meleg/hideg*
with/without sugar	*cukorral/cukor nélkül*
with/without ice	*jéggel/jég nélkül*

DRINKS
Nonalcoholic Drinks

almalé – apple juice
ásvány víz – mineral water
cappuccino – coffee with whipped cream (see *tejes kávé*)
limonádé – lemonade
narancslé – orange juice
tejes kávé – cappuccino (milky coffee with froth)
üdítő ital – soft drink

Alcoholic Drinks

barackpálinka – apricot brandy
barna sör – dark beer/stout
bor – wine
borozó – wine bar
borpince – wine cellar
csapolt sör – draught beer
édes bor – sweet wine
egészségére! – cheers!
fehér bor – white wine
fél barna sör – dark lager
félédes bor – semisweet wine
félszáraz bor – semidry/medium wine
fröccs – spritzer/wine cooler
itallap – drinks/wine list
korsó sör – mug (half litre) or beer
körtepálinka – pear brandy
őszibarack pálinka – peach brandy
pezsgő – champagne/sparkling wine
pohár bor – glass of wine (size varies)
pohár sör – glass (one-third litre) of beer
sör – beer
söröző – pub/beer hall
szilvapálinka – plum brandy
világos sör – lager
üveg – bottle
vörös bor – red wine

Glossary

If you can't find the word you're looking for in the Glossary, try the previous Language section.

ÁEV – United Forest Railways
ÁFA – value-added tax (VAT)
Alföld – see *Nagyalföld* and *puszta*
Ausgleich – German for 'reconciliation'; the Compromise of 1867
autóbusz – bus
áutóbuszállomás – bus station
Avars – a people of the Caucasus who invaded Europe in the 6th century
ÁVO – Rákosi's hated secret police; later renamed ÁVH

bal – left
bejárat – entrance
borozó – wine bar
BKV – Budapest's city transport company
bolhapiac – flea market
Bp – abbreviation for Budapest
búcsú – farewell; also, a church patronal festival
büfé – snack bar

centrum – town or city centre
Compromise of 1867 – agreement which created the dual monarchy of Austria-Hungary
Copf – a transitional architectural style between late baroque and neoclassicism (see *Zopf*)
csárda – a Hungarian-style inn and/or restaurant
csatorna – canal
csikós – cowboy from the *puszta*
csomagmegőrző – left-luggage office
cukrászda – cake shop or cafe

D – abbreviation for *dél* (south)
Dacia – Roman name for Romania and lands east of the Tisza River
db or **drb** – piece (measurement used in markets)
de – am (in the morning)
du – pm (in the afternoon)

É – abbreviation for *észak* (north)
Eclectic – an art style popular in Hungary in the Romantic period, drawing from varied sources
élelmiszer – grocery shop, provisions
előszoba – vestibule or anteroom; one of three rooms in a traditional Hungarian cottage
em – abbreviation for *emelet* (floor or storey)
erdő – forest
érkezés – arrivals
eszpresszó or **presszó** – coffee shop, often also selling alcoholic drinks and snacks; strong, black coffee
étterem – restaurant

falu – village
fasor – boulevard, avenue
felvilágosítás – information
fogas – pike-perch fish of Lake Balaton
földszint – ground floor
folyó – river
főváros – main city or capital
fsz – abbreviation for földszint or ground floor
Ft – forint (see also *HUF*)

gyógyfürdő – bath or spa
gyógyvíz – medicinal drinking water
gyűjtemény – collection
gyula – chief military commander of the early Magyar

hajdúk – Hungarian for Heyducks or Haiduks
hajó – boat
hajóállomás – ferry pier or landing
ház – house
hegy – hill, mountain
HÉV – suburban commuter train in Budapest
Heyducks – drovers and outlaws from the *puszta* who fought as mercenaries and artisans against the Habsburgs
helyi autóbusz pályaudvar – local bus station
híd – bridge
HNTO – Hungarian National Tourism Office

hőforrás – thermal spring
honfoglalás – conquest of the Carpathian Basin by the early Magyars in the late 9th century
HUF – Hungarian forint (international currency code)
Huns – a Mongol tribe that swept across Europe, notably under Attila, in the 5th century AD

Ibusz – Hungarian national network of travel agencies
ifjúsági szálló – youth hostel
illeték – duty on tax
indulás – departures

jobb – right

K – abbreviation for *kelet* (east)
kamra – workshop or shed; one of three rooms in a traditional Hungarian cottage
kastély – manor house, mansion (see *vár*)
kb – approximately
kékfestő – cotton fabric dyed a rich indigo blue
kemping – camping ground
KEOKH – foreigners' registration office
képtár – picture or gallery
kerület – district
khas – towns of the Ottoman period under direct rule of the sultan
kijárat – exit
kincstár – treasury
Kiskörút – the 'Little Ring Road' in Budapest
kocsma – pub or saloon
kolostor – monastery or cloister
komp – ferry
könyvesbolt – bookshop
könyvtár – library
kórház – hospital
körút – ring road
korzó – embankment, promenade
köz – alley, mews, lane
központ – town or city centre
krt – see *körút*
kúria – mansion, country house
kuruc – Hungarian mercenaries, partisans or insurrectionists who resisted the expansion of Habsburg rule in Hungary after the withdrawal of the Turks (late 17th/early 18th centuries)

lángos – deep-fried dough with toppings
lekvár – fruit jam
lépcső – stairs, steps
liget – park

Mahart – Hungarian passenger ferry company
Malév – Hungary's national airline
MÁV – Hungarian State Railways
megye – county
menetrend – timetable
mihrab – Mecca-oriented prayer niche
MNB – National Bank of Hungary
Moorish Romantic – an art style popular in the decoration of 19th-century synagogues
mozi – cinema
műemlék – memorial, monument

Nagyalföld – the Great Plain (also called the *Alföld* and *puszta*)
Nagykörút – the 'Big Ring Road' in Budapest
Nonius – Hungarian horse breed
nosztalgiavonat – MÁV vintage steam train
Ny – abbreviation for *nyugat* (west)
nyitva – open

ó – abbreviation for *óra*
önkiszolgáló – self-service
óra – hour, o'clock
oszt – abbreviation for *osztály* (department)
OTP – National Savings Bank
Ottoman Empire – the Turkish empire that took over from the Byzantine Empire when it captured Constantinople (Istanbul) in 1453, and expanded into south-eastern Europe right up to the gates of Vienna

pálinka – Hungarian fruit brandy
palota – palace
pályaudvar – train station
Pannonia – Roman name for the lands south and west of the Danube River
panzió – pension, guesthouse
part – embankment
patika – pharmacy
patyolat – laundry
pénztár – cashier
pénzváltó – exchange office
piac – market
pince – wine cellar
plébánia – rectory, parish house

polgármester – mayor

porta – type of farmhouse in Transdanubia

presszó – see *eszpresszó*

pu – abbreviation for *pályaudvar* (train station)

puli – Hungarian breed of sheepdog with shaggy coat

puszta – literally deserted; other name for the Great Plain (see *Alföld* and *Nagyalföld*)

puttony – the number of 'butts' of sweet *aszú* essence added to other base wines in making Tokaj wine

racka – *puszta* sheep with distinctive corkscrew horns

rakpart – quay, embankment

rendőrkapitányság – police station

repülőtér – airport

Romany – the language and culture of the Roma (Gypsy) people

Secessionism – art and architectural style similar to Art Nouveau

sedile (sedilia) – medieval stone niche(s) with seats

sétány – walkway, promenade

skanzen – open-air museum displaying village architecture

söröző – beer bar or pub

stb – abbreviation equivalent to English 'etc'

strand – grassy 'beach' near a river or lake

sugárút – avenue

szálló, szálloda – hotel

székesegyház – cathedral

sziget – island

színház – theatre

szoba kiadó – room for rent

szűr – long embroidered felt cloak or cape worn by traditional Hungarian shepherds

Tanácsköztársaság – the 1919 Communist Republic of Councils under Béla Kun

táncház – an evening of folk music and dance

tanya – homestead or ranch

távolsági autóbusz pályaudvar – long-distance bus station

templom – church

tér – town or market square

tere – genitive form of *tér* as in *Hősök tere* (Square of the Heroes)

tilos – prohibited

tista szoba – parlour; one of three rooms in a traditional Hungarian cottage

tó – lake

toalett – toilet

Trianon Treaty – 1920 treaty imposed on Hungary by the victorious Allies, which reduced the country to one-third of its former size, allowing for the creation of new countries like Yugoslavia and Czechoslovakia

Triple Alliance – 1882-1914 alliance between Germany, Austria-Hungary and Italy – not to be confused with the WWI Allies (members of the *Triple Entente* and their supporters)

Triple Entente – agreement between Britain, France and Russia, intended as a counterbalance to the *Triple Alliance*, lasting until the Russian Revolution of 1917

turul – eagle-like totem of the ancient Magyars and now a national symbol

u – abbreviation for *utca*

udvar – court

ünnep – public holiday

úszoda – swimming pool

út – road

utca – street

utcája – genitive form of *utca* as in *Ferencesek utcája* (Street of the Franciscans)

útja – genitive form of *út* as in *Mártíroká útja* (Street of the Martyrs)

üzlet – shop

va – abbreviations for *vasútállomás*

vágány – platform

vár – castle (see *kastély*)

város – city

városház, városháza – town hall

vasútállomás – train station

vendéglő – a type of restaurant

vm – abbreviations for *vasútállomás*

Volán – Hungarian bus company

vonat – train

WC – toilet (see *toalett*)

zárva – closed

Zimmer frei – German for 'room for rent'

Zopf – German and more commonly used word for *Copf*

Alternative Place Names

The following abbreviations are used:
(C) Croatian
(E) English
(G) German
(H) Hungarian
(R) Romanian
(S) Serbian
(Slk) Slovak
(Slo) Slovene
(U) Ukrainian

Alba Iulia (R) – Gyula Fehérvár (H),
Karlsburg/Weissenburg (G)

Baia Mare (R) – Nagybánya (H)
Balaton (H) – Plattensee (G)
Belgrade (E) – Beograd (S),
Nándorfehérvár (H)
Beregovo (U) – Beregszász (H)
Braşov (R) – Brassó (H), Kronstadt (G)
Bratislava (Slk) – Pozsony (H), Pressburg (G)

Carei (R) – Magykároly (H)
Cluj-Napoca (R) – Kolozsvár (H),
Klausenburg (G)

Danube (E) – Duna (H), Donau (G)
Danube Bend (E) – Dunakanyar (H),
Donauknie (G)
Debrecen (H) – Debrezin (G)

Eger (H) – Erlau (G)
Eisenstadt (G) – Kismárton (H)
Esztergom (H) – Gran (G)

Great Plain (E) – Nagyalföld, Alföld or
Puszta (H)
Győr (H) – Raab (G)

Hungary (E) – Magyarország (H),
Ungarn (G)

Kisalföld (H) – Little Plain (E)
Komárom (H) – Komárno (Slk)
Košice (Slk) – Kassa (H), Kaschau (G)
Kőszeg (H) – Güns (G)

Lendava (Slo) – Lendva (H)
Lučenec (Slk) – Losonc (H)

Mukačevo (U) – Munkács (H)
Murska Sobota (Slo) – Muraszombat (H)

Northern Uplands (E) – Északi Felföld (H)

Oradea (R) – Nagyvárad (H),
Grosswardein (G)
Osijek (C) – Eszék (H)

Pécs (H) – Fünfkirchen (G)

Rožnava (Slk) – Rozsnyó (H)

Satu Mare (R) – Szatmárnémeti (H)
Senta (S) – Zenta (H)
Sibiu (R) – Nagyszében (H),
Hermannstadt (G)
Sic (R) – Szék (H)
Sighişoara (R) – Szegesvár (H),
Schässburg (G)
Sopron (H) – Ödenburg (G)
Štúrovo (Slk) – Párkány (H)
Subotica (S) – Szabadka (H)
Szeged (H) – Segedin (G)
Székesfehérvár (H) – Stuhlweissenburg (G)
Szombathely (H) – Steinamanger (G)

Tata (H) – Totis (G)
Timişoara (R) – Temesvár (H)
Tirgu Mureş (R) – Marosvásárhely (H)
Transdanubia (E) – Dunántúl (H)
Transylvania (R) – Erdély (H),
Siebenbürgen (G)
Trnava (Slk) – Nagyszombat (H)

Užgorod (U) – Ungvár (H)

Vác (H) – Wartzen (G)
Vienna (E) – Wien (G), Bécs (H)
Villány (H) – Wieland (G)
Villánykövesd (H) – Growisch (G)

Wiener Neustadt (G) – Bécsújhely (H)

Acknowledgements

THANKS

Many thanks to those travellers who used the last edition and wrote to us with helpful hints, useful advice and interesting anecdotes:

Ade Allen, Adrian Mather, Agi Nagy, Alexander Matskevich, Amy McKay, Amy Paden, Andras Gefferth, Andy Praserthdam, Ann Mari Michaels, Annamaira Gutierrez Sandbekken, Anne Berit Haugsnes, Anthony Hull, Ardath Cade, B Stoney, Balazs Vajda, Ben Crelling, Beverley Lucock, Brian Payne, Bryan Glendon, Bryne Moy, Caitlin Brice, Caroline & Martin Evans, Caroline Newhouse, Charmian Bakker, Cheryl Hodson, Chris Kidd, Christin Bjergbakke, Coreto Vicente , Courtney Rae Peterson, Csaba Szinell, Danidlle Snellen, Dave McAllister, David F Johnson, David Ridge, Dickie Knee, Duan Ambagtsheer, Eric Hood, Esther Bankuti, Fabrice Mathieu, Ferga Solleveld, Fizh Mike, Francois Cimon, Frank Shaerf, Fred Walther, Garrett Prestage, George Birsic, George Rady, Ghewy Philip, Gottfried Knott, Greg Mills, Hamish Gregor, Heather Watts, Hua Hong Koh, Ilya Shapiro, Inga Schedlbauer, Itamar Raz, J Ayres, J R Hough, Jamie Marley, Jamie Roth, Jan Gunnar, Jay Russian, Jeanne Bortolot, Jessica Stalley, Johanna Souck, Johannes Fabo, John O'Flynn, Jonathan Chilvers, Jonathan Shultz, Juliet Lehair, K P Norris, K Seto, Karen Hilditch, Karen Walker, Kathryn Grose, Keith Baumwald, Kenneth G Allen, Kevin Howard, Kim Wilson, Kristin Joynt, Krystyna Drywa, Lacey Bishop, Lassi Gyorffy, Laura Dixon, Lawrence Rappoport, Luis Migel Mendes , Maja Krause, Maria Catalinatherino, Mariane Breuer, Mary Smith, Mary-Anne Carmedy, Melissa Michels, Mike Lillico, Nacho Rojo, Nagy Attila Gyorgy, Nathalie Ollier, Neil Audley, Nicholas Weaver, Patric Langevin, Paul Vary, Paula Vilen, Perttu Tuomi , Petra Thorbrietz, Rebecca Lennen, Riberiu de Almeick, Ricardo Gonzalez Elespuru, Ricardo Roding, Ricardo Rodrigues, Richard Grainger, Rob Yeager, Robyn Park, Roger Firth, Sarah Tibbattes, Simon McFadden, Sipos Attila, Steffan de Turck, Sule Gabor, Suzi Asmus, Tim Houghton, Tom Anderson, Tom Haten, Tom Vander Elst, Toni Hoffman, Tony Gordon, Tunde Schliszka, Warren Browning, Wendy Graham, Zoe Gibbs , Zoltan Szrenko,

LONELY PLANET

You already know that Lonely Planet produces more than this one guidebook, but you might not be aware of the other products we have on this region. Here is a selection of titles which you may want to check out as well:

Budapest Map
ISBN 1 86450 077 8
US$5.95 • UK£3.99 • 39FF

Budapest
ISBN 1 86450 118 9
US$14.99 • UK£9.99 • 119FF

Europe on a shoestring
ISBN 0 86442 648 8
US$24.95 • UK£14.99 • 180FF

Eastern Europe
ISBN 0 86442 136 7
US$24.95 • UK£14.99 • 180FF

Eastern Europe phrasebook
ISBN 0 86442 260 1
US$6.95 • UK£4.50 • 55FF

Read this First
ISBN 1 86450 136 7
US$14.99 • UK£8.99 • 99FF

Central Europe
ISBN 0 86442 608 9
US$24.95 • UK£14.99 • 180FF

Central Europe phrasebook
ISBN 0 86442 259 8
US$6.95 • UK£4.50 • 55FF

Available wherever books are sold.

LONELY PLANET

Guides by Region

Lonely Planet is known worldwide for publishing practical, reliable and no-nonsense travel information in our guides and on our web site. The Lonely Planet list covers just about every accessible part of the world. Currently there are fifteen series: travel guides, Shoestrings, Condensed, Phrasebooks, Read This First, Healthy Travel, Walking guides, Cycling guides, Pisces Diving & Snorkeling guides, City Maps, Travel Atlases, Out to Eat, World Food, Journeys travel literature and Pictorials.

AFRICA Africa on a shoestring • Africa – the South • Arabic (Egyptian) phrasebook • Arabic (Moroccan) phrasebook • Cairo • Cape Town • Cape Town city map • Central Africa • East Africa • Egypt • Egypt travel atlas • Ethiopian (Amharic) phrasebook • The Gambia & Senegal • Healthy Travel Africa • Kenya • Kenya travel atlas • Malawi, Mozambique & Zambia • Morocco • North Africa • Read This First Africa • South Africa, Lesotho & Swaziland • South Africa, Lesotho & Swaziland travel atlas • Swahili phrasebook • Tanzania, Zanzibar & Pemba • Trekking in East Africa • Tunisia • West Africa • Zimbabwe, Botswana & Namibia • Zimbabwe, Botswana & Nambia Travel Atlas • World Food Morocco
Travel Literature: The Rainbird: A Central African Journey • Songs to an African Sunset: A Zimbabwean Story • Mali Blues: Traveling to an African Beat

AUSTRALIA & THE PACIFIC Auckland • Australia • Australian phrasebook • Bushwalking in Australia • Bushwalking in Papua New Guinea • Fiji • Fijian phrasebook • Healthy Travel Australia, NZ and the Pacific • Islands of Australia's Great Barrier Reef • Melbourne • Melbourne city map • Micronesia • New Caledonia • New South Wales & the ACT • New Zealand • Northern Territory • Outback Australia • Out To Eat – Melbourne • Out to Eat – Sydney • Papua New Guinea • Pidgin phrasebook • Queensland • Rarotonga & the Cook Islands • Samoa • Solomon Islands • South Australia • South Pacific • South Pacific Languages phrasebook • Sydney • Sydney city map • Sydney Condensed • Tahiti & French Polynesia • Tasmania • Tonga • Tramping in New Zealand • Vanuatu • Victoria • Western Australia
Travel Literature: Islands in the Clouds • Kiwi Tracks: A New Zealand Journey • Sean & David's Long Drive

CENTRAL AMERICA & THE CARIBBEAN Bahamas, Turks & Caicos • Bermuda • Central America on a shoestring • Costa Rica • Cuba • Dominican Republic & Haiti • Eastern Caribbean • Guatemala, Belize & Yucatán: La Ruta Maya • Jamaica • Mexico • Mexico City • Panama • Puerto Rico • Read This First Central & South America • World Food Mexico
Travel Literature: Green Dreams: Travels in Central America

EUROPE Amsterdam • Amsterdam city map • Andalucía • Austria • Baltic States phrasebook • Barcelona • Berlin • Berlin city map • Britain • British phrasebook • Brussels, Bruges & Antwerp • Budapest city map • Canary Islands • Central Europe • Central Europe phrasebook • Corfu & Ionians • Corsica • Crete • Crete Condensed • Croatia • Cyprus • Czech & Slovak Republics • Denmark • Dublin • Eastern Europe • Eastern Europe phrasebook • Edinburgh • Estonia, Latvia & Lithuania • Europe on a shoestring • Finland • Florence • France • French phrasebook • Germany • German phrasebook • Greece • Greek Islands • Greek phrasebook • Hungary • Iceland, Greenland & the Faroe Islands • Ireland • Italian phrasebook • Italy • Krakow • Lisbon • The Loire • London • London city map • London Condensed • Mediterranean Europe • Mediterranean Europe phrasebook • Munich • Norway • Paris • Paris city map • Paris Condensed • Poland • Portugal • Portugese phrasebook • Portugal travel atlas • Prague • Prague city map • Provence & the Côte d'Azur • Read This First Europe • Romania & Moldova • Rome • Russia, Ukraine & Belarus • Russian phrasebook • Scandinavian & Baltic Europe • Scandinavian Europe phrasebook • Scotland • Slovenia • Spain • Spanish phrasebook • St Petersburg • Sweden • Switzerland • Trekking in Spain • Tuscany • Ukrainian phrasebook • Venice • Vienna • Walking in Britain • Walking in Ireland • Walking in Italy • Walking in Spain • Walking in Switzerland • Western Europe • Western Europe phrasebook • World Food Ireland • World Food Italy • World Food Spain
Travel Literature: The Olive Grove: Travels in Greece

INDIAN SUBCONTINENT Bangladesh • Bengali phrasebook • Bhutan • Delhi • Goa • Hindi & Urdu phrasebook • India • India & Bangladesh travel atlas • Indian Himalaya • Karakoram Highway • Kerala • Mumbai (Bombay) • Nepal • Nepali phrasebook • Pakistan • Rajasthan • Read This First: Asia & India • South India • Sri Lanka • Sri Lanka phrasebook • Trekking in the Indian Himalaya • Trekking in the Karakoram & Hindukush • Trekking in the Nepal Himalaya
Travel Literature: In Rajasthan • Shopping for Buddhas • The Age Of Kali

LONELY PLANET

Mail Order

Lonely Planet products are distributed worldwide. They are also available by mail order from Lonely Planet, so if you have difficulty finding a title please write to us. North and South American residents should write to 150 Linden St, Oakland CA 94607, USA; European and African residents should write to 10a Spring Place, London, NW5 3BH; and residents of other countries to PO Box 617, Hawthorn, Victoria 3122, Australia.

ISLANDS OF THE INDIAN OCEAN Madagascar & Comoros • Maldives • Mauritius, Réunion & Seychelles

MIDDLE EAST & CENTRAL ASIA Bahrain, Kuwait & Qatar • Central Asia • Central Asia phrasebook • Dubai • Hebrew phrasebook • Iran • Israel & the Palestinian Territories • Israel & the Palestinian Territories travel atlas • Istanbul • Istanbul City Map • Istanbul to Cairo on a shoestring • Jerusalem • Jerusalem City Map • Jordan • Jordan, Syria & Lebanon travel atlas • Lebanon • Middle East • Oman & the United Arab Emirates • Syria • Turkey • Turkey travel atlas • Turkish phrasebook • World Food Turkey • Yemen
Travel Literature: The Gates of Damascus • Kingdom of the Film Stars: Journey into Jordan • Black on Black: Iran Revisited

NORTH AMERICA Alaska • Backpacking in Alaska • Baja California • California & Nevada • California Condensed • Canada • Chicago • Chicago city map • Deep South • Florida • Hawaii • Honolulu • Las Vegas • Los Angeles • Miami • New England • New Orleans • New York City • New York city map • New York Condensed • New York, New Jersey & Pennsylvania • Oahu • Pacific Northwest USA • Puerto Rico • Rocky Mountain • San Francisco • San Francisco city map • Seattle • Southwest USA • Texas • USA • USA phrasebook • Vancouver • Washington, DC & the Capital Region • Washington DC city map
Travel Literature: Drive Thru America

NORTH-EAST ASIA Beijing • Cantonese phrasebook • China • Hong Kong • Hong Kong city map • Hong Kong, Macau & Guangzhou • Japan • Japanese phrasebook • Japanese audio pack • Korea • Korean phrasebook • Kyoto • Mandarin phrasebook • Mongolia • Mongolian phrasebook • North-East Asia on a shoestring • Seoul • South-West China • Taiwan • Tibet • Tibetan phrasebook • Tokyo
Travel Literature: Lost Japan • In Xanadu

SOUTH AMERICA Argentina, Uruguay & Paraguay • Bolivia • Brazil • Brazilian phrasebook • Buenos Aires • Chile & Easter Island • Chile & Easter Island travel atlas • Colombia • Ecuador & the Galapagos Islands • Healthy Travel Central & South America • Latin American Spanish phrasebook • Peru • Quechua phrasebook • Rio de Janeiro • Rio de Janeiro city map • South America on a shoestring • Trekking in the Patagonian Andes • Venezuela
Travel Literature: Full Circle: A South American Journey

SOUTH-EAST ASIA Bali & Lombok • Bangkok • Bangkok city map • Burmese phrasebook • Cambodia • Hanoi • Healthy Travel Asia & India • Hill Tribes phrasebook • Ho Chi Minh City • Indonesia • Indonesia's Eastern Islands • Indonesian phrasebook • Indonesian audio pack • Jakarta • Java • Laos • Lao phrasebook • Laos travel atlas • Malay phrasebook • Malaysia, Singapore & Brunei • Myanmar (Burma) • Philippines • Pilipino (Tagalog) phrasebook • Read This First Asia & India • Singapore • South-East Asia on a shoestring • South-East Asia phrasebook • Thailand • Thailand's Islands & Beaches • Thailand travel atlas • Thai phrasebook • Thai audio pack • Vietnam • Vietnamese phrasebook • Vietnam travel atlas • World Food Thailand • World Food Vietnam

ALSO AVAILABLE: Antarctica • The Arctic • Brief Encounters: Stories of Love, Sex & Travel • Chasing Rickshaws • Lonely Planet Unpacked • Not the Only Planet: Travel Stories from Science Fiction • Sacred India • Travel with Children • Traveller's Tales

Index

Text

Bold indicates maps.

Bold indicates maps.

Boxed Text